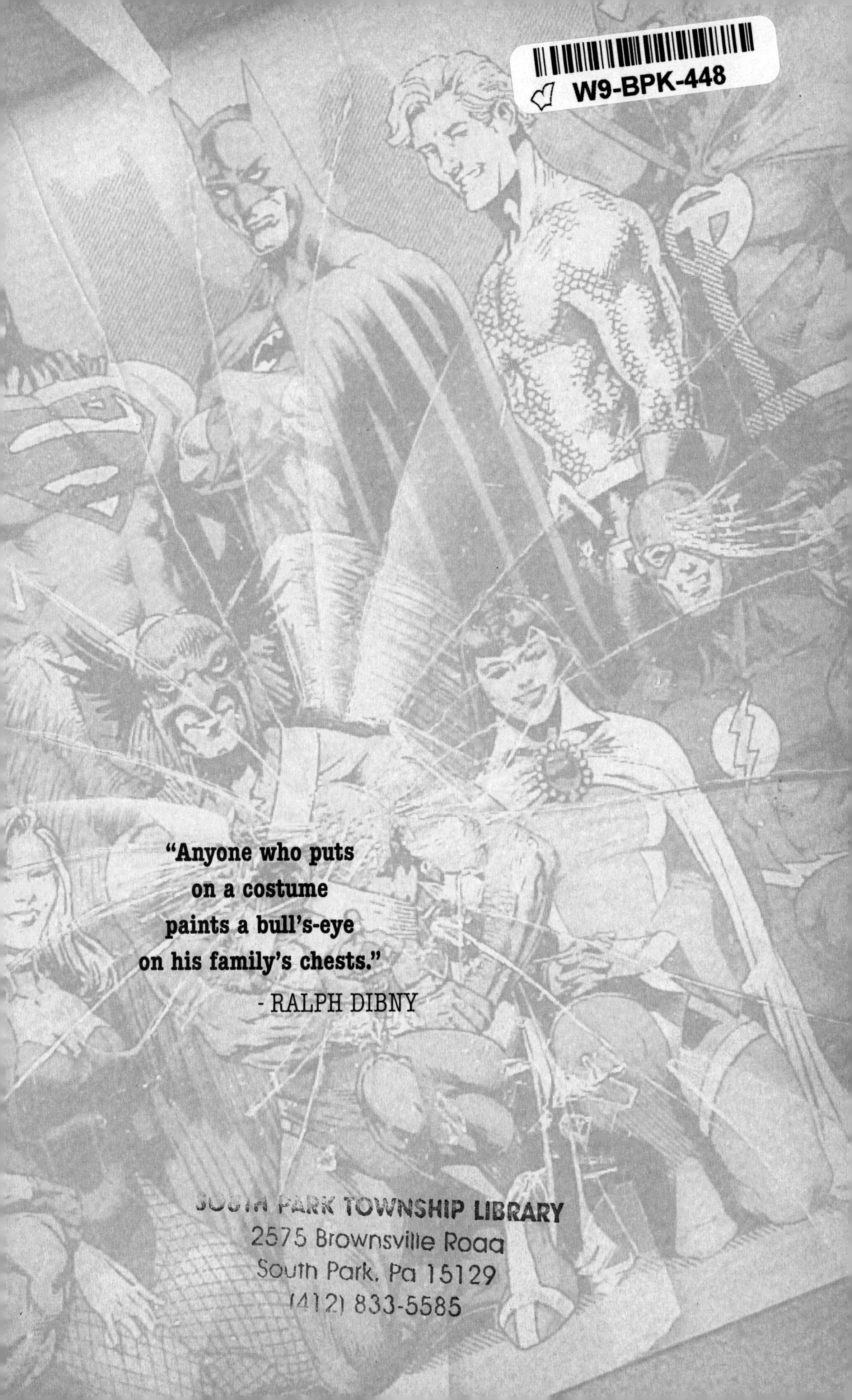

"Anyone who puts
on a costume
paints a bull's-eye
on his family's chests."

- RALPH DIBNY

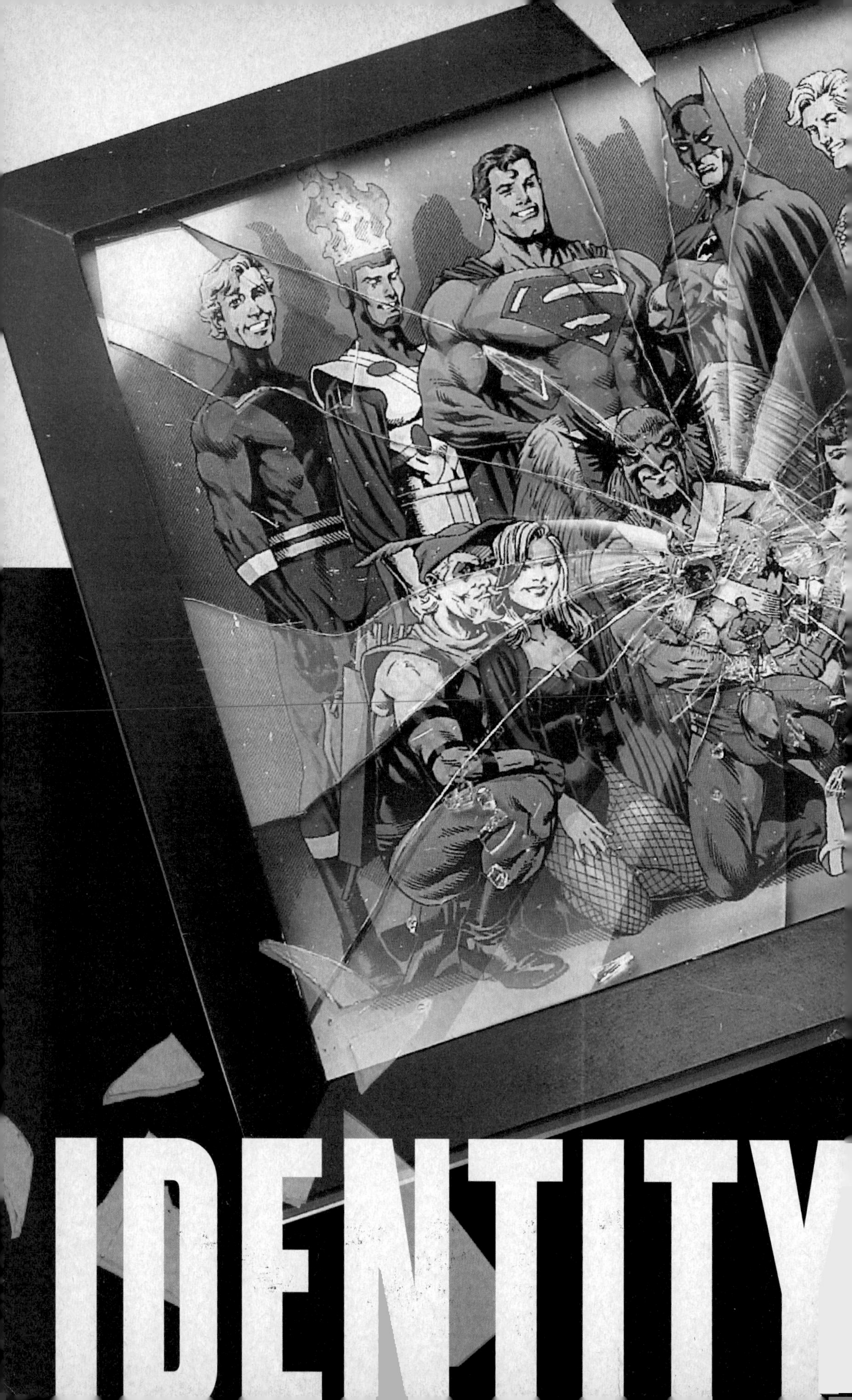

IDENTITY

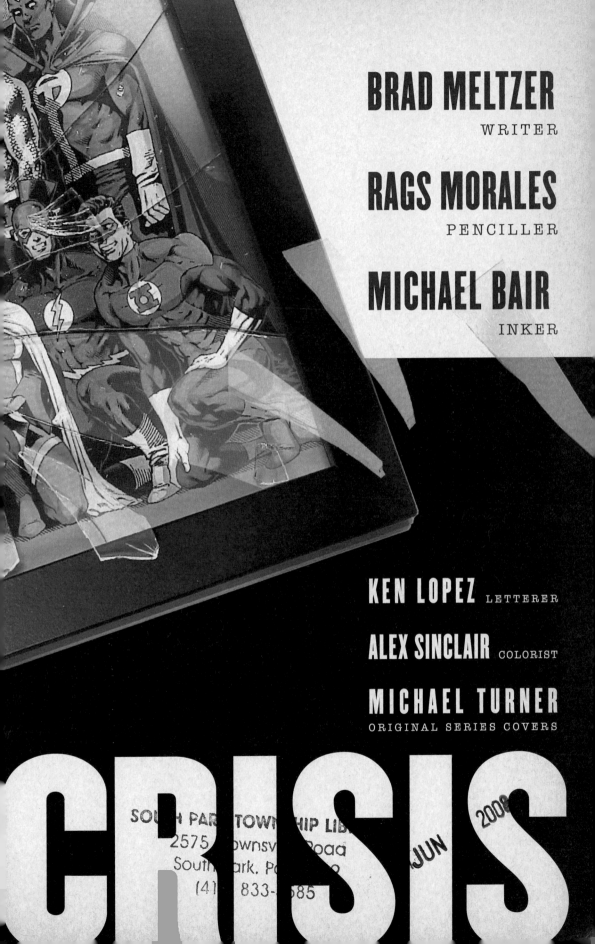

BRAD MELTZER
WRITER

RAGS MORALES
PENCILLER

MICHAEL BAIR
INKER

KEN LOPEZ LETTERER

ALEX SINCLAIR COLORIST

MICHAEL TURNER
ORIGINAL SERIES COVERS

CRISIS

IDENTITY CRISIS. Published by DC Comics.

Cover, introduction, and compilation copyright © 2005 DC Comics.

Originally published in single magazine form as IDENTITY CRISIS 1-7. Copyright © 2004, 2005 DC Comics. All Rights Reserved. All characters the distinctive likenesses thereof and related elements are trademarks of DC Comics. The stories, characters, and incidents featured in this publication are entirely fictional. DC Comics does not read or accept unsolicited submissions of ideas, stories or artwork.

DC Comics, 1700 Broadway, New York, NY 10019.

A Warner Bros. Entertainment Company

Printed in Canada. Second Printing.

ISBN: 1-4012-0458-9.

ISBN 13: 978-1-4012-0458-7.

Cover illustration by Rags Morales and Michael Bair.

Cover photography by Geoff Spear.

Logo designed by Brainchild Studios/NYC.

Publication design by Amie Brockway-Metcalf.

BY JOSS WHEDON

INTRODUCTION

The nature of epiphany is that it changes the universe without moving a hair. Everything before you is cast in a new light, a light so revealing it sometimes hurts. So it is with great mainstream comic book writing. Mainstream comics (particularly the Two Titans, DC and that other one) **are** a universe, one that is as established and often unfathomable as the real one. A great novel or film might take you to a new world, but books like *Identity Crisis* have a much more complex criterion. They have to make you feel you're seeing something new without destroying the familiar. Not killin' Supes. Not revealing that everything since 1972 was all a dream. Just shining that light, and showing us what we should have seen all along. Humanity.

Brad Meltzer and Rags Morales are students of humanity. You will see heroes, streamlined and dynamic, but Rags's pencils always keep them human, lived-in. It's a style that evokes the artists of the forties as well as it does the modern, which is perfect for a book built to light up the whole history of the DC universe. You will read epic battles and gripping mysteries, but Brad Meltzer does much more than move chess pieces around with brilliant precision (which is, in itself, really hard for the rest of us). He humanizes. He sees the smallest quirks, the darkest passions, the matter-of-fact absurdity that is inevitably the life of a super-powered person.

You start at the beginning. Even if you're a lifelong fan of DC, it's unlikely that Elongated Man is your favorite-ever character. But halfway into issue one he was certainly mine. Brad and Rags paint a portrait of a man — and a marriage — that is so unassumingly lovely, it's unbearable to think anything bad might happen to either. And inevitable that it will. What follows is a story so genuinely tragic it **does** change the universe — at least for a few characters. But what makes this book great (this is a great book, in case I wasn't being clear) is that the tragedy is rooted in the past, in the existing structure of the DC Universe. In the terrible actions of great heroes. Actions they not only might have taken, but inevitably would have, **must** have. That fact was sitting there, secret and silent, until in that blinding moment of epiphany, it was revealed.

Not by me, though. You have to read the book to find out. And even if you know what happens, you have to live through it. That's the feeling this book gives you — of living with these people, through their pain and triumph and madness, and did I mention the pain? You will come through it with a new understanding of the world before you. You will **see**.

Joss Whedon is an award-winning writer and creator of the television series Buffy the Vampire Slayer, Angel *and* Firefly. *He makes his feature film directing debut with* Serenity, *based on* Firefly. *Joss is currently writing a* Wonder Woman *feature film, which he will direct for Warner Bros.*

DEDICATIONS

For Ben Rubin,
my Poppy,
who used to make up the best
Batman stories just because
he knew I loved hearing them.

— BRAD MELTZER

Dedicated to Ralph, Flerida and Lisa.
To Kyra, Lorraine, Devon, Isabel and Gwendolyn.
For friends, and a family's love and support;
in the end that is what this story is about.
And to the naysayers because this book
speaks of perseverance as well.
Dad, chapter five is for us.
I love you all.

— RAGS MORALES

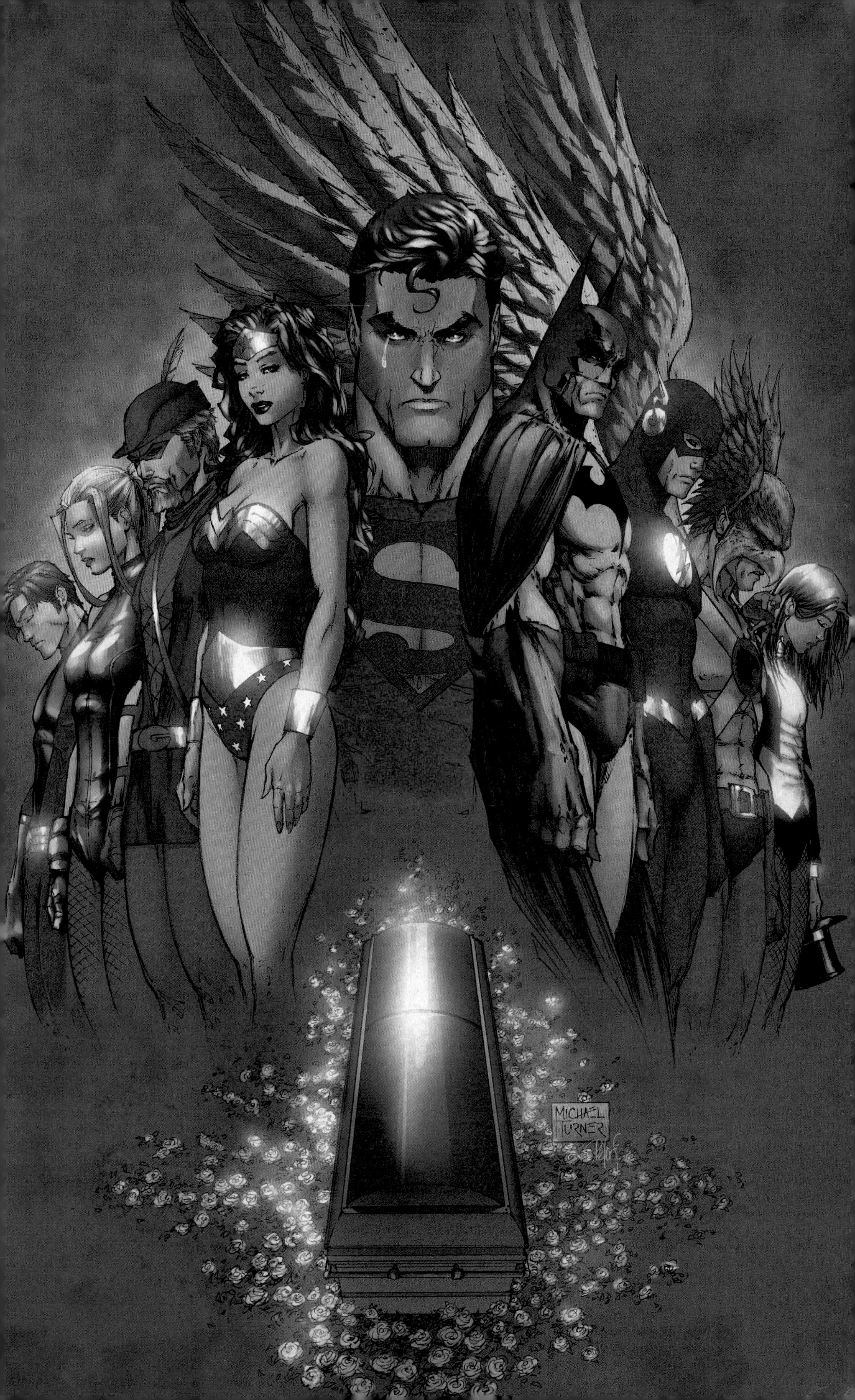
MICHAEL TURNER

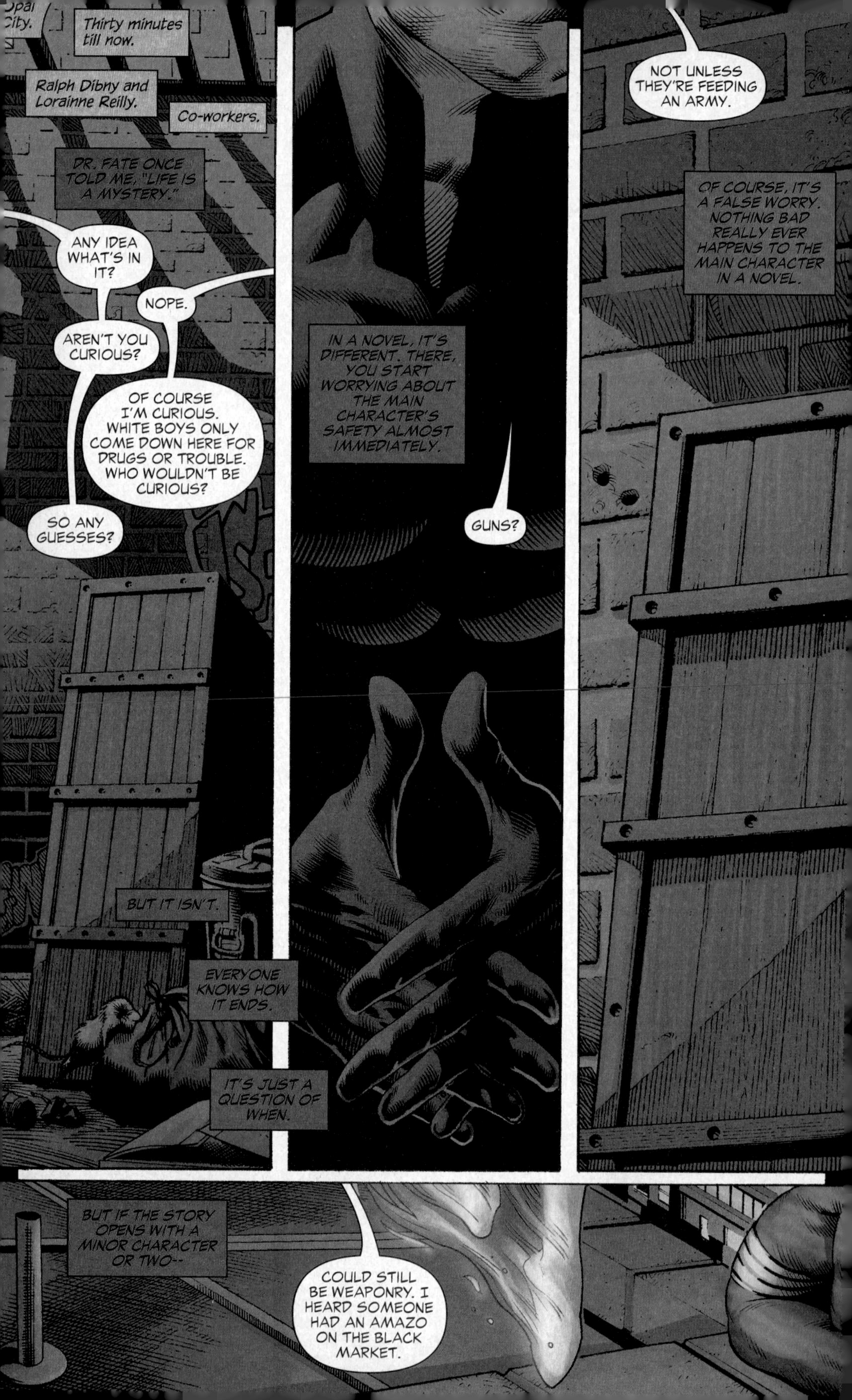
Opal City.
Thirty minutes till now.
Ralph Dibny and Lorainne Reilly.
Co-workers.
DR. FATE ONCE TOLD ME, "LIFE IS A MYSTERY."
ANY IDEA WHAT'S IN IT?
NOPE.
AREN'T YOU CURIOUS?
OF COURSE I'M CURIOUS. WHITE BOYS ONLY COME DOWN HERE FOR DRUGS OR TROUBLE. WHO WOULDN'T BE CURIOUS?
SO ANY GUESSES?
IN A NOVEL, IT'S DIFFERENT. THERE, YOU START WORRYING ABOUT THE MAIN CHARACTER'S SAFETY ALMOST IMMEDIATELY.
GUNS?
NOT UNLESS THEY'RE FEEDING AN ARMY.
OF COURSE, IT'S A FALSE WORRY. NOTHING BAD REALLY EVER HAPPENS TO THE MAIN CHARACTER IN A NOVEL.
BUT IT ISN'T.
EVERYONE KNOWS HOW IT ENDS.
IT'S JUST A QUESTION OF WHEN.
BUT IF THE STORY OPENS WITH A MINOR CHARACTER OR TWO--
COULD STILL BE WEAPONRY. I HEARD SOMEONE HAD AN AMAZO ON THE BLACK MARKET.

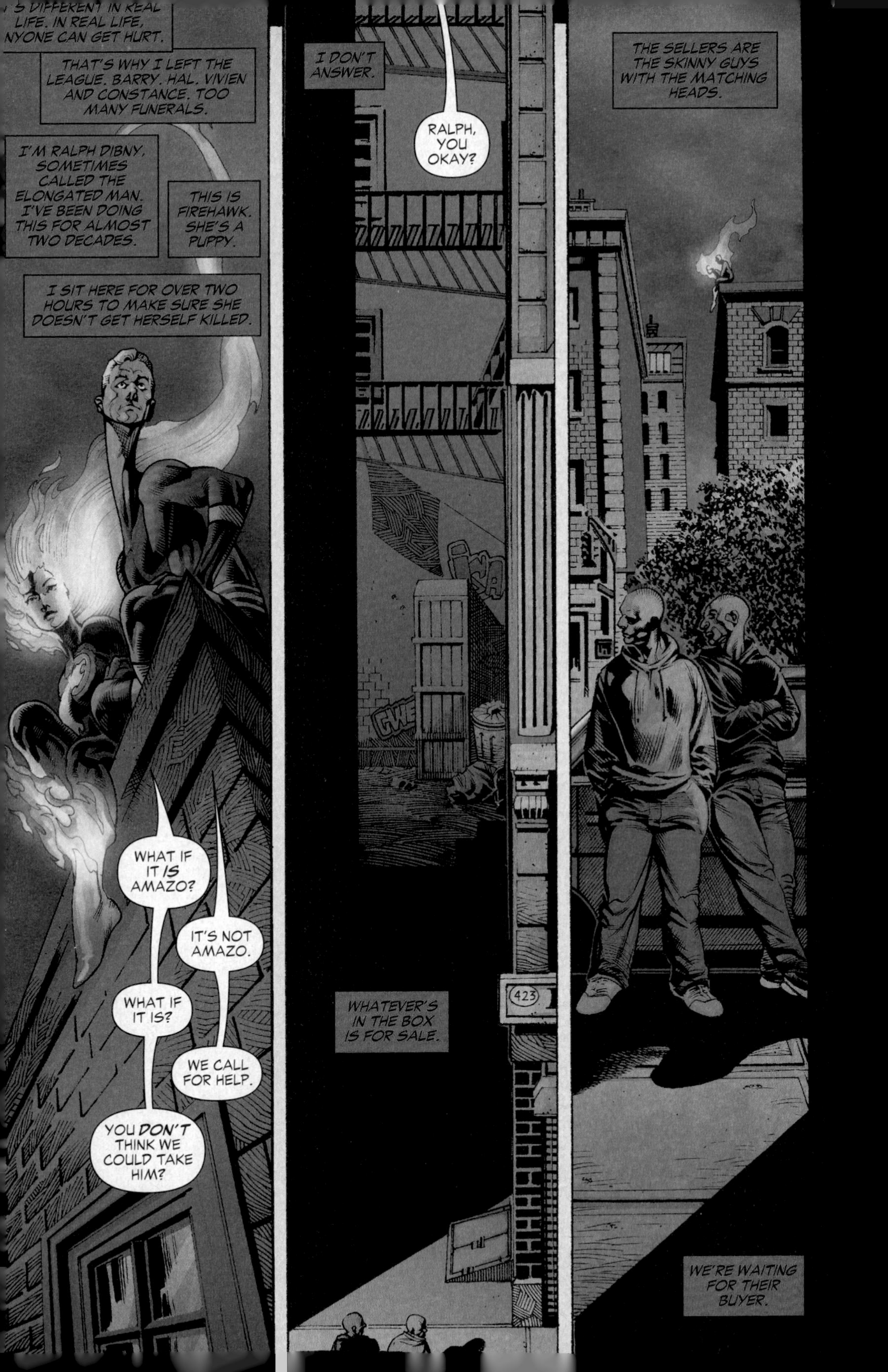
'S DIFFERENT IN REAL LIFE. IN REAL LIFE, NYONE CAN GET HURT.
THAT'S WHY I LEFT THE LEAGUE. BARRY. HAL. VIVIEN AND CONSTANCE. TOO MANY FUNERALS.
I'M RALPH DIBNY, SOMETIMES CALLED THE ELONGATED MAN. I'VE BEEN DOING THIS FOR ALMOST TWO DECADES.
THIS IS FIREHAWK. SHE'S A PUPPY.
I SIT HERE FOR OVER TWO HOURS TO MAKE SURE SHE DOESN'T GET HERSELF KILLED.
WHAT IF IT *IS* AMAZO?
IT'S NOT AMAZO.
WHAT IF IT IS?
WE CALL FOR HELP.
YOU ***DON'T*** THINK WE COULD TAKE HIM?
I DON'T ANSWER.
RALPH, YOU OKAY?
WHATEVER'S IN THE BOX IS FOR SALE.
423
THE SELLERS ARE THE SKINNY GUYS WITH THE MATCHING HEADS.
WE'RE WAITING FOR THEIR BUYER.

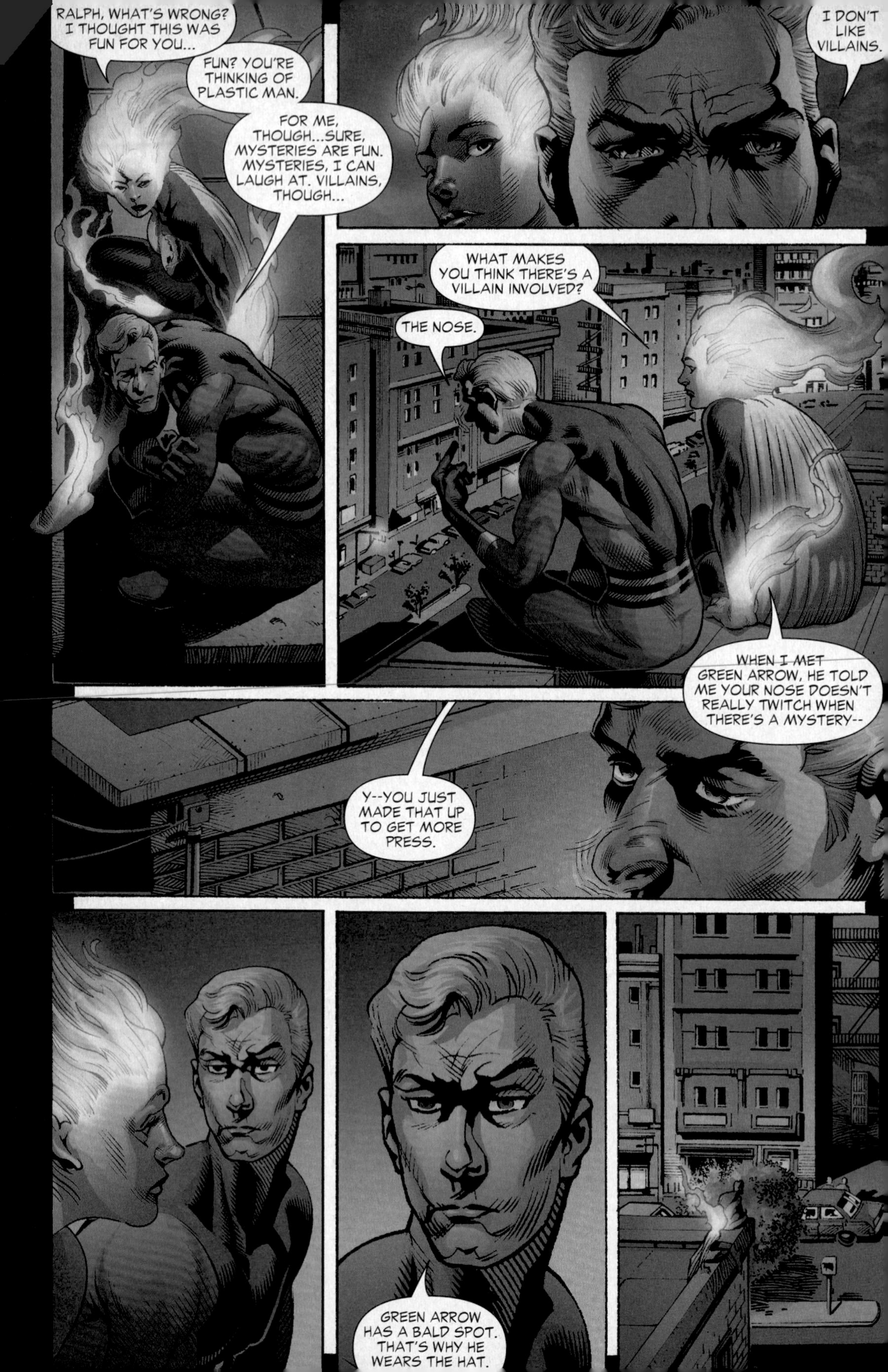
RALPH, WHAT'S WRONG? I THOUGHT THIS WAS FUN FOR YOU...
FUN? YOU'RE THINKING OF PLASTIC MAN.
FOR ME, THOUGH...SURE, MYSTERIES ARE FUN. MYSTERIES, I CAN LAUGH AT. VILLAINS, THOUGH...
I DON'T LIKE VILLAINS.
WHAT MAKES YOU THINK THERE'S A VILLAIN INVOLVED?
THE NOSE.
WHEN I MET GREEN ARROW, HE TOLD ME YOUR NOSE DOESN'T REALLY TWITCH WHEN THERE'S A MYSTERY--
Y--YOU JUST MADE THAT UP TO GET MORE PRESS.
GREEN ARROW HAS A BALD SPOT. THAT'S WHY HE WEARS THE HAT.

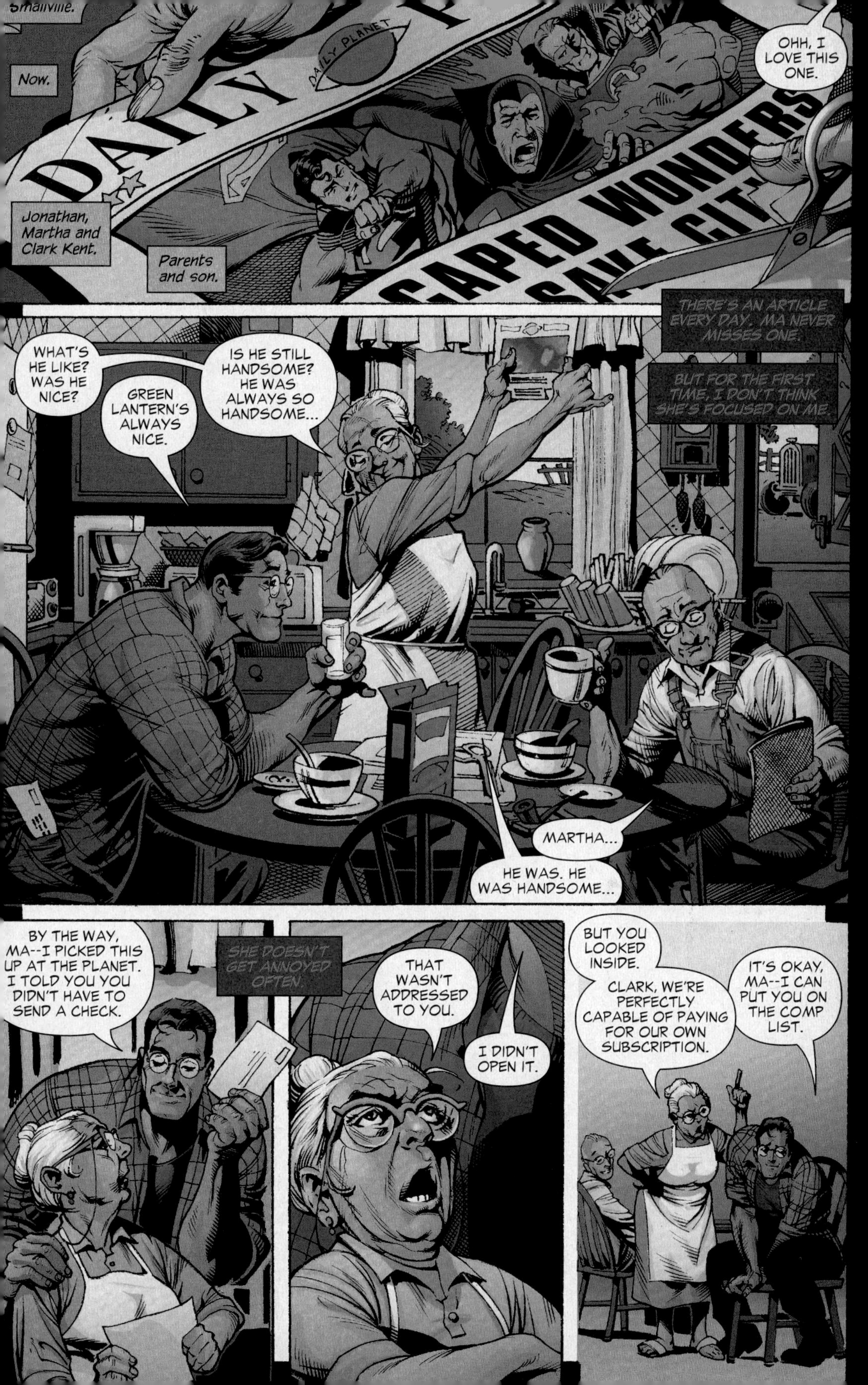
Smallville.
Now.
DAILY
DAILY PLANET
CAPED WONDERS
OHH, I LOVE THIS ONE.
Jonathan, Martha and Clark Kent.
Parents and son.
THERE'S AN ARTICLE EVERY DAY. MA NEVER MISSES ONE.
BUT FOR THE FIRST TIME, I DON'T THINK SHE'S FOCUSED ON ME.
WHAT'S HE LIKE? WAS HE NICE?
GREEN LANTERN'S ALWAYS NICE.
IS HE STILL HANDSOME? HE WAS ALWAYS SO HANDSOME...
MARTHA...
HE WAS. HE WAS HANDSOME...
BY THE WAY, MA--I PICKED THIS UP AT THE PLANET. I TOLD YOU YOU DIDN'T HAVE TO SEND A CHECK.
SHE DOESN'T GET ANNOYED OFTEN.
THAT WASN'T ADDRESSED TO YOU.
I DIDN'T OPEN IT.
BUT YOU LOOKED INSIDE.
CLARK, WE'RE PERFECTLY CAPABLE OF PAYING FOR OUR OWN SUBSCRIPTION.
IT'S OKAY, MA--I CAN PUT YOU ON THE COMP LIST.

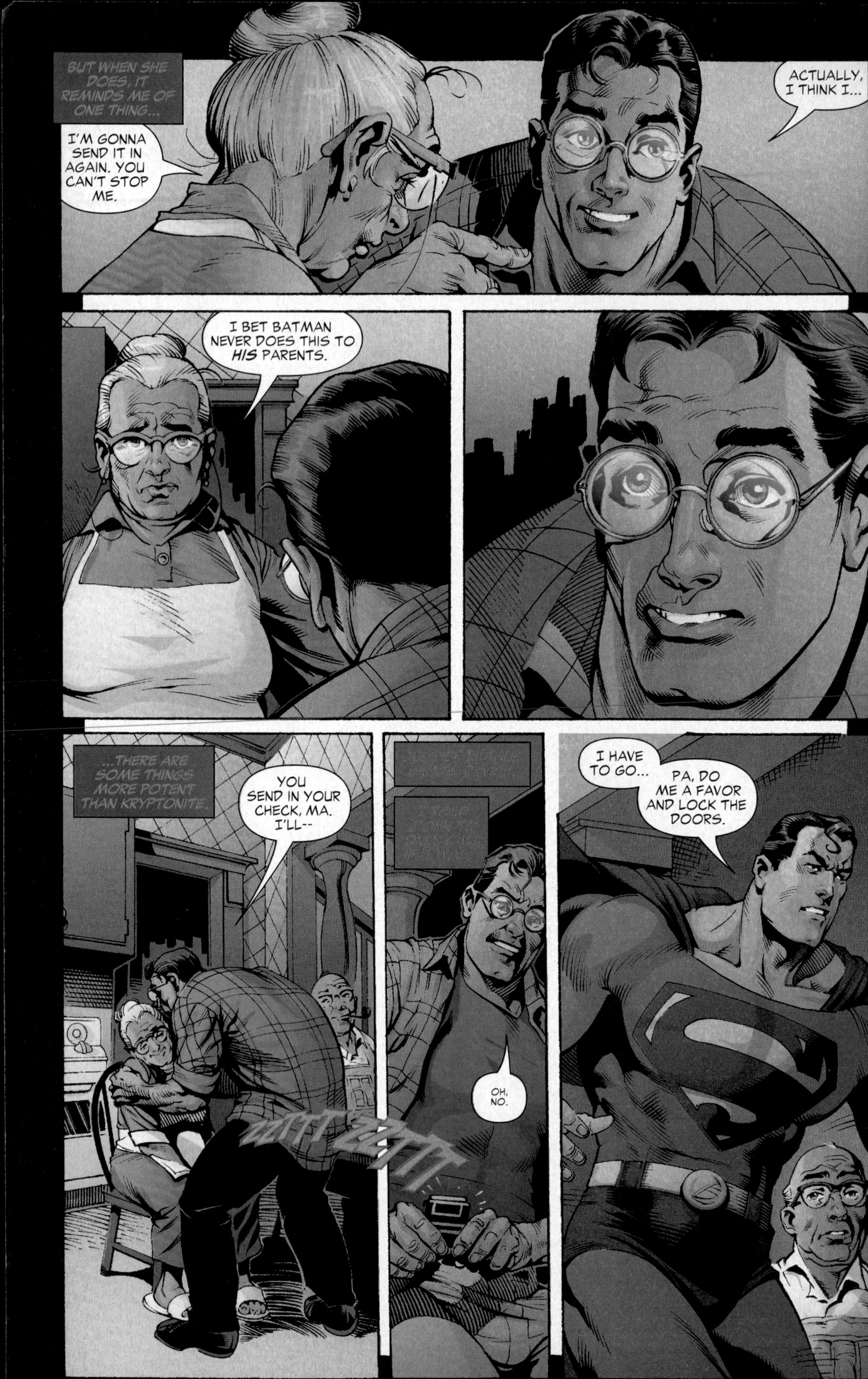
BUT WHEN SHE DOES, IT REMINDS ME OF ONE THING...
I'M GONNA SEND IT IN AGAIN. YOU CAN'T STOP ME.
ACTUALLY, I THINK I...
I BET BATMAN NEVER DOES THIS TO HIS PARENTS.
...THERE ARE SOME THINGS MORE POTENT THAN KRYPTONITE.
YOU SEND IN YOUR CHECK, MA. I'LL--
ZZTTT ZZTTT
JUSTICE LEAGUE SIGNAL DEVICE.
I TOLD J'ONN TO ONLY CALL IF IT WAS--
OH, NO.
I HAVE TO GO...
PA, DO ME A FAVOR AND LOCK THE DOORS.

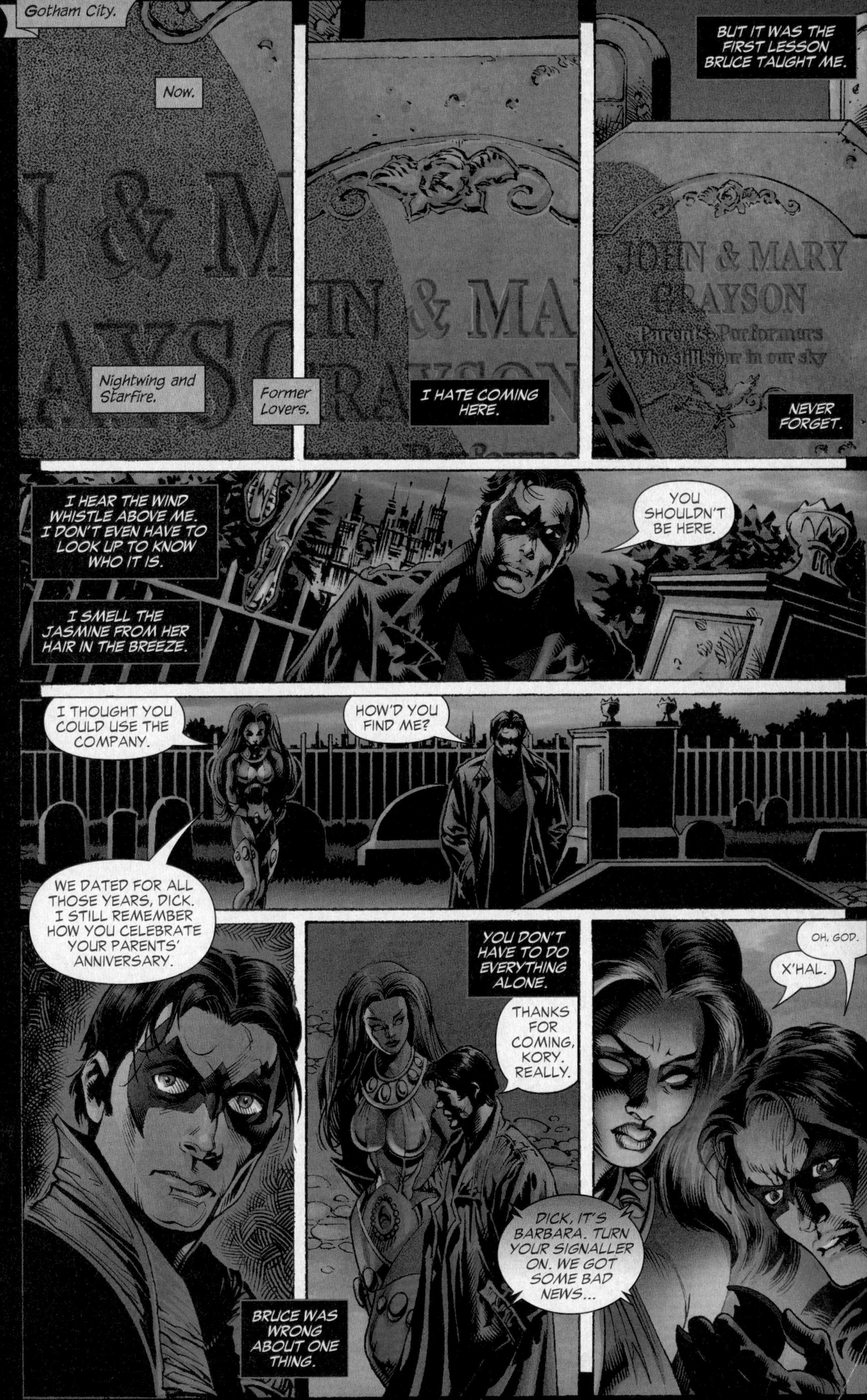
Gotham City.
Now.
Nightwing and Starfire.
Former Lovers.
I HATE COMING HERE.
BUT IT WAS THE FIRST LESSON BRUCE TAUGHT ME.
JOHN & MARY GRAYSON
Parents & Performers
Who still soar in our sky
NEVER FORGET.
I HEAR THE WIND WHISTLE ABOVE ME. I DON'T EVEN HAVE TO LOOK UP TO KNOW WHO IT IS.
I SMELL THE JASMINE FROM HER HAIR IN THE BREEZE.
YOU SHOULDN'T BE HERE.
I THOUGHT YOU COULD USE THE COMPANY.
HOW'D YOU FIND ME?
WE DATED FOR ALL THOSE YEARS, DICK. I STILL REMEMBER HOW YOU CELEBRATE YOUR PARENTS' ANNIVERSARY.
YOU DON'T HAVE TO DO EVERYTHING ALONE.
THANKS FOR COMING, KORY. REALLY.
DICK, IT'S BARBARA. TURN YOUR SIGNALLER ON. WE GOT SOME BAD NEWS...
BRUCE WAS WRONG ABOUT ONE THING.
OH, GOD.
X'HAL.

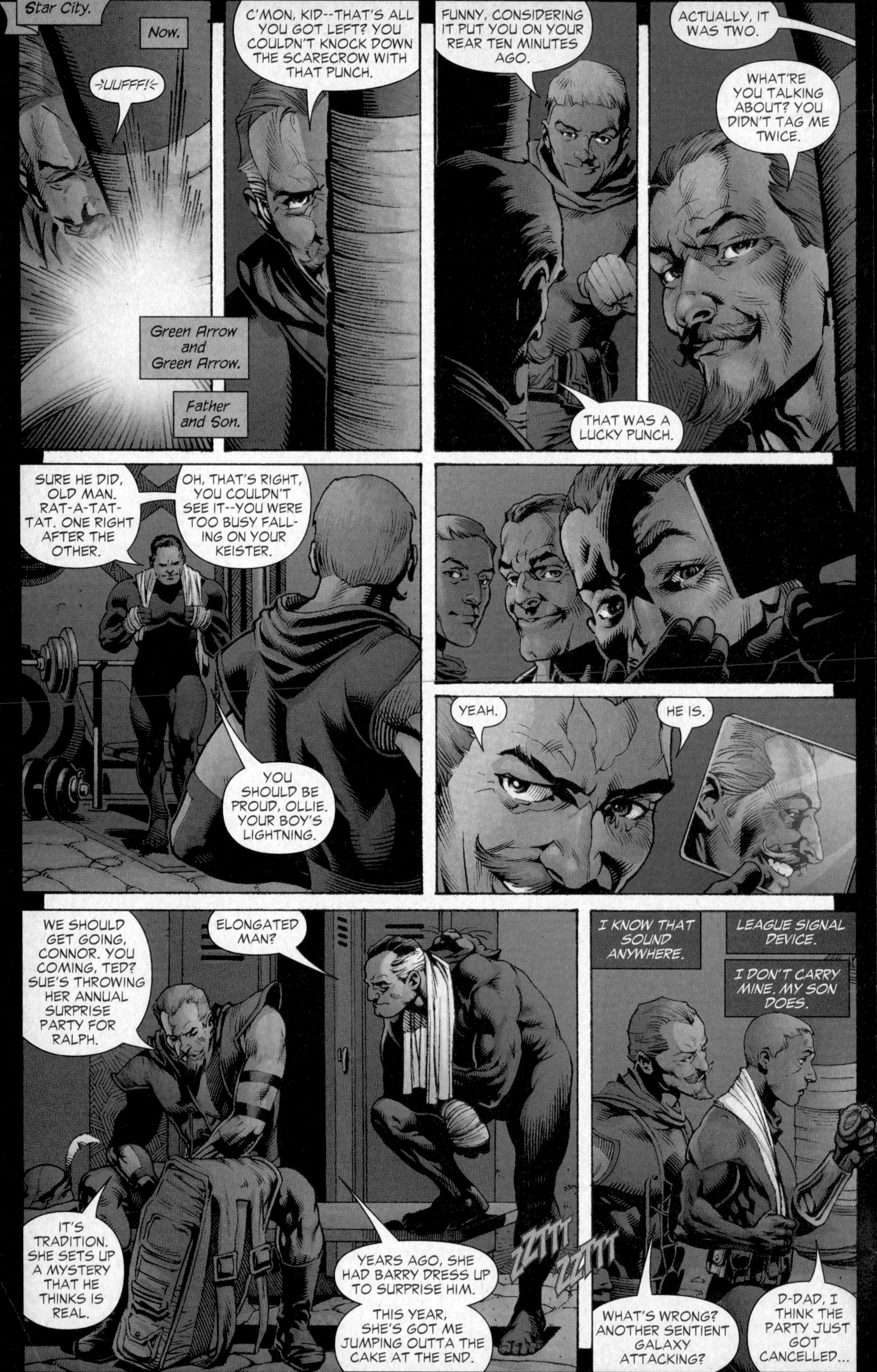
Star City.
Now.
>UUFFF!<
Green Arrow and Green Arrow.
Father and Son.
C'MON, KID--THAT'S ALL YOU GOT LEFT? YOU COULDN'T KNOCK DOWN THE SCARECROW WITH THAT PUNCH.
FUNNY, CONSIDERING IT PUT YOU ON YOUR REAR TEN MINUTES AGO.
THAT WAS A LUCKY PUNCH.
ACTUALLY, IT WAS TWO.
WHAT'RE YOU TALKING ABOUT? YOU DIDN'T TAG ME TWICE.
SURE HE DID, OLD MAN. RAT-A-TAT-TAT. ONE RIGHT AFTER THE OTHER.
OH, THAT'S RIGHT, YOU COULDN'T SEE IT--YOU WERE TOO BUSY FALLING ON YOUR KEISTER.
YOU SHOULD BE PROUD, OLLIE. YOUR BOY'S LIGHTNING.
YEAH.
HE IS.
WE SHOULD GET GOING, CONNOR. YOU COMING, TED? SUE'S THROWING HER ANNUAL SURPRISE PARTY FOR RALPH.
ELONGATED MAN?
IT'S TRADITION. SHE SETS UP A MYSTERY THAT HE THINKS IS REAL.
YEARS AGO, SHE HAD BARRY DRESS UP TO SURPRISE HIM.
THIS YEAR, SHE'S GOT ME JUMPING OUTTA THE CAKE AT THE END.
ZZTTT
ZZTTT
I KNOW THAT SOUND ANYWHERE.
LEAGUE SIGNAL DEVICE.
I DON'T CARRY MINE. MY SON DOES.
WHAT'S WRONG? ANOTHER SENTIENT GALAXY ATTACKING?
D-DAD, I THINK THE PARTY JUST GOT CANCELLED...

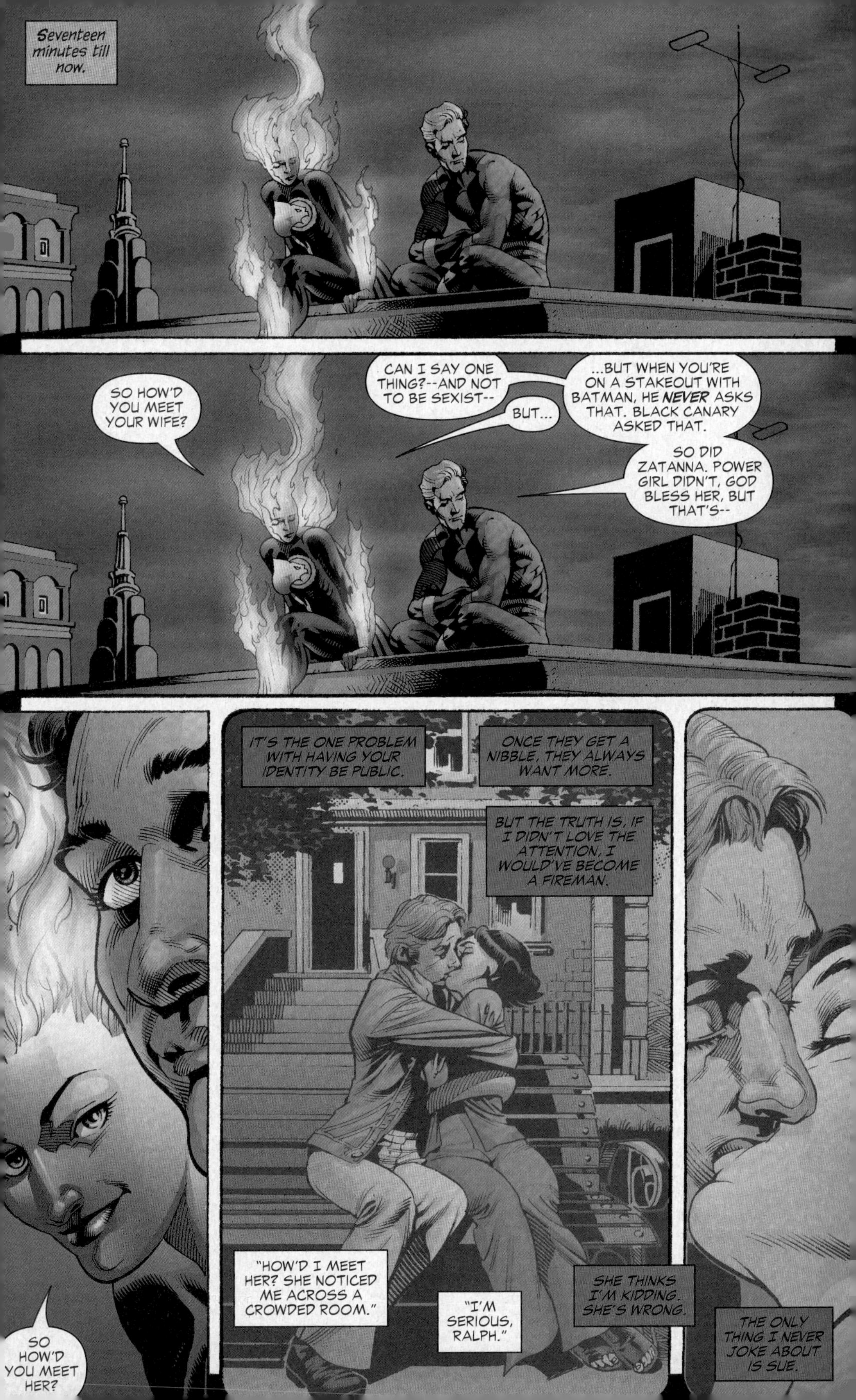
Seventeen minutes till now.
SO HOW'D YOU MEET YOUR WIFE?
CAN I SAY ONE THING?--AND NOT TO BE SEXIST--
BUT...
...BUT WHEN YOU'RE ON A STAKEOUT WITH BATMAN, HE NEVER ASKS THAT. BLACK CANARY ASKED THAT.
SO DID ZATANNA. POWER GIRL DIDN'T, GOD BLESS HER, BUT THAT'S--
IT'S THE ONE PROBLEM WITH HAVING YOUR IDENTITY BE PUBLIC.
ONCE THEY GET A NIBBLE, THEY ALWAYS WANT MORE.
BUT THE TRUTH IS, IF I DIDN'T LOVE THE ATTENTION, I WOULD'VE BECOME A FIREMAN.
SO HOW'D YOU MEET HER?
"HOW'D I MEET HER? SHE NOTICED ME ACROSS A CROWDED ROOM."
"I'M SERIOUS, RALPH."
SHE THINKS I'M KIDDING. SHE'S WRONG.
THE ONLY THING I NEVER JOKE ABOUT IS SUE.

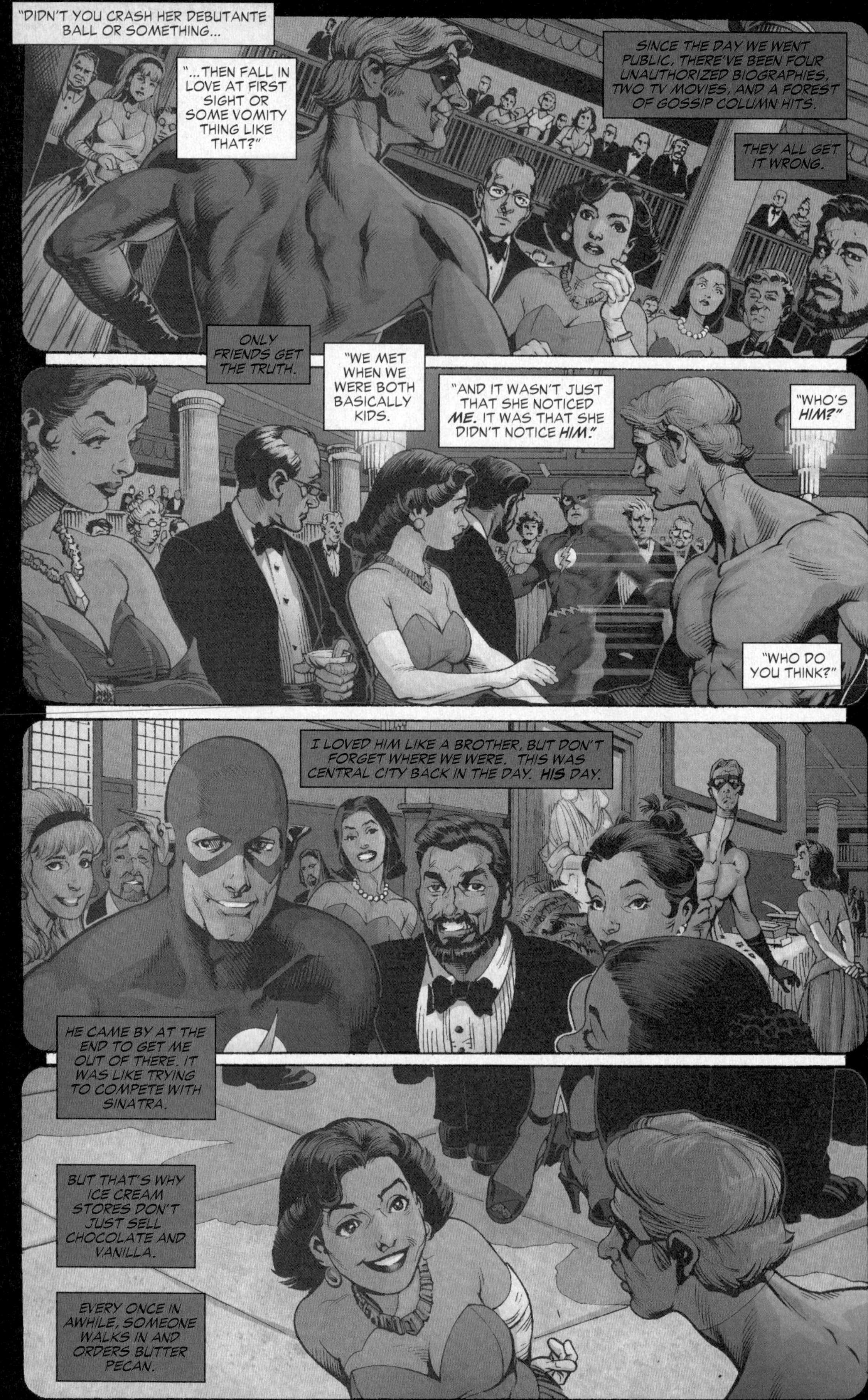
"DIDN'T YOU CRASH HER DEBUTANTE BALL OR SOMETHING...
"...THEN FALL IN LOVE AT FIRST SIGHT OR SOME VOMITY THING LIKE THAT?"
SINCE THE DAY WE WENT PUBLIC, THERE'VE BEEN FOUR UNAUTHORIZED BIOGRAPHIES, TWO TV MOVIES, AND A FOREST OF GOSSIP COLUMN HITS.
THEY ALL GET IT WRONG.
ONLY FRIENDS GET THE TRUTH.
"WE MET WHEN WE WERE BOTH BASICALLY KIDS.
"AND IT WASN'T JUST THAT SHE NOTICED *ME*. IT WAS THAT SHE DIDN'T NOTICE *HIM*."
"WHO'S *HIM?*"
"WHO DO YOU THINK?"
I LOVED HIM LIKE A BROTHER, BUT DON'T FORGET WHERE WE WERE. THIS WAS CENTRAL CITY BACK IN THE DAY. *HIS* DAY.
HE CAME BY AT THE END TO GET ME OUT OF THERE. IT WAS LIKE TRYING TO COMPETE WITH SINATRA.
BUT THAT'S WHY ICE CREAM STORES DON'T JUST SELL CHOCOLATE AND VANILLA.
EVERY ONCE IN AWHILE, SOMEONE WALKS IN AND ORDERS BUTTER PECAN.

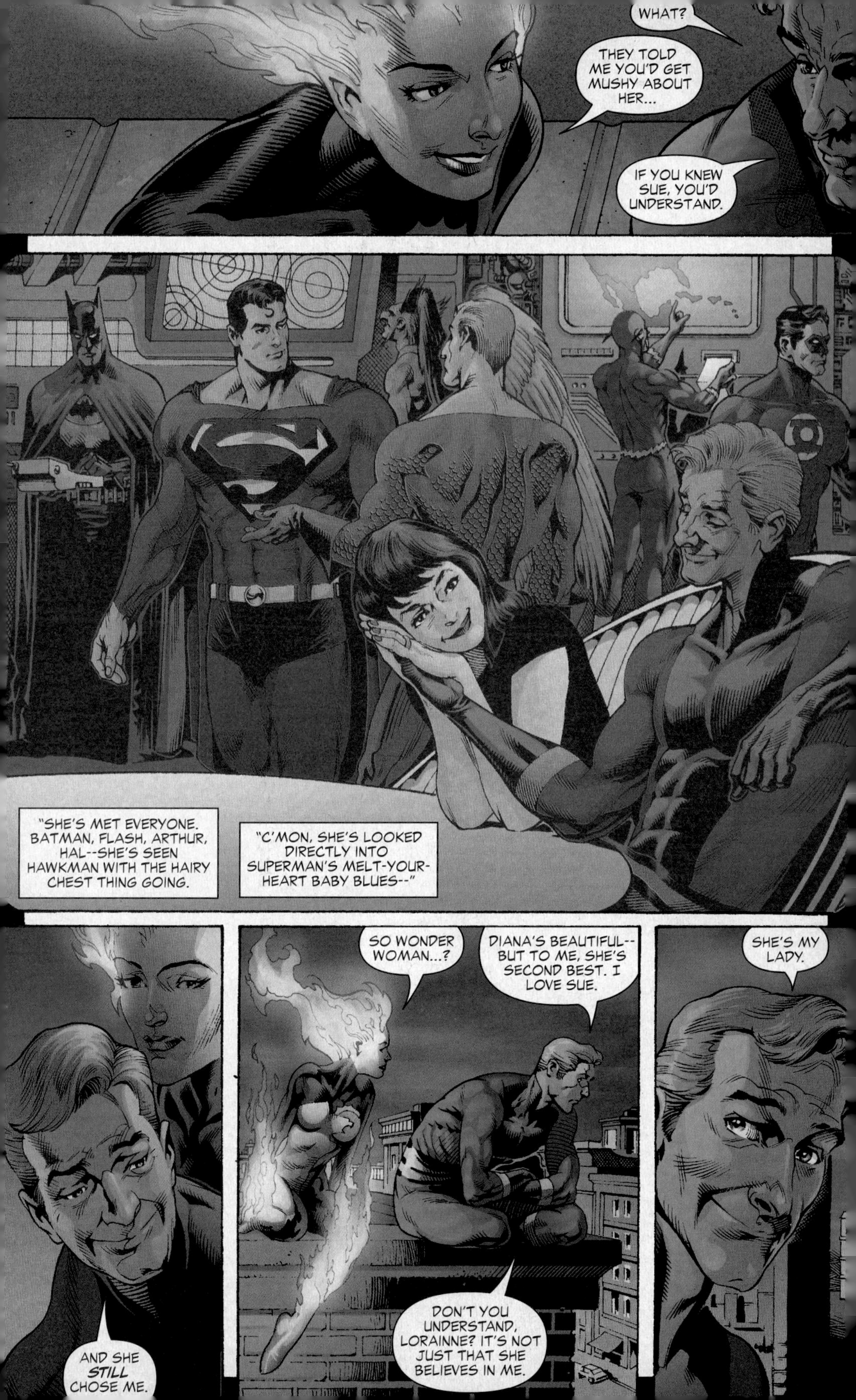
WHAT?
THEY TOLD ME YOU'D GET MUSHY ABOUT HER...
IF YOU KNEW SUE, YOU'D UNDERSTAND.
"SHE'S MET EVERYONE. BATMAN, FLASH, ARTHUR, HAL--SHE'S SEEN HAWKMAN WITH THE HAIRY CHEST THING GOING.
"C'MON, SHE'S LOOKED DIRECTLY INTO SUPERMAN'S MELT-YOUR-HEART BABY BLUES--"
AND SHE STILL CHOSE ME.
SO WONDER WOMAN...?
DIANA'S BEAUTIFUL--BUT TO ME, SHE'S SECOND BEST. I LOVE SUE.
DON'T YOU UNDERSTAND, LORAINNE? IT'S NOT JUST THAT SHE BELIEVES IN ME.
SHE'S MY LADY.

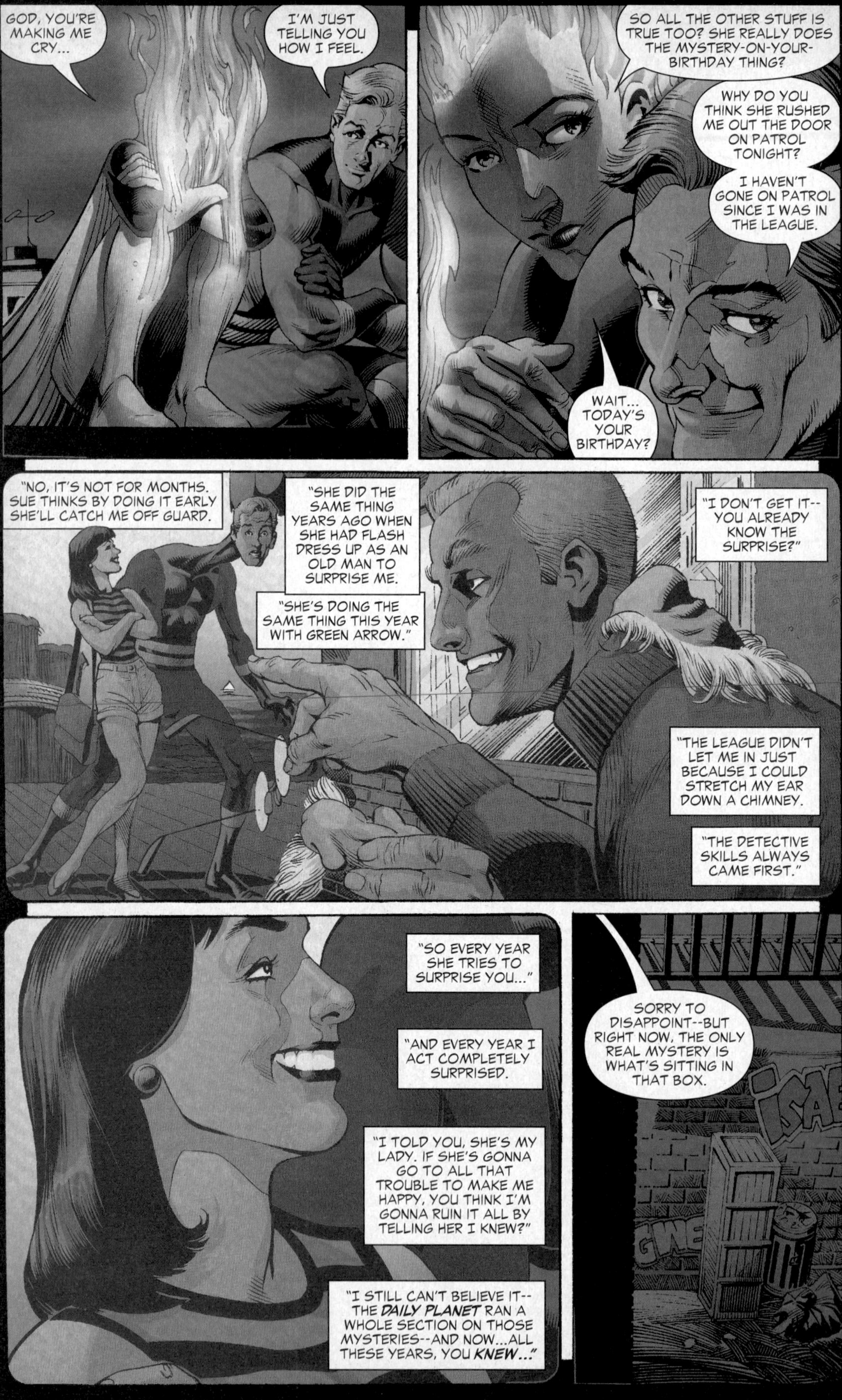
GOD, YOU'RE MAKING ME CRY...
I'M JUST TELLING YOU HOW I FEEL.
SO ALL THE OTHER STUFF IS TRUE TOO? SHE REALLY DOES THE MYSTERY-ON-YOUR-BIRTHDAY THING?
WHY DO YOU THINK SHE RUSHED ME OUT THE DOOR ON PATROL TONIGHT?
I HAVEN'T GONE ON PATROL SINCE I WAS IN THE LEAGUE.
WAIT... TODAY'S YOUR BIRTHDAY?
"NO, IT'S NOT FOR MONTHS. SUE THINKS BY DOING IT EARLY SHE'LL CATCH ME OFF GUARD.
"SHE DID THE SAME THING YEARS AGO WHEN SHE HAD FLASH DRESS UP AS AN OLD MAN TO SURPRISE ME.
"SHE'S DOING THE SAME THING THIS YEAR WITH GREEN ARROW."
"I DON'T GET IT-- YOU ALREADY KNOW THE SURPRISE?"
"THE LEAGUE DIDN'T LET ME IN JUST BECAUSE I COULD STRETCH MY EAR DOWN A CHIMNEY.
"THE DETECTIVE SKILLS ALWAYS CAME FIRST."
"SO EVERY YEAR SHE TRIES TO SURPRISE YOU..."
"AND EVERY YEAR I ACT COMPLETELY SURPRISED.
"I TOLD YOU, SHE'S MY LADY. IF SHE'S GONNA GO TO ALL THAT TROUBLE TO MAKE ME HAPPY, YOU THINK I'M GONNA RUIN IT ALL BY TELLING HER I KNEW?"
"I STILL CAN'T BELIEVE IT-- THE *DAILY PLANET* RAN A WHOLE SECTION ON THOSE MYSTERIES--AND NOW...ALL THESE YEARS, YOU ***KNEW...***"
SORRY TO DISAPPOINT--BUT RIGHT NOW, THE ONLY REAL MYSTERY IS WHAT'S SITTING IN THAT BOX.

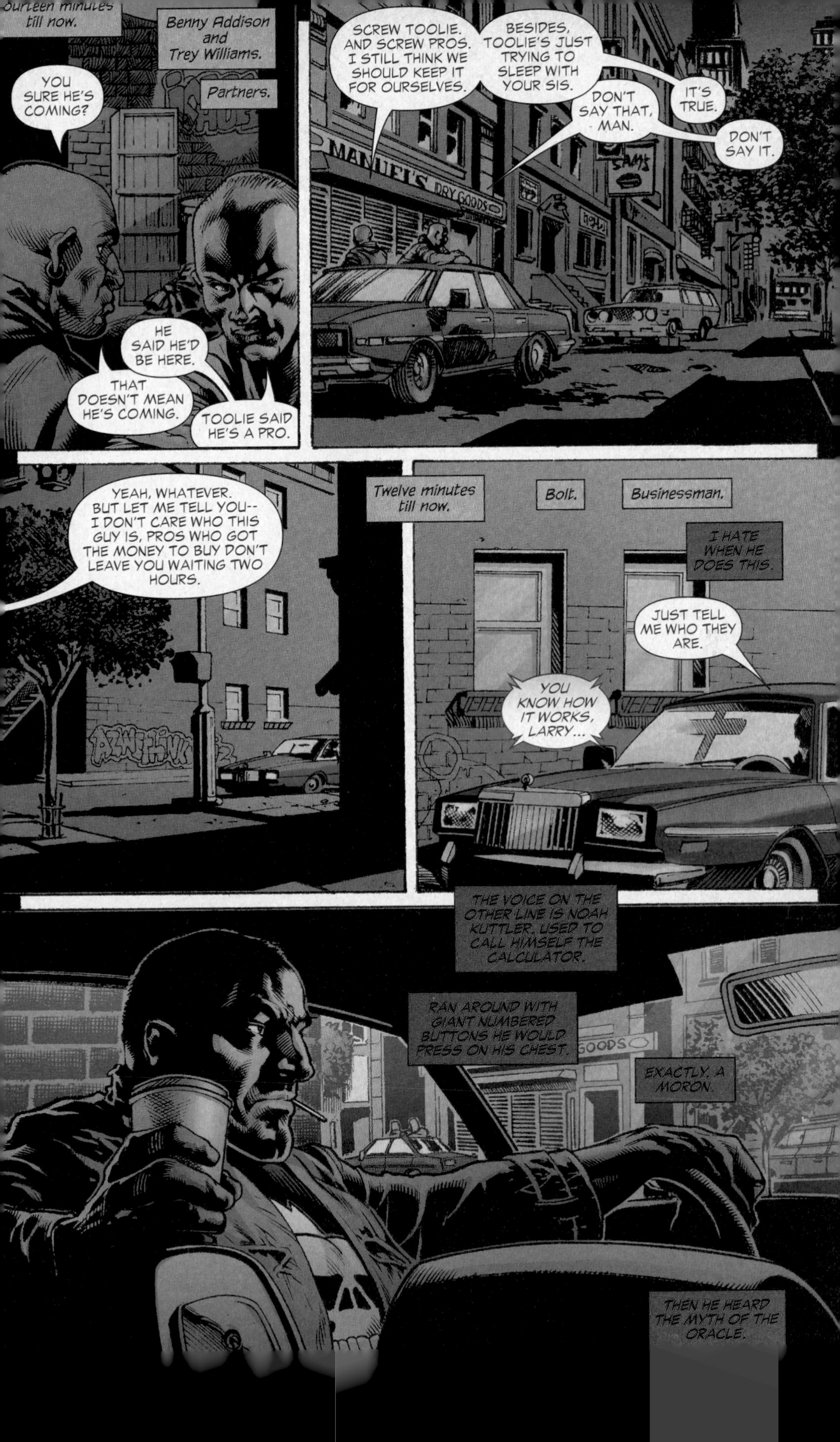

ourteen minutes till now.
Benny Addison and Trey Williams.
Partners.
YOU SURE HE'S COMING?
HE SAID HE'D BE HERE.
THAT DOESN'T MEAN HE'S COMING.
TOOLIE SAID HE'S A PRO.
SCREW TOOLIE. AND SCREW PROS. I STILL THINK WE SHOULD KEEP IT FOR OURSELVES.
BESIDES, TOOLIE'S JUST TRYING TO SLEEP WITH YOUR SIS.
IT'S TRUE.
DON'T SAY THAT, MAN.
DON'T SAY IT.
MANUEL'S DRY GOODS
SAM'S
YEAH, WHATEVER. BUT LET ME TELL YOU-- I DON'T CARE WHO THIS GUY IS, PROS WHO GOT THE MONEY TO BUY DON'T LEAVE YOU WAITING TWO HOURS.
Twelve minutes till now.
Bolt.
Businessman.
I HATE WHEN HE DOES THIS.
JUST TELL ME WHO THEY ARE.
YOU KNOW HOW IT WORKS, LARRY...
THE VOICE ON THE OTHER LINE IS NOAH KUTTLER. USED TO CALL HIMSELF THE CALCULATOR.
RAN AROUND WITH GIANT NUMBERED BUTTONS HE WOULD PRESS ON HIS CHEST.
EXACTLY. A MORON.
THEN HE HEARD THE MYTH OF THE ORACLE.

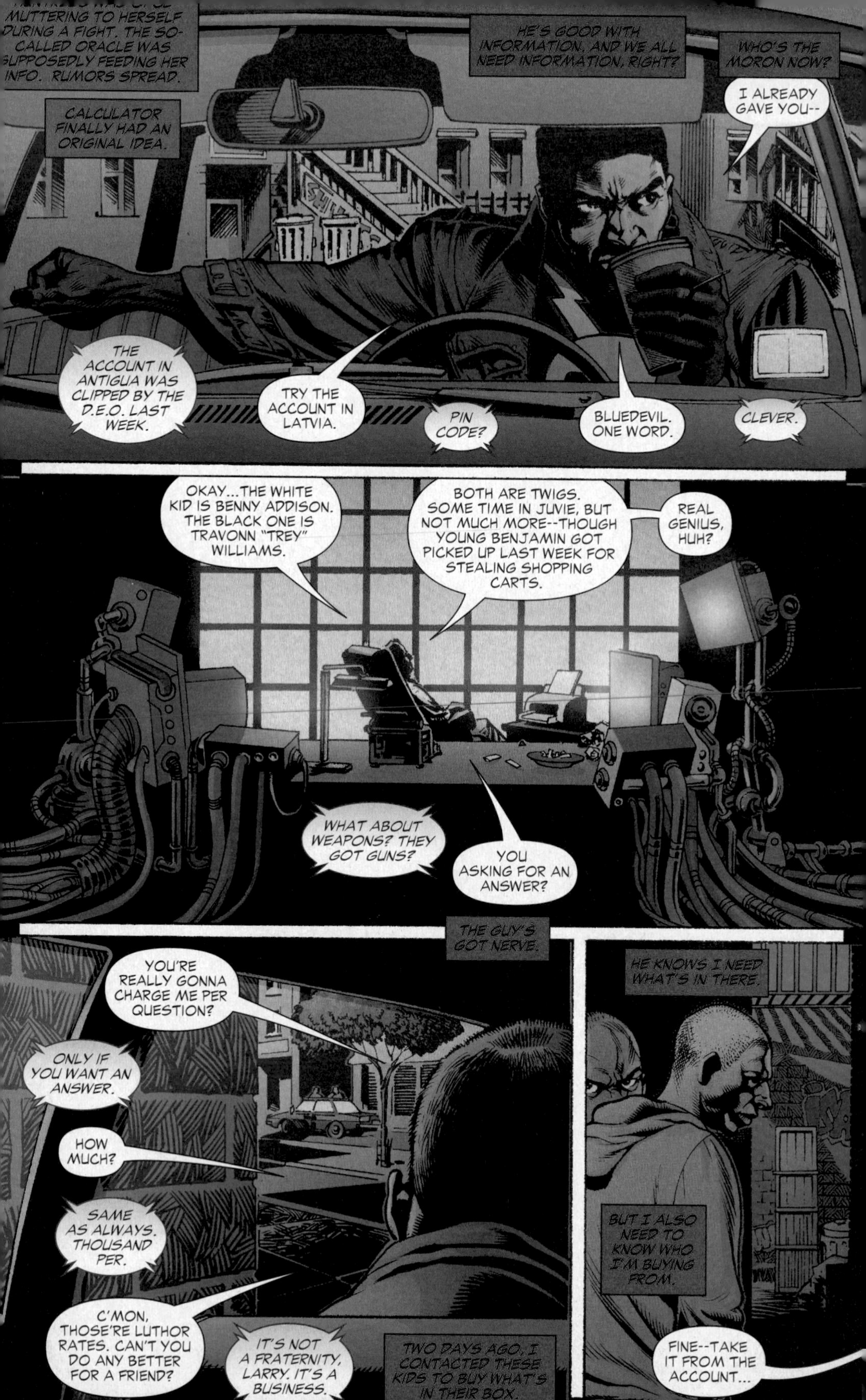
MUTTERING TO HERSELF DURING A FIGHT. THE SO-CALLED ORACLE WAS SUPPOSEDLY FEEDING HER INFO. RUMORS SPREAD.
CALCULATOR FINALLY HAD AN ORIGINAL IDEA.
HE'S GOOD WITH INFORMATION, AND WE ALL NEED INFORMATION, RIGHT?
WHO'S THE MORON NOW?
I ALREADY GAVE YOU--
THE ACCOUNT IN ANTIGUA WAS CLIPPED BY THE D.E.O. LAST WEEK.
TRY THE ACCOUNT IN LATVIA.
PIN CODE?
BLUEDEVIL. ONE WORD.
CLEVER.
OKAY...THE WHITE KID IS BENNY ADDISON. THE BLACK ONE IS TRAVONN "TREY" WILLIAMS.
BOTH ARE TWIGS. SOME TIME IN JUVIE, BUT NOT MUCH MORE--THOUGH YOUNG BENJAMIN GOT PICKED UP LAST WEEK FOR STEALING SHOPPING CARTS.
REAL GENIUS, HUH?
WHAT ABOUT WEAPONS? THEY GOT GUNS?
YOU ASKING FOR AN ANSWER?
THE GUY'S GOT NERVE.
YOU'RE REALLY GONNA CHARGE ME PER QUESTION?
ONLY IF YOU WANT AN ANSWER.
HOW MUCH?
SAME AS ALWAYS. THOUSAND PER.
C'MON, THOSE'RE LUTHOR RATES. CAN'T YOU DO ANY BETTER FOR A FRIEND?
IT'S NOT A FRATERNITY, LARRY. IT'S A BUSINESS.
TWO DAYS AGO, I CONTACTED THESE KIDS TO BUY WHAT'S IN THEIR BOX.
HE KNOWS I NEED WHAT'S IN THERE.
BUT I ALSO NEED TO KNOW WHO I'M BUYING FROM.
FINE--TAKE IT FROM THE ACCOUNT...

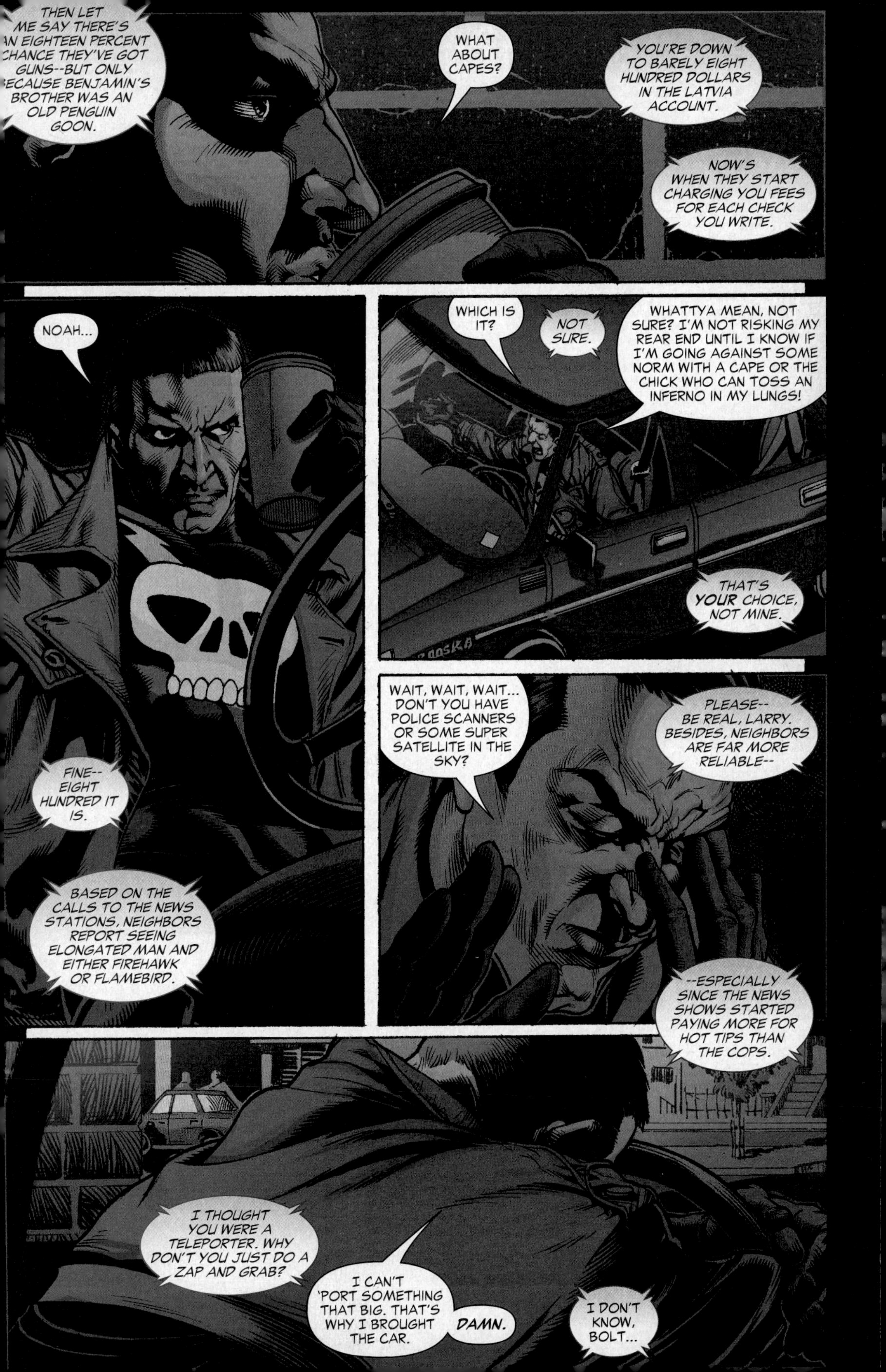
THEN LET ME SAY THERE'S AN EIGHTEEN PERCENT CHANCE THEY'VE GOT GUNS--BUT ONLY BECAUSE BENJAMIN'S BROTHER WAS AN OLD PENGUIN GOON.
WHAT ABOUT CAPES?
YOU'RE DOWN TO BARELY EIGHT HUNDRED DOLLARS IN THE LATVIA ACCOUNT.
NOW'S WHEN THEY START CHARGING YOU FEES FOR EACH CHECK YOU WRITE.
NOAH...
FINE-- EIGHT HUNDRED IT IS.
BASED ON THE CALLS TO THE NEWS STATIONS, NEIGHBORS REPORT SEEING ELONGATED MAN AND EITHER FIREHAWK OR FLAMEBIRD.
WHICH IS IT?
NOT SURE.
WHATTYA MEAN, NOT SURE? I'M NOT RISKING MY REAR END UNTIL I KNOW IF I'M GOING AGAINST SOME NORM WITH A CAPE OR THE CHICK WHO CAN TOSS AN INFERNO IN MY LUNGS!
THAT'S YOUR CHOICE, NOT MINE.
WAIT, WAIT, WAIT... DON'T YOU HAVE POLICE SCANNERS OR SOME SUPER SATELLITE IN THE SKY?
PLEASE-- BE REAL, LARRY. BESIDES, NEIGHBORS ARE FAR MORE RELIABLE--
--ESPECIALLY SINCE THE NEWS SHOWS STARTED PAYING MORE FOR HOT TIPS THAN THE COPS.
I THOUGHT YOU WERE A TELEPORTER. WHY DON'T YOU JUST DO A ZAP AND GRAB?
I CAN'T 'PORT SOMETHING THAT BIG. THAT'S WHY I BROUGHT THE CAR.
DAMN.
I DON'T KNOW, BOLT...

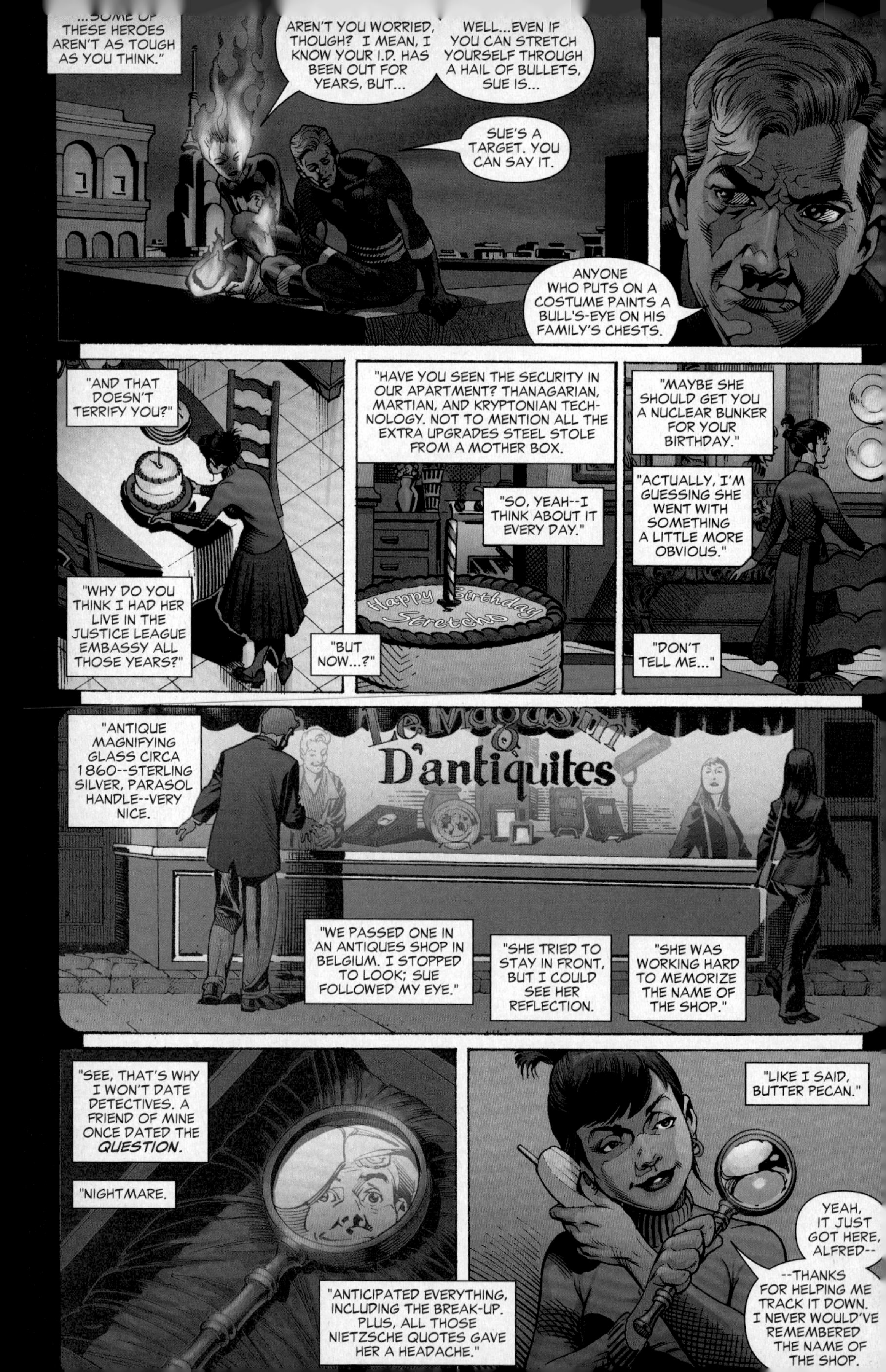

...SOME OF THESE HEROES AREN'T AS TOUGH AS YOU THINK."
AREN'T YOU WORRIED, THOUGH? I MEAN, I KNOW YOUR I.D. HAS BEEN OUT FOR YEARS, BUT...
WELL...EVEN IF YOU CAN STRETCH YOURSELF THROUGH A HAIL OF BULLETS, SUE IS...
SUE'S A TARGET. YOU CAN SAY IT.
ANYONE WHO PUTS ON A COSTUME PAINTS A BULL'S-EYE ON HIS FAMILY'S CHESTS.
"AND THAT DOESN'T TERRIFY YOU?"
"WHY DO YOU THINK I HAD HER LIVE IN THE JUSTICE LEAGUE EMBASSY ALL THOSE YEARS?"
"HAVE YOU SEEN THE SECURITY IN OUR APARTMENT? THANAGARIAN, MARTIAN, AND KRYPTONIAN TECH-NOLOGY. NOT TO MENTION ALL THE EXTRA UPGRADES STEEL STOLE FROM A MOTHER BOX.
"SO, YEAH--I THINK ABOUT IT EVERY DAY."
Happy Birthday
"BUT NOW...?"
"MAYBE SHE SHOULD GET YOU A NUCLEAR BUNKER FOR YOUR BIRTHDAY."
"ACTUALLY, I'M GUESSING SHE WENT WITH SOMETHING A LITTLE MORE OBVIOUS."
"DON'T TELL ME..."
"ANTIQUE MAGNIFYING GLASS CIRCA 1860--STERLING SILVER, PARASOL HANDLE--VERY NICE.
D'antiquites
"WE PASSED ONE IN AN ANTIQUES SHOP IN BELGIUM. I STOPPED TO LOOK; SUE FOLLOWED MY EYE."
"SHE TRIED TO STAY IN FRONT, BUT I COULD SEE HER REFLECTION.
"SHE WAS WORKING HARD TO MEMORIZE THE NAME OF THE SHOP."
"SEE, THAT'S WHY I WON'T DATE DETECTIVES. A FRIEND OF MINE ONCE DATED THE ***QUESTION.***
"NIGHTMARE.
"ANTICIPATED EVERYTHING, INCLUDING THE BREAK-UP. PLUS, ALL THOSE NIETZSCHE QUOTES GAVE HER A HEADACHE."
"LIKE I SAID, BUTTER PECAN."
YEAH, IT JUST GOT HERE, ALFRED--
--THANKS FOR HELPING ME TRACK IT DOWN. I NEVER WOULD'VE REMEMBERED THE NAME OF THE SHOP.

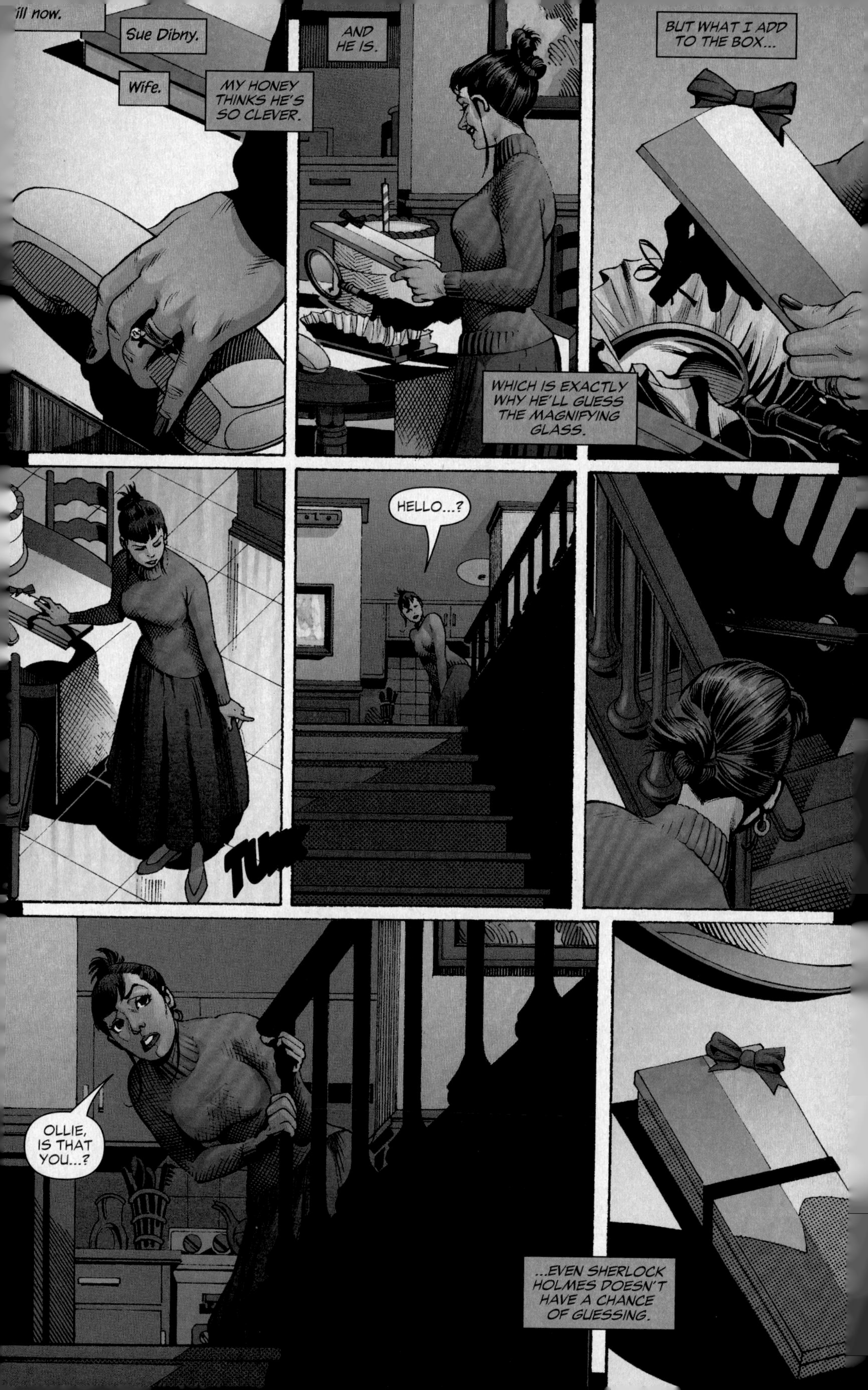

ill now.
Sue Dibny.
Wife.
MY HONEY THINKS HE'S SO CLEVER.
AND HE IS.
WHICH IS EXACTLY WHY HE'LL GUESS THE MAGNIFYING GLASS.
BUT WHAT I ADD TO THE BOX...
TUMP
HELLO...?
OLLIE, IS THAT YOU...?
...EVEN SHERLOCK HOLMES DOESN'T HAVE A CHANCE OF GUESSING.

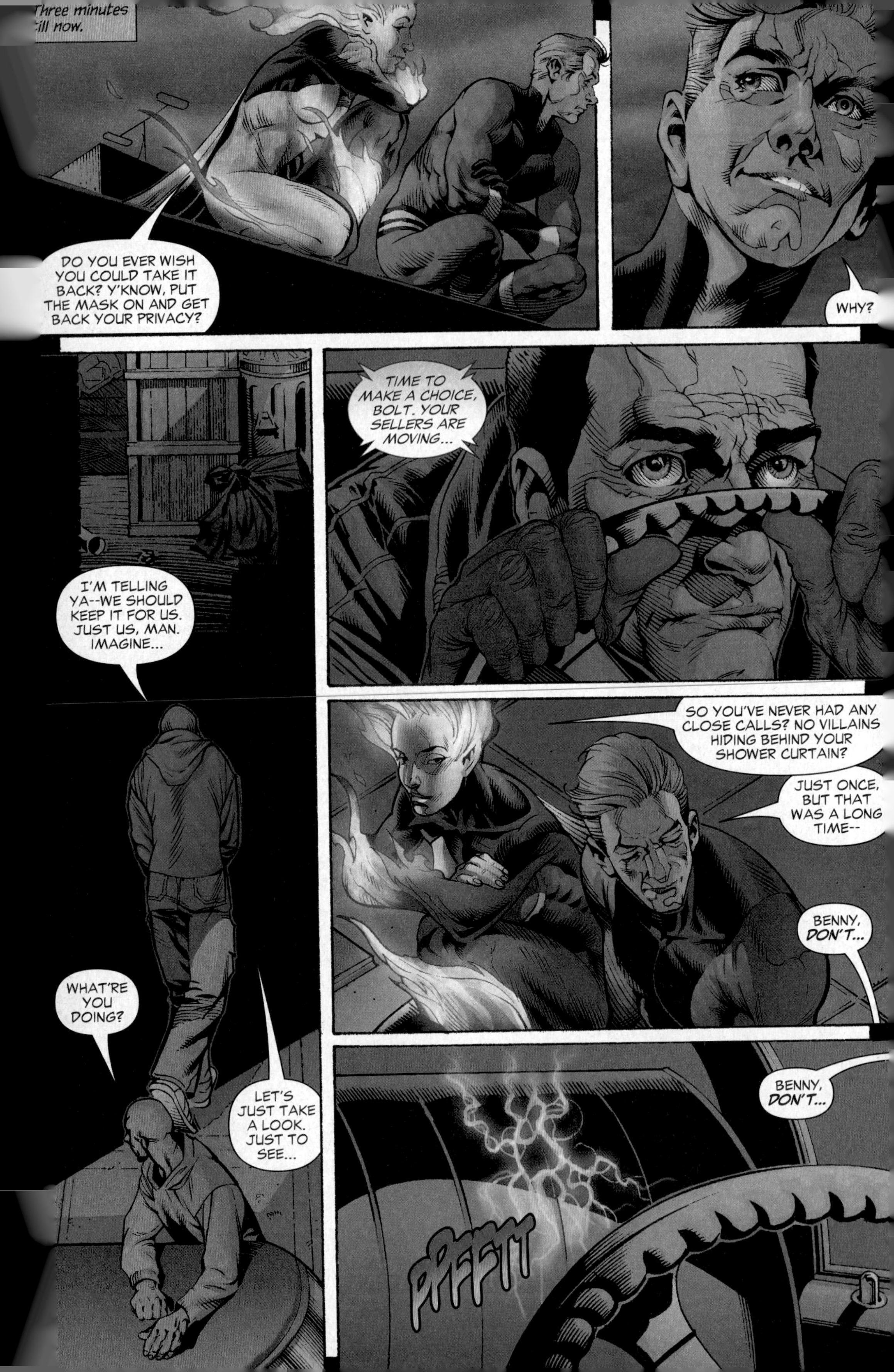

Three minutes till now.
DO YOU EVER WISH YOU COULD TAKE IT BACK? Y'KNOW, PUT THE MASK ON AND GET BACK YOUR PRIVACY?
WHY?
TIME TO MAKE A CHOICE, BOLT. YOUR SELLERS ARE MOVING...
I'M TELLING YA--WE SHOULD KEEP IT FOR US. JUST US, MAN. IMAGINE...
SO YOU'VE NEVER HAD ANY CLOSE CALLS? NO VILLAINS HIDING BEHIND YOUR SHOWER CURTAIN?
JUST ONCE, BUT THAT WAS A LONG TIME--
BENNY, DON'T...
WHAT'RE YOU DOING?
LET'S JUST TAKE A LOOK. JUST TO SEE...
BENNY, DON'T...
PFFTT

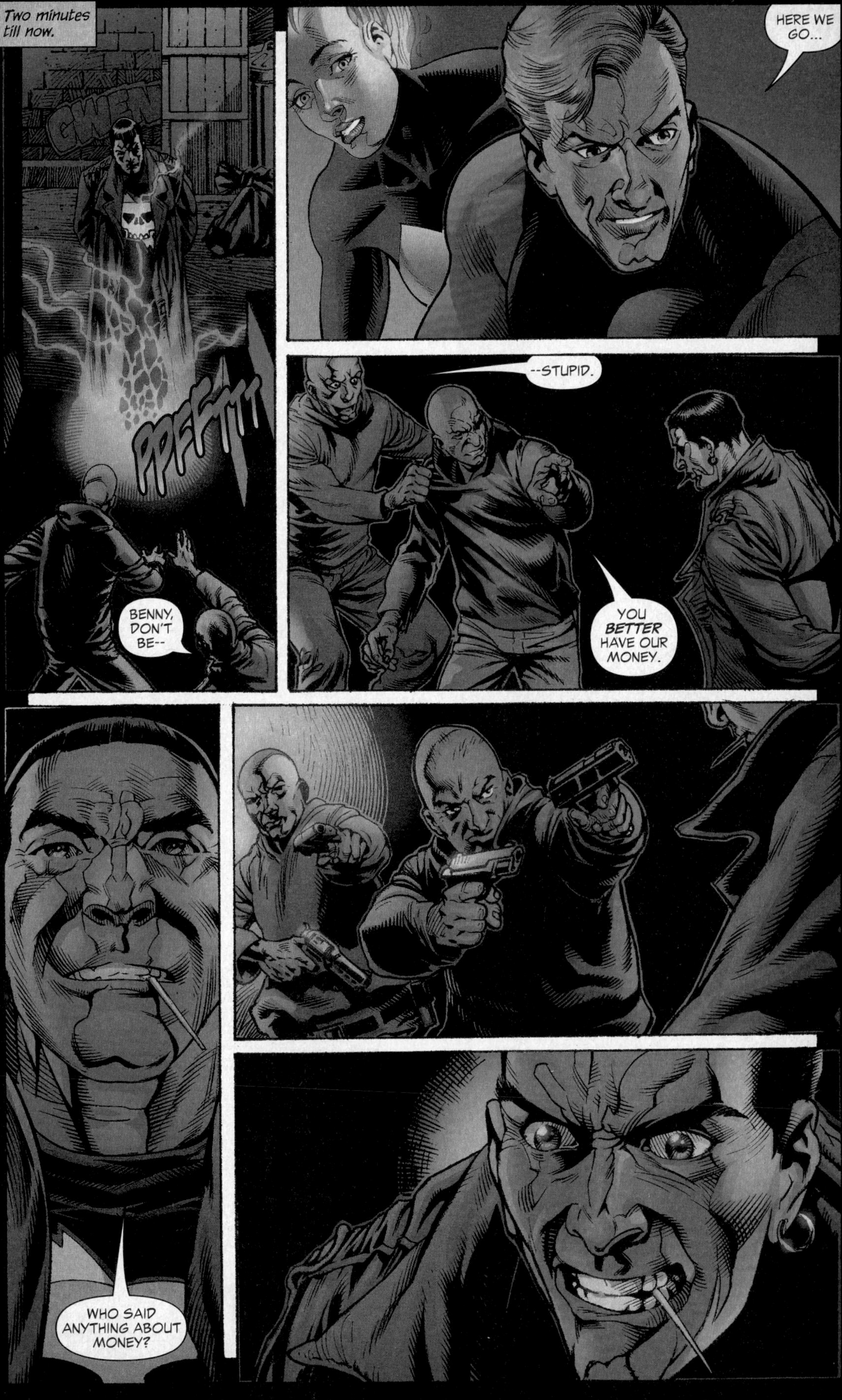
Two minutes till now.
GWEN
PPFFTTT
BENNY, DON'T BE--
--STUPID.
YOU BETTER HAVE OUR MONEY.
HERE WE GO...
WHO SAID ANYTHING ABOUT MONEY?

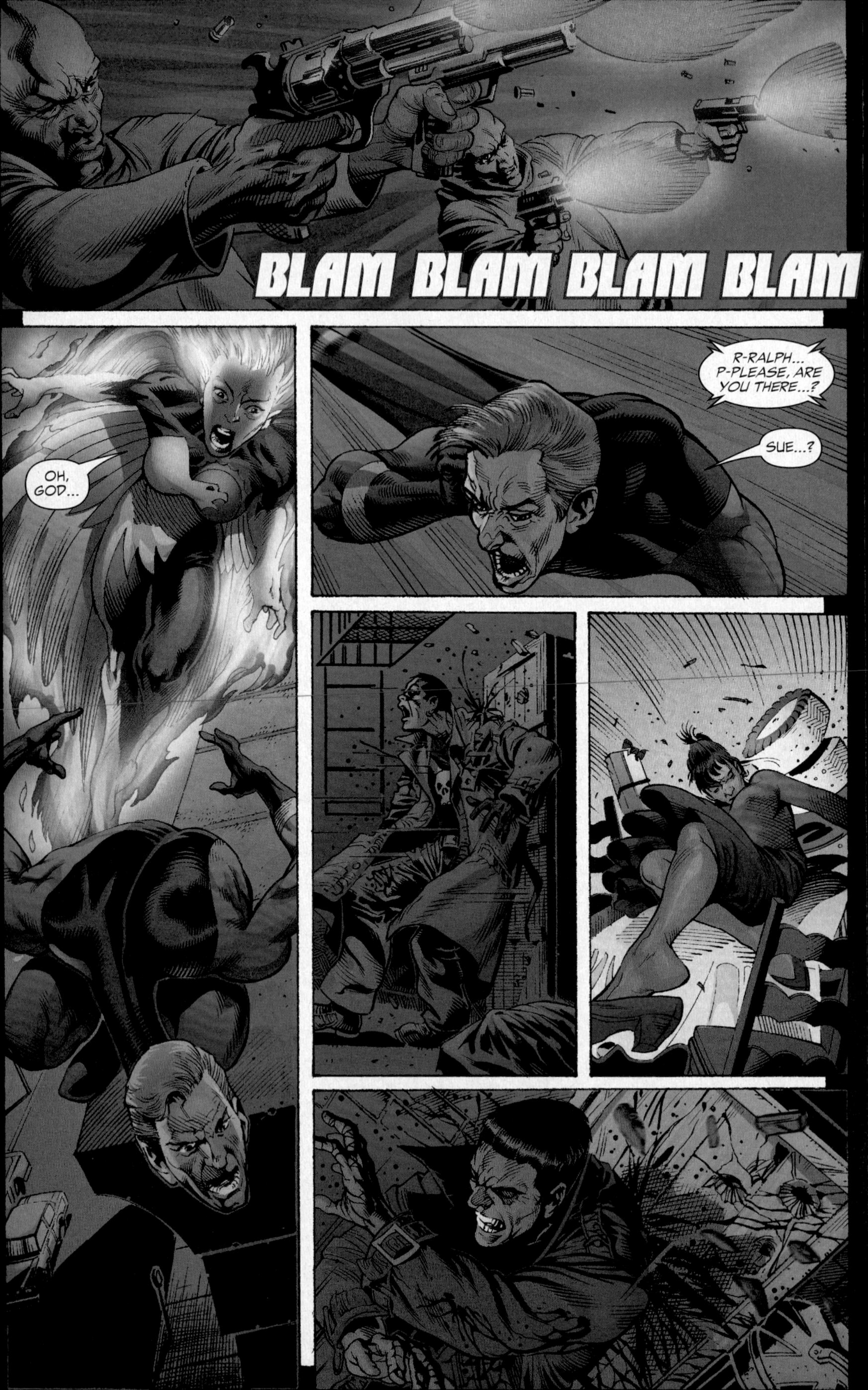
BLAM BLAM BLAM BLAM
OH, GOD...
R-RALPH... P-PLEASE, ARE YOU THERE...?
SUE...?

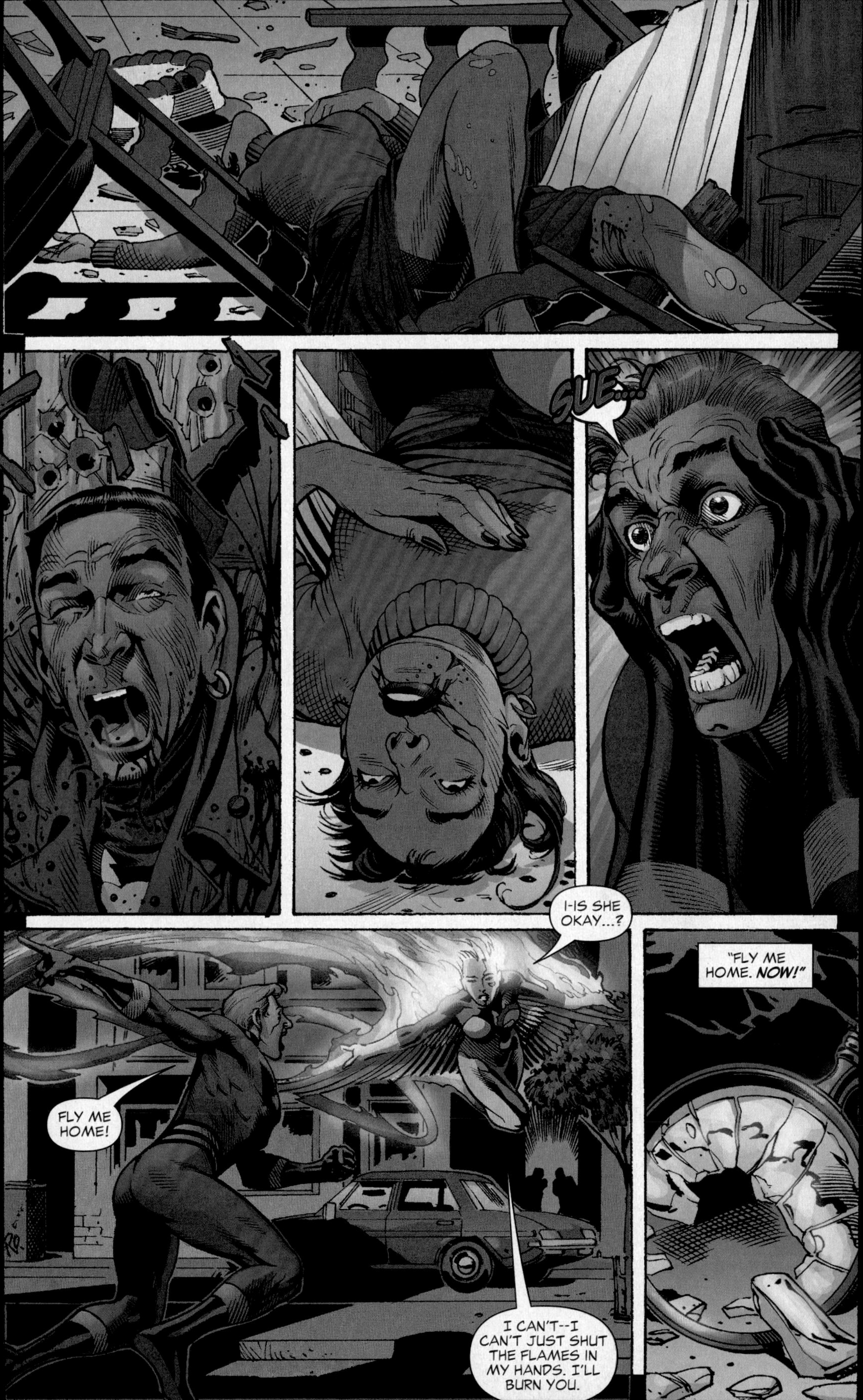
SUE...!
I-IS SHE OKAY...?
FLY ME HOME!
I CAN'T--I CAN'T JUST SHUT THE FLAMES IN MY HANDS. I'LL BURN YOU.
"FLY ME HOME. NOW!"

GOODBYE, SUE...

->HUUUK...
HUUK...
HUUK...<-

FWOOOOOSH!

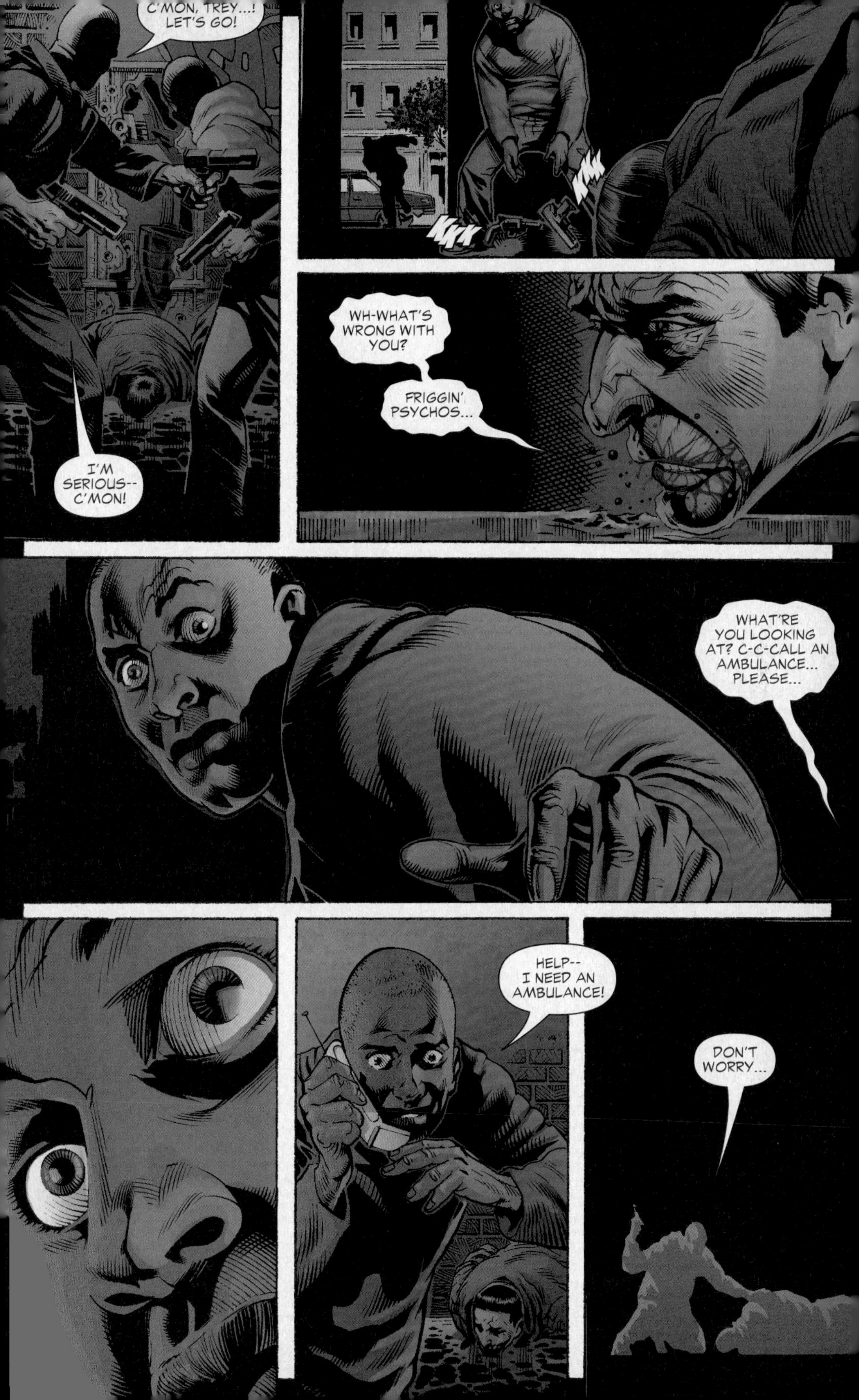
C'MON, TREY...! LET'S GO!
I'M SERIOUS-- C'MON!
KKK
KKK
WH-WHAT'S WRONG WITH YOU?
FRIGGIN' PSYCHOS...
WHAT'RE YOU LOOKING AT? C-C-CALL AN AMBULANCE... PLEASE...
HELP-- I NEED AN AMBULANCE!
DON'T WORRY...

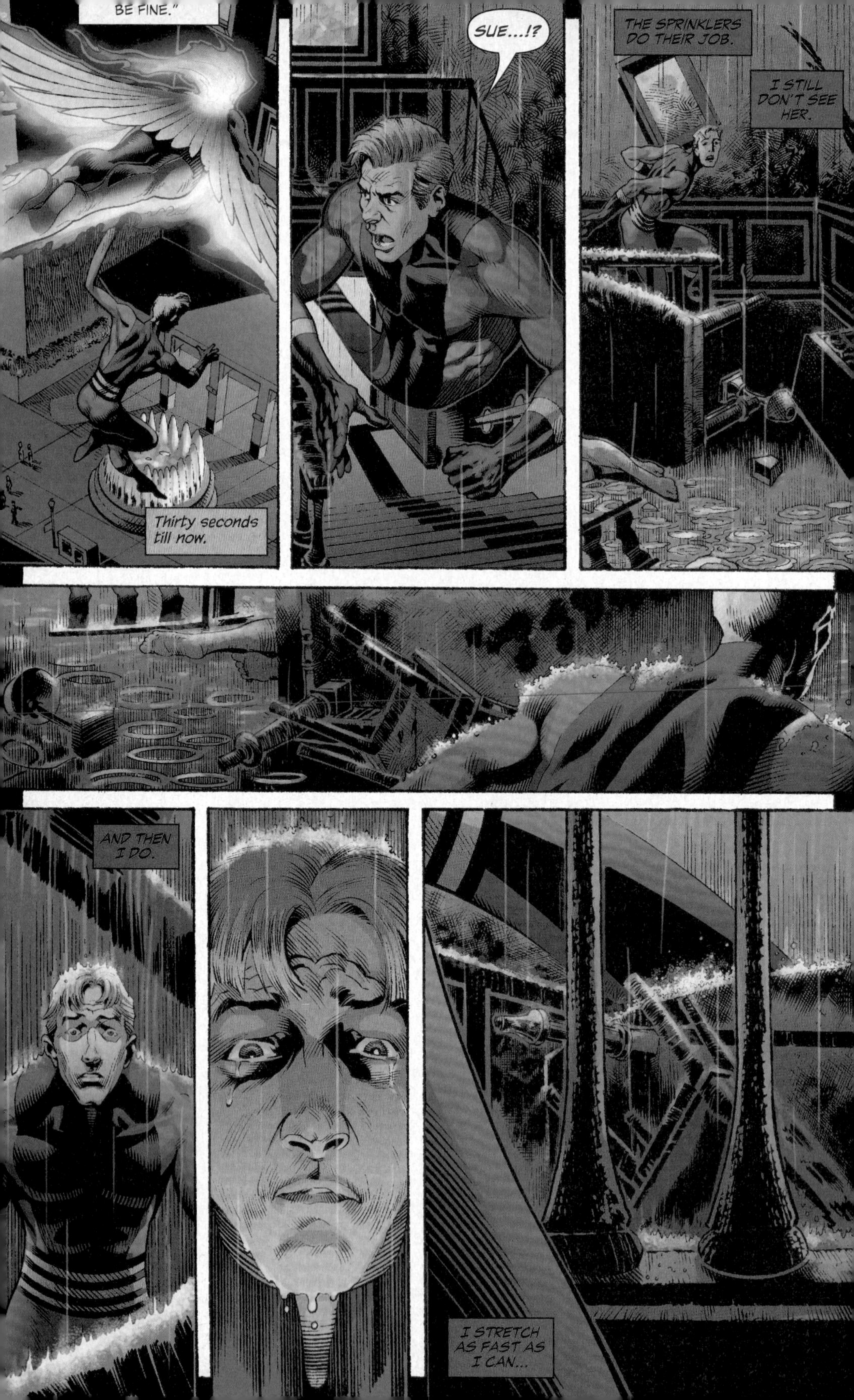
BE FINE."
Thirty seconds
till now.
SUE...!?
THE SPRINKLERS
DO THEIR JOB.
I STILL
DON'T SEE
HER.
AND THEN
I DO.
I STRETCH
AS FAST AS
I CAN...

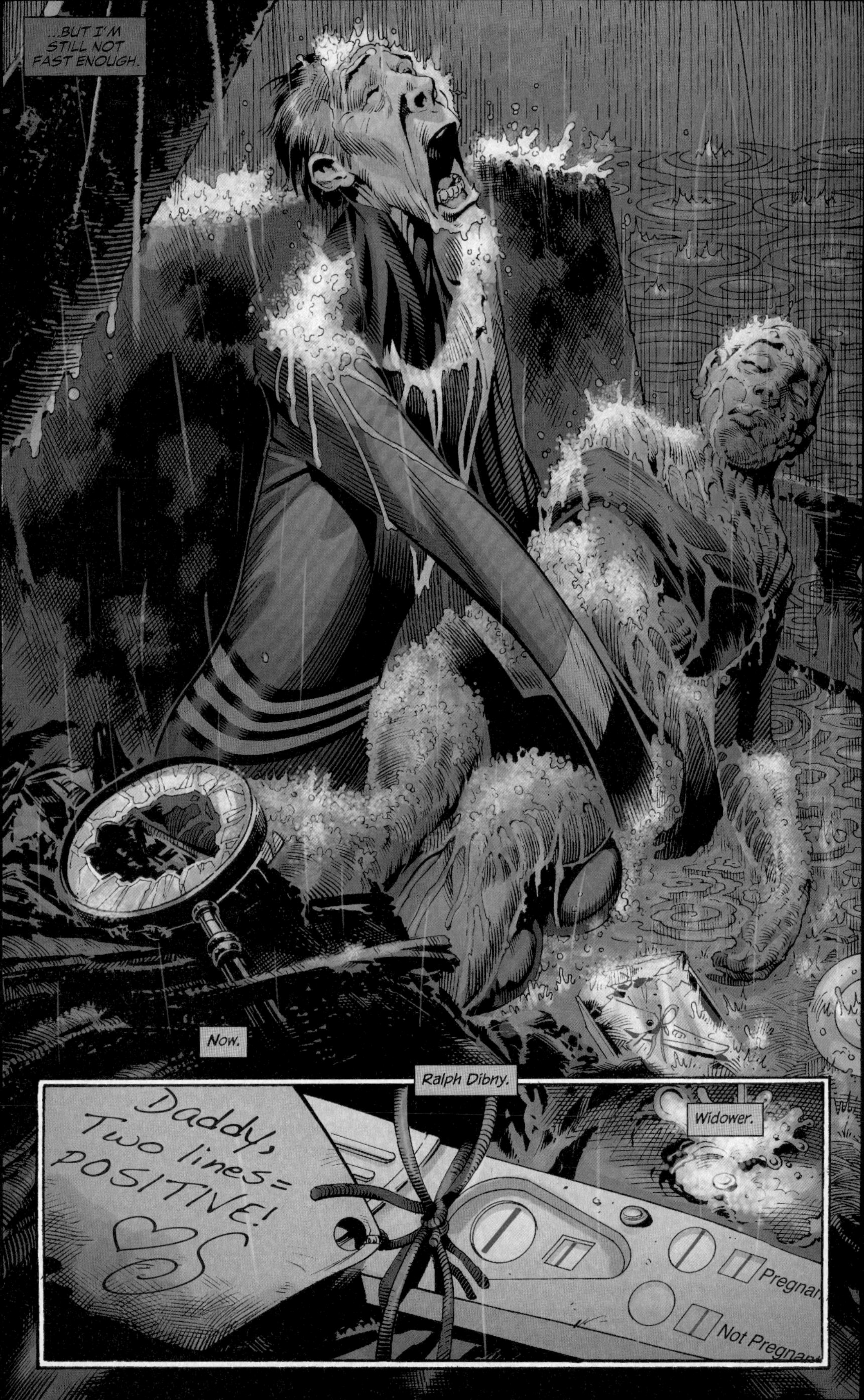
...BUT I'M STILL NOT FAST ENOUGH.
Now.
Ralph Dibny.
Widower.
Daddy, Two lines = POSITIVE!
S
Pregnan
Not Pregnan

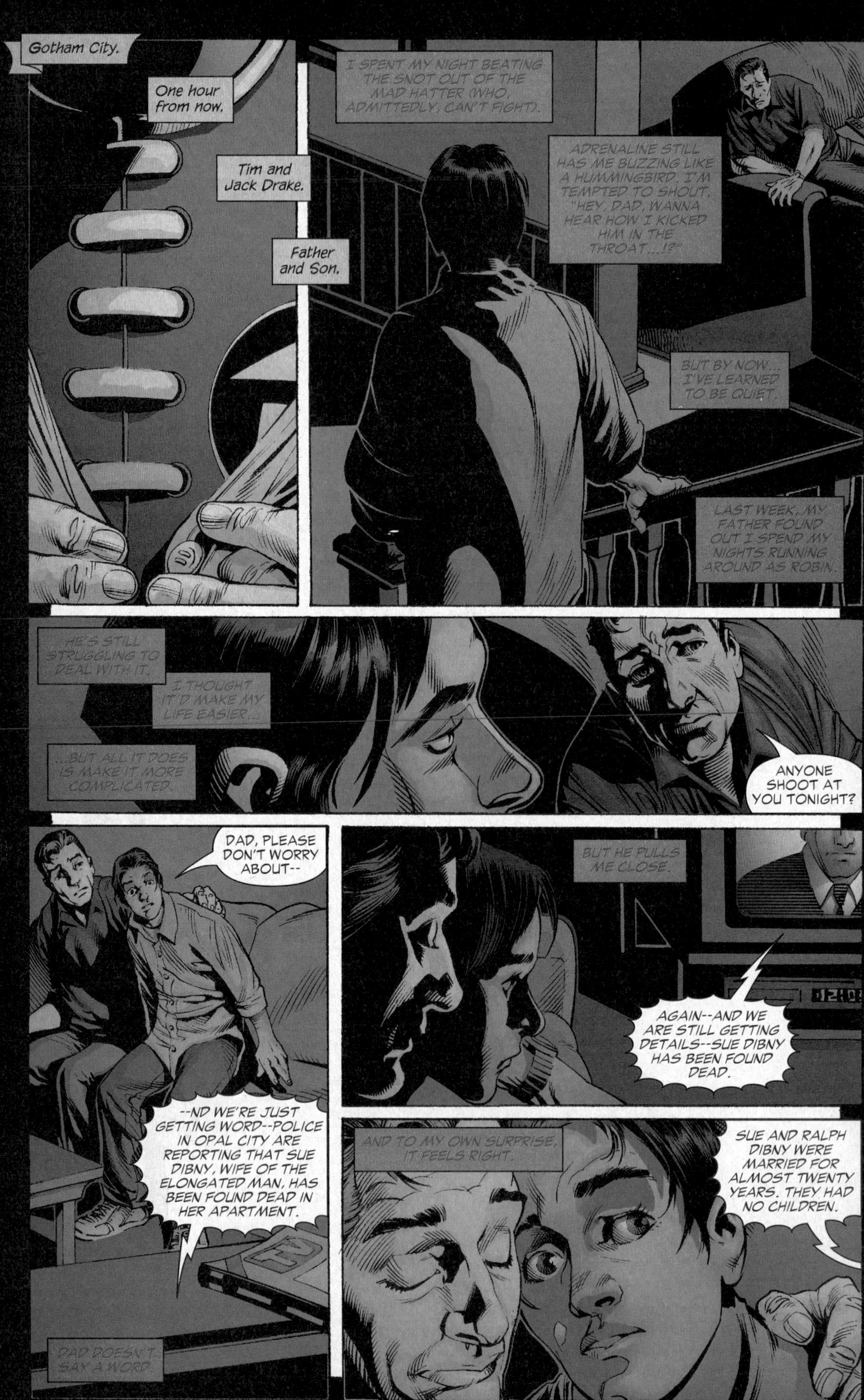
Gotham City.
One hour from now.
Tim and Jack Drake.
Father and Son.
I SPENT MY NIGHT BEATING THE SNOT OUT OF THE MAD HATTER (WHO, ADMITTEDLY, CAN'T FIGHT).
ADRENALINE STILL HAS ME BUZZING LIKE A HUMMINGBIRD. I'M TEMPTED TO SHOUT, "HEY, DAD, WANNA HEAR HOW I KICKED HIM IN THE THROAT...!?"
BUT BY NOW... I'VE LEARNED TO BE QUIET.
LAST WEEK, MY FATHER FOUND OUT I SPEND MY NIGHTS RUNNING AROUND AS ROBIN.
HE'S STILL STRUGGLING TO DEAL WITH IT.
I THOUGHT IT'D MAKE MY LIFE EASIER...
...BUT ALL IT DOES IS MAKE IT MORE COMPLICATED.
ANYONE SHOOT AT YOU TONIGHT?
DAD, PLEASE DON'T WORRY ABOUT--
--ND WE'RE JUST GETTING WORD--POLICE IN OPAL CITY ARE REPORTING THAT SUE DIBNY, WIFE OF THE ELONGATED MAN, HAS BEEN FOUND DEAD IN HER APARTMENT.
DAD DOESN'T SAY A WORD.
BUT HE PULLS ME CLOSE.
AGAIN--AND WE ARE STILL GETTING DETAILS--SUE DIBNY HAS BEEN FOUND DEAD.
AND TO MY OWN SURPRISE, IT FEELS RIGHT.
SUE AND RALPH DIBNY WERE MARRIED FOR ALMOST TWENTY YEARS. THEY HAD NO CHILDREN.

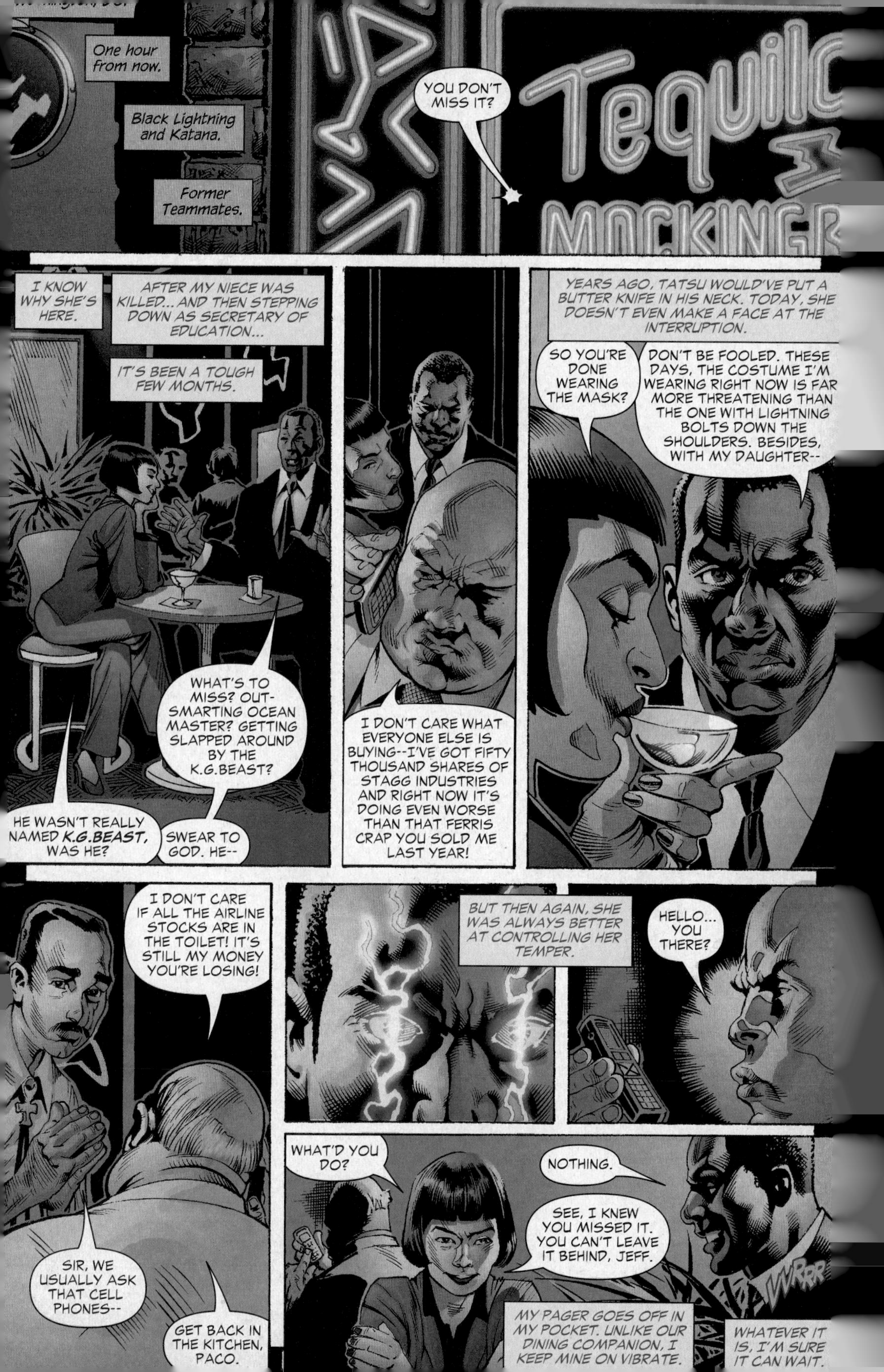
One hour from now.
Black Lightning and Katana.
Former Teammates.
YOU DON'T MISS IT?
Tequila
MOCKINGB
I KNOW WHY SHE'S HERE.
AFTER MY NIECE WAS KILLED... AND THEN STEPPING DOWN AS SECRETARY OF EDUCATION...
IT'S BEEN A TOUGH FEW MONTHS.
WHAT'S TO MISS? OUT-SMARTING OCEAN MASTER? GETTING SLAPPED AROUND BY THE K.G.BEAST?
HE WASN'T REALLY NAMED **K.G.BEAST,** WAS HE?
SWEAR TO GOD. HE--
I DON'T CARE WHAT EVERYONE ELSE IS BUYING--I'VE GOT FIFTY THOUSAND SHARES OF STAGG INDUSTRIES AND RIGHT NOW IT'S DOING EVEN WORSE THAN THAT FERRIS CRAP YOU SOLD ME LAST YEAR!
YEARS AGO, TATSU WOULD'VE PUT A BUTTER KNIFE IN HIS NECK. TODAY, SHE DOESN'T EVEN MAKE A FACE AT THE INTERRUPTION.
SO YOU'RE DONE WEARING THE MASK?
DON'T BE FOOLED. THESE DAYS, THE COSTUME I'M WEARING RIGHT NOW IS FAR MORE THREATENING THAN THE ONE WITH LIGHTNING BOLTS DOWN THE SHOULDERS. BESIDES, WITH MY DAUGHTER--
I DON'T CARE IF ALL THE AIRLINE STOCKS ARE IN THE TOILET! IT'S STILL MY MONEY YOU'RE LOSING!
SIR, WE USUALLY ASK THAT CELL PHONES--
GET BACK IN THE KITCHEN, PACO.
BUT THEN AGAIN, SHE WAS ALWAYS BETTER AT CONTROLLING HER TEMPER.
HELLO... YOU THERE?
WHAT'D YOU DO?
NOTHING.
SEE, I KNEW YOU MISSED IT. YOU CAN'T LEAVE IT BEHIND, JEFF.
VVRRR
MY PAGER GOES OFF IN MY POCKET. UNLIKE OUR DINING COMPANION, I KEEP MINE ON VIBRATE.
WHATEVER IT IS, I'M SURE IT CAN WAIT.

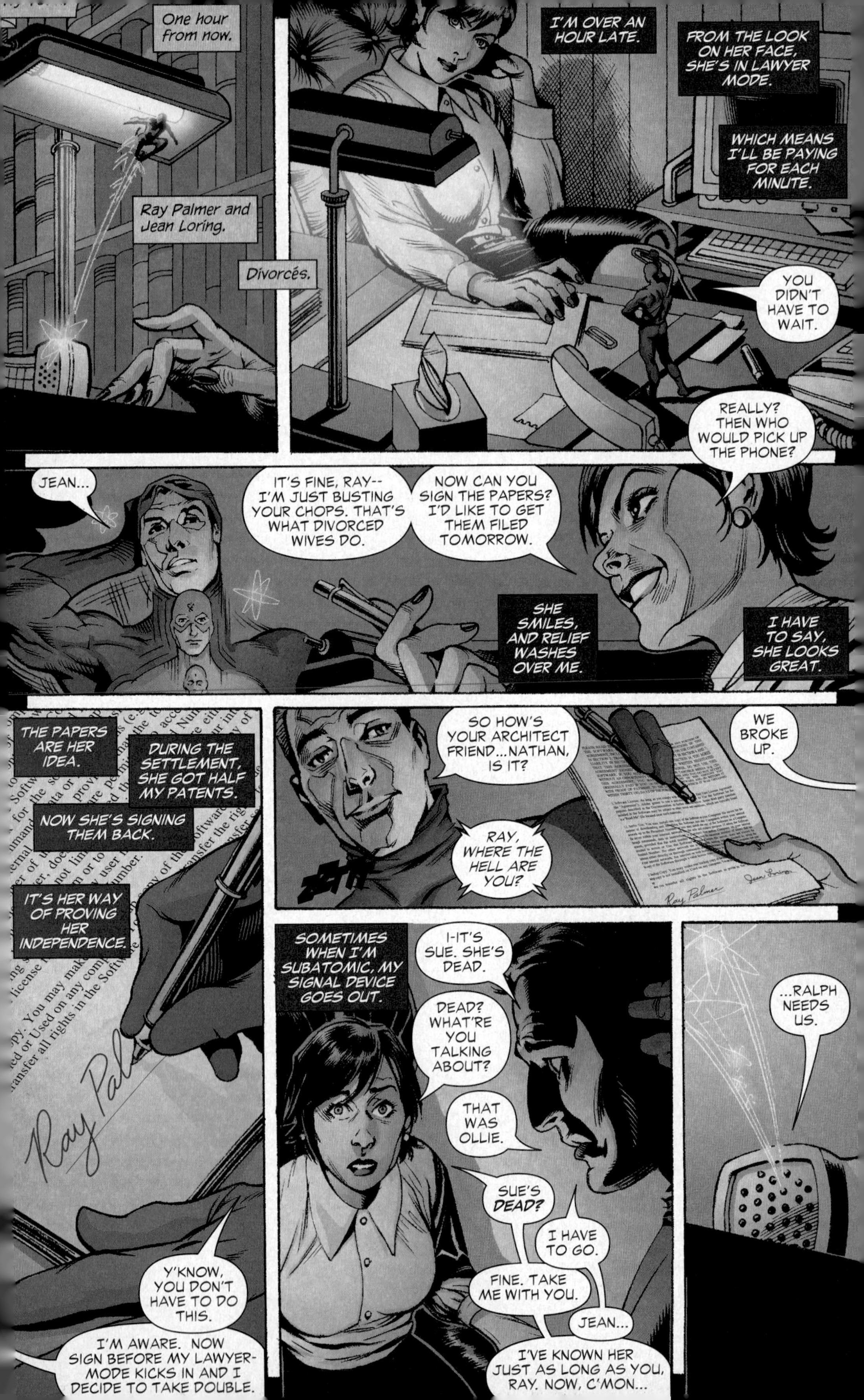
One hour from now.
Ray Palmer and Jean Loring.
Divorcés.
I'M OVER AN HOUR LATE.
FROM THE LOOK ON HER FACE, SHE'S IN LAWYER MODE.
WHICH MEANS I'LL BE PAYING FOR EACH MINUTE.
YOU DIDN'T HAVE TO WAIT.
REALLY? THEN WHO WOULD PICK UP THE PHONE?
JEAN...
IT'S FINE, RAY-- I'M JUST BUSTING YOUR CHOPS. THAT'S WHAT DIVORCED WIVES DO.
NOW CAN YOU SIGN THE PAPERS? I'D LIKE TO GET THEM FILED TOMORROW.
SHE SMILES, AND RELIEF WASHES OVER ME.
I HAVE TO SAY, SHE LOOKS GREAT.
THE PAPERS ARE HER IDEA.
DURING THE SETTLEMENT, SHE GOT HALF MY PATENTS.
NOW SHE'S SIGNING THEM BACK.
IT'S HER WAY OF PROVING HER INDEPENDENCE.
Ray Pal
Y'KNOW, YOU DON'T HAVE TO DO THIS.
I'M AWARE. NOW SIGN BEFORE MY LAWYER-MODE KICKS IN AND I DECIDE TO TAKE DOUBLE.
SO HOW'S YOUR ARCHITECT FRIEND...NATHAN, IS IT?
WE BROKE UP.
RAY, WHERE THE HELL ARE YOU?
Ray Palmer
Jean Loring
SOMETIMES WHEN I'M SUBATOMIC, MY SIGNAL DEVICE GOES OUT.
I-IT'S SUE. SHE'S DEAD.
DEAD? WHAT'RE YOU TALKING ABOUT?
THAT WAS OLLIE.
SUE'S DEAD?
I HAVE TO GO.
FINE. TAKE ME WITH YOU.
JEAN...
I'VE KNOWN HER JUST AS LONG AS YOU, RAY. NOW, C'MON...
...RALPH NEEDS US.

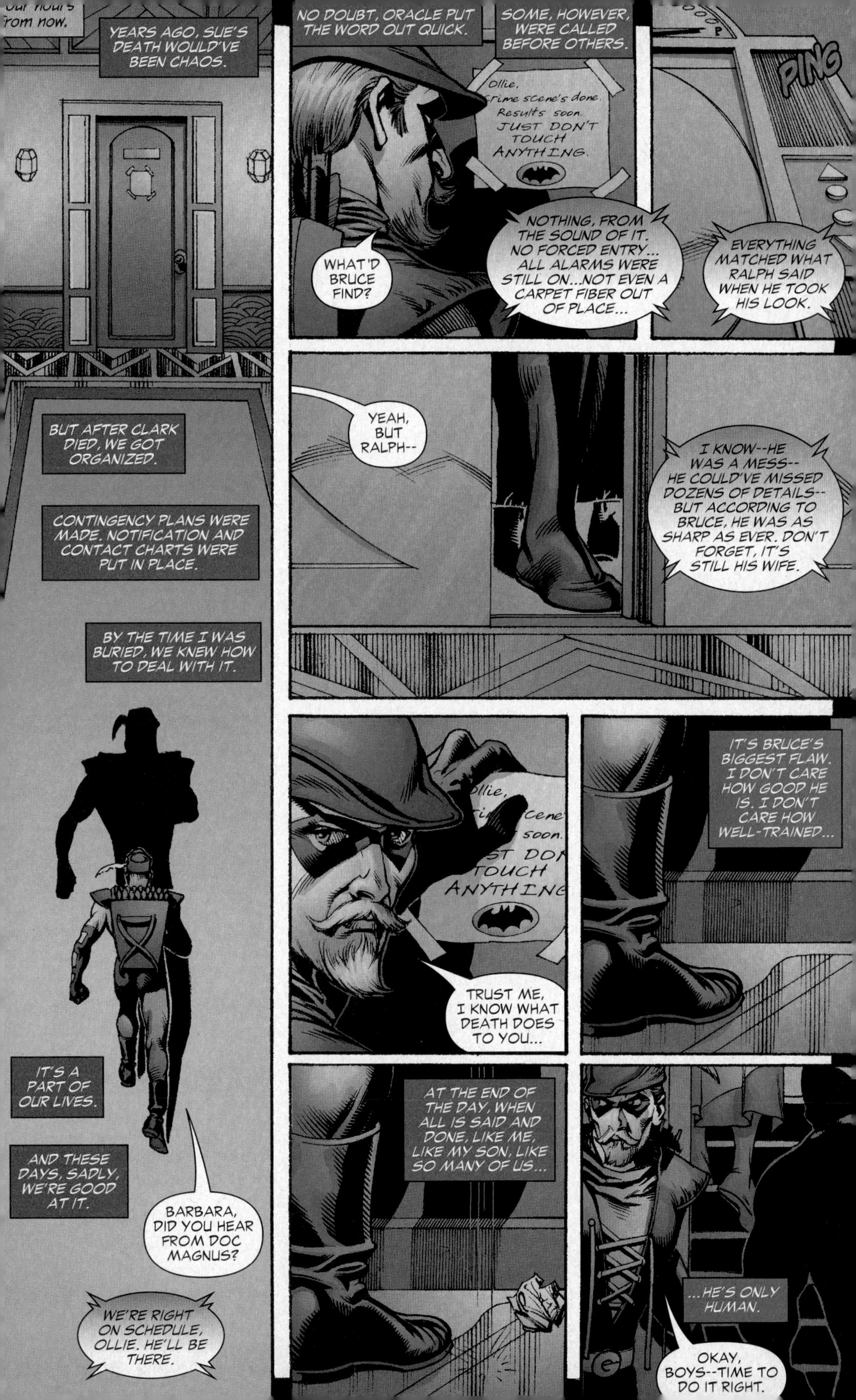
from now.
YEARS AGO, SUE'S DEATH WOULD'VE BEEN CHAOS.
BUT AFTER CLARK DIED, WE GOT ORGANIZED.
CONTINGENCY PLANS WERE MADE. NOTIFICATION AND CONTACT CHARTS WERE PUT IN PLACE.
BY THE TIME I WAS BURIED, WE KNEW HOW TO DEAL WITH IT.
IT'S A PART OF OUR LIVES.
AND THESE DAYS, SADLY, WE'RE GOOD AT IT.
BARBARA, DID YOU HEAR FROM DOC MAGNUS?
WE'RE RIGHT ON SCHEDULE, OLLIE. HE'LL BE THERE.
NO DOUBT, ORACLE PUT THE WORD OUT QUICK.
SOME, HOWEVER, WERE CALLED BEFORE OTHERS.
Ollie, Crime scene's done. Results soon. JUST DON'T TOUCH ANYTHING.
WHAT'D BRUCE FIND?
NOTHING, FROM THE SOUND OF IT. NO FORCED ENTRY... ALL ALARMS WERE STILL ON...NOT EVEN A CARPET FIBER OUT OF PLACE...
PING
EVERYTHING MATCHED WHAT RALPH SAID WHEN HE TOOK HIS LOOK.
YEAH, BUT RALPH--
I KNOW--HE WAS A MESS-- HE COULD'VE MISSED DOZENS OF DETAILS-- BUT ACCORDING TO BRUCE, HE WAS AS SHARP AS EVER. DON'T FORGET, IT'S STILL HIS WIFE.
TRUST ME, I KNOW WHAT DEATH DOES TO YOU...
IT'S BRUCE'S BIGGEST FLAW. I DON'T CARE HOW GOOD HE IS. I DON'T CARE HOW WELL-TRAINED...
AT THE END OF THE DAY, WHEN ALL IS SAID AND DONE, LIKE ME, LIKE MY SON, LIKE SO MANY OF US...
...HE'S ONLY HUMAN.
OKAY, BOYS--TIME TO DO IT RIGHT.

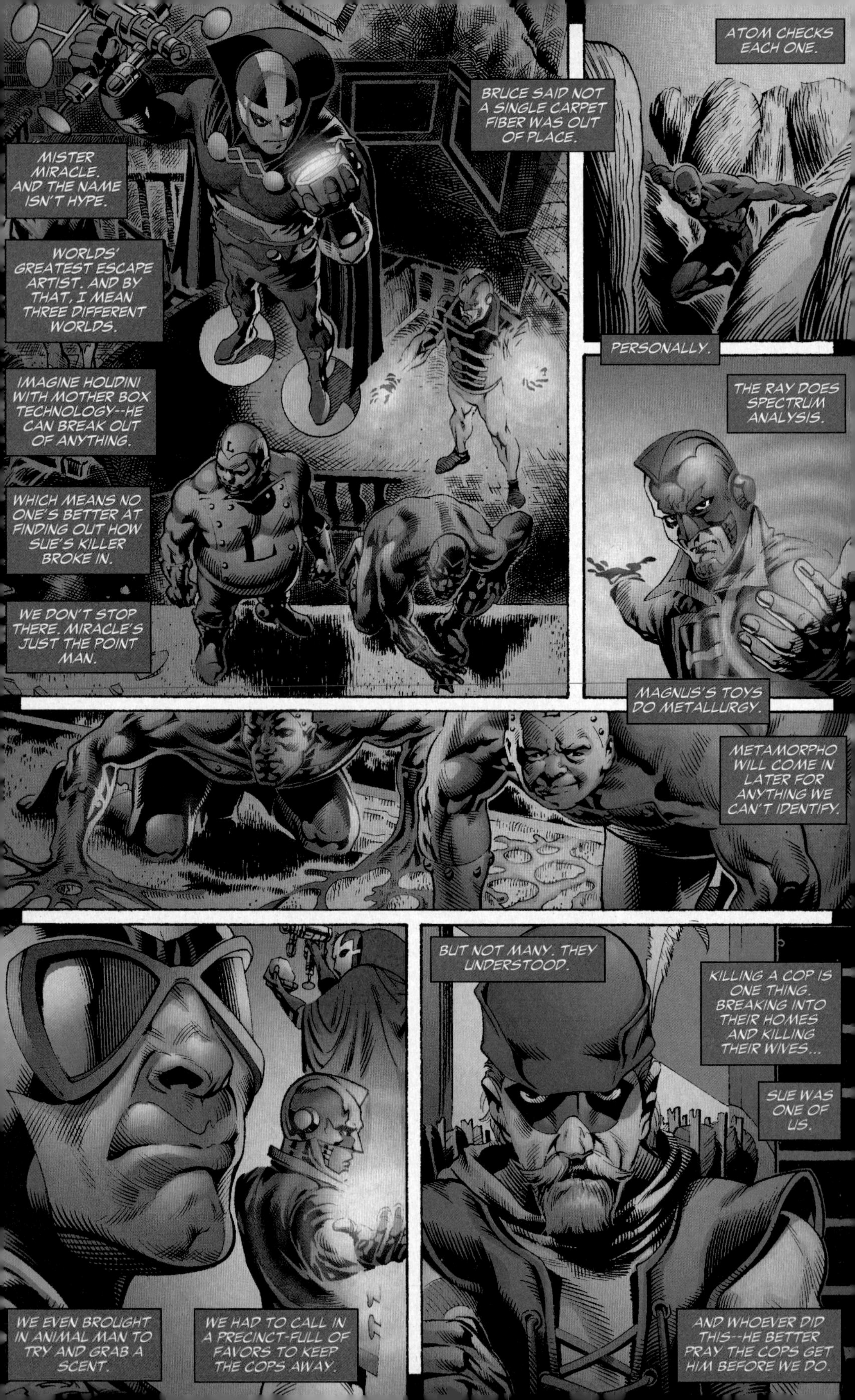
MISTER MIRACLE. AND THE NAME ISN'T HYPE.
WORLDS' GREATEST ESCAPE ARTIST. AND BY THAT, I MEAN THREE DIFFERENT WORLDS.
IMAGINE HOUDINI WITH MOTHER BOX TECHNOLOGY--HE CAN BREAK OUT OF ANYTHING.
WHICH MEANS NO ONE'S BETTER AT FINDING OUT HOW SUE'S KILLER BROKE IN.
WE DON'T STOP THERE. MIRACLE'S JUST THE POINT MAN.
BRUCE SAID NOT A SINGLE CARPET FIBER WAS OUT OF PLACE.
ATOM CHECKS EACH ONE.
PERSONALLY.
THE RAY DOES SPECTRUM ANALYSIS.
MAGNUS'S TOYS DO METALLURGY.
METAMORPHO WILL COME IN LATER FOR ANYTHING WE CAN'T IDENTIFY.
WE EVEN BROUGHT IN ANIMAL MAN TO TRY AND GRAB A SCENT.
WE HAD TO CALL IN A PRECINCT-FULL OF FAVORS TO KEEP THE COPS AWAY.
BUT NOT MANY. THEY UNDERSTOOD.
KILLING A COP IS ONE THING. BREAKING INTO THEIR HOMES AND KILLING THEIR WIVES...
SUE WAS ONE OF US.
AND WHOEVER DID THIS--HE BETTER PRAY THE COPS GET HIM BEFORE WE DO.

Forty-eight hours from now.

THE FUNERAL'S CALLED FOR NOON.

RALPH WANTED IT IN CENTRAL CITY.

WHERE THEY MET.

STILL, SUE'S UNCLE ASKED IF HE COULD TAKE THE BACK CORNER.

WHERE IT'S HEAVIEST.

ON THREE...   ONE...   TWO...

THE FUNERAL HOME GAVE US THE OPTION OF ROLLING IT IN.

WE REFUSED.

TO BE HONEST, CARTER COULD LIFT IT BY HIMSELF.

WE DON'T ARGUE.

WE LIFT TOGETHER.

TO NO ONE'S SURPRISE, MOURNERS CAME FROM AS FAR AWAY AS STAR CITY.

SOME ARE THERE TO HONOR SUE.

LIKE A TEAM.

...THREE.

OTHERS ARE PAYING THEIR RESPECTS TO RALPH.

AND, SAD TO SAY, OTHERS ARE THERE--

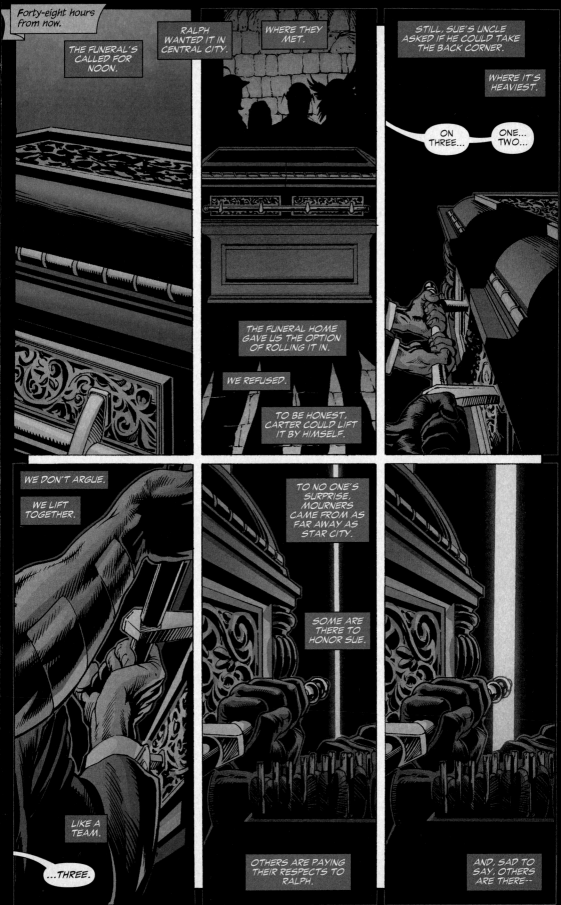

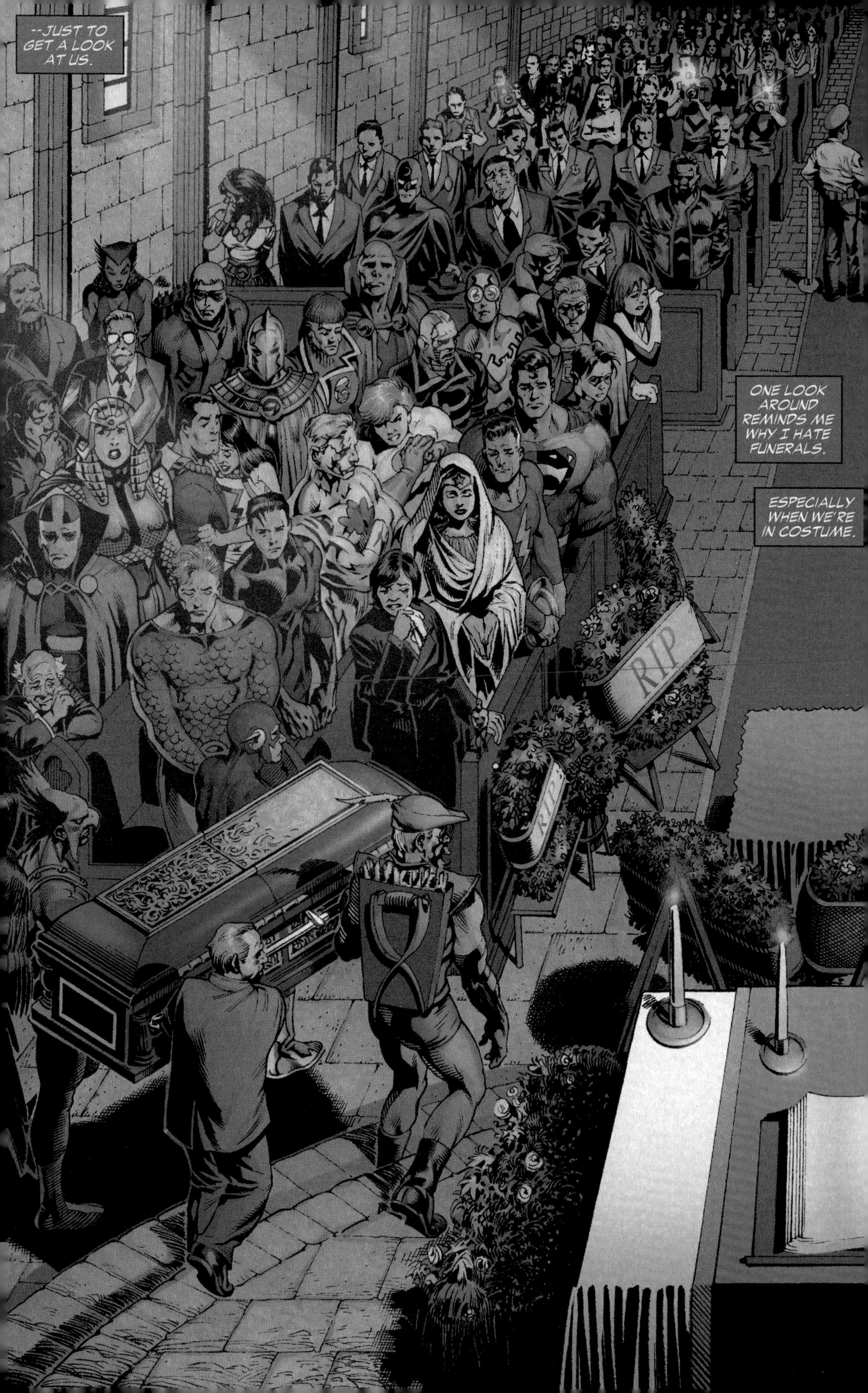
--JUST TO GET A LOOK AT US.
ONE LOOK AROUND REMINDS ME WHY I HATE FUNERALS.
ESPECIALLY WHEN WE'RE IN COSTUME.
RIP
RIP

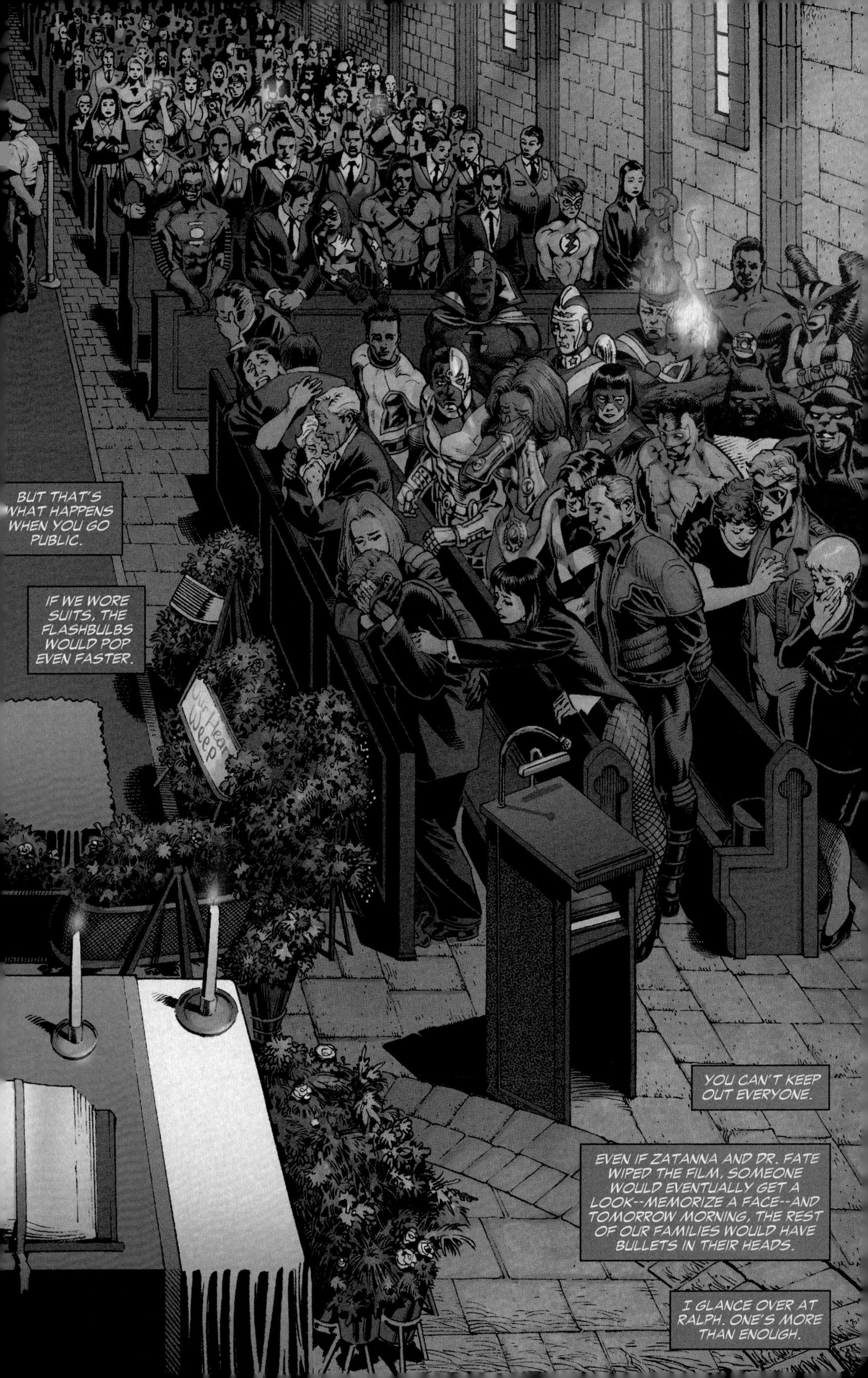
BUT THAT'S WHAT HAPPENS WHEN YOU GO PUBLIC.
IF WE WORE SUITS, THE FLASHBULBS WOULD POP EVEN FASTER.
YOU CAN'T KEEP OUT EVERYONE.
EVEN IF ZATANNA AND DR. FATE WIPED THE FILM, SOMEONE WOULD EVENTUALLY GET A LOOK--MEMORIZE A FACE--AND TOMORROW MORNING, THE REST OF OUR FAMILIES WOULD HAVE BULLETS IN THEIR HEADS.
I GLANCE OVER AT RALPH. ONE'S MORE THAN ENOUGH.

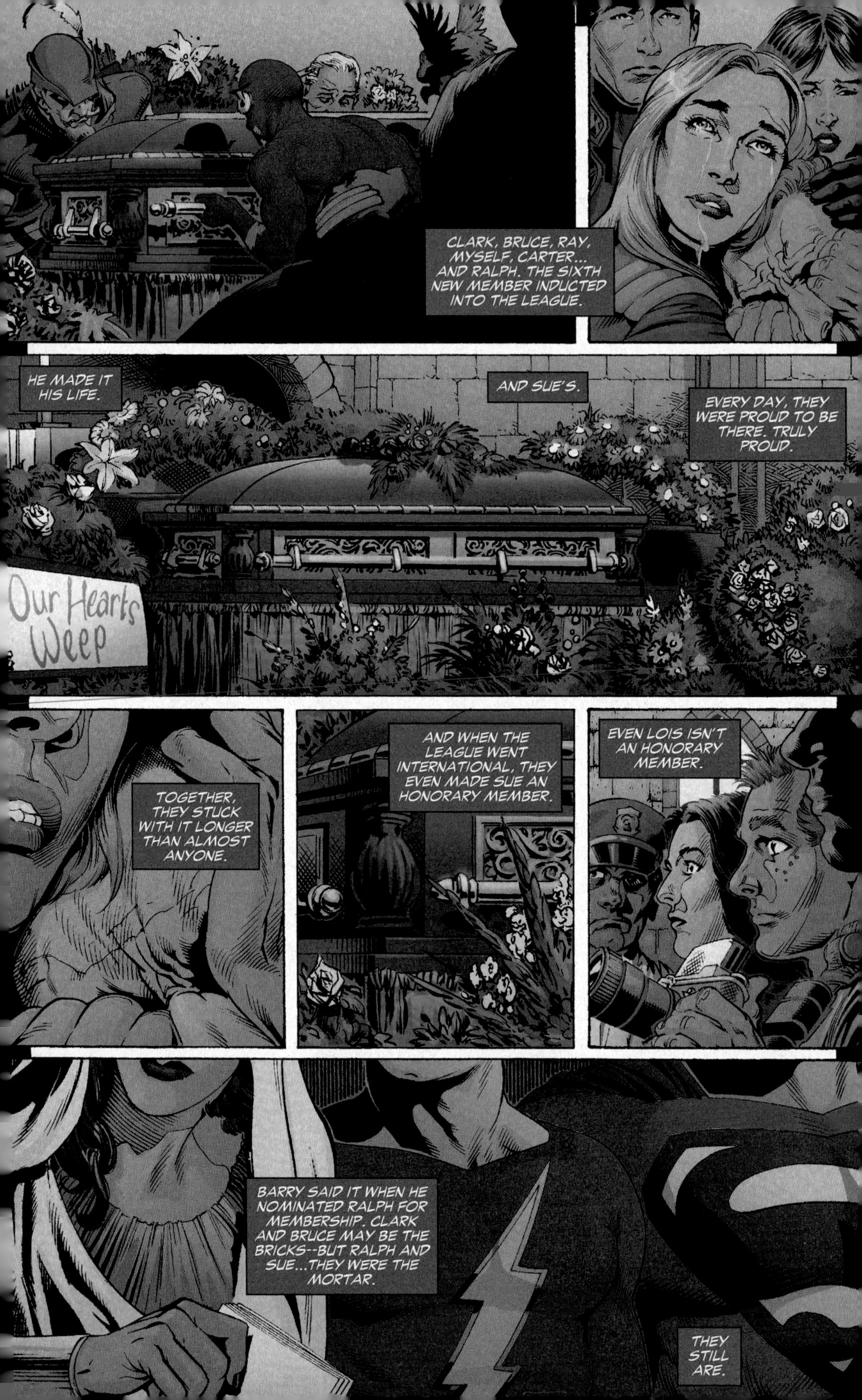
CLARK, BRUCE, RAY, MYSELF, CARTER... AND RALPH. THE SIXTH NEW MEMBER INDUCTED INTO THE LEAGUE.
HE MADE IT HIS LIFE.
AND SUE'S.
EVERY DAY, THEY WERE PROUD TO BE THERE. TRULY PROUD.
Our Hearts Weep
TOGETHER, THEY STUCK WITH IT LONGER THAN ALMOST ANYONE.
AND WHEN THE LEAGUE WENT INTERNATIONAL, THEY EVEN MADE SUE AN HONORARY MEMBER.
EVEN LOIS ISN'T AN HONORARY MEMBER.
BARRY SAID IT WHEN HE NOMINATED RALPH FOR MEMBERSHIP. CLARK AND BRUCE MAY BE THE BRICKS--BUT RALPH AND SUE...THEY WERE THE MORTAR.
THEY STILL ARE.

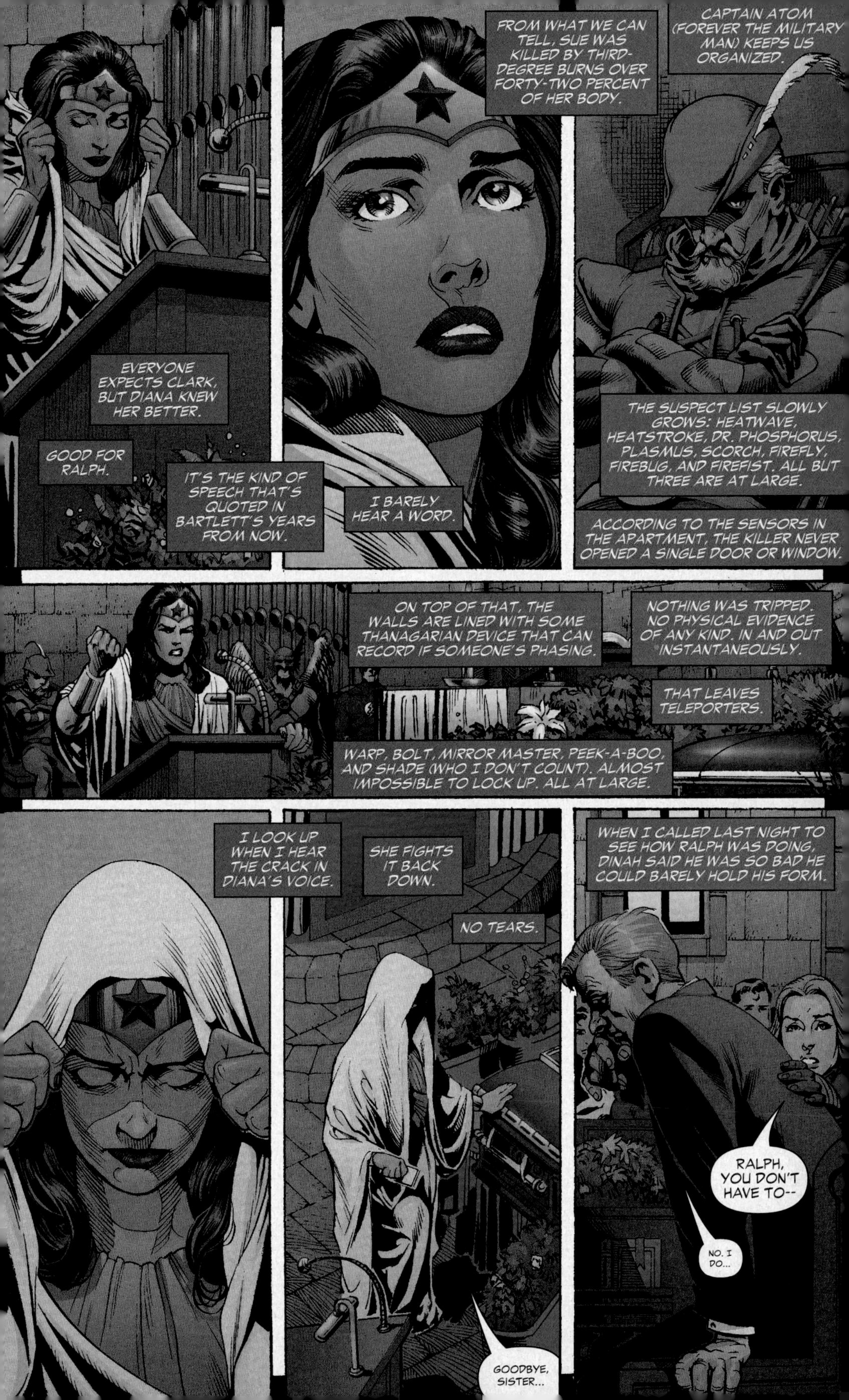
EVERYONE EXPECTS CLARK, BUT DIANA KNEW HER BETTER.
GOOD FOR RALPH.
IT'S THE KIND OF SPEECH THAT'S QUOTED IN BARTLETT'S YEARS FROM NOW.
I BARELY HEAR A WORD.
FROM WHAT WE CAN TELL, SUE WAS KILLED BY THIRD-DEGREE BURNS OVER FORTY-TWO PERCENT OF HER BODY.
CAPTAIN ATOM (FOREVER THE MILITARY MAN) KEEPS US ORGANIZED.
THE SUSPECT LIST SLOWLY GROWS: HEATWAVE, HEATSTROKE, DR. PHOSPHORUS, PLASMUS, SCORCH, FIREFLY, FIREBUG, AND FIREFIST. ALL BUT THREE ARE AT LARGE.
ACCORDING TO THE SENSORS IN THE APARTMENT, THE KILLER NEVER OPENED A SINGLE DOOR OR WINDOW.
ON TOP OF THAT, THE WALLS ARE LINED WITH SOME THANAGARIAN DEVICE THAT CAN RECORD IF SOMEONE'S PHASING.
NOTHING WAS TRIPPED. NO PHYSICAL EVIDENCE OF ANY KIND. IN AND OUT INSTANTANEOUSLY.
THAT LEAVES TELEPORTERS.
WARP, BOLT, MIRROR MASTER, PEEK-A-BOO, AND SHADE (WHO I DON'T COUNT). ALMOST IMPOSSIBLE TO LOCK UP. ALL AT LARGE.
I LOOK UP WHEN I HEAR THE CRACK IN DIANA'S VOICE.
SHE FIGHTS IT BACK DOWN.
NO TEARS.
GOODBYE, SISTER...
WHEN I CALLED LAST NIGHT TO SEE HOW RALPH WAS DOING, DINAH SAID HE WAS SO BAD HE COULD BARELY HOLD HIS FORM.
RALPH, YOU DON'T HAVE TO--
NO. I DO...

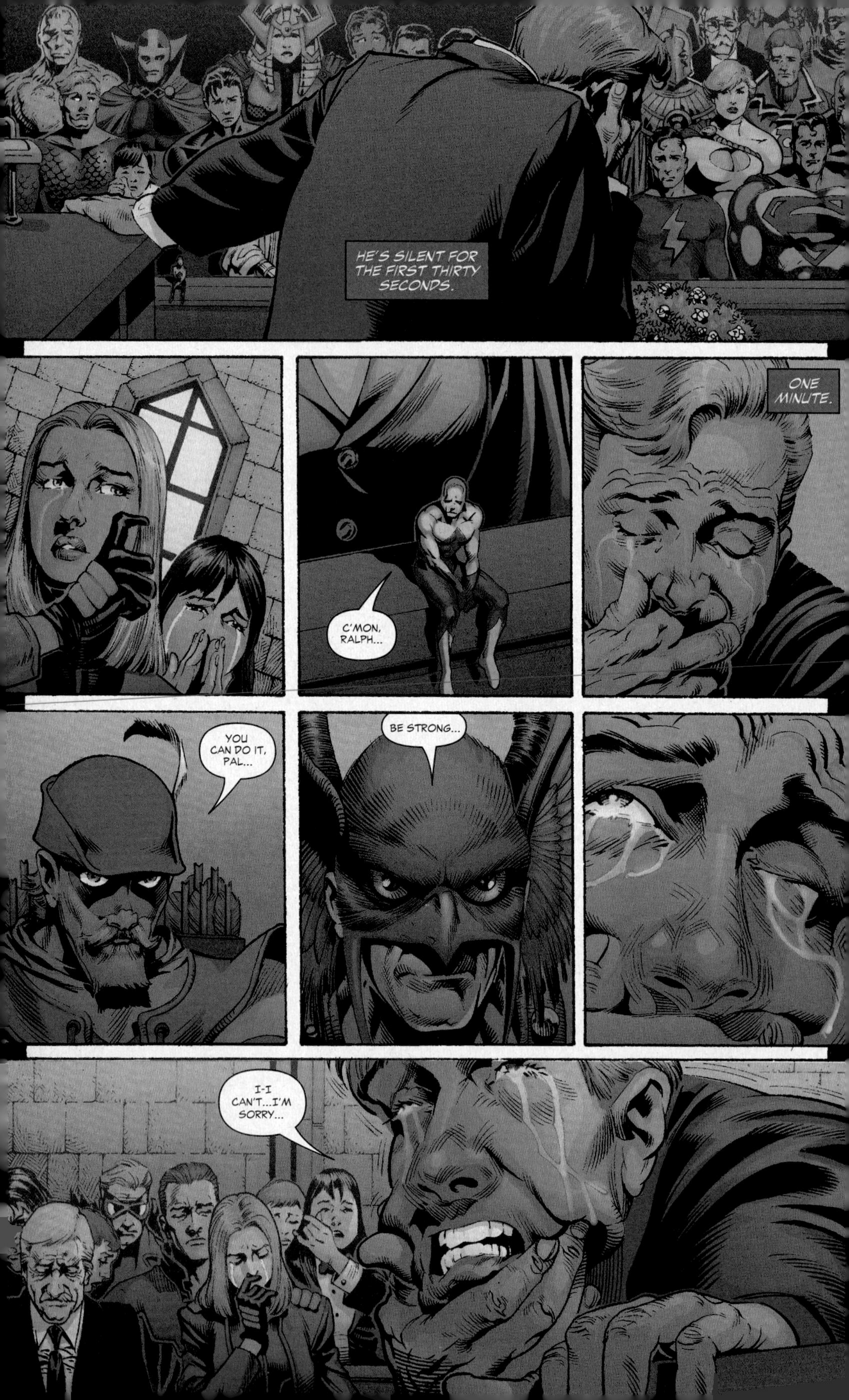
HE'S SILENT FOR THE FIRST THIRTY SECONDS.
C'MON, RALPH...
ONE MINUTE.
YOU CAN DO IT, PAL...
BE STRONG...
I-I CAN'T...I'M SORRY...

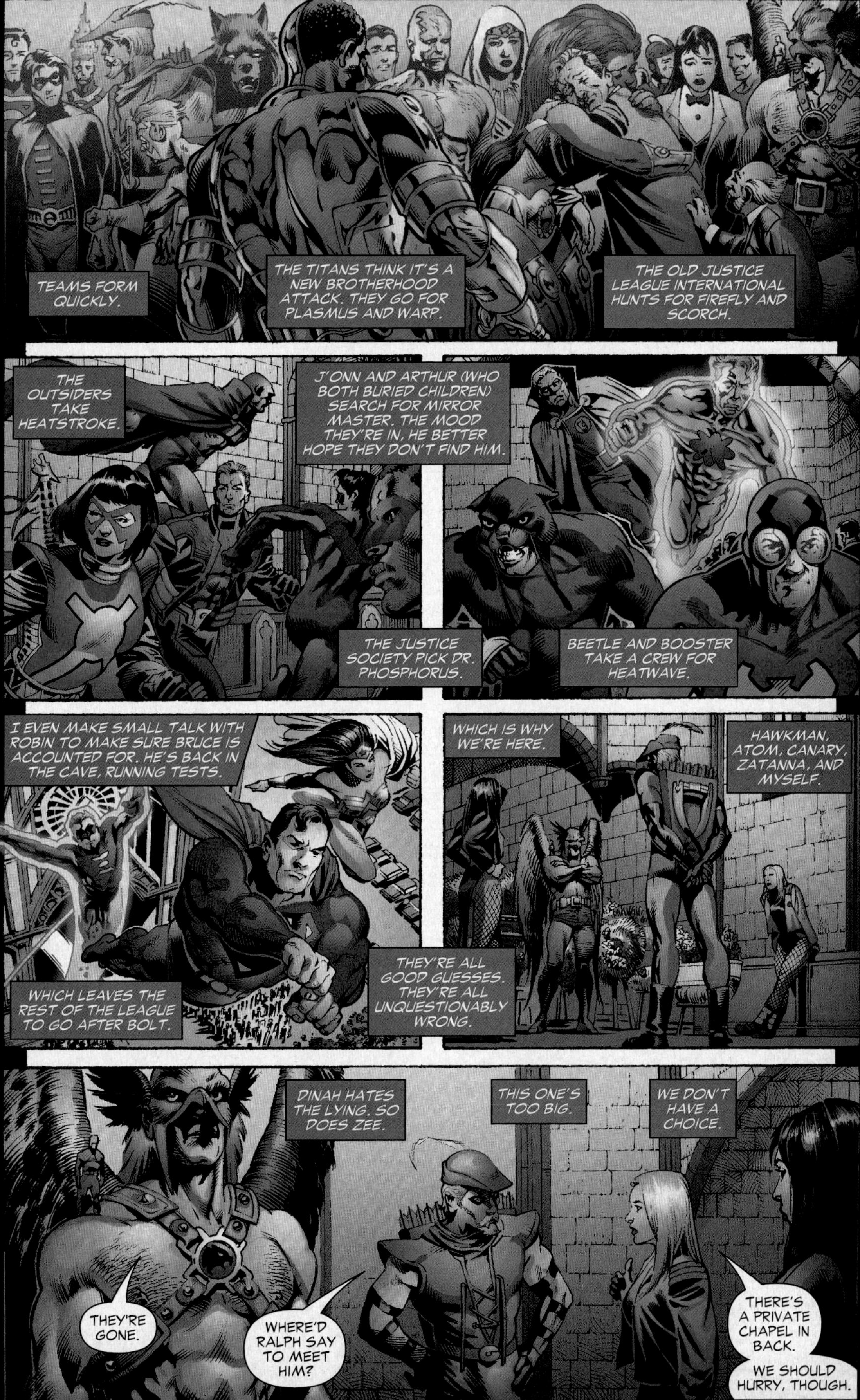
TEAMS FORM QUICKLY.
THE TITANS THINK IT'S A NEW BROTHERHOOD ATTACK. THEY GO FOR PLASMUS AND WARP.
THE OLD JUSTICE LEAGUE INTERNATIONAL HUNTS FOR FIREFLY AND SCORCH.
THE OUTSIDERS TAKE HEATSTROKE.
J'ONN AND ARTHUR (WHO BOTH BURIED CHILDREN) SEARCH FOR MIRROR MASTER. THE MOOD THEY'RE IN, HE BETTER HOPE THEY DON'T FIND HIM.
THE JUSTICE SOCIETY PICK DR. PHOSPHORUS.
BEETLE AND BOOSTER TAKE A CREW FOR HEATWAVE.
I EVEN MAKE SMALL TALK WITH ROBIN TO MAKE SURE BRUCE IS ACCOUNTED FOR. HE'S BACK IN THE CAVE, RUNNING TESTS.
WHICH LEAVES THE REST OF THE LEAGUE TO GO AFTER BOLT.
THEY'RE ALL GOOD GUESSES. THEY'RE ALL UNQUESTIONABLY WRONG.
WHICH IS WHY WE'RE HERE.
HAWKMAN, ATOM, CANARY, ZATANNA, AND MYSELF.
DINAH HATES THE LYING. SO DOES ZEE.
THIS ONE'S TOO BIG.
WE DON'T HAVE A CHOICE.
THEY'RE GONE.
WHERE'D RALPH SAY TO MEET HIM?
THERE'S A PRIVATE CHAPEL IN BACK.
WE SHOULD HURRY, THOUGH.

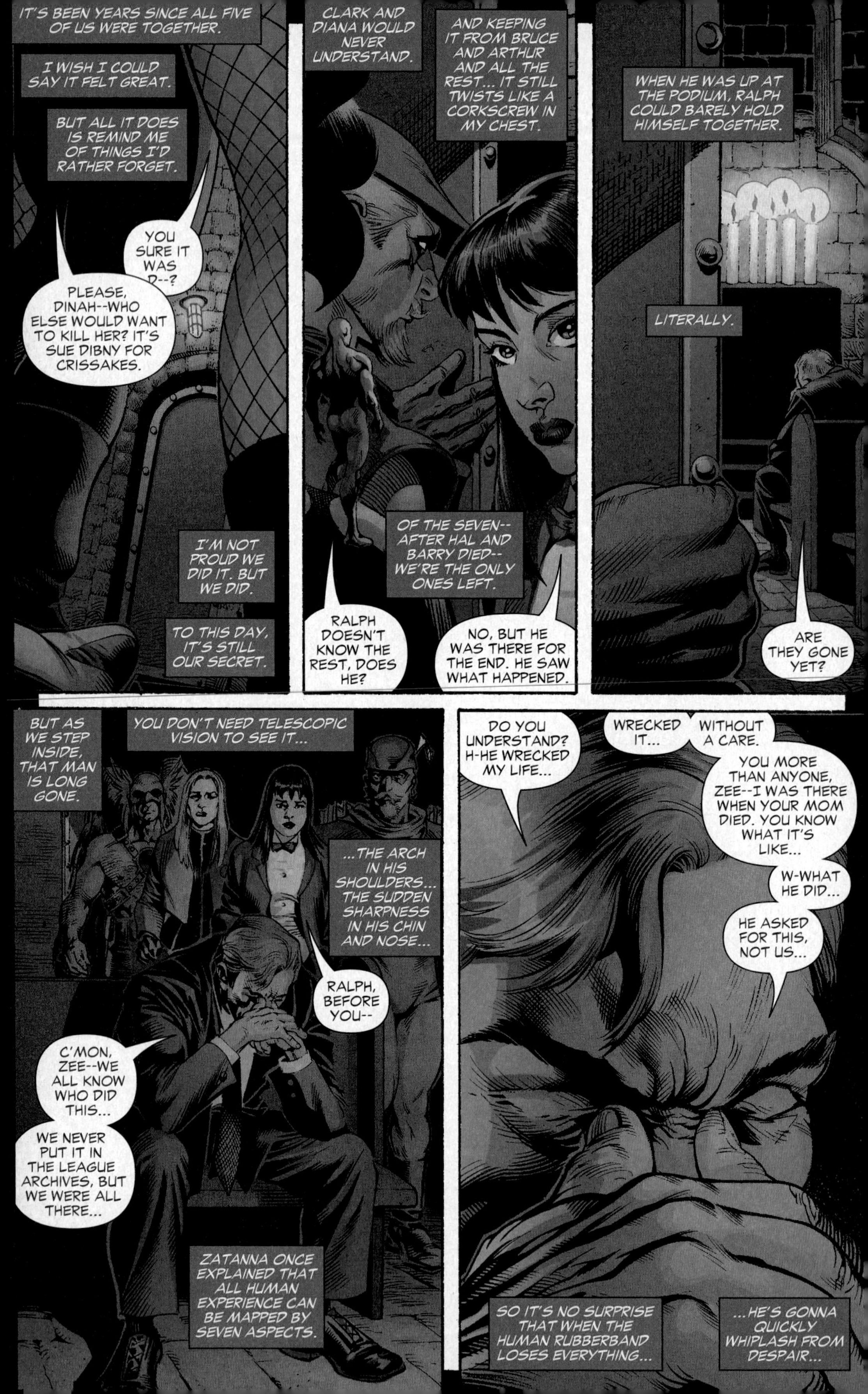
IT'S BEEN YEARS SINCE ALL FIVE OF US WERE TOGETHER.
I WISH I COULD SAY IT FELT GREAT.
BUT ALL IT DOES IS REMIND ME OF THINGS I'D RATHER FORGET.
YOU SURE IT WAS D--?
PLEASE, DINAH--WHO ELSE WOULD WANT TO KILL HER? IT'S SUE DIBNY FOR CRISSAKES.
I'M NOT PROUD WE DID IT. BUT WE DID.
TO THIS DAY, IT'S STILL OUR SECRET.
CLARK AND DIANA WOULD NEVER UNDERSTAND.
AND KEEPING IT FROM BRUCE AND ARTHUR AND ALL THE REST... IT STILL TWISTS LIKE A CORKSCREW IN MY CHEST.
OF THE SEVEN-- AFTER HAL AND BARRY DIED-- WE'RE THE ONLY ONES LEFT.
RALPH DOESN'T KNOW THE REST, DOES HE?
NO, BUT HE WAS THERE FOR THE END. HE SAW WHAT HAPPENED.
WHEN HE WAS UP AT THE PODIUM, RALPH COULD BARELY HOLD HIMSELF TOGETHER.
LITERALLY.
ARE THEY GONE YET?
BUT AS WE STEP INSIDE, THAT MAN IS LONG GONE.
YOU DON'T NEED TELESCOPIC VISION TO SEE IT...
...THE ARCH IN HIS SHOULDERS... THE SUDDEN SHARPNESS IN HIS CHIN AND NOSE...
RALPH, BEFORE YOU--
C'MON, ZEE--WE ALL KNOW WHO DID THIS...
WE NEVER PUT IT IN THE LEAGUE ARCHIVES, BUT WE WERE ALL THERE...
ZATANNA ONCE EXPLAINED THAT ALL HUMAN EXPERIENCE CAN BE MAPPED BY SEVEN ASPECTS.
DO YOU UNDERSTAND? H-HE WRECKED MY LIFE...
WRECKED IT...
WITHOUT A CARE.
YOU MORE THAN ANYONE, ZEE--I WAS THERE WHEN YOUR MOM DIED. YOU KNOW WHAT IT'S LIKE...
W-WHAT HE DID...
HE ASKED FOR THIS, NOT US...
SO IT'S NO SURPRISE THAT WHEN THE HUMAN RUBBERBAND LOSES EVERYTHING...
...HE'S GONNA QUICKLY WHIPLASH FROM DESPAIR...

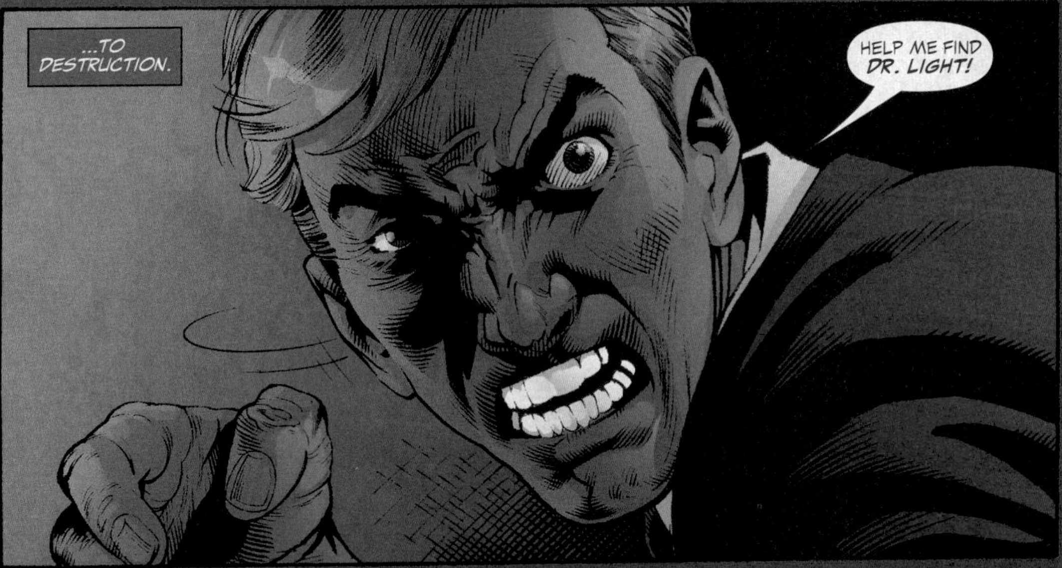
...TO DESTRUCTION.
HELP ME FIND DR. LIGHT!

CHAPTER ONE

COFFIN

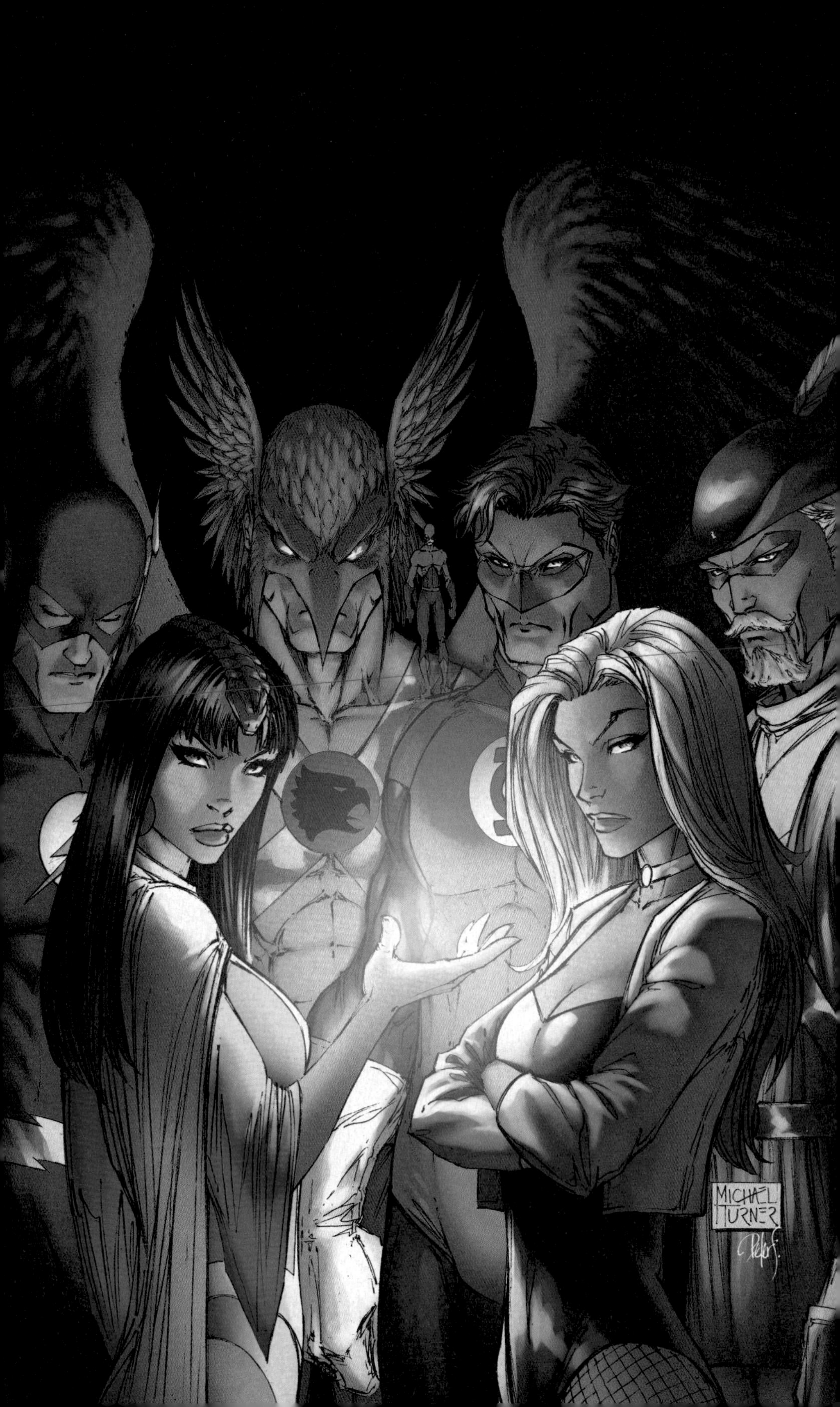
MICHAEL TURNER

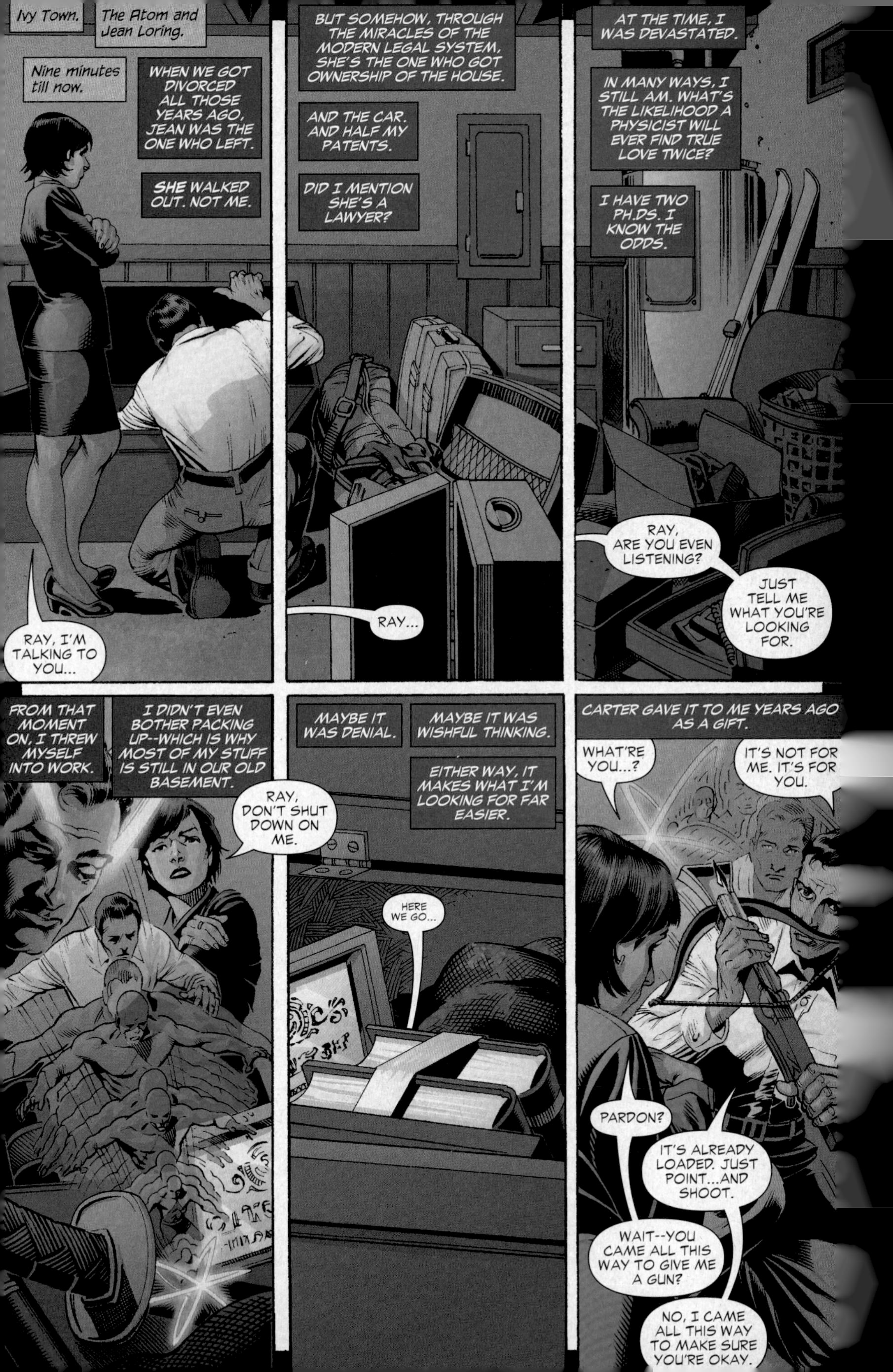

Ivy Town.
The Atom and Jean Loring.
Nine minutes till now.
WHEN WE GOT DIVORCED ALL THOSE YEARS AGO, JEAN WAS THE ONE WHO LEFT.
SHE WALKED OUT. NOT ME.
RAY, I'M TALKING TO YOU...
BUT SOMEHOW, THROUGH THE MIRACLES OF THE MODERN LEGAL SYSTEM, SHE'S THE ONE WHO GOT OWNERSHIP OF THE HOUSE.
AND THE CAR. AND HALF MY PATENTS.
DID I MENTION SHE'S A LAWYER?
RAY...
AT THE TIME, I WAS DEVASTATED.
IN MANY WAYS, I STILL AM. WHAT'S THE LIKELIHOOD A PHYSICIST WILL EVER FIND TRUE LOVE TWICE?
I HAVE TWO PH.DS. I KNOW THE ODDS.
RAY, ARE YOU EVEN LISTENING?
JUST TELL ME WHAT YOU'RE LOOKING FOR.
FROM THAT MOMENT ON, I THREW MYSELF INTO WORK.
I DIDN'T EVEN BOTHER PACKING UP--WHICH IS WHY MOST OF MY STUFF IS STILL IN OUR OLD BASEMENT.
RAY, DON'T SHUT DOWN ON ME.
MAYBE IT WAS DENIAL.
MAYBE IT WAS WISHFUL THINKING.
EITHER WAY, IT MAKES WHAT I'M LOOKING FOR FAR EASIER.
HERE WE GO...
CARTER GAVE IT TO ME YEARS AGO AS A GIFT.
WHAT'RE YOU...?
IT'S NOT FOR ME. IT'S FOR YOU.
PARDON?
IT'S ALREADY LOADED. JUST POINT...AND SHOOT.
WAIT--YOU CAME ALL THIS WAY TO GIVE ME A GUN?
NO, I CAME ALL THIS WAY TO MAKE SURE YOU'RE OKAY.

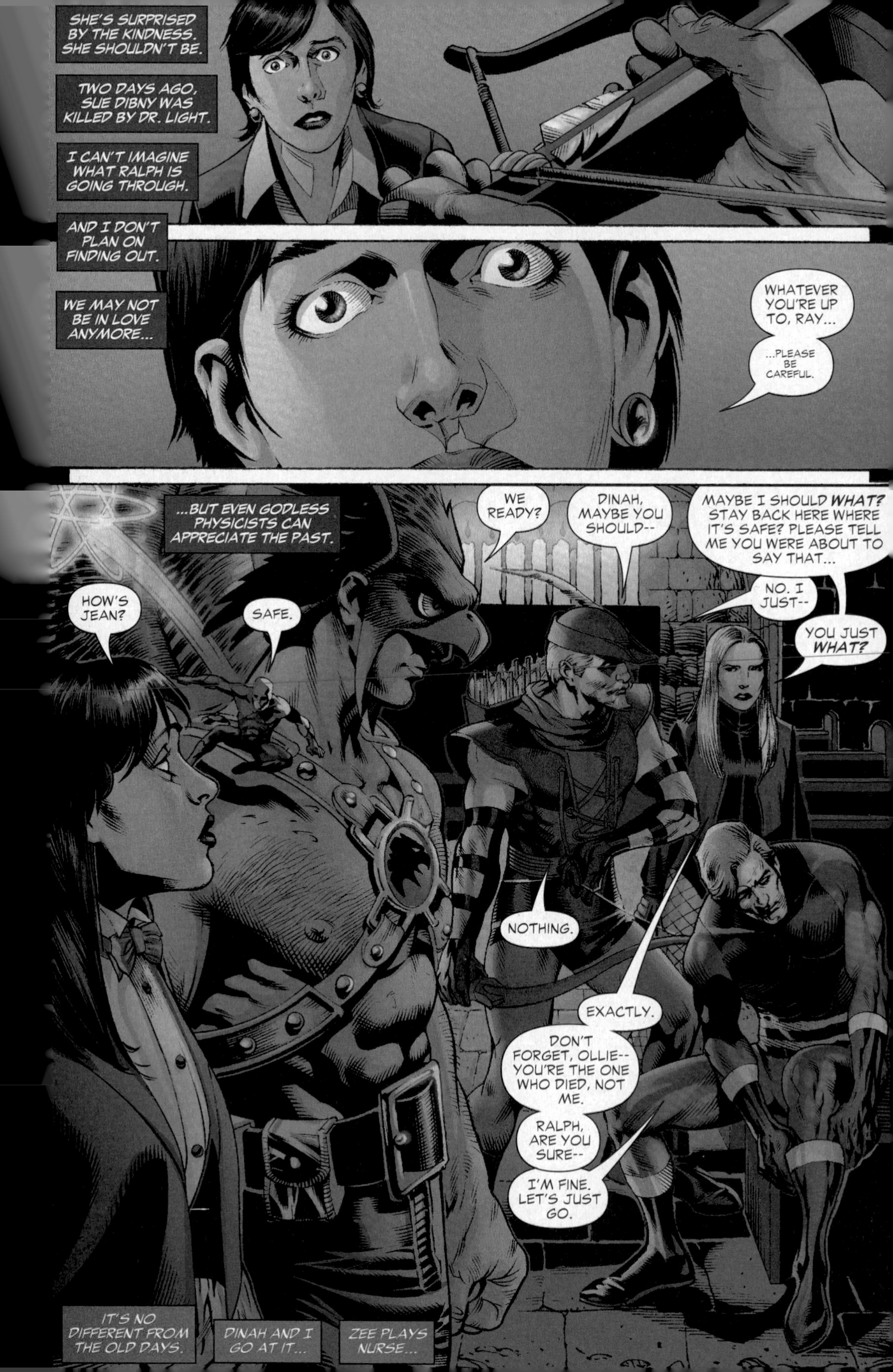
SHE'S SURPRISED BY THE KINDNESS. SHE SHOULDN'T BE.
TWO DAYS AGO, SUE DIBNY WAS KILLED BY DR. LIGHT.
I CAN'T IMAGINE WHAT RALPH IS GOING THROUGH.
AND I DON'T PLAN ON FINDING OUT.
WE MAY NOT BE IN LOVE ANYMORE...
WHATEVER YOU'RE UP TO, RAY...
...PLEASE BE CAREFUL.
...BUT EVEN GODLESS PHYSICISTS CAN APPRECIATE THE PAST.
HOW'S JEAN?
SAFE.
WE READY?
DINAH, MAYBE YOU SHOULD--
MAYBE I SHOULD WHAT? STAY BACK HERE WHERE IT'S SAFE? PLEASE TELL ME YOU WERE ABOUT TO SAY THAT...
NO. I JUST--
YOU JUST WHAT?
NOTHING.
EXACTLY.
DON'T FORGET, OLLIE--YOU'RE THE ONE WHO DIED, NOT ME.
RALPH, ARE YOU SURE--
I'M FINE. LET'S JUST GO.
IT'S NO DIFFERENT FROM THE OLD DAYS.
DINAH AND I GO AT IT...
ZEE PLAYS NURSE...

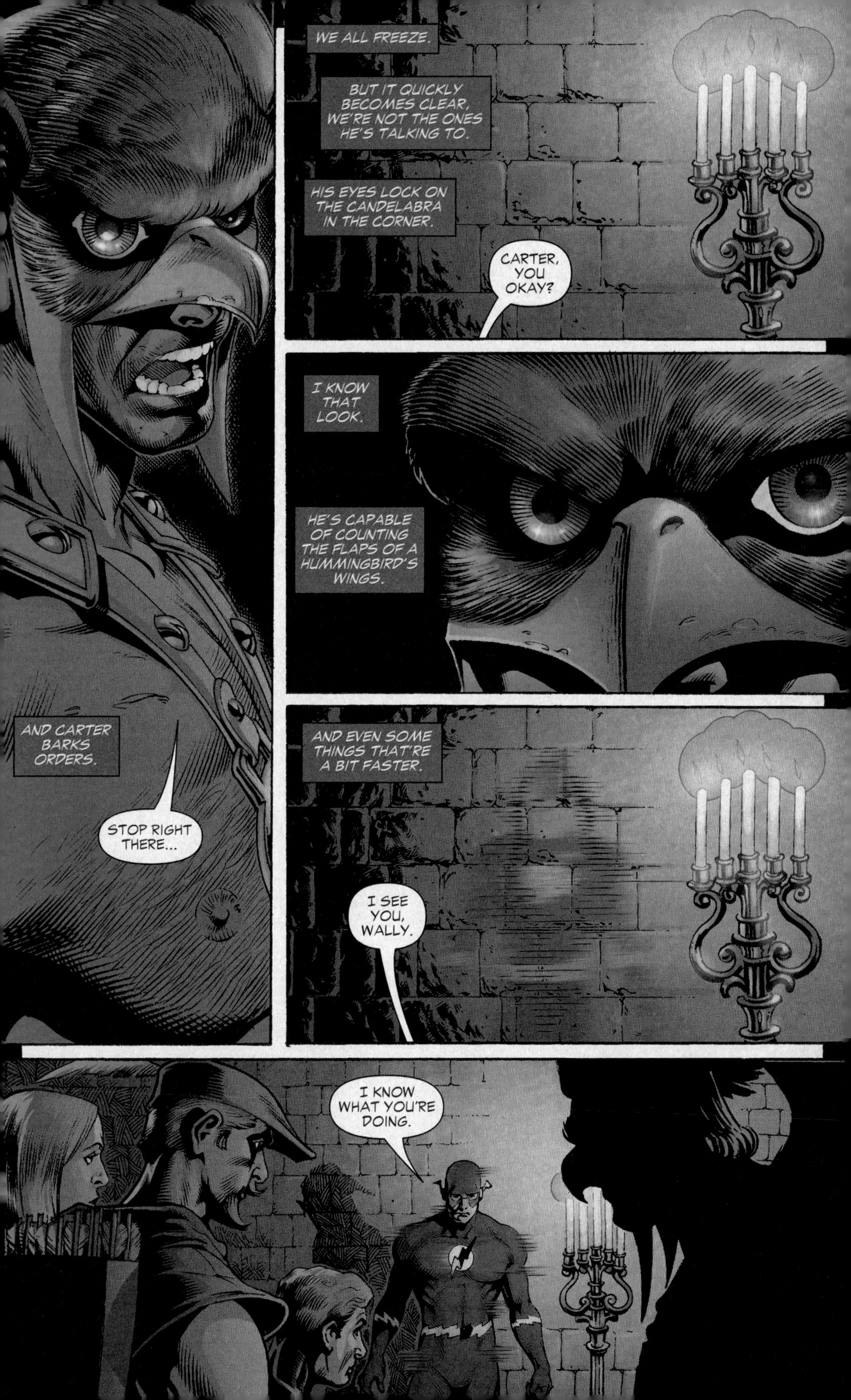
WE ALL FREEZE.
BUT IT QUICKLY BECOMES CLEAR, WE'RE NOT THE ONES HE'S TALKING TO.
HIS EYES LOCK ON THE CANDELABRA IN THE CORNER.
CARTER, YOU OKAY?
I KNOW THAT LOOK.
HE'S CAPABLE OF COUNTING THE FLAPS OF A HUMMINGBIRD'S WINGS.
AND CARTER BARKS ORDERS.
STOP RIGHT THERE...
AND EVEN SOME THINGS THAT'RE A BIT FASTER.
I SEE YOU, WALLY.
I KNOW WHAT YOU'RE DOING.

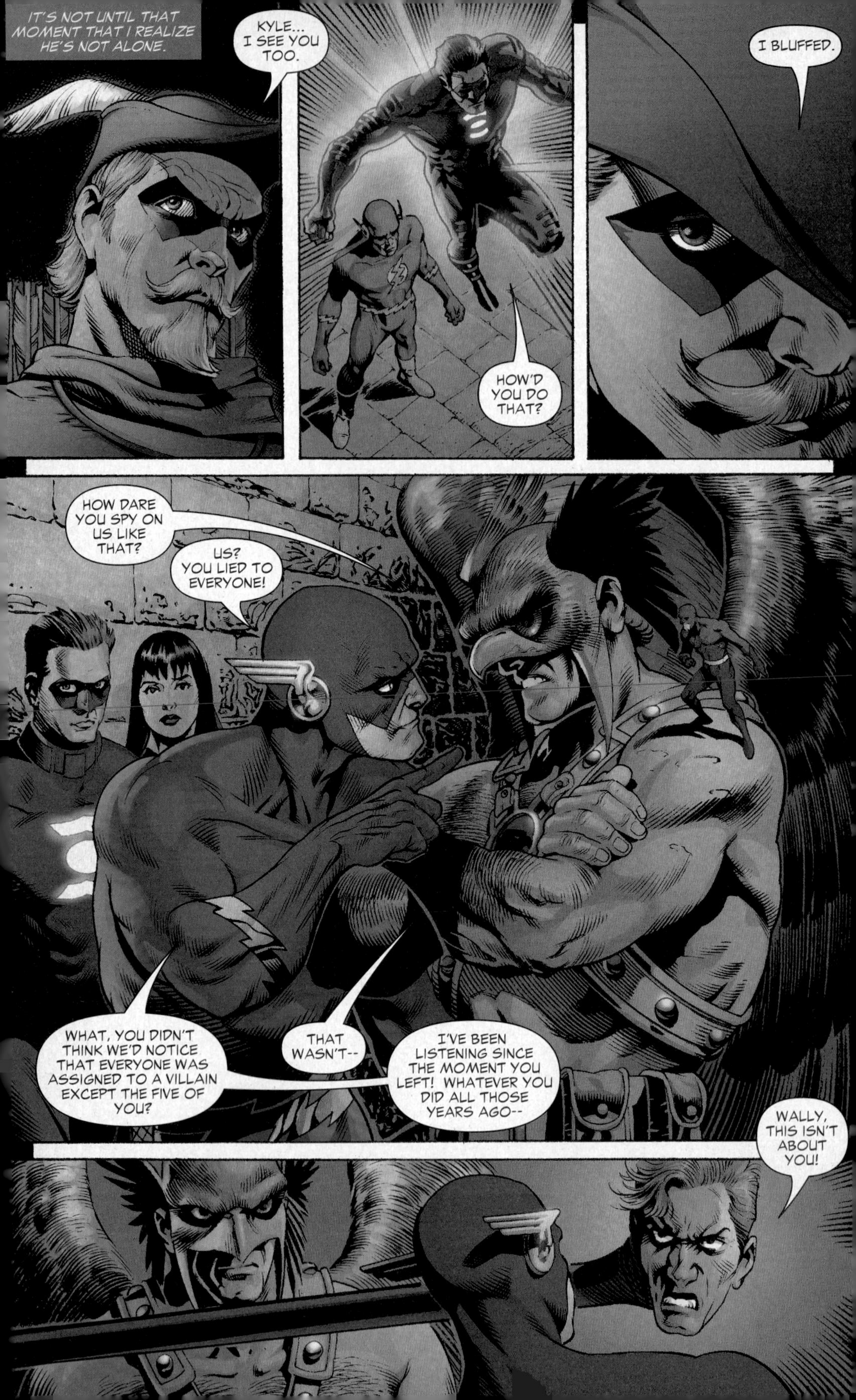
IT'S NOT UNTIL THAT MOMENT THAT I REALIZE HE'S NOT ALONE.
KYLE... I SEE YOU TOO.
HOW'D YOU DO THAT?
I BLUFFED.
HOW DARE YOU SPY ON US LIKE THAT?
US? YOU LIED TO EVERYONE!
WHAT, YOU DIDN'T THINK WE'D NOTICE THAT EVERYONE WAS ASSIGNED TO A VILLAIN EXCEPT THE FIVE OF YOU?
THAT WASN'T--
I'VE BEEN LISTENING SINCE THE MOMENT YOU LEFT! WHATEVER YOU DID ALL THOSE YEARS AGO--
WALLY, THIS ISN'T ABOUT YOU!

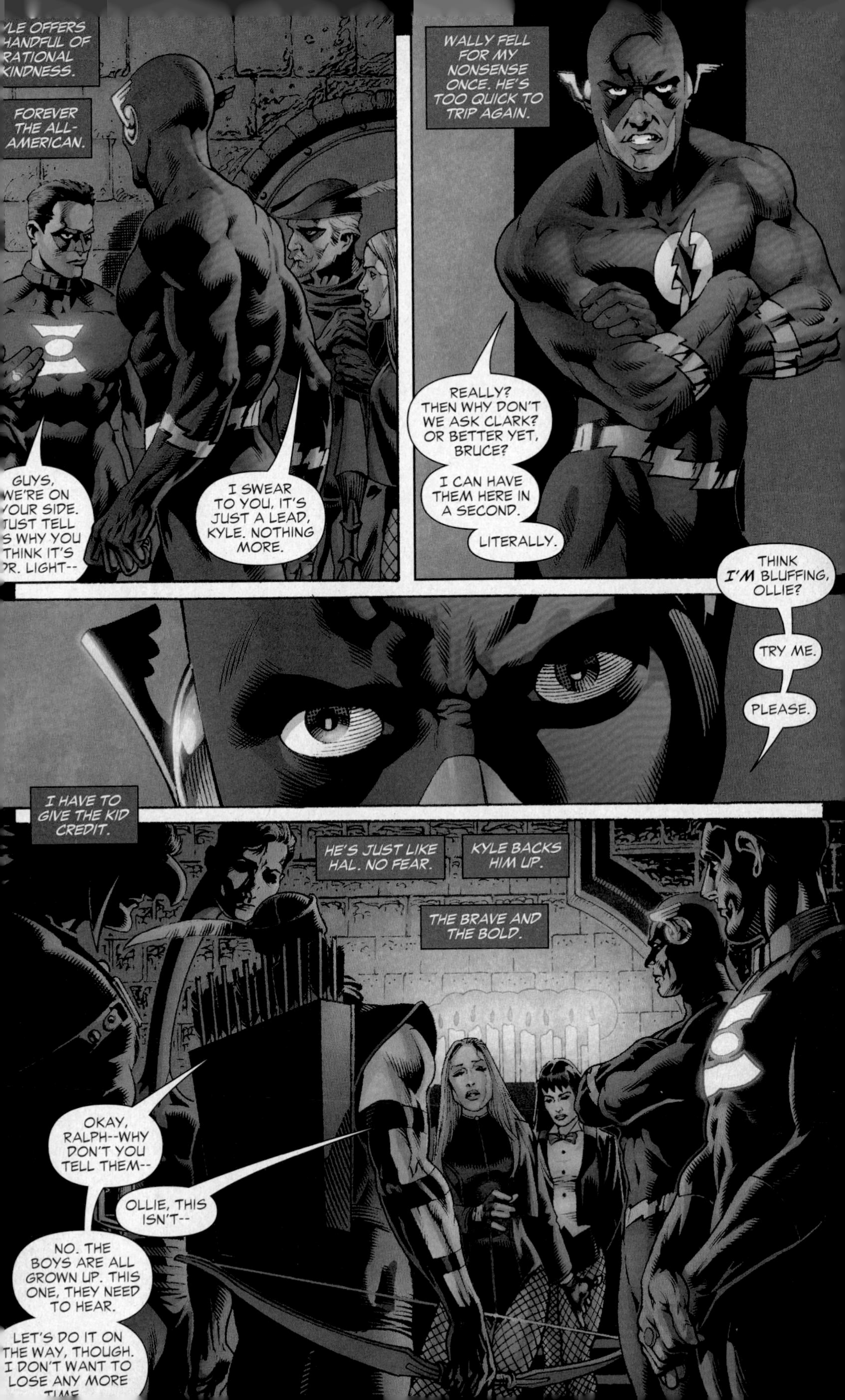

YLE OFFERS HANDFUL OF RATIONAL KINDNESS.
FOREVER THE ALL-AMERICAN.
GUYS, WE'RE ON YOUR SIDE. JUST TELL S WHY YOU THINK IT'S DR. LIGHT--
I SWEAR TO YOU, IT'S JUST A LEAD, KYLE. NOTHING MORE.
WALLY FELL FOR MY NONSENSE ONCE. HE'S TOO QUICK TO TRIP AGAIN.
REALLY? THEN WHY DON'T WE ASK CLARK? OR BETTER YET, BRUCE?
I CAN HAVE THEM HERE IN A SECOND.
LITERALLY.
THINK *I'M* BLUFFING, OLLIE?
TRY ME.
PLEASE.
I HAVE TO GIVE THE KID CREDIT.
HE'S JUST LIKE HAL. NO FEAR.
KYLE BACKS HIM UP.
THE BRAVE AND THE BOLD.
OKAY, RALPH--WHY DON'T YOU TELL THEM--
OLLIE, THIS ISN'T--
NO. THE BOYS ARE ALL GROWN UP. THIS ONE, THEY NEED TO HEAR.
LET'S DO IT ON THE WAY, THOUGH. I DON'T WANT TO LOSE ANY MORE

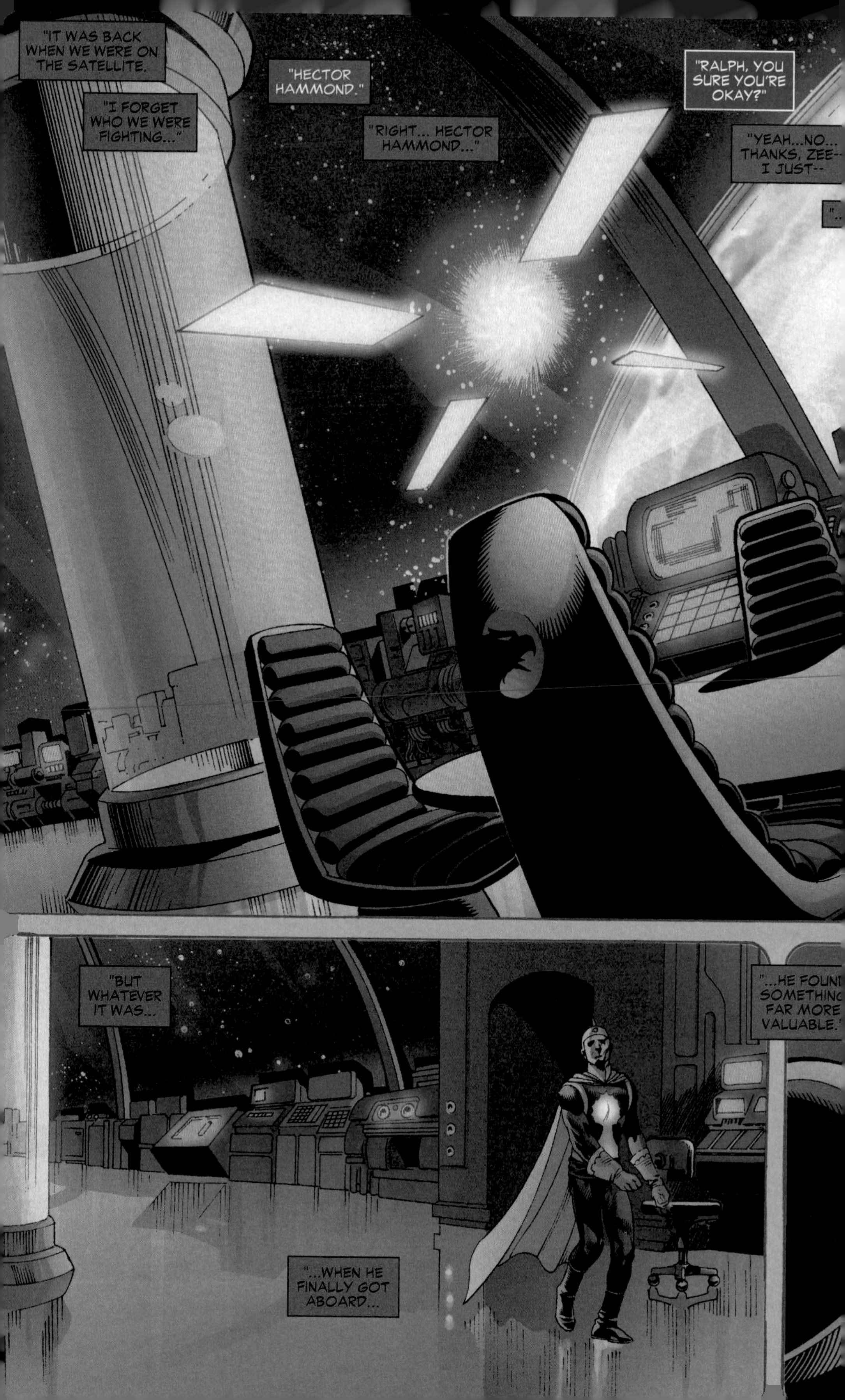
"IT WAS BACK WHEN WE WERE ON THE SATELLITE.
"I FORGET WHO WE WERE FIGHTING..."
"HECTOR HAMMOND."
"RIGHT... HECTOR HAMMOND..."
"RALPH, YOU SURE YOU'RE OKAY?"
"YEAH...NO... THANKS, ZEE-- I JUST--
"BUT WHATEVER IT WAS...
"...WHEN HE FINALLY GOT ABOARD...
"...HE FOUND SOMETHING FAR MORE VALUABLE."

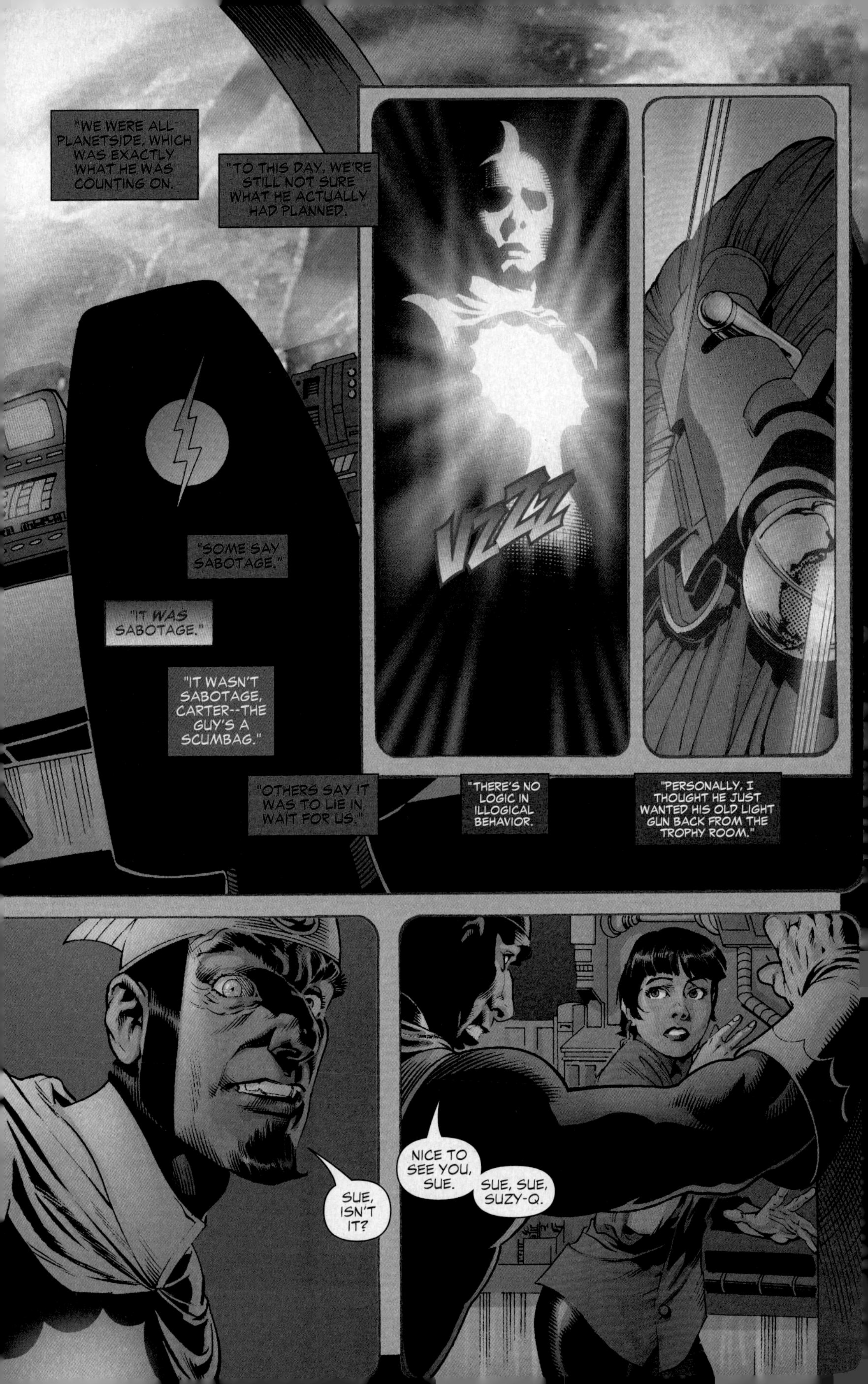
"WE WERE ALL PLANETSIDE, WHICH WAS EXACTLY WHAT HE WAS COUNTING ON.
"TO THIS DAY, WE'RE STILL NOT SURE WHAT HE ACTUALLY HAD PLANNED.
VZZZ
"SOME SAY SABOTAGE."
"IT WAS SABOTAGE."
"IT WASN'T SABOTAGE, CARTER--THE GUY'S A SCUMBAG."
"OTHERS SAY IT WAS TO LIE IN WAIT FOR US."
"THERE'S NO LOGIC IN ILLOGICAL BEHAVIOR.
"PERSONALLY, I THOUGHT HE JUST WANTED HIS OLD LIGHT GUN BACK FROM THE TROPHY ROOM."
SUE, ISN'T IT?
NICE TO SEE YOU, SUE.
SUE, SUE, SUZY-Q.

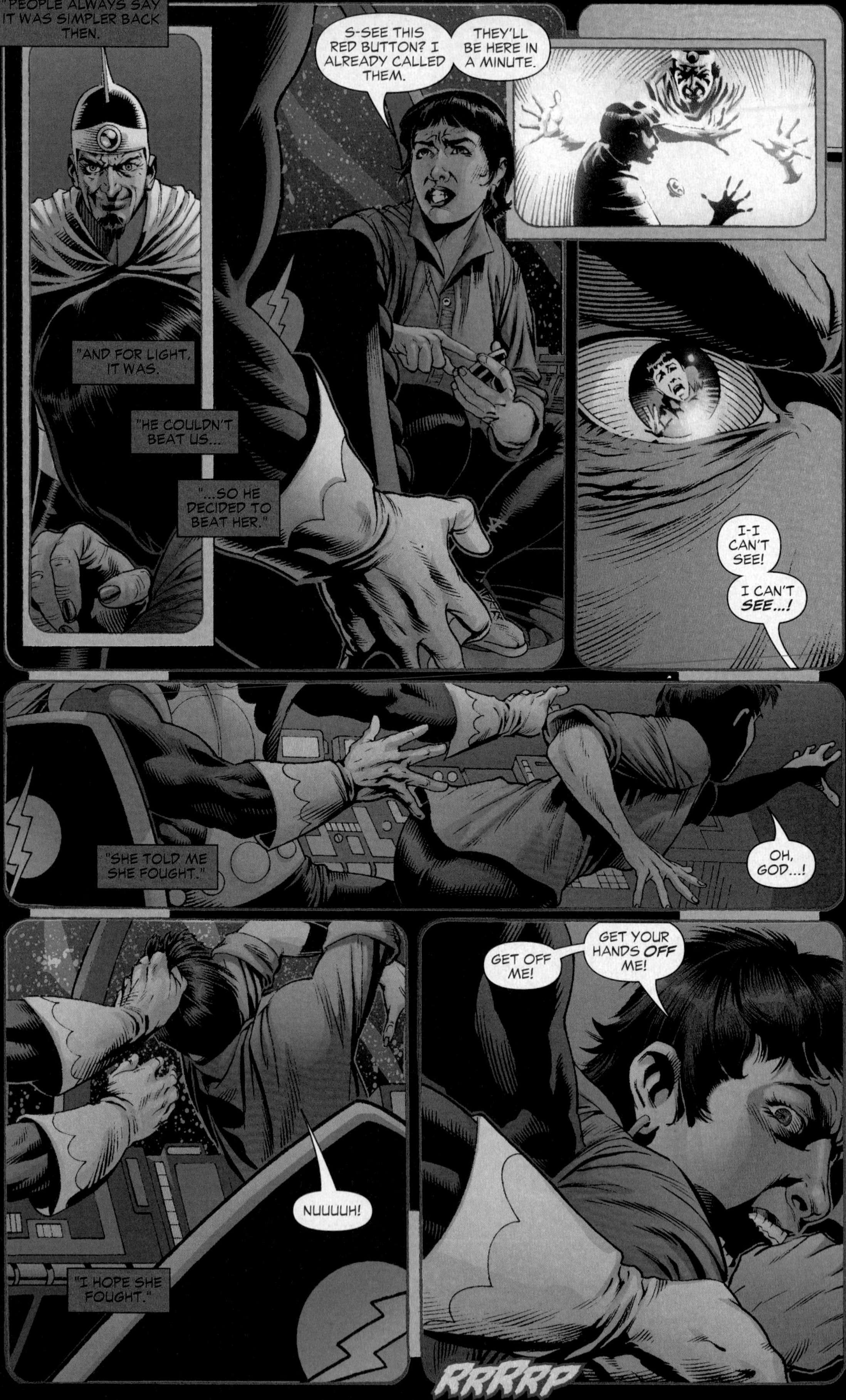
"PEOPLE ALWAYS SAY IT WAS SIMPLER BACK THEN.
"AND FOR LIGHT, IT WAS.
"HE COULDN'T BEAT US...
"...SO HE DECIDED TO BEAT HER."
S-SEE THIS RED BUTTON? I ALREADY CALLED THEM.
THEY'LL BE HERE IN A MINUTE.
I-I CAN'T SEE!
I CAN'T ***SEE...!***
"SHE TOLD ME SHE FOUGHT."
OH, GOD...!
NUUUUH!
"I HOPE SHE FOUGHT."
GET OFF ME!
GET YOUR HANDS ***OFF*** ME!
RRRRP

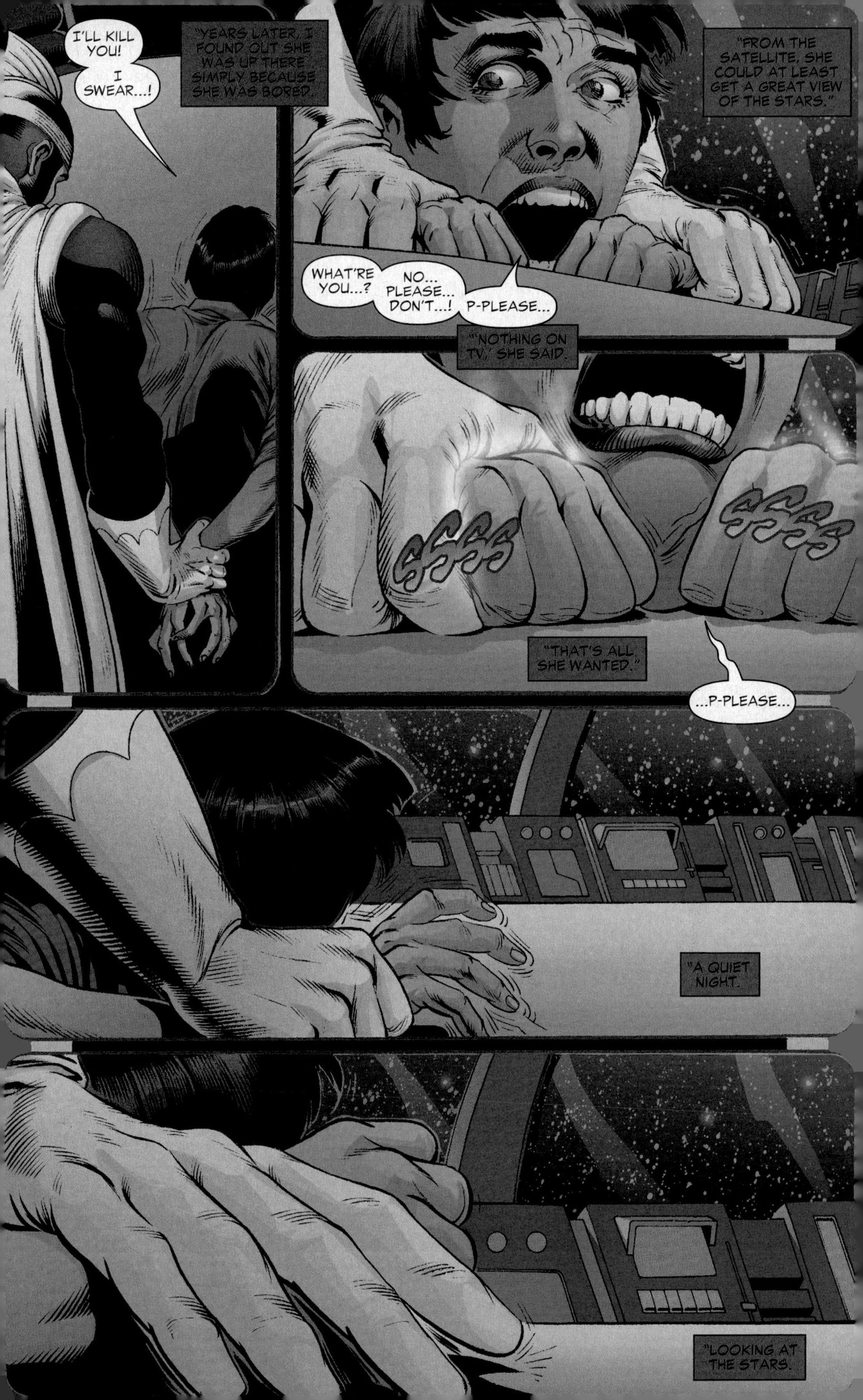
I'LL KILL YOU!
I SWEAR...!
"YEARS LATER, I FOUND OUT SHE WAS UP THERE SIMPLY BECAUSE SHE WAS BORED.
"FROM THE SATELLITE, SHE COULD AT LEAST GET A GREAT VIEW OF THE STARS."
WHAT'RE YOU...?
NO... PLEASE... DON'T...!
P-PLEASE...
"'NOTHING ON TV,' SHE SAID.
"THAT'S ALL SHE WANTED."
...P-PLEASE...
"A QUIET NIGHT.
"LOOKING AT THE STARS.

"NATURALLY, BARRY GOT BACK FIRST."

OH GOD...

IT'S YOUR WEAKNESS, ISN'T IT?

I FINALLY GOT IT...

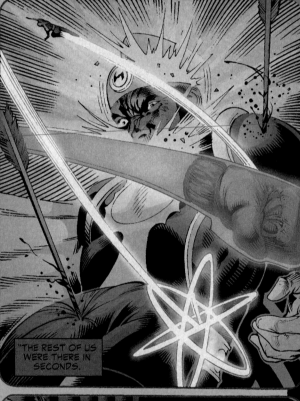

"THE REST OF US WERE THERE IN SECONDS."

"BUT BY THAT POINT, HE WAS PURE ADRENALINE.

"ALL THAT POWER...

"IT WAS LIKE TRYING TO TACKLE AN ELEPHANT."

I'LL FIND HER AGAIN, YOU KNOW...

THEN I'LL FIND ALL OF YOURS.

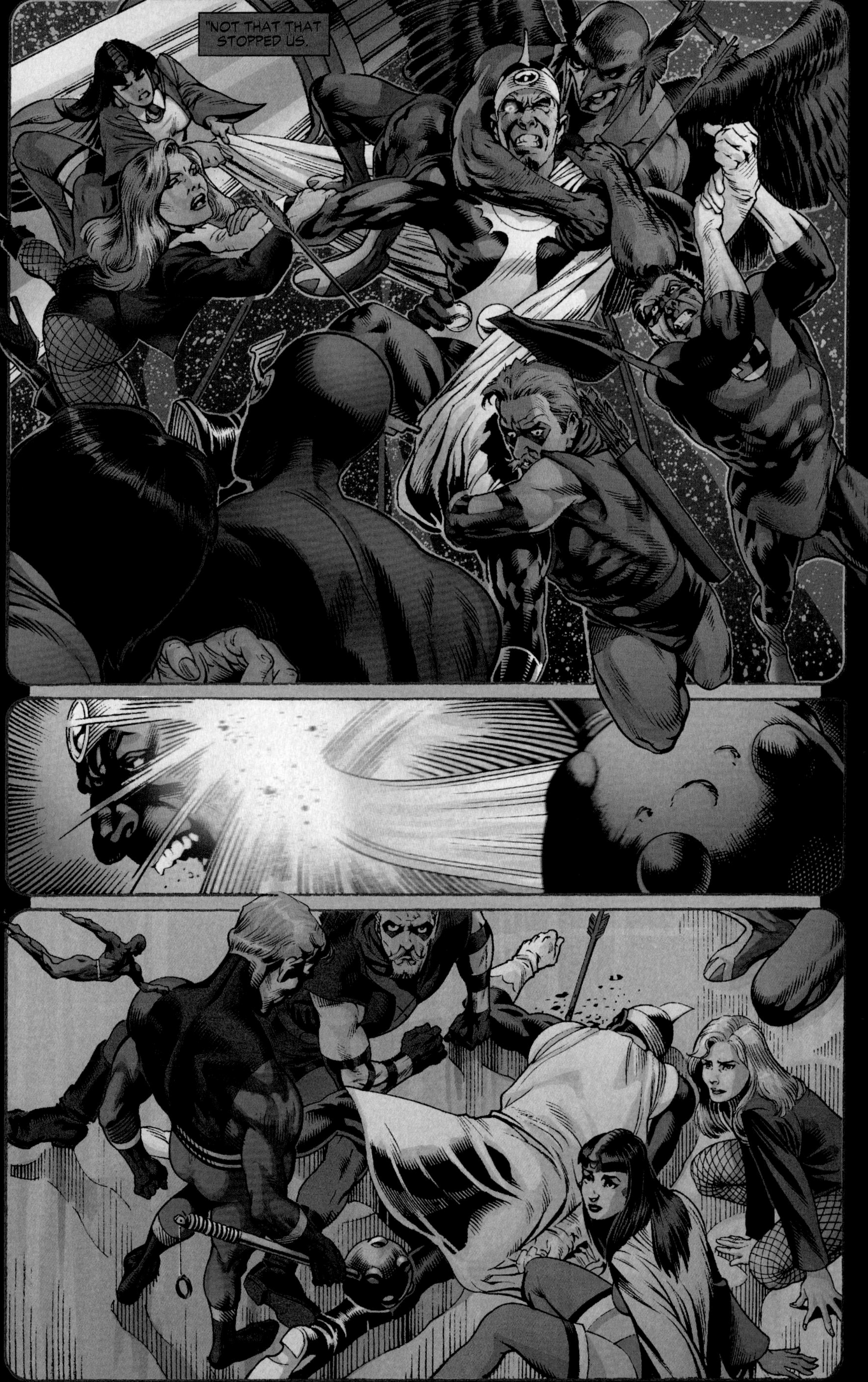
"NOT THAT THAT STOPPED US.

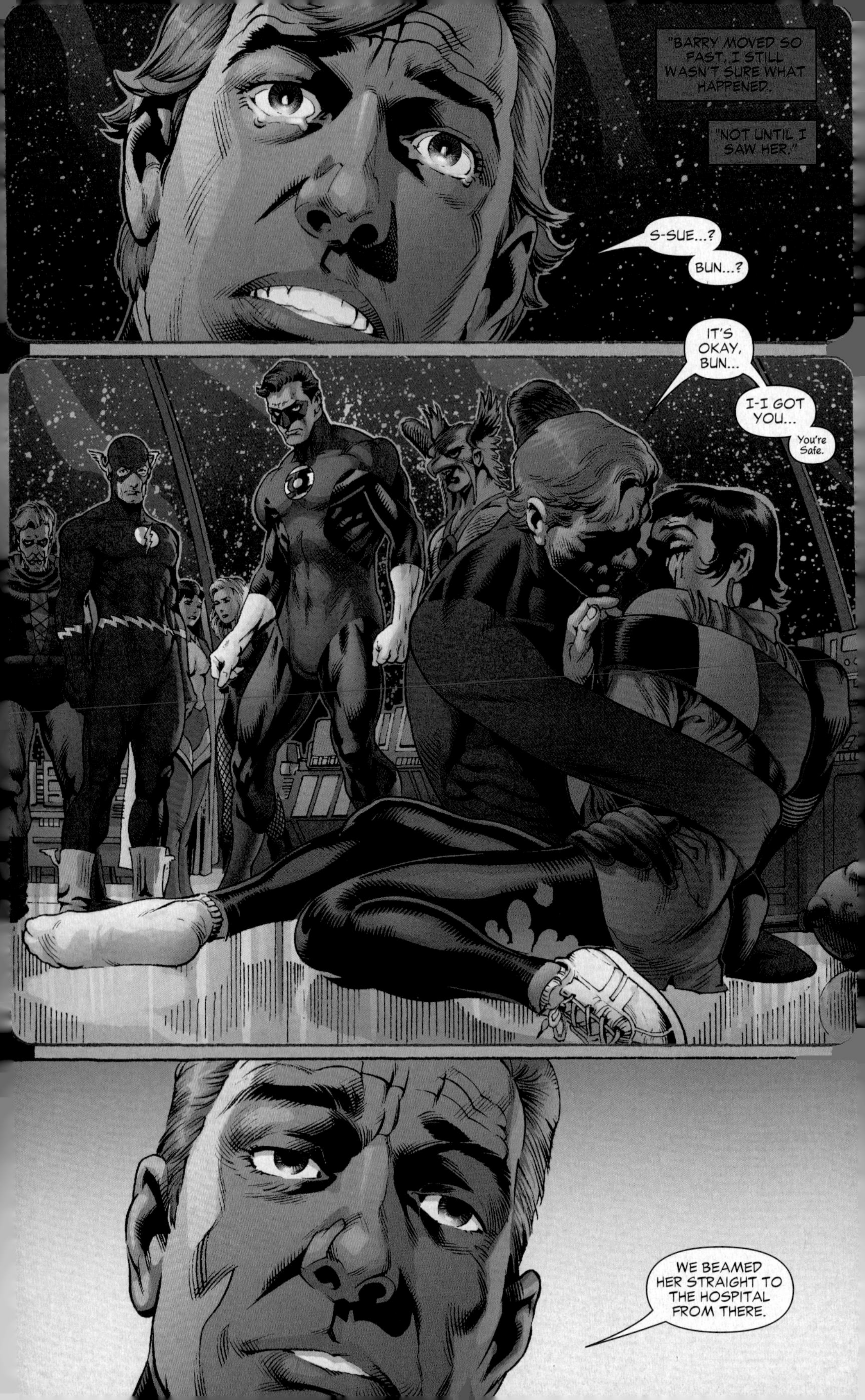
"BARRY MOVED SO FAST, I STILL WASN'T SURE WHAT HAPPENED.
"NOT UNTIL I SAW HER."
S-SUE...?
BUN...?
IT'S OKAY, BUN...
I-I GOT YOU...
You're Safe.
WE BEAMED HER STRAIGHT TO THE HOSPITAL FROM THERE.

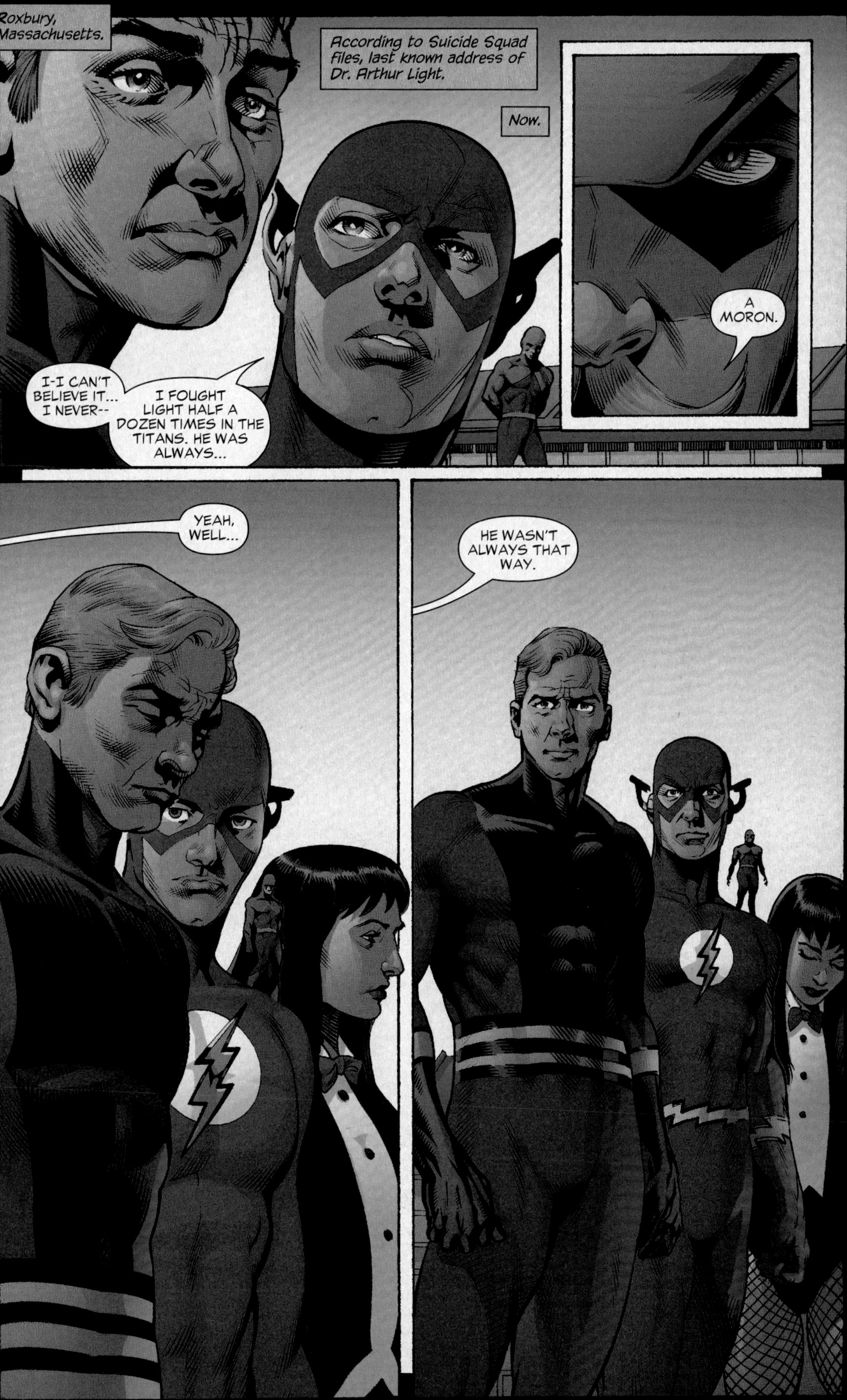
Roxbury, Massachusetts.
According to Suicide Squad files, last known address of Dr. Arthur Light.
Now.
I-I CAN'T BELIEVE IT... I NEVER--
I FOUGHT LIGHT HALF A DOZEN TIMES IN THE TITANS. HE WAS ALWAYS...
A MORON.
YEAH, WELL...
HE WASN'T ALWAYS THAT WAY.

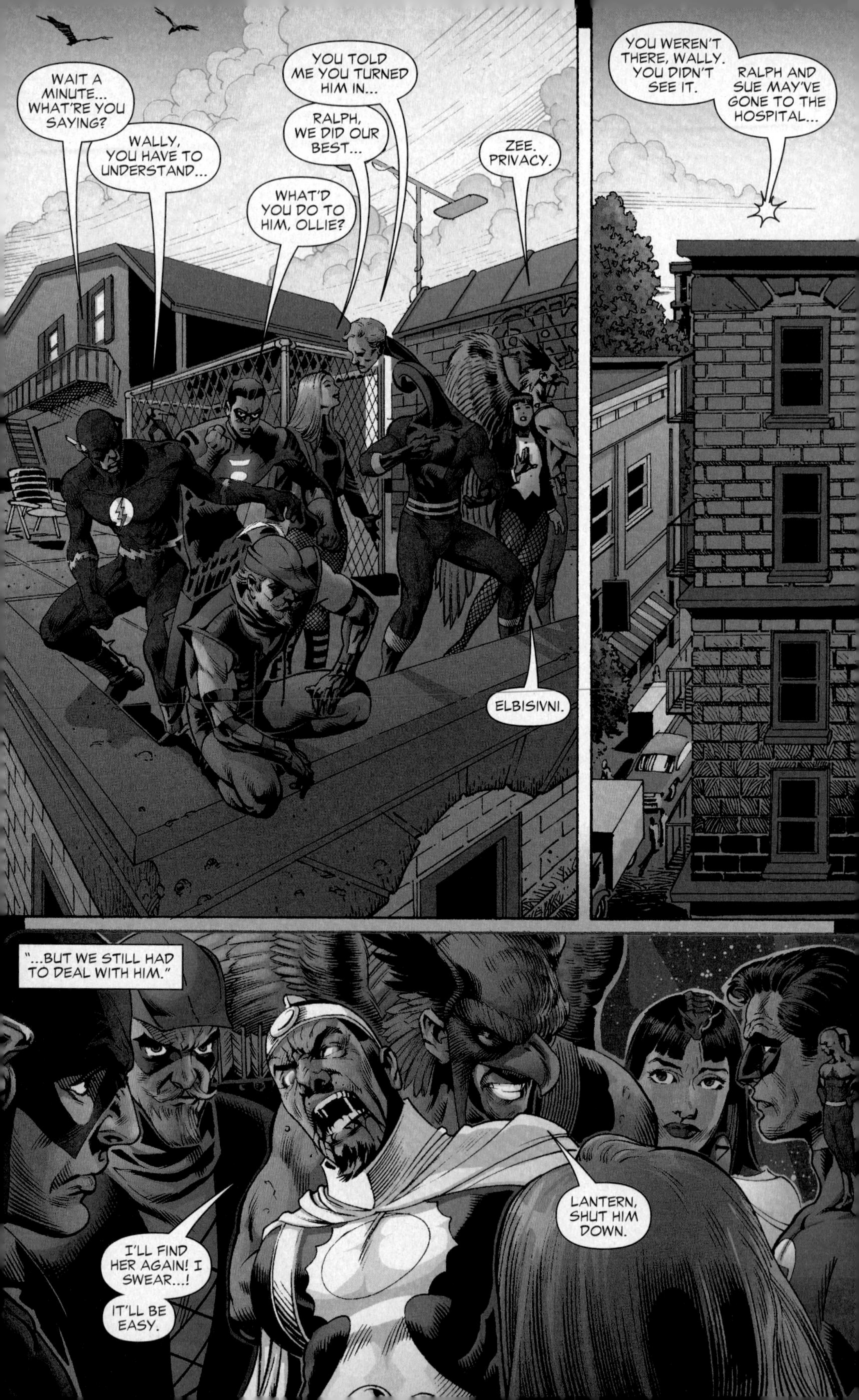
WAIT A MINUTE... WHAT'RE YOU SAYING?
WALLY, YOU HAVE TO UNDERSTAND...
YOU TOLD ME YOU TURNED HIM IN...
RALPH, WE DID OUR BEST...
WHAT'D YOU DO TO HIM, OLLIE?
ZEE. PRIVACY.
ELBISIVNI.
YOU WEREN'T THERE, WALLY. YOU DIDN'T SEE IT.
RALPH AND SUE MAY'VE GONE TO THE HOSPITAL...
"...BUT WE STILL HAD TO DEAL WITH HIM."
I'LL FIND HER AGAIN! I SWEAR...!
IT'LL BE EASY.
LANTERN, SHUT HIM DOWN.

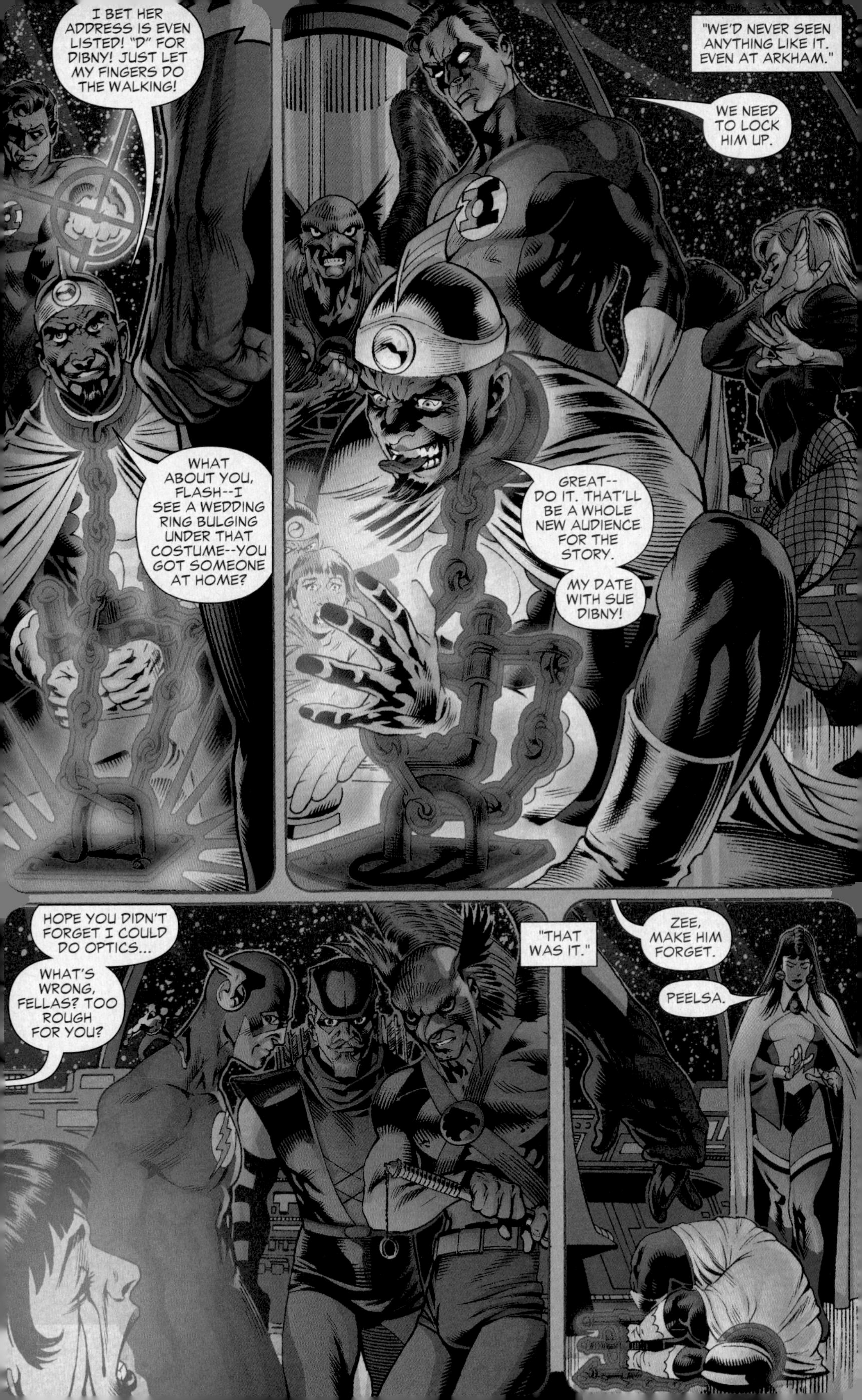
I BET HER ADDRESS IS EVEN LISTED! "D" FOR DIBNY! JUST LET MY FINGERS DO THE WALKING!
WHAT ABOUT YOU, FLASH--I SEE A WEDDING RING BULGING UNDER THAT COSTUME--YOU GOT SOMEONE AT HOME?
"WE'D NEVER SEEN ANYTHING LIKE IT. EVEN AT ARKHAM."
WE NEED TO LOCK HIM UP.
GREAT-- DO IT. THAT'LL BE A WHOLE NEW AUDIENCE FOR THE STORY.
MY DATE WITH SUE DIBNY!
HOPE YOU DIDN'T FORGET I COULD DO OPTICS...
WHAT'S WRONG, FELLAS? TOO ROUGH FOR YOU?
"THAT WAS IT."
ZEE, MAKE HIM FORGET.
PEELSA.

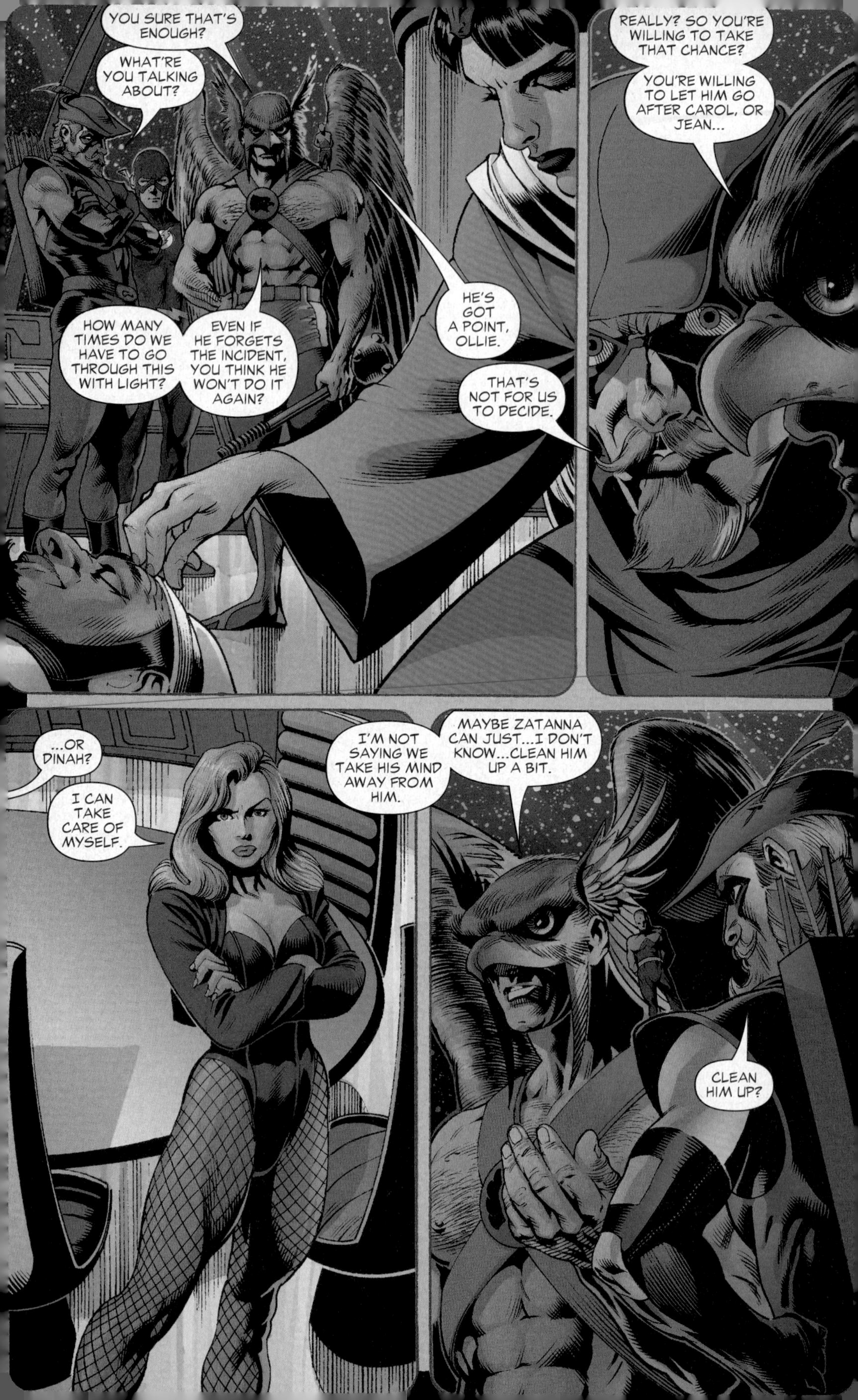
YOU SURE THAT'S ENOUGH?
WHAT'RE YOU TALKING ABOUT?
HOW MANY TIMES DO WE HAVE TO GO THROUGH THIS WITH LIGHT?
EVEN IF HE FORGETS THE INCIDENT, YOU THINK HE WON'T DO IT AGAIN?
HE'S GOT A POINT, OLLIE.
THAT'S NOT FOR US TO DECIDE.
REALLY? SO YOU'RE WILLING TO TAKE THAT CHANCE?
YOU'RE WILLING TO LET HIM GO AFTER CAROL, OR JEAN...
...OR DINAH?
I CAN TAKE CARE OF MYSELF.
I'M NOT SAYING WE TAKE HIS MIND AWAY FROM HIM.
MAYBE ZATANNA CAN JUST...I DON'T KNOW...CLEAN HIM UP A BIT.
CLEAN HIM UP?

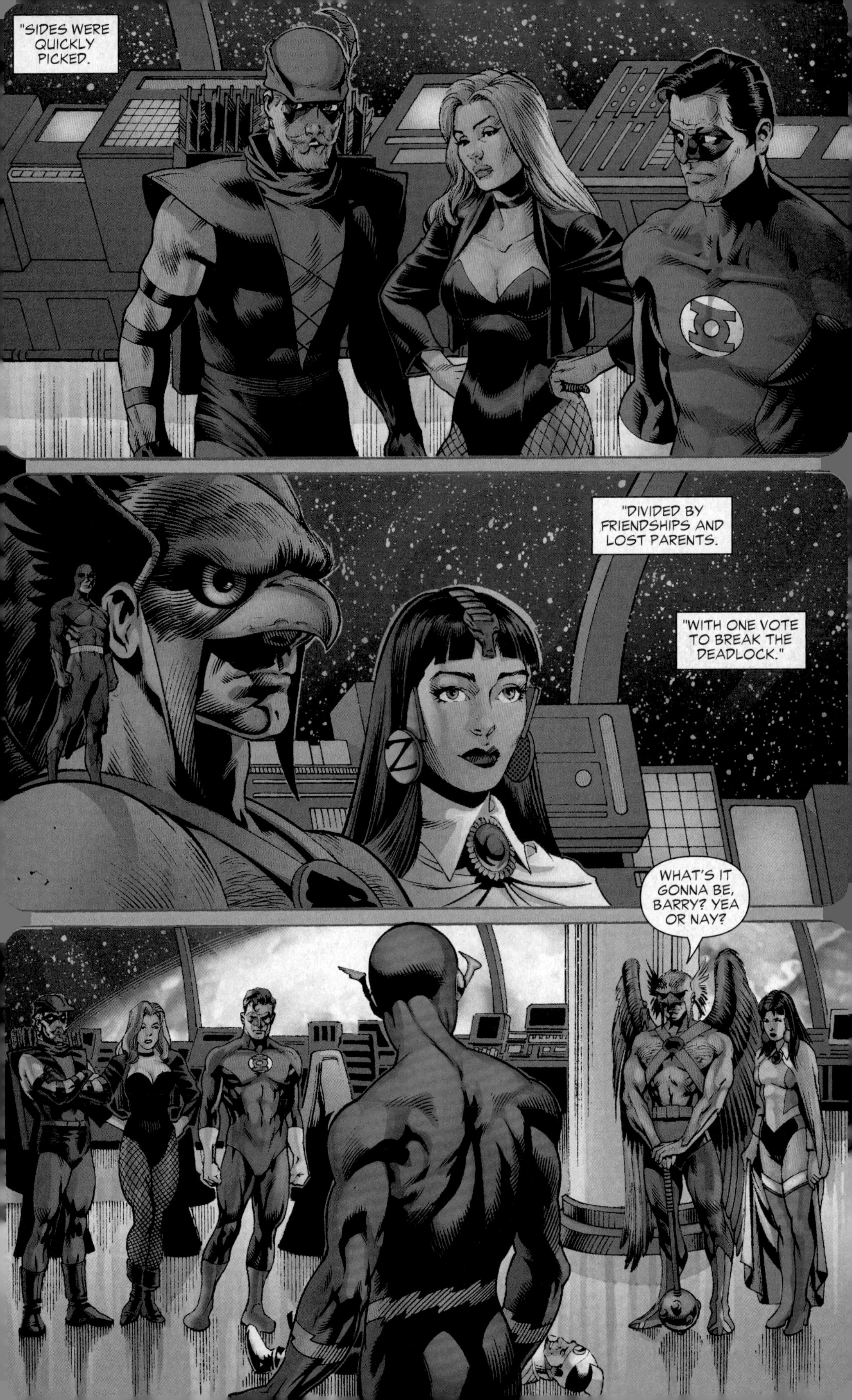
"SIDES WERE QUICKLY PICKED.
"DIVIDED BY FRIENDSHIPS AND LOST PARENTS.
"WITH ONE VOTE TO BREAK THE DEADLOCK."
WHAT'S IT GONNA BE, BARRY? YEA OR NAY?

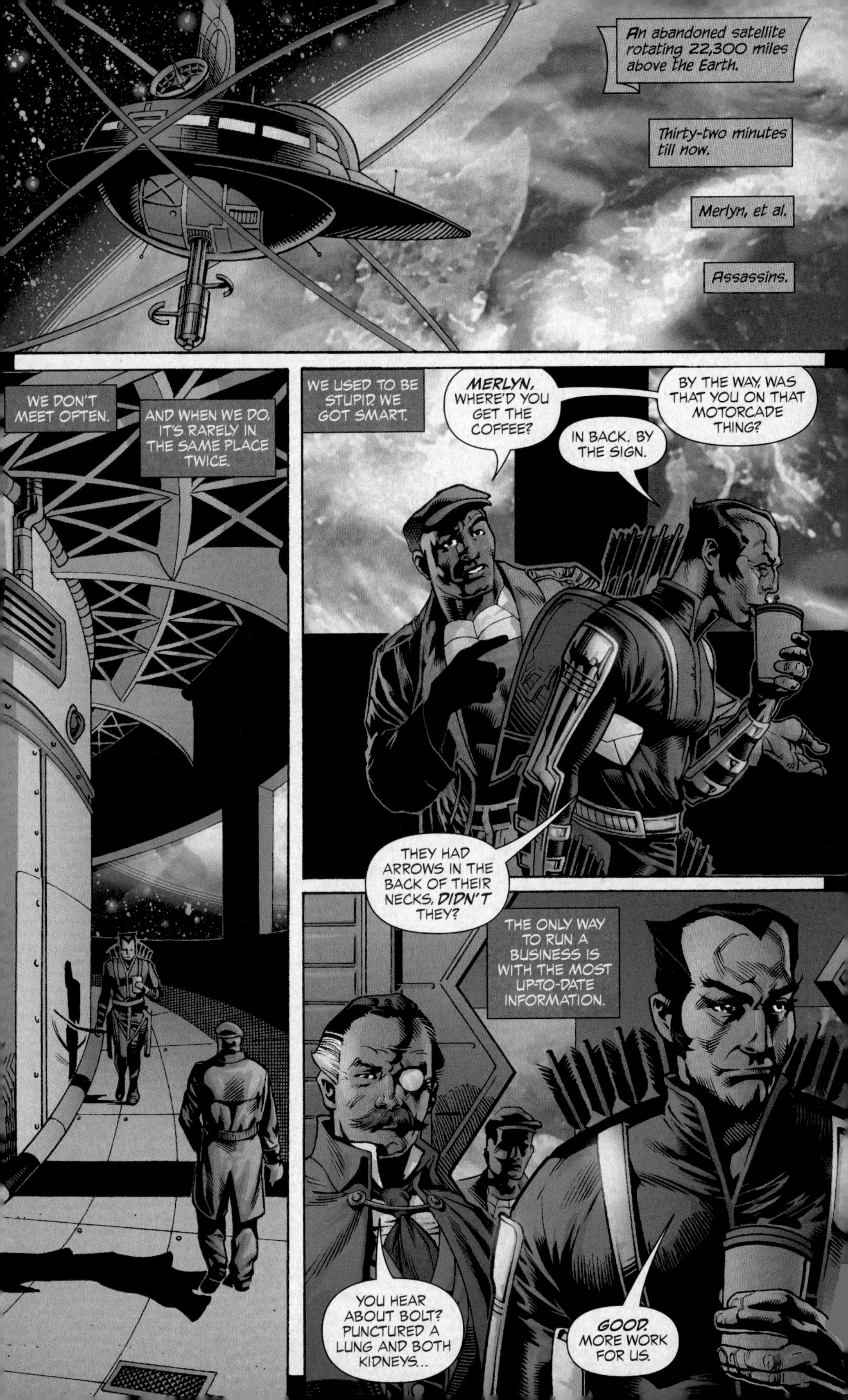
An abandoned satellite rotating 22,300 miles above the Earth.
Thirty-two minutes till now.
Merlyn, et al.
Assassins.
WE DON'T MEET OFTEN.
AND WHEN WE DO, IT'S RARELY IN THE SAME PLACE TWICE.
WE USED TO BE STUPID. WE GOT SMART.
MERLYN, WHERE'D YOU GET THE COFFEE?
BY THE WAY, WAS THAT YOU ON THAT MOTORCADE THING?
IN BACK. BY THE SIGN.
THEY HAD ARROWS IN THE BACK OF THEIR NECKS, DIDN'T THEY?
THE ONLY WAY TO RUN A BUSINESS IS WITH THE MOST UP-TO-DATE INFORMATION.
YOU HEAR ABOUT BOLT? PUNCTURED A LUNG AND BOTH KIDNEYS...
GOOD. MORE WORK FOR US.

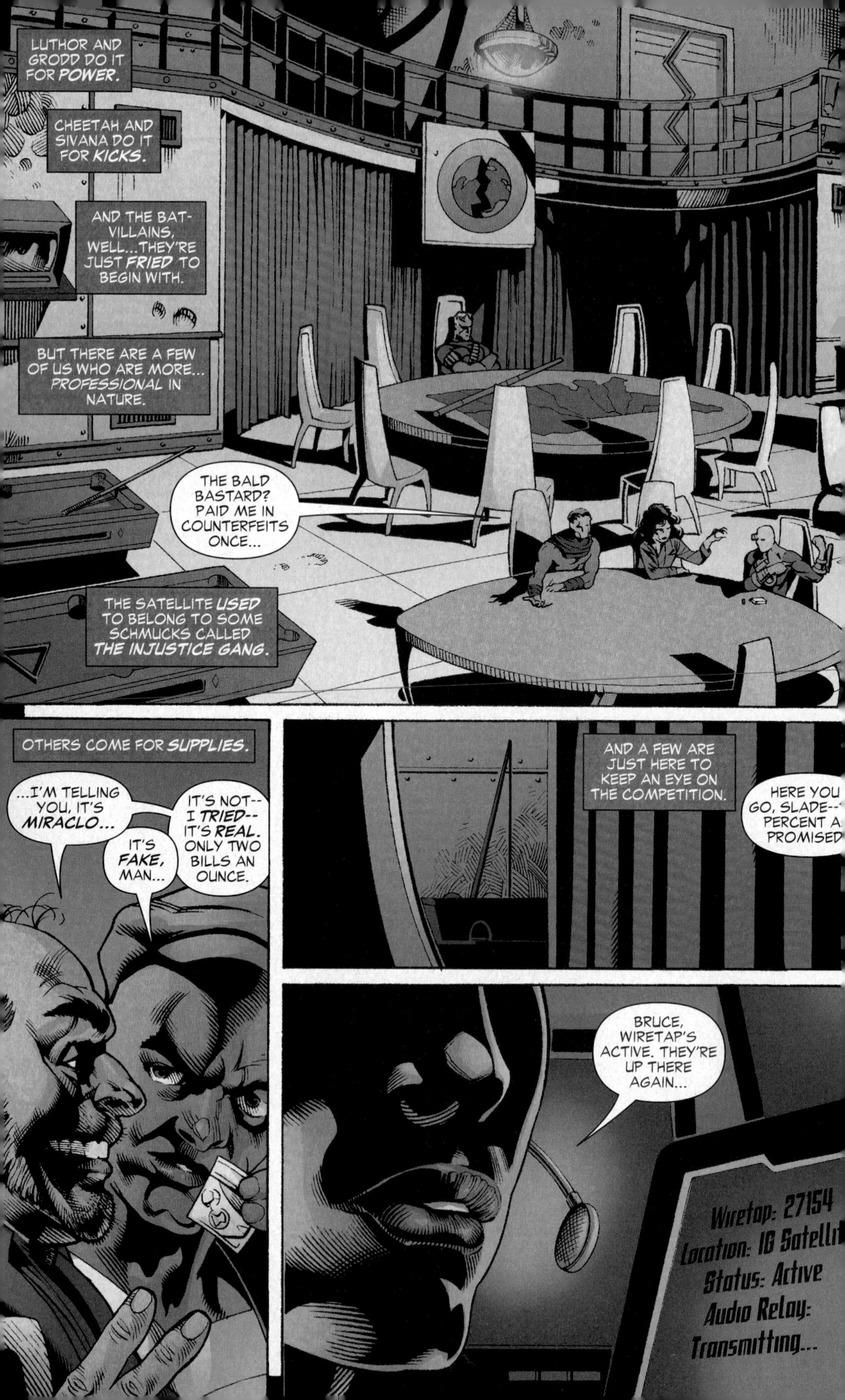

LUTHOR AND GRODD DO IT FOR POWER.
CHEETAH AND SIVANA DO IT FOR KICKS.
AND THE BAT-VILLAINS, WELL...THEY'RE JUST FRIED TO BEGIN WITH.
BUT THERE ARE A FEW OF US WHO ARE MORE... PROFESSIONAL IN NATURE.
THE BALD BASTARD? PAID ME IN COUNTERFEITS ONCE...
THE SATELLITE USED TO BELONG TO SOME SCHMUCKS CALLED THE INJUSTICE GANG.
OTHERS COME FOR SUPPLIES.
...I'M TELLING YOU, IT'S MIRACLO...
IT'S FAKE, MAN...
IT'S NOT-- I TRIED-- IT'S REAL. ONLY TWO BILLS AN OUNCE.
AND A FEW ARE JUST HERE TO KEEP AN EYE ON THE COMPETITION.
HERE YOU GO, SLADE-- PERCENT A PROMISED
BRUCE, WIRETAP'S ACTIVE. THEY'RE UP THERE AGAIN...
Wiretap: 27154
Location: IG Satellit
Status: Active
Audio Relay:
Transmitting...

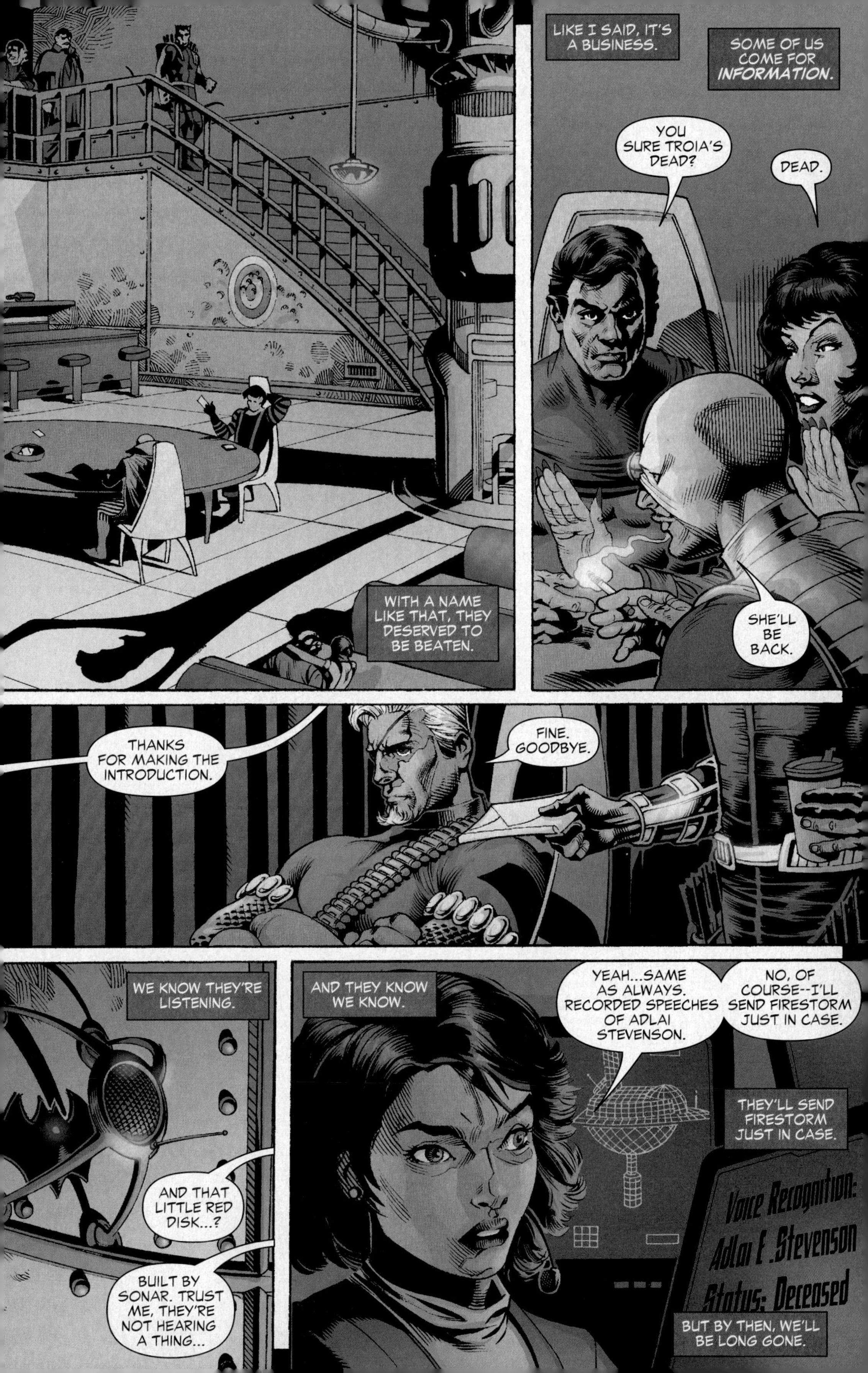
WITH A NAME LIKE THAT, THEY DESERVED TO BE BEATEN.
LIKE I SAID, IT'S A BUSINESS.
SOME OF US COME FOR *INFORMATION*.
YOU SURE TROIA'S DEAD?
DEAD.
SHE'LL BE BACK.
THANKS FOR MAKING THE INTRODUCTION.
FINE. GOODBYE.
WE KNOW THEY'RE LISTENING.
AND THAT LITTLE RED DISK...?
BUILT BY SONAR. TRUST ME, THEY'RE NOT HEARING A THING...
AND THEY KNOW WE KNOW.
YEAH...SAME AS ALWAYS. RECORDED SPEECHES OF ADLAI STEVENSON.
NO, OF COURSE--I'LL SEND FIRESTORM JUST IN CASE.
THEY'LL SEND FIRESTORM JUST IN CASE.
Voice Recognition: Adlai E. Stevenson Status: Deceased
BUT BY THEN, WE'LL BE LONG GONE.

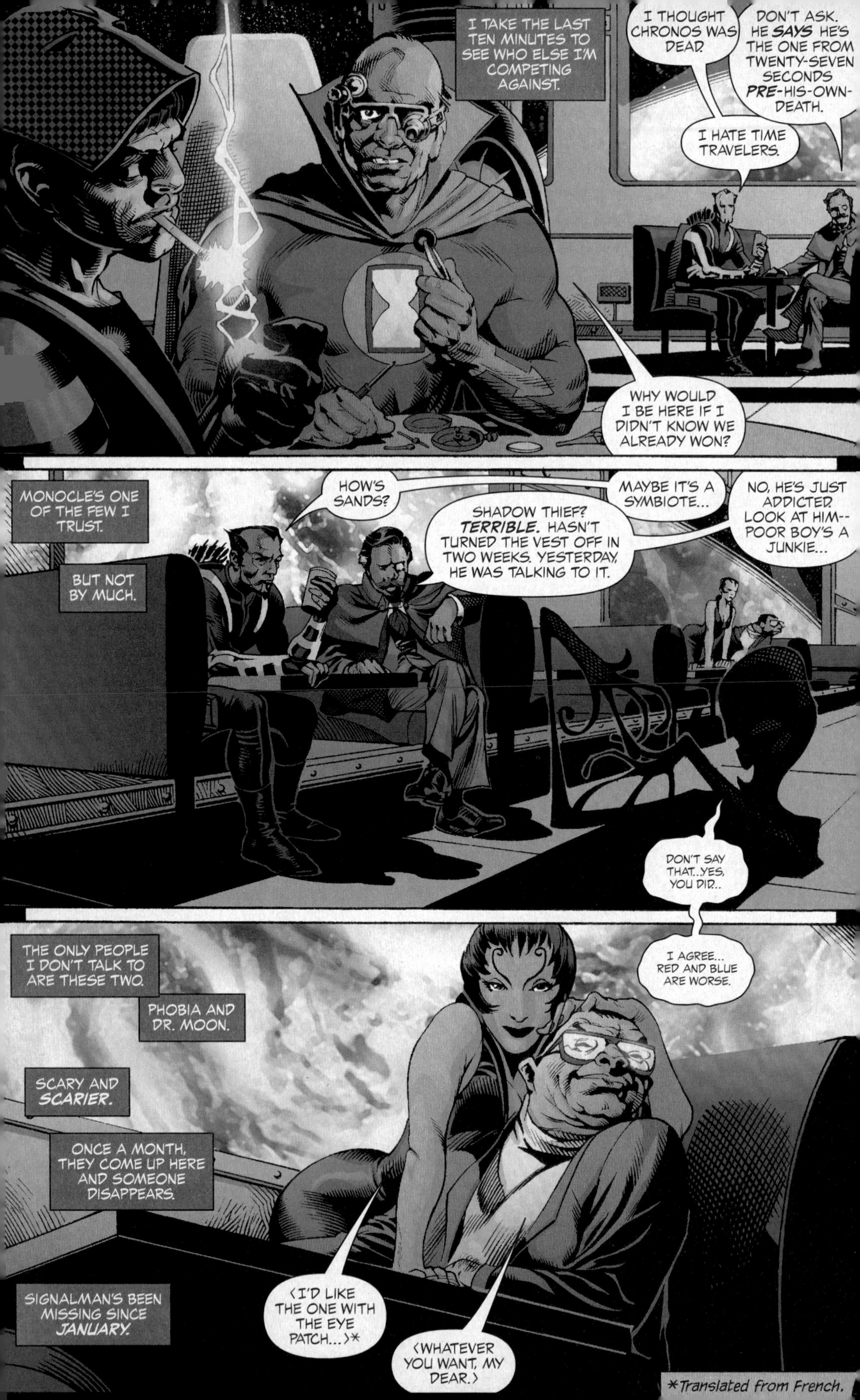
I TAKE THE LAST TEN MINUTES TO SEE WHO ELSE I'M COMPETING AGAINST.
I THOUGHT CHRONOS WAS DEAD.
DON'T ASK. HE SAYS HE'S THE ONE FROM TWENTY-SEVEN SECONDS PRE-HIS-OWN-DEATH.
I HATE TIME TRAVELERS.
WHY WOULD I BE HERE IF I DIDN'T KNOW WE ALREADY WON?
MONOCLE'S ONE OF THE FEW I TRUST.
BUT NOT BY MUCH.
HOW'S SANDS?
SHADOW THIEF? TERRIBLE. HASN'T TURNED THE VEST OFF IN TWO WEEKS. YESTERDAY, HE WAS TALKING TO IT.
MAYBE IT'S A SYMBIOTE...
NO, HE'S JUST ADDICTED. LOOK AT HIM-- POOR BOY'S A JUNKIE...
DON'T SAY THAT...YES, YOU DID...
THE ONLY PEOPLE I DON'T TALK TO ARE THESE TWO.
PHOBIA AND DR. MOON.
SCARY AND SCARIER.
ONCE A MONTH, THEY COME UP HERE AND SOMEONE DISAPPEARS.
I AGREE... RED AND BLUE ARE WORSE.
SIGNALMAN'S BEEN MISSING SINCE JANUARY.
‹I'D LIKE THE ONE WITH THE EYE PATCH...›*
‹WHATEVER YOU WANT, MY DEAR.›
*Translated from French.

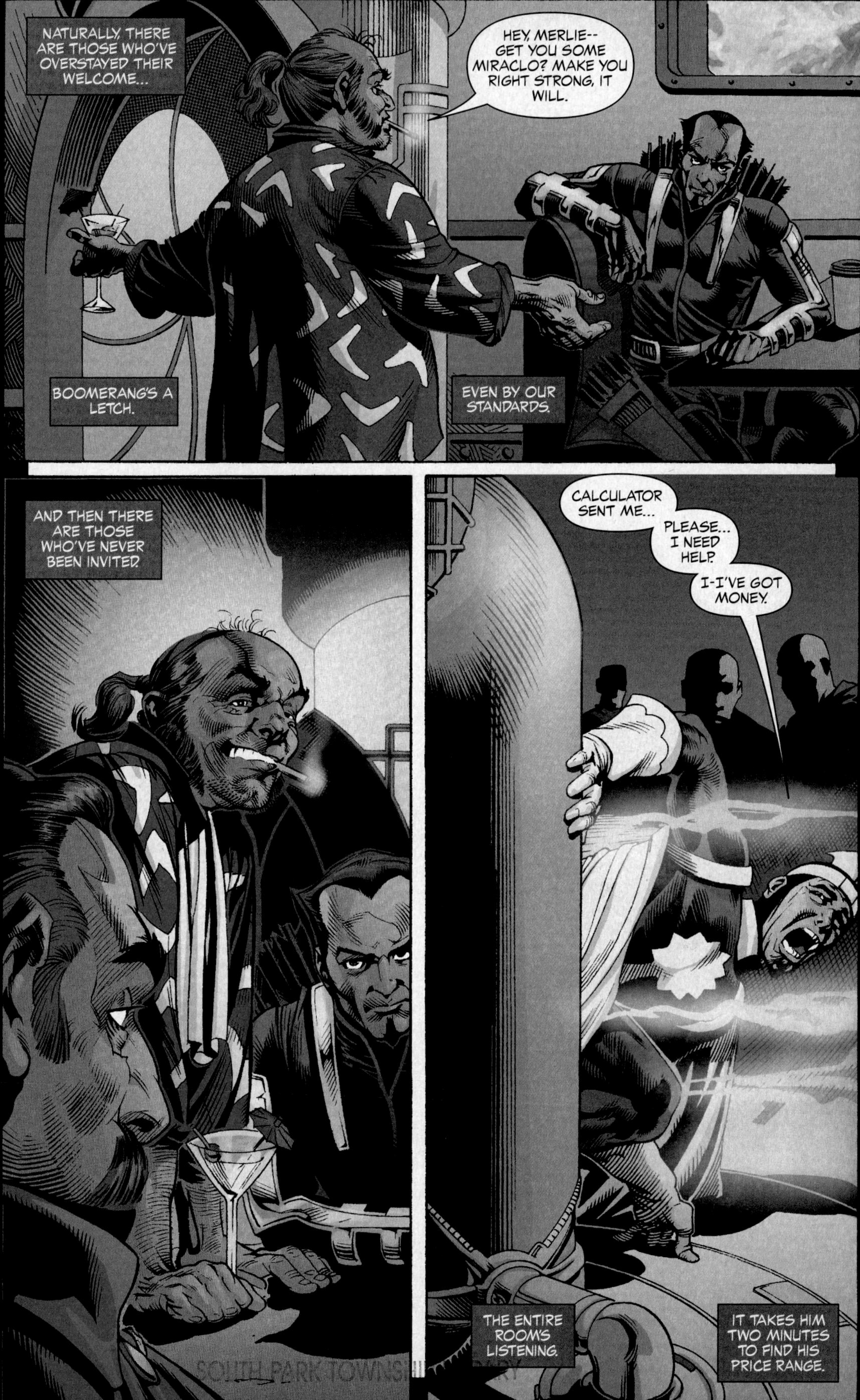
NATURALLY, THERE ARE THOSE WHO'VE OVERSTAYED THEIR WELCOME...
HEY, MERLIE-- GET YOU SOME MIRACLO? MAKE YOU RIGHT STRONG, IT WILL.
BOOMERANG'S A LETCH.
EVEN BY OUR STANDARDS.
AND THEN THERE ARE THOSE WHO'VE NEVER BEEN INVITED.
CALCULATOR SENT ME...
PLEASE... I NEED HELP.
I-I'VE GOT MONEY.
THE ENTIRE ROOM'S LISTENING.
IT TAKES HIM TWO MINUTES TO FIND HIS PRICE RANGE.

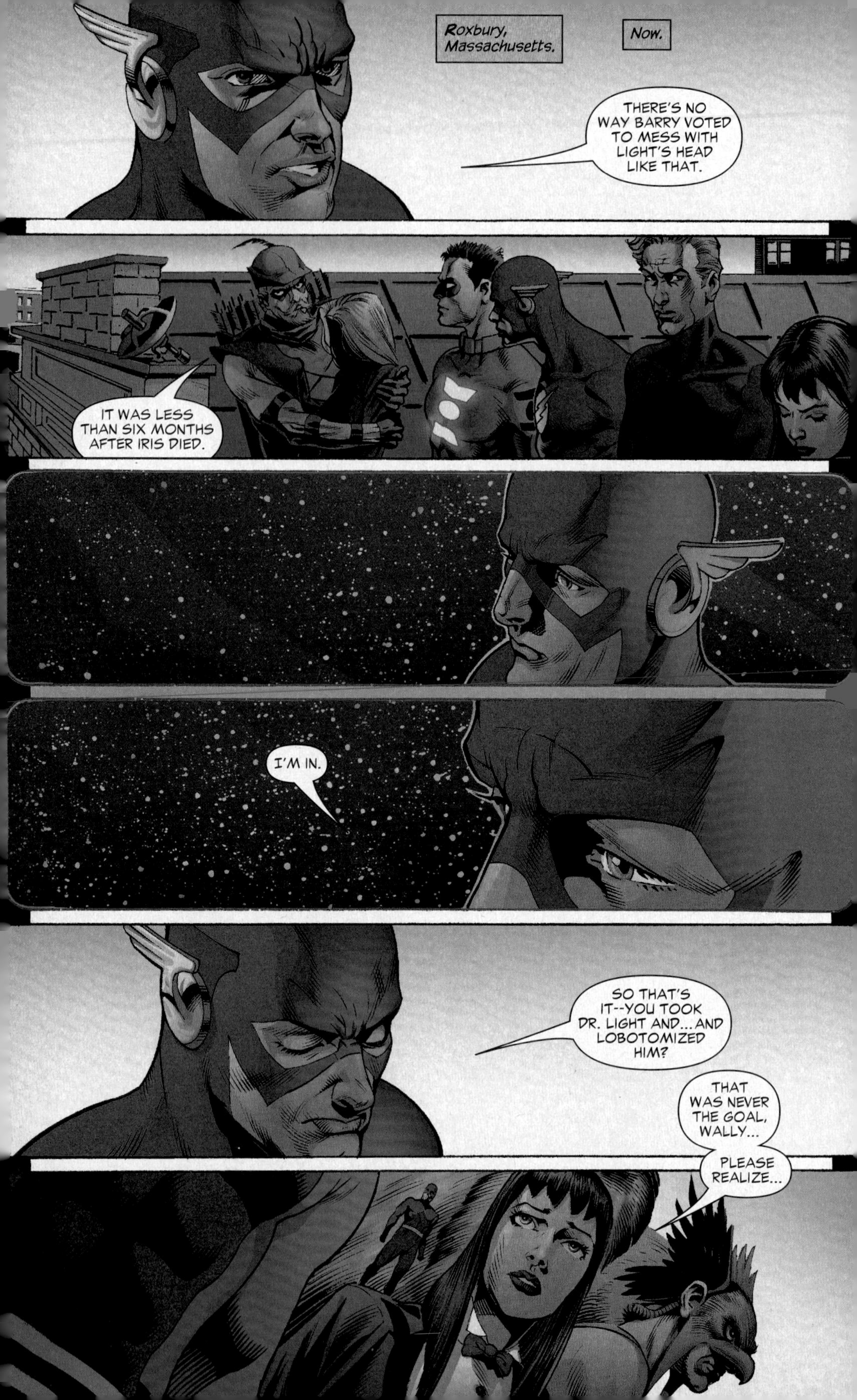
Roxbury, Massachusetts.
Now.
THERE'S NO WAY BARRY VOTED TO MESS WITH LIGHT'S HEAD LIKE THAT.
IT WAS LESS THAN SIX MONTHS AFTER IRIS DIED.
I'M IN.
SO THAT'S IT--YOU TOOK DR. LIGHT AND...AND LOBOTOMIZED HIM?
THAT WAS NEVER THE GOAL, WALLY...
PLEASE REALIZE...

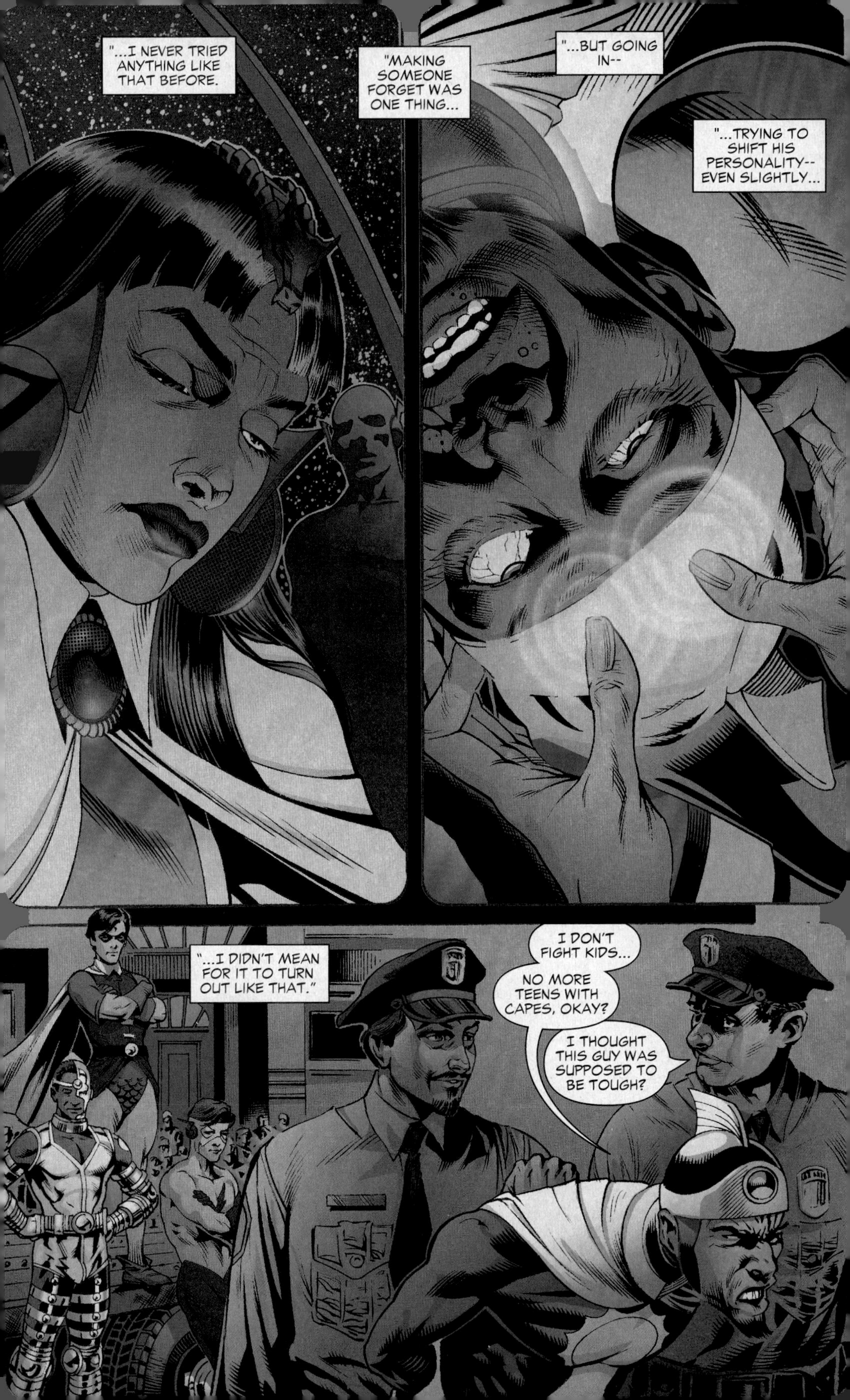
"...I NEVER TRIED ANYTHING LIKE THAT BEFORE.
"MAKING SOMEONE FORGET WAS ONE THING...
"...BUT GOING IN--
"...TRYING TO SHIFT HIS PERSONALITY-- EVEN SLIGHTLY...
"...I DIDN'T MEAN FOR IT TO TURN OUT LIKE THAT."
I DON'T FIGHT KIDS...
NO MORE TEENS WITH CAPES, OKAY?
I THOUGHT THIS GUY WAS SUPPOSED TO BE TOUGH?

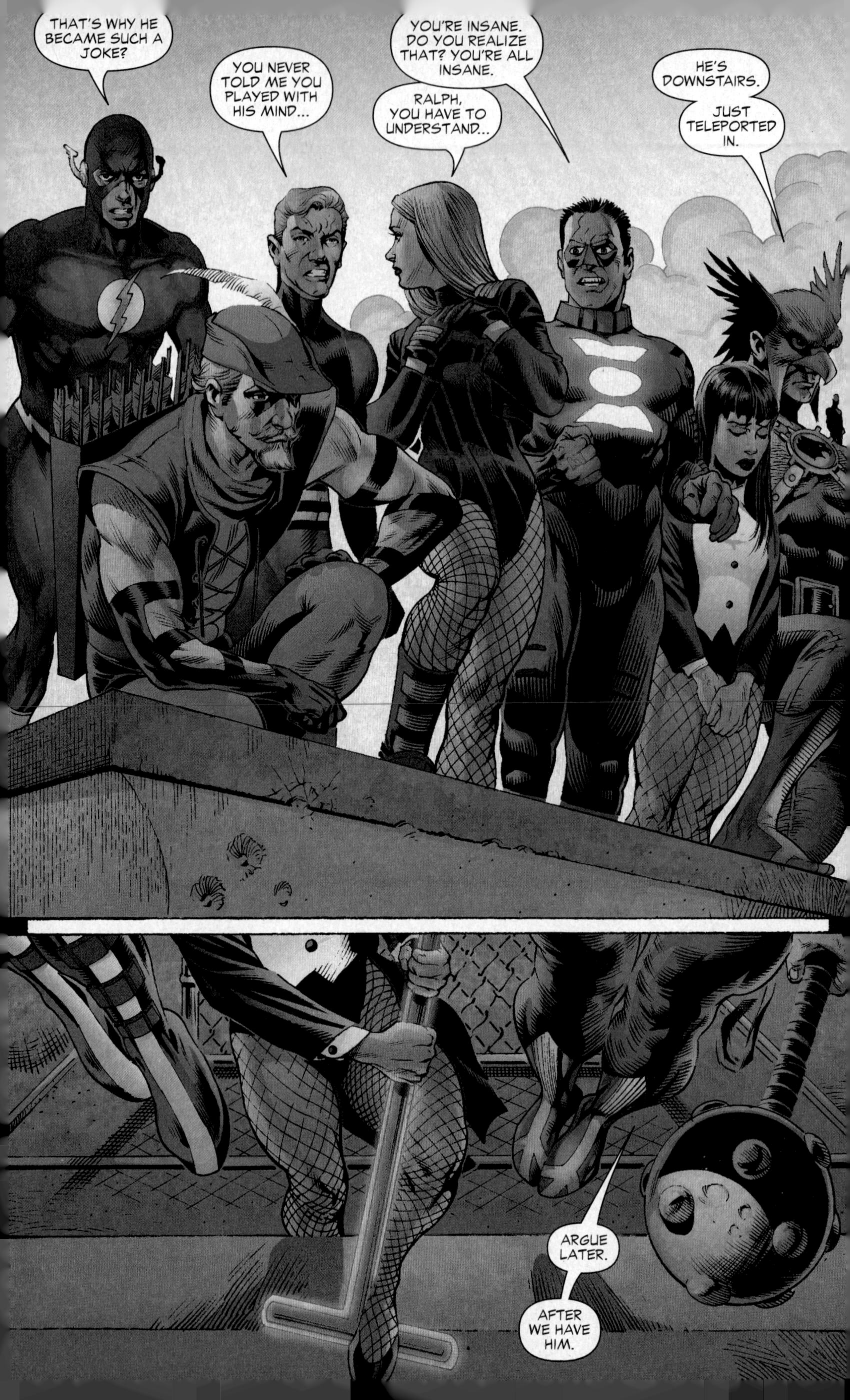
THAT'S WHY HE BECAME SUCH A JOKE?
YOU NEVER TOLD ME YOU PLAYED WITH HIS MIND...
YOU'RE INSANE. DO YOU REALIZE THAT? YOU'RE ALL INSANE.
RALPH, YOU HAVE TO UNDERSTAND...
HE'S DOWNSTAIRS.
JUST TELEPORTED IN.
ARGUE LATER.
AFTER WE HAVE HIM.

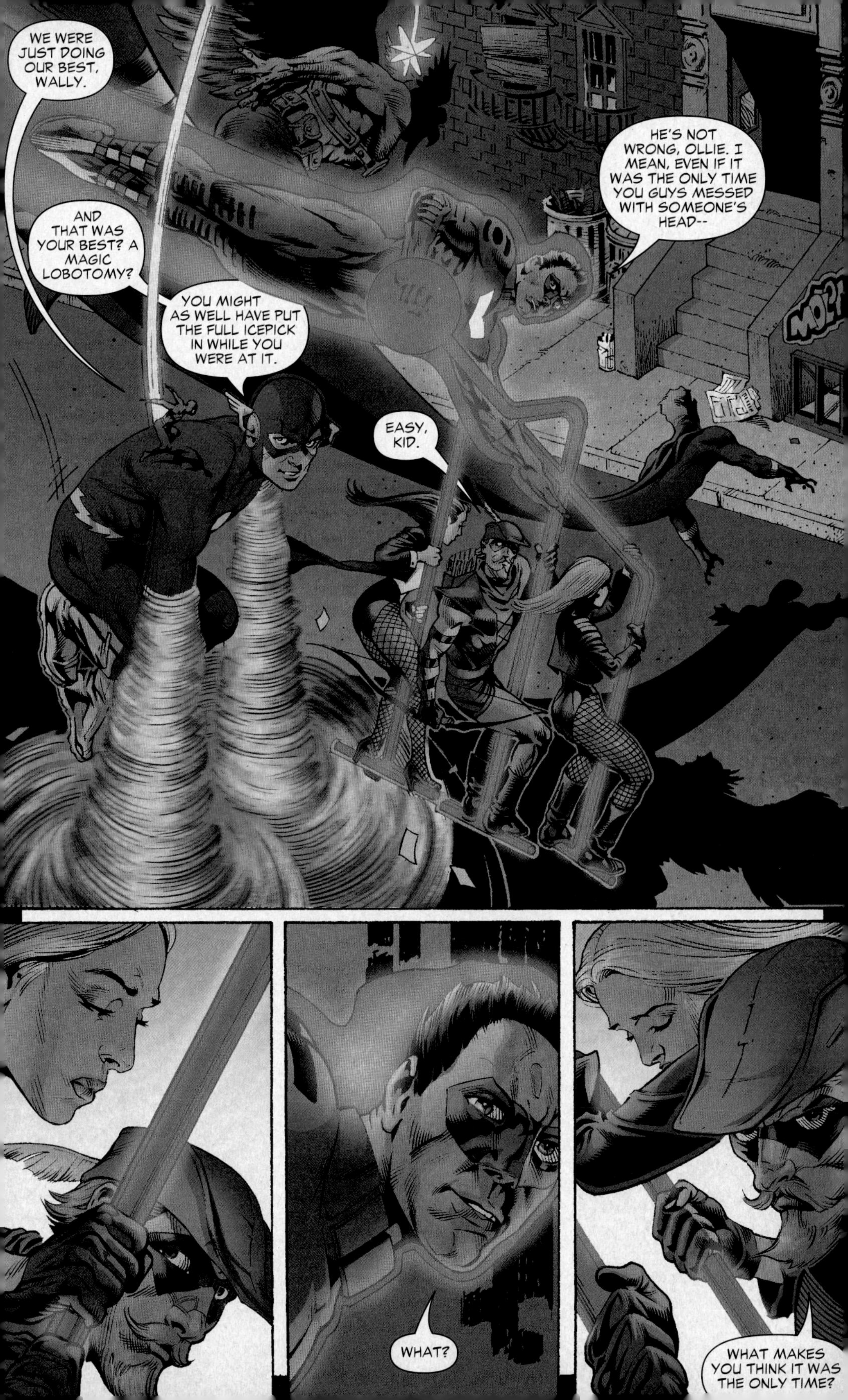
WE WERE JUST DOING OUR BEST, WALLY.
AND THAT WAS YOUR BEST? A MAGIC LOBOTOMY?
YOU MIGHT AS WELL HAVE PUT THE FULL ICEPICK IN WHILE YOU WERE AT IT.
HE'S NOT WRONG, OLLIE. I MEAN, EVEN IF IT WAS THE ONLY TIME YOU GUYS MESSED WITH SOMEONE'S HEAD--
EASY, KID.
WHAT?
WHAT MAKES YOU THINK IT WAS THE ONLY TIME?

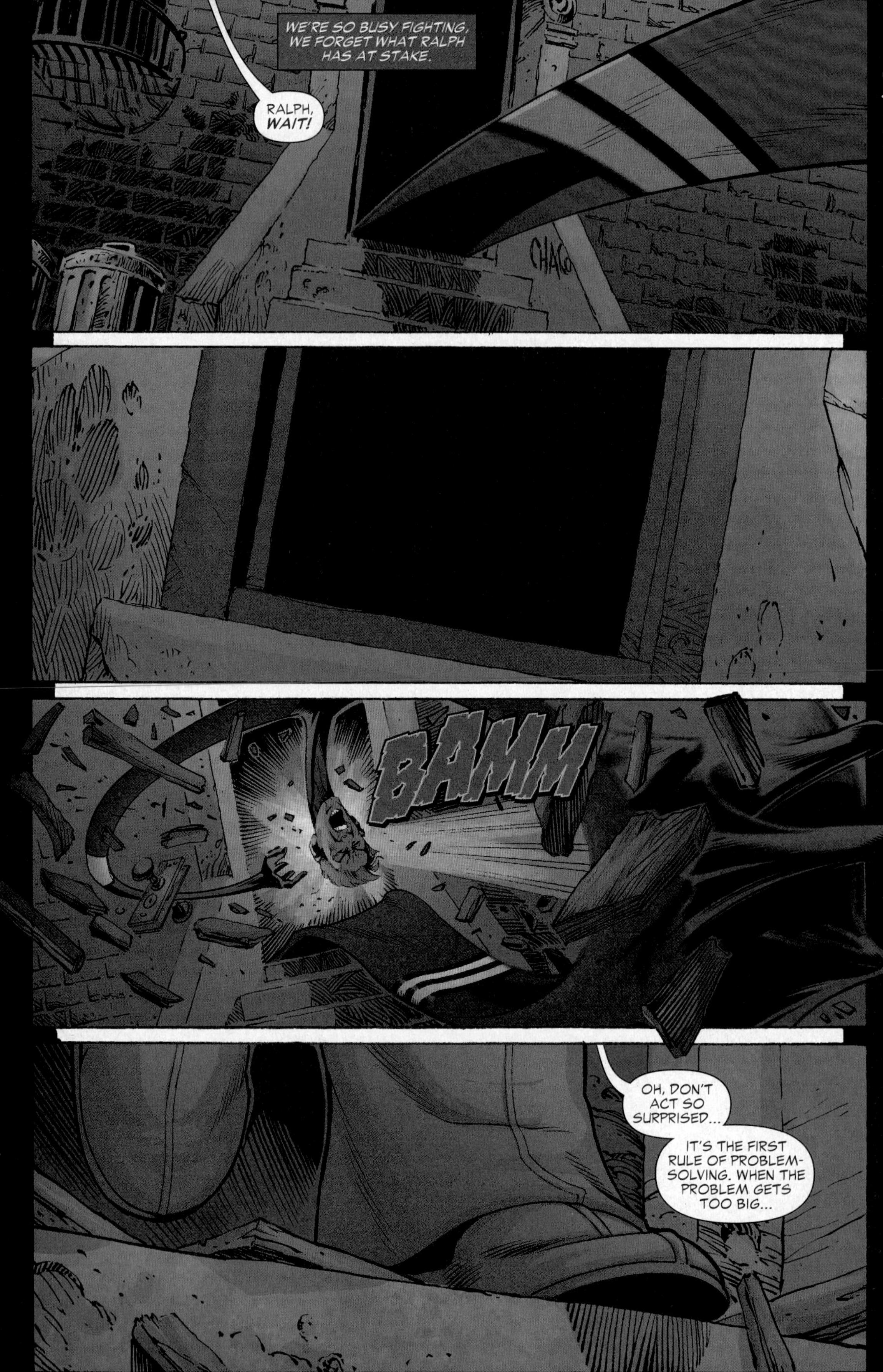
WE'RE SO BUSY FIGHTING, WE FORGET WHAT RALPH HAS AT STAKE.
RALPH, WAIT!
CHAGO
BAMM
OH, DON'T ACT SO SURPRISED...
IT'S THE FIRST RULE OF PROBLEM-SOLVING. WHEN THE PROBLEM GETS TOO BIG...

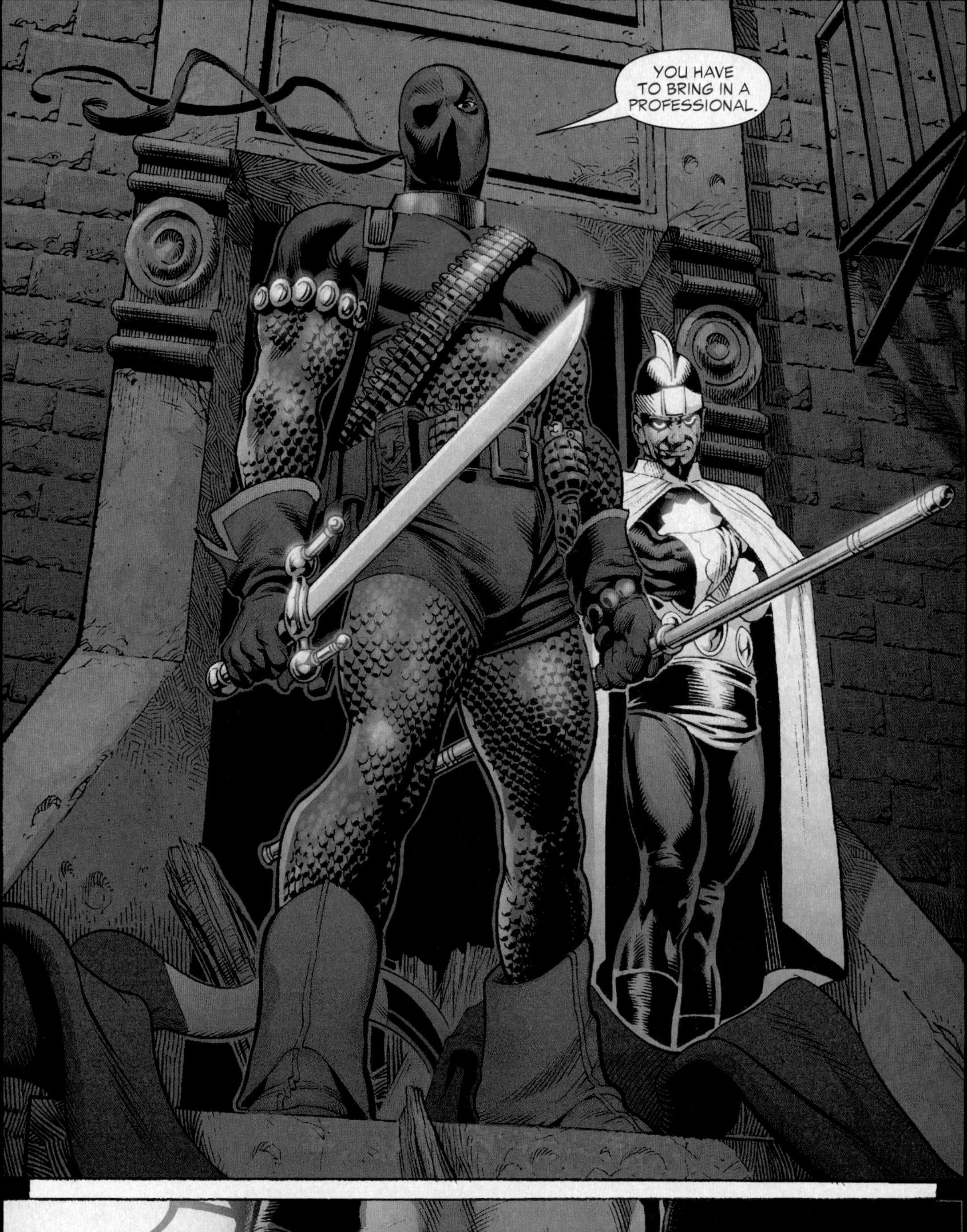
YOU HAVE TO BRING IN A PROFESSIONAL.

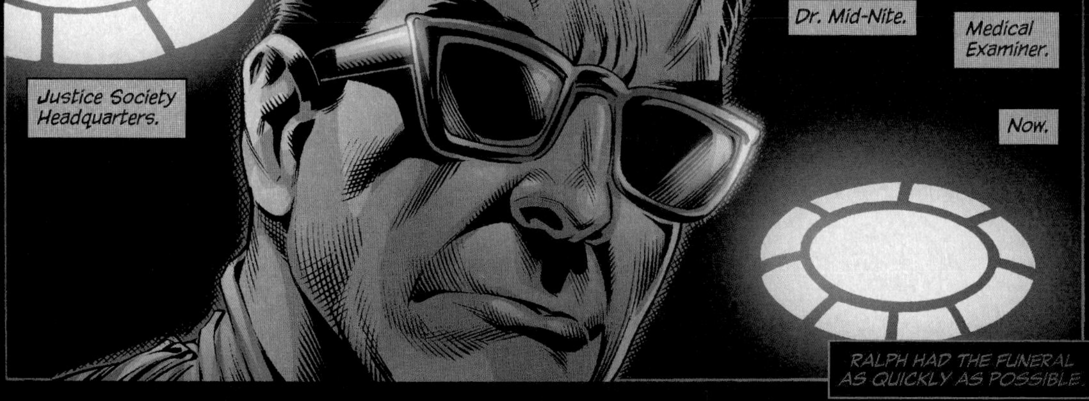
Justice Society Headquarters.
Dr. Mid-Nite.
Medical Examiner.
Now.
RALPH HAD THE FUNERAL AS QUICKLY AS POSSIBLE.

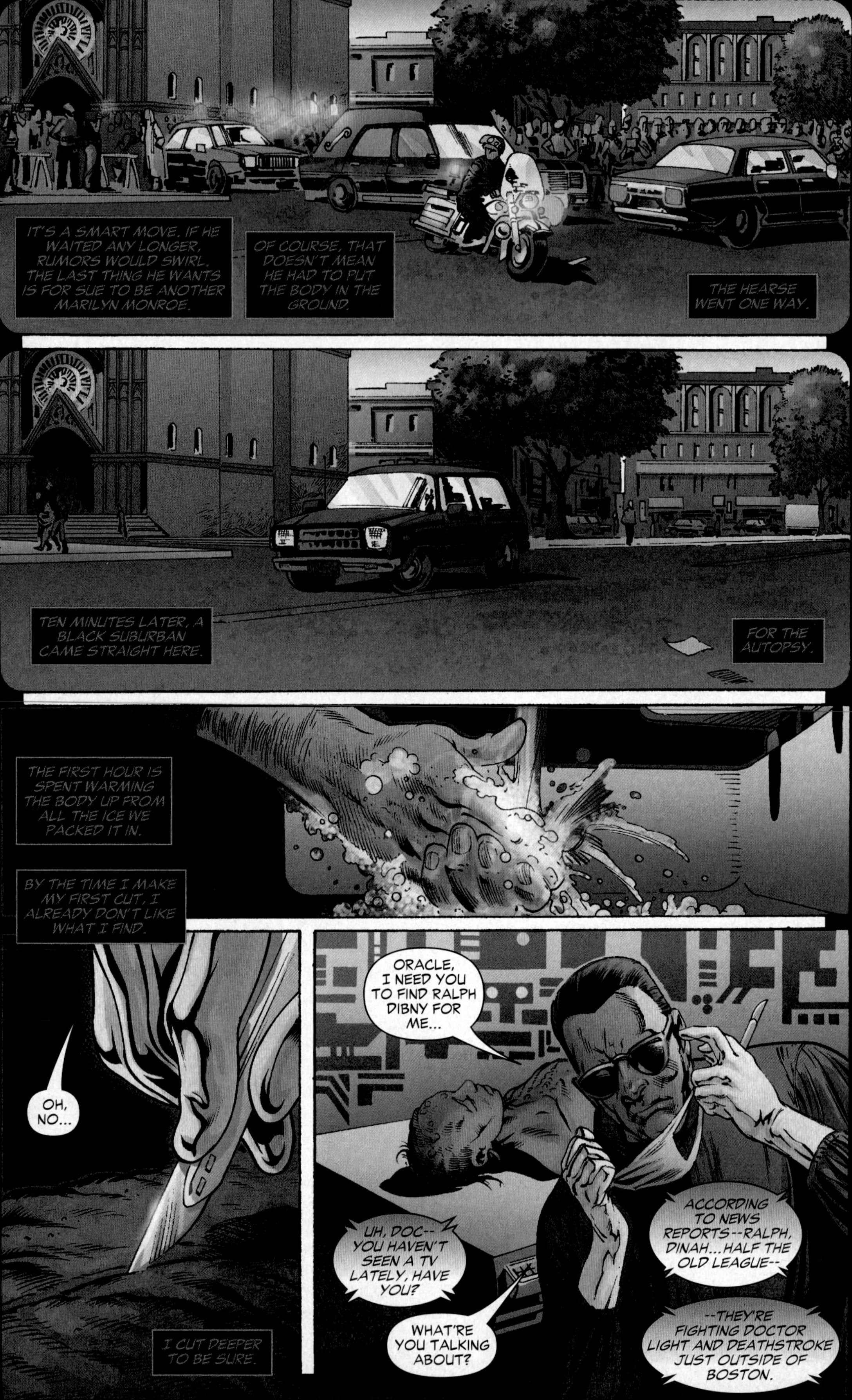
IT'S A SMART MOVE. IF HE WAITED ANY LONGER, RUMORS WOULD SWIRL. THE LAST THING HE WANTS IS FOR SUE TO BE ANOTHER MARILYN MONROE.
OF COURSE, THAT DOESN'T MEAN HE HAD TO PUT THE BODY IN THE GROUND.
THE HEARSE WENT ONE WAY.
TEN MINUTES LATER, A BLACK SUBURBAN CAME STRAIGHT HERE.
FOR THE AUTOPSY.
THE FIRST HOUR IS SPENT WARMING THE BODY UP FROM ALL THE ICE WE PACKED IT IN.
BY THE TIME I MAKE MY FIRST CUT, I ALREADY DON'T LIKE WHAT I FIND.
OH, NO...
I CUT DEEPER TO BE SURE.
ORACLE, I NEED YOU TO FIND RALPH DIBNY FOR ME...
UH, DOC--YOU HAVEN'T SEEN A TV LATELY, HAVE YOU?
WHAT'RE YOU TALKING ABOUT?
ACCORDING TO NEWS REPORTS--RALPH, DINAH...HALF THE OLD LEAGUE--
--THEY'RE FIGHTING DOCTOR LIGHT AND DEATHSTROKE JUST OUTSIDE OF BOSTON.

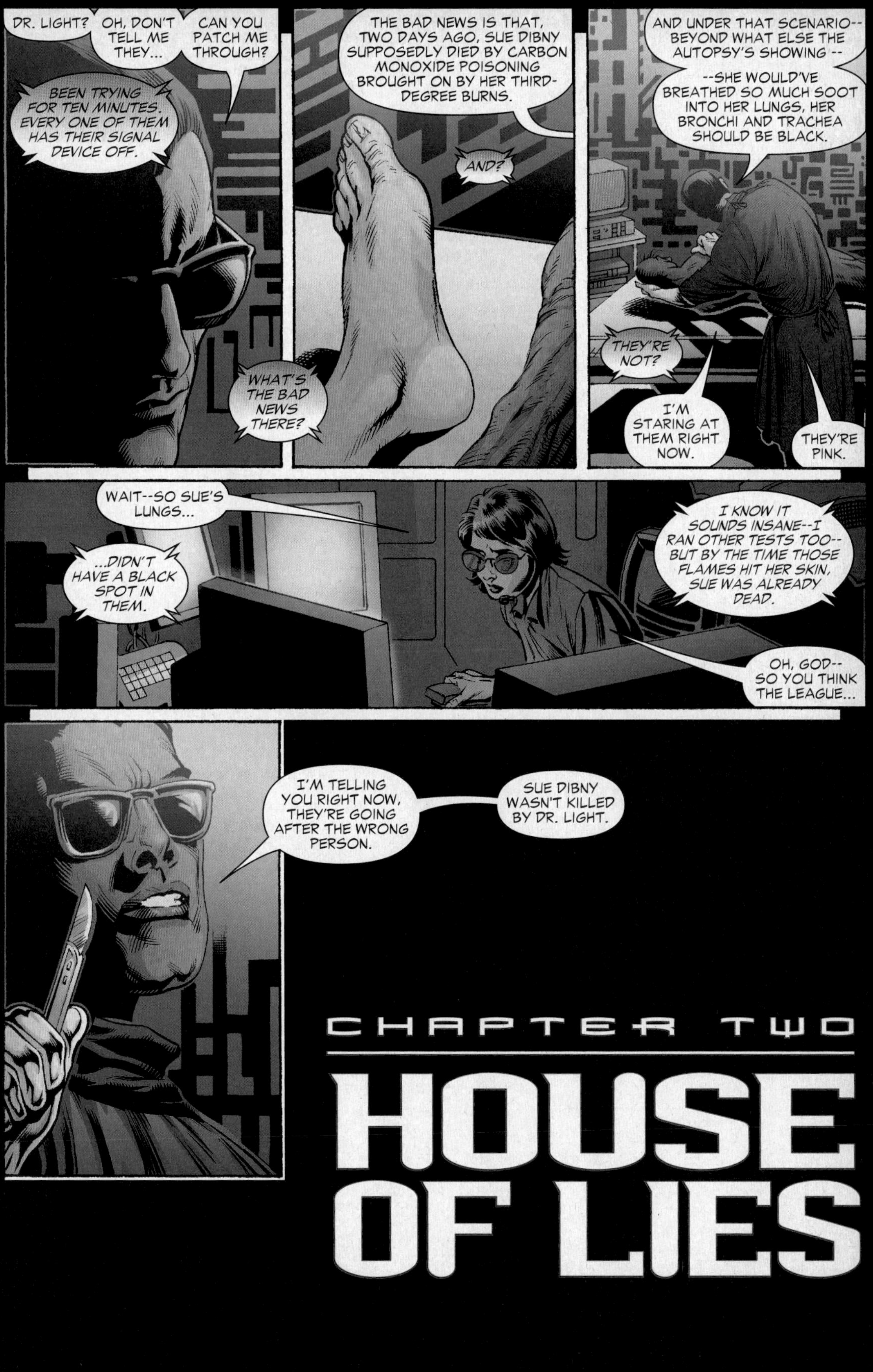
DR. LIGHT?
OH, DON'T TELL ME THEY...
BEEN TRYING FOR TEN MINUTES. EVERY ONE OF THEM HAS THEIR SIGNAL DEVICE OFF.
CAN YOU PATCH ME THROUGH?
WHAT'S THE BAD NEWS THERE?
THE BAD NEWS IS THAT, TWO DAYS AGO, SUE DIBNY SUPPOSEDLY DIED BY CARBON MONOXIDE POISONING BROUGHT ON BY HER THIRD-DEGREE BURNS.
AND?
AND UNDER THAT SCENARIO--BEYOND WHAT ELSE THE AUTOPSY'S SHOWING --
--SHE WOULD'VE BREATHED SO MUCH SOOT INTO HER LUNGS, HER BRONCHI AND TRACHEA SHOULD BE BLACK.
THEY'RE NOT?
I'M STARING AT THEM RIGHT NOW.
THEY'RE PINK.
WAIT--SO SUE'S LUNGS...
...DIDN'T HAVE A BLACK SPOT IN THEM.
I KNOW IT SOUNDS INSANE--I RAN OTHER TESTS TOO--BUT BY THE TIME THOSE FLAMES HIT HER SKIN, SUE WAS ALREADY DEAD.
OH, GOD--SO YOU THINK THE LEAGUE...
I'M TELLING YOU RIGHT NOW, THEY'RE GOING AFTER THE WRONG PERSON.
SUE DIBNY WASN'T KILLED BY DR. LIGHT.
CHAPTER TWO
HOUSE OF LIES

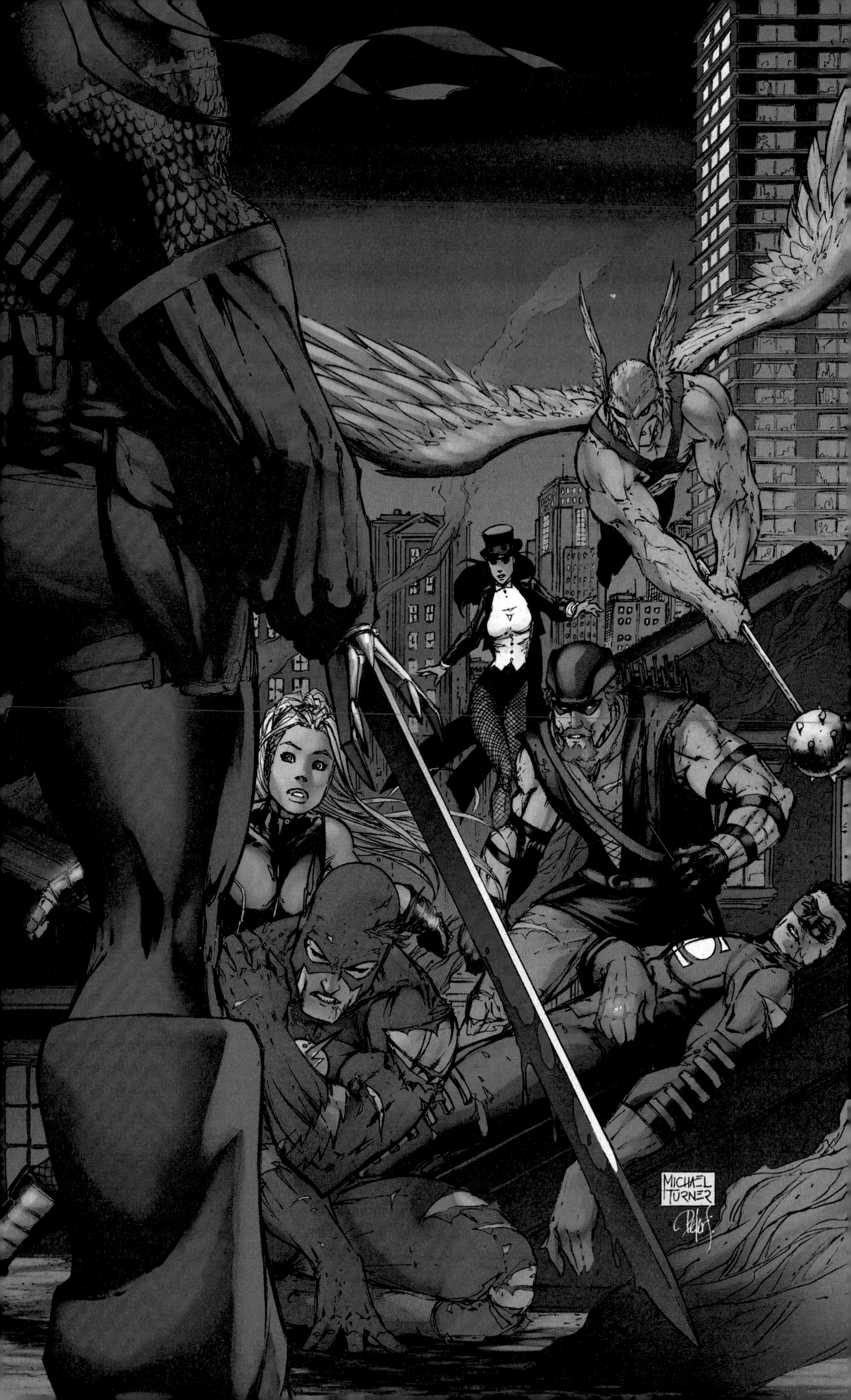
MICHAEL TURNER

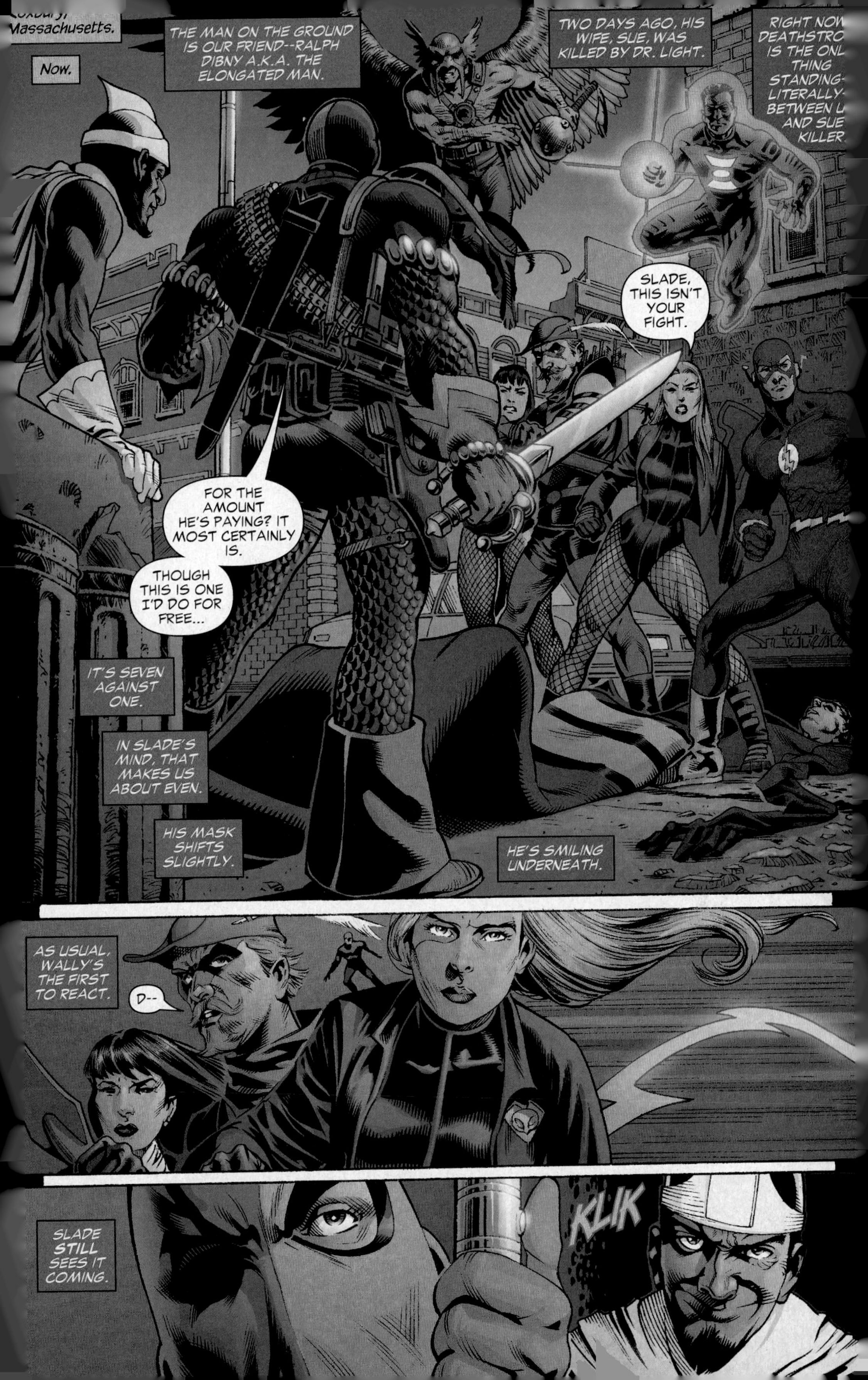
oxbury, Massachusetts.
Now.
THE MAN ON THE GROUND IS OUR FRIEND--RALPH DIBNY A.K.A. THE ELONGATED MAN.
TWO DAYS AGO, HIS WIFE, SUE, WAS KILLED BY DR. LIGHT.
RIGHT NOW DEATHSTRO IS THE ONL THING STANDING- LITERALLY- BETWEEN U AND SUE KILLER.
SLADE, THIS ISN'T YOUR FIGHT.
FOR THE AMOUNT HE'S PAYING? IT MOST CERTAINLY IS.
THOUGH THIS IS ONE I'D DO FOR FREE...
IT'S SEVEN AGAINST ONE.
IN SLADE'S MIND, THAT MAKES US ABOUT EVEN.
HIS MASK SHIFTS SLIGHTLY.
HE'S SMILING UNDERNEATH.
AS USUAL, WALLY'S THE FIRST TO REACT.
D--
SLADE STILL SEES IT COMING.
KLIK

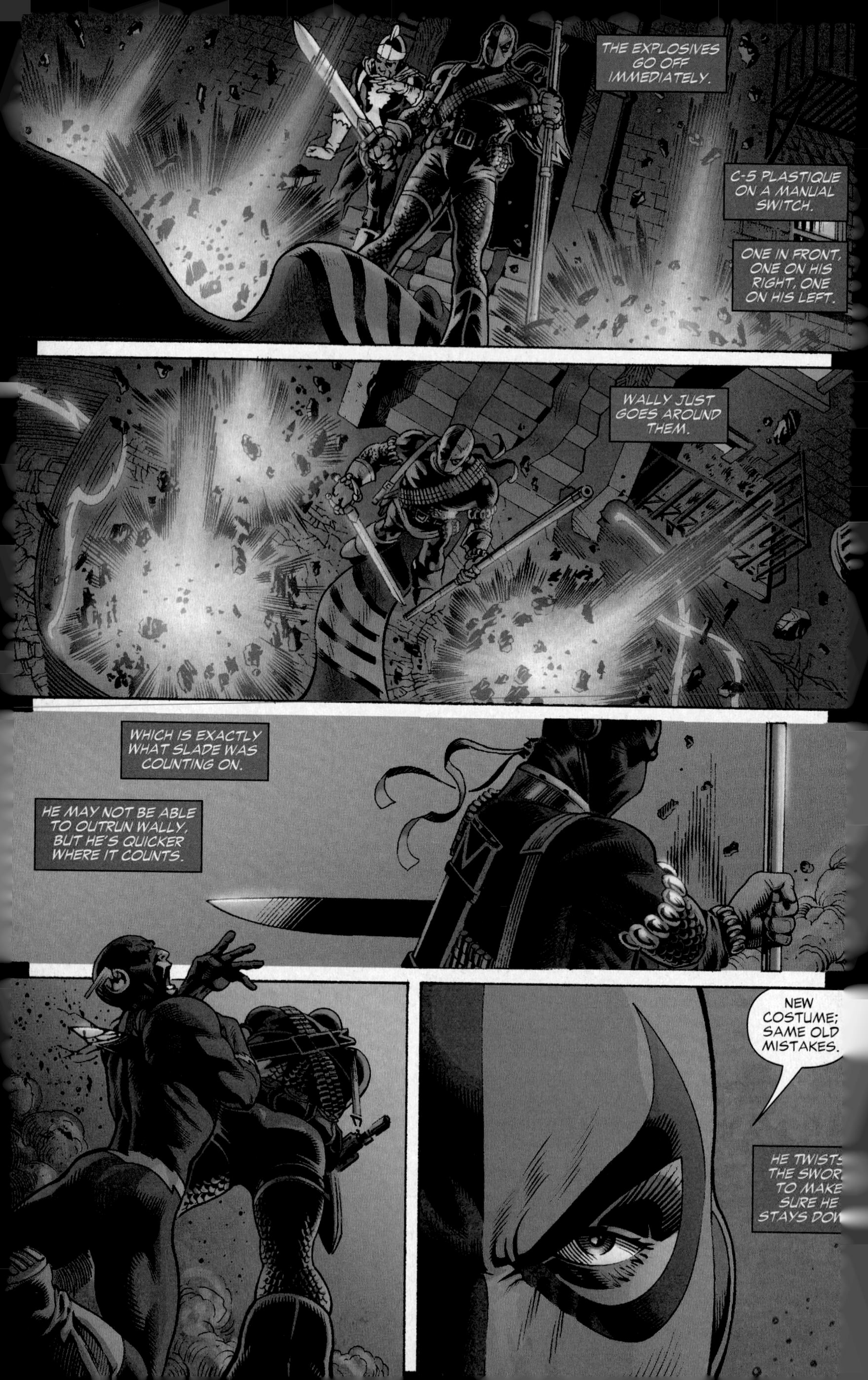
THE EXPLOSIVES GO OFF IMMEDIATELY.
C-5 PLASTIQUE ON A MANUAL SWITCH.
ONE IN FRONT, ONE ON HIS RIGHT, ONE ON HIS LEFT.
WALLY JUST GOES AROUND THEM.
WHICH IS EXACTLY WHAT SLADE WAS COUNTING ON.
HE MAY NOT BE ABLE TO OUTRUN WALLY, BUT HE'S QUICKER WHERE IT COUNTS.
NEW COSTUME; SAME OLD MISTAKES.
HE TWISTS THE SWOR TO MAKE SURE HE STAYS DOW

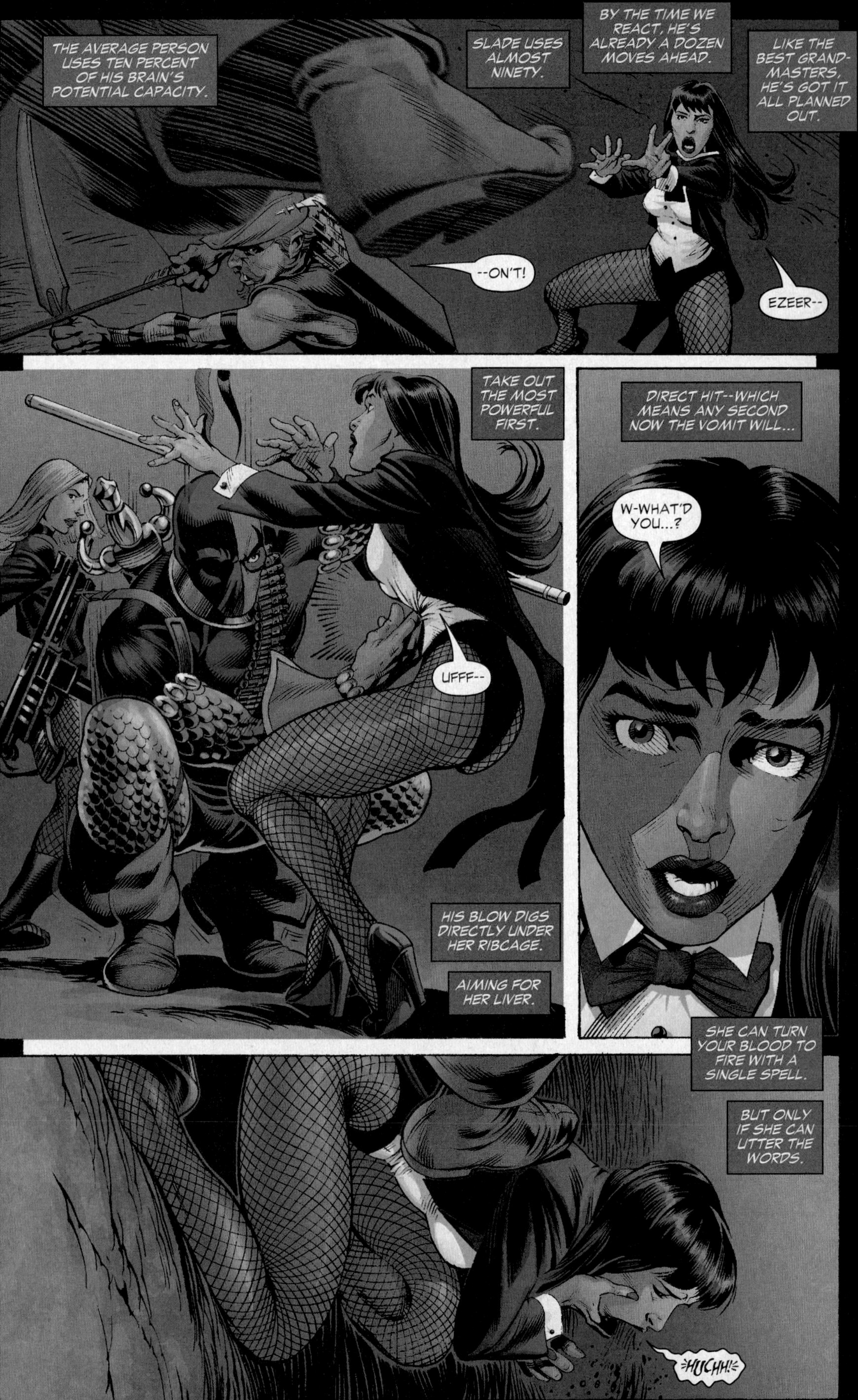
THE AVERAGE PERSON USES TEN PERCENT OF HIS BRAIN'S POTENTIAL CAPACITY.
SLADE USES ALMOST NINETY.
BY THE TIME WE REACT, HE'S ALREADY A DOZEN MOVES AHEAD.
LIKE THE BEST GRAND-MASTERS, HE'S GOT IT ALL PLANNED OUT.
--ON'T!
EZEER--
TAKE OUT THE MOST POWERFUL FIRST.
UFFF--
HIS BLOW DIGS DIRECTLY UNDER HER RIBCAGE.
AIMING FOR HER LIVER.
DIRECT HIT--WHICH MEANS ANY SECOND NOW THE VOMIT WILL...
W-WHAT'D YOU...?
SHE CAN TURN YOUR BLOOD TO FIRE WITH A SINGLE SPELL.
BUT ONLY IF SHE CAN UTTER THE WORDS.
HUCHH!

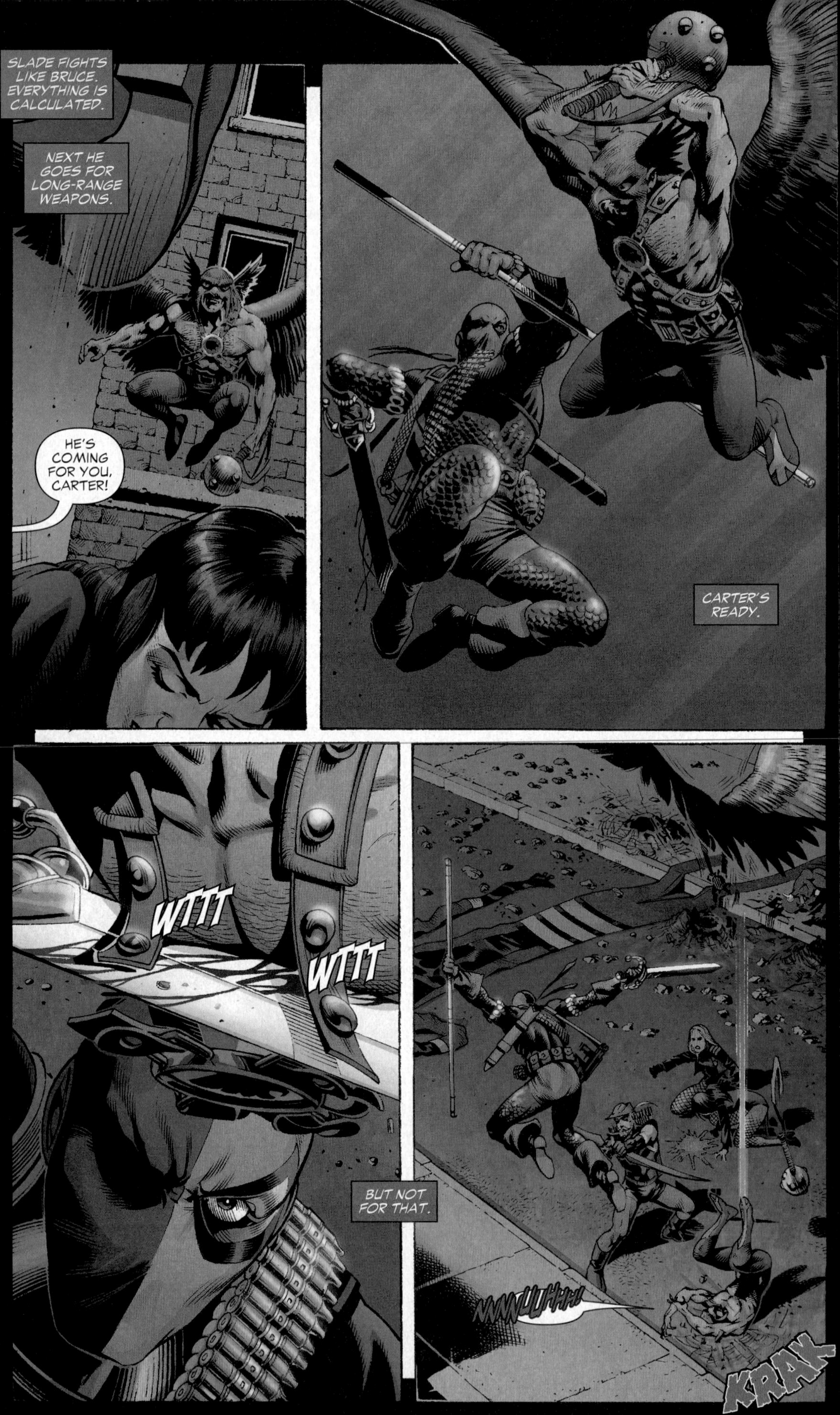
SLADE FIGHTS LIKE BRUCE. EVERYTHING IS CALCULATED.
NEXT HE GOES FOR LONG-RANGE WEAPONS.
HE'S COMING FOR YOU, CARTER!
CARTER'S READY.
WTTT
WTTT
BUT NOT FOR THAT.
NNNNUUHHH!
KRAK

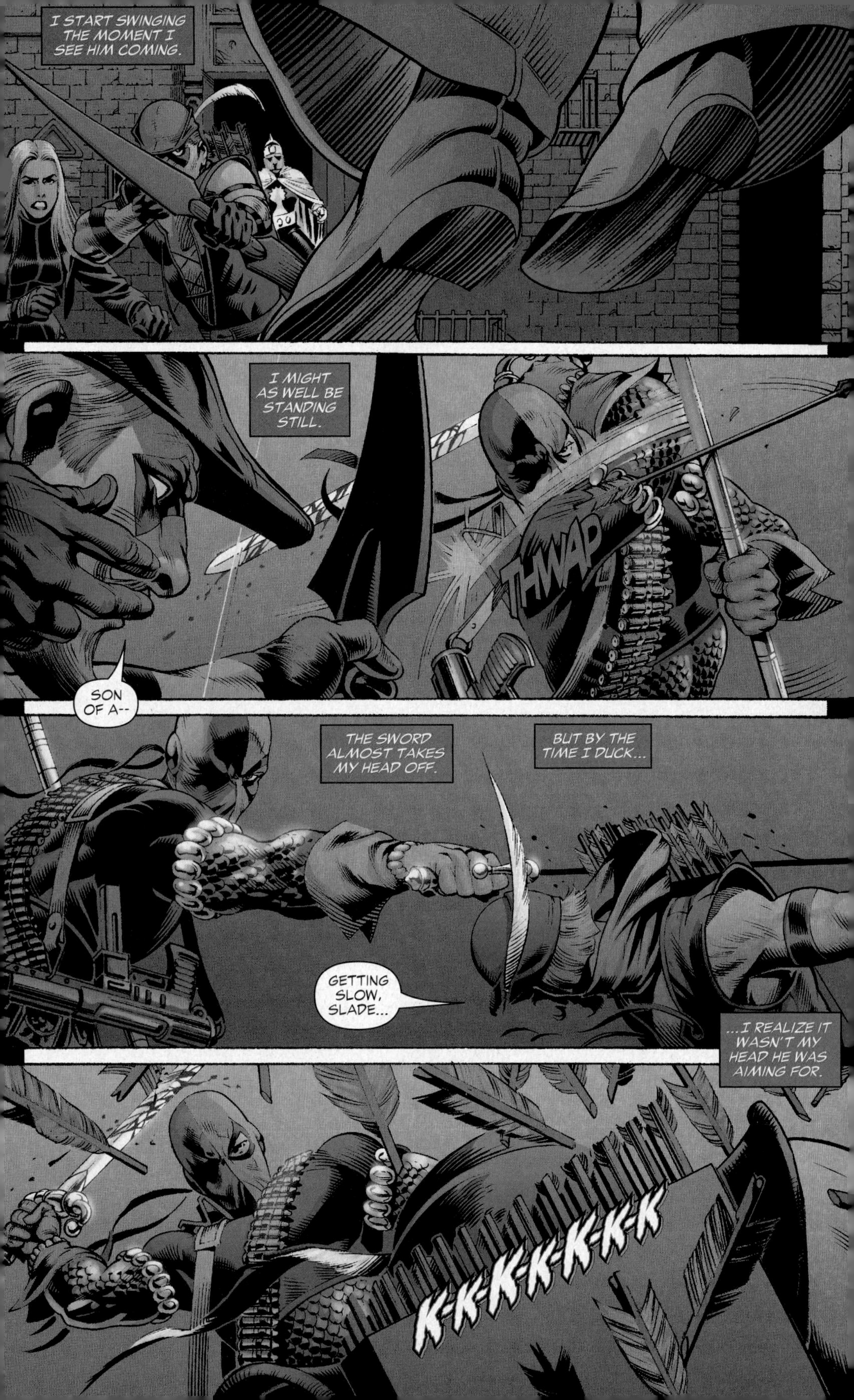
I START SWINGING THE MOMENT I SEE HIM COMING.
I MIGHT AS WELL BE STANDING STILL.
THWAP
SON OF A--
THE SWORD ALMOST TAKES MY HEAD OFF.
BUT BY THE TIME I DUCK...
GETTING SLOW, SLADE...
...I REALIZE IT WASN'T MY HEAD HE WAS AIMING FOR.
K-K-K-K-K-K-K-K

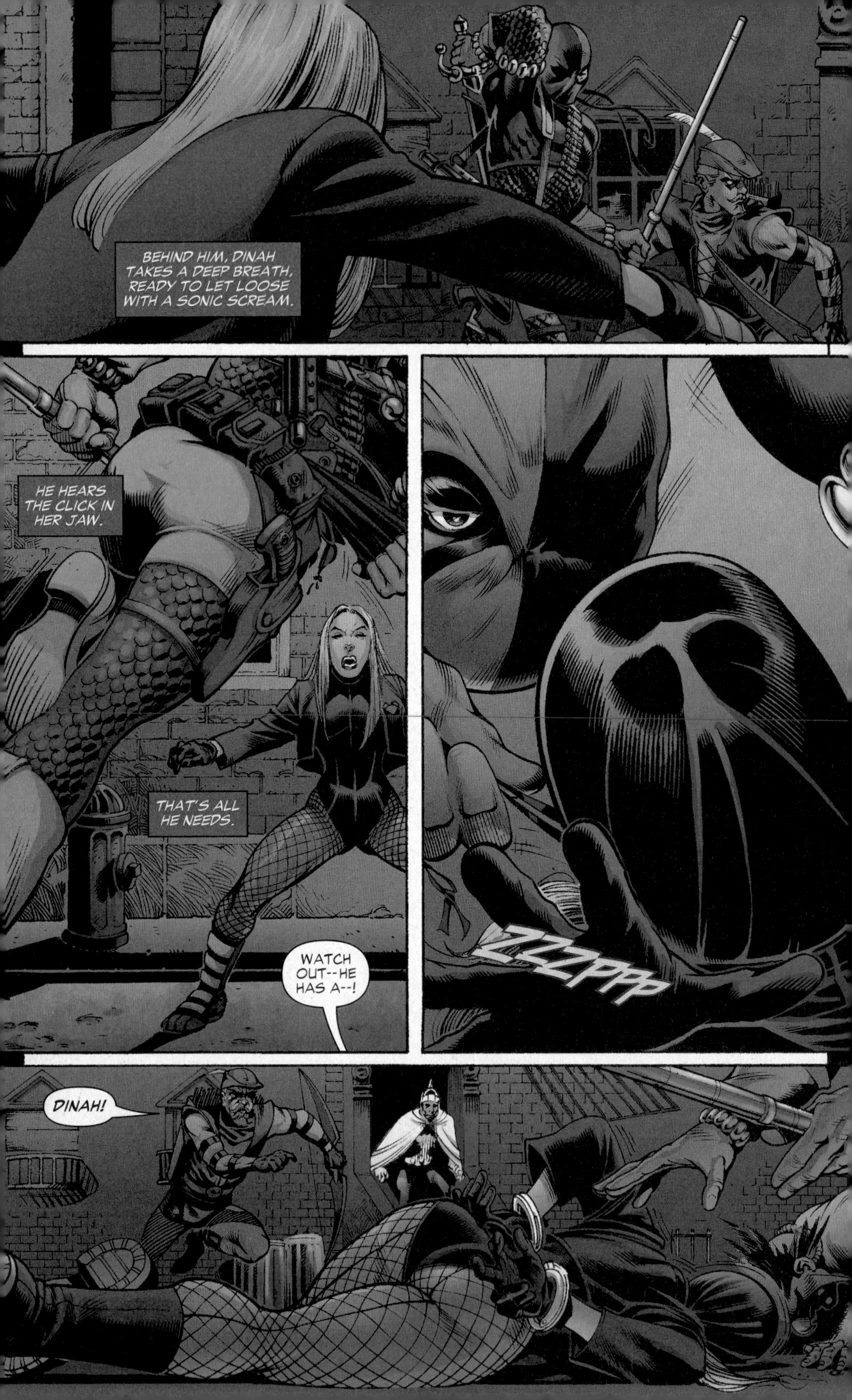
BEHIND HIM, DINAH TAKES A DEEP BREATH, READY TO LET LOOSE WITH A SONIC SCREAM.
HE HEARS THE CLICK IN HER JAW.
THAT'S ALL HE NEEDS.
WATCH OUT--HE HAS A--!
ZZZPPPP
DINAH!

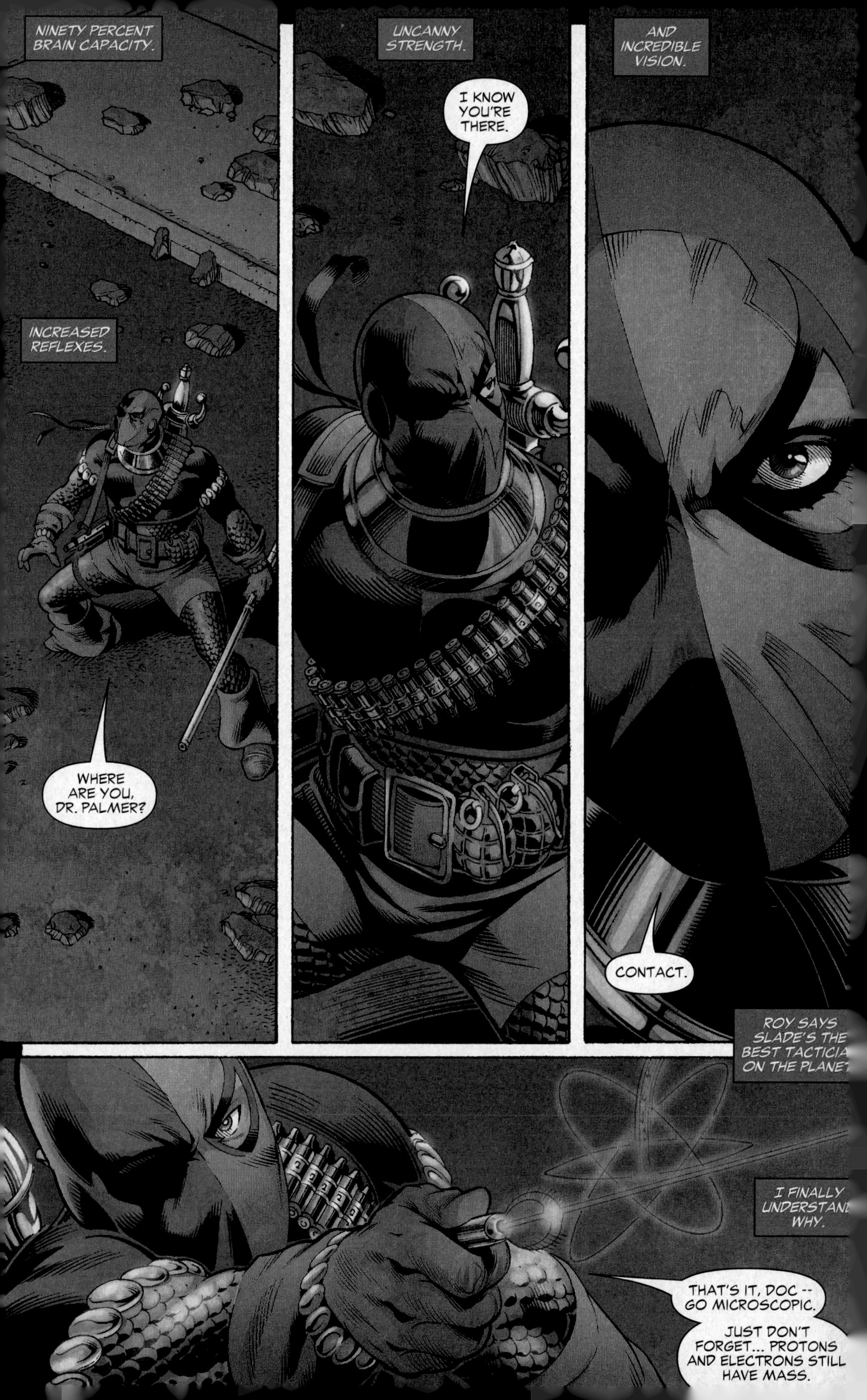
NINETY PERCENT BRAIN CAPACITY.
INCREASED REFLEXES.
WHERE ARE YOU, DR. PALMER?
UNCANNY STRENGTH.
I KNOW YOU'RE THERE.
AND INCREDIBLE VISION.
CONTACT.
ROY SAYS SLADE'S THE BEST TACTICIA ON THE PLANE
I FINALLY UNDERSTAN WHY.
THAT'S IT, DOC -- GO MICROSCOPIC.
JUST DON'T FORGET... PROTONS AND ELECTRONS STILL HAVE MASS.

BY THE TIME RAY
REALIZES WHAT'S
APPENING, HE'S LIKE
A FEATHER BEING
SPRAYED BY A FIRE
HOSE.

UHHHH!

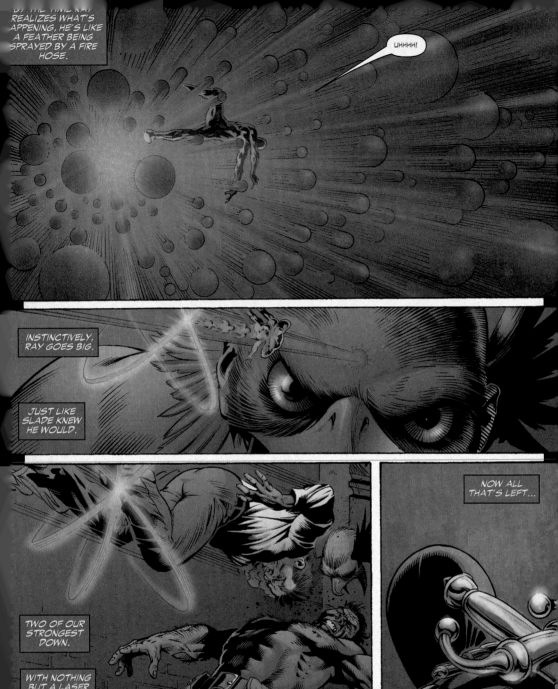

INSTINCTIVELY,
RAY GOES BIG.

JUST LIKE
SLADE KNEW
HE WOULD.

NOW ALL
THAT'S LEFT...

TWO OF OUR
STRONGEST
DOWN.

WITH NOTHING
BUT A LASER
POINTER.

UUUFFF!

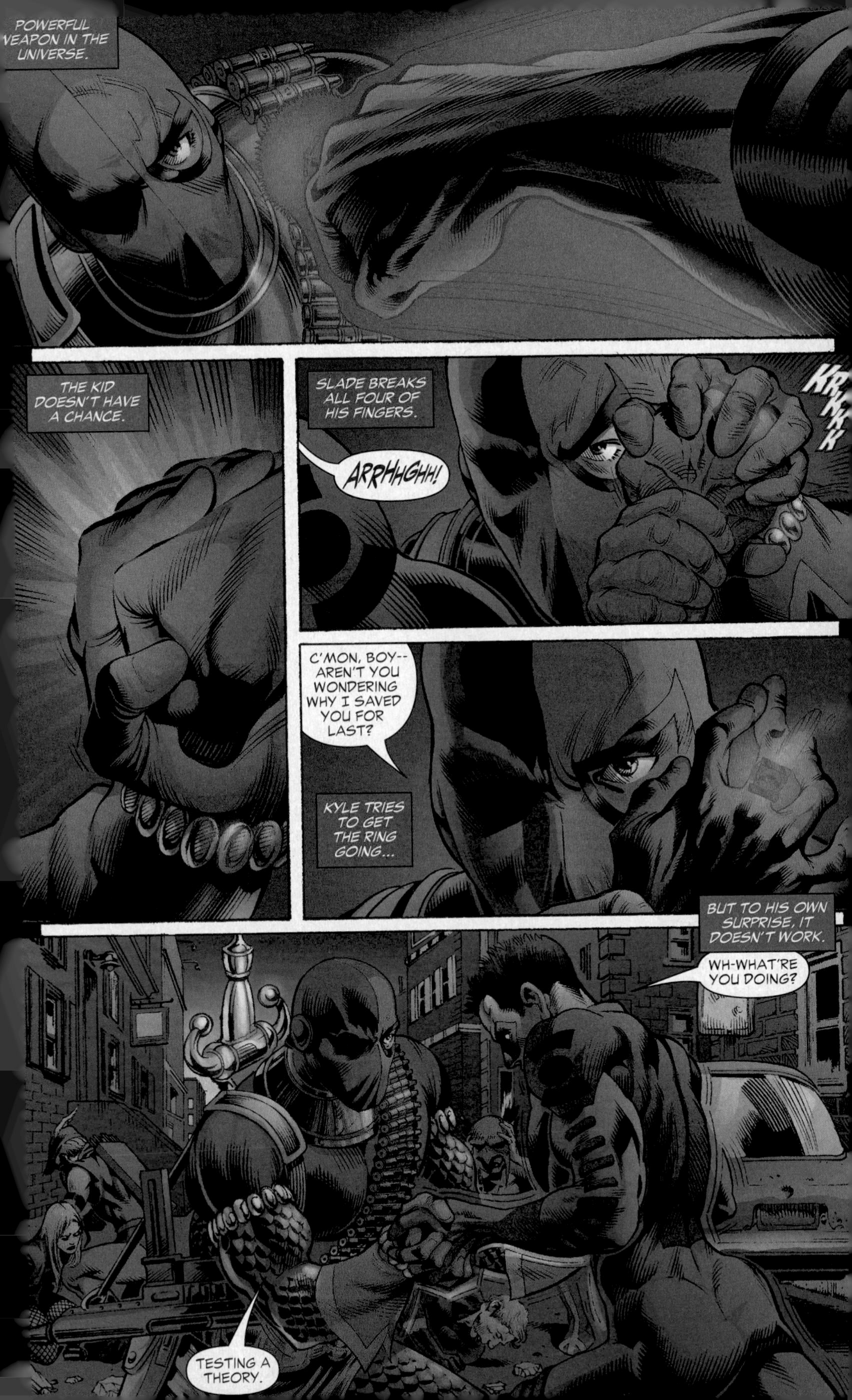
POWERFUL WEAPON IN THE UNIVERSE.
THE KID DOESN'T HAVE A CHANCE.
SLADE BREAKS ALL FOUR OF HIS FINGERS.
KRKKK
ARRHHGHH!
C'MON, BOY-- AREN'T YOU WONDERING WHY I SAVED YOU FOR LAST?
KYLE TRIES TO GET THE RING GOING...
BUT TO HIS OWN SURPRISE, IT DOESN'T WORK.
WH-WHAT'RE YOU DOING?
TESTING A THEORY.

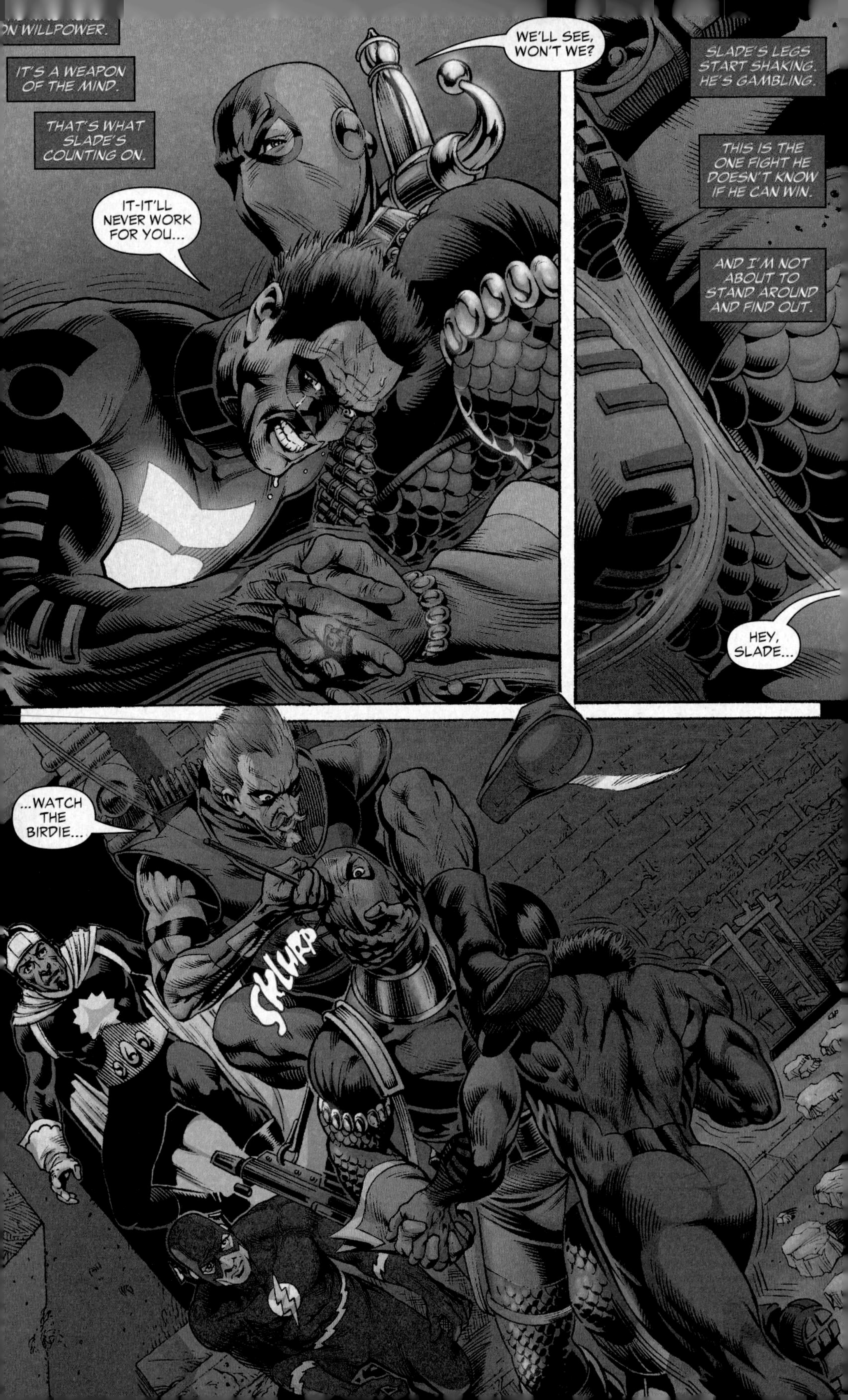

ON WILLPOWER.
IT'S A WEAPON OF THE MIND.
THAT'S WHAT SLADE'S COUNTING ON.
IT-IT'LL NEVER WORK FOR YOU...
WE'LL SEE, WON'T WE?
SLADE'S LEGS START SHAKING. HE'S GAMBLING.
THIS IS THE ONE FIGHT HE DOESN'T KNOW IF HE CAN WIN.
AND I'M NOT ABOUT TO STAND AROUND AND FIND OUT.
HEY, SLADE...
...WATCH THE BIRDIE...
SKLURP

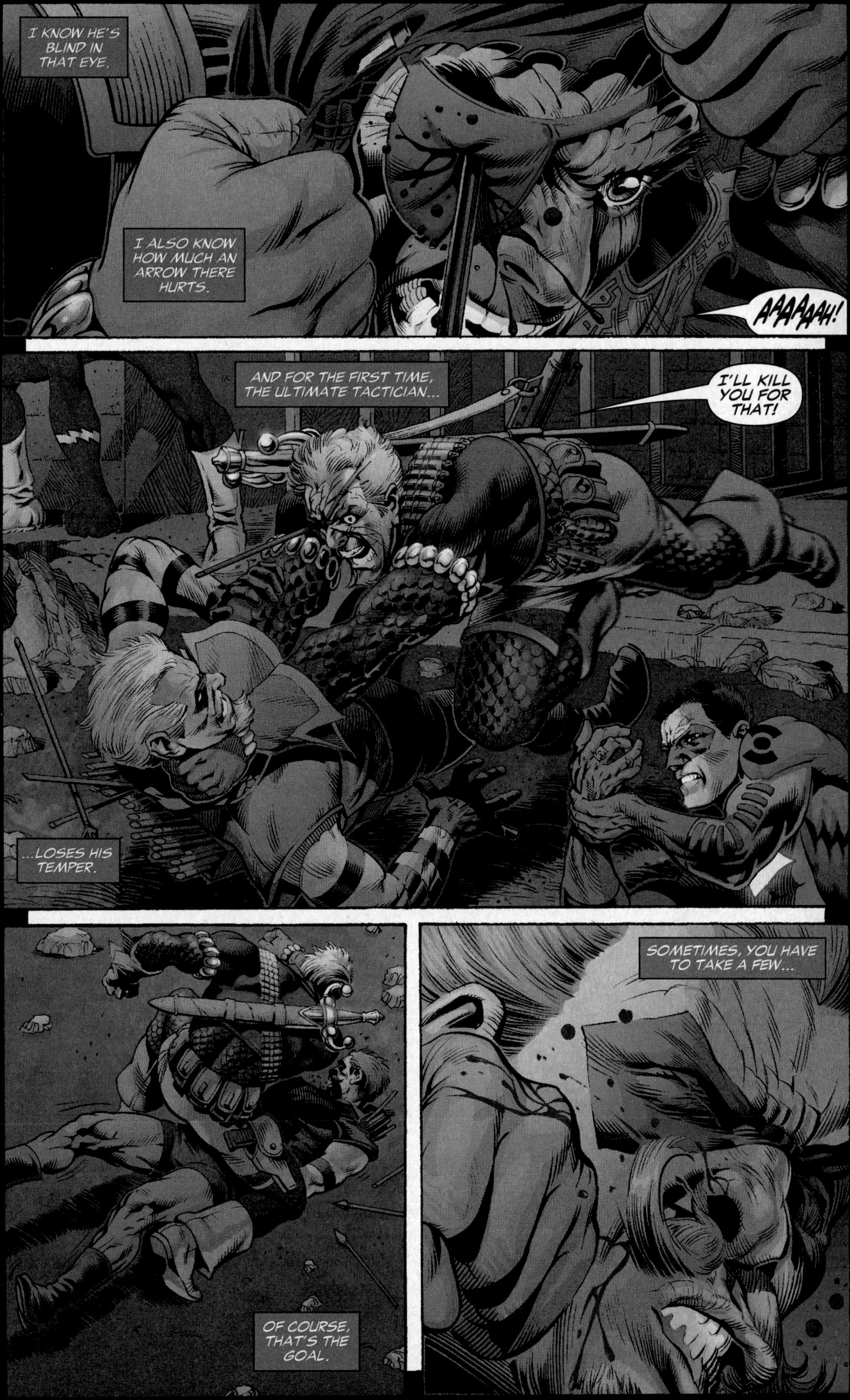
I KNOW HE'S BLIND IN THAT EYE.
I ALSO KNOW HOW MUCH AN ARROW THERE HURTS.
AAAAAAH!
AND FOR THE FIRST TIME, THE ULTIMATE TACTICIAN...
I'LL KILL YOU FOR THAT!
...LOSES HIS TEMPER.
OF COURSE, THAT'S THE GOAL.
SOMETIMES, YOU HAVE TO TAKE A FEW...

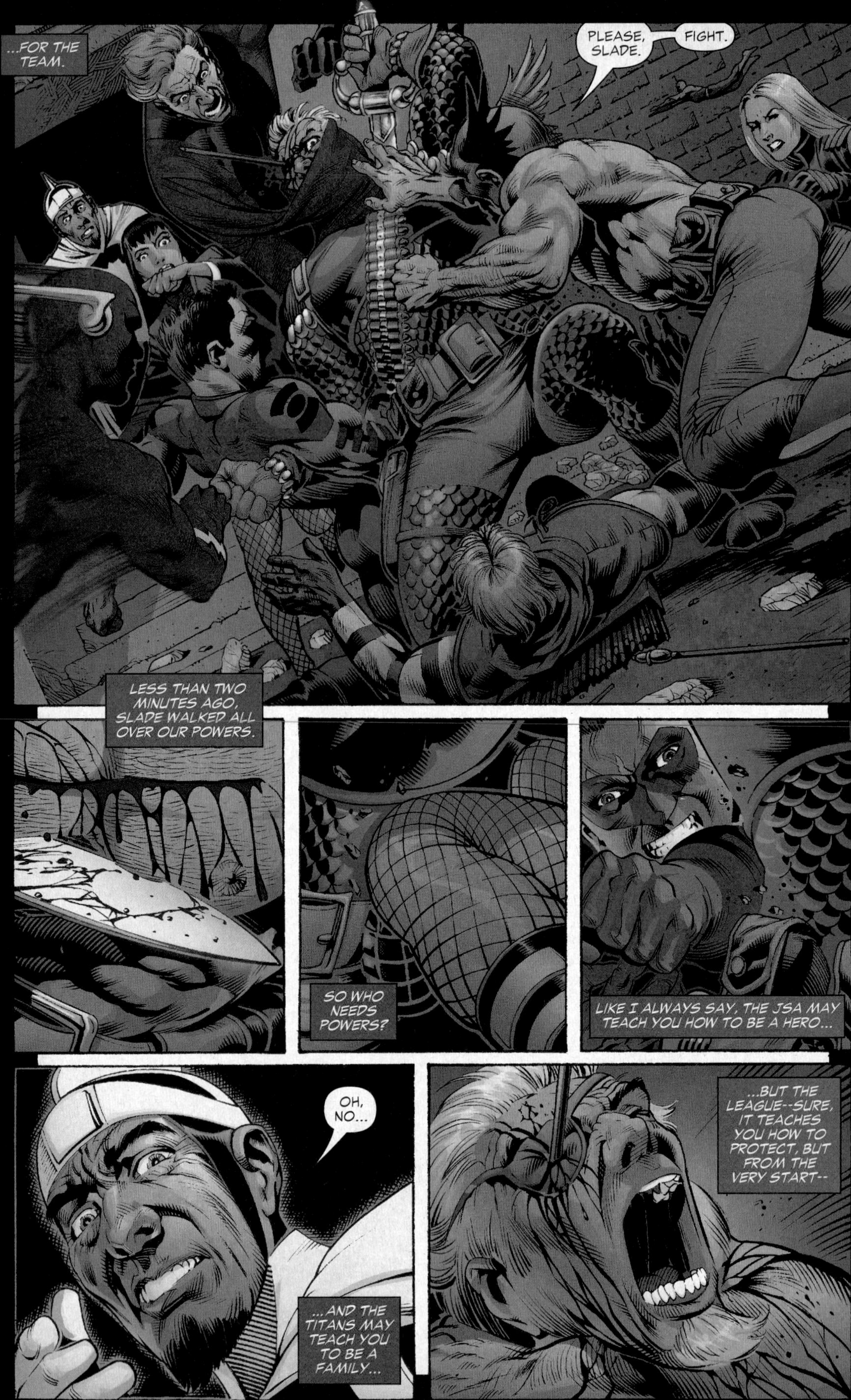
...FOR THE TEAM.
PLEASE, SLADE.
FIGHT.
LESS THAN TWO MINUTES AGO, SLADE WALKED ALL OVER OUR POWERS.
SO WHO NEEDS POWERS?
LIKE I ALWAYS SAY, THE JSA MAY TEACH YOU HOW TO BE A HERO...
OH, NO...
...AND THE TITANS MAY TEACH YOU TO BE A FAMILY...
...BUT THE LEAGUE--SURE, IT TEACHES YOU HOW TO PROTECT, BUT FROM THE VERY START--

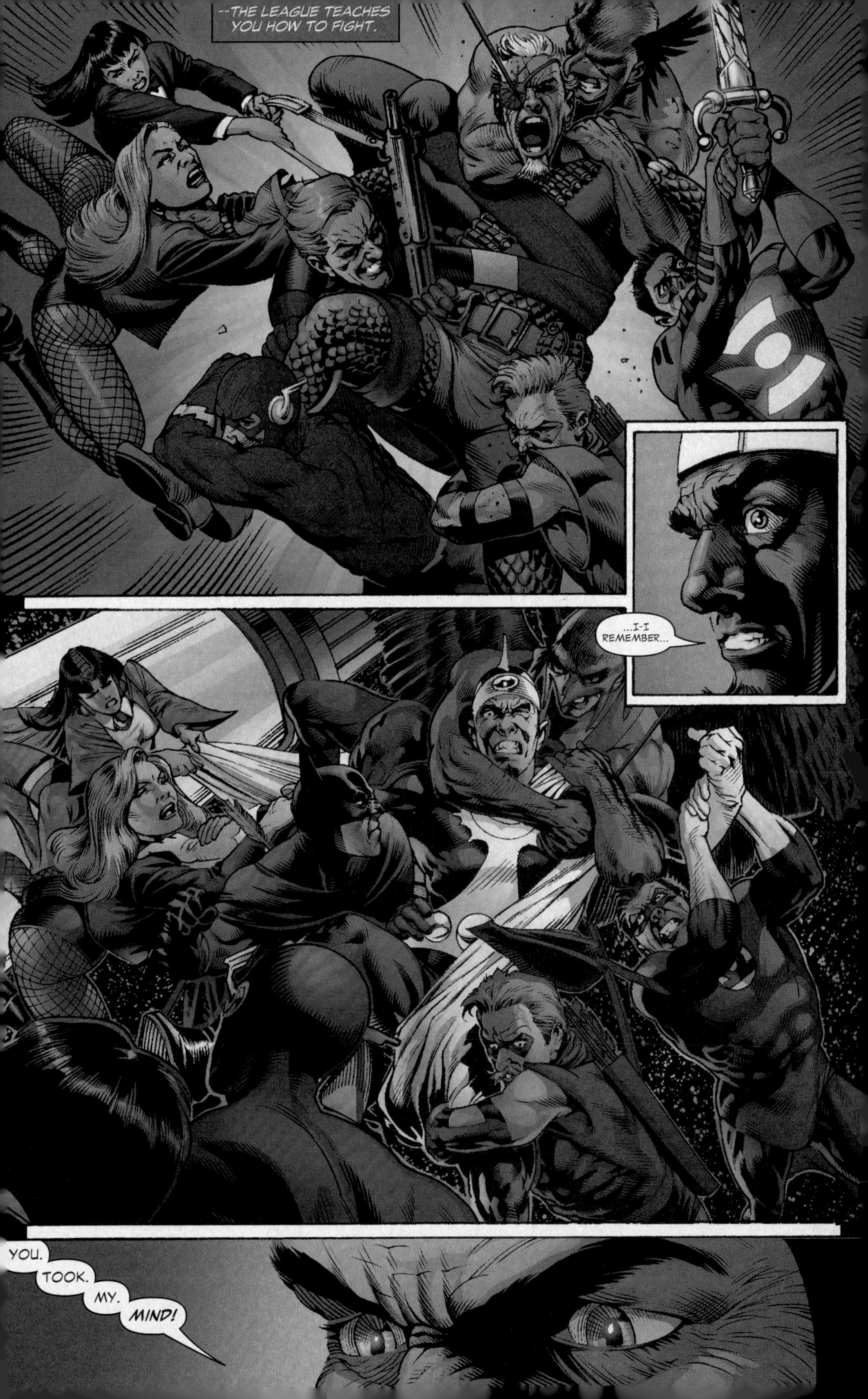
--THE LEAGUE TEACHES YOU HOW TO FIGHT.
...I-I REMEMBER...
YOU.
TOOK.
MY.
MIND!

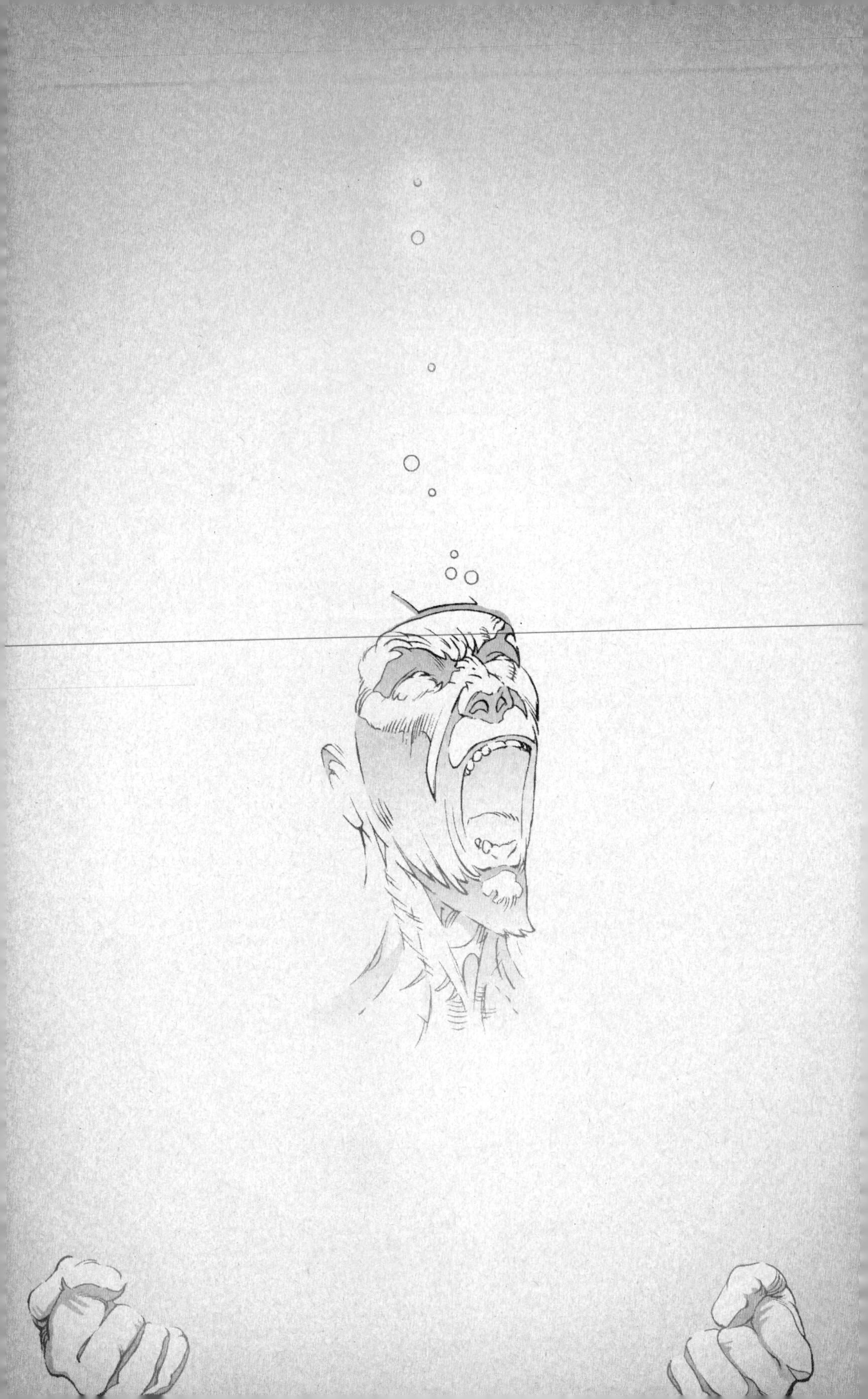

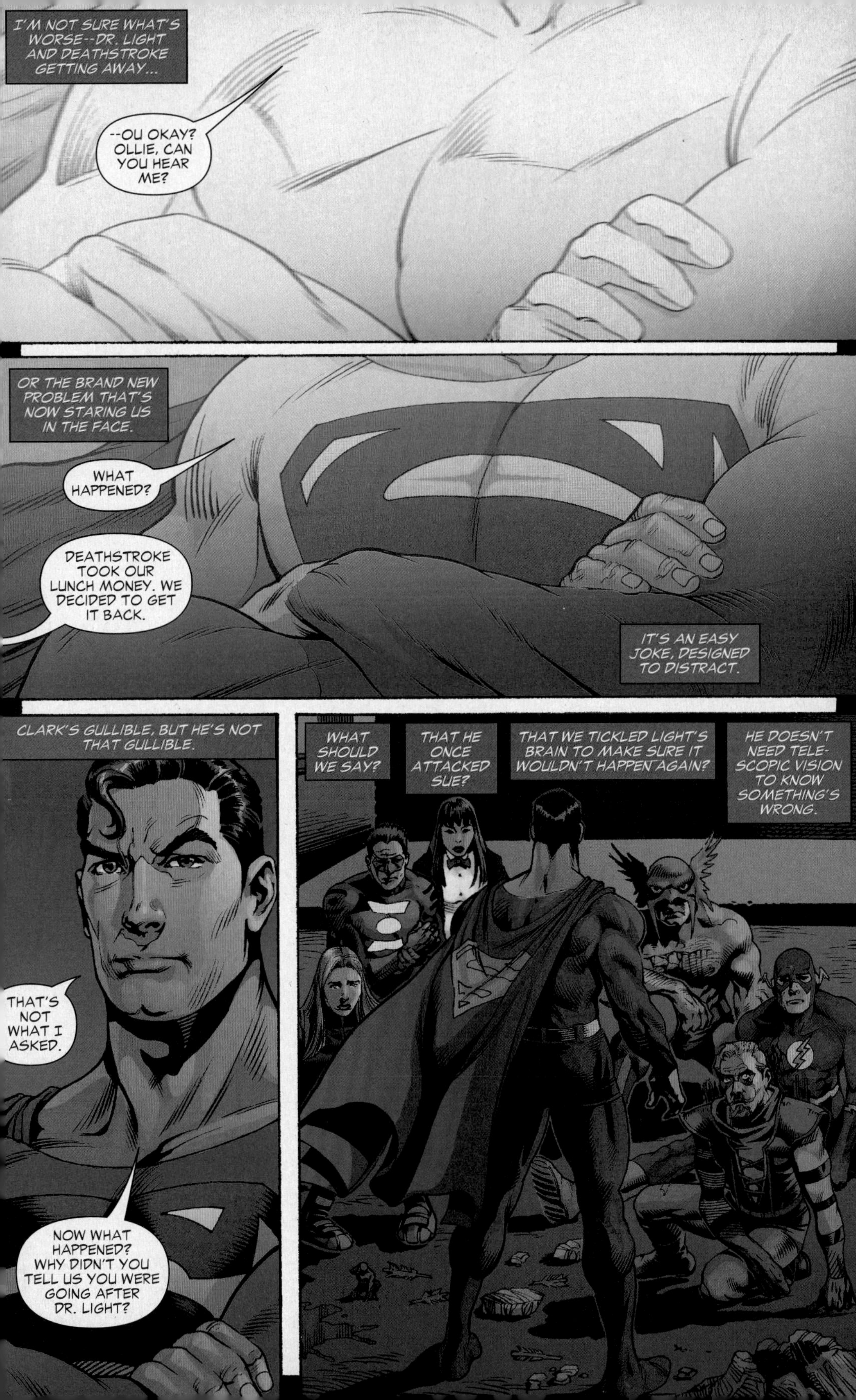
I'M NOT SURE WHAT'S WORSE--DR. LIGHT AND DEATHSTROKE GETTING AWAY...
--OU OKAY? OLLIE, CAN YOU HEAR ME?
OR THE BRAND NEW PROBLEM THAT'S NOW STARING US IN THE FACE.
WHAT HAPPENED?
DEATHSTROKE TOOK OUR LUNCH MONEY. WE DECIDED TO GET IT BACK.
IT'S AN EASY JOKE, DESIGNED TO DISTRACT.
CLARK'S GULLIBLE, BUT HE'S NOT THAT GULLIBLE.
THAT'S NOT WHAT I ASKED.
NOW WHAT HAPPENED? WHY DIDN'T YOU TELL US YOU WERE GOING AFTER DR. LIGHT?
WHAT SHOULD WE SAY?
THAT HE ONCE ATTACKED SUE?
THAT WE TICKLED LIGHT'S BRAIN TO MAKE SURE IT WOULDN'T HAPPEN AGAIN?
HE DOESN'T NEED TELE-SCOPIC VISION TO KNOW SOMETHING'S WRONG.

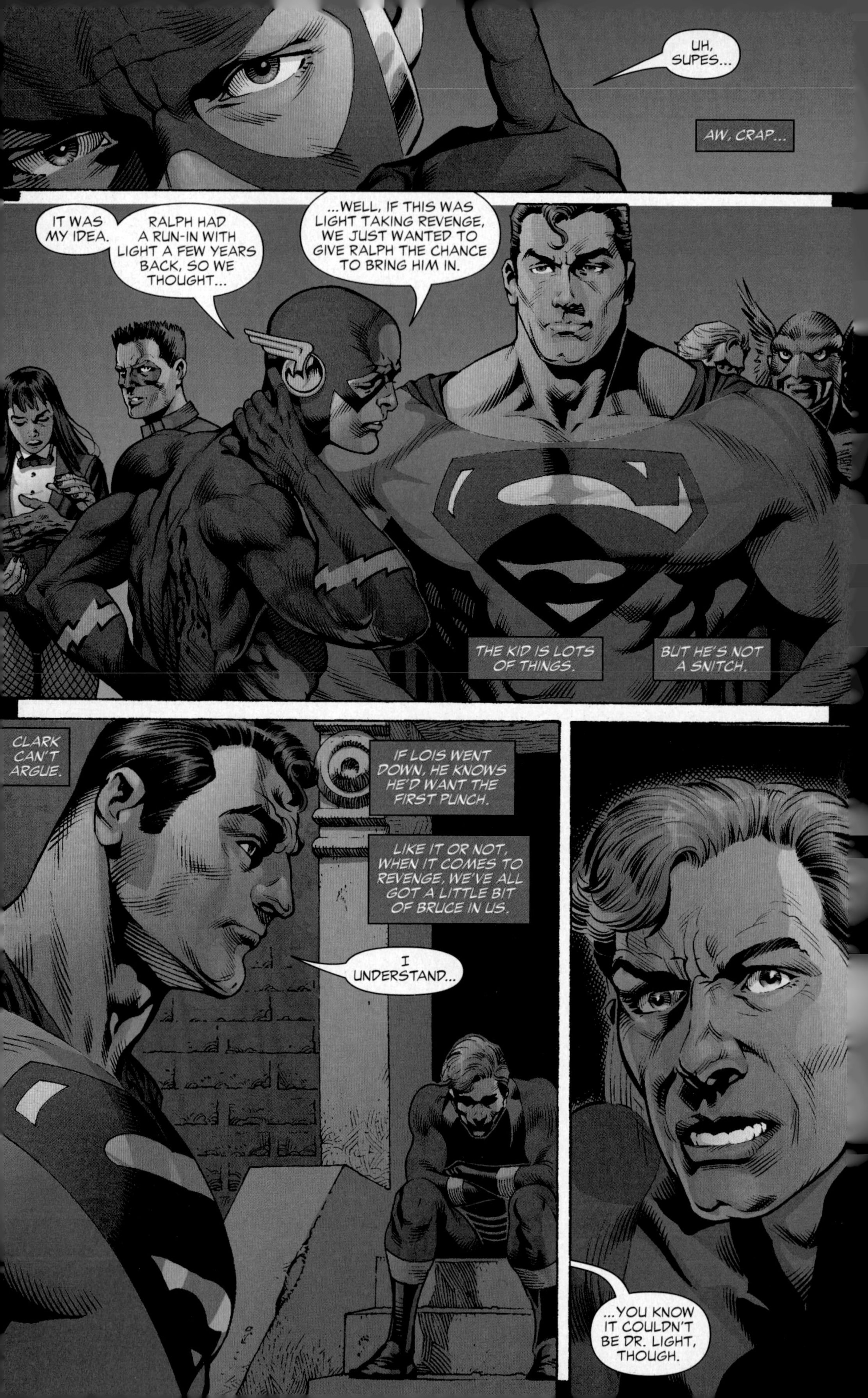
UH, SUPES...
AW, CRAP...
IT WAS MY IDEA.
RALPH HAD A RUN-IN WITH LIGHT A FEW YEARS BACK, SO WE THOUGHT...
...WELL, IF THIS WAS LIGHT TAKING REVENGE, WE JUST WANTED TO GIVE RALPH THE CHANCE TO BRING HIM IN.
THE KID IS LOTS OF THINGS.
BUT HE'S NOT A SNITCH.
CLARK CAN'T ARGUE.
IF LOIS WENT DOWN, HE KNOWS HE'D WANT THE FIRST PUNCH.
LIKE IT OR NOT, WHEN IT COMES TO REVENGE, WE'VE ALL GOT A LITTLE BIT OF BRUCE IN US.
I UNDERSTAND...
...YOU KNOW IT COULDN'T BE DR. LIGHT, THOUGH.

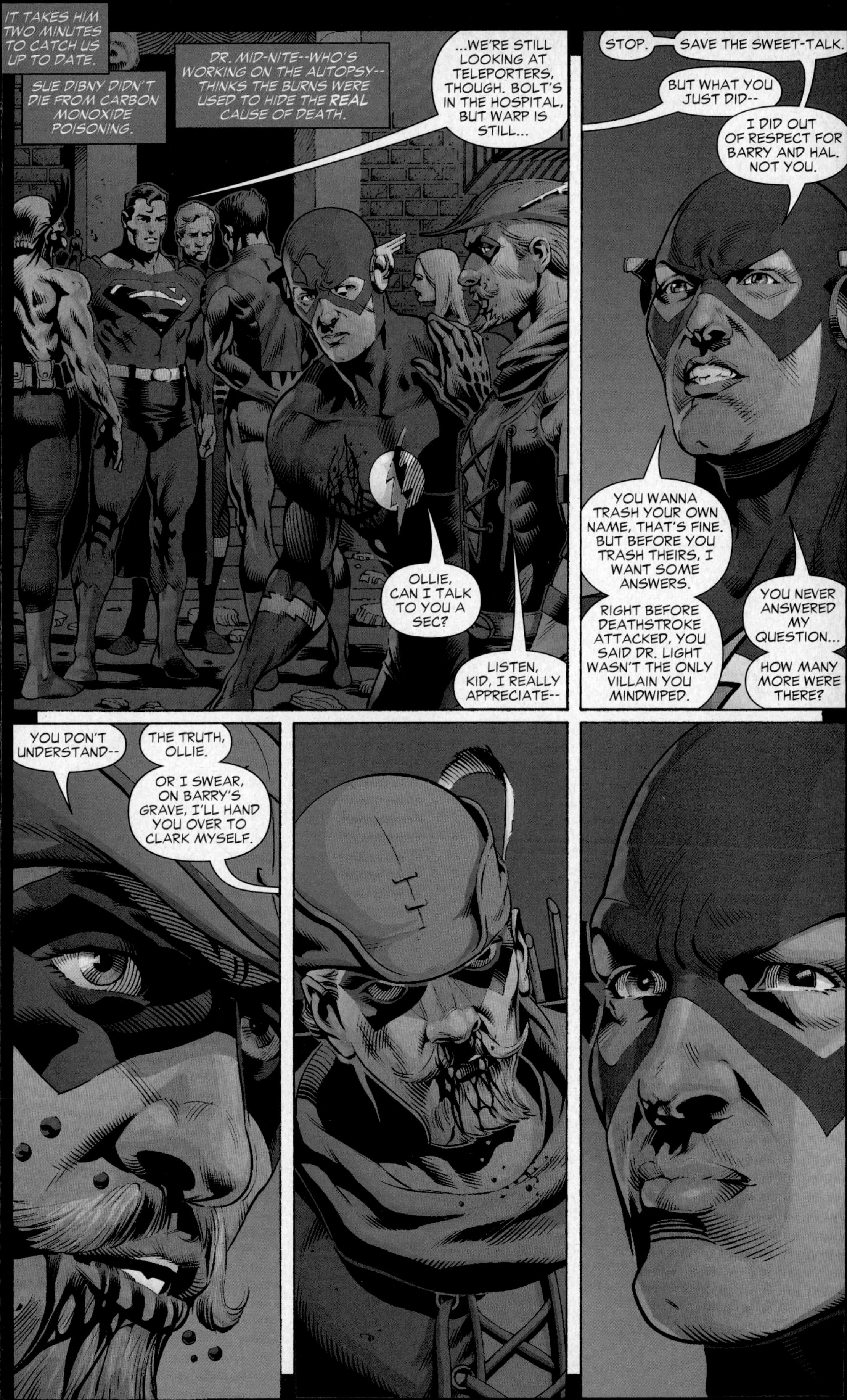
IT TAKES HIM TWO MINUTES TO CATCH US UP TO DATE.
SUE DIBNY DIDN'T DIE FROM CARBON MONOXIDE POISONING.
DR. MID-NITE--WHO'S WORKING ON THE AUTOPSY--THINKS THE BURNS WERE USED TO HIDE THE REAL CAUSE OF DEATH.
...WE'RE STILL LOOKING AT TELEPORTERS, THOUGH. BOLT'S IN THE HOSPITAL, BUT WARP IS STILL...
OLLIE, CAN I TALK TO YOU A SEC?
LISTEN, KID, I REALLY APPRECIATE--
STOP.
SAVE THE SWEET-TALK.
BUT WHAT YOU JUST DID--
I DID OUT OF RESPECT FOR BARRY AND HAL. NOT YOU.
YOU WANNA TRASH YOUR OWN NAME, THAT'S FINE. BUT BEFORE YOU TRASH THEIRS, I WANT SOME ANSWERS.
RIGHT BEFORE DEATHSTROKE ATTACKED, YOU SAID DR. LIGHT WASN'T THE ONLY VILLAIN YOU MINDWIPED.
YOU NEVER ANSWERED MY QUESTION...
HOW MANY MORE WERE THERE?
YOU DON'T UNDERSTAND--
THE TRUTH, OLLIE.
OR I SWEAR, ON BARRY'S GRAVE, I'LL HAND YOU OVER TO CLARK MYSELF.

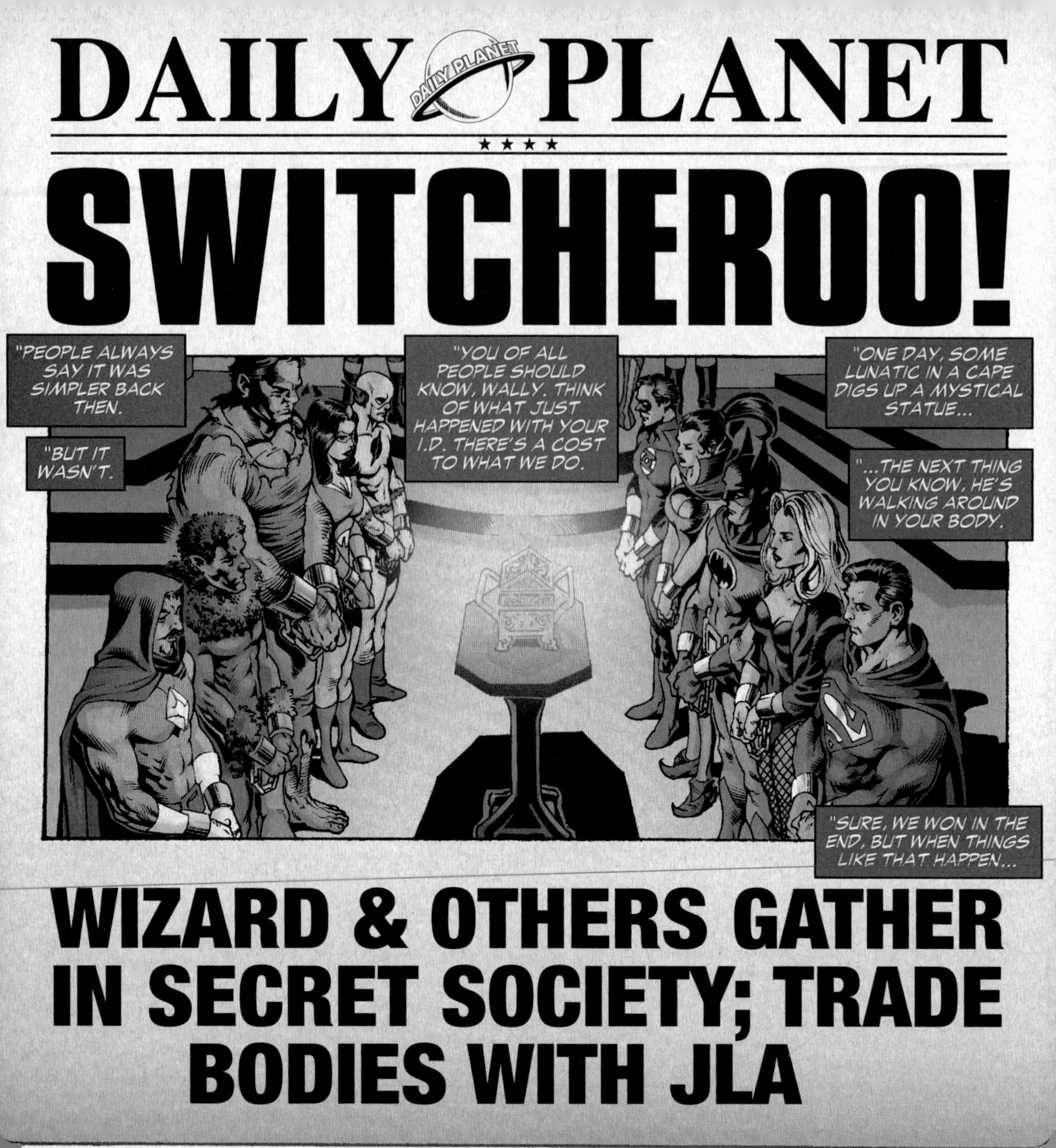
DAILY PLANET
DAILY PLANET
SWITCHEROO!
"PEOPLE ALWAYS SAY IT WAS SIMPLER BACK THEN.
"BUT IT WASN'T.
"YOU OF ALL PEOPLE SHOULD KNOW, WALLY. THINK OF WHAT JUST HAPPENED WITH YOUR I.D. THERE'S A COST TO WHAT WE DO.
"ONE DAY, SOME LUNATIC IN A CAPE DIGS UP A MYSTICAL STATUE...
"...THE NEXT THING YOU KNOW, HE'S WALKING AROUND IN YOUR BODY.
"SURE, WE WON IN THE END, BUT WHEN THINGS LIKE THAT HAPPEN...
WIZARD & OTHERS GATHER IN SECRET SOCIETY; TRADE BODIES WITH JLA
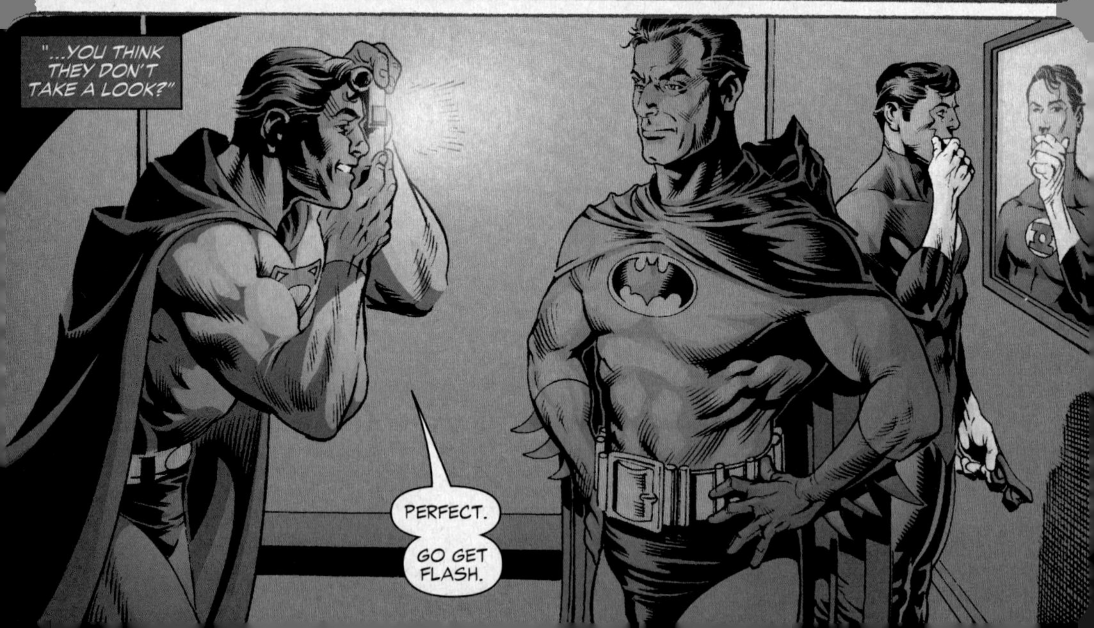
"...YOU THINK THEY DON'T TAKE A LOOK?"
PERFECT.
GO GET FLASH.

"EVEN WHEN IT'S OVER..."

"ALL THE BIGSHOTS CARE ABOUT IS THE NEXT FIGHT."

LUTHOR IS--

GO...

JOKER JUST--

WE'VE GOT IT HERE.

"NO ONE UNDERSTANDS THE CLEAN-UP."

SO WHERE YOU TAKING US...HAL?

"AND BELIEVE ME, THERE'S ALWAYS CLEAN-UP."

OH, BARRY, DON'T LOOK SO SAD.

"SO YOU JUST--"

"YOU WEREN'T THERE, WALLY..."

"WE'D JUST BURIED A FATHER..."

LAWRENCE LANCE

Devoted husband
Proud father

"...A MOTHER..."

SINDELLA

Mother - Wife who brought magic to our lives

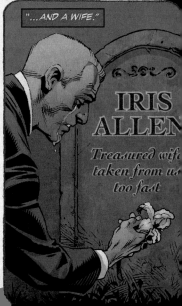

"...AND A WIFE."

IRIS ALLEN

Treasured wife taken from us too fast

IT WAS ENOUGH.

"OLLIE, YOU CROSSED THE LINE."

"WE MADE A CHOICE.

"AND THERE'S NOT A CAPE OUT THERE WHO WOULDN'T DO THE SAME.

"GUYS LIKE THE WIZARD--OR LIGHT--OR ANY OF THE OTHERS--

"THEY'D LOVE NOTHING MORE THAN TO KNOW WHERE OUR WIVES ARE...WHERE OUR CHILDREN SLEEP...

"IF THEY KNEW WHERE YOUR MOTHER LIVED, THEY'D SLICE HER THROAT, THEN GO OUT FOR A BEER.

"PEOPLE MAKE FUN OF SECRET IDENTITIES-- WONDERING HOW WE KEPT THEM UP FOR SO LONG."

T'S BECAUSE WE WORKED AT IT.

ALL THOSE YEARS...IT WASN'T COINCIDENCE.

YOU THINK BRAINWAVE JUST FORGOT WHO BARRY WAS?

YOU THINK DR. DESTINY FORGOT THE TIME HE INVADED OUR DREAMS?

IT DIDN'T JUST HAPPEN BY ITSELF.

WE MADE IT HAPPEN.

AND WE WERE OKAY WITH IT.

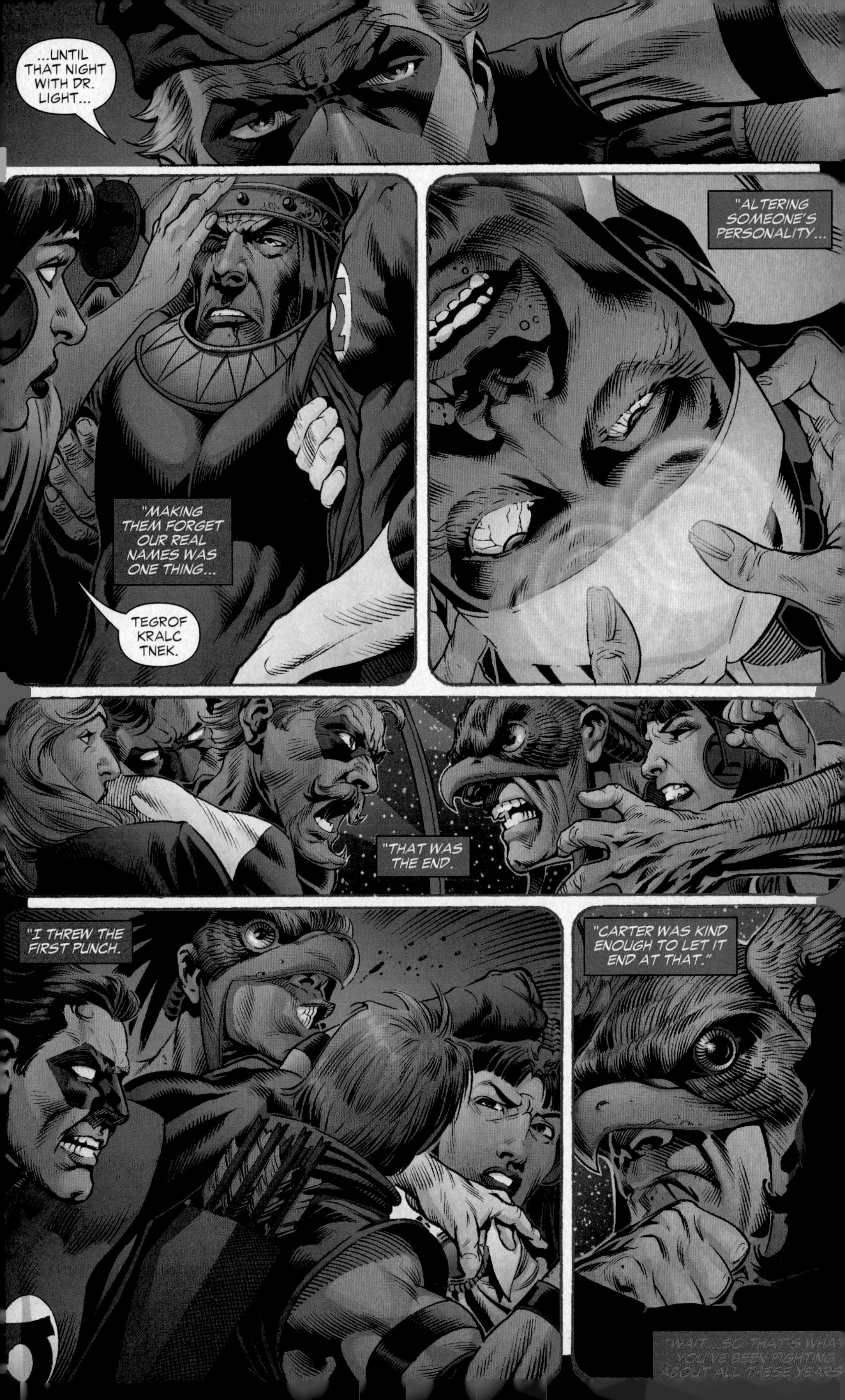
...UNTIL THAT NIGHT WITH DR. LIGHT...
"MAKING THEM FORGET OUR REAL NAMES WAS ONE THING...
TEGROF KRALC TNEK.
"ALTERING SOMEONE'S PERSONALITY...
"THAT WAS THE END.
"I THREW THE FIRST PUNCH.
"CARTER WAS KIND ENOUGH TO LET IT END AT THAT."
"WAIT...SO THAT'S WHAT YOU'VE BEEN FIGHTING ABOUT ALL THESE YEARS

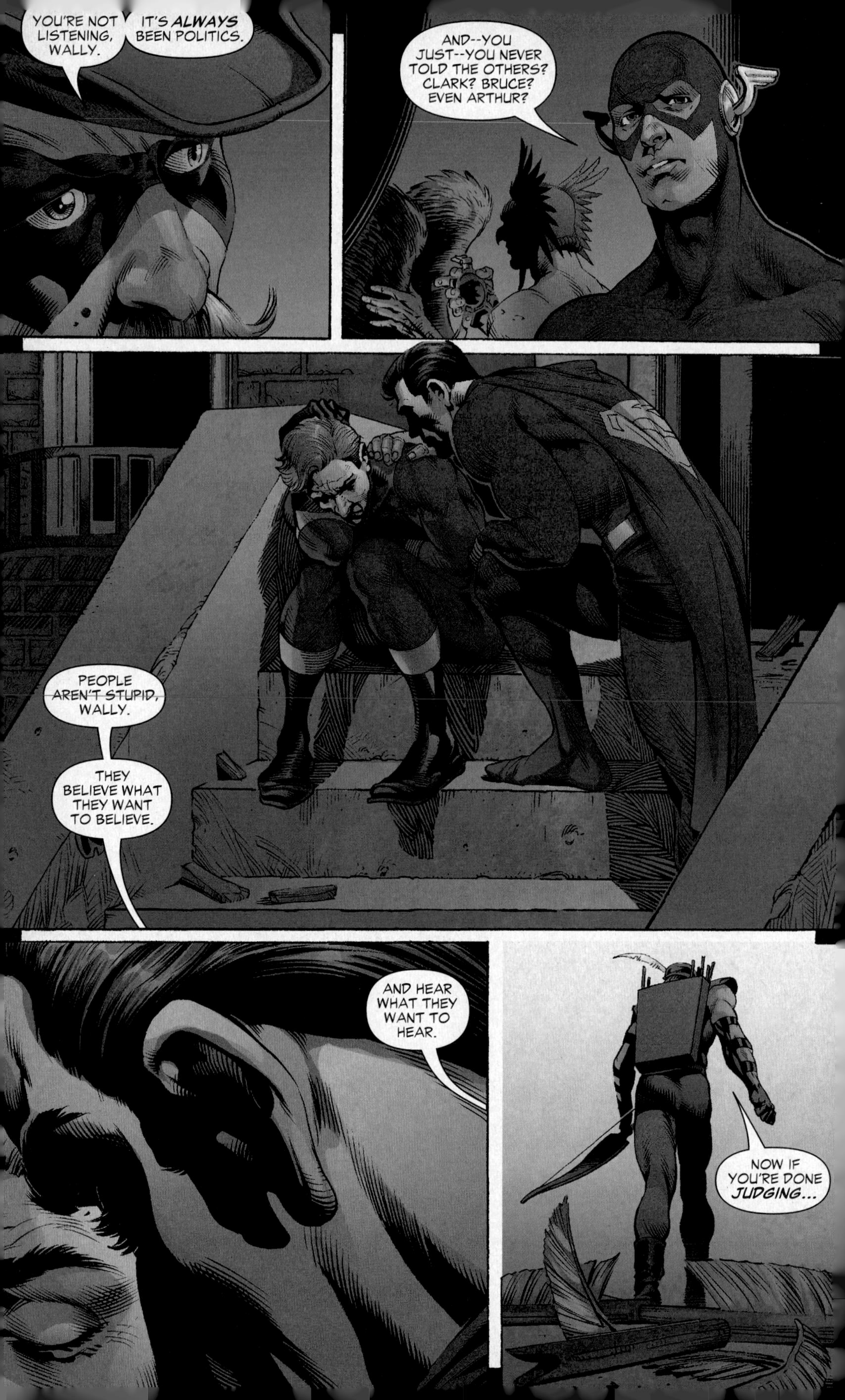
YOU'RE NOT LISTENING, WALLY.
IT'S *ALWAYS* BEEN POLITICS.
AND--YOU JUST--YOU NEVER TOLD THE OTHERS? CLARK? BRUCE? EVEN ARTHUR?
PEOPLE AREN'T STUPID, WALLY.
THEY BELIEVE WHAT THEY WANT TO BELIEVE.
AND HEAR WHAT THEY WANT TO HEAR.
NOW IF YOU'RE DONE *JUDGING*...

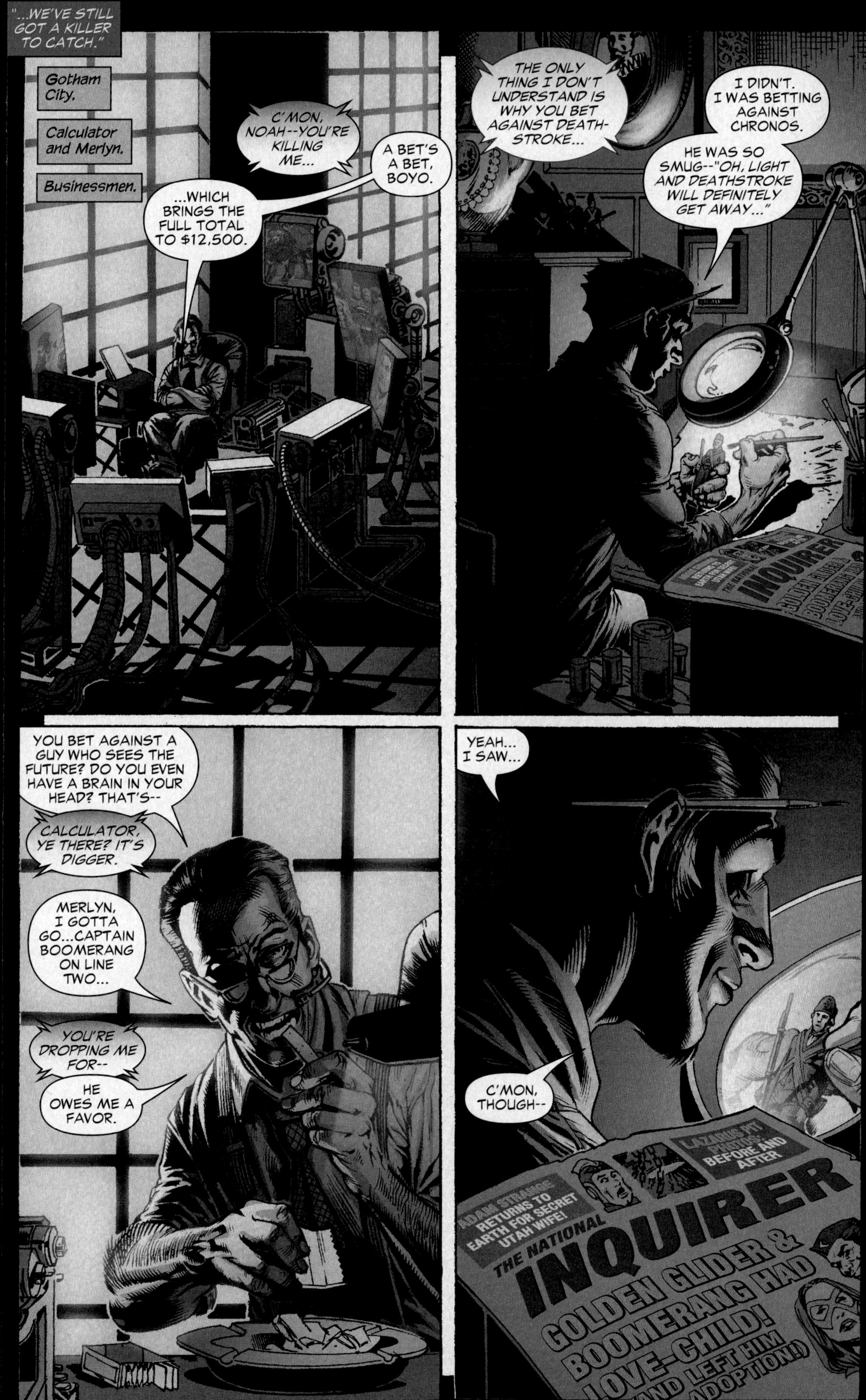

"...WE'VE STILL GOT A KILLER TO CATCH."
Gotham City.
Calculator and Merlyn.
Businessmen.
C'MON, NOAH--YOU'RE KILLING ME...
A BET'S A BET, BOYO.
...WHICH BRINGS THE FULL TOTAL TO $12,500.
THE ONLY THING I DON'T UNDERSTAND IS WHY YOU BET AGAINST DEATHSTROKE...
I DIDN'T. I WAS BETTING AGAINST CHRONOS.
HE WAS SO SMUG--"OH, LIGHT AND DEATHSTROKE WILL DEFINITELY GET AWAY..."
YOU BET AGAINST A GUY WHO SEES THE FUTURE? DO YOU EVEN HAVE A BRAIN IN YOUR HEAD? THAT'S--
CALCULATOR, YE THERE? IT'S DIGGER.
MERLYN, I GOTTA GO...CAPTAIN BOOMERANG ON LINE TWO...
YOU'RE DROPPING ME FOR--
HE OWES ME A FAVOR.
YEAH... I SAW...
C'MON, THOUGH--
ADAM STRANGE RETURNS TO EARTH FOR SECRET UTAH WIFE!
LAZARUS PIT PHOTOS BEFORE AND AFTER
THE NATIONAL INQUIRER
GOLDEN GLIDER & BOOMERANG HAD LOVE-CHILD!
(AND LEFT HIM
ADOPTION!)

"--LIKE HE COULD EVER GET GLIDER INTO BED ANYWAY."

OH, CAPTAIN, MY CAPTAIN! HOW ARE YOU?

THIS IS FUN FOR YOU, ISN'T IT, NOAH?

I'M JUST A SMALL ENTREPRENEUR. I TAKE NO PLEASURE IN PAIN.

THAT'S WHAT YOU PAID FOR, ISN'T IT?

RIGHT.

YOU'RE SURE THIS IS THE RIGHT ADDRESS?

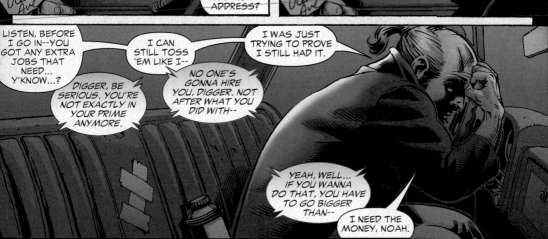

LISTEN, BEFORE I GO IN--YOU GOT ANY EXTRA JOBS THAT NEED... Y'KNOW...?

I CAN STILL TOSS 'EM LIKE I--

I WAS JUST TRYING TO PROVE I STILL HAD IT.

DIGGER, BE SERIOUS. YOU'RE NOT EXACTLY IN YOUR PRIME ANYMORE.

NO ONE'S GONNA HIRE YOU, DIGGER. NOT AFTER WHAT YOU DID WITH--

YEAH, WELL... IF YOU WANNA DO THAT, YOU HAVE TO GO BIGGER THAN--

I NEED THE MONEY, NOAH.

DO ME A FAVOR--FOCUS ON WHAT'S IN FRONT OF YOU.

BUT THE--

JUST FOCUS.

ALL YOU GOTTA DO IS GO UP AND SAY HELLO. GET ONE PART OF YOUR LIFE TOGETHER.

SOME ADOPTED KIDS HAVE A REAL NEED TO MEET THEIR BIOLOGICALS...

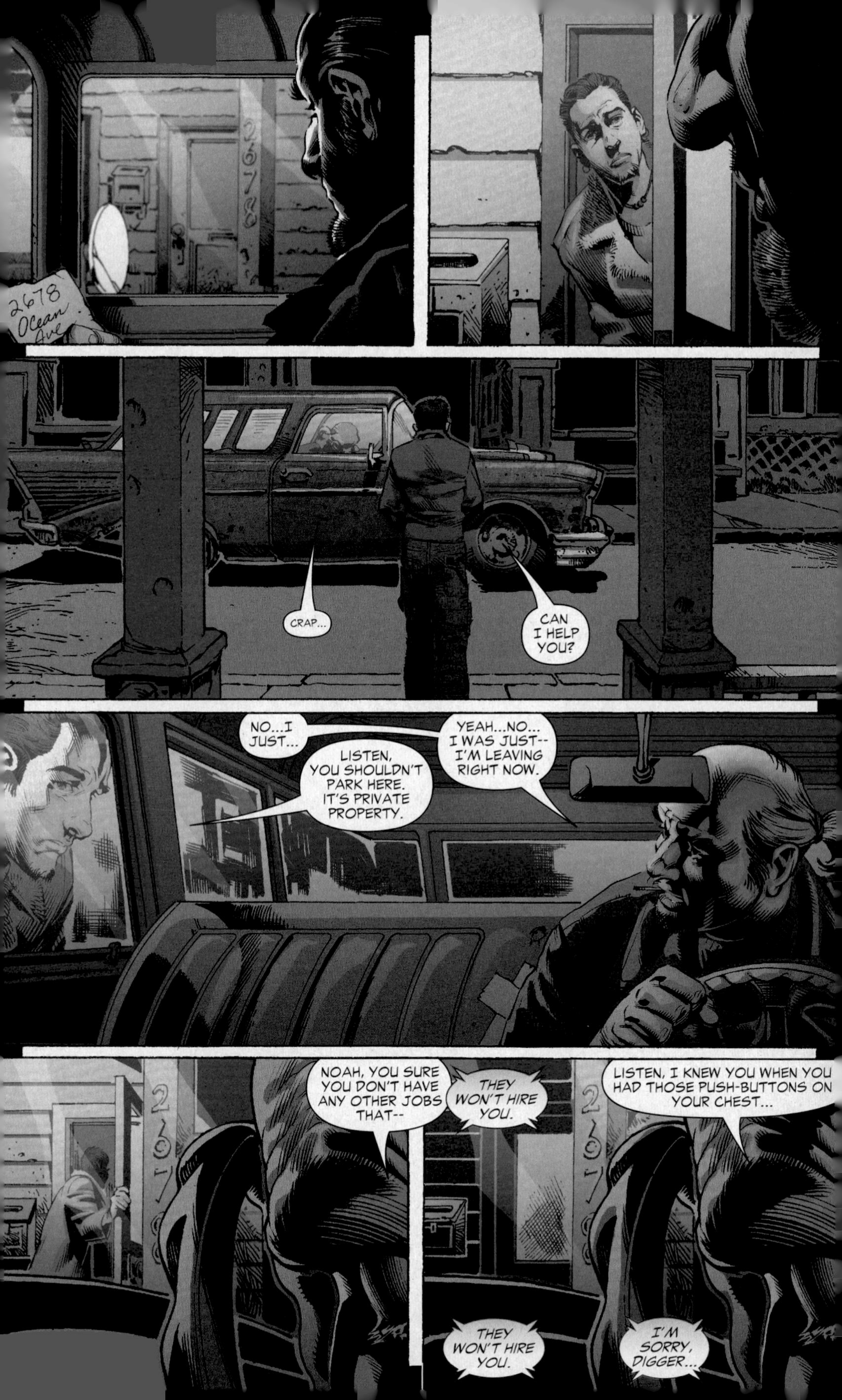
2678
Ocean
Ave
CRAP...
CAN I HELP YOU?
NO...I JUST...
YEAH...NO... I WAS JUST-- I'M LEAVING RIGHT NOW.
LISTEN, YOU SHOULDN'T PARK HERE. IT'S PRIVATE PROPERTY.
NOAH, YOU SURE YOU DON'T HAVE ANY OTHER JOBS THAT--
THEY WON'T HIRE YOU.
LISTEN, I KNEW YOU WHEN YOU HAD THOSE PUSH-BUTTONS ON YOUR CHEST...
THEY WON'T HIRE YOU.
I'M SORRY, DIGGER...

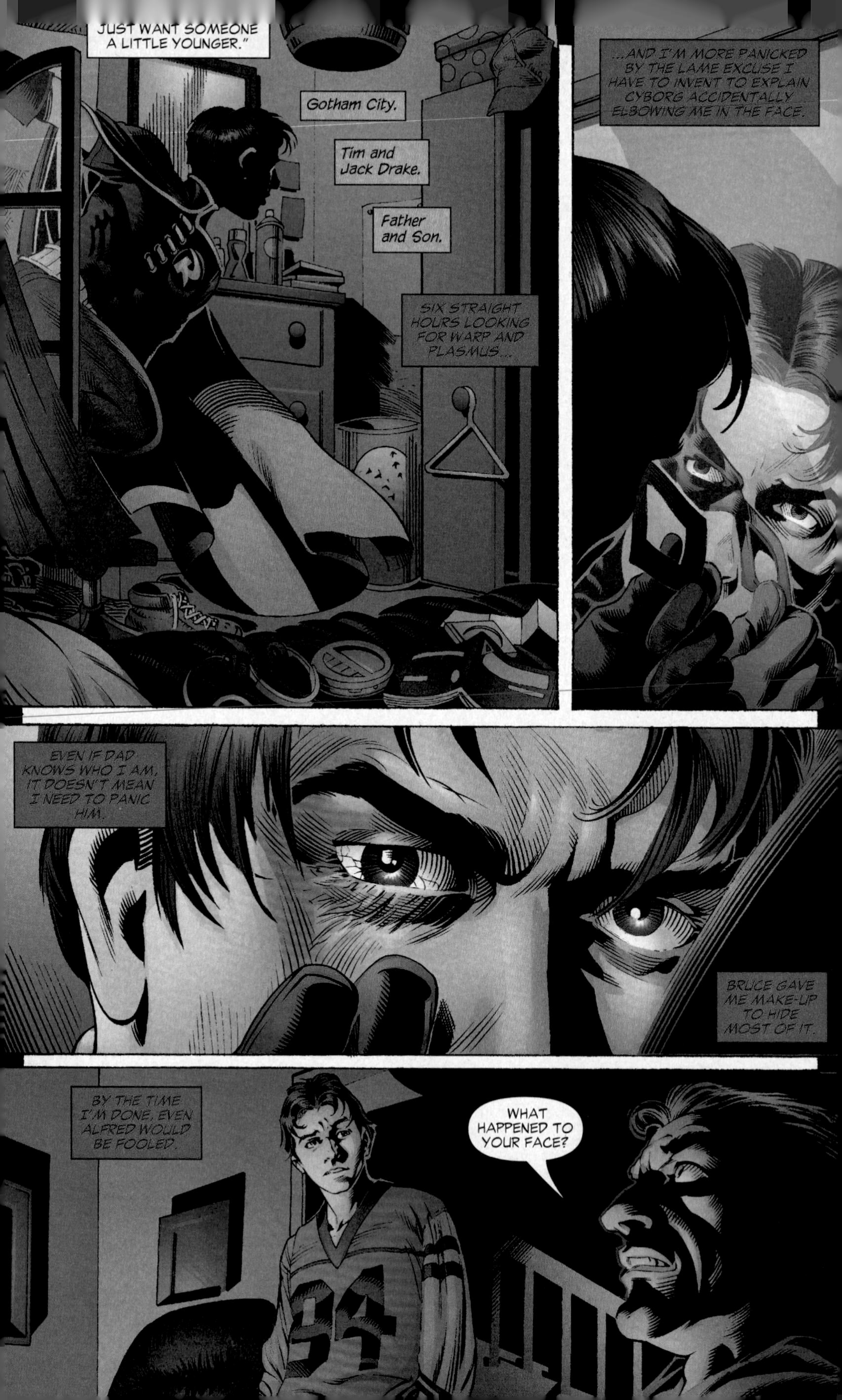
JUST WANT SOMEONE A LITTLE YOUNGER."
Gotham City.
Tim and Jack Drake.
Father and Son.
SIX STRAIGHT HOURS LOOKING FOR WARP AND PLASMUS...
...AND I'M MORE PANICKED BY THE LAME EXCUSE I HAVE TO INVENT TO EXPLAIN CYBORG ACCIDENTALLY ELBOWING ME IN THE FACE.
EVEN IF DAD KNOWS WHO I AM, IT DOESN'T MEAN I NEED TO PANIC HIM.
BRUCE GAVE ME MAKE-UP TO HIDE MOST OF IT.
BY THE TIME I'M DONE, EVEN ALFRED WOULD BE FOOLED.
WHAT HAPPENED TO YOUR FACE?

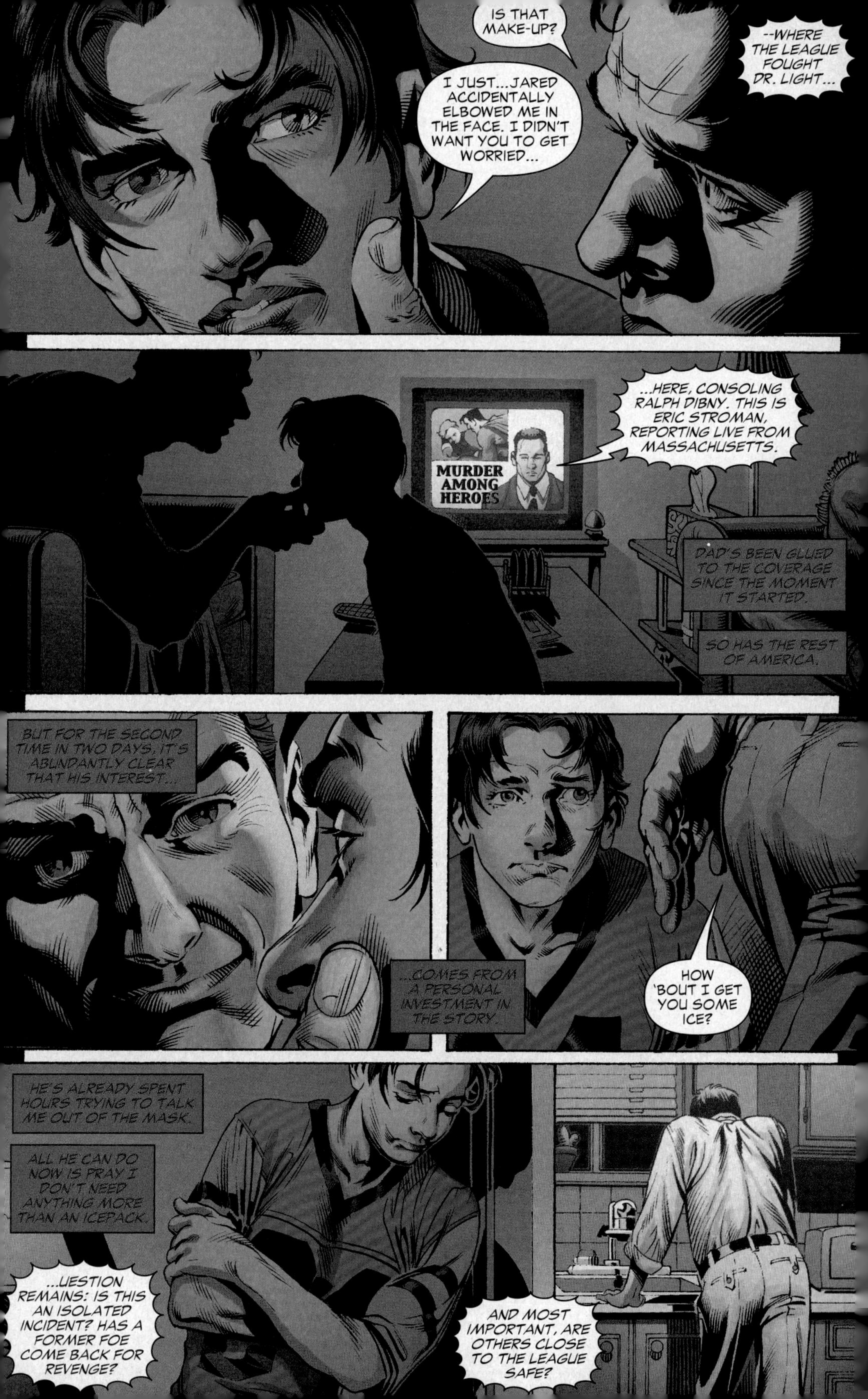
IS THAT MAKE-UP?
--WHERE THE LEAGUE FOUGHT DR. LIGHT...
I JUST...JARED ACCIDENTALLY ELBOWED ME IN THE FACE. I DIDN'T WANT YOU TO GET WORRIED...
MURDER AMONG HEROES
...HERE, CONSOLING RALPH DIBNY. THIS IS ERIC STROMAN, REPORTING LIVE FROM MASSACHUSETTS.
DAD'S BEEN GLUED TO THE COVERAGE SINCE THE MOMENT IT STARTED.
SO HAS THE REST OF AMERICA.
BUT FOR THE SECOND TIME IN TWO DAYS, IT'S ABUNDANTLY CLEAR THAT HIS INTEREST...
...COMES FROM A PERSONAL INVESTMENT IN THE STORY.
HOW 'BOUT I GET YOU SOME ICE?
HE'S ALREADY SPENT HOURS TRYING TO TALK ME OUT OF THE MASK.
ALL HE CAN DO NOW IS PRAY I DON'T NEED ANYTHING MORE THAN AN ICEPACK.
...UESTION REMAINS: IS THIS AN ISOLATED INCIDENT? HAS A FORMER FOE COME BACK FOR REVENGE?
AND MOST IMPORTANT, ARE OTHERS CLOSE TO THE LEAGUE SAFE?

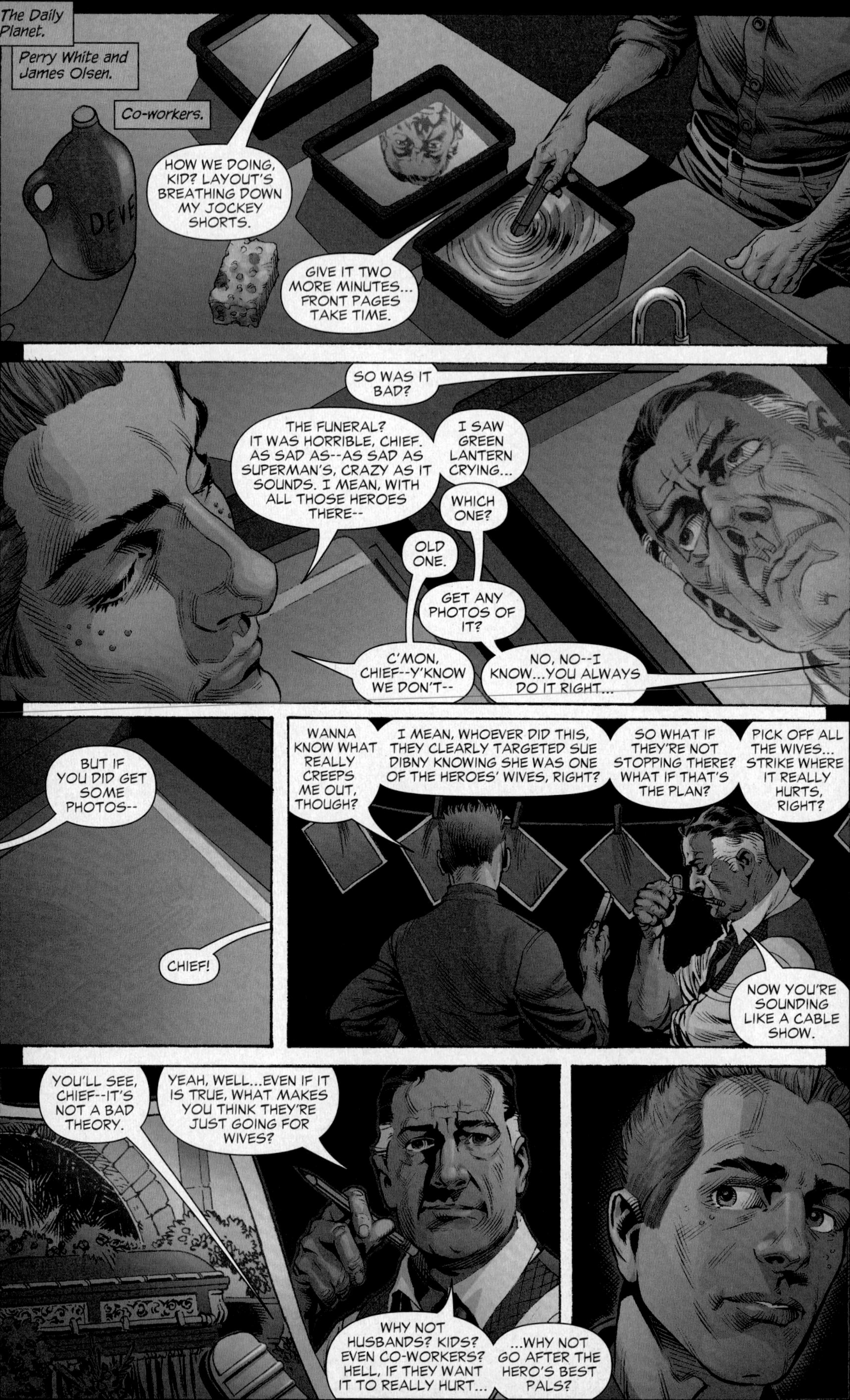
The Daily Planet.
Perry White and James Olsen.
Co-workers.
HOW WE DOING, KID? LAYOUT'S BREATHING DOWN MY JOCKEY SHORTS.
GIVE IT TWO MORE MINUTES... FRONT PAGES TAKE TIME.
DEVE
SO WAS IT BAD?
THE FUNERAL? IT WAS HORRIBLE, CHIEF. AS SAD AS--AS SAD AS SUPERMAN'S, CRAZY AS IT SOUNDS. I MEAN, WITH ALL THOSE HEROES THERE--
I SAW GREEN LANTERN CRYING...
WHICH ONE?
OLD ONE.
GET ANY PHOTOS OF IT?
C'MON, CHIEF--Y'KNOW WE DON'T--
NO, NO--I KNOW...YOU ALWAYS DO IT RIGHT...
BUT IF YOU DID GET SOME PHOTOS--
CHIEF!
WANNA KNOW WHAT REALLY CREEPS ME OUT, THOUGH?
I MEAN, WHOEVER DID THIS, THEY CLEARLY TARGETED SUE DIBNY KNOWING SHE WAS ONE OF THE HEROES' WIVES, RIGHT?
SO WHAT IF THEY'RE NOT STOPPING THERE? WHAT IF THAT'S THE PLAN?
PICK OFF ALL THE WIVES... STRIKE WHERE IT REALLY HURTS, RIGHT?
NOW YOU'RE SOUNDING LIKE A CABLE SHOW.
YOU'LL SEE, CHIEF--IT'S NOT A BAD THEORY.
YEAH, WELL...EVEN IF IT IS TRUE, WHAT MAKES YOU THINK THEY'RE JUST GOING FOR WIVES?
WHY NOT HUSBANDS? KIDS? EVEN CO-WORKERS? HELL, IF THEY WANT IT TO REALLY HURT...
...WHY NOT GO AFTER THE HERO'S BEST PALS?

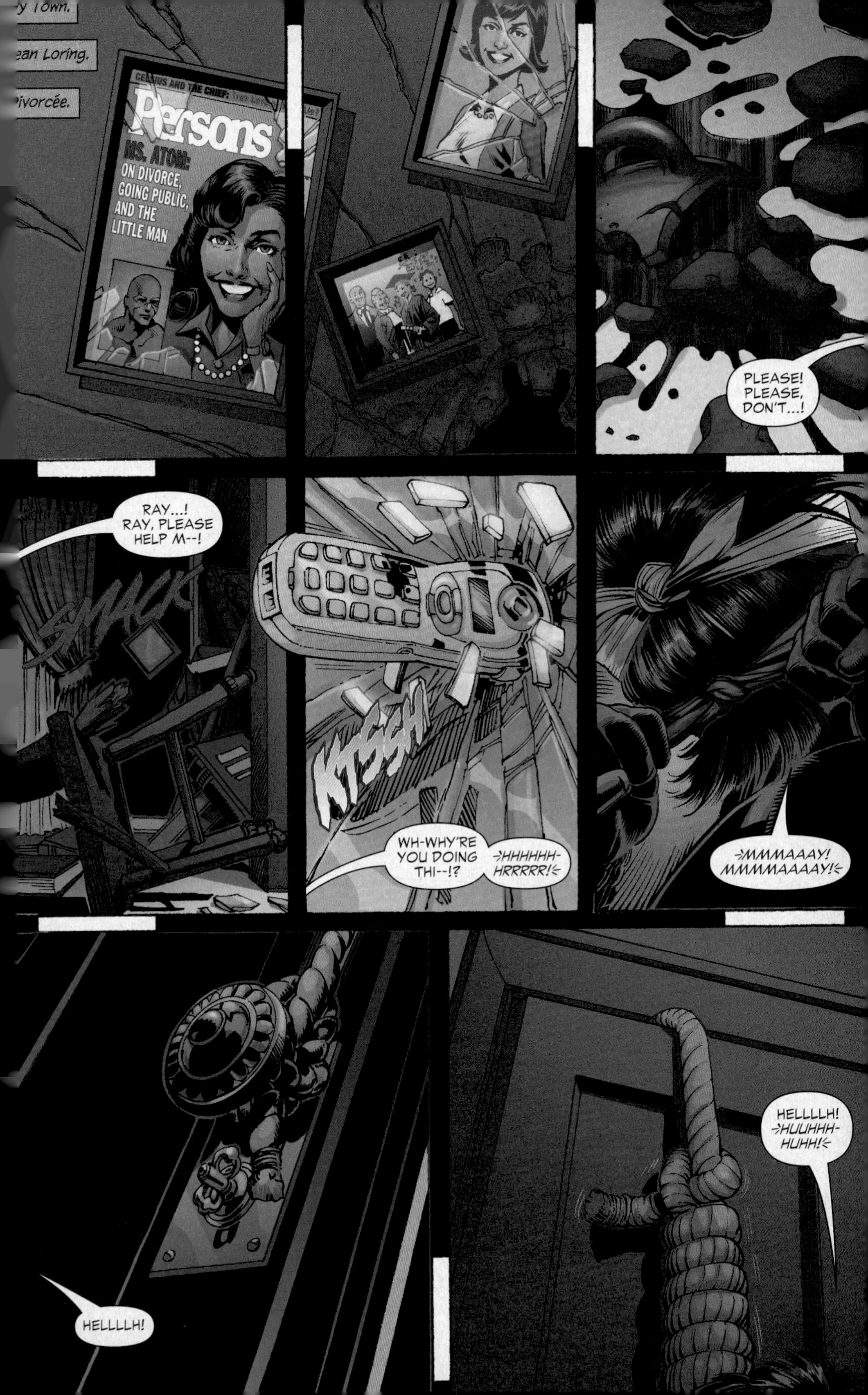
...y Town.
...ean Loring.
...Divorcée.
CELSIUS AND THE CHIEF:
Persons
MS. ATOM: ON DIVORCE, GOING PUBLIC, AND THE LITTLE MAN
PLEASE! PLEASE, DON'T...!
RAY...! RAY, PLEASE HELP M--!
SMACK
KTSSH
WH-WHY'RE YOU DOING THI--!?
HHHHHH-HRRRRR!
MMMAAAY! MMMMAAAAY!
HELLLLH!
HELLLLH! HUUHHH-HUHH!

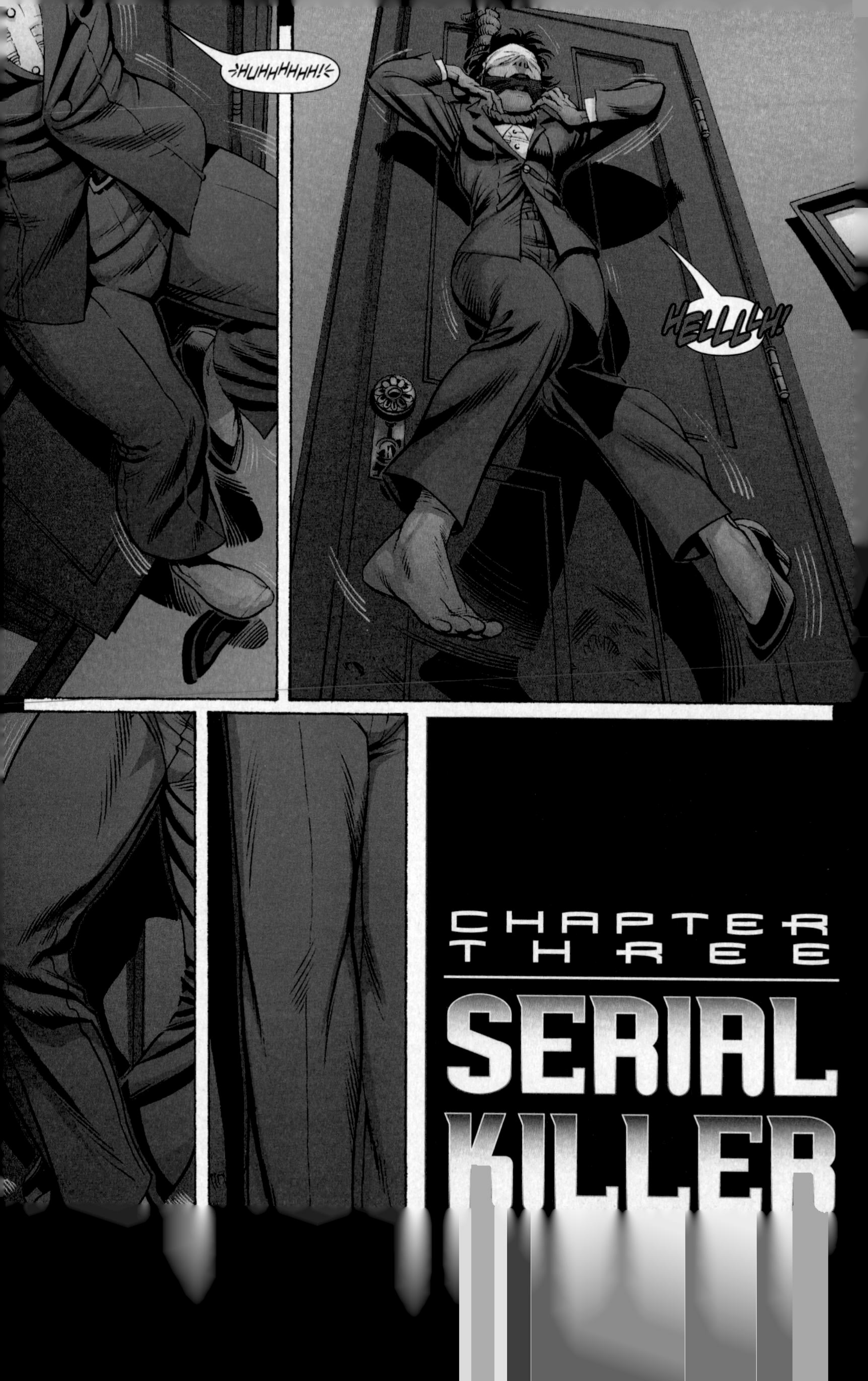

HUHHHHHH!
HELLLLH!
CHAPTER THREE
SERIAL KILLER

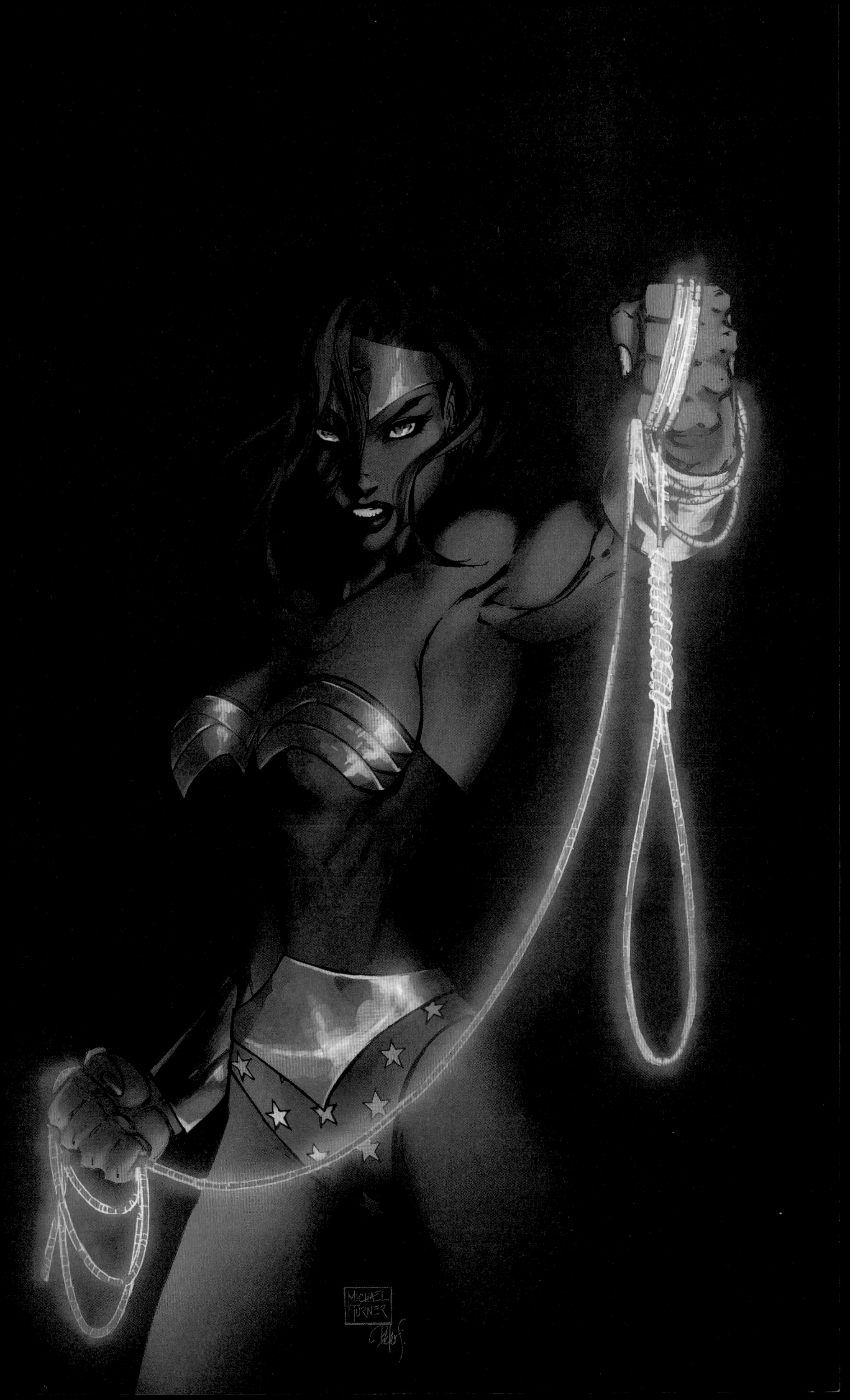
MICHAEL TURNER

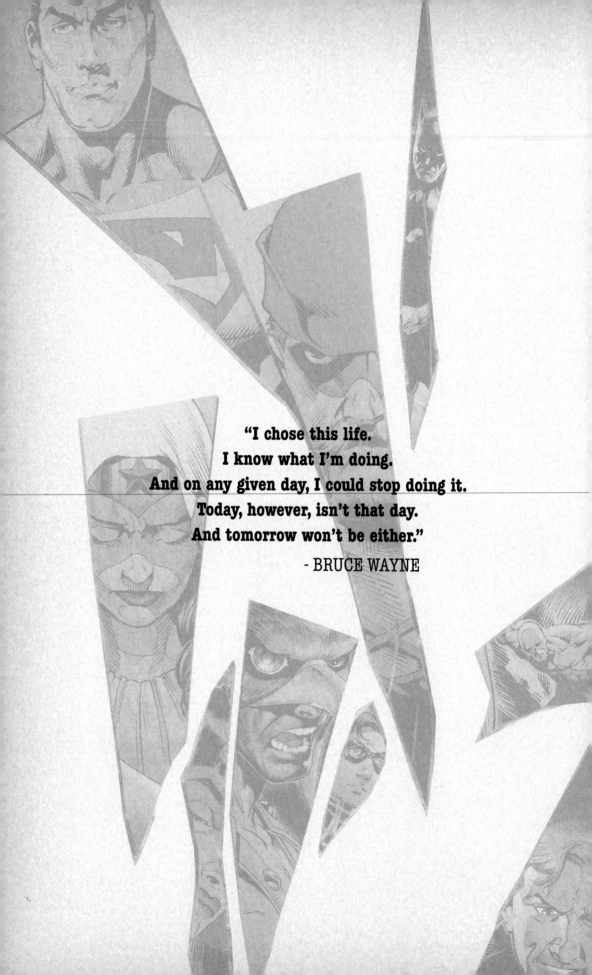

"I chose this life.
I know what I'm doing.
And on any given day, I could stop doing it.
Today, however, isn't that day.
And tomorrow won't be either."

— BRUCE WAYNE

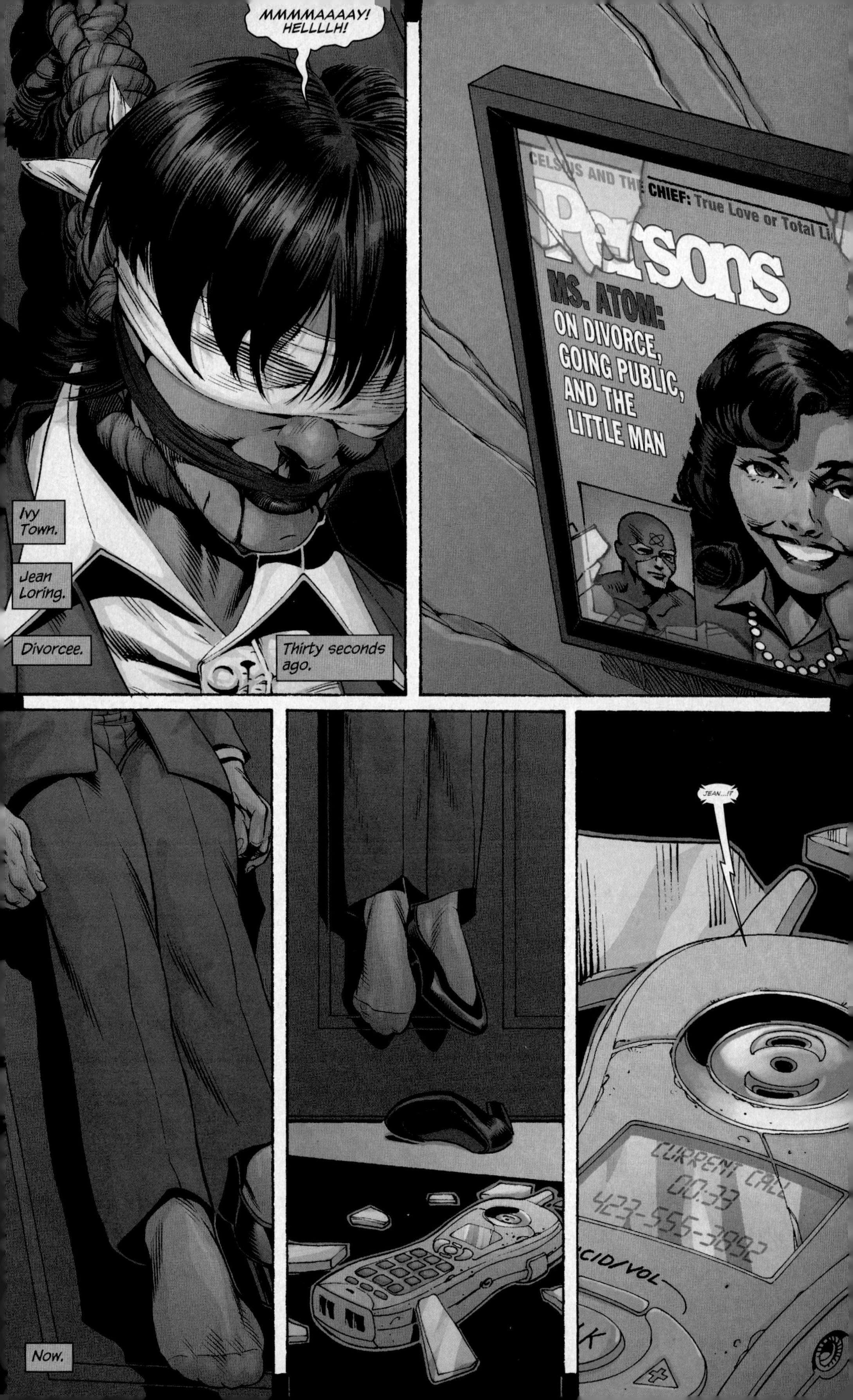
MMMMAAAAY! HELLLLH!
Ivy Town.
Jean Loring.
Divorcee.
Thirty seconds ago.
CELSUS AND THE CHIEF: True Love or Total
Persons
MS. ATOM: ON DIVORCE, GOING PUBLIC, AND THE LITTLE MAN
Now.
JEAN...!?
CURRENT CALL
00:33
423-555-3892
CID/VOL

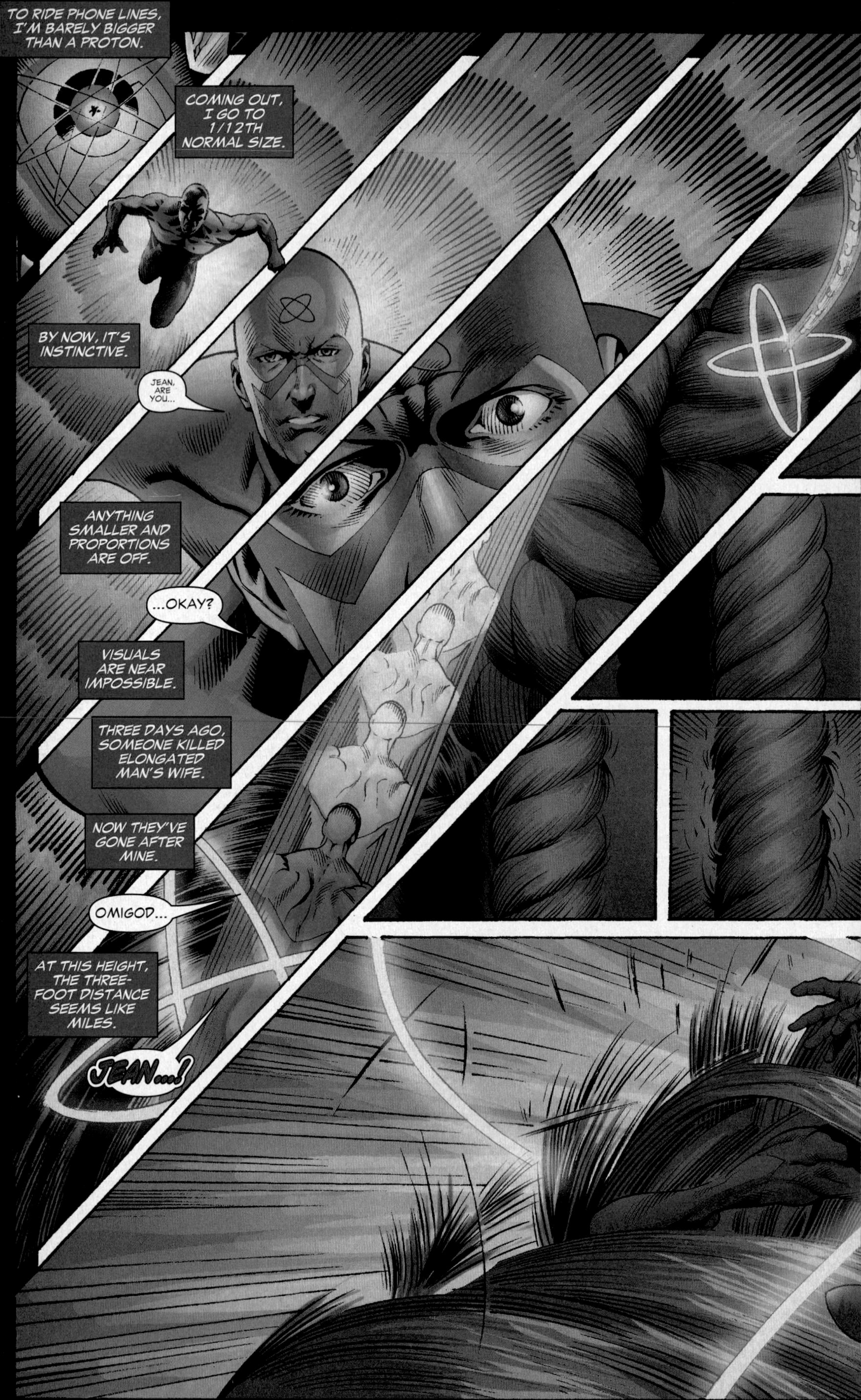
TO RIDE PHONE LINES, I'M BARELY BIGGER THAN A PROTON.
COMING OUT, I GO TO 1/12TH NORMAL SIZE.
BY NOW, IT'S INSTINCTIVE.
JEAN, ARE YOU...
ANYTHING SMALLER AND PROPORTIONS ARE OFF.
...OKAY?
VISUALS ARE NEAR IMPOSSIBLE.
THREE DAYS AGO, SOMEONE KILLED ELONGATED MAN'S WIFE.
NOW THEY'VE GONE AFTER MINE.
OMIGOD...
AT THIS HEIGHT, THE THREE-FOOT DISTANCE SEEMS LIKE MILES.
JEAN...!

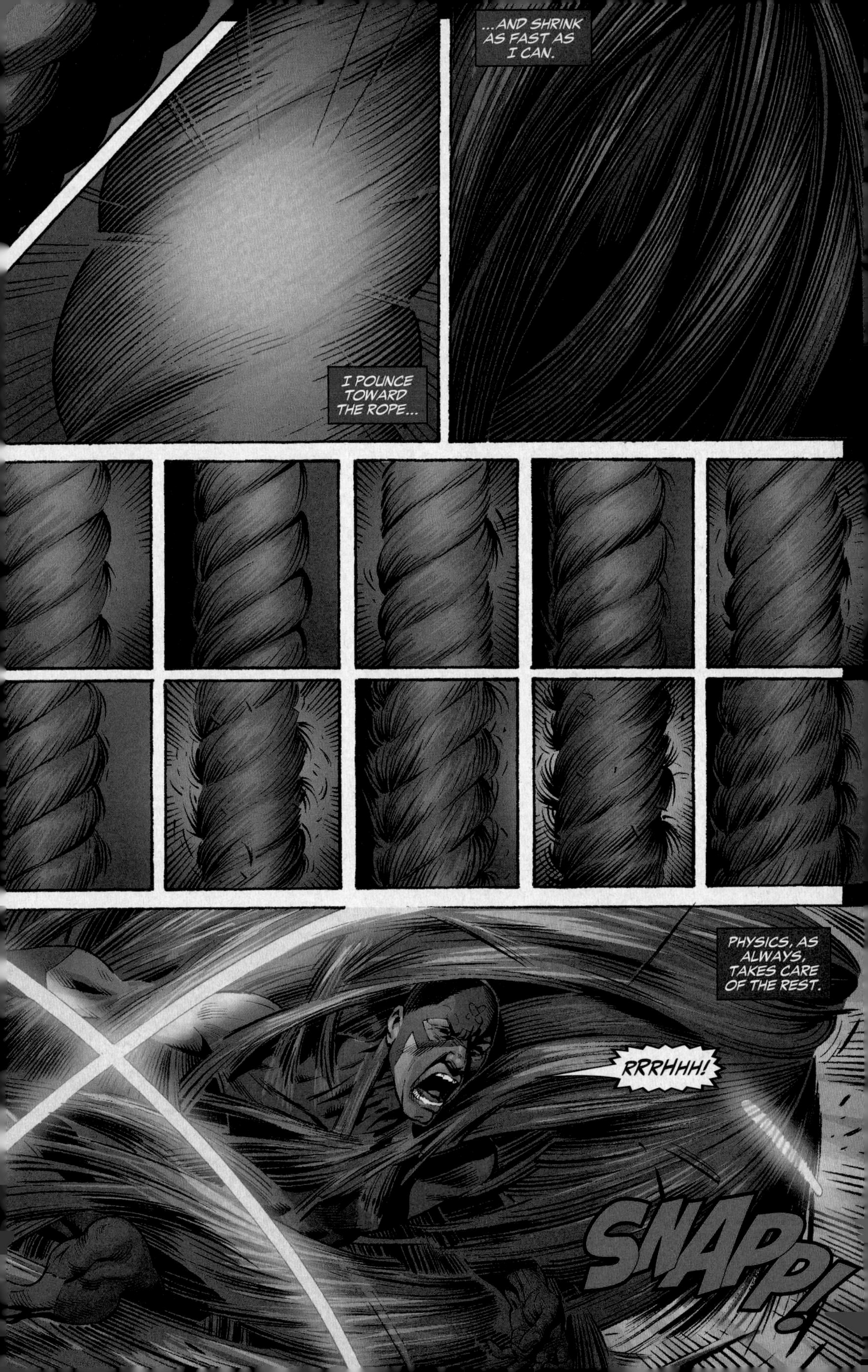
I POUNCE TOWARD THE ROPE...
...AND SHRINK AS FAST AS I CAN.
PHYSICS, AS ALWAYS, TAKES CARE OF THE REST.
RRRHHH!
SNAPP!

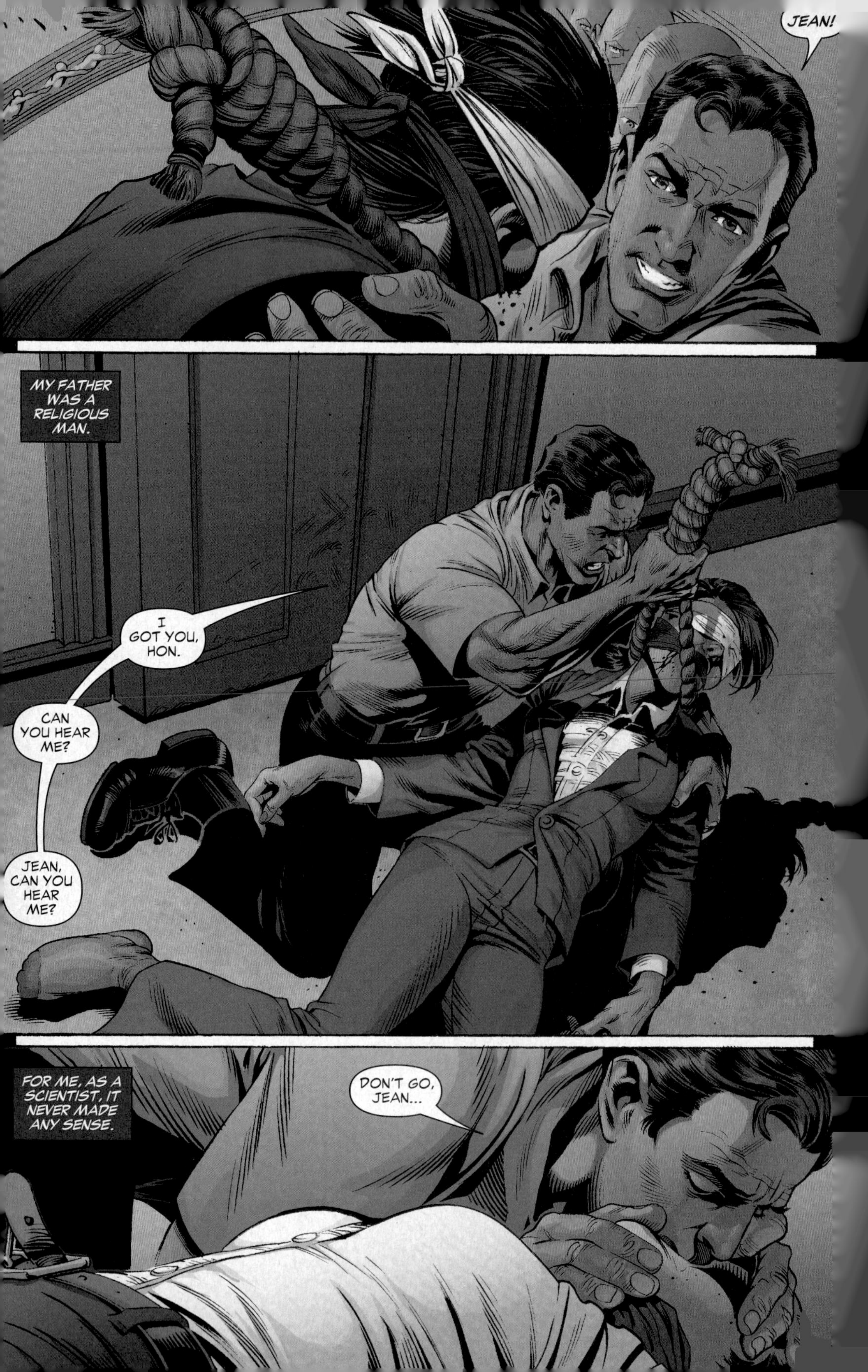
JEAN!
MY FATHER WAS A RELIGIOUS MAN.
I GOT YOU, HON.
CAN YOU HEAR ME?
JEAN, CAN YOU HEAR ME?
FOR ME, AS A SCIENTIST, IT NEVER MADE ANY SENSE.
DON'T GO, JEAN...

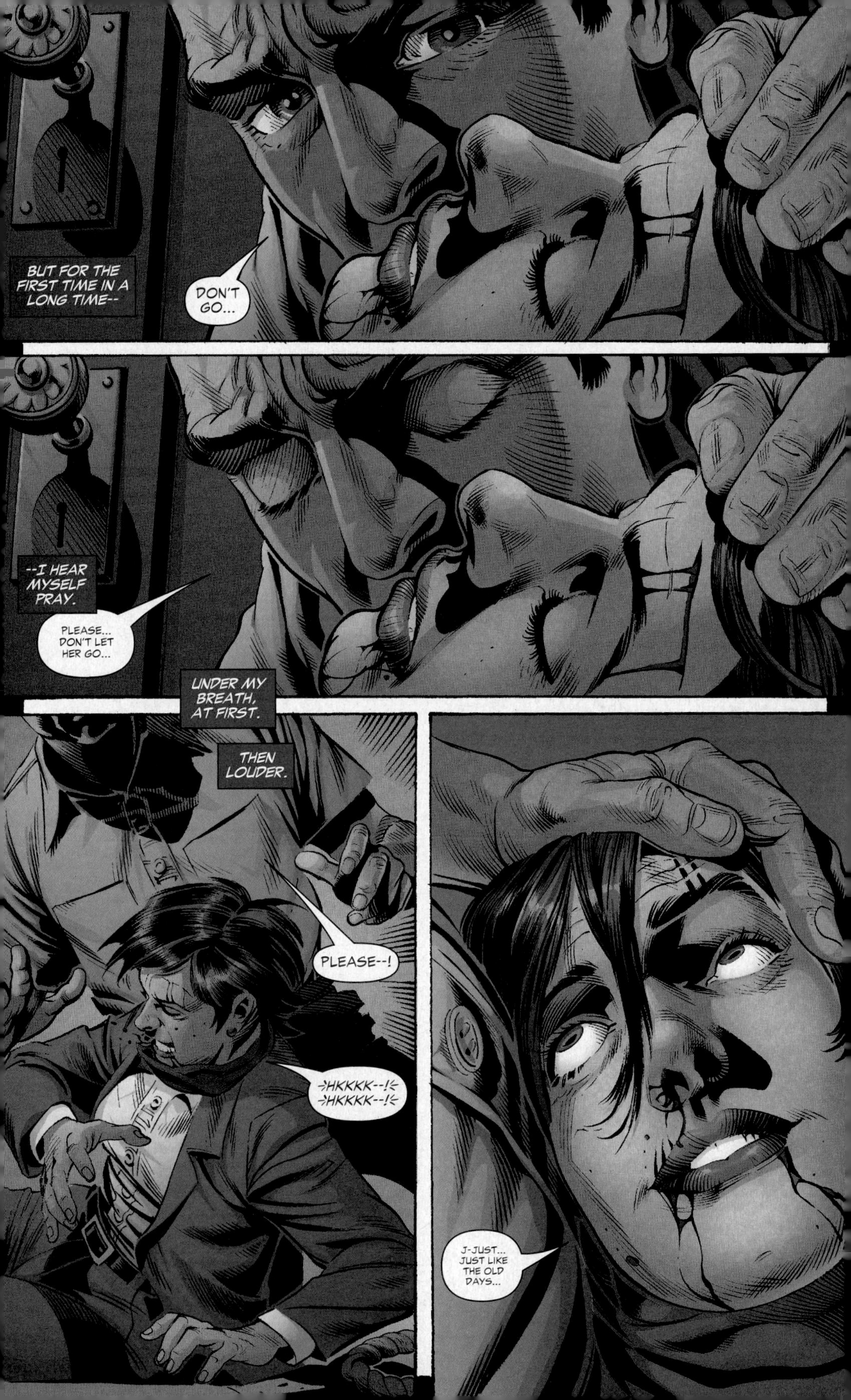
BUT FOR THE FIRST TIME IN A LONG TIME--
DON'T GO...
--I HEAR MYSELF PRAY.
PLEASE... DON'T LET HER GO...
UNDER MY BREATH, AT FIRST.
THEN LOUDER.
PLEASE--!
HKKKK--!
HKKKK--!
J-JUST... JUST LIKE THE OLD DAYS...

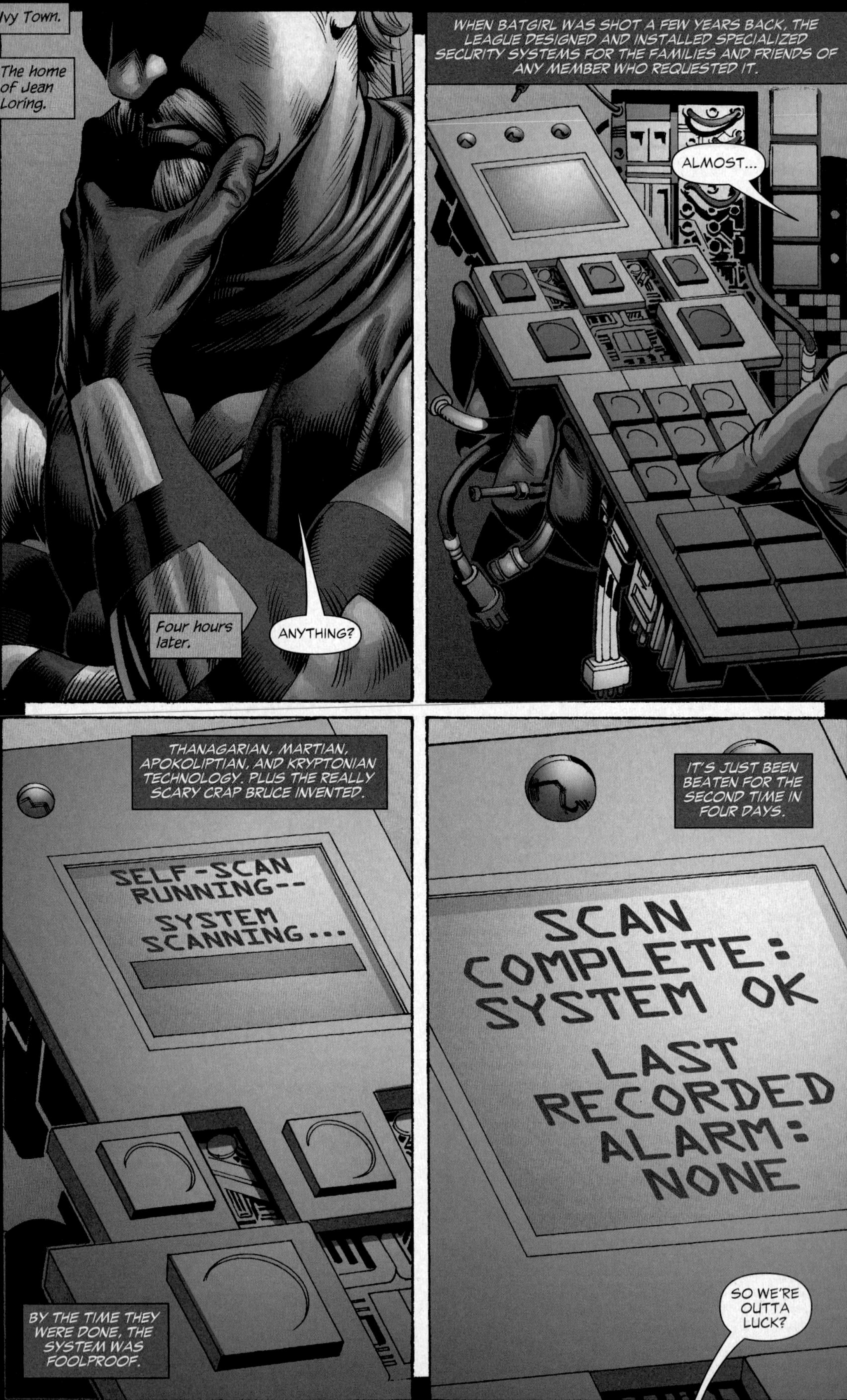
Ivy Town.
The home of Jean Loring.
Four hours later.
ANYTHING?
WHEN BATGIRL WAS SHOT A FEW YEARS BACK, THE LEAGUE DESIGNED AND INSTALLED SPECIALIZED SECURITY SYSTEMS FOR THE FAMILIES AND FRIENDS OF ANY MEMBER WHO REQUESTED IT.
ALMOST...
THANAGARIAN, MARTIAN, APOKOLIPTIAN, AND KRYPTONIAN TECHNOLOGY. PLUS THE REALLY SCARY CRAP BRUCE INVENTED.
SELF-SCAN RUNNING--
SYSTEM SCANNING...
BY THE TIME THEY WERE DONE, THE SYSTEM WAS FOOLPROOF.
IT'S JUST BEEN BEATEN FOR THE SECOND TIME IN FOUR DAYS.
SCAN COMPLETE: SYSTEM OK
LAST RECORDED ALARM: NONE
SO WE'RE OUTTA LUCK?

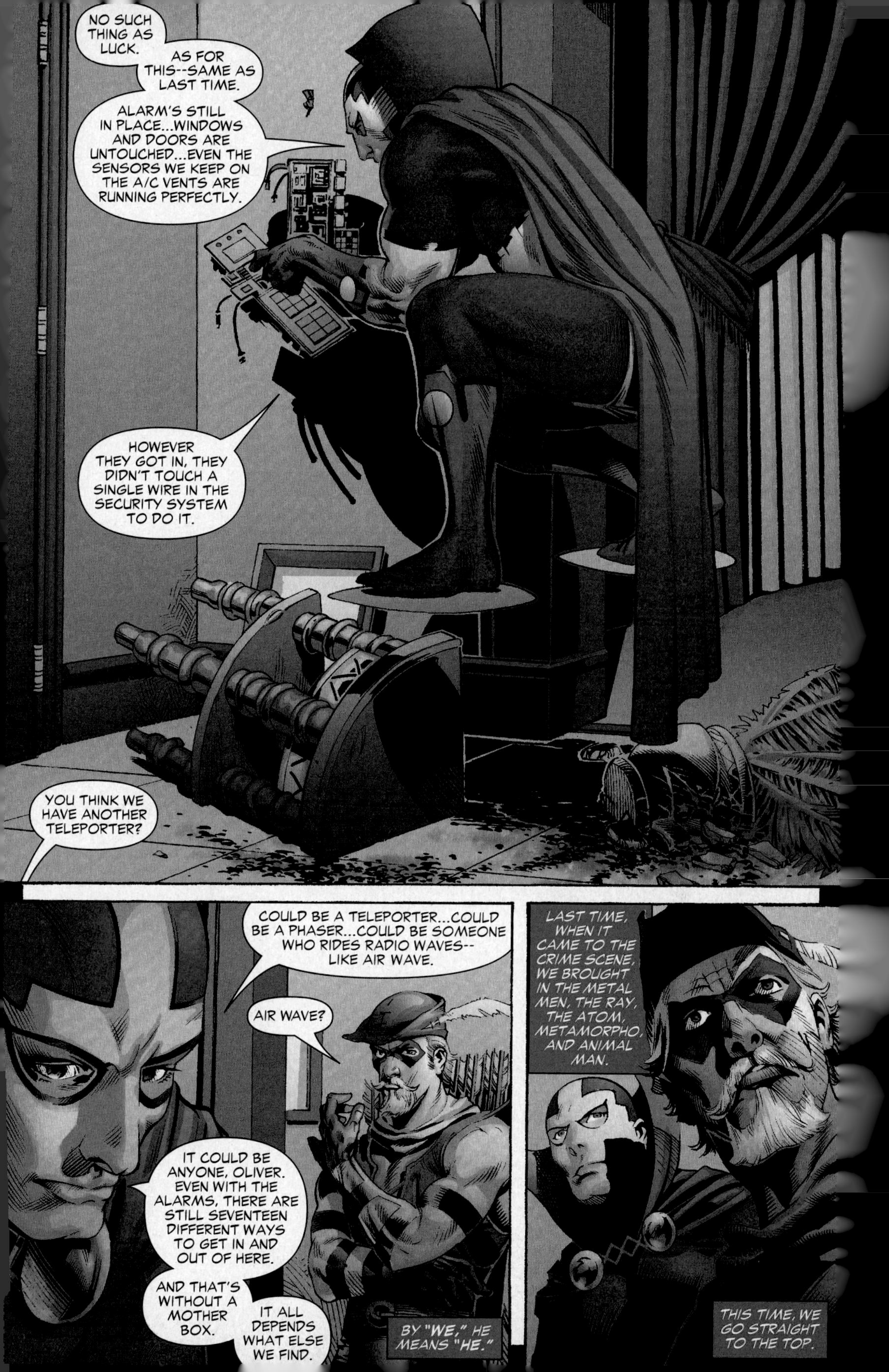
NO SUCH THING AS LUCK.
AS FOR THIS--SAME AS LAST TIME.
ALARM'S STILL IN PLACE...WINDOWS AND DOORS ARE UNTOUCHED...EVEN THE SENSORS WE KEEP ON THE A/C VENTS ARE RUNNING PERFECTLY.
HOWEVER THEY GOT IN, THEY DIDN'T TOUCH A SINGLE WIRE IN THE SECURITY SYSTEM TO DO IT.
YOU THINK WE HAVE ANOTHER TELEPORTER?
COULD BE A TELEPORTER...COULD BE A PHASER...COULD BE SOMEONE WHO RIDES RADIO WAVES--LIKE AIR WAVE.
AIR WAVE?
IT COULD BE ANYONE, OLIVER. EVEN WITH THE ALARMS, THERE ARE STILL SEVENTEEN DIFFERENT WAYS TO GET IN AND OUT OF HERE.
AND THAT'S WITHOUT A MOTHER BOX.
IT ALL DEPENDS WHAT ELSE WE FIND.
BY "WE," HE MEANS "HE."
LAST TIME, WHEN IT CAME TO THE CRIME SCENE, WE BROUGHT IN THE METAL MEN, THE RAY, THE ATOM, METAMORPHO, AND ANIMAL MAN.
THIS TIME, WE GO STRAIGHT TO THE TOP.

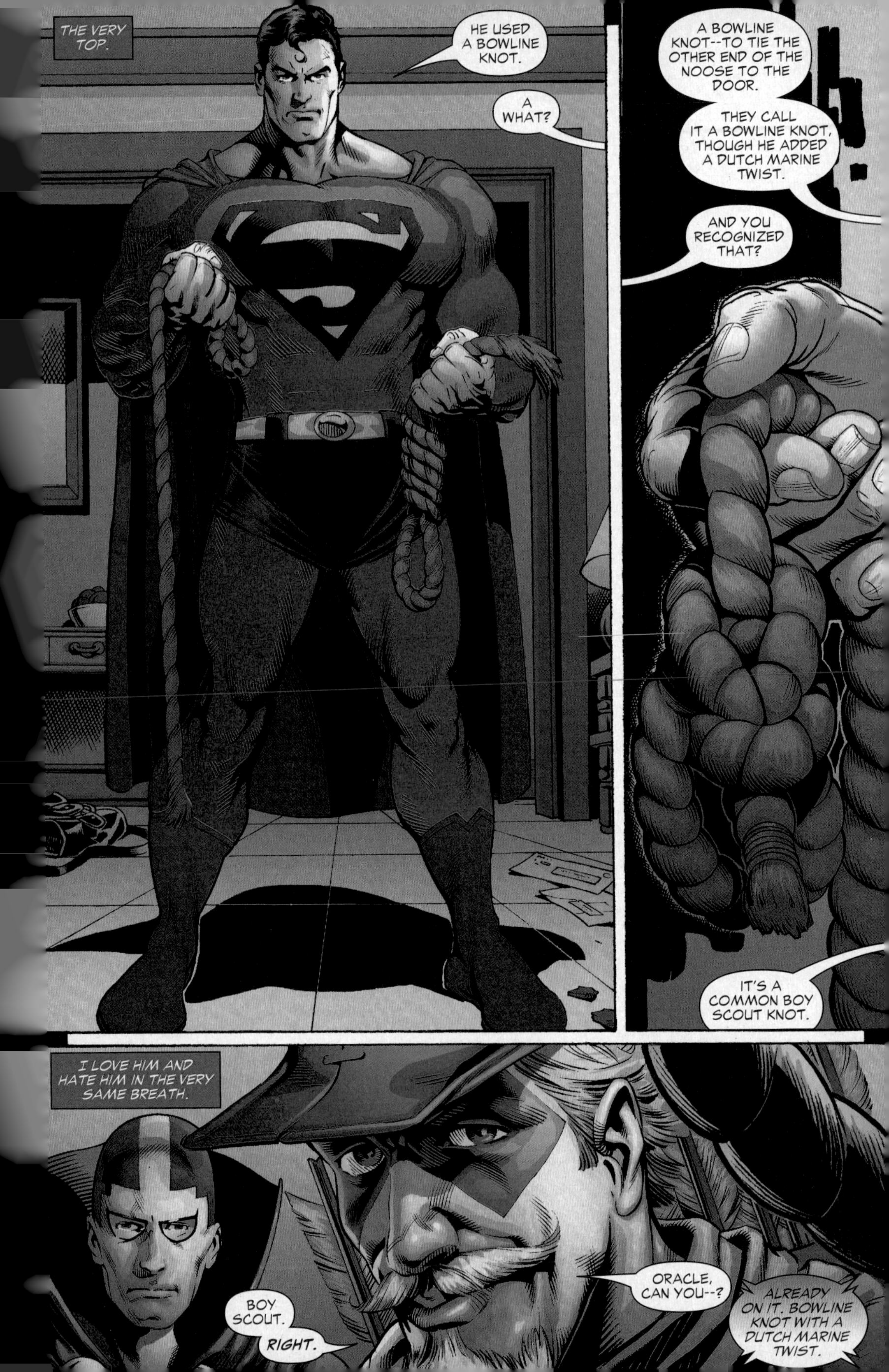
THE VERY TOP.
HE USED A BOWLINE KNOT.
A WHAT?
A BOWLINE KNOT--TO TIE THE OTHER END OF THE NOOSE TO THE DOOR.
THEY CALL IT A BOWLINE KNOT, THOUGH HE ADDED A DUTCH MARINE TWIST.
AND YOU RECOGNIZED THAT?
IT'S A COMMON BOY SCOUT KNOT.
I LOVE HIM AND HATE HIM IN THE VERY SAME BREATH.
BOY SCOUT.
RIGHT.
ORACLE, CAN YOU--?
ALREADY ON IT. BOWLINE KNOT WITH A DUTCH MARINE TWIST.

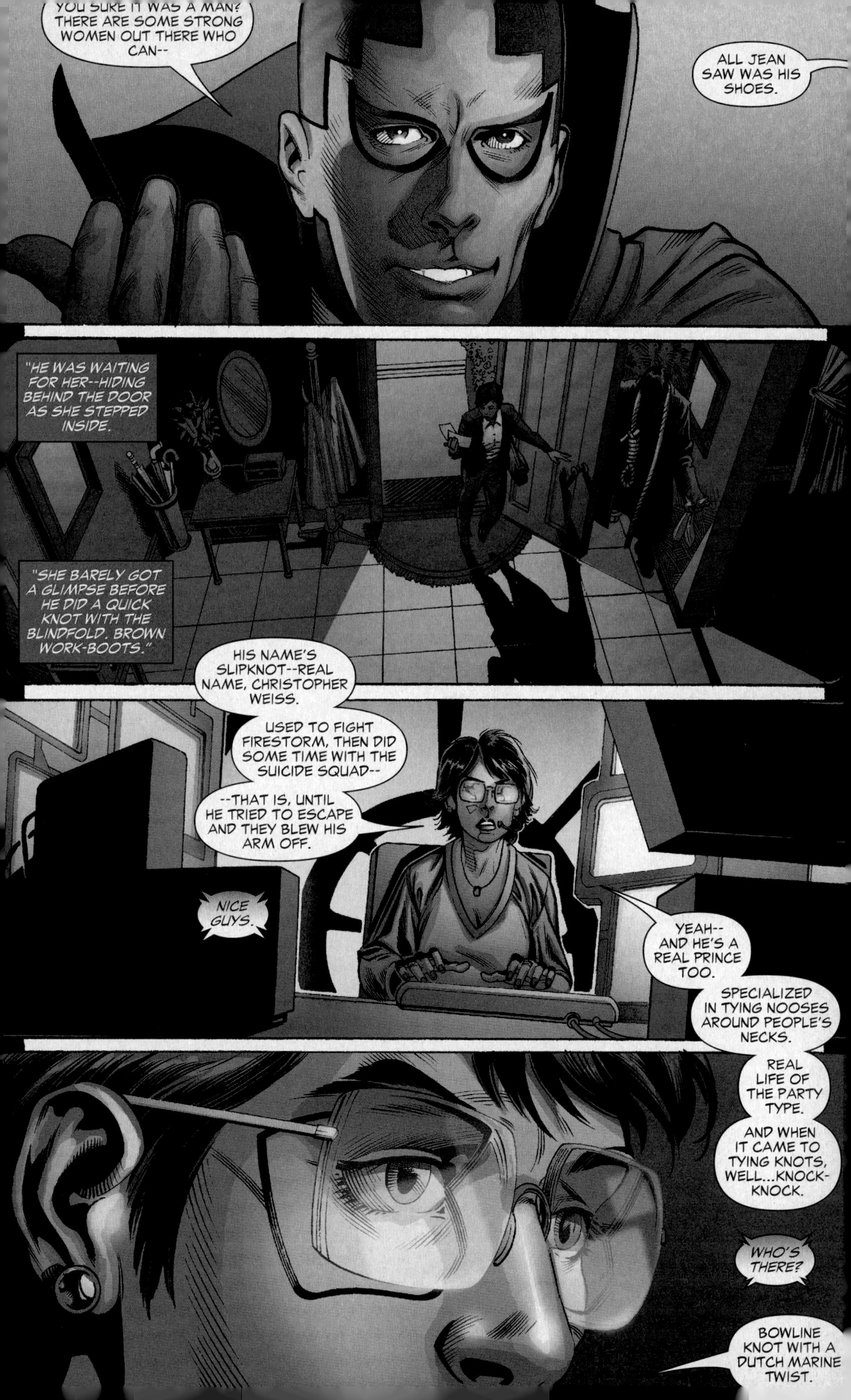
YOU SURE IT WAS A MAN? THERE ARE SOME STRONG WOMEN OUT THERE WHO CAN--
ALL JEAN SAW WAS HIS SHOES.
"HE WAS WAITING FOR HER--HIDING BEHIND THE DOOR AS SHE STEPPED INSIDE.
"SHE BARELY GOT A GLIMPSE BEFORE HE DID A QUICK KNOT WITH THE BLINDFOLD. BROWN WORK-BOOTS."
HIS NAME'S SLIPKNOT--REAL NAME, CHRISTOPHER WEISS.
USED TO FIGHT FIRESTORM, THEN DID SOME TIME WITH THE SUICIDE SQUAD--
--THAT IS, UNTIL HE TRIED TO ESCAPE AND THEY BLEW HIS ARM OFF.
NICE GUYS.
YEAH-- AND HE'S A REAL PRINCE TOO.
SPECIALIZED IN TYING NOOSES AROUND PEOPLE'S NECKS.
REAL LIFE OF THE PARTY TYPE.
AND WHEN IT CAME TO TYING KNOTS, WELL...KNOCK-KNOCK.
WHO'S THERE?
BOWLINE KNOT WITH A DUTCH MARINE TWIST.

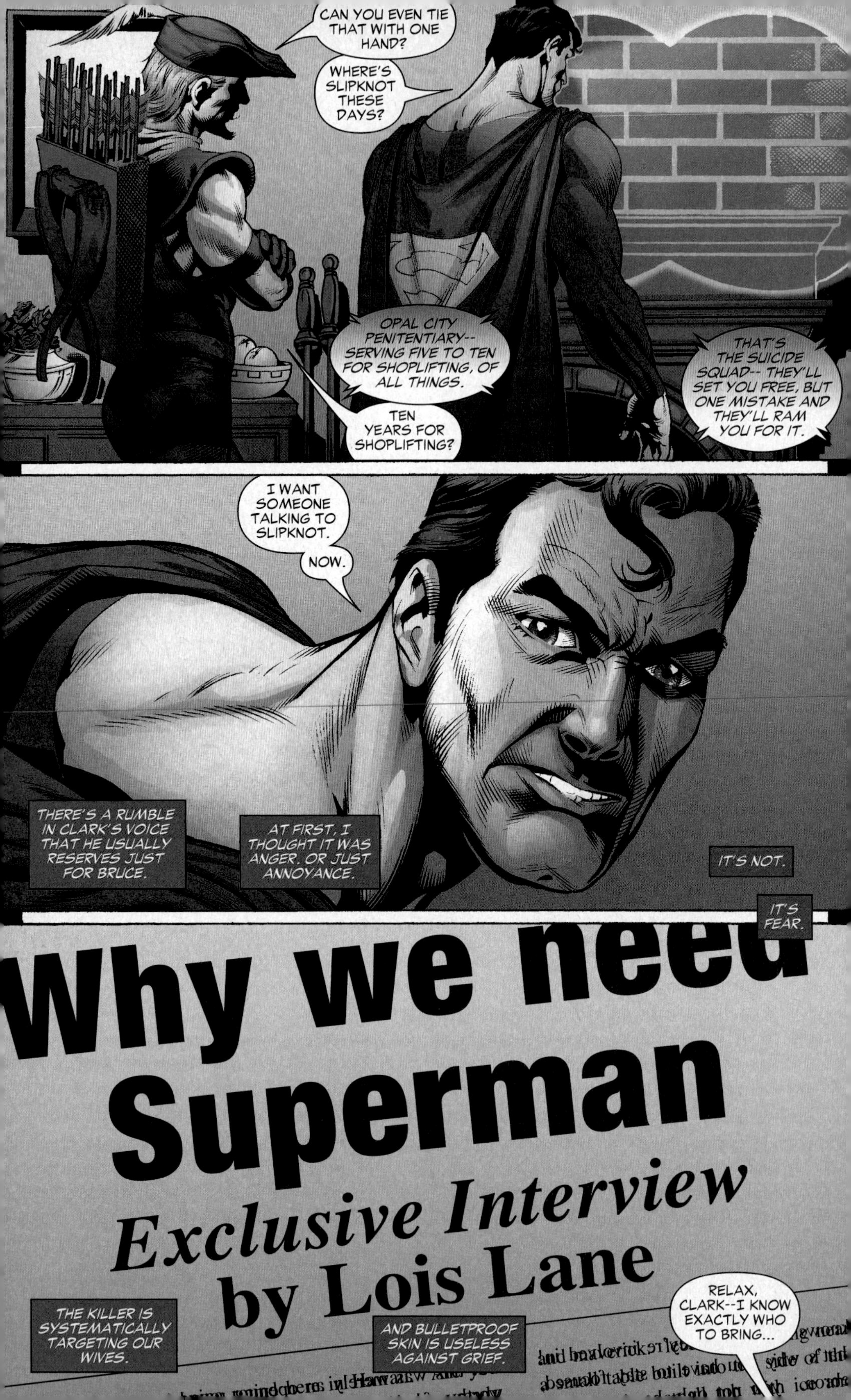

CAN YOU EVEN TIE THAT WITH ONE HAND?
WHERE'S SLIPKNOT THESE DAYS?
OPAL CITY PENITENTIARY-- SERVING FIVE TO TEN FOR SHOPLIFTING, OF ALL THINGS.
TEN YEARS FOR SHOPLIFTING?
THAT'S THE SUICIDE SQUAD-- THEY'LL SET YOU FREE, BUT ONE MISTAKE AND THEY'LL RAM YOU FOR IT.
I WANT SOMEONE TALKING TO SLIPKNOT.
NOW.
THERE'S A RUMBLE IN CLARK'S VOICE THAT HE USUALLY RESERVES JUST FOR BRUCE.
AT FIRST, I THOUGHT IT WAS ANGER. OR JUST ANNOYANCE.
IT'S NOT.
IT'S FEAR.
Why we need Superman
Exclusive Interview by Lois Lane
THE KILLER IS SYSTEMATICALLY TARGETING OUR WIVES.
AND BULLETPROOF SKIN IS USELESS AGAINST GRIEF.
RELAX, CLARK--I KNOW EXACTLY WHO TO BRING...

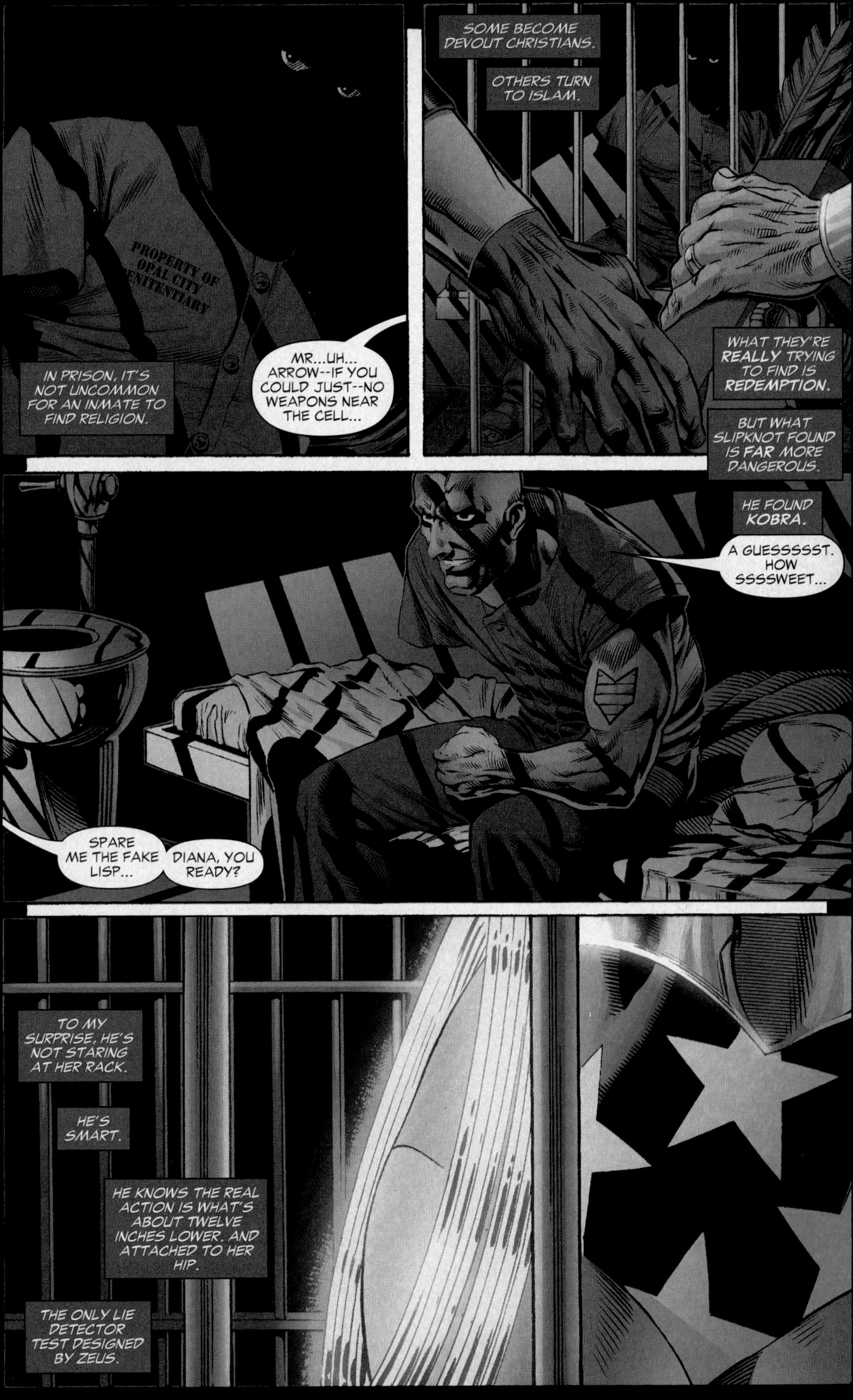
PROPERTY OF OPAL CITY PENITENTIARY
IN PRISON, IT'S NOT UNCOMMON FOR AN INMATE TO FIND RELIGION.
MR...UH... ARROW--IF YOU COULD JUST--NO WEAPONS NEAR THE CELL...
SOME BECOME DEVOUT CHRISTIANS.
OTHERS TURN TO ISLAM.
WHAT THEY'RE REALLY TRYING TO FIND IS REDEMPTION.
BUT WHAT SLIPKNOT FOUND IS FAR MORE DANGEROUS.
HE FOUND KOBRA.
A GUESSSSST. HOW SSSSWEET...
SPARE ME THE FAKE LISP...
DIANA, YOU READY?
TO MY SURPRISE, HE'S NOT STARING AT HER RACK.
HE'S SMART.
HE KNOWS THE REAL ACTION IS WHAT'S ABOUT TWELVE INCHES LOWER. AND ATTACHED TO HER HIP.
THE ONLY LIE DETECTOR TEST DESIGNED BY ZEUS.

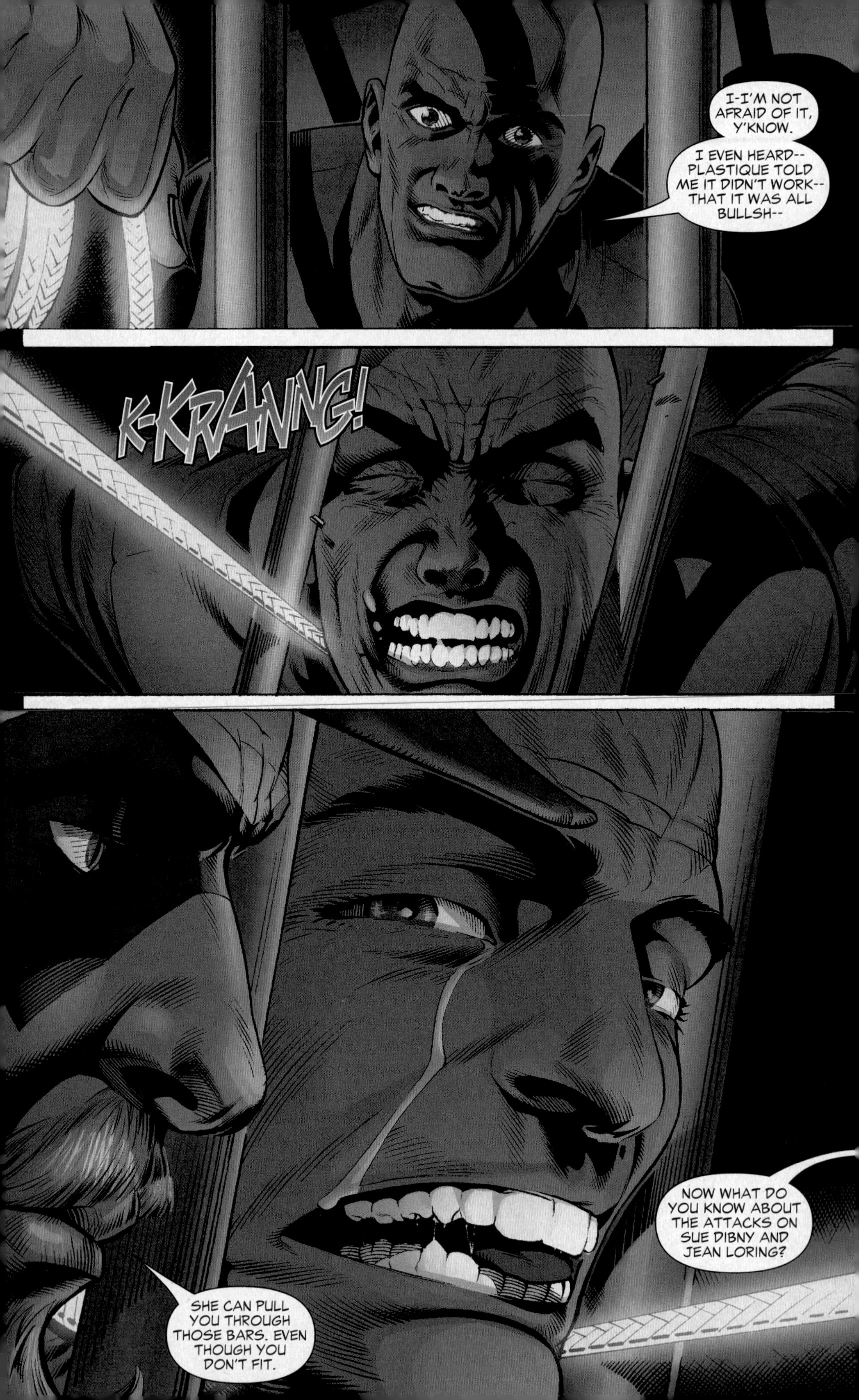
I-I'M NOT AFRAID OF IT, Y'KNOW.
I EVEN HEARD-- PLASTIQUE TOLD ME IT DIDN'T WORK-- THAT IT WAS ALL BULLSH--
K-KRANNG!
NOW WHAT DO YOU KNOW ABOUT THE ATTACKS ON SUE DIBNY AND JEAN LORING?
SHE CAN PULL YOU THROUGH THOSE BARS. EVEN THOUGH YOU DON'T FIT.

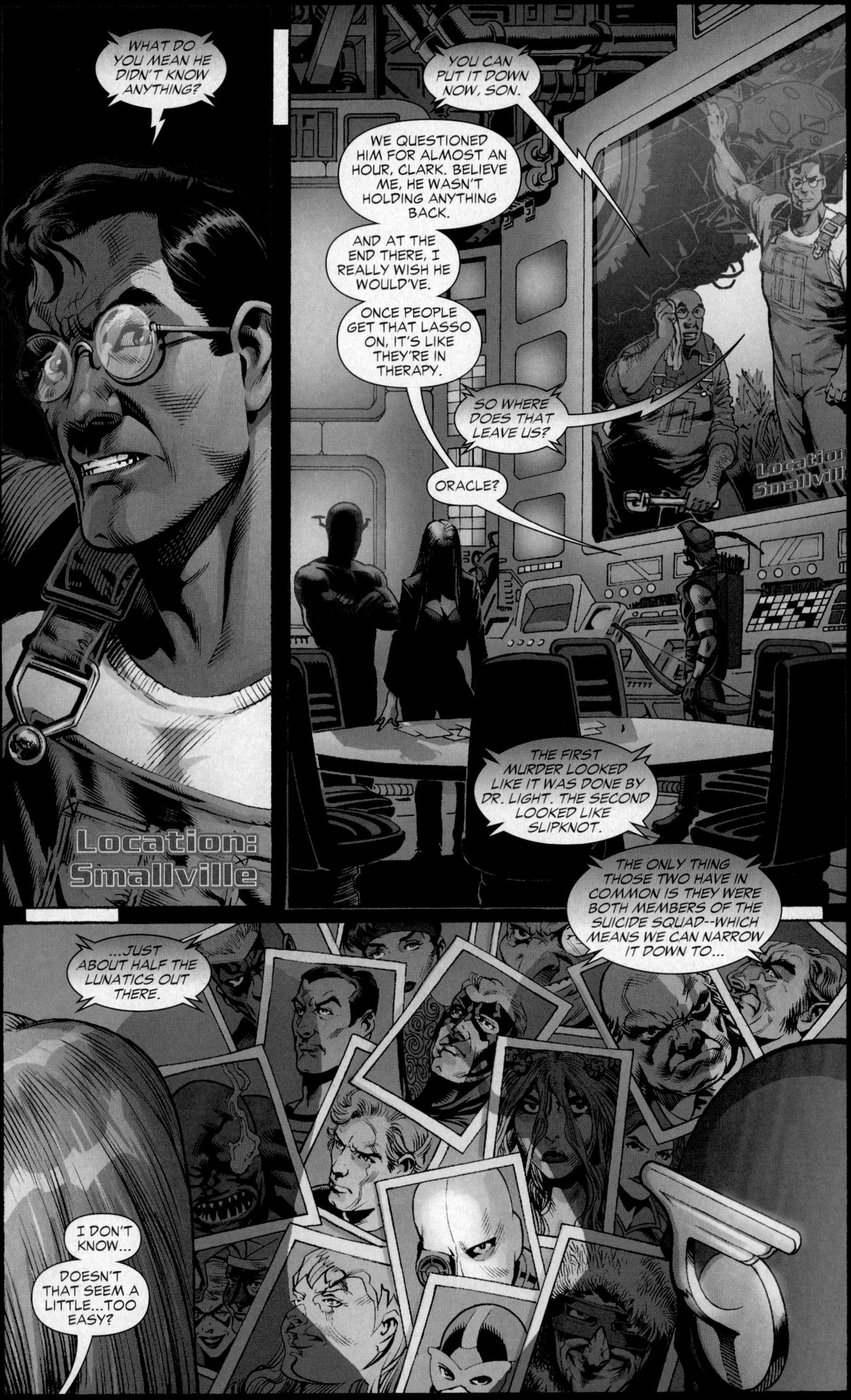
WHAT DO YOU MEAN HE DIDN'T KNOW ANYTHING?
Location: Smallville
YOU CAN PUT IT DOWN NOW, SON.
WE QUESTIONED HIM FOR ALMOST AN HOUR, CLARK. BELIEVE ME, HE WASN'T HOLDING ANYTHING BACK.
AND AT THE END THERE, I REALLY WISH HE WOULD'VE.
ONCE PEOPLE GET THAT LASSO ON, IT'S LIKE THEY'RE IN THERAPY.
SO WHERE DOES THAT LEAVE US?
ORACLE?
THE FIRST MURDER LOOKED LIKE IT WAS DONE BY DR. LIGHT. THE SECOND LOOKED LIKE SLIPKNOT.
THE ONLY THING THOSE TWO HAVE IN COMMON IS THEY WERE BOTH MEMBERS OF THE SUICIDE SQUAD--WHICH MEANS WE CAN NARROW IT DOWN TO...
...JUST ABOUT HALF THE LUNATICS OUT THERE.
I DON'T KNOW...
DOESN'T THAT SEEM A LITTLE...TOO EASY?

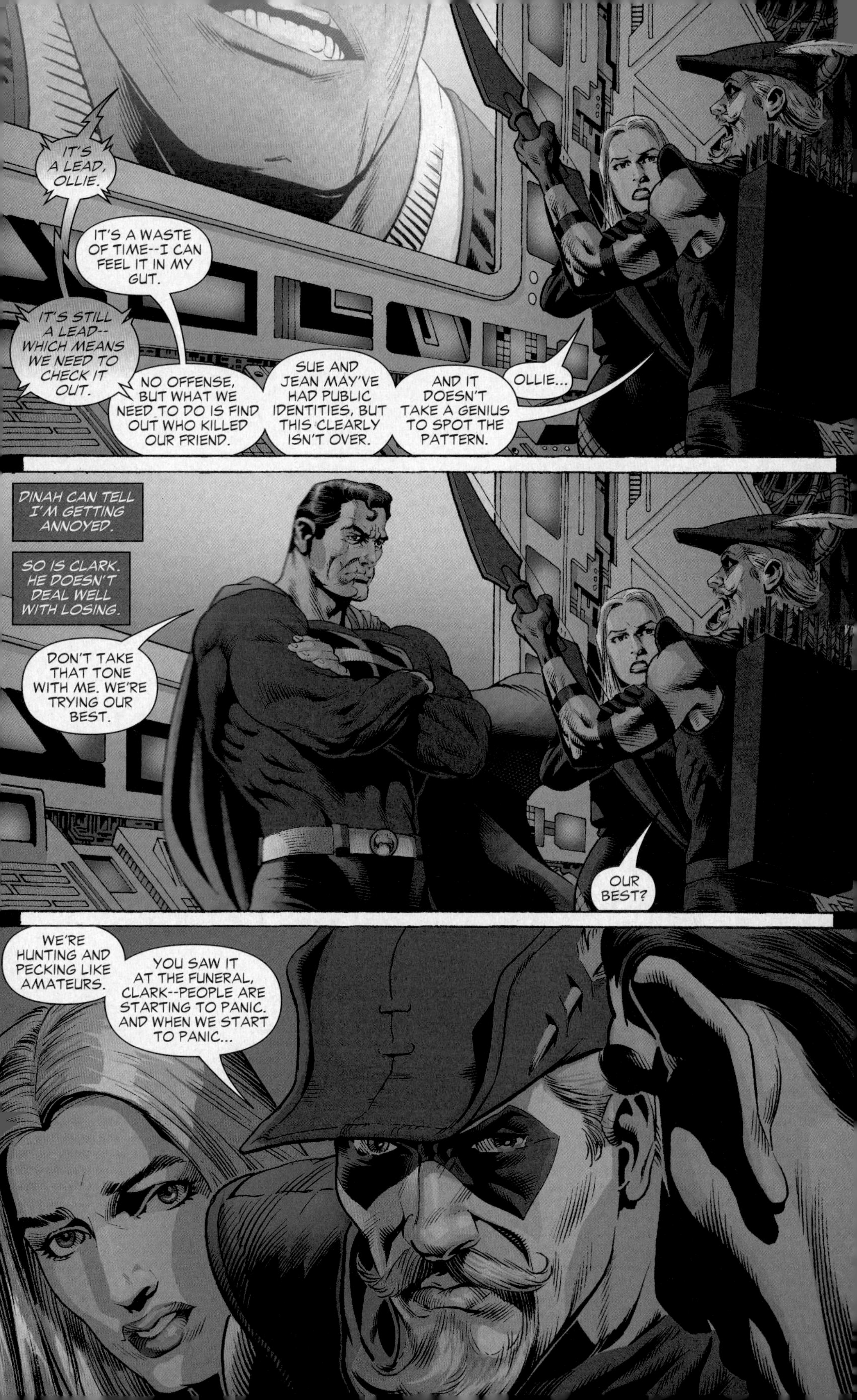
IT'S A LEAD, OLLIE.
IT'S A WASTE OF TIME--I CAN FEEL IT IN MY GUT.
IT'S STILL A LEAD--WHICH MEANS WE NEED TO CHECK IT OUT.
NO OFFENSE, BUT WHAT WE NEED TO DO IS FIND OUT WHO KILLED OUR FRIEND.
SUE AND JEAN MAY'VE HAD PUBLIC IDENTITIES, BUT THIS CLEARLY ISN'T OVER.
AND IT DOESN'T TAKE A GENIUS TO SPOT THE PATTERN.
OLLIE...
DINAH CAN TELL I'M GETTING ANNOYED.
SO IS CLARK. HE DOESN'T DEAL WELL WITH LOSING.
DON'T TAKE THAT TONE WITH ME. WE'RE TRYING OUR BEST.
OUR BEST?
WE'RE HUNTING AND PECKING LIKE AMATEURS.
YOU SAW IT AT THE FUNERAL, CLARK--PEOPLE ARE STARTING TO PANIC. AND WHEN WE START TO PANIC...

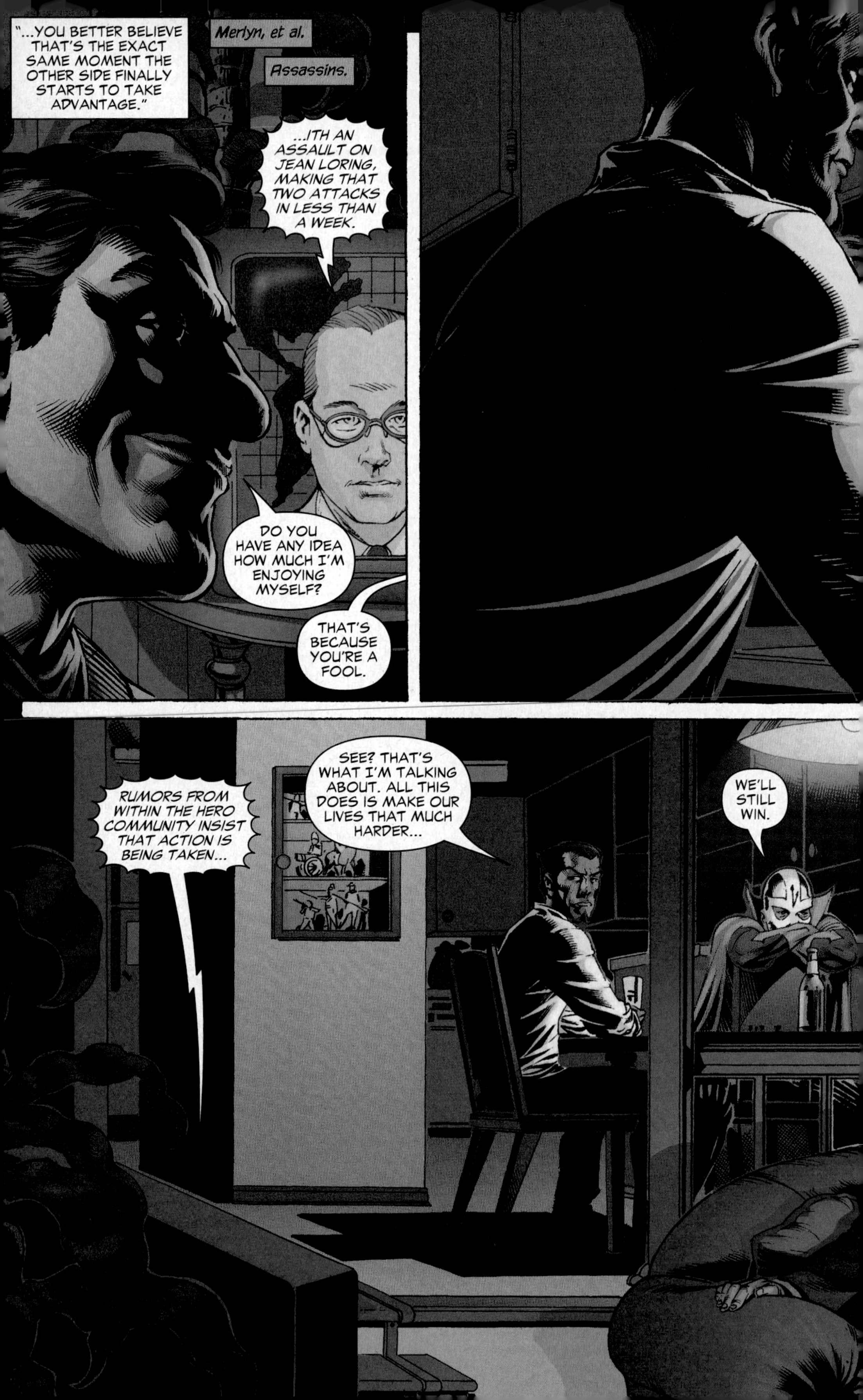
"...YOU BETTER BELIEVE THAT'S THE EXACT SAME MOMENT THE OTHER SIDE FINALLY STARTS TO TAKE ADVANTAGE."
Merlyn, et al.
Assassins.
...ITH AN ASSAULT ON JEAN LORING, MAKING THAT TWO ATTACKS IN LESS THAN A WEEK.
DO YOU HAVE ANY IDEA HOW MUCH I'M ENJOYING MYSELF?
THAT'S BECAUSE YOU'RE A FOOL.
RUMORS FROM WITHIN THE HERO COMMUNITY INSIST THAT ACTION IS BEING TAKEN...
SEE? THAT'S WHAT I'M TALKING ABOUT. ALL THIS DOES IS MAKE OUR LIVES THAT MUCH HARDER...
WE'LL STILL WIN.

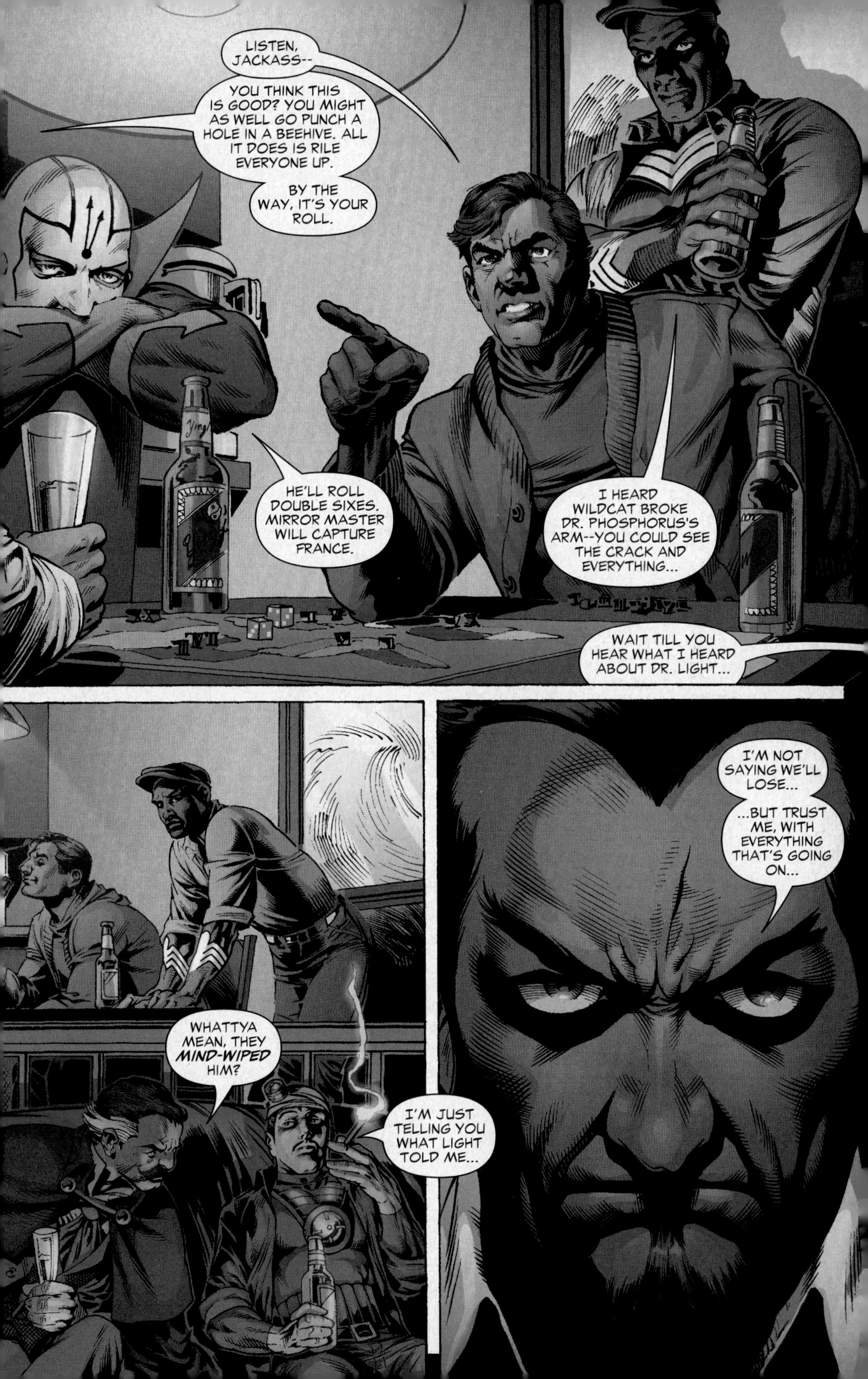
LISTEN, JACKASS--
YOU THINK THIS IS GOOD? YOU MIGHT AS WELL GO PUNCH A HOLE IN A BEEHIVE. ALL IT DOES IS RILE EVERYONE UP.
BY THE WAY, IT'S YOUR ROLL.
HE'LL ROLL DOUBLE SIXES. MIRROR MASTER WILL CAPTURE FRANCE.
I HEARD WILDCAT BROKE DR. PHOSPHORUS'S ARM--YOU COULD SEE THE CRACK AND EVERYTHING...
WAIT TILL YOU HEAR WHAT I HEARD ABOUT DR. LIGHT...
WHATTYA MEAN, THEY *MIND-WIPED* HIM?
I'M JUST TELLING YOU WHAT LIGHT TOLD ME...
I'M NOT SAYING WE'LL LOSE...
...BUT TRUST ME, WITH EVERYTHING THAT'S GOING ON...

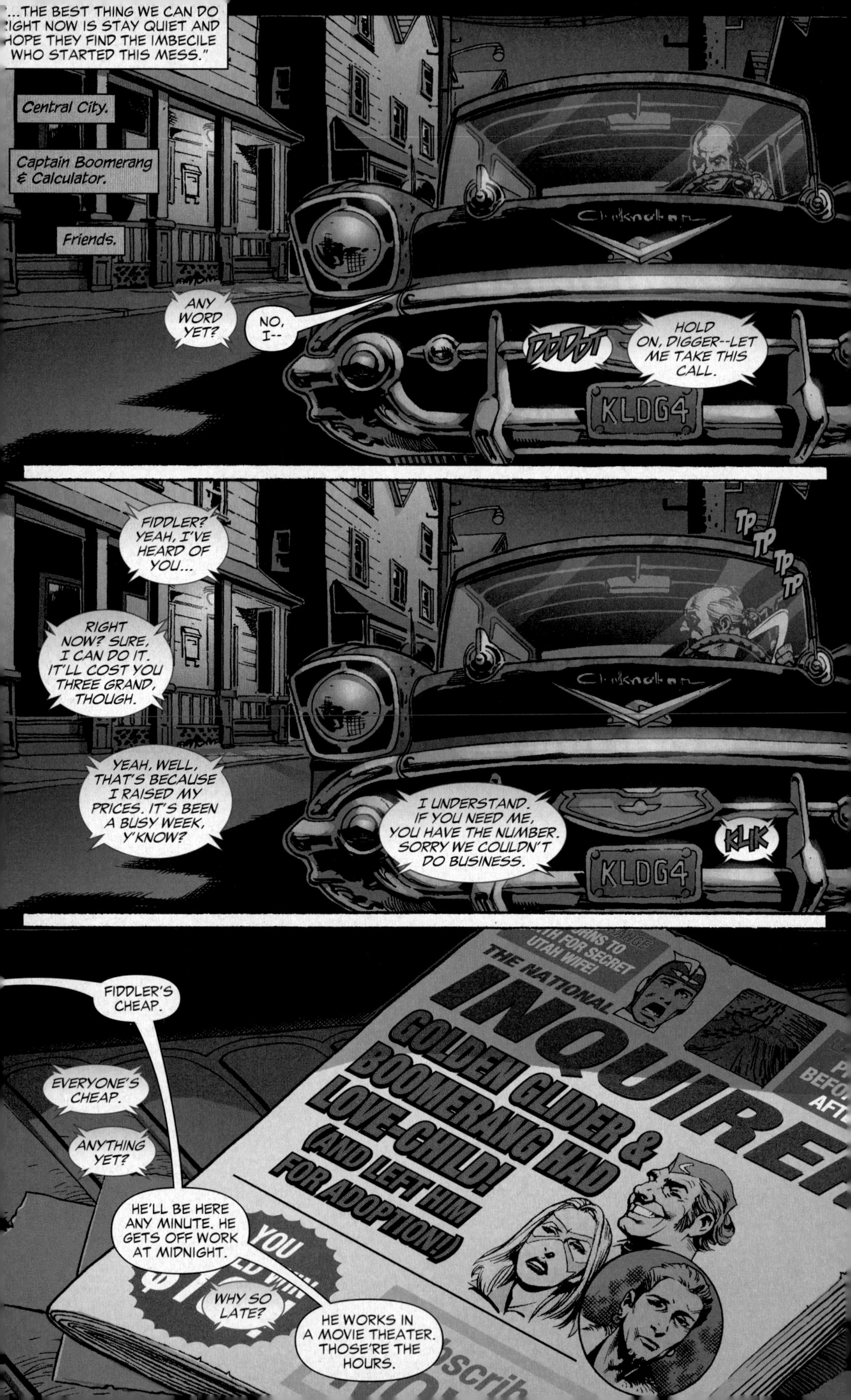

"...THE BEST THING WE CAN DO RIGHT NOW IS STAY QUIET AND HOPE THEY FIND THE IMBECILE WHO STARTED THIS MESS."
Central City.
Captain Boomerang & Calculator.
Friends.
ANY WORD YET?
NO, I--
DDDDT
HOLD ON, DIGGER--LET ME TAKE THIS CALL.
KLDG4
FIDDLER? YEAH, I'VE HEARD OF YOU...
TP TP TP TP
RIGHT NOW? SURE, I CAN DO IT. IT'LL COST YOU THREE GRAND, THOUGH.
YEAH, WELL, THAT'S BECAUSE I RAISED MY PRICES. IT'S BEEN A BUSY WEEK, Y'KNOW?
I UNDERSTAND. IF YOU NEED ME, YOU HAVE THE NUMBER. SORRY WE COULDN'T DO BUSINESS.
KLIK
KLDG4
THE NATIONAL INQUIRE
GOLDEN GLIDER & BOOMERANG HAD LOVE-CHILD! (AND LEFT HIM FOR ADOPTION!)
FIDDLER'S CHEAP.
EVERYONE'S CHEAP.
ANYTHING YET?
HE'LL BE HERE ANY MINUTE. HE GETS OFF WORK AT MIDNIGHT.
WHY SO LATE?
HE WORKS IN A MOVIE THEATER. THOSE'RE THE HOURS.

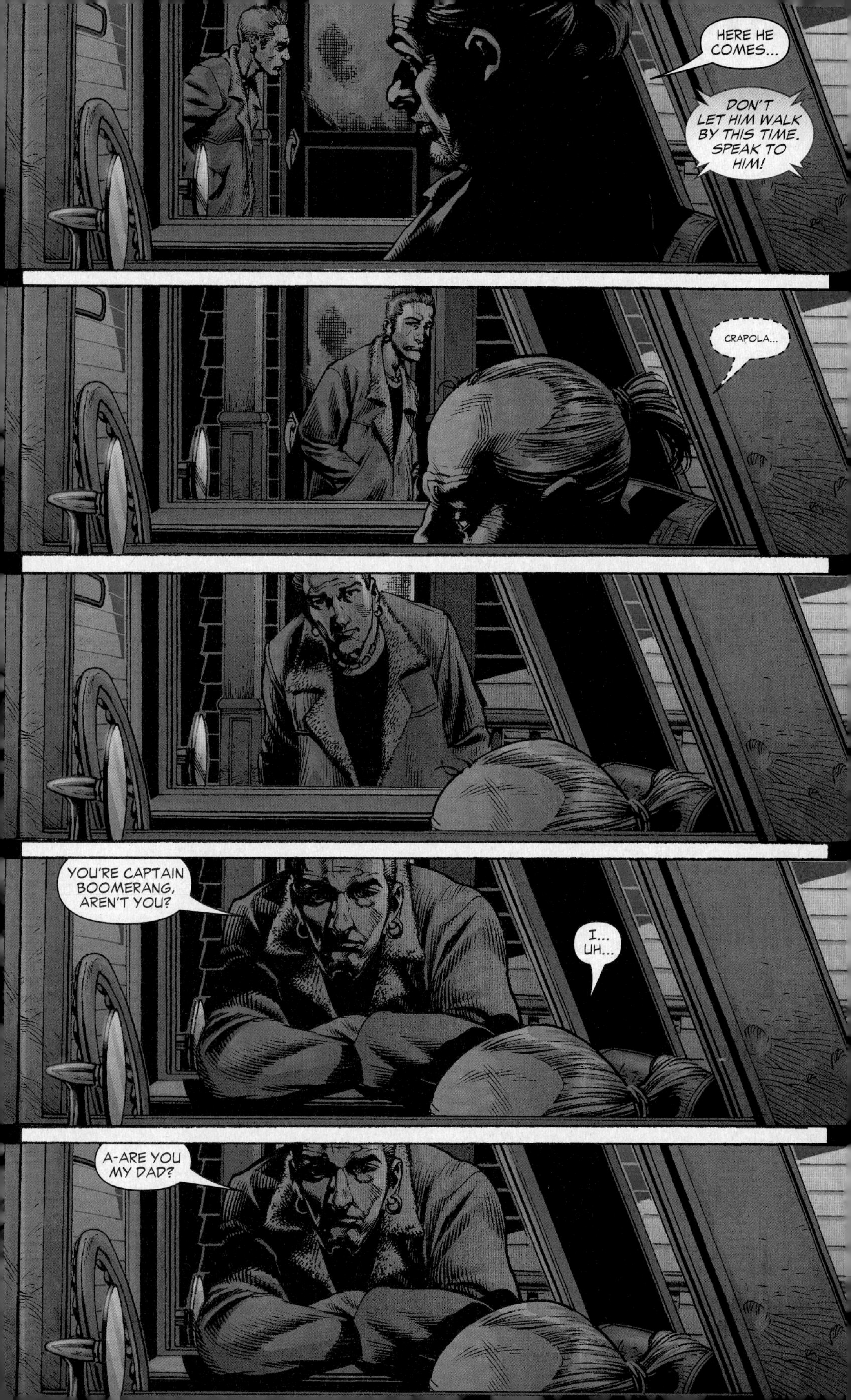
HERE HE COMES...
DON'T LET HIM WALK BY THIS TIME. SPEAK TO HIM!
CRAPOLA...
YOU'RE CAPTAIN BOOMERANG, AREN'T YOU?
I... UH...
A-ARE YOU MY DAD?

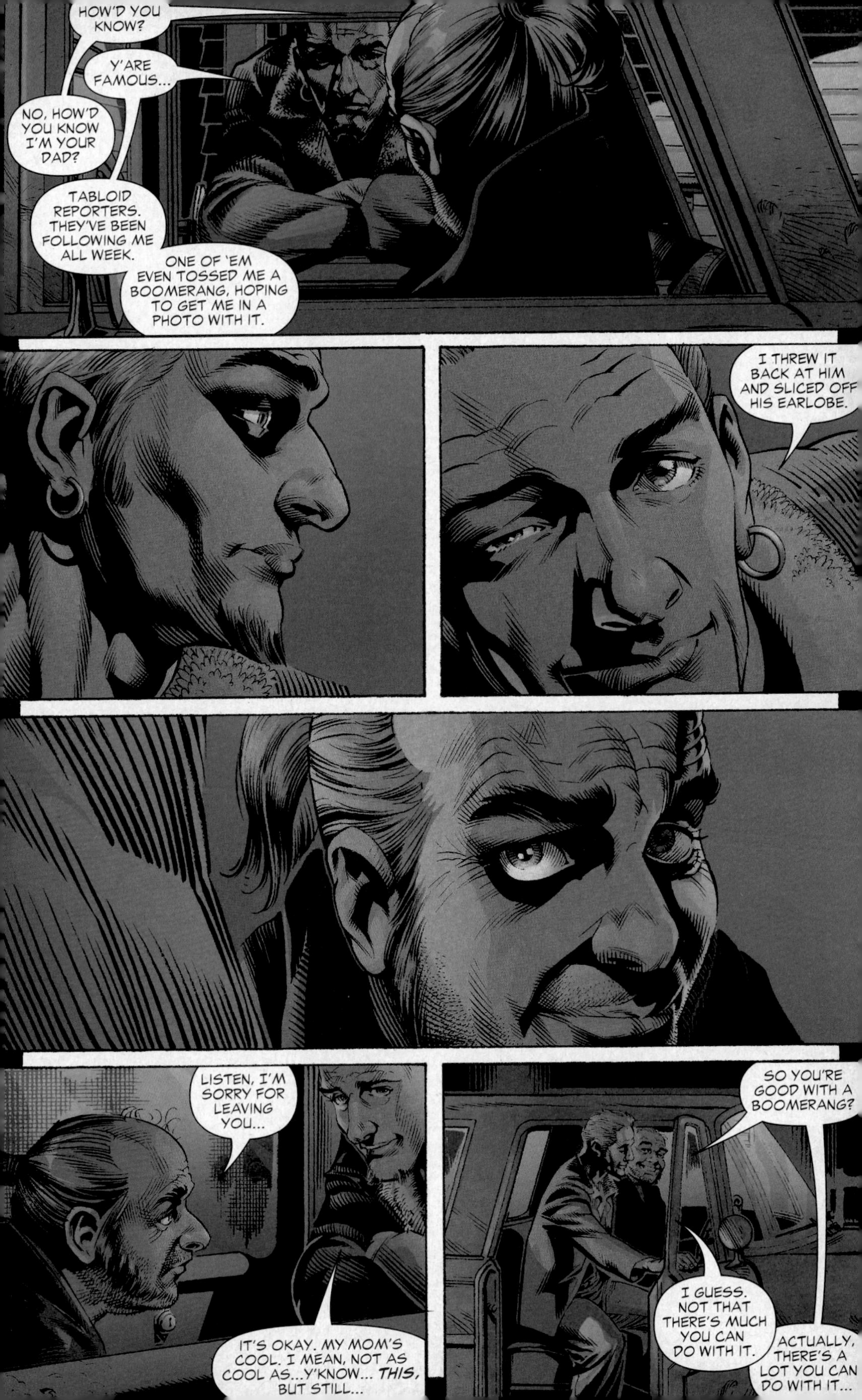
HOW'D YOU KNOW?
Y'ARE FAMOUS...
NO, HOW'D YOU KNOW I'M YOUR DAD?
TABLOID REPORTERS. THEY'VE BEEN FOLLOWING ME ALL WEEK.
ONE OF 'EM EVEN TOSSED ME A BOOMERANG, HOPING TO GET ME IN A PHOTO WITH IT.
I THREW IT BACK AT HIM AND SLICED OFF HIS EARLOBE.
LISTEN, I'M SORRY FOR LEAVING YOU...
IT'S OKAY. MY MOM'S COOL. I MEAN, NOT AS COOL AS...Y'KNOW... *THIS,* BUT STILL...
SO YOU'RE GOOD WITH A BOOMERANG?
I GUESS. NOT THAT THERE'S MUCH YOU CAN DO WITH IT.
ACTUALLY, THERE'S A LOT YOU CAN DO WITH IT...

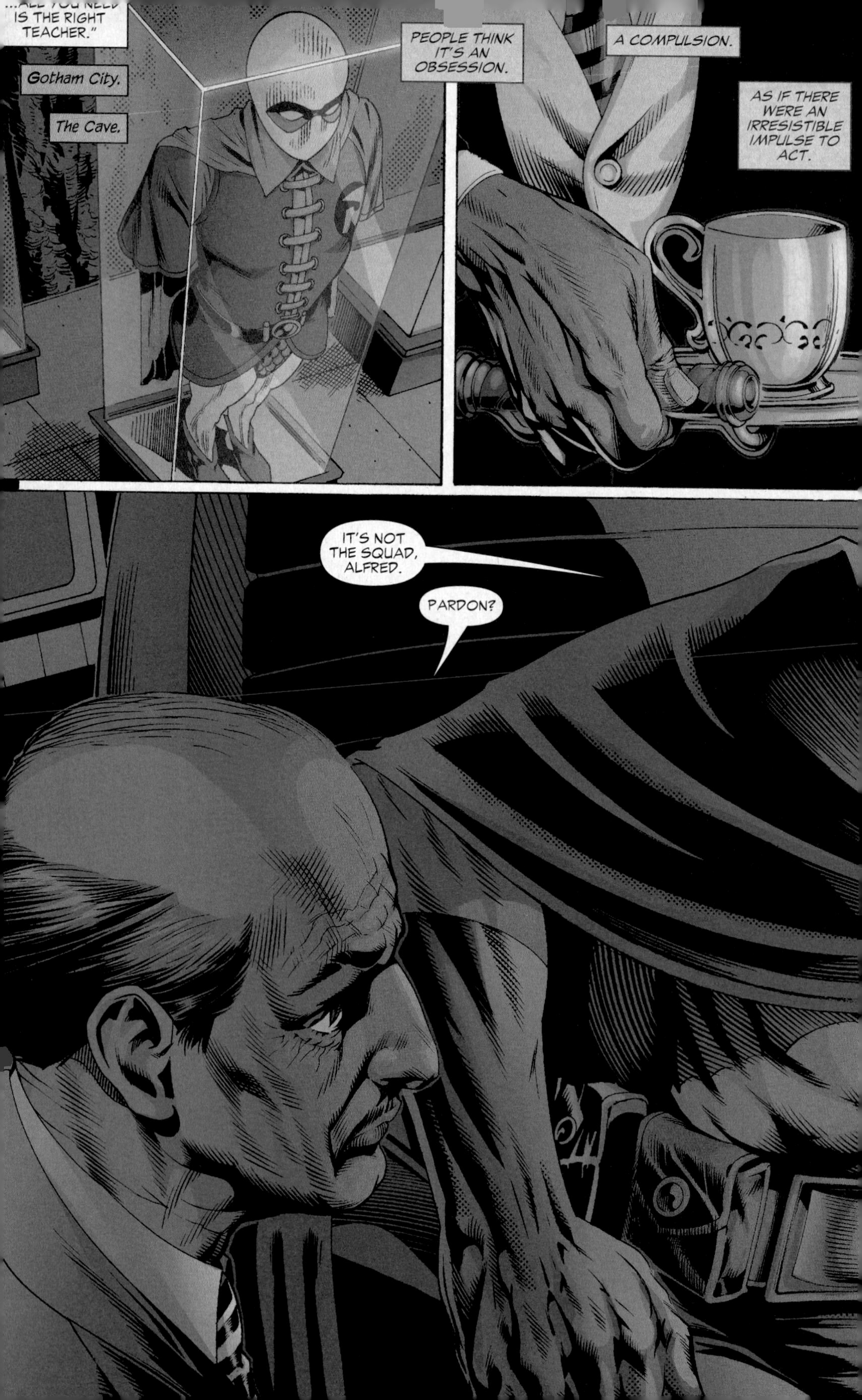

IS THE RIGHT TEACHER."
Gotham City.
The Cave.
PEOPLE THINK IT'S AN OBSESSION.
A COMPULSION.
AS IF THERE WERE AN IRRESISTIBLE IMPULSE TO ACT.
IT'S NOT THE SQUAD, ALFRED.
PARDON?

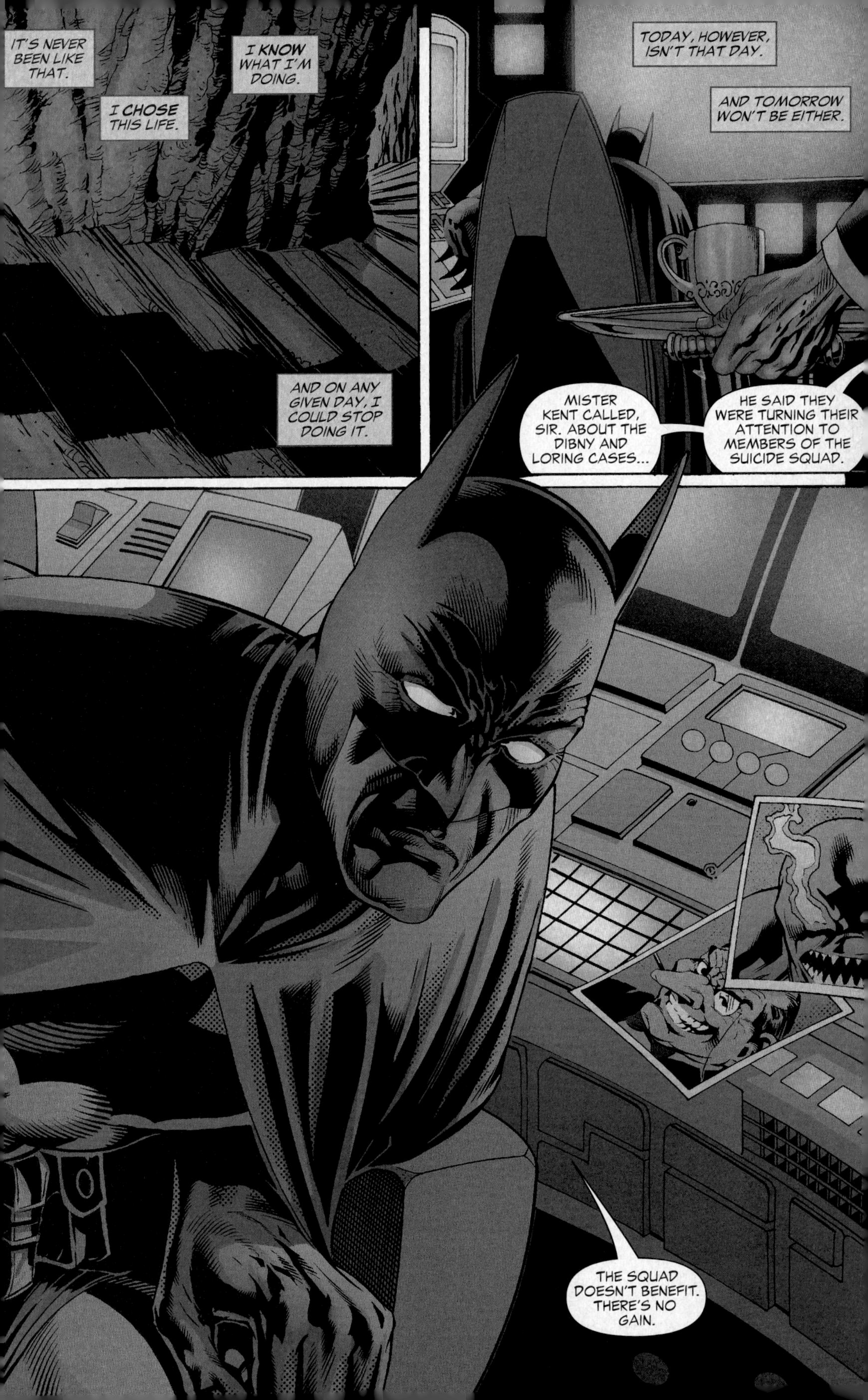
IT'S NEVER BEEN LIKE THAT.
I CHOSE THIS LIFE.
I KNOW WHAT I'M DOING.
AND ON ANY GIVEN DAY, I COULD STOP DOING IT.
TODAY, HOWEVER, ISN'T THAT DAY.
AND TOMORROW WON'T BE EITHER.
MISTER KENT CALLED, SIR. ABOUT THE DIBNY AND LORING CASES...
HE SAID THEY WERE TURNING THEIR ATTENTION TO MEMBERS OF THE SUICIDE SQUAD.
THE SQUAD DOESN'T BENEFIT. THERE'S NO GAIN.

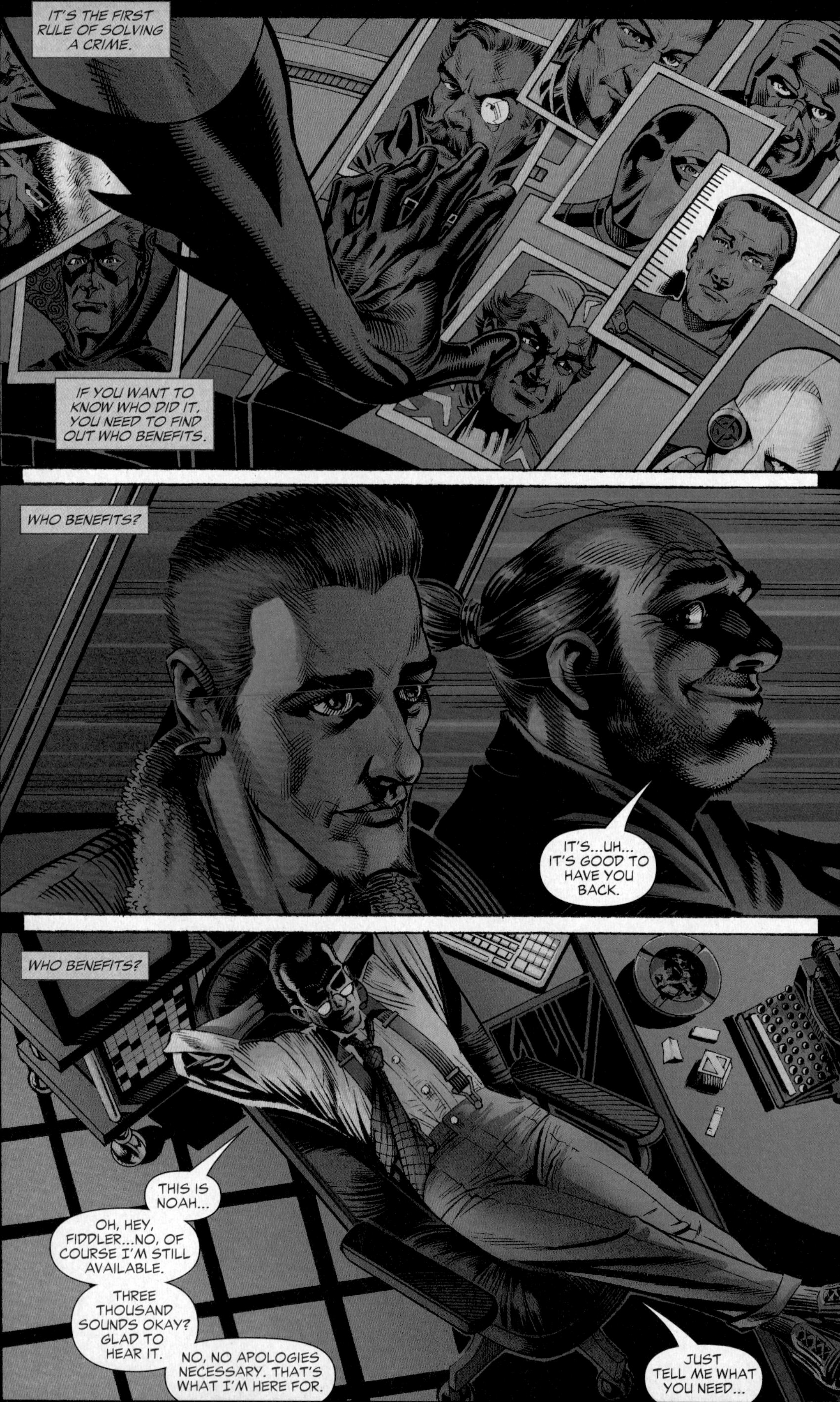
IT'S THE FIRST RULE OF SOLVING A CRIME.
IF YOU WANT TO KNOW WHO DID IT, YOU NEED TO FIND OUT WHO BENEFITS.
WHO BENEFITS?
IT'S...UH... IT'S GOOD TO HAVE YOU BACK.
WHO BENEFITS?
THIS IS NOAH...
OH, HEY, FIDDLER...NO, OF COURSE I'M STILL AVAILABLE.
THREE THOUSAND SOUNDS OKAY? GLAD TO HEAR IT.
NO, NO APOLOGIES NECESSARY. THAT'S WHAT I'M HERE FOR.
JUST TELL ME WHAT YOU NEED...

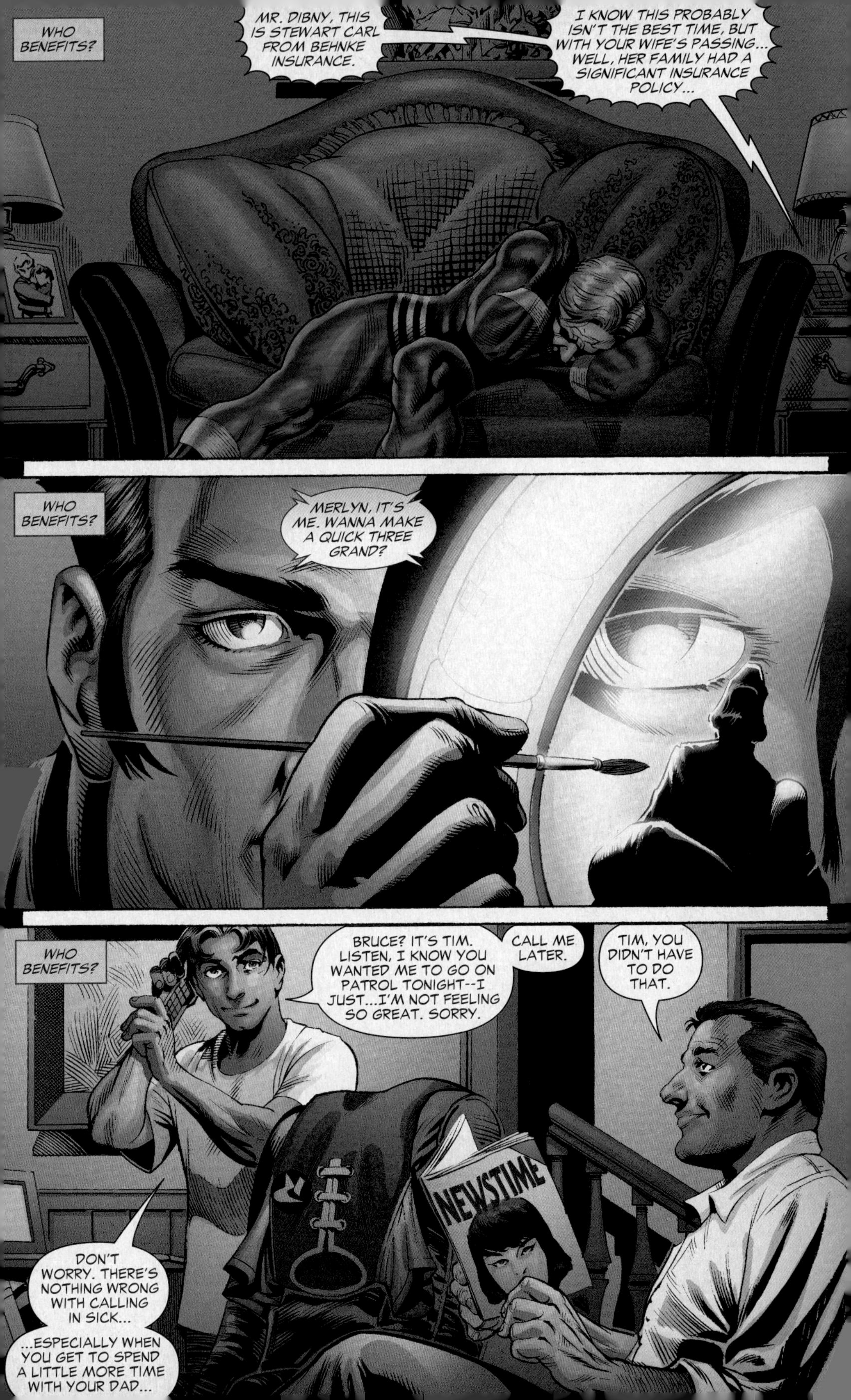
WHO BENEFITS?
MR. DIBNY, THIS IS STEWART CARL FROM BEHNKE INSURANCE.
I KNOW THIS PROBABLY ISN'T THE BEST TIME, BUT WITH YOUR WIFE'S PASSING... WELL, HER FAMILY HAD A SIGNIFICANT INSURANCE POLICY...
WHO BENEFITS?
MERLYN, IT'S ME. WANNA MAKE A QUICK THREE GRAND?
WHO BENEFITS?
BRUCE? IT'S TIM. LISTEN, I KNOW YOU WANTED ME TO GO ON PATROL TONIGHT--I JUST...I'M NOT FEELING SO GREAT. SORRY.
CALL ME LATER.
TIM, YOU DIDN'T HAVE TO DO THAT.
NEWSTIME
DON'T WORRY. THERE'S NOTHING WRONG WITH CALLING IN SICK...
...ESPECIALLY WHEN YOU GET TO SPEND A LITTLE MORE TIME WITH YOUR DAD...

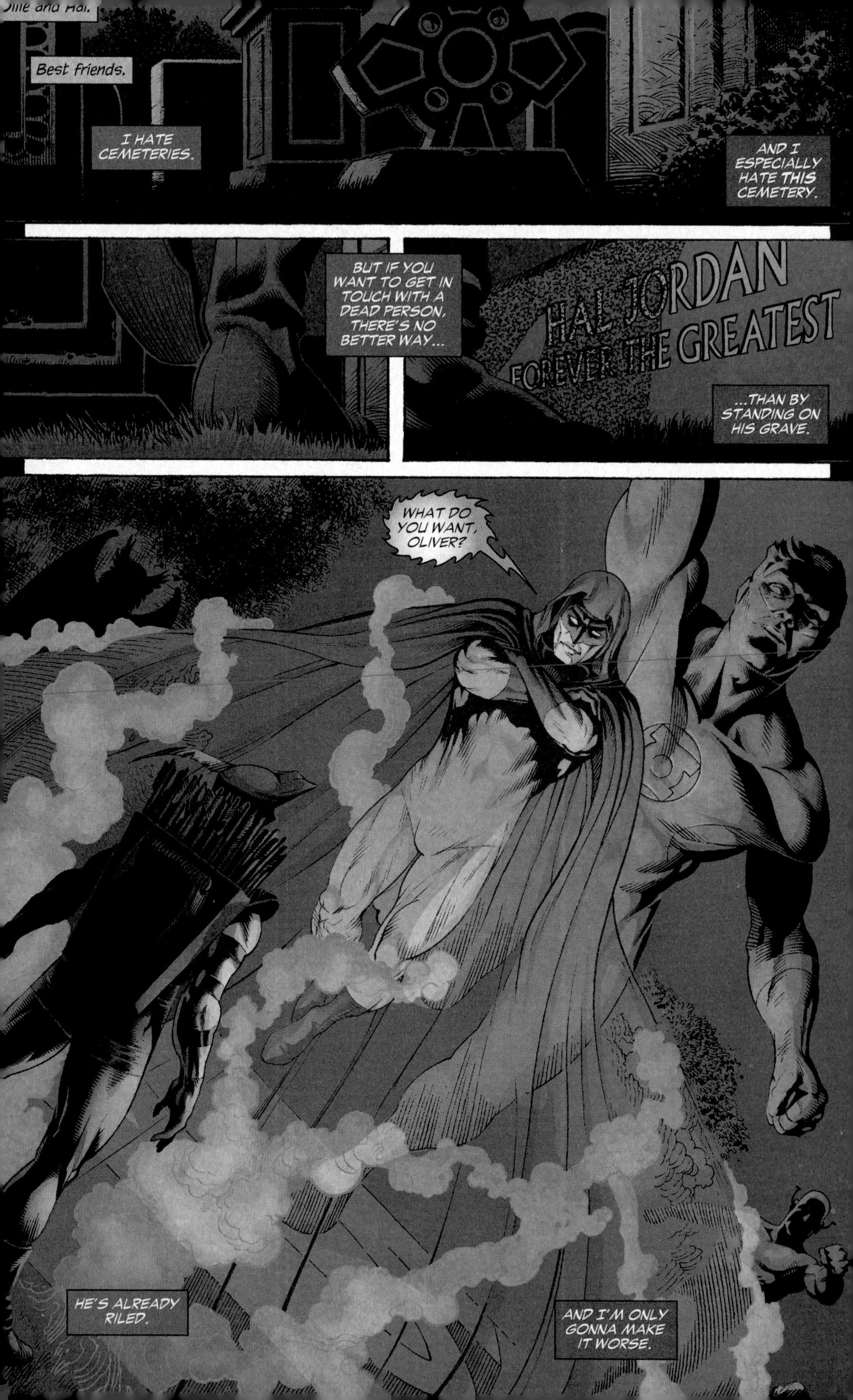
and Hal.
Best friends.
I HATE CEMETERIES.
AND I ESPECIALLY HATE THIS CEMETERY.
BUT IF YOU WANT TO GET IN TOUCH WITH A DEAD PERSON, THERE'S NO BETTER WAY...
HAL JORDAN
FOREVER THE GREATEST
...THAN BY STANDING ON HIS GRAVE.
WHAT DO YOU WANT, OLIVER?
HE'S ALREADY RILED.
AND I'M ONLY GONNA MAKE IT WORSE.

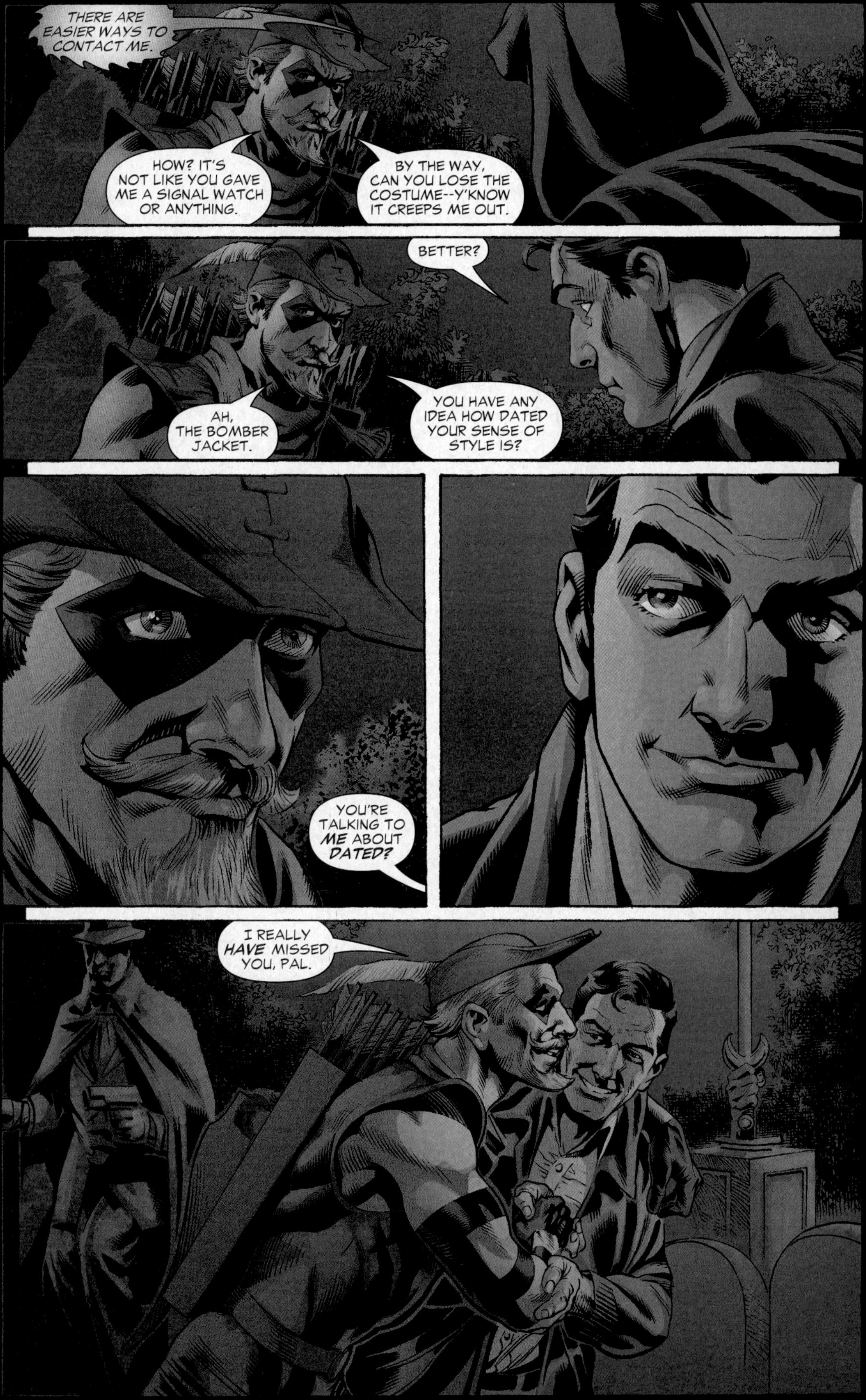
THERE ARE EASIER WAYS TO CONTACT ME.
HOW? IT'S NOT LIKE YOU GAVE ME A SIGNAL WATCH OR ANYTHING.
BY THE WAY, CAN YOU LOSE THE COSTUME--Y'KNOW IT CREEPS ME OUT.
BETTER?
AH, THE BOMBER JACKET.
YOU HAVE ANY IDEA HOW DATED YOUR SENSE OF STYLE IS?
YOU'RE TALKING TO ME ABOUT DATED?
I REALLY HAVE MISSED YOU, PAL.

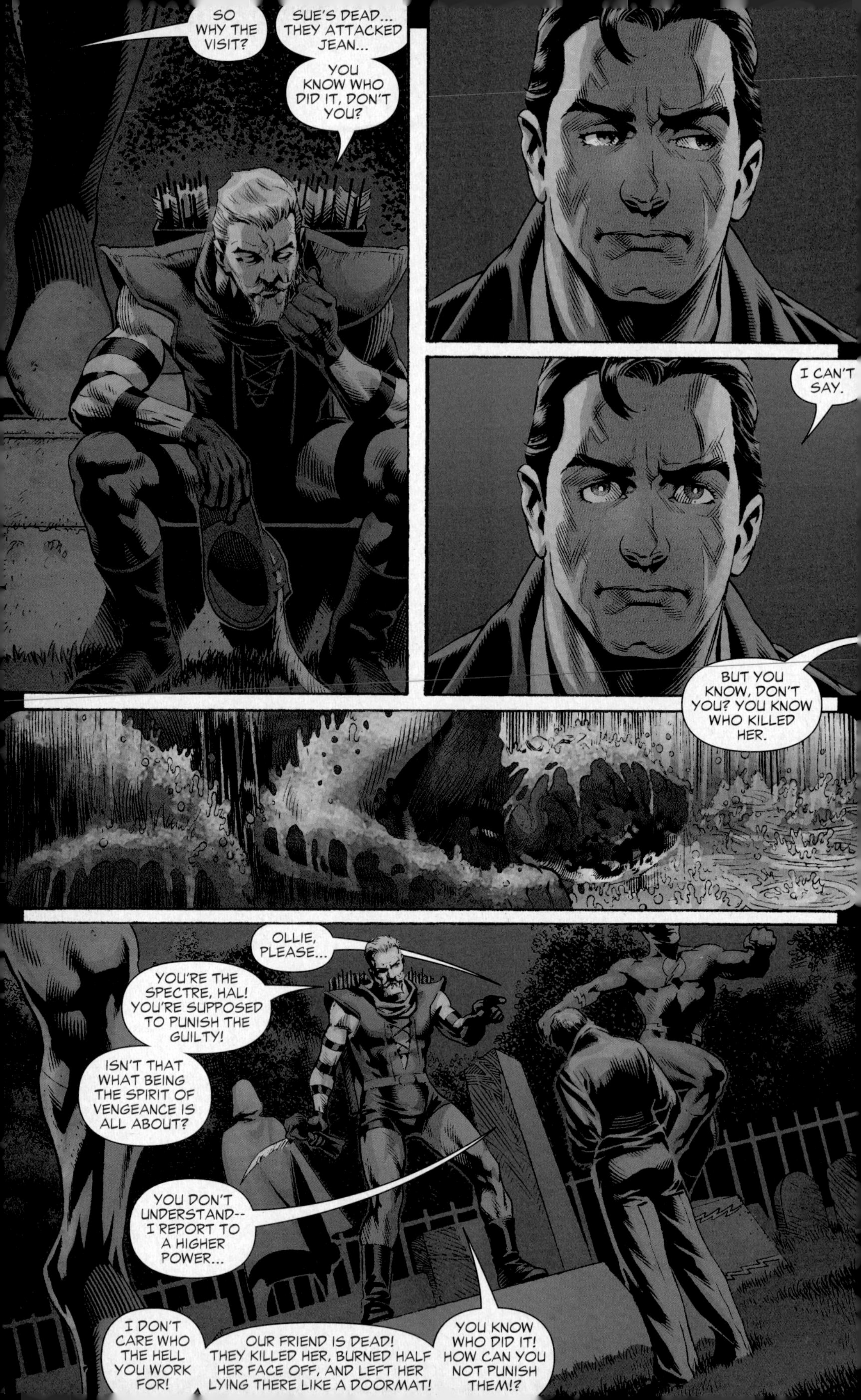
SO WHY THE VISIT?
SUE'S DEAD... THEY ATTACKED JEAN...
YOU KNOW WHO DID IT, DON'T YOU?
I CAN'T SAY.
BUT YOU KNOW, DON'T YOU? YOU KNOW WHO KILLED HER.
OLLIE, PLEASE...
YOU'RE THE SPECTRE, HAL! YOU'RE SUPPOSED TO PUNISH THE GUILTY!
ISN'T THAT WHAT BEING THE SPIRIT OF VENGEANCE IS ALL ABOUT?
YOU DON'T UNDERSTAND-- I REPORT TO A HIGHER POWER...
I DON'T CARE WHO THE HELL YOU WORK FOR!
OUR FRIEND IS DEAD! THEY KILLED HER, BURNED HALF HER FACE OFF, AND LEFT HER LYING THERE LIKE A DOORMAT!
YOU KNOW WHO DID IT! HOW CAN YOU NOT PUNISH THEM!?

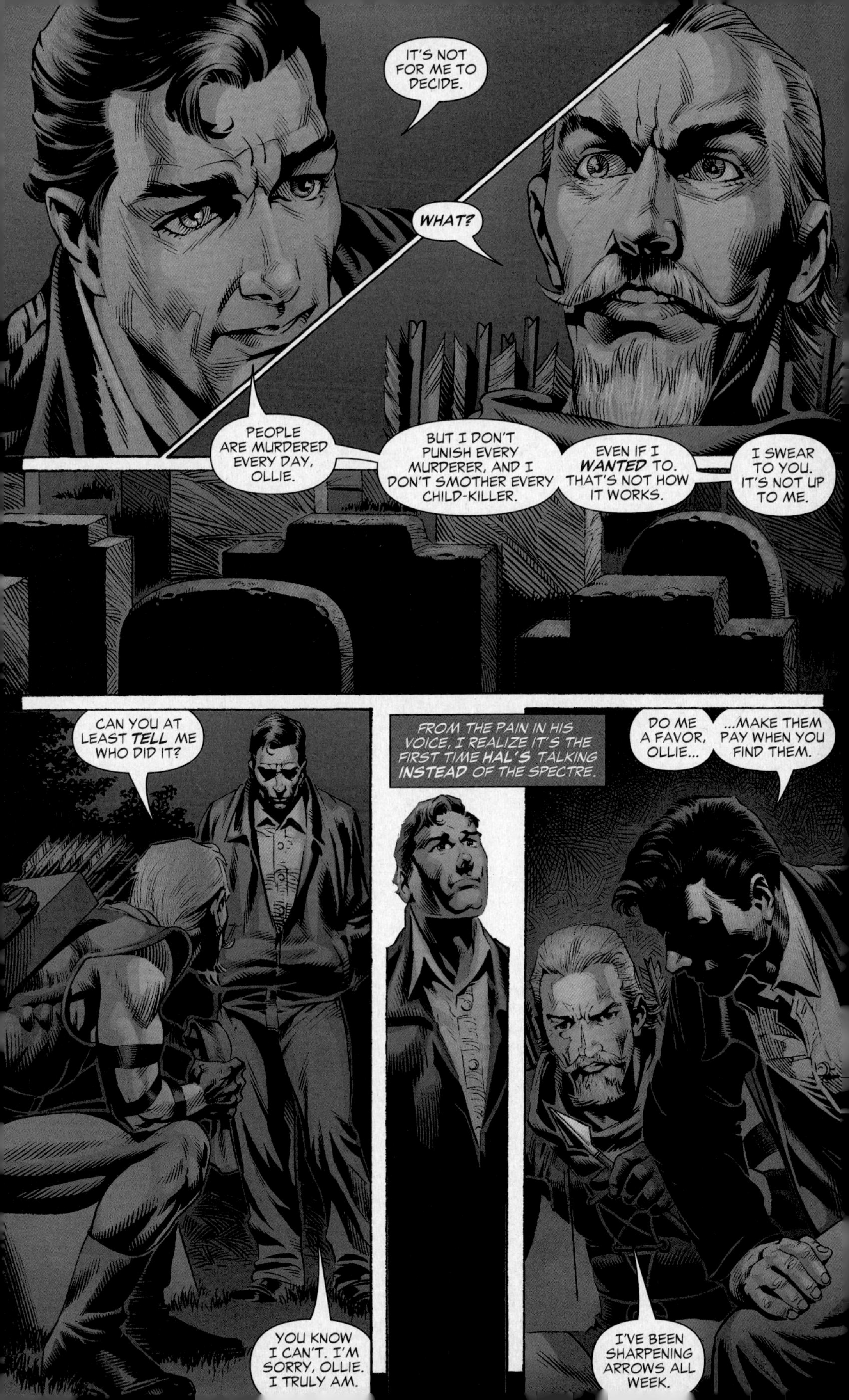
IT'S NOT FOR ME TO DECIDE.
WHAT?
PEOPLE ARE MURDERED EVERY DAY, OLLIE.
BUT I DON'T PUNISH EVERY MURDERER, AND I DON'T SMOTHER EVERY CHILD-KILLER.
EVEN IF I WANTED TO. THAT'S NOT HOW IT WORKS.
I SWEAR TO YOU. IT'S NOT UP TO ME.
CAN YOU AT LEAST TELL ME WHO DID IT?
YOU KNOW I CAN'T. I'M SORRY, OLLIE. I TRULY AM.
FROM THE PAIN IN HIS VOICE, I REALIZE IT'S THE FIRST TIME HAL'S TALKING INSTEAD OF THE SPECTRE.
DO ME A FAVOR, OLLIE...
...MAKE THEM PAY WHEN YOU FIND THEM.
I'VE BEEN SHARPENING ARROWS ALL WEEK.

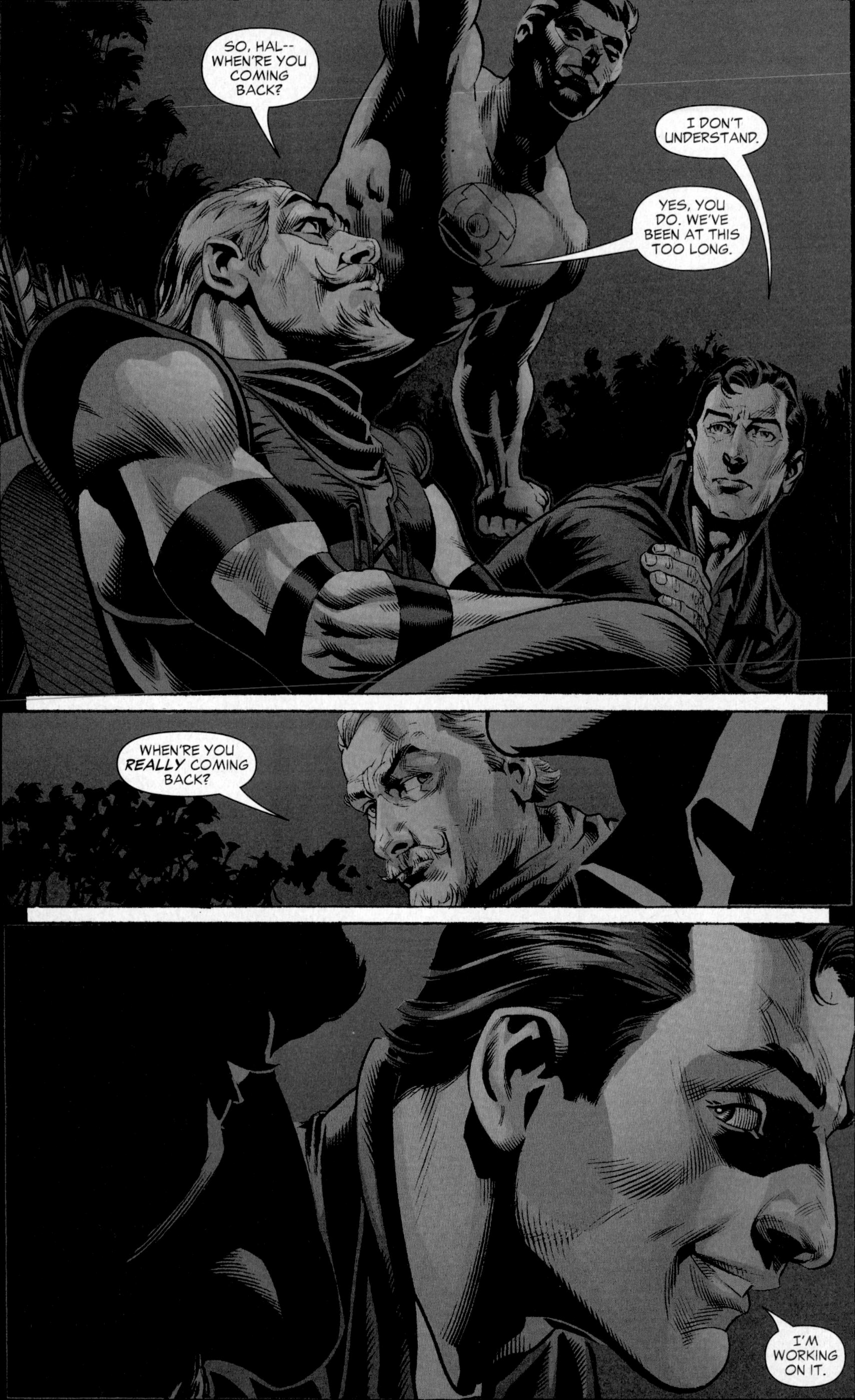
SO, HAL--
WHEN'RE YOU COMING BACK?
I DON'T UNDERSTAND.
YES, YOU DO. WE'VE BEEN AT THIS TOO LONG.
WHEN'RE YOU *REALLY* COMING BACK?
I'M WORKING ON IT.

Lois Lane.

Soul mate.

WHEN IT COMES TO BRAVE FACES, CLARK HAS A GOOD ONE.

MAYBE THE BEST ONE.

LOWELL, YOU SEE *THE STAR* THIS MORNING?

THEY EVEN SAY "PICTURES INSIDE"-- BUT ALL THEY'VE GOT IS AN AUTHOR PHOTO FROM LORING'S BOOK JACKET.

HE'S BEEN BACK TO HIS PARENTS' HOUSE THREE DAYS IN A ROW.

DAILY PLANET
CAPED WONDER SAVES

DAILY
HE'
EA

DAILY STAR
LORING ATTACKED WHO'S NEXT

ALL CLASS.

BUT THERE ARE SOME THINGS GLASSES AND A SPIT CURL CAN'T HIDE.

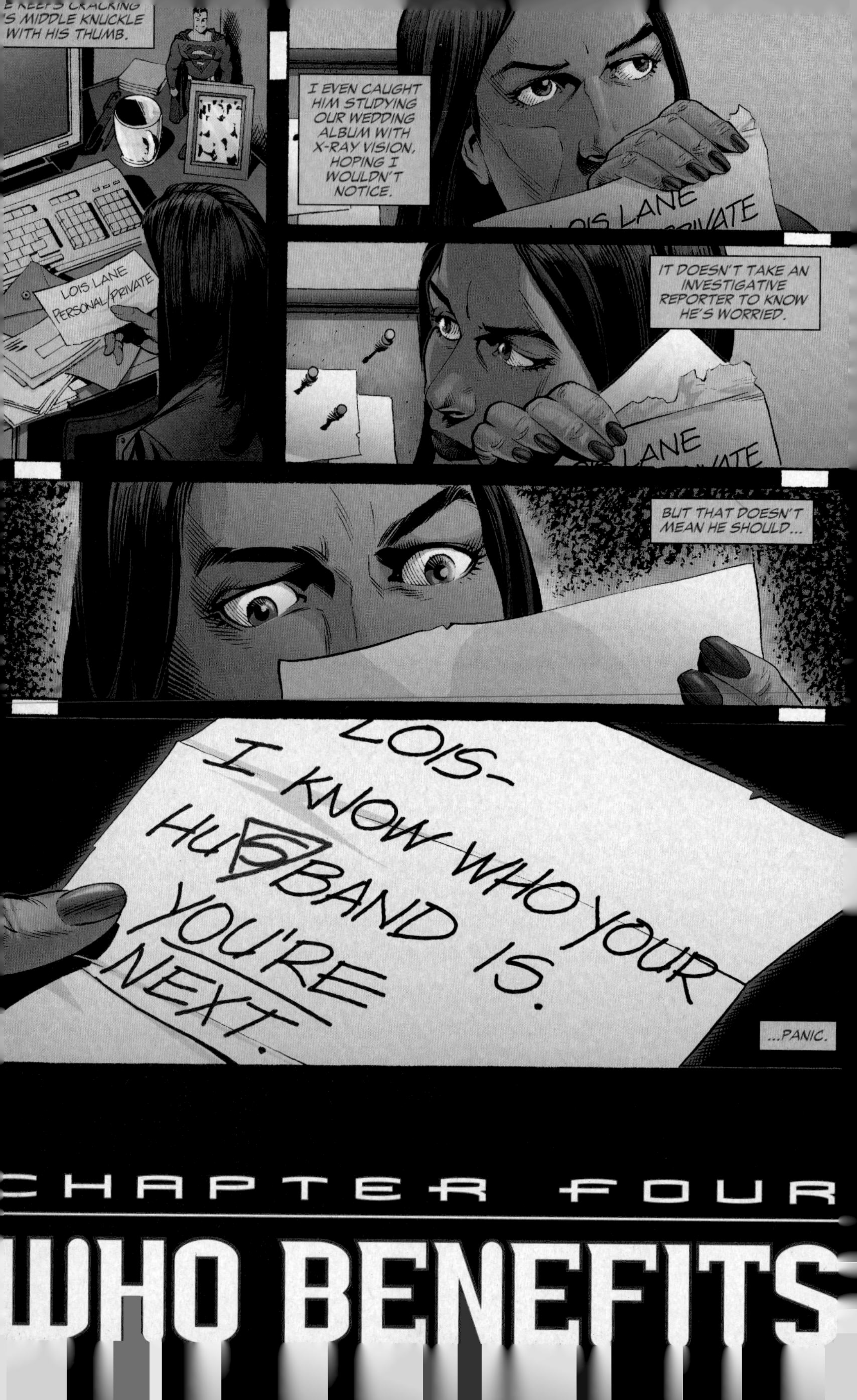
KEEPS CRACKING 'S MIDDLE KNUCKLE WITH HIS THUMB.
LOIS LANE PERSONAL/PRIVATE
I EVEN CAUGHT HIM STUDYING OUR WEDDING ALBUM WITH X-RAY VISION, HOPING I WOULDN'T NOTICE.
LOIS LANE
IT DOESN'T TAKE AN INVESTIGATIVE REPORTER TO KNOW HE'S WORRIED.
BUT THAT DOESN'T MEAN HE SHOULD...
LOIS-
I KNOW WHO YOUR HUSBAND IS.
YOU'RE NEXT.
...PANIC.

CHAPTER FOUR

WHO BENEFITS

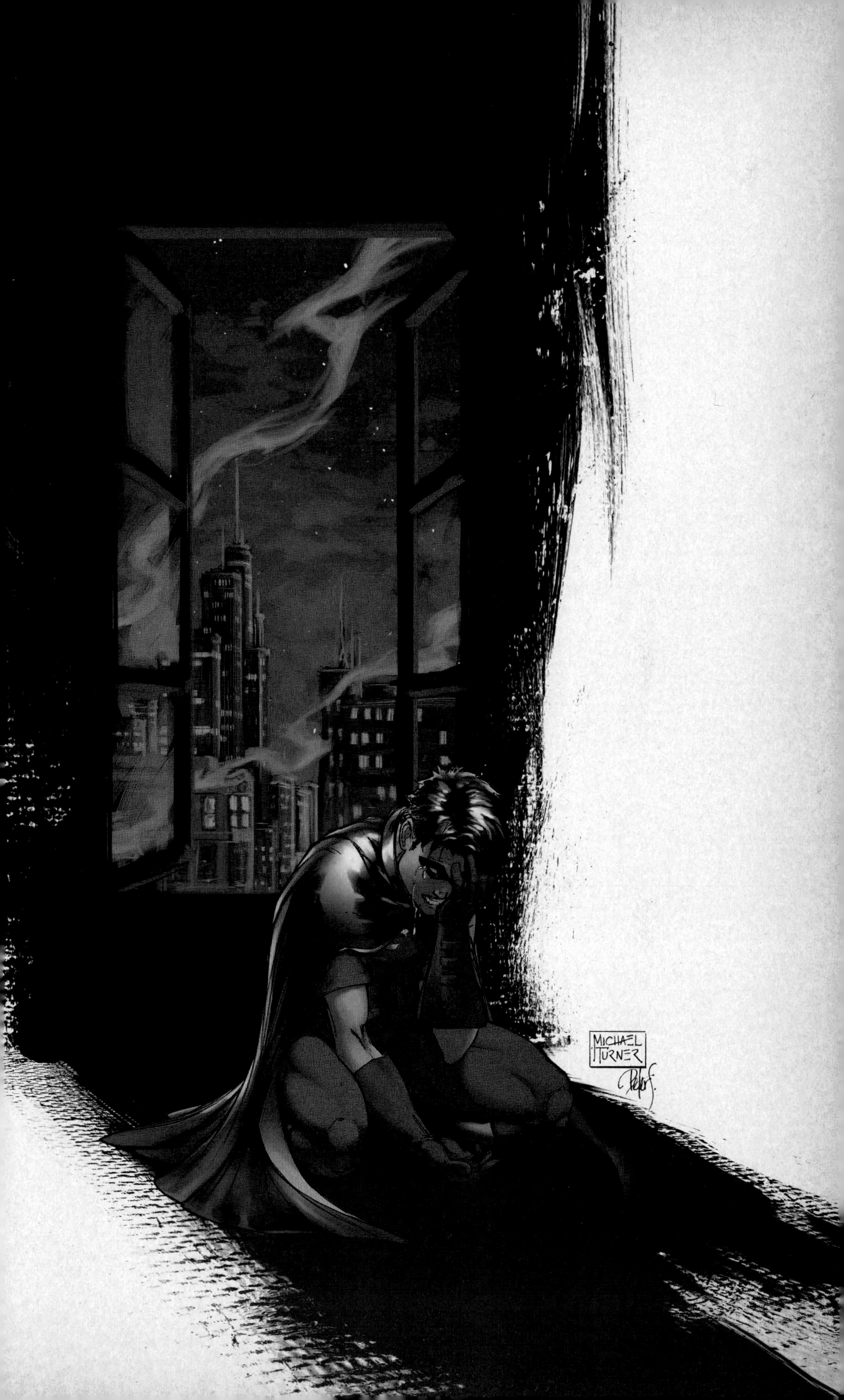
MICHAEL TURNER

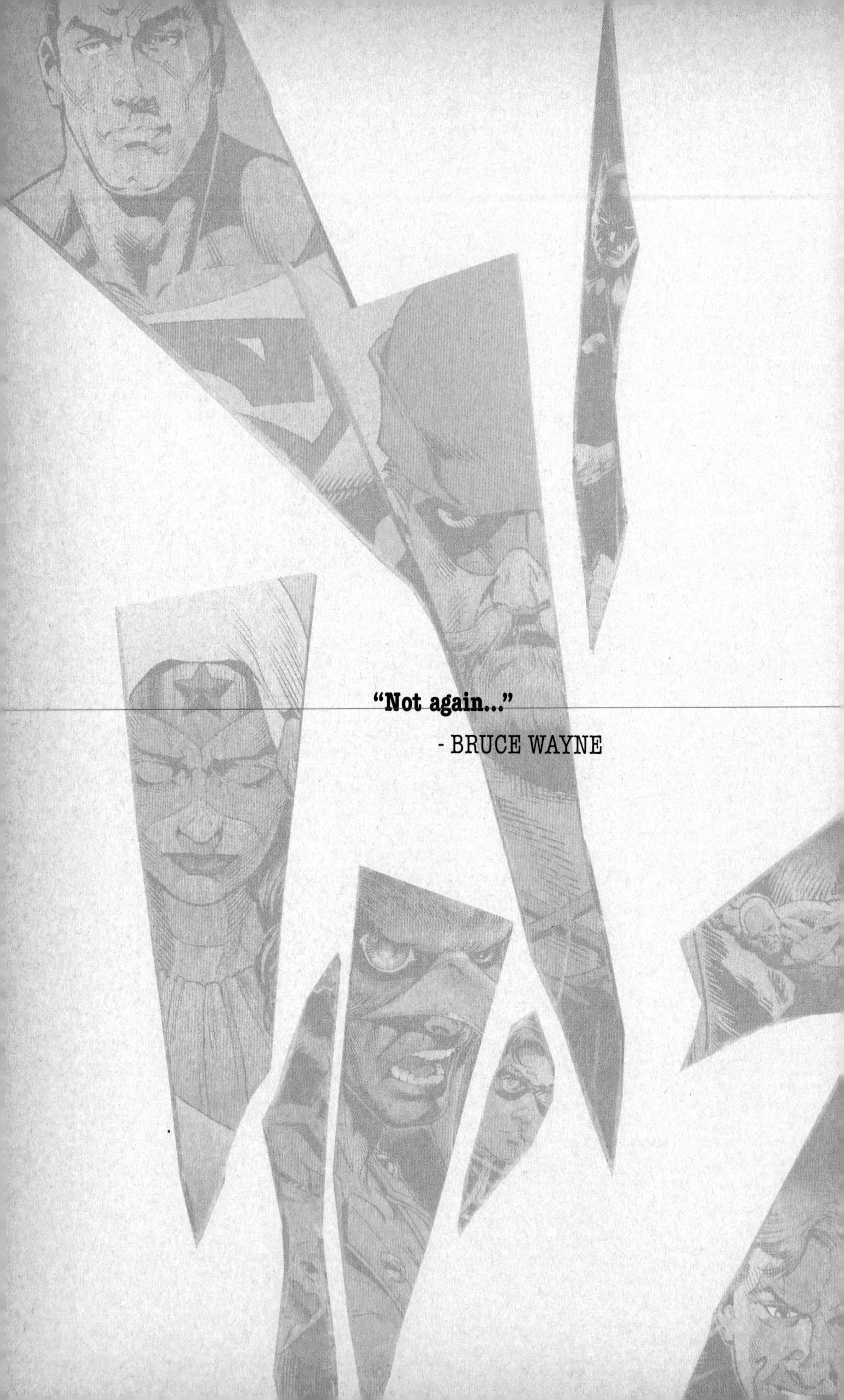

"Not again..."

- BRUCE WAYNE

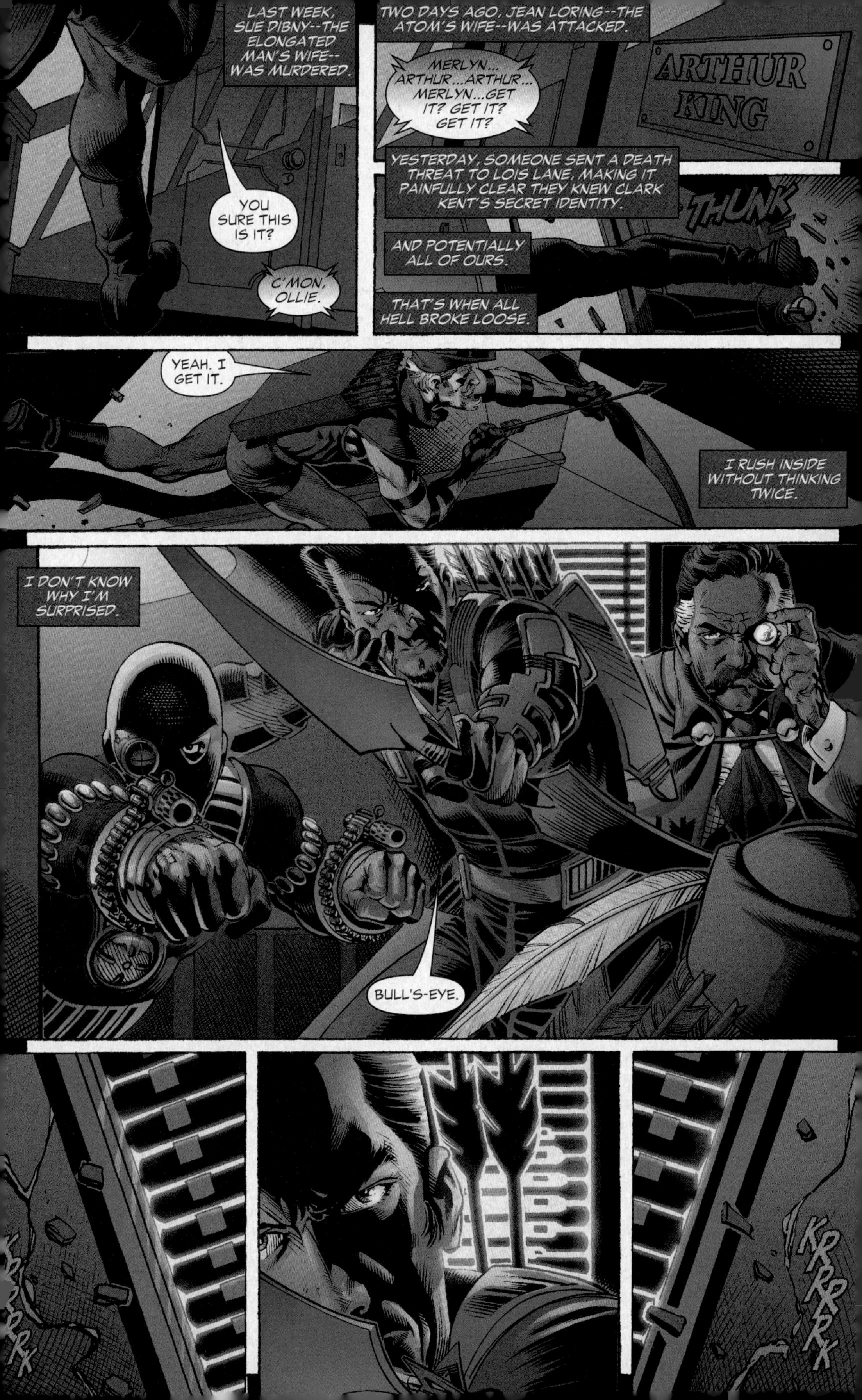
LAST WEEK, SUE DIBNY--THE ELONGATED MAN'S WIFE--WAS MURDERED.
YOU SURE THIS IS IT?
C'MON, OLLIE.
TWO DAYS AGO, JEAN LORING--THE ATOM'S WIFE--WAS ATTACKED.
MERLYN... ARTHUR...ARTHUR... MERLYN...GET IT? GET IT? GET IT?
ARTHUR KING
YESTERDAY, SOMEONE SENT A DEATH THREAT TO LOIS LANE, MAKING IT PAINFULLY CLEAR THEY KNEW CLARK KENT'S SECRET IDENTITY.
AND POTENTIALLY ALL OF OURS.
THUNK
THAT'S WHEN ALL HELL BROKE LOOSE.
YEAH. I GET IT.
I RUSH INSIDE WITHOUT THINKING TWICE.
I DON'T KNOW WHY I'M SURPRISED.
BULL'S-EYE.
KRRRRK

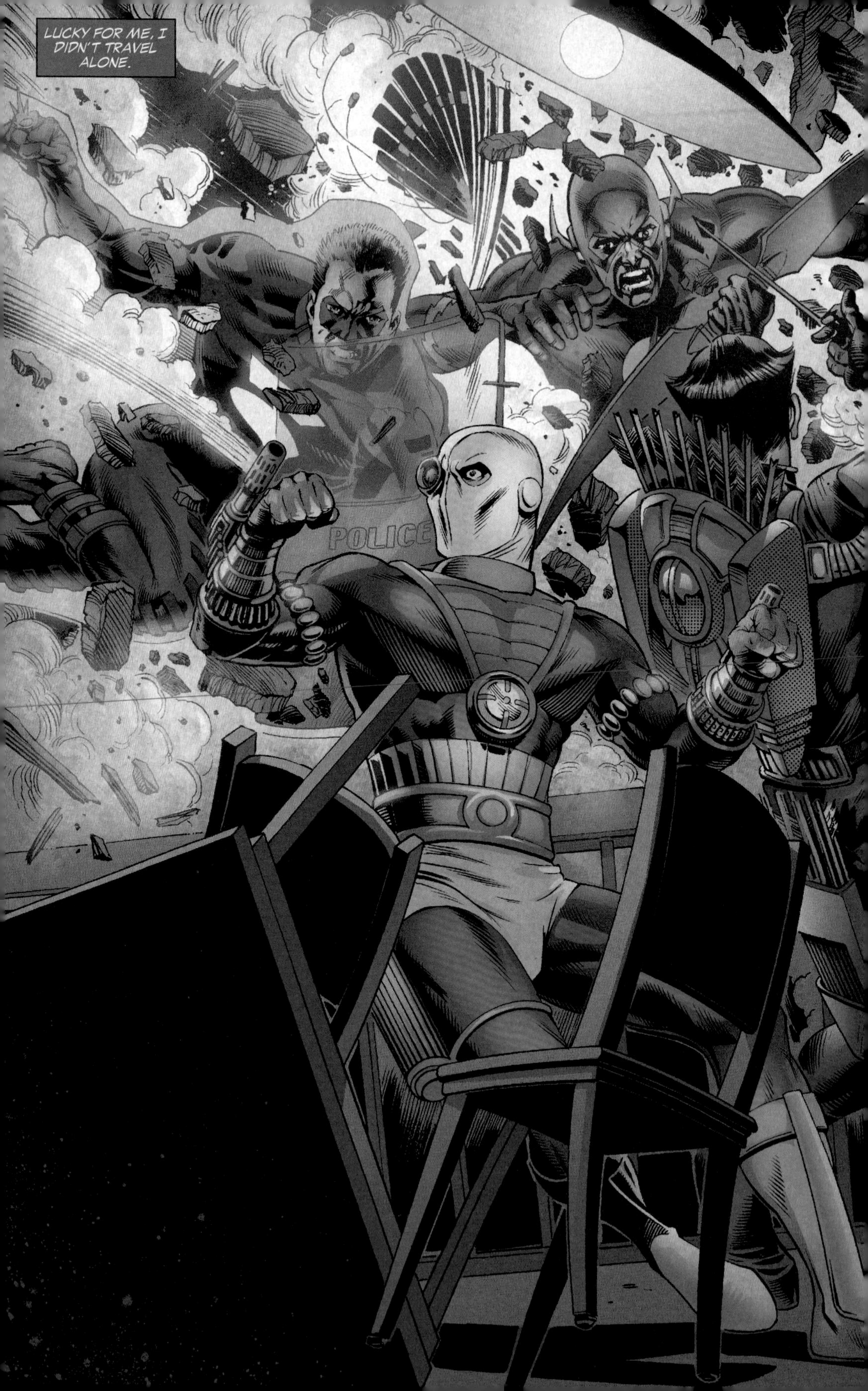
LUCKY FOR ME, I DIDN'T TRAVEL ALONE.
POLICE

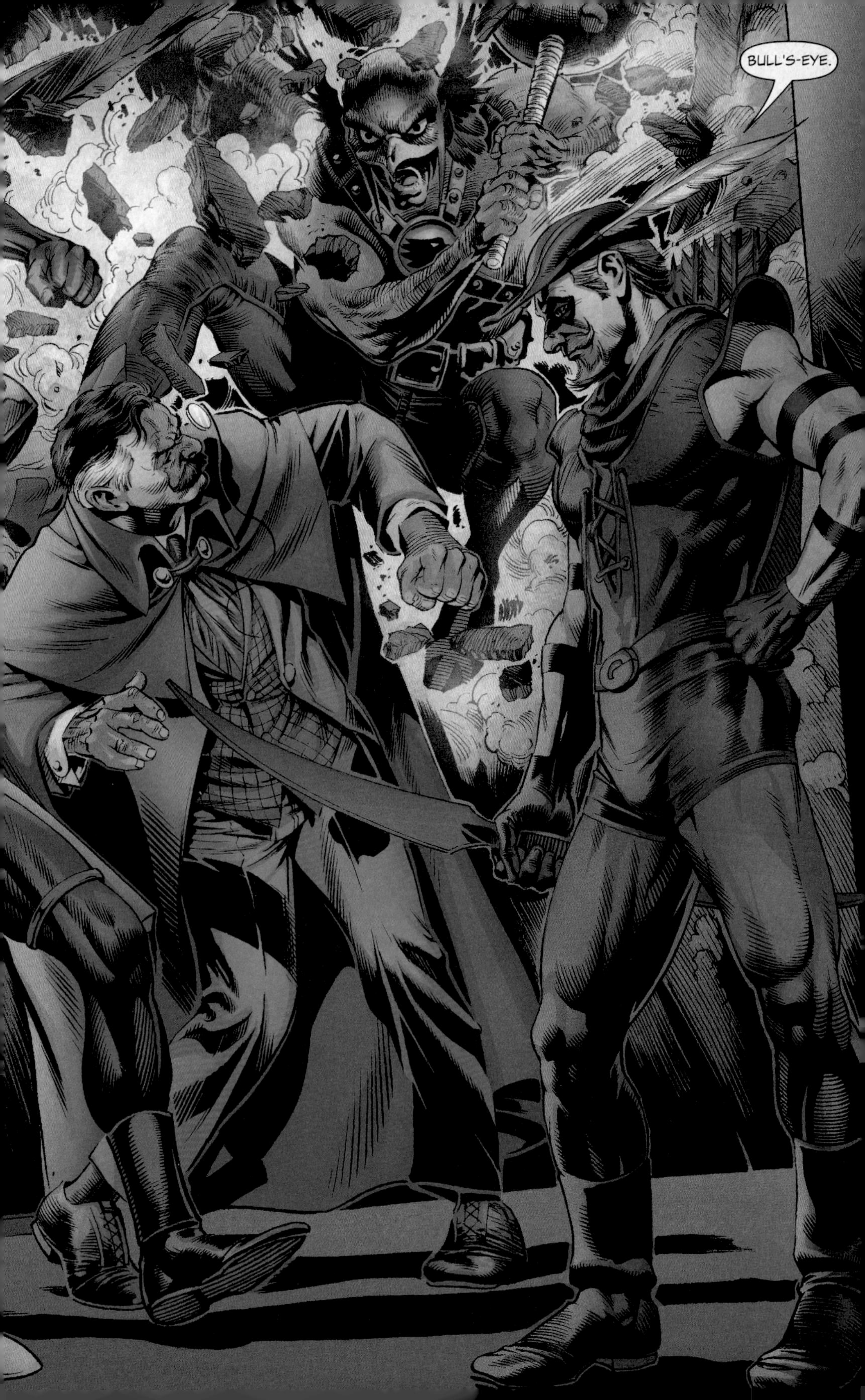
BULL'S-EYE.

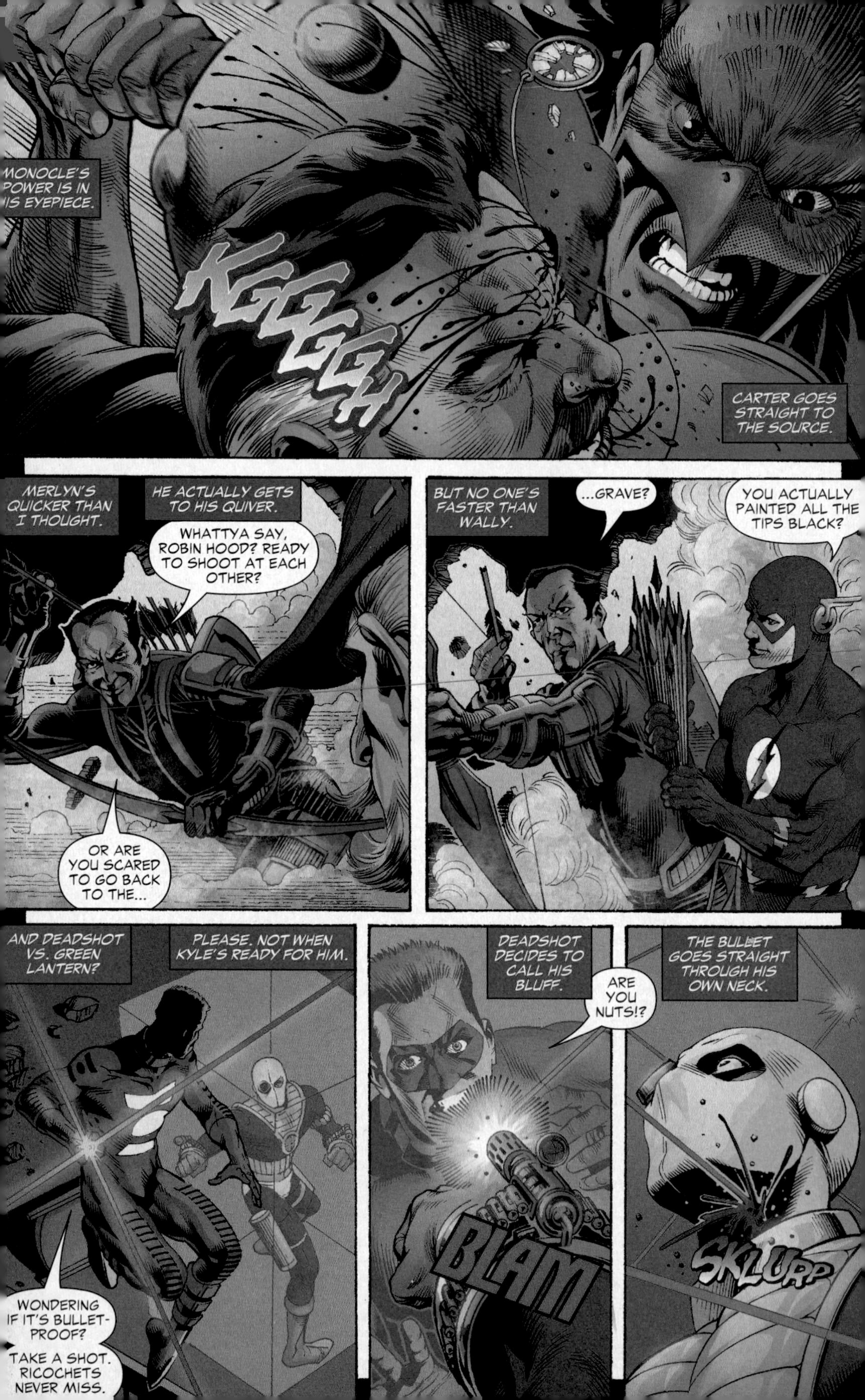
MONOCLE'S POWER IS IN HIS EYEPIECE.
KGGGGH
CARTER GOES STRAIGHT TO THE SOURCE.
MERLYN'S QUICKER THAN I THOUGHT.
HE ACTUALLY GETS TO HIS QUIVER.
WHATTYA SAY, ROBIN HOOD? READY TO SHOOT AT EACH OTHER?
OR ARE YOU SCARED TO GO BACK TO THE...
BUT NO ONE'S FASTER THAN WALLY.
...GRAVE?
YOU ACTUALLY PAINTED ALL THE TIPS BLACK?
AND DEADSHOT VS. GREEN LANTERN?
PLEASE. NOT WHEN KYLE'S READY FOR HIM.
WONDERING IF IT'S BULLET-PROOF?
TAKE A SHOT. RICOCHETS NEVER MISS.
DEADSHOT DECIDES TO CALL HIS BLUFF.
ARE YOU NUTS!?
BLAM
THE BULLET GOES STRAIGHT THROUGH HIS OWN NECK.
SKLURP

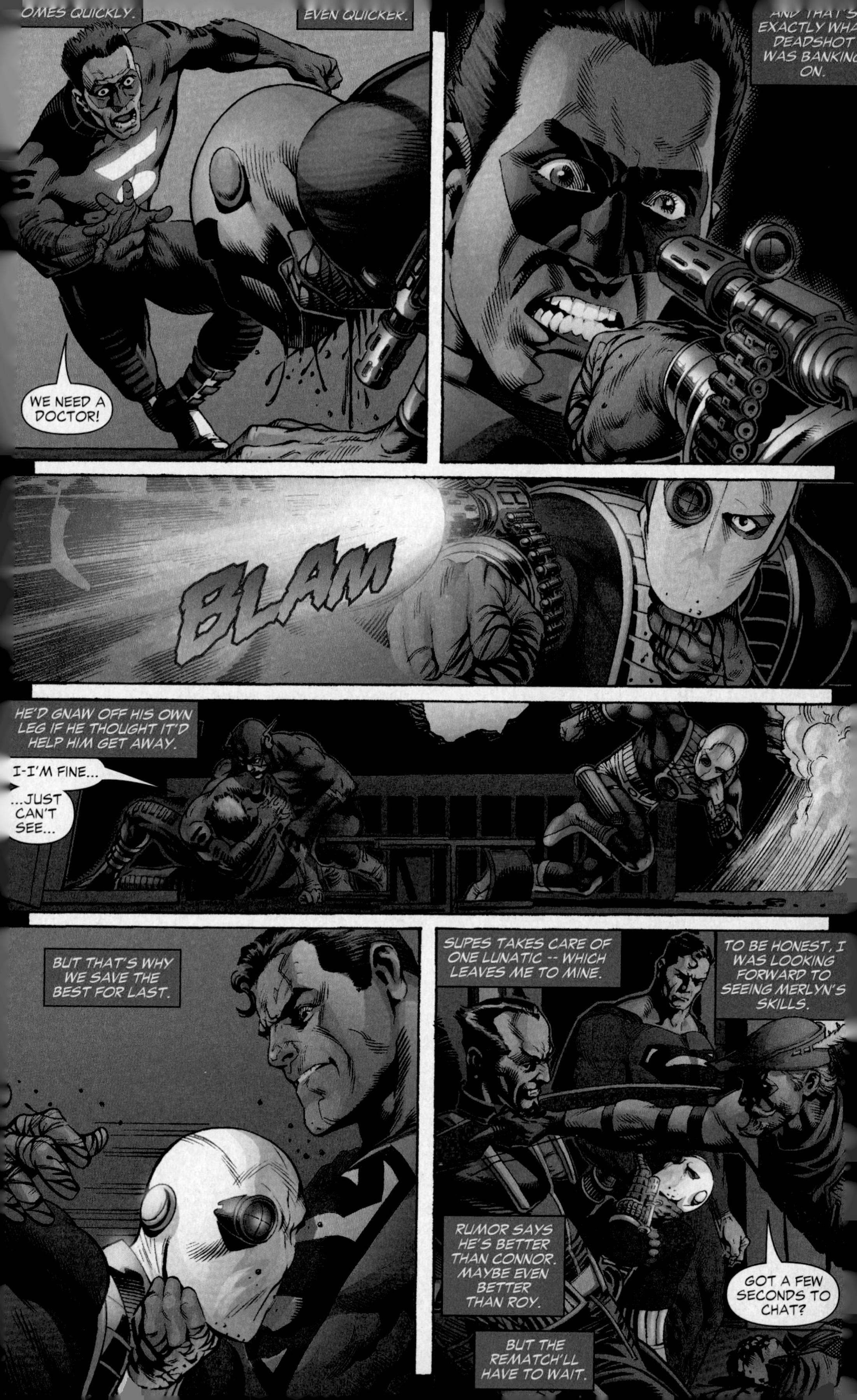

OMES QUICKLY.
EVEN QUICKER.
WE NEED A DOCTOR!
AND THAT'S EXACTLY WHA DEADSHOT WAS BANKING ON.
BLAM
HE'D GNAW OFF HIS OWN LEG IF HE THOUGHT IT'D HELP HIM GET AWAY.
I-I'M FINE...
...JUST CAN'T SEE...
BUT THAT'S WHY WE SAVE THE BEST FOR LAST.
SUPES TAKES CARE OF ONE LUNATIC -- WHICH LEAVES ME TO MINE.
TO BE HONEST, I WAS LOOKING FORWARD TO SEEING MERLYN'S SKILLS.
RUMOR SAYS HE'S BETTER THAN CONNOR. MAYBE EVEN BETTER THAN ROY.
GOT A FEW SECONDS TO CHAT?
BUT THE REMATCH'LL HAVE TO WAIT.

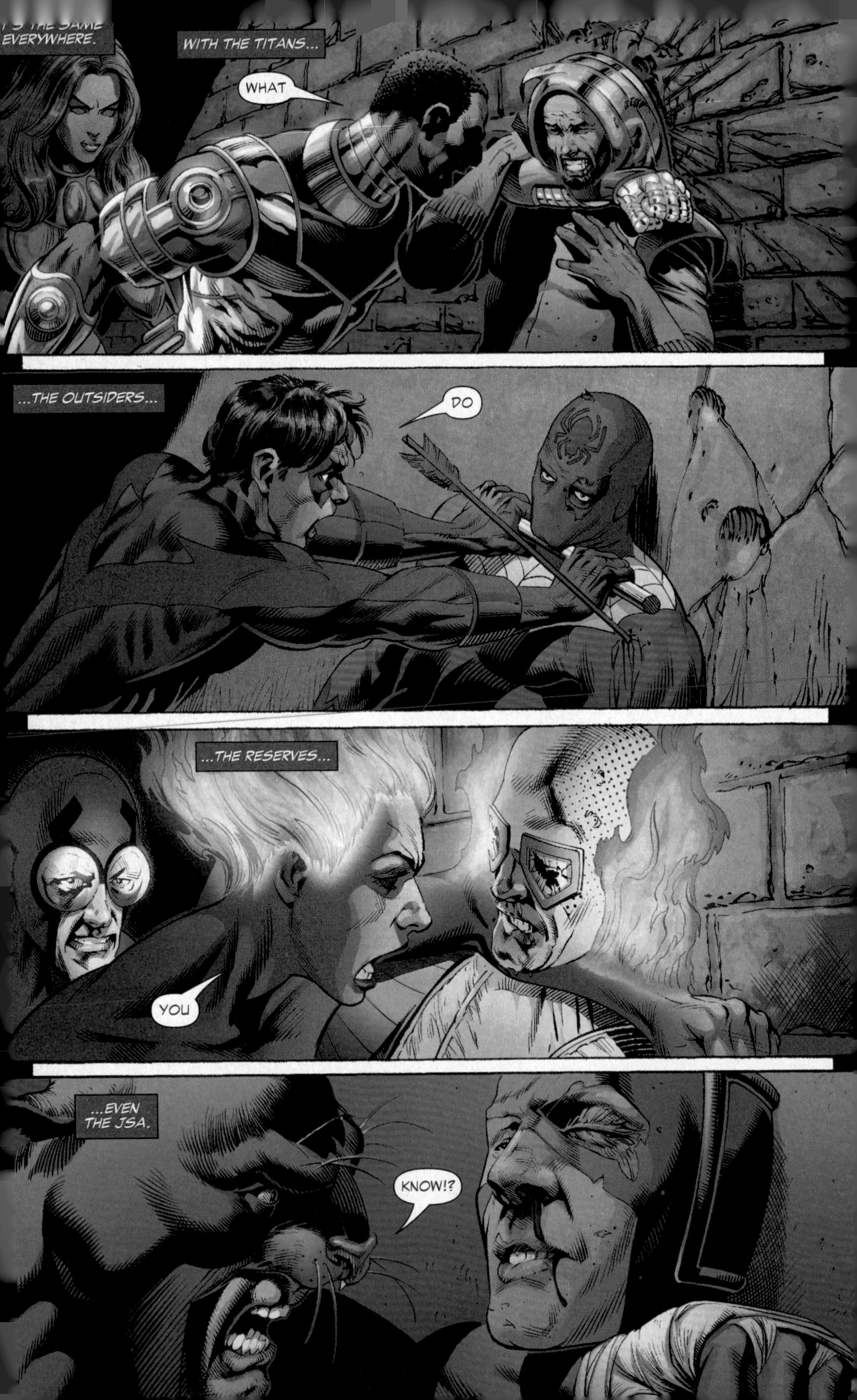
IT'S THE SAME EVERYWHERE.
WITH THE TITANS...
WHAT
...THE OUTSIDERS...
DO
...THE RESERVES...
YOU
...EVEN THE JSA.
KNOW!?

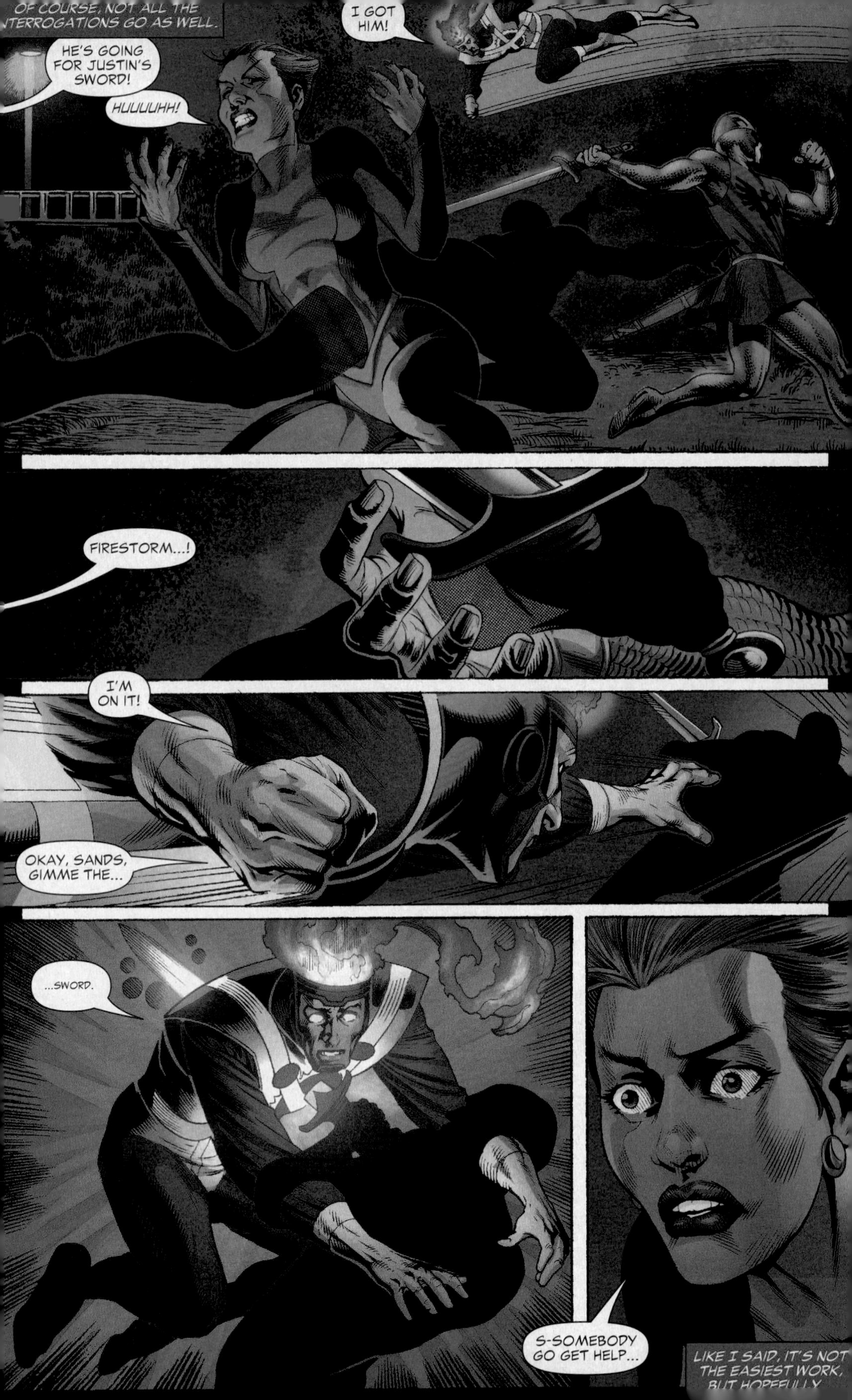
OF COURSE, NOT ALL THE INTERROGATIONS GO AS WELL.
HE'S GOING FOR JUSTIN'S SWORD!
HUUUUHH!
I GOT HIM!
FIRESTORM...!
I'M ON IT!
OKAY, SANDS, GIMME THE...
...SWORD.
S-SOMEBODY GO GET HELP...
LIKE I SAID, IT'S NOT THE EASIEST WORK, BUT HOPEFULLY

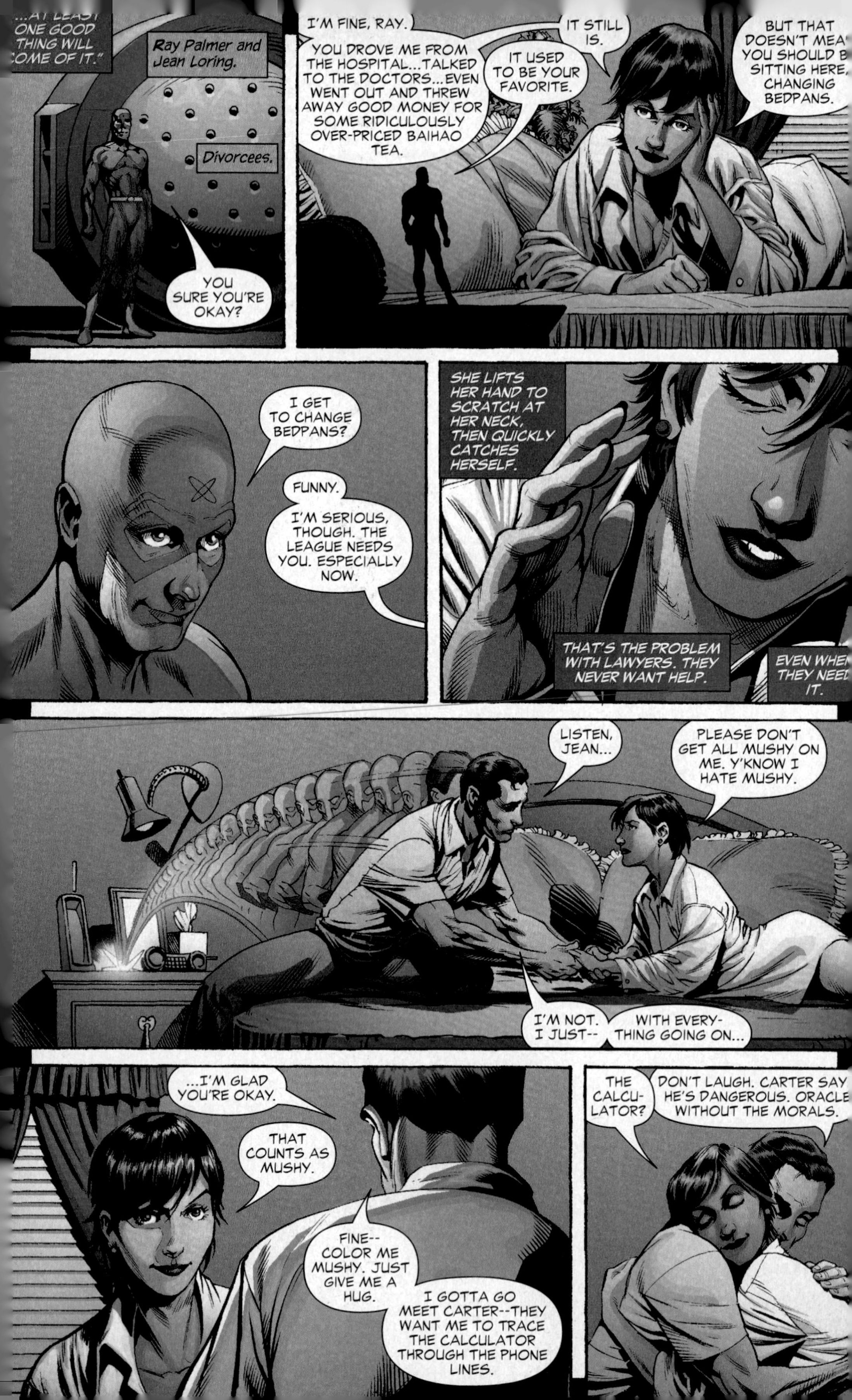
...AT LEAST ONE GOOD THING WILL COME OF IT."
Ray Palmer and Jean Loring.
Divorcees.
YOU SURE YOU'RE OKAY?
I'M FINE, RAY.
YOU DROVE ME FROM THE HOSPITAL...TALKED TO THE DOCTORS...EVEN WENT OUT AND THREW AWAY GOOD MONEY FOR SOME RIDICULOUSLY OVER-PRICED BAIHAO TEA.
IT USED TO BE YOUR FAVORITE.
IT STILL IS.
BUT THAT DOESN'T MEA YOU SHOULD B SITTING HERE, CHANGING BEDPANS.
I GET TO CHANGE BEDPANS?
FUNNY.
I'M SERIOUS, THOUGH. THE LEAGUE NEEDS YOU. ESPECIALLY NOW.
SHE LIFTS HER HAND TO SCRATCH AT HER NECK, THEN QUICKLY CATCHES HERSELF.
THAT'S THE PROBLEM WITH LAWYERS. THEY NEVER WANT HELP.
EVEN WHE THEY NEED IT.
LISTEN, JEAN...
PLEASE DON'T GET ALL MUSHY ON ME. Y'KNOW I HATE MUSHY.
I'M NOT. I JUST--
WITH EVERY-THING GOING ON...
...I'M GLAD YOU'RE OKAY.
THAT COUNTS AS MUSHY.
FINE--COLOR ME MUSHY. JUST GIVE ME A HUG.
I GOTTA GO MEET CARTER--THEY WANT ME TO TRACE THE CALCULATOR THROUGH THE PHONE LINES.
THE CALCU-LATOR?
DON'T LAUGH. CARTER SAY HE'S DANGEROUS. ORACLE WITHOUT THE MORALS.

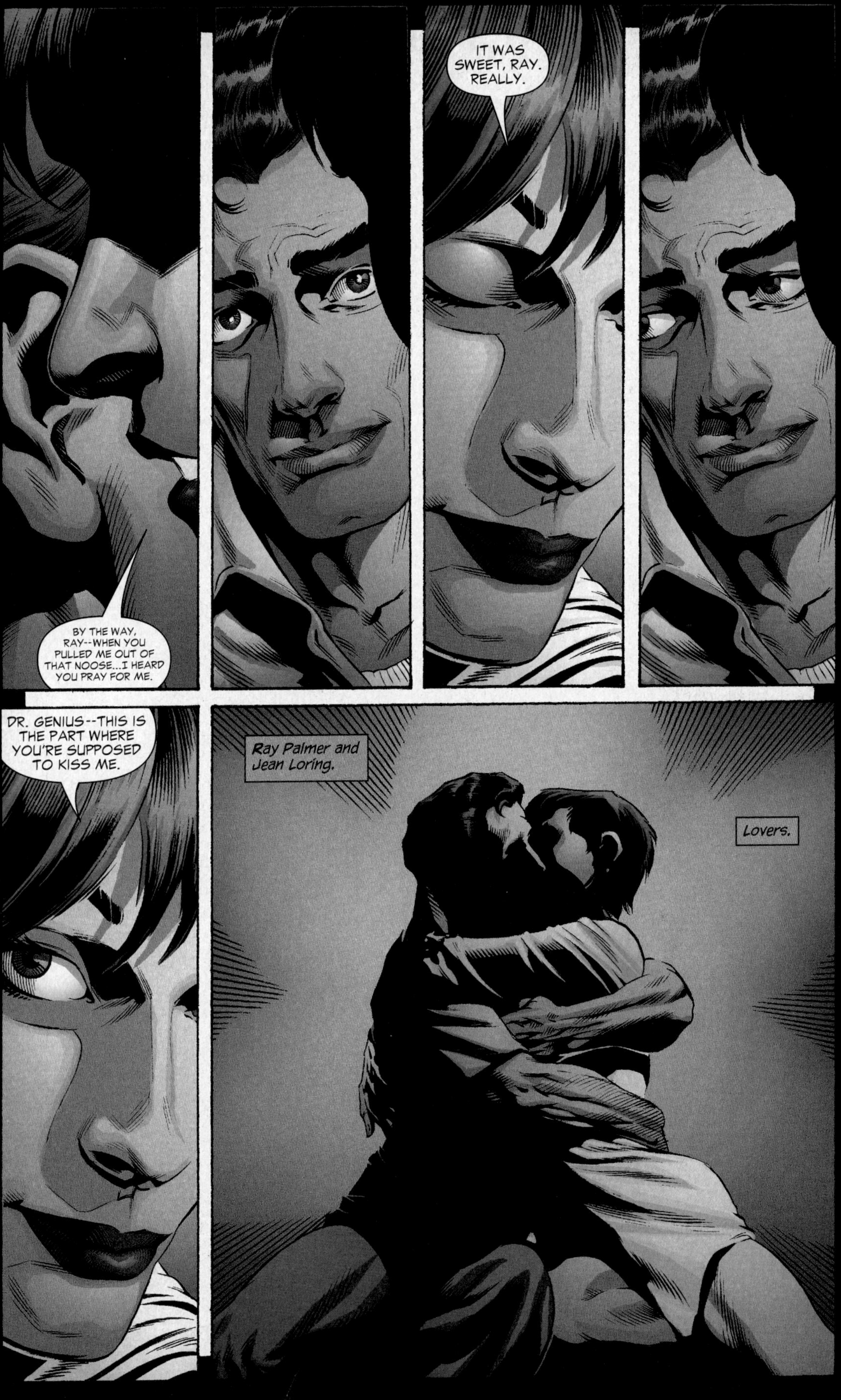

BY THE WAY, RAY--WHEN YOU PULLED ME OUT OF THAT NOOSE...I HEARD YOU PRAY FOR ME.
IT WAS SWEET, RAY. REALLY.
DR. GENIUS--THIS IS THE PART WHERE YOU'RE SUPPOSED TO KISS ME.
Ray Palmer and Jean Loring.
Lovers.

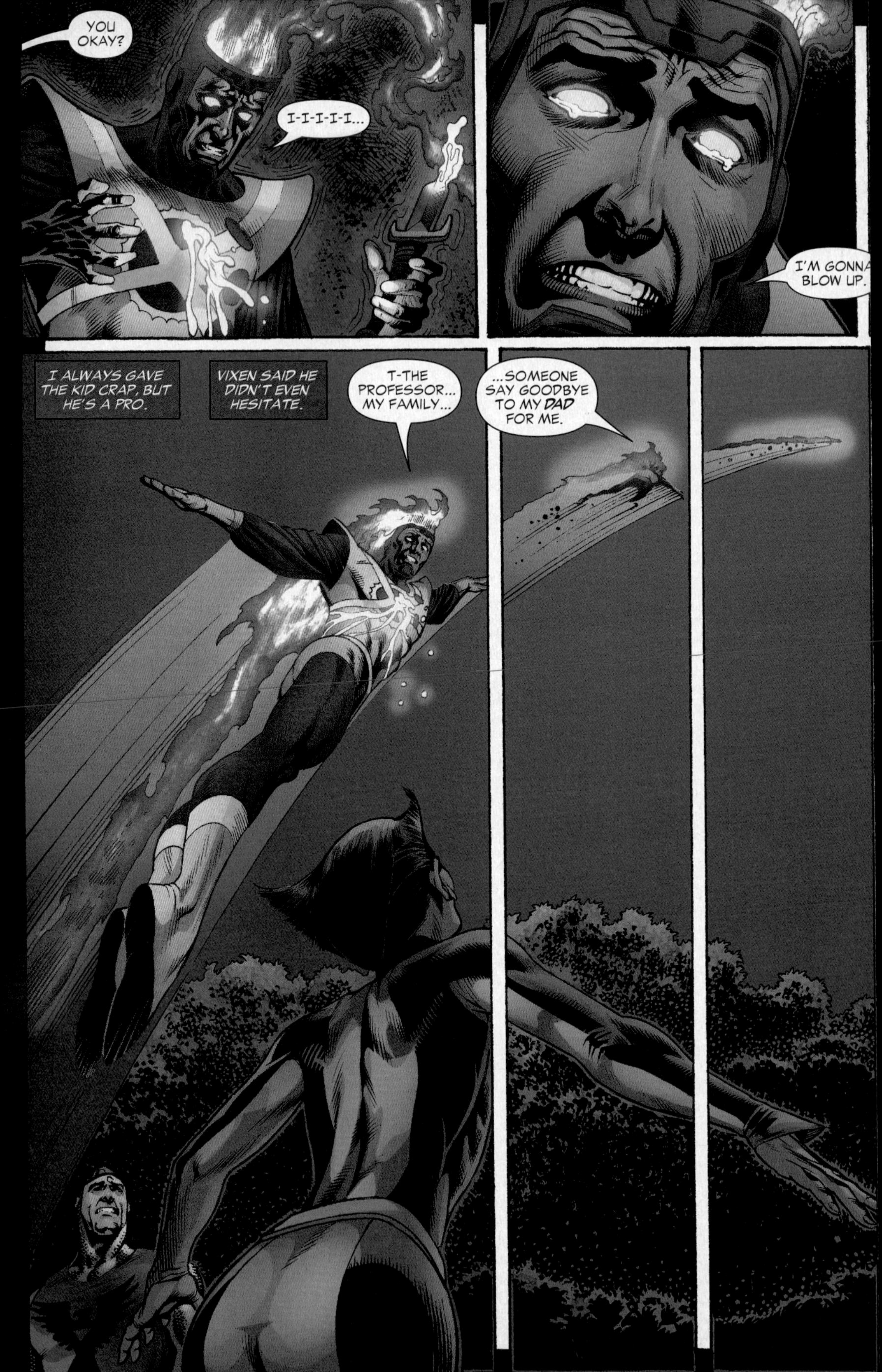
YOU OKAY?
I-I-I-I-I...
I'M GONNA BLOW UP.
I ALWAYS GAVE THE KID CRAP, BUT HE'S A PRO.
VIXEN SAID HE DIDN'T EVEN HESITATE.
T-THE PROFESSOR... MY FAMILY...
...SOMEONE SAY GOODBYE TO MY DAD FOR ME.

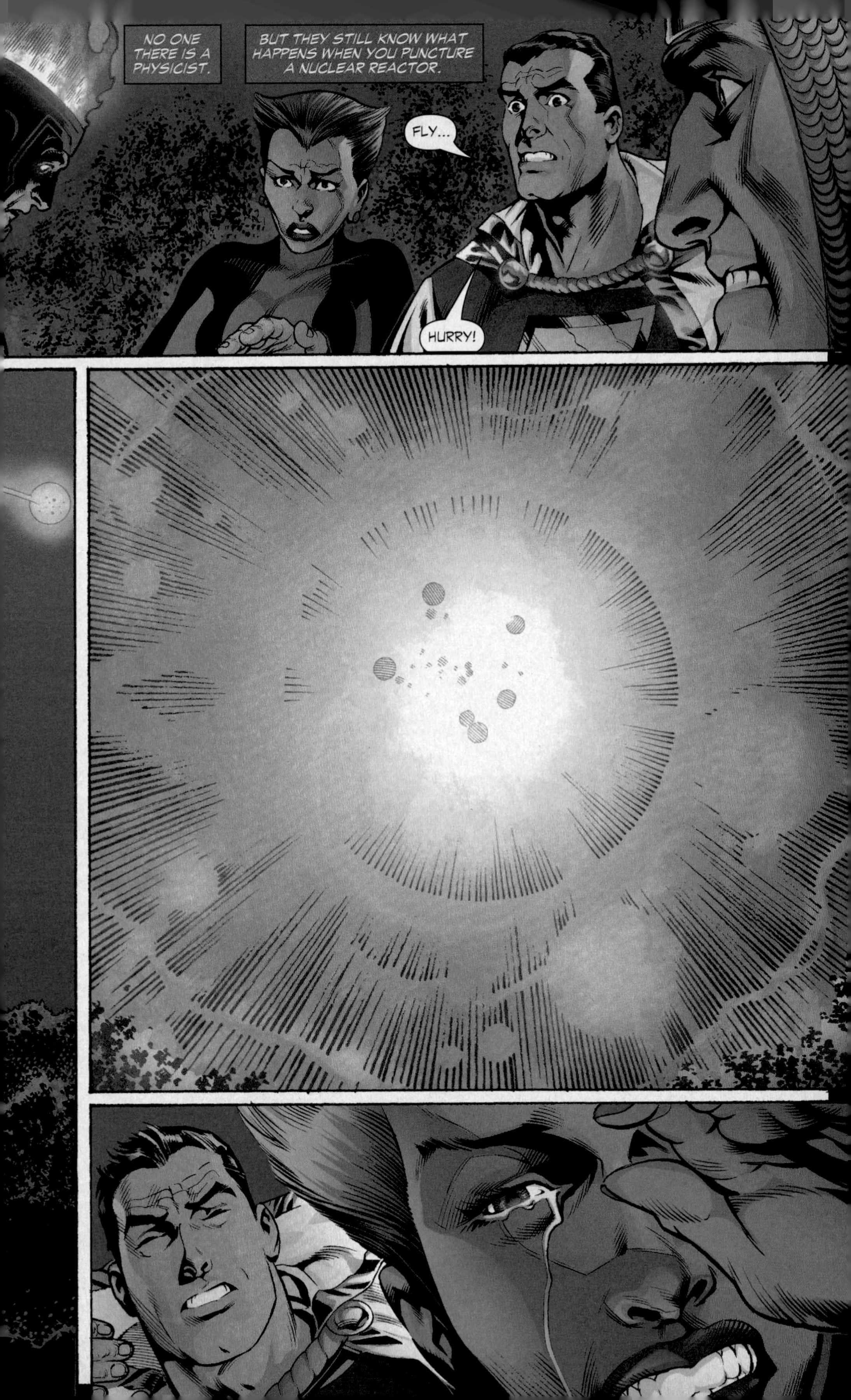
NO ONE THERE IS A PHYSICIST.
BUT THEY STILL KNOW WHAT HAPPENS WHEN YOU PUNCTURE A NUCLEAR REACTOR.
FLY...
HURRY!

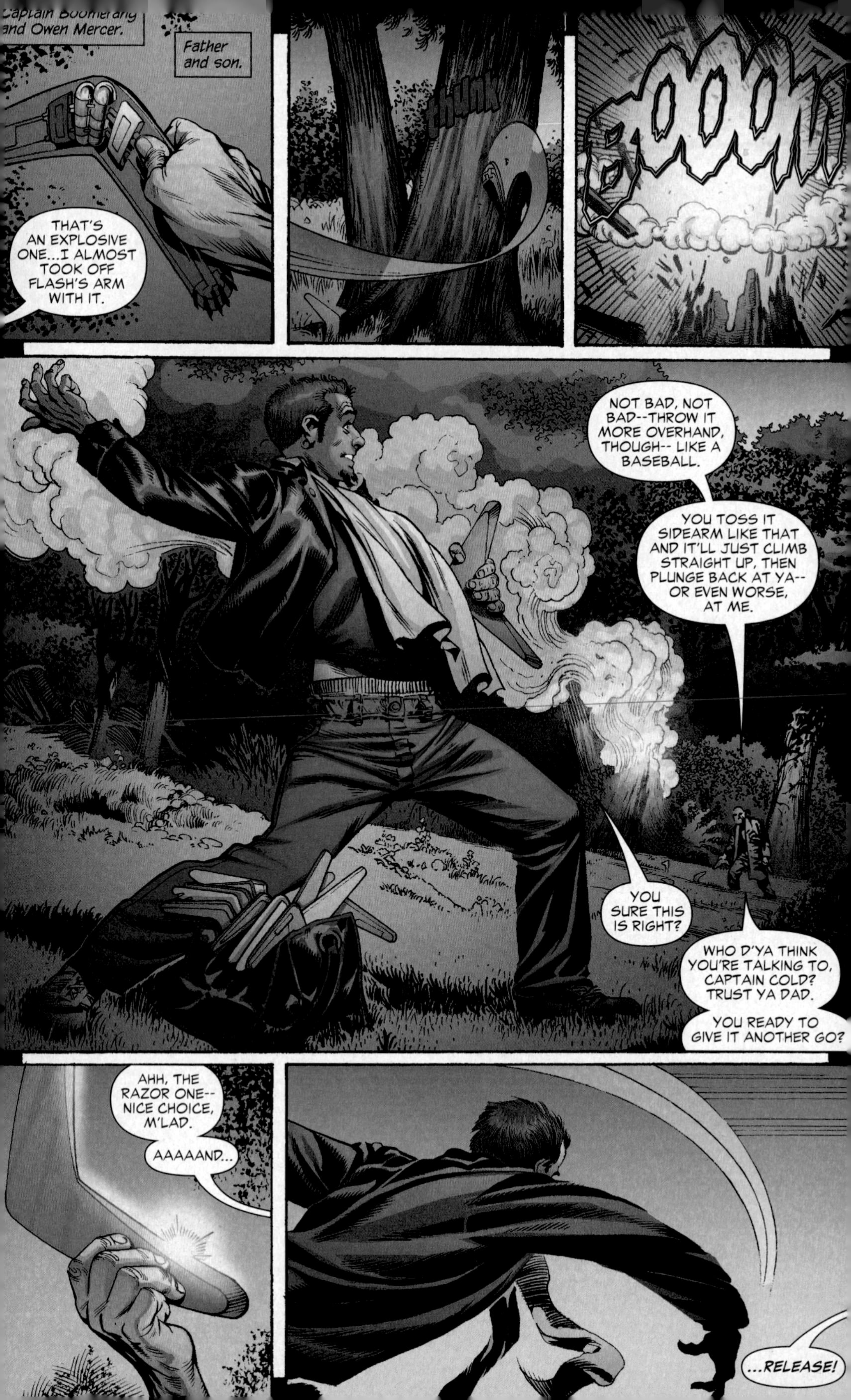
Captain Boomerang and Owen Mercer.
Father and son.
THAT'S AN EXPLOSIVE ONE...I ALMOST TOOK OFF FLASH'S ARM WITH IT.
THUNK
BOOOOM
NOT BAD, NOT BAD--THROW IT MORE OVERHAND, THOUGH-- LIKE A BASEBALL.
YOU TOSS IT SIDEARM LIKE THAT AND IT'LL JUST CLIMB STRAIGHT UP, THEN PLUNGE BACK AT YA-- OR EVEN WORSE, AT ME.
YOU SURE THIS IS RIGHT?
WHO D'YA THINK YOU'RE TALKING TO, CAPTAIN COLD? TRUST YA DAD.
YOU READY TO GIVE IT ANOTHER GO?
AHH, THE RAZOR ONE-- NICE CHOICE, M'LAD.
AAAAAND...
...RELEASE!

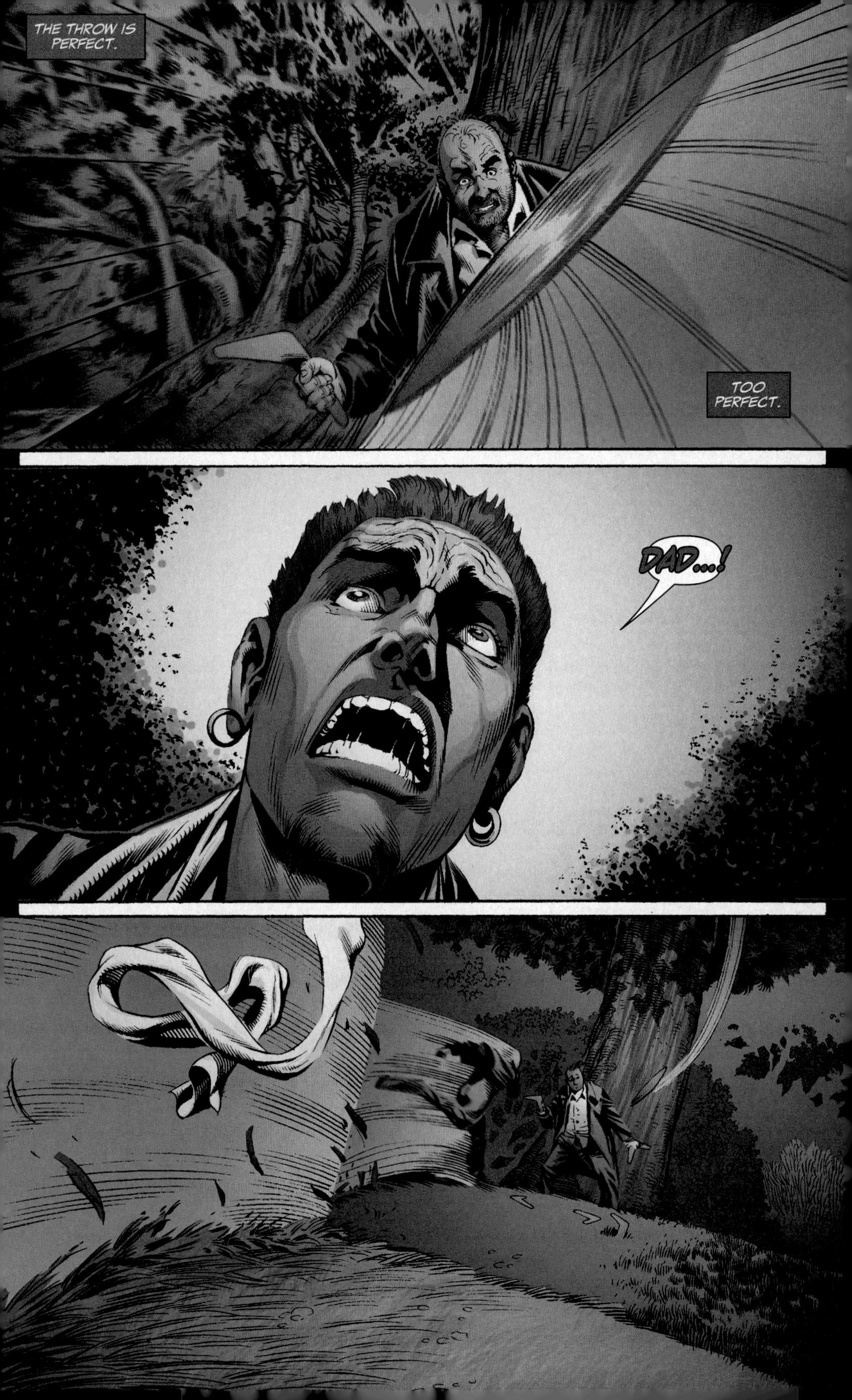
THE THROW IS PERFECT.
TOO PERFECT.
DAD...!

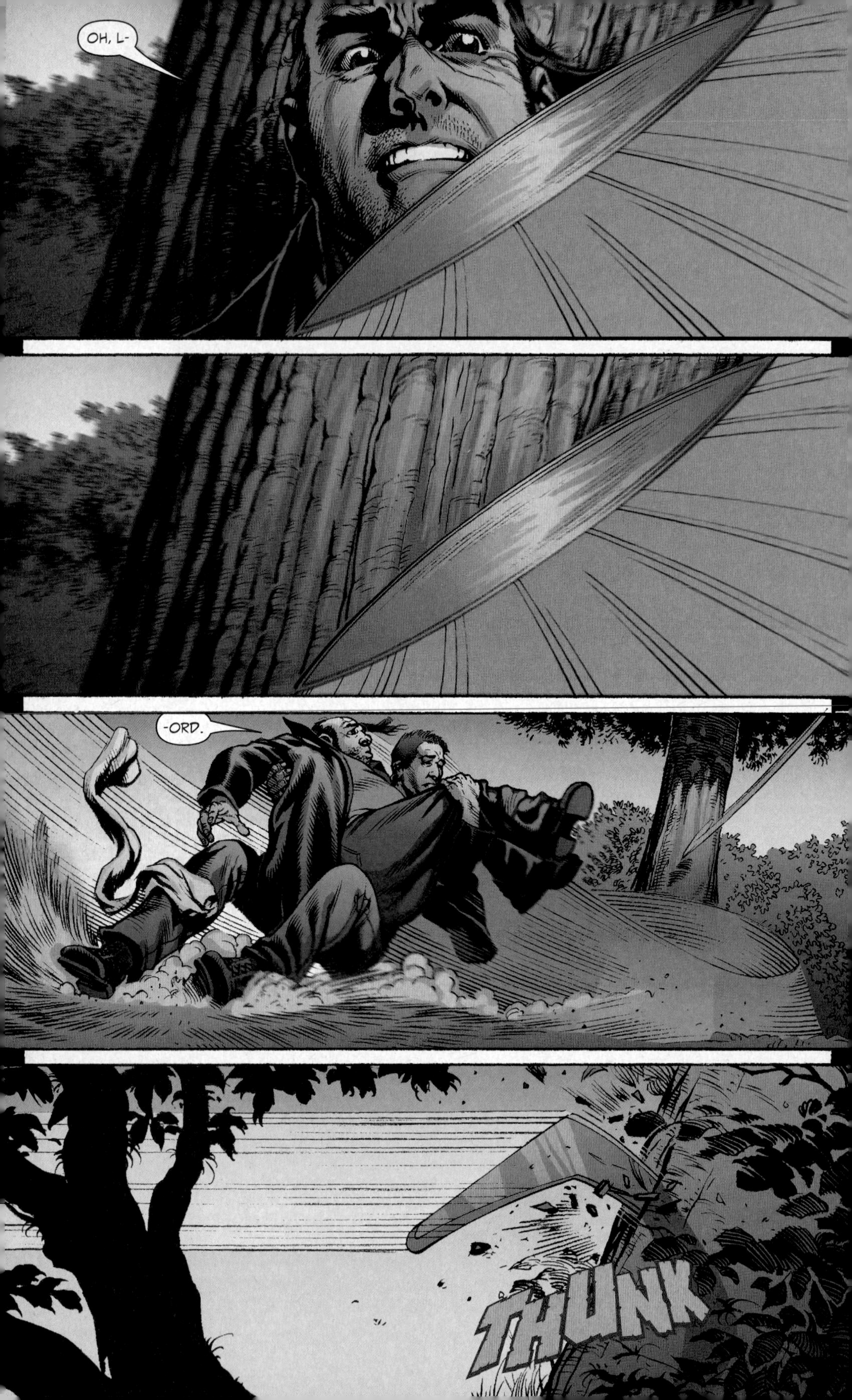
OH, L-
-ORD.
THUNK

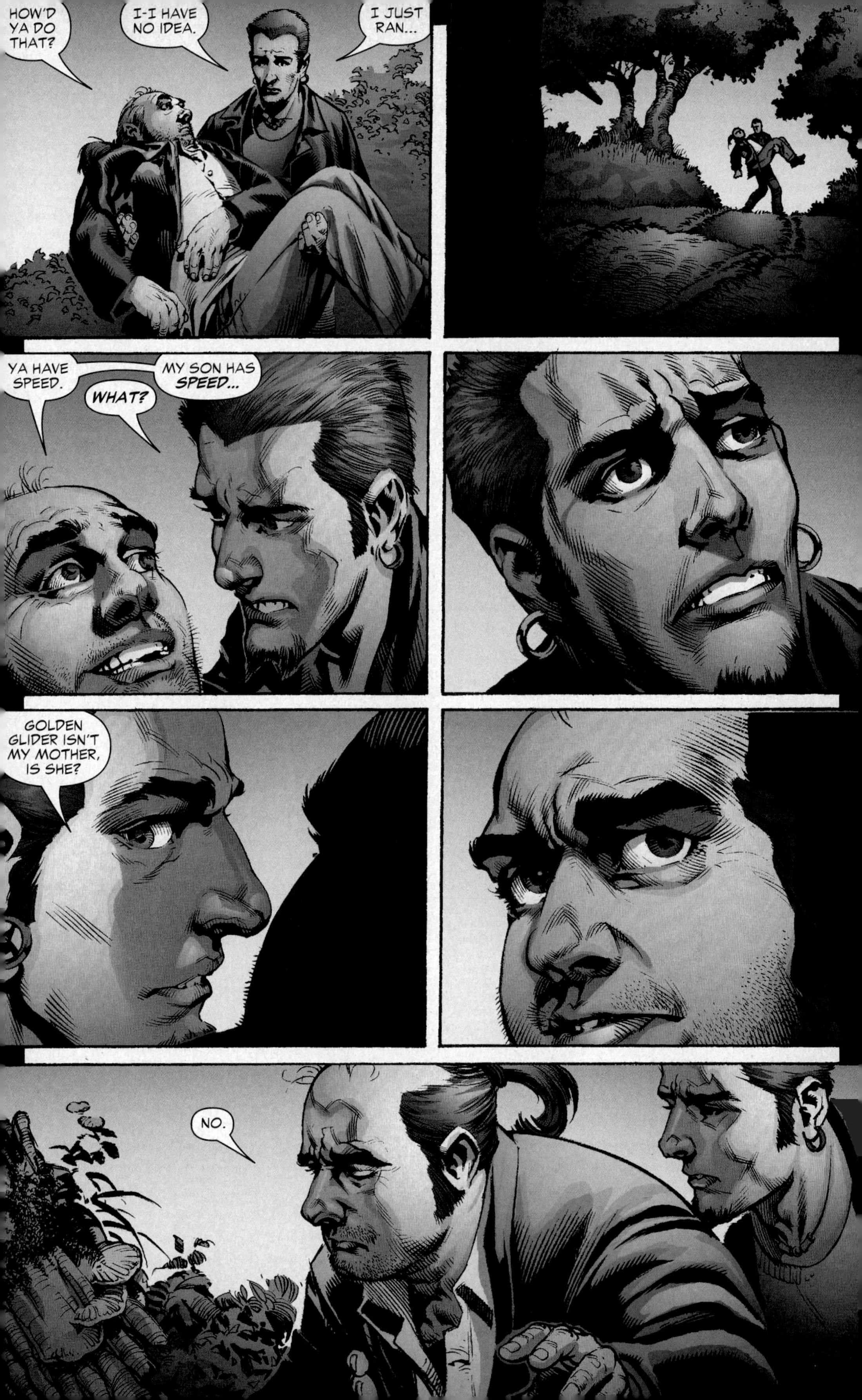
HOW'D YA DO THAT?
I-I HAVE NO IDEA.
I JUST RAN...
YA HAVE SPEED.
WHAT?
MY SON HAS SPEED...
GOLDEN GLIDER ISN'T MY MOTHER, IS SHE?
NO.

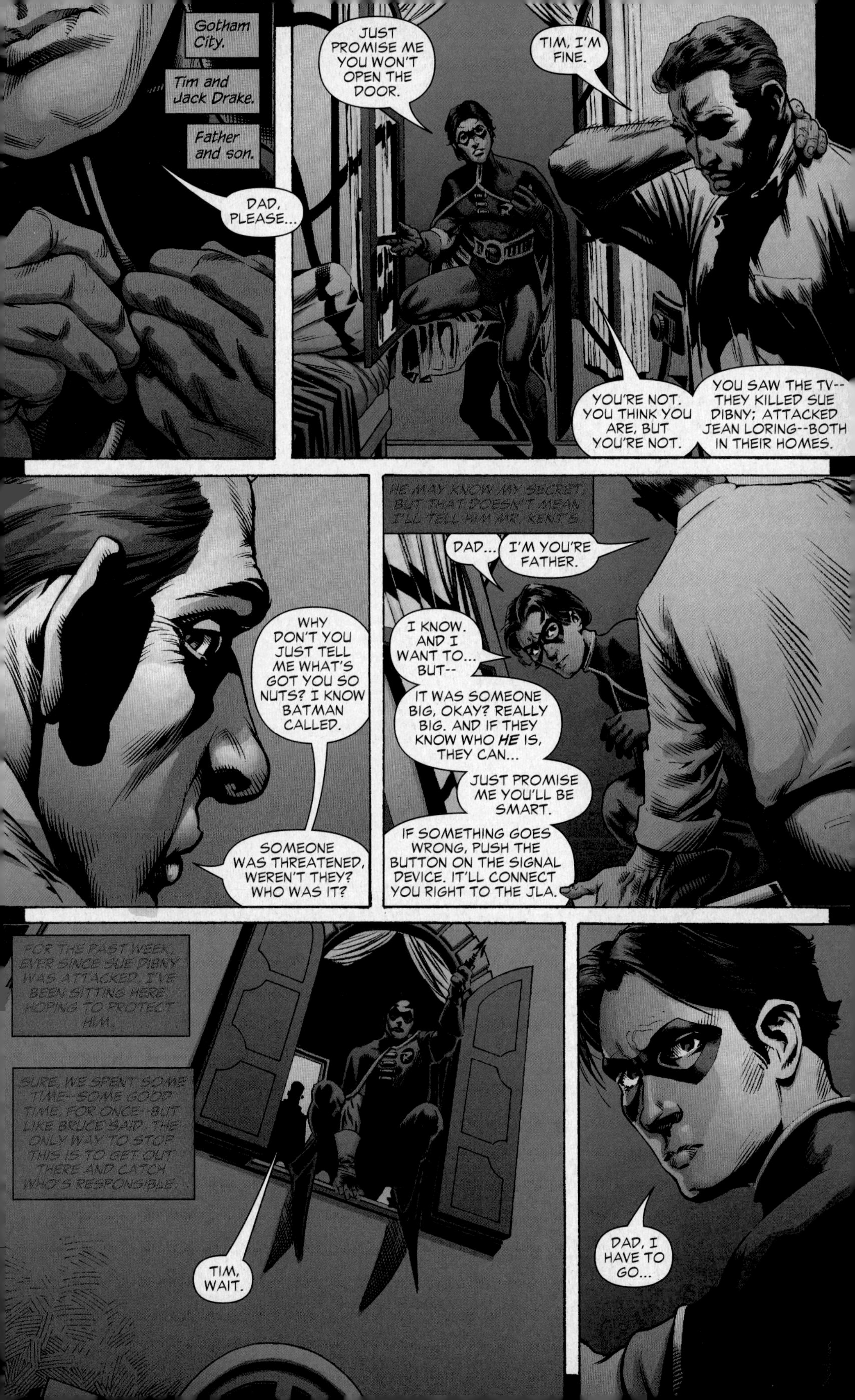
Gotham City.
Tim and Jack Drake.
Father and son.
DAD, PLEASE...
JUST PROMISE ME YOU WON'T OPEN THE DOOR.
TIM, I'M FINE.
YOU'RE NOT. YOU THINK YOU ARE, BUT YOU'RE NOT.
YOU SAW THE TV-- THEY KILLED SUE DIBNY; ATTACKED JEAN LORING--BOTH IN THEIR HOMES.
WHY DON'T YOU JUST TELL ME WHAT'S GOT YOU SO NUTS? I KNOW BATMAN CALLED.
SOMEONE WAS THREATENED, WEREN'T THEY? WHO WAS IT?
HE MAY KNOW MY SECRET, BUT THAT DOESN'T MEAN I'LL TELL HIM MR. KENT'S.
DAD...
I'M YOU'RE FATHER.
I KNOW. AND I WANT TO... BUT--
IT WAS SOMEONE BIG, OKAY? REALLY BIG. AND IF THEY KNOW WHO *HE* IS, THEY CAN...
JUST PROMISE ME YOU'LL BE SMART.
IF SOMETHING GOES WRONG, PUSH THE BUTTON ON THE SIGNAL DEVICE. IT'LL CONNECT YOU RIGHT TO THE JLA.
FOR THE PAST WEEK, EVER SINCE SUE DIBNY WAS ATTACKED, I'VE BEEN SITTING HERE HOPING TO PROTECT HIM.
SURE, WE SPENT SOME TIME--SOME GOOD TIME, FOR ONCE--BUT LIKE BRUCE SAID, THE ONLY WAY TO STOP THIS IS TO GET OUT THERE AND CATCH WHO'S RESPONSIBLE.
TIM, WAIT.
DAD, I HAVE TO GO...

Y'KNOW, I'VE TRIED TO BE GOOD ABOUT THIS...

BETTER THAN MOST PARENTS-- IN FACT, BETTER THAN *ANY* PARENT. I MEAN, MY THERAPY BILLS ALONE--

I'M JUST SAYING, I KNOW HE CHOSE YOU FOR A REASON--AND I RESPECT THAT. YOU OBVIOUSLY HAVE A GIFT.

BUT DON'T THINK IT MAKES IT ANY EASIER FOR ME TO WATCH MY SON GO OUT THERE AND PURPOSELY PUT HIMSELF IN HARM'S WAY.

I KNOW, I JUST...

I WORRY ABOUT YOU, TIM.

I WORRY ABOUT YOU TOO. OBVIOUSLY...

MAYBE IT'D BE BETTER IF YOU STAYED IN TONIGHT.

I MEAN, YOU'R SIXTEEN YEARS O YOU SHOULDN'T RUNNING AROUN A MASK AND CAPE.

YOU REALLY THINK I SHOULD STAY? BE HONEST, DAD.

YOU REALLY THINK I'M BETTER OFF SITTING HERE, WATCHING ALL THIS HAPPEN ON THE NEWS?

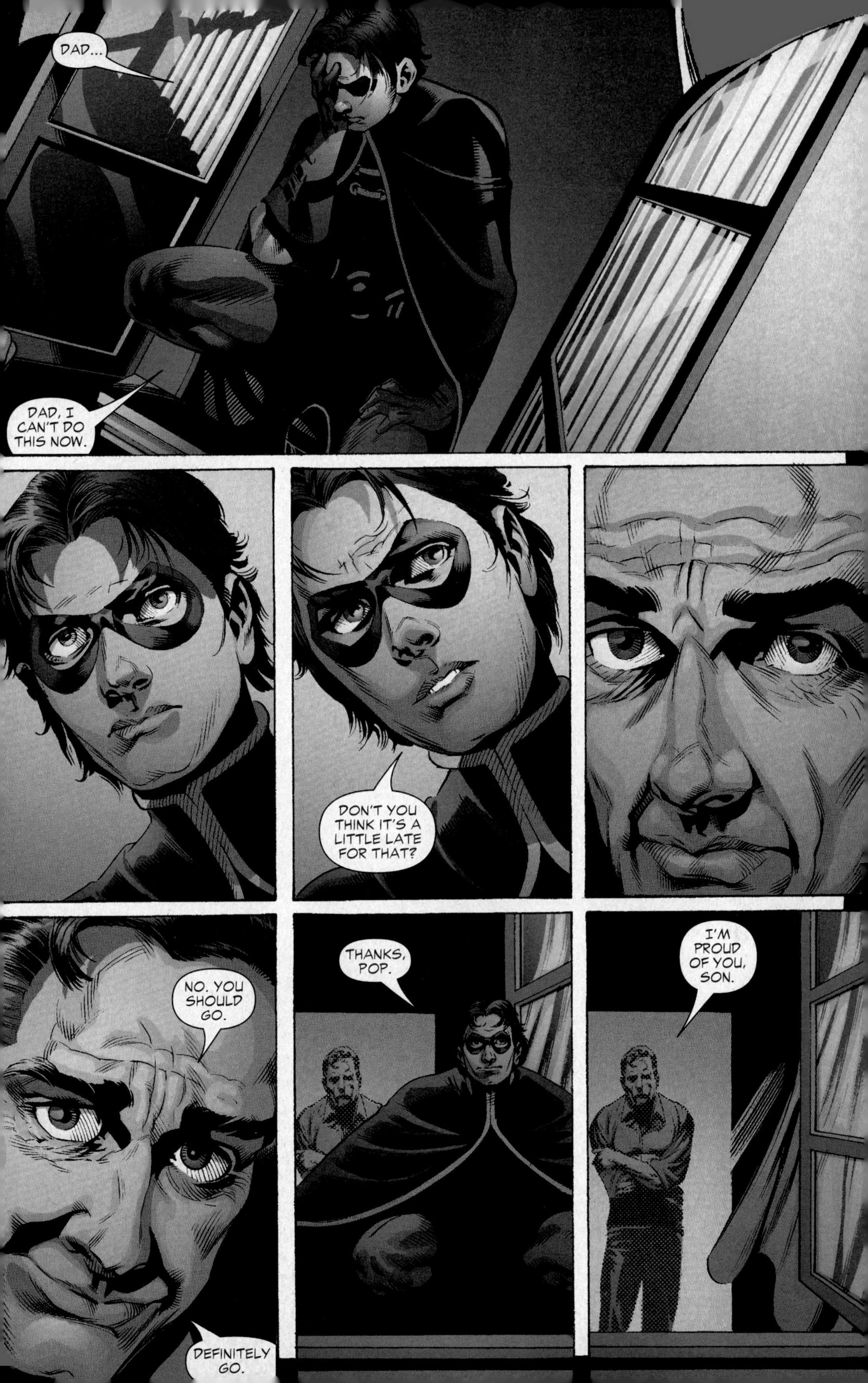
DAD...
DAD, I CAN'T DO THIS NOW.
DON'T YOU THINK IT'S A LITTLE LATE FOR THAT?
NO. YOU SHOULD GO.
DEFINITELY GO.
THANKS, POP.
I'M PROUD OF YOU, SON.

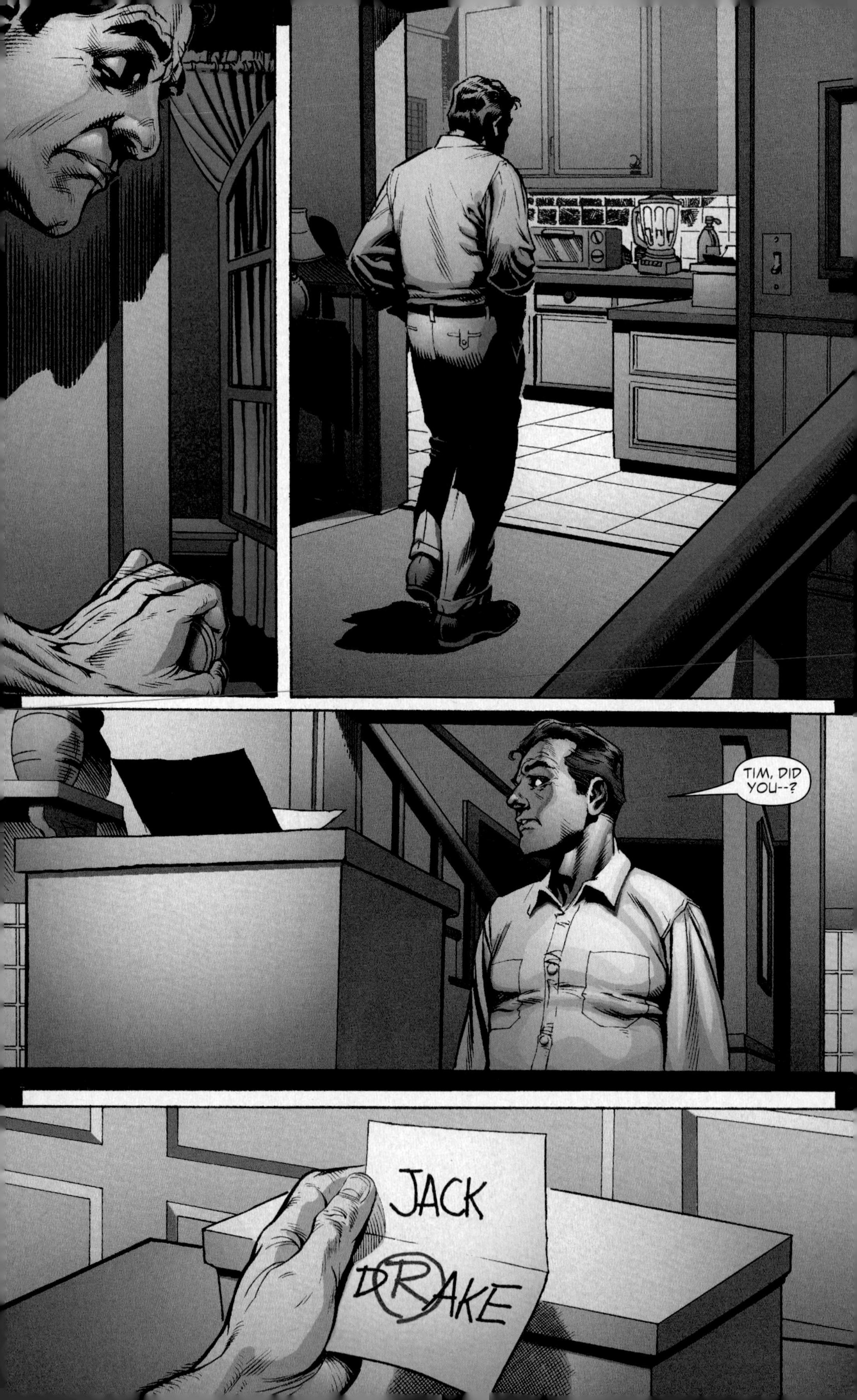
TIM, DID YOU--?
JACK
DRAKE

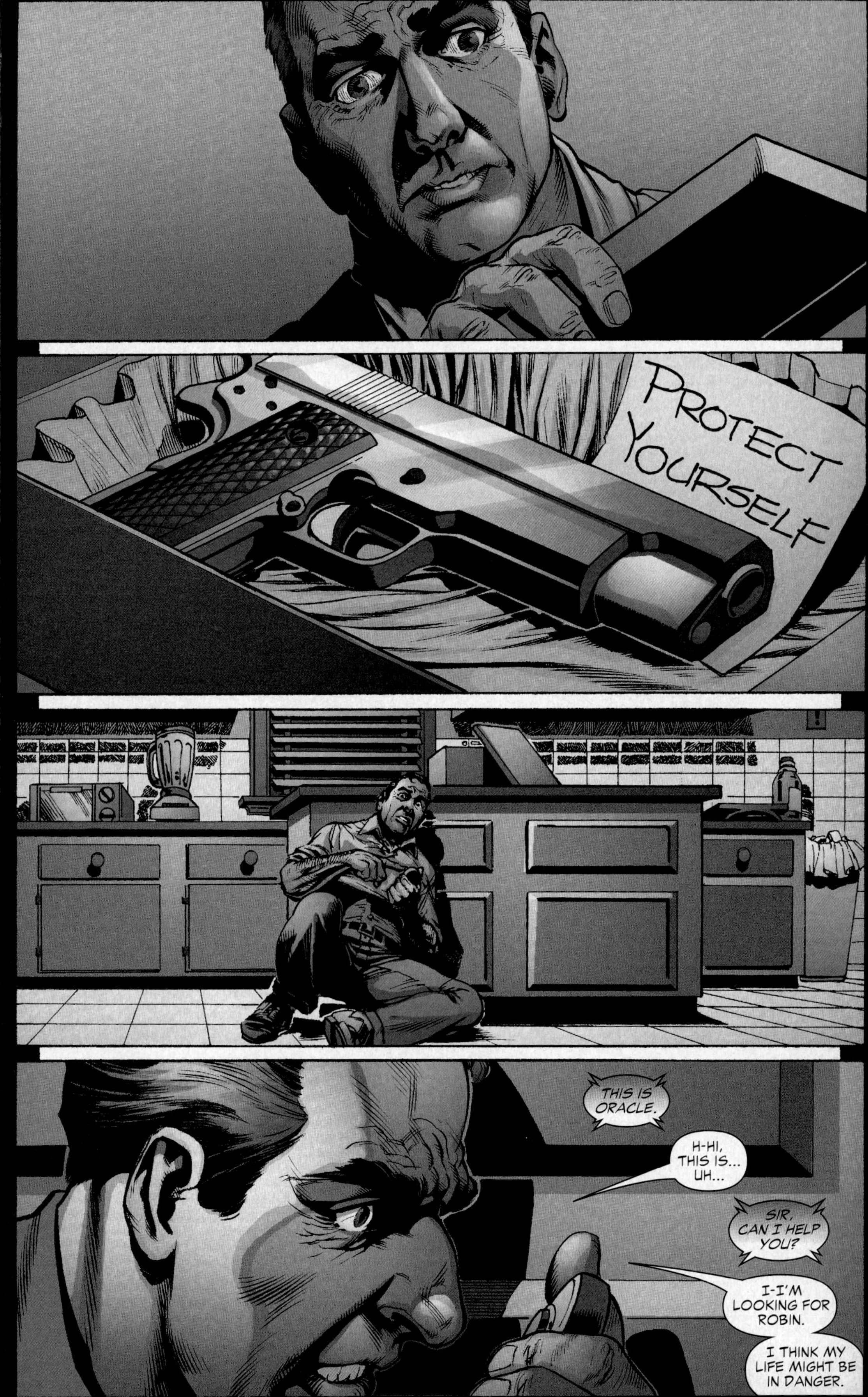
PROTECT YOURSELF
THIS IS ORACLE.
H-HI, THIS IS... UH...
SIR, CAN I HELP YOU?
I-I'M LOOKING FOR ROBIN.
I THINK MY LIFE MIGHT BE IN DANGER.

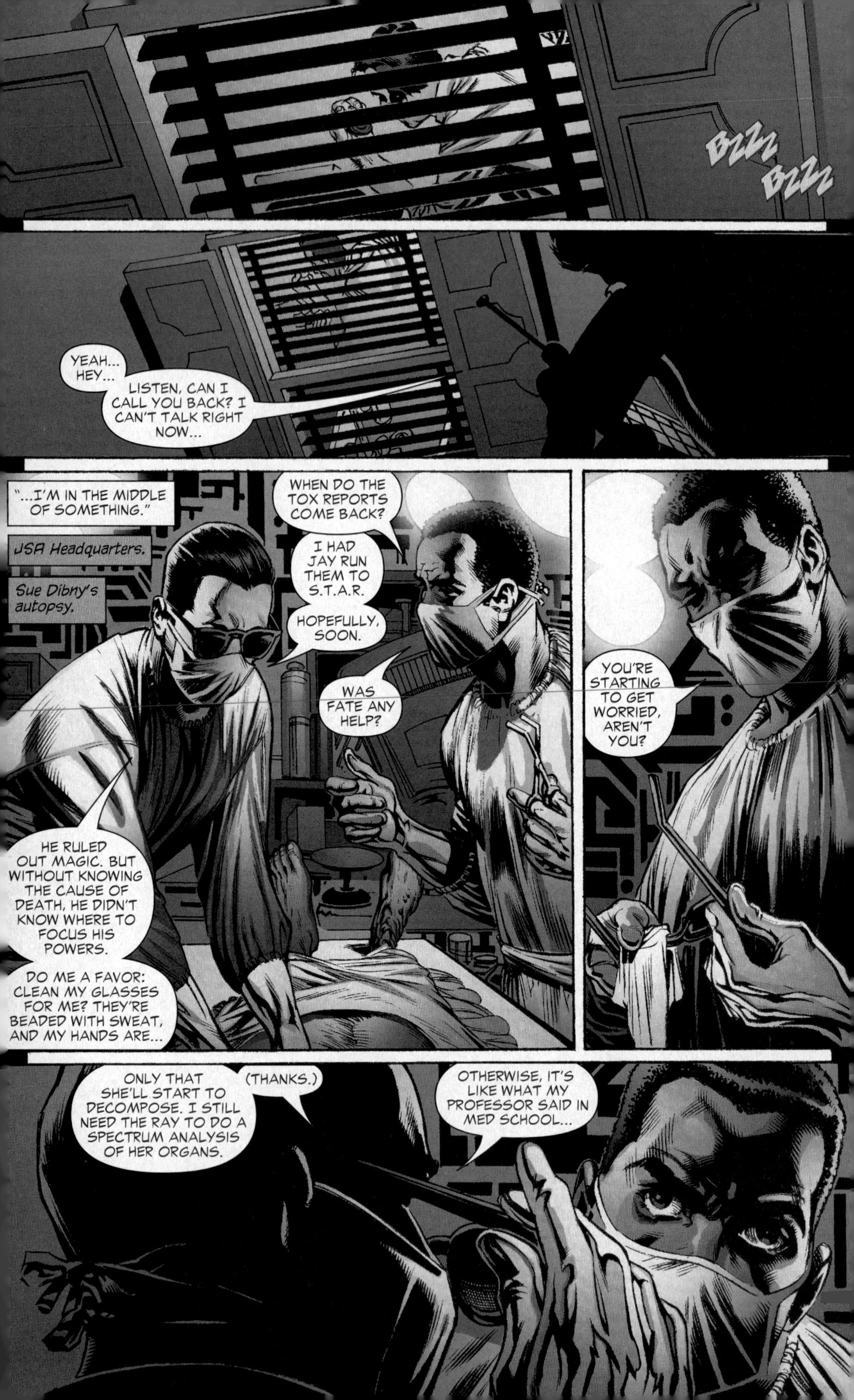
BZZZ BZZZ
YEAH... HEY...
LISTEN, CAN I CALL YOU BACK? I CAN'T TALK RIGHT NOW...
"...I'M IN THE MIDDLE OF SOMETHING."
JSA Headquarters.
Sue Dibny's autopsy.
WHEN DO THE TOX REPORTS COME BACK?
I HAD JAY RUN THEM TO S.T.A.R.
HOPEFULLY, SOON.
WAS FATE ANY HELP?
HE RULED OUT MAGIC. BUT WITHOUT KNOWING THE CAUSE OF DEATH, HE DIDN'T KNOW WHERE TO FOCUS HIS POWERS.
DO ME A FAVOR: CLEAN MY GLASSES FOR ME? THEY'RE BEADED WITH SWEAT, AND MY HANDS ARE...
YOU'RE STARTING TO GET WORRIED, AREN'T YOU?
ONLY THAT SHE'LL START TO DECOMPOSE. I STILL NEED THE RAY TO DO A SPECTRUM ANALYSIS OF HER ORGANS.
(THANKS.)
OTHERWISE, IT'S LIKE WHAT MY PROFESSOR SAID IN MED SCHOOL...

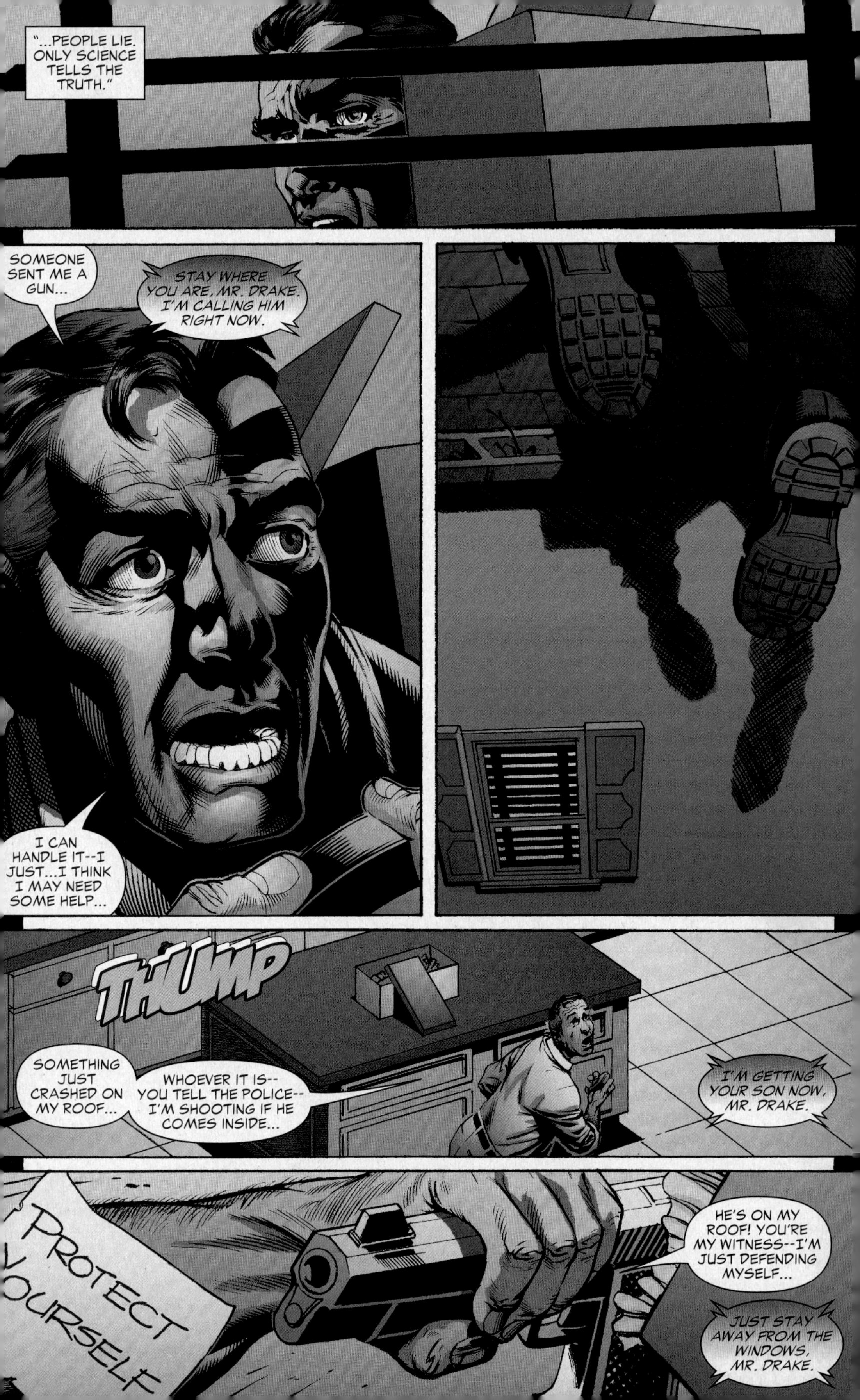
"...PEOPLE LIE. ONLY SCIENCE TELLS THE TRUTH."
SOMEONE SENT ME A GUN...
STAY WHERE YOU ARE, MR. DRAKE. I'M CALLING HIM RIGHT NOW.
I CAN HANDLE IT--I JUST...I THINK I MAY NEED SOME HELP...
THUMP
SOMETHING JUST CRASHED ON MY ROOF...
WHOEVER IT IS-- YOU TELL THE POLICE-- I'M SHOOTING IF HE COMES INSIDE...
I'M GETTING YOUR SON NOW, MR. DRAKE.
PROTECT YOURSELF
HE'S ON MY ROOF! YOU'RE MY WITNESS--I'M JUST DEFENDING MYSELF...
JUST STAY AWAY FROM THE WINDOWS, MR. DRAKE.

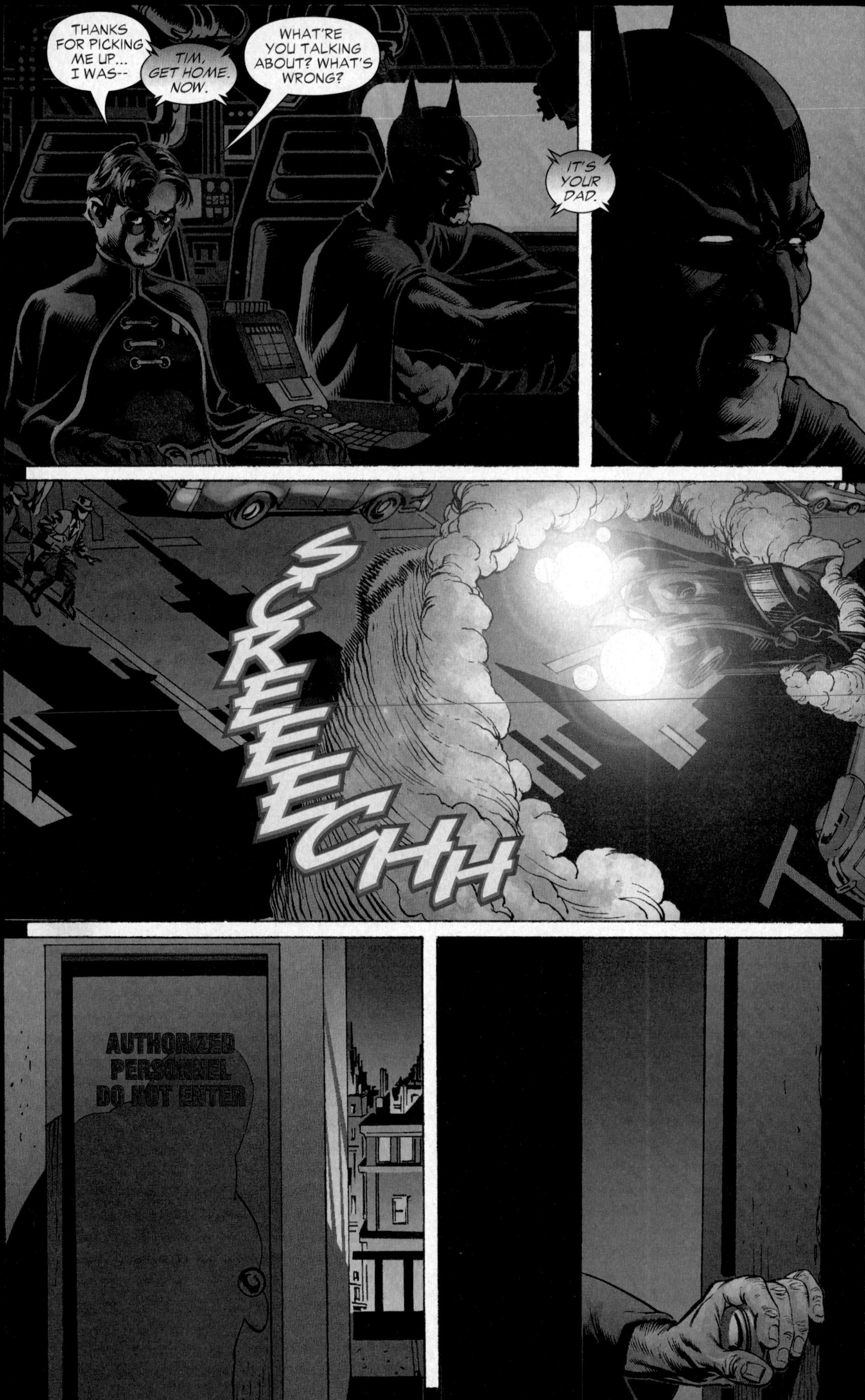
THANKS FOR PICKING ME UP... I WAS--
TIM, GET HOME. NOW.
WHAT'RE YOU TALKING ABOUT? WHAT'S WRONG?
IT'S YOUR DAD.
SCREEECHH
AUTHORIZED PERSONNEL DO NOT ENTER

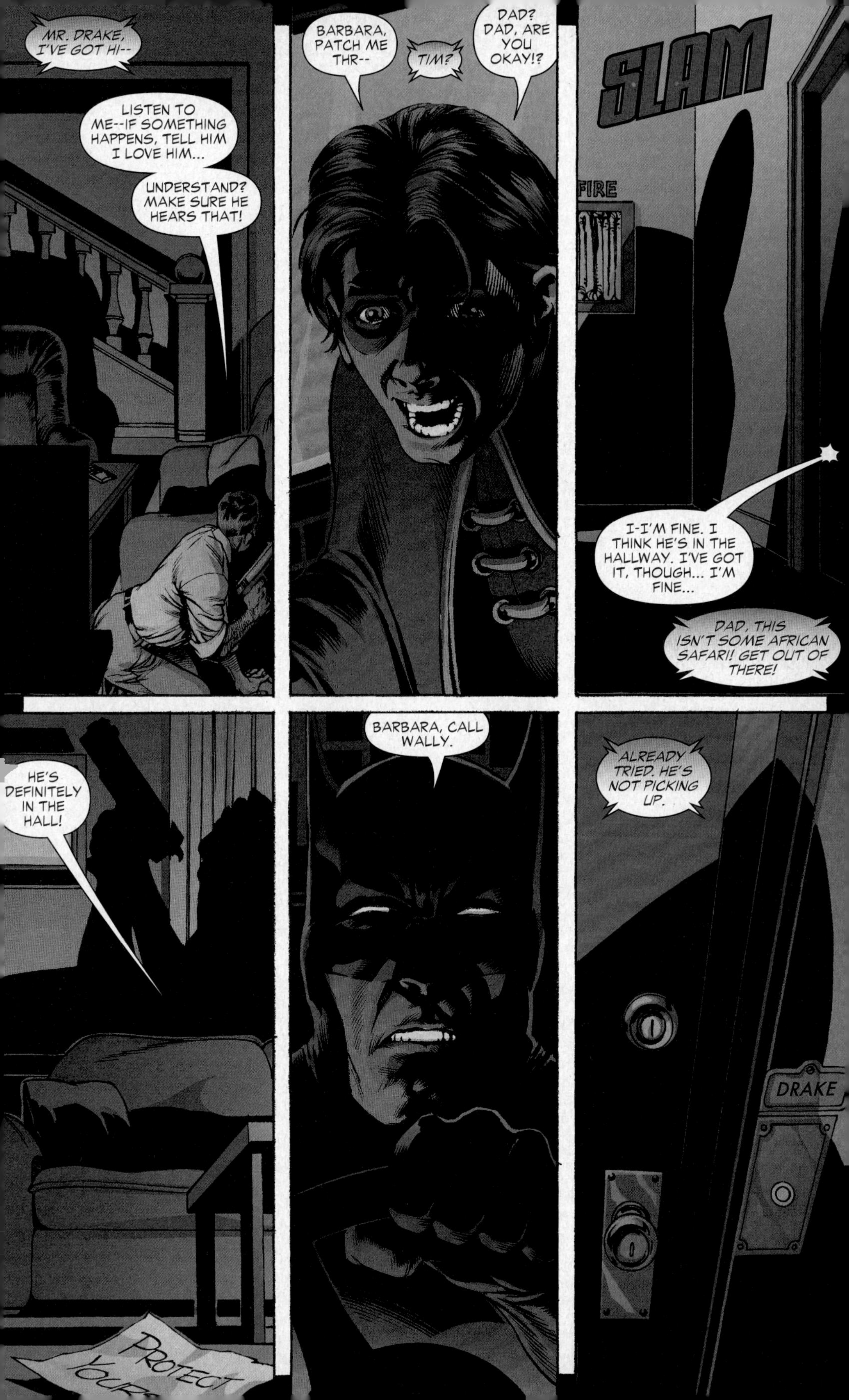
MR. DRAKE, I'VE GOT HI--
LISTEN TO ME--IF SOMETHING HAPPENS, TELL HIM I LOVE HIM...
UNDERSTAND? MAKE SURE HE HEARS THAT!
BARBARA, PATCH ME THR--
TIM?
DAD? DAD, ARE YOU OKAY!?
SLAM
FIRE
I-I'M FINE. I THINK HE'S IN THE HALLWAY. I'VE GOT IT, THOUGH... I'M FINE...
DAD, THIS ISN'T SOME AFRICAN SAFARI! GET OUT OF THERE!
HE'S DEFINITELY IN THE HALL!
BARBARA, CALL WALLY.
ALREADY TRIED. HE'S NOT PICKING UP.
DRAKE
PROTECT YOURS

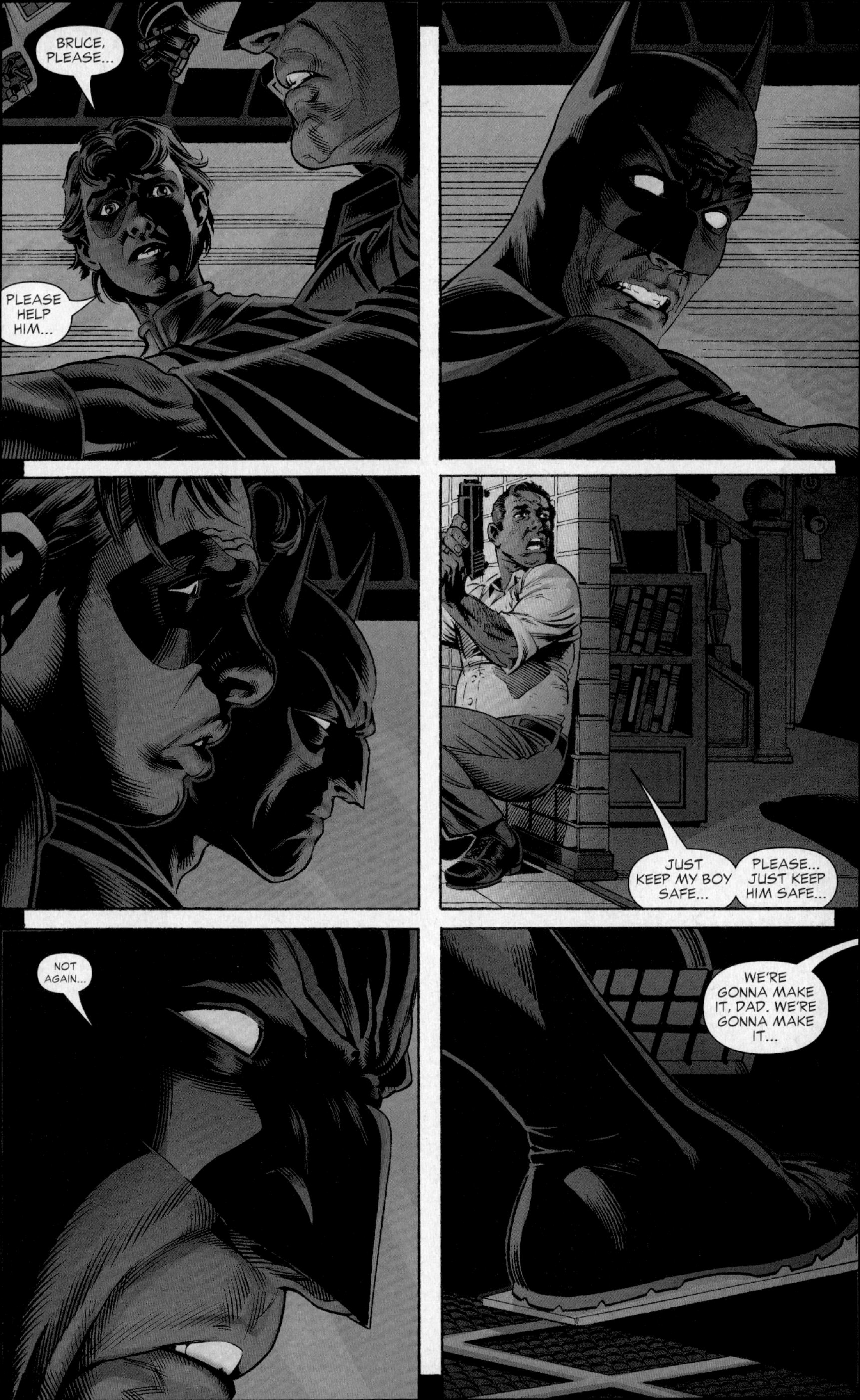
BRUCE, PLEASE...
PLEASE HELP HIM...
JUST KEEP MY BOY SAFE...
PLEASE... JUST KEEP HIM SAFE...
NOT AGAIN...
WE'RE GONNA MAKE IT, DAD. WE'RE GONNA MAKE IT...

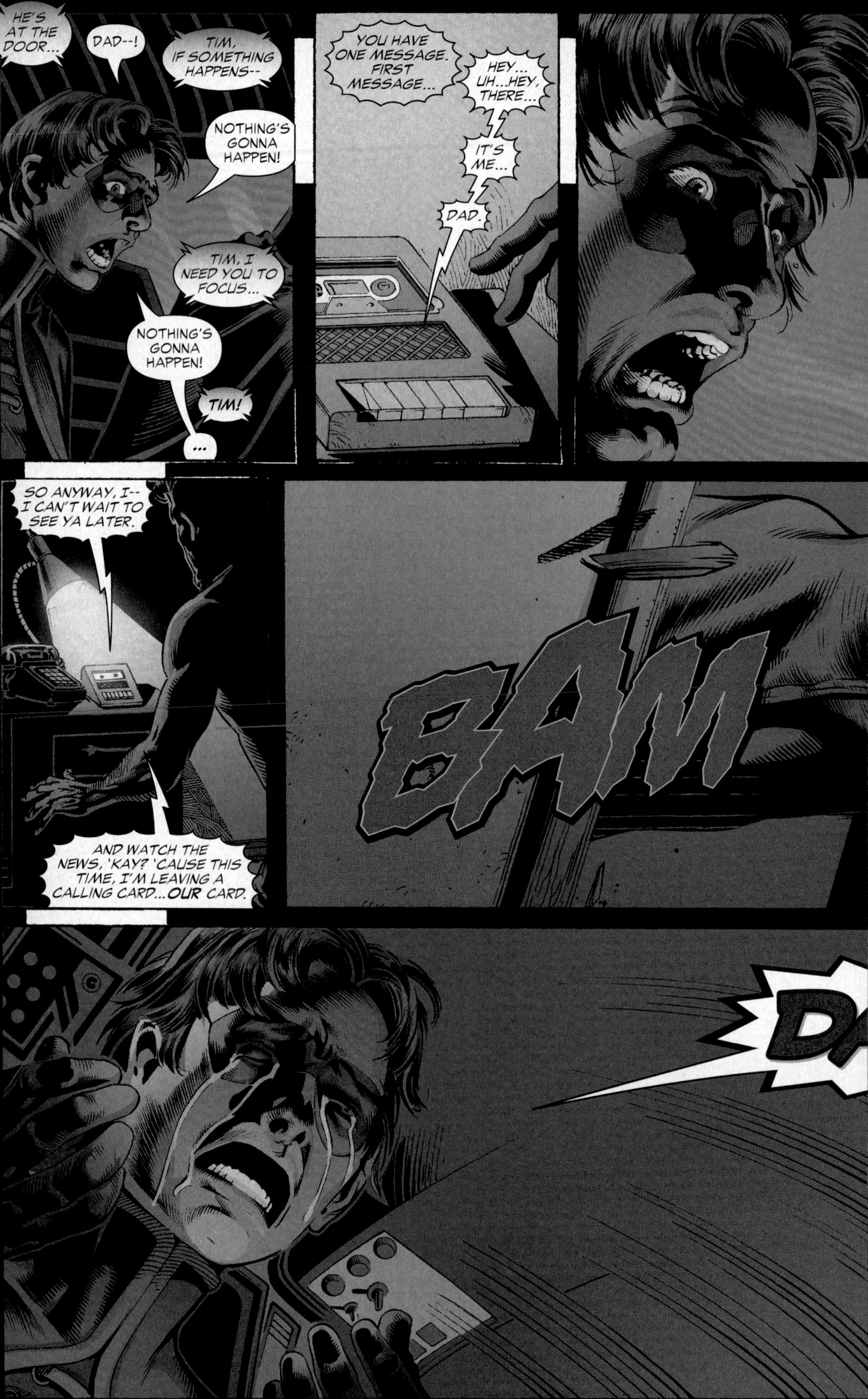

HE'S AT THE DOOR...
DAD--!
TIM, IF SOMETHING HAPPENS--
NOTHING'S GONNA HAPPEN!
TIM, I NEED YOU TO FOCUS...
NOTHING'S GONNA HAPPEN!
TIM!
...
YOU HAVE ONE MESSAGE. FIRST MESSAGE...
HEY... UH...HEY, THERE...
IT'S ME...
DAD.
SO ANYWAY, I-- I CAN'T WAIT TO SEE YA LATER.
AND WATCH THE NEWS, 'KAY? 'CAUSE THIS TIME, I'M LEAVING A CALLING CARD...OUR CARD.
BAM

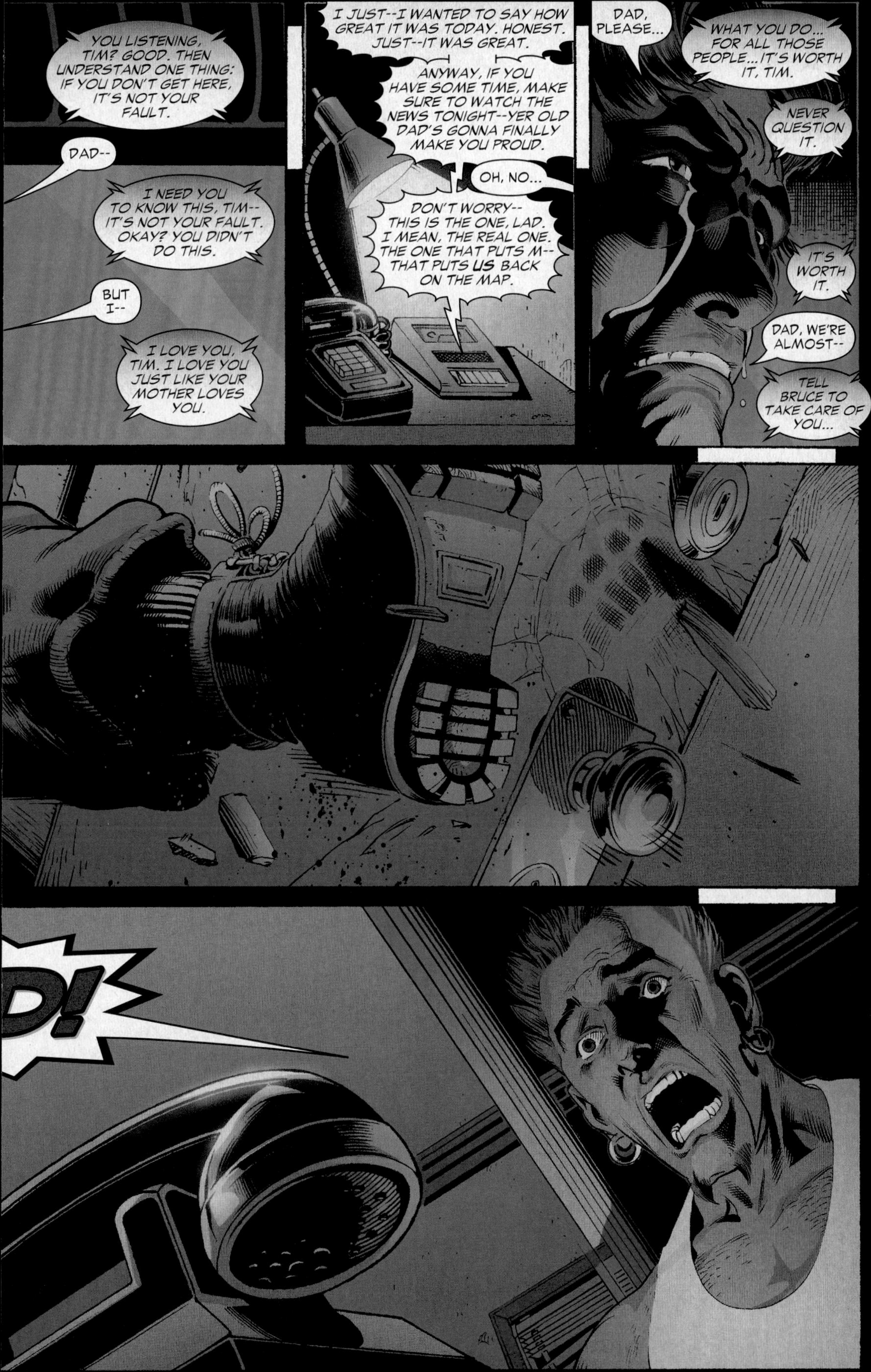
YOU LISTENING, TIM? GOOD. THEN UNDERSTAND ONE THING: IF YOU DON'T GET HERE, IT'S NOT YOUR FAULT.
DAD--
I NEED YOU TO KNOW THIS, TIM-- IT'S NOT YOUR FAULT. OKAY? YOU DIDN'T DO THIS.
BUT I--
I LOVE YOU, TIM. I LOVE YOU JUST LIKE YOUR MOTHER LOVES YOU.
I JUST--I WANTED TO SAY HOW GREAT IT WAS TODAY. HONEST. JUST--IT WAS GREAT.
ANYWAY, IF YOU HAVE SOME TIME, MAKE SURE TO WATCH THE NEWS TONIGHT--YER OLD DAD'S GONNA FINALLY MAKE YOU PROUD.
OH, NO...
DON'T WORRY-- THIS IS THE ONE, LAD. I MEAN, THE REAL ONE. THE ONE THAT PUTS M-- THAT PUTS **US** BACK ON THE MAP.
DAD, PLEASE...
WHAT YOU DO... FOR ALL THOSE PEOPLE... IT'S WORTH IT, TIM.
NEVER QUESTION IT.
IT'S WORTH IT.
DAD, WE'RE ALMOST--
TELL BRUCE TO TAKE CARE OF YOU...
D!

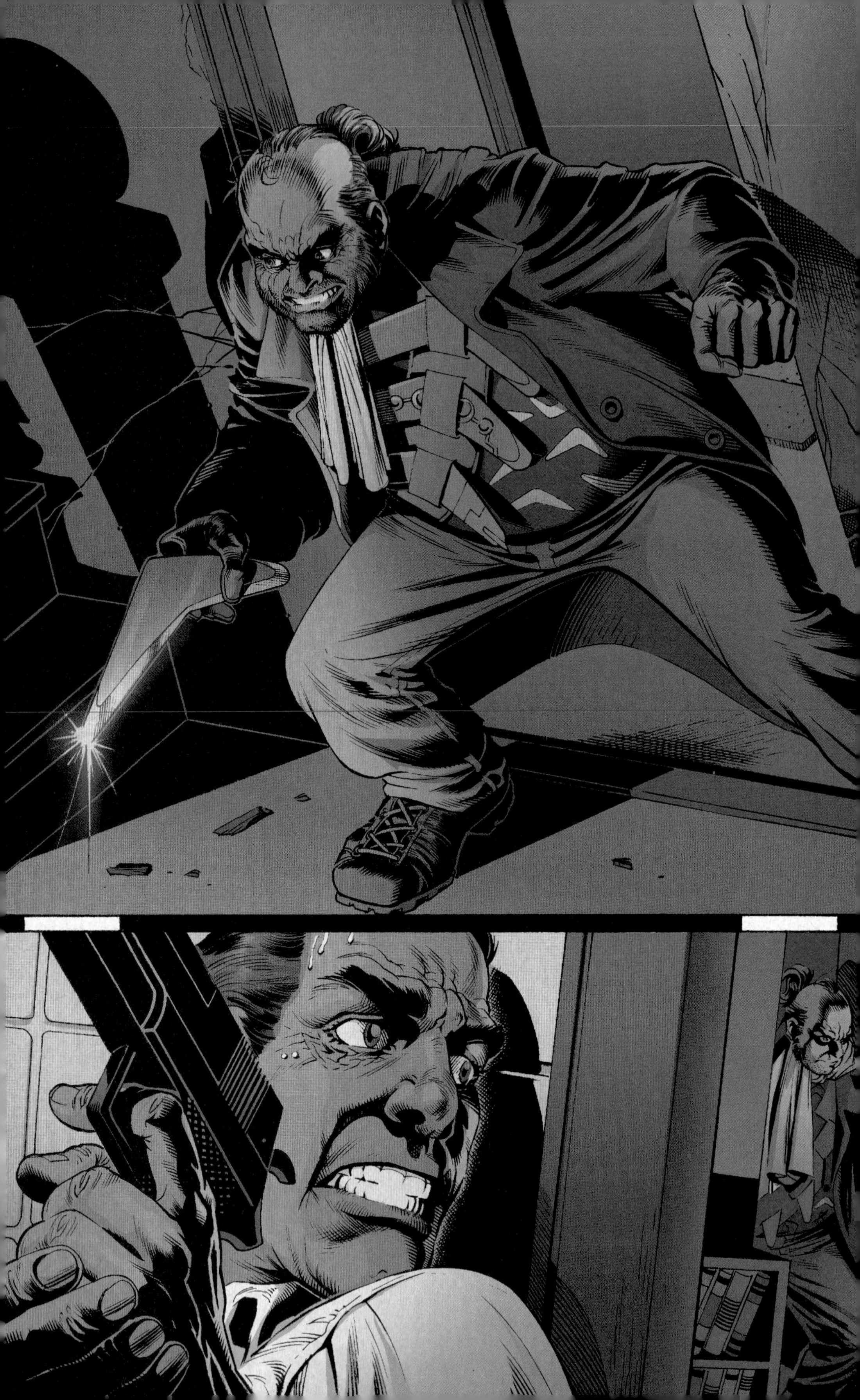

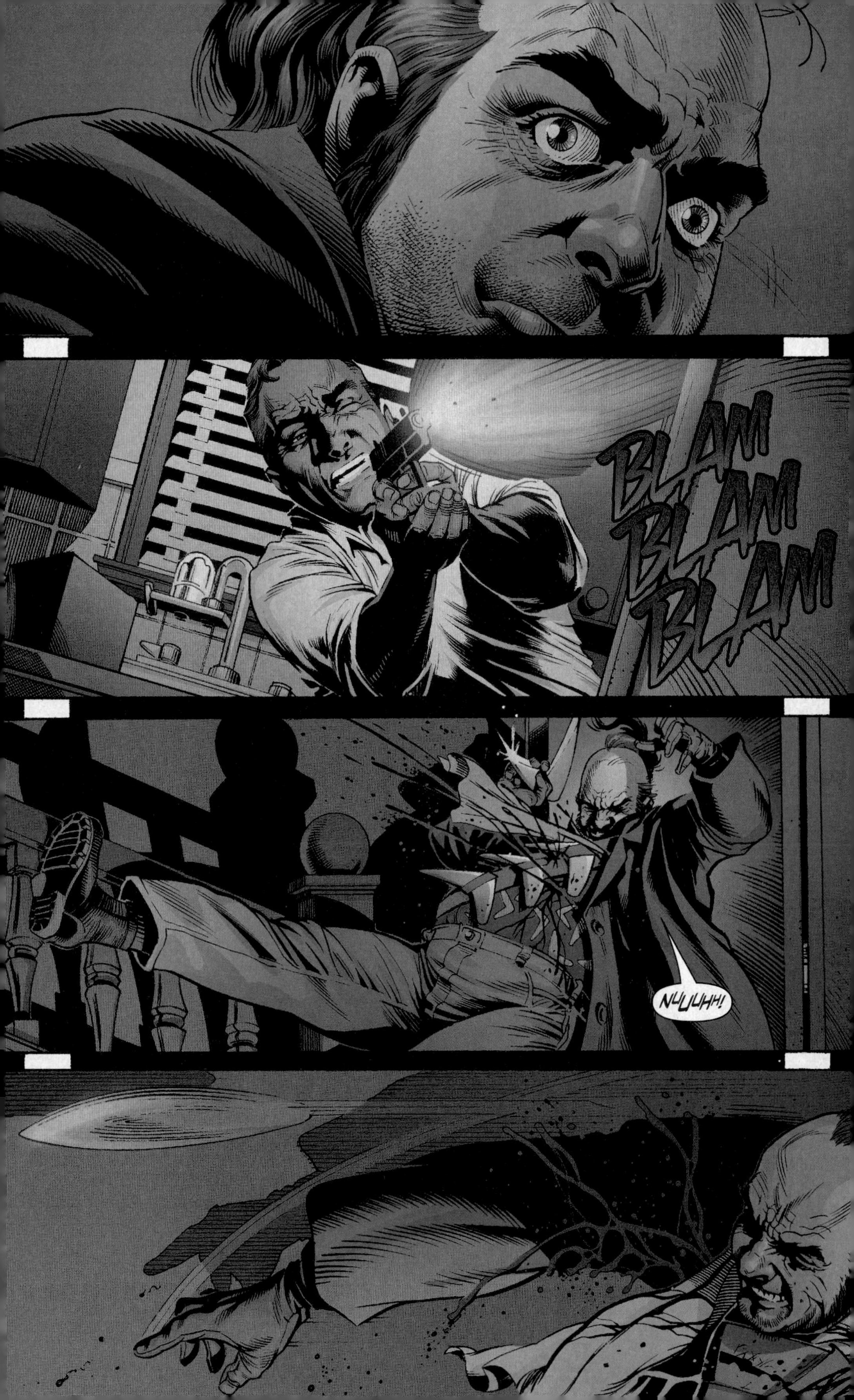
BLAM
BLAM
BLAM
NUUUHH!

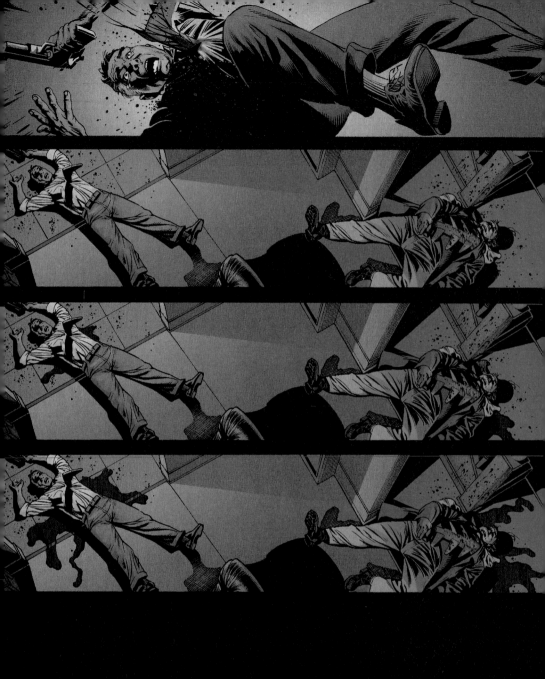

CHAPTER FIVE
FATHER'S DAY

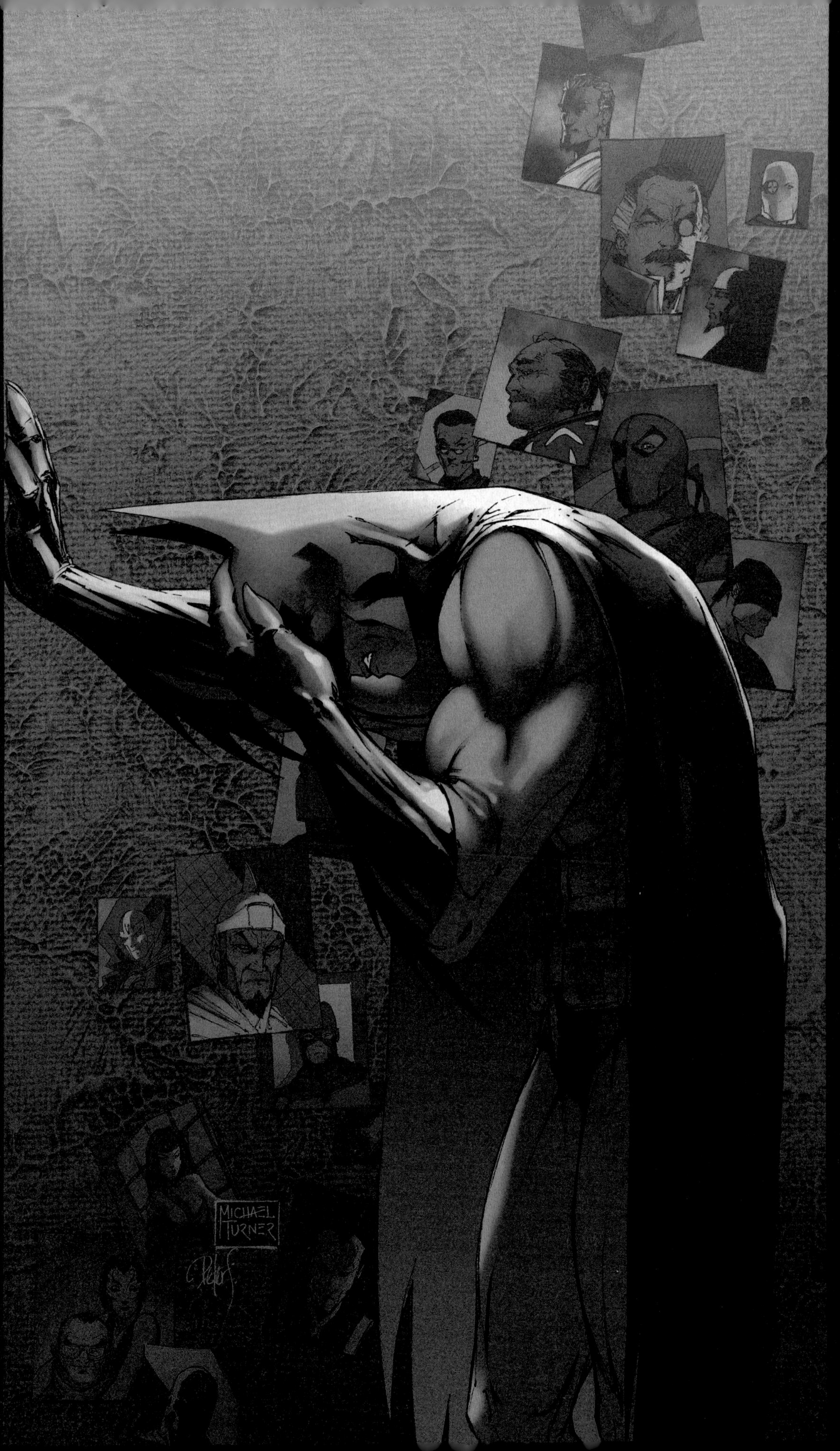
MICHAEL TURNER

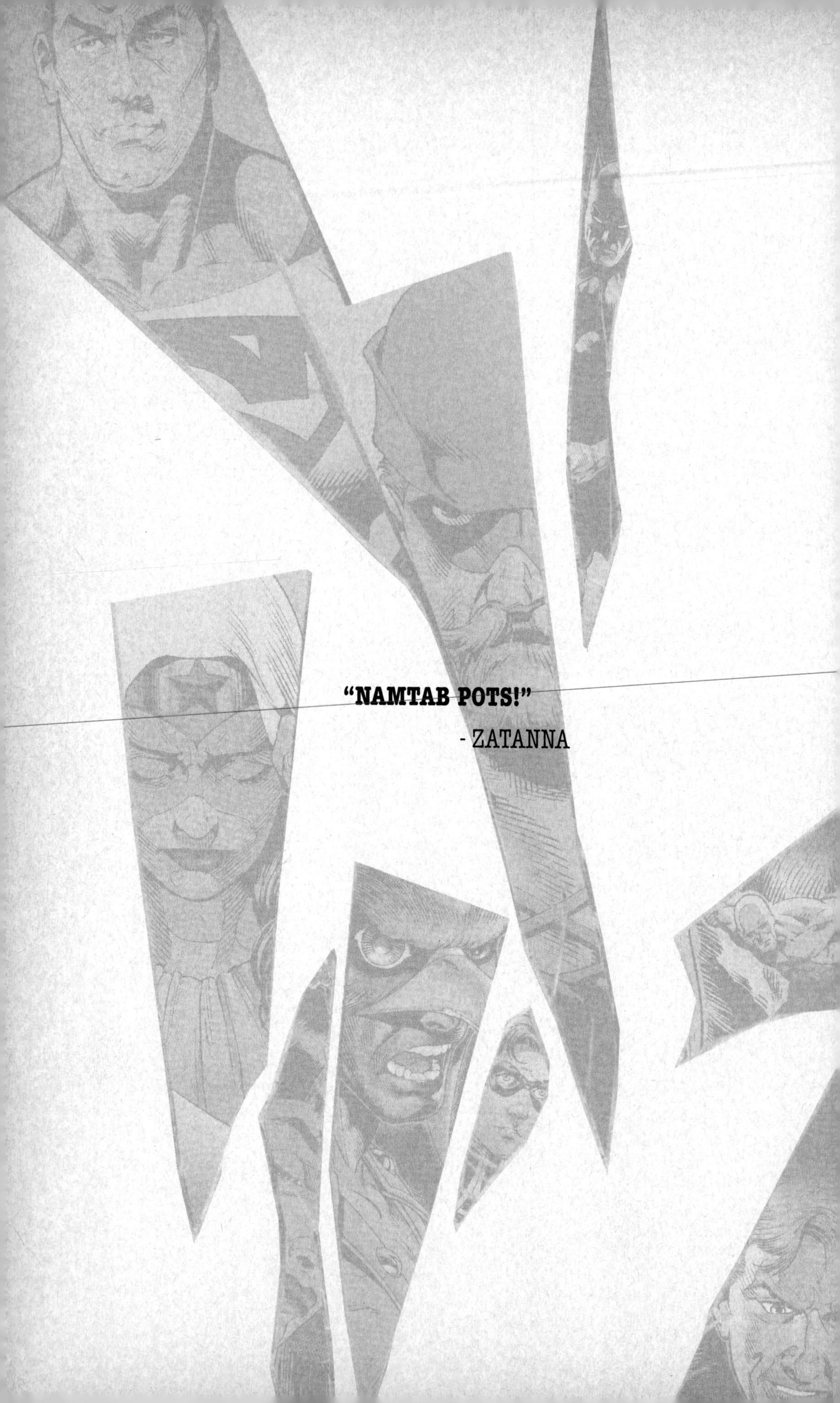

"NAMTAB POTS!"

- ZATANNA

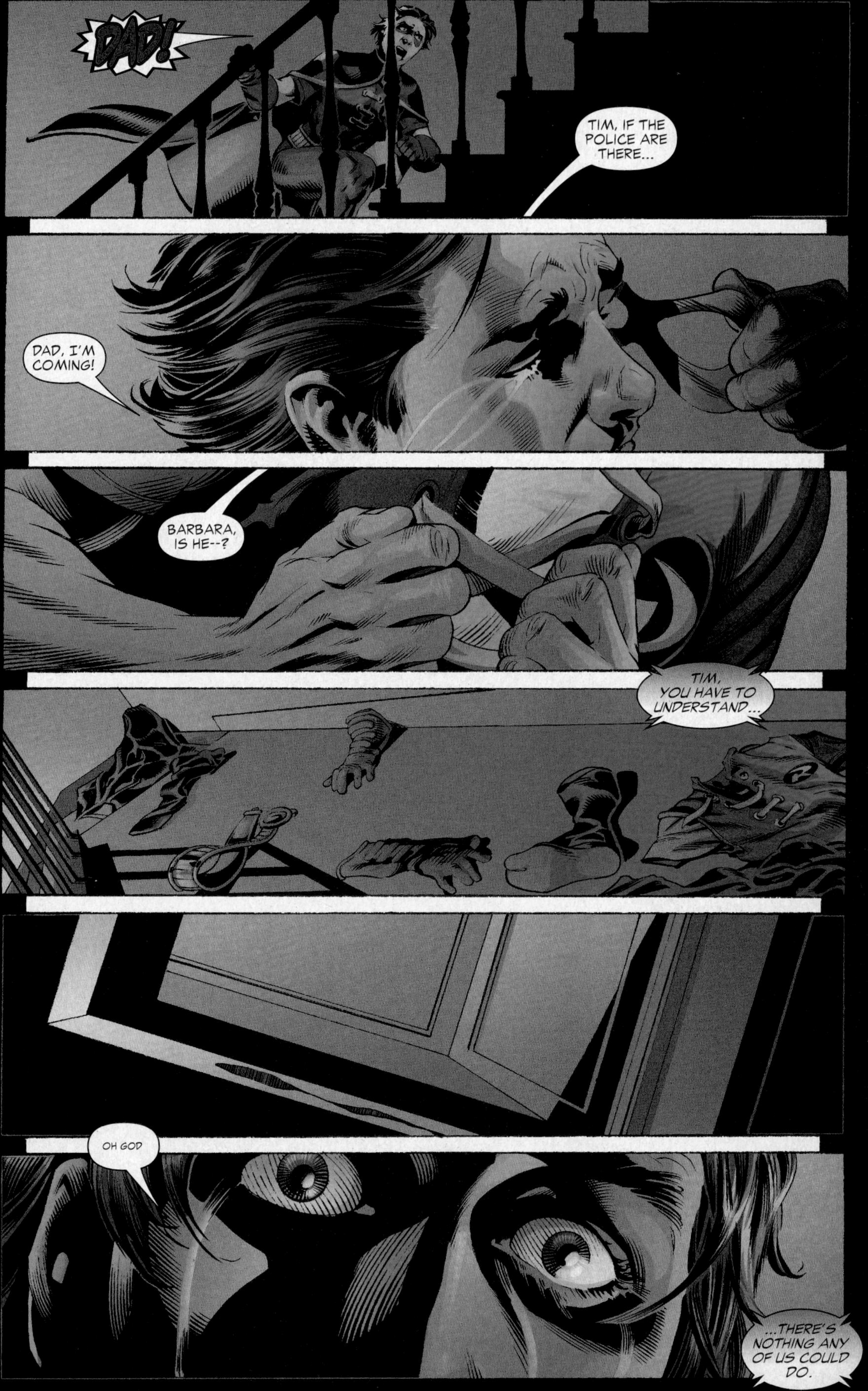
DAD!
TIM, IF THE POLICE ARE THERE...
DAD, I'M COMING!
BARBARA, IS HE--?
TIM, YOU HAVE TO UNDERSTAND...
OH GOD
...THERE'S NOTHING ANY OF US COULD DO.

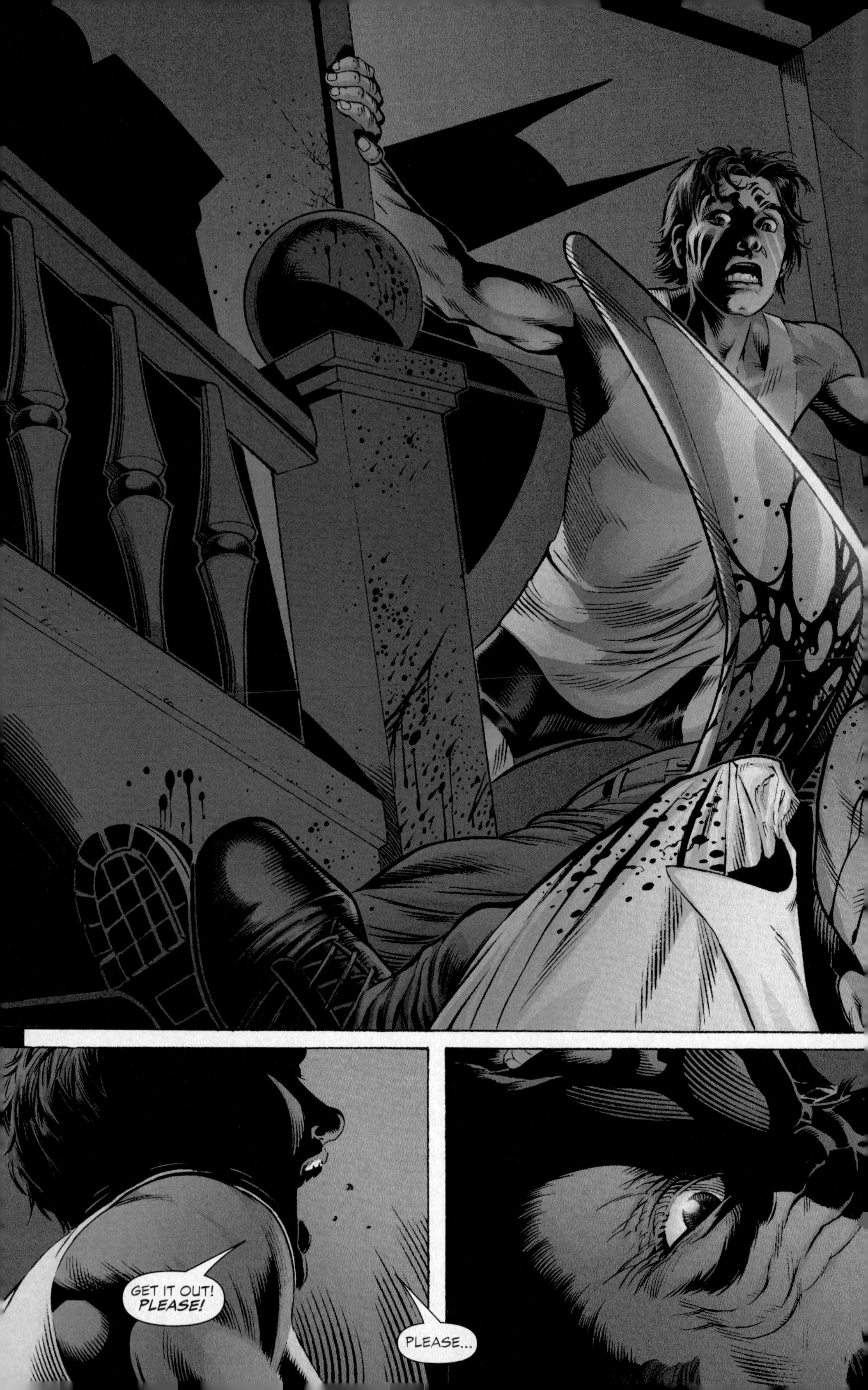
GET IT OUT! PLEASE!
PLEASE...

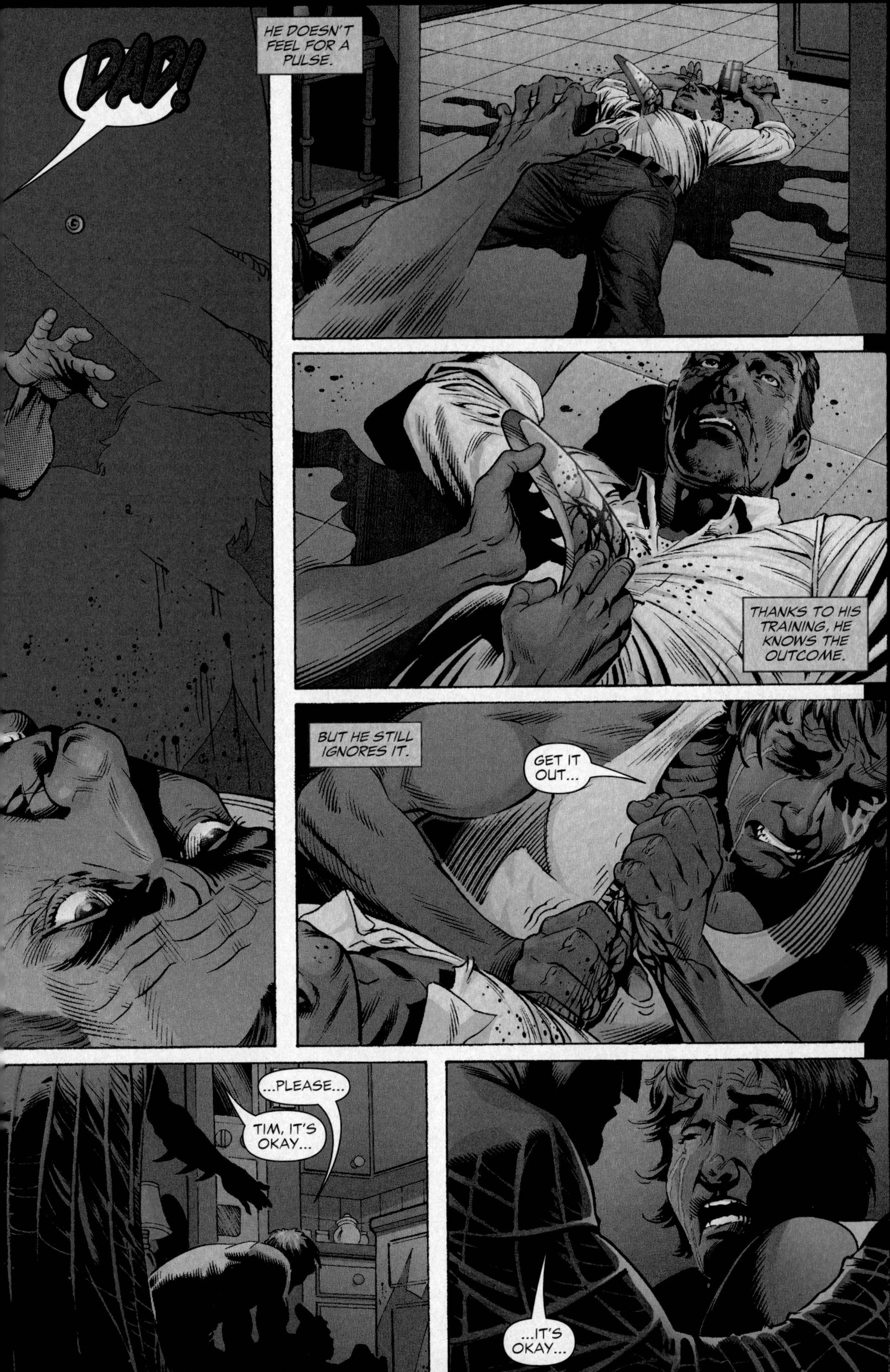
DAD!
HE DOESN'T FEEL FOR A PULSE.
THANKS TO HIS TRAINING, HE KNOWS THE OUTCOME.
BUT HE STILL IGNORES IT.
GET IT OUT...
...PLEASE...
TIM, IT'S OKAY...
...IT'S OKAY...

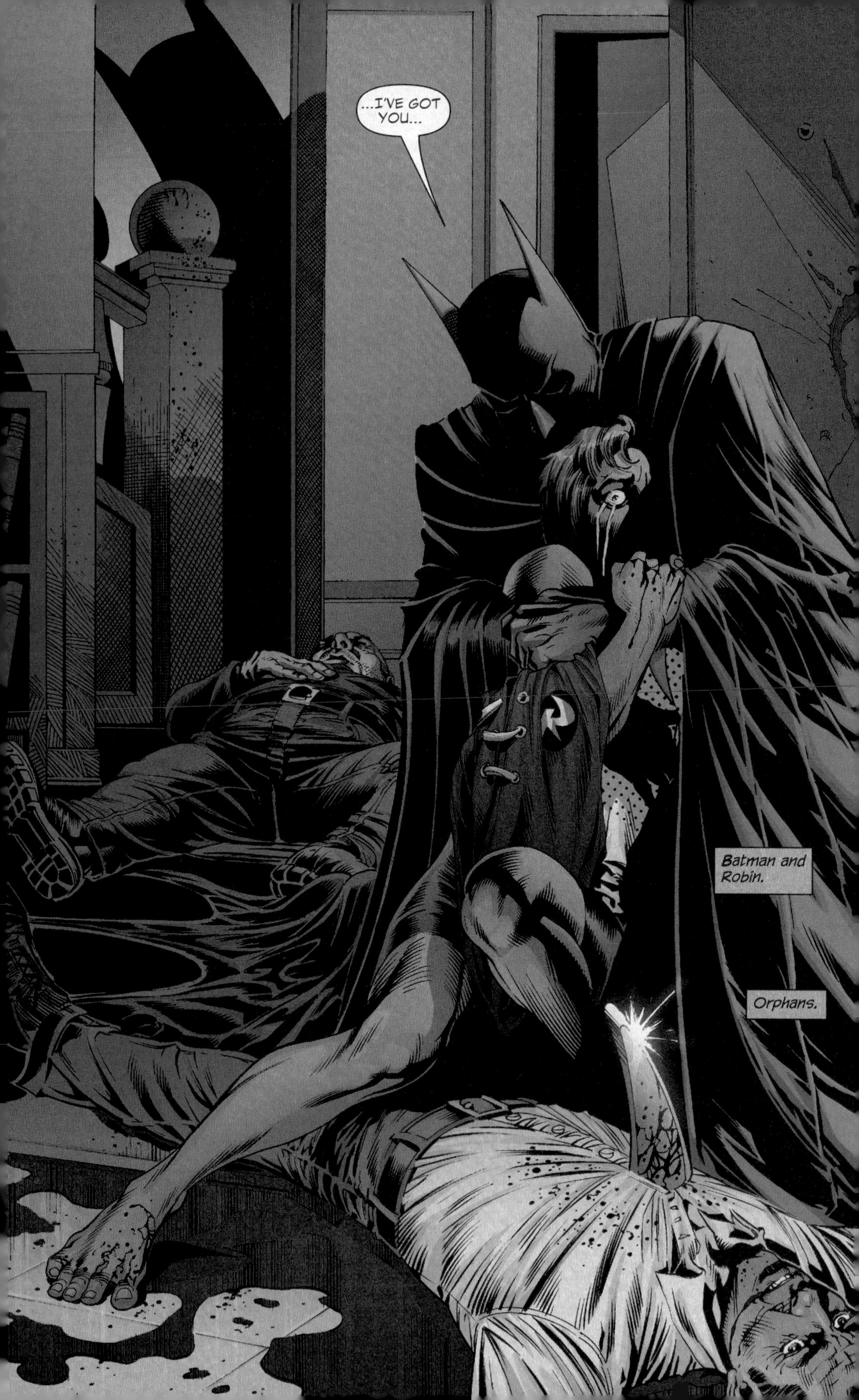
...I'VE GOT YOU...
Batman and Robin.
Orphans.

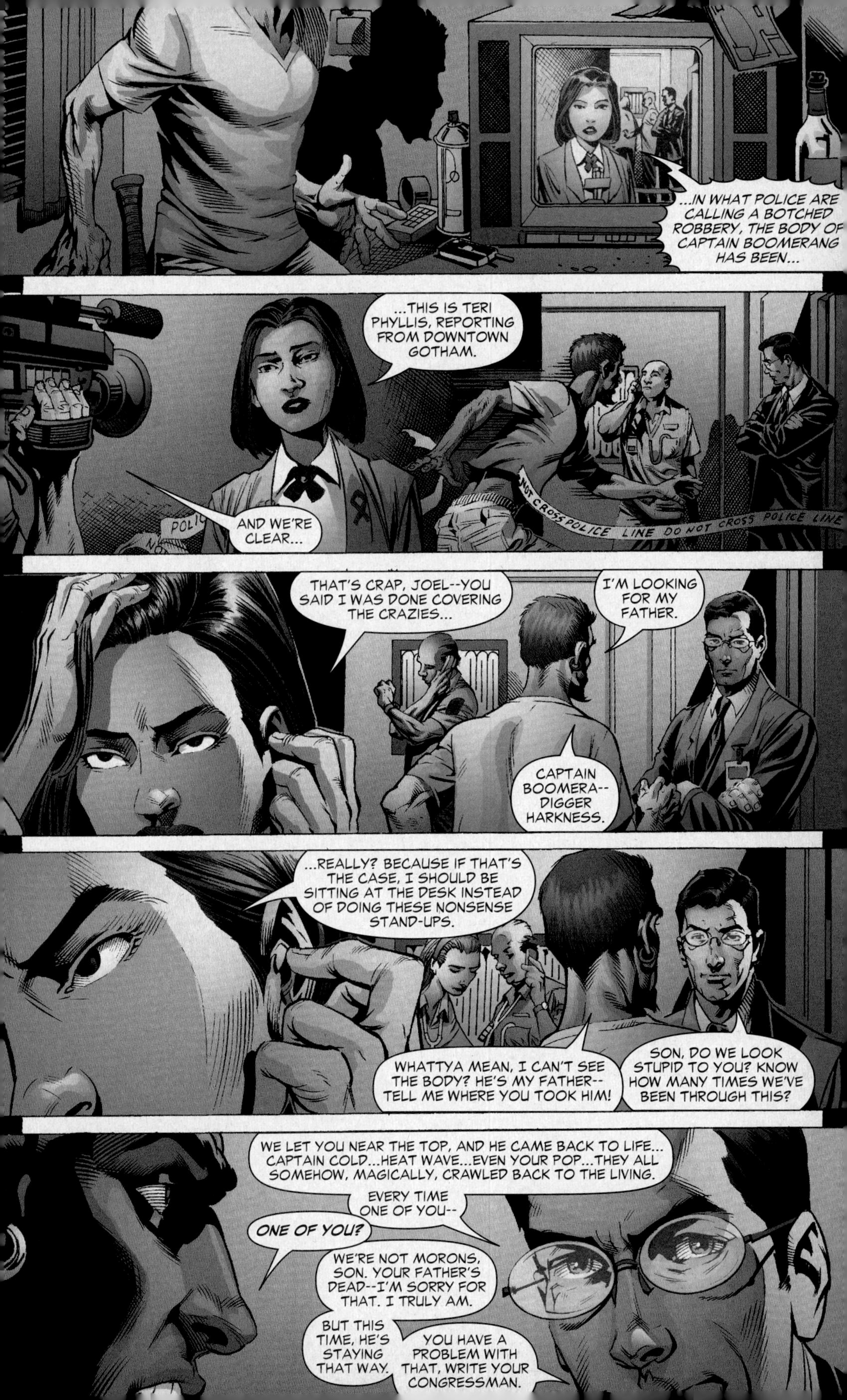
...IN WHAT POLICE ARE CALLING A BOTCHED ROBBERY, THE BODY OF CAPTAIN BOOMERANG HAS BEEN...
...THIS IS TERI PHYLLIS, REPORTING FROM DOWNTOWN GOTHAM.
AND WE'RE CLEAR...
NOT CROSS POLICE LINE DO NOT CROSS POLICE LINE
THAT'S CRAP, JOEL--YOU SAID I WAS DONE COVERING THE CRAZIES...
I'M LOOKING FOR MY FATHER.
CAPTAIN BOOMERA-- DIGGER HARKNESS.
...REALLY? BECAUSE IF THAT'S THE CASE, I SHOULD BE SITTING AT THE DESK INSTEAD OF DOING THESE NONSENSE STAND-UPS.
WHATTYA MEAN, I CAN'T SEE THE BODY? HE'S MY FATHER-- TELL ME WHERE YOU TOOK HIM!
SON, DO WE LOOK STUPID TO YOU? KNOW HOW MANY TIMES WE'VE BEEN THROUGH THIS?
WE LET YOU NEAR THE TOP, AND HE CAME BACK TO LIFE... CAPTAIN COLD...HEAT WAVE...EVEN YOUR POP...THEY ALL SOMEHOW, MAGICALLY, CRAWLED BACK TO THE LIVING.
EVERY TIME ONE OF YOU--
ONE OF YOU?
WE'RE NOT MORONS, SON. YOUR FATHER'S DEAD--I'M SORRY FOR THAT. I TRULY AM.
BUT THIS TIME, HE'S STAYING THAT WAY.
YOU HAVE A PROBLEM WITH THAT, WRITE YOUR CONGRESSMAN.

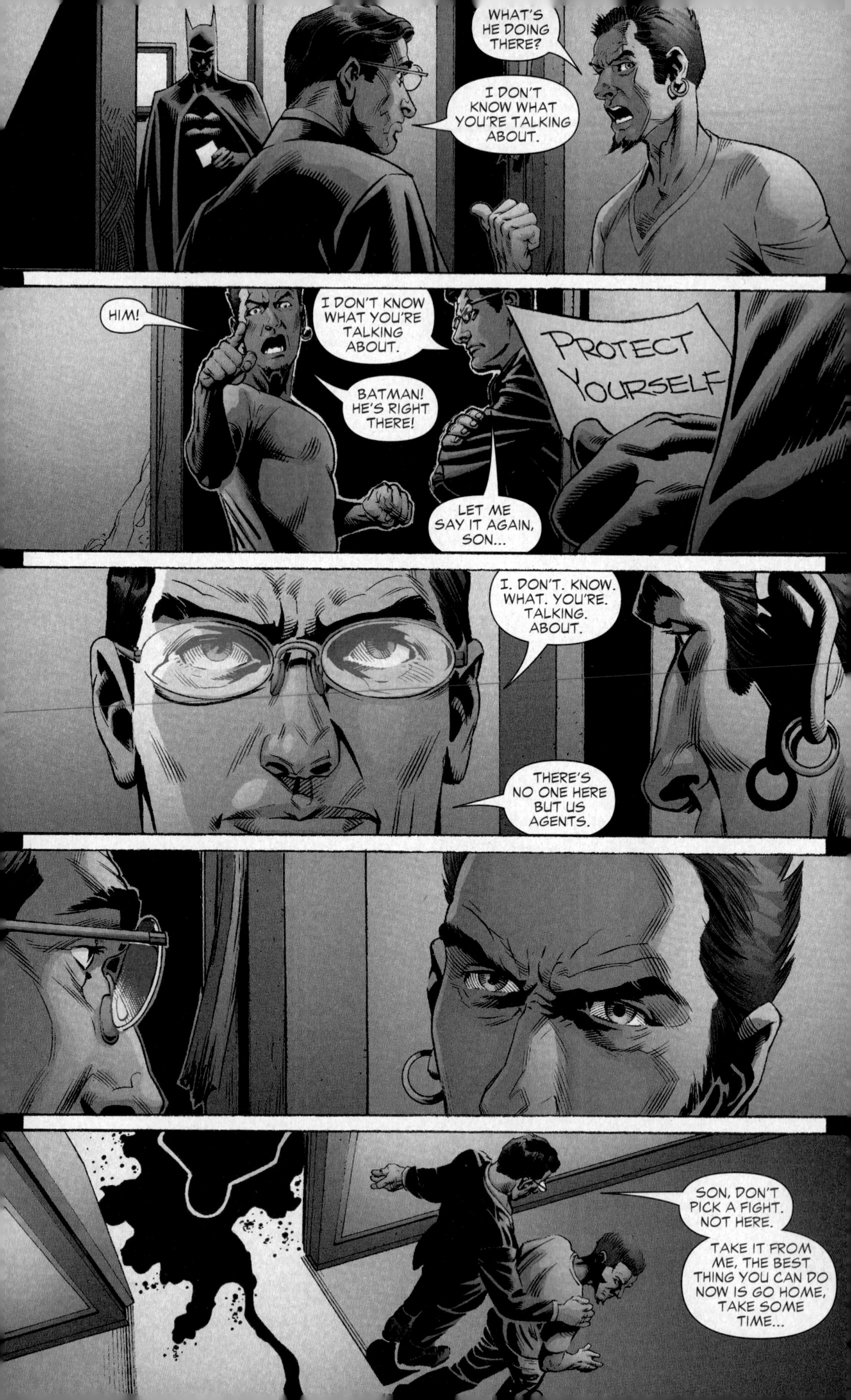
WHAT'S HE DOING THERE?
I DON'T KNOW WHAT YOU'RE TALKING ABOUT.
HIM!
I DON'T KNOW WHAT YOU'RE TALKING ABOUT.
BATMAN! HE'S RIGHT THERE!
PROTECT YOURSELF
LET ME SAY IT AGAIN, SON...
I. DON'T. KNOW. WHAT. YOU'RE. TALKING. ABOUT.
THERE'S NO ONE HERE BUT US AGENTS.
SON, DON'T PICK A FIGHT. NOT HERE.
TAKE IT FROM ME, THE BEST THING YOU CAN DO NOW IS GO HOME, TAKE SOME TIME...

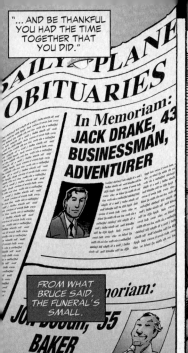

"... AND BE THANKFUL YOU HAD THE TIME TOGETHER THAT YOU DID."

DAILY PLANE OBITUARIES

In Memoriam:
JACK DRAKE, 43
BUSINESSMAN,
ADVENTURER

FROM WHAT BRUCE SAID, THE FUNERAL'S SMALL.

In Memoriam:
JO... DOOR, 55
BAKER

MOST OF US AREN'T INVITED.

CONNOR, COME HERE...

Hot Head

YOU'RE STILL NOT DRESSED? I THOUGHT WE WERE GOING TO TED'S?

He's survived by his son, Ti

NO...NO FIGHTING TODAY.

YOU KNOW HOW MUCH I--?

DAAAD...

JUST DO ME A FAVOR--SHUT UP AND HUG.

BUT THAT DOESN'T MEAN WE DON'T MOURN IN OUR OWN WAYS.

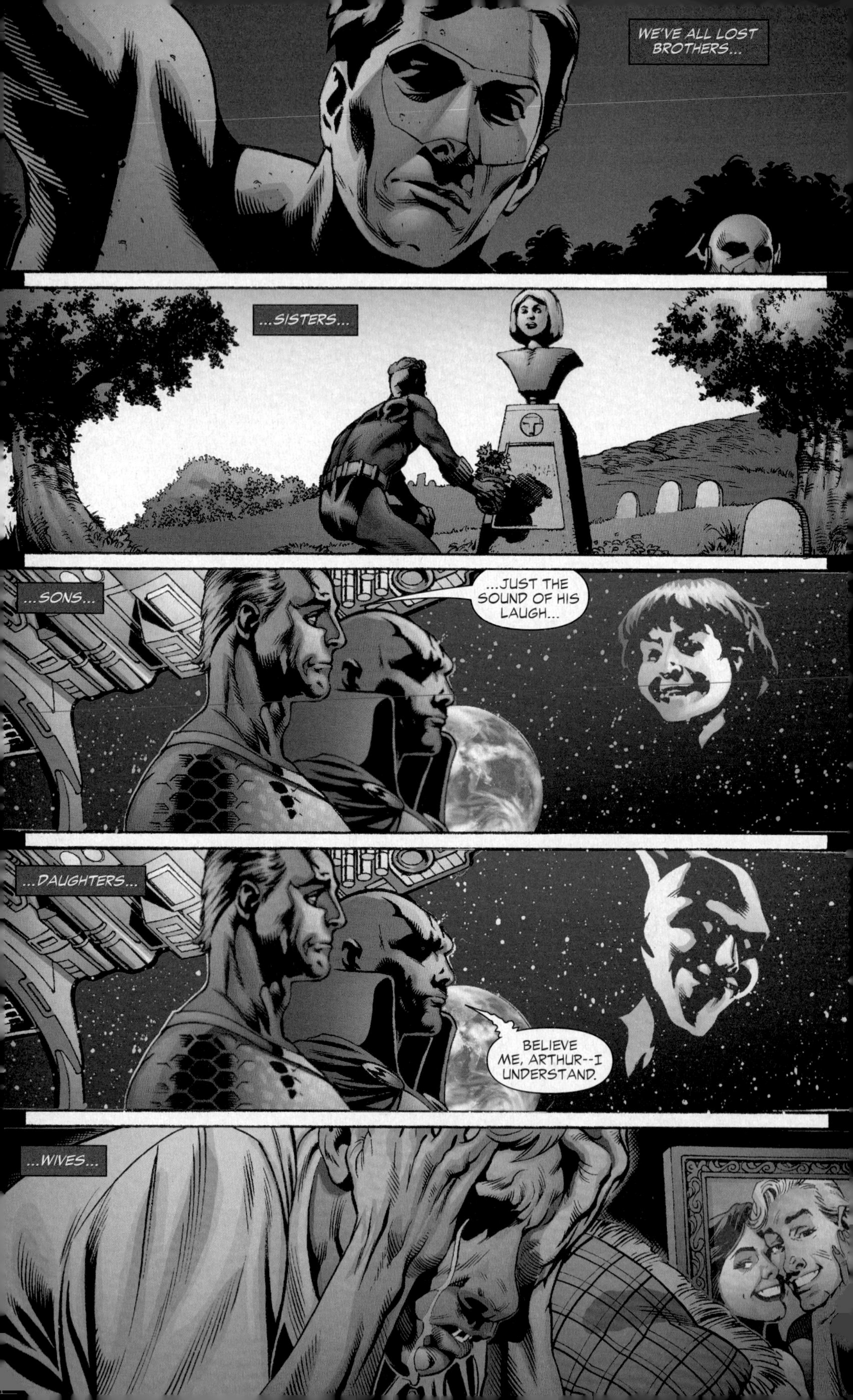
WE'VE ALL LOST BROTHERS...
...SISTERS...
...SONS...
...JUST THE SOUND OF HIS LAUGH...
...DAUGHTERS...
BELIEVE ME, ARTHUR--I UNDERSTAND.
...WIVES...

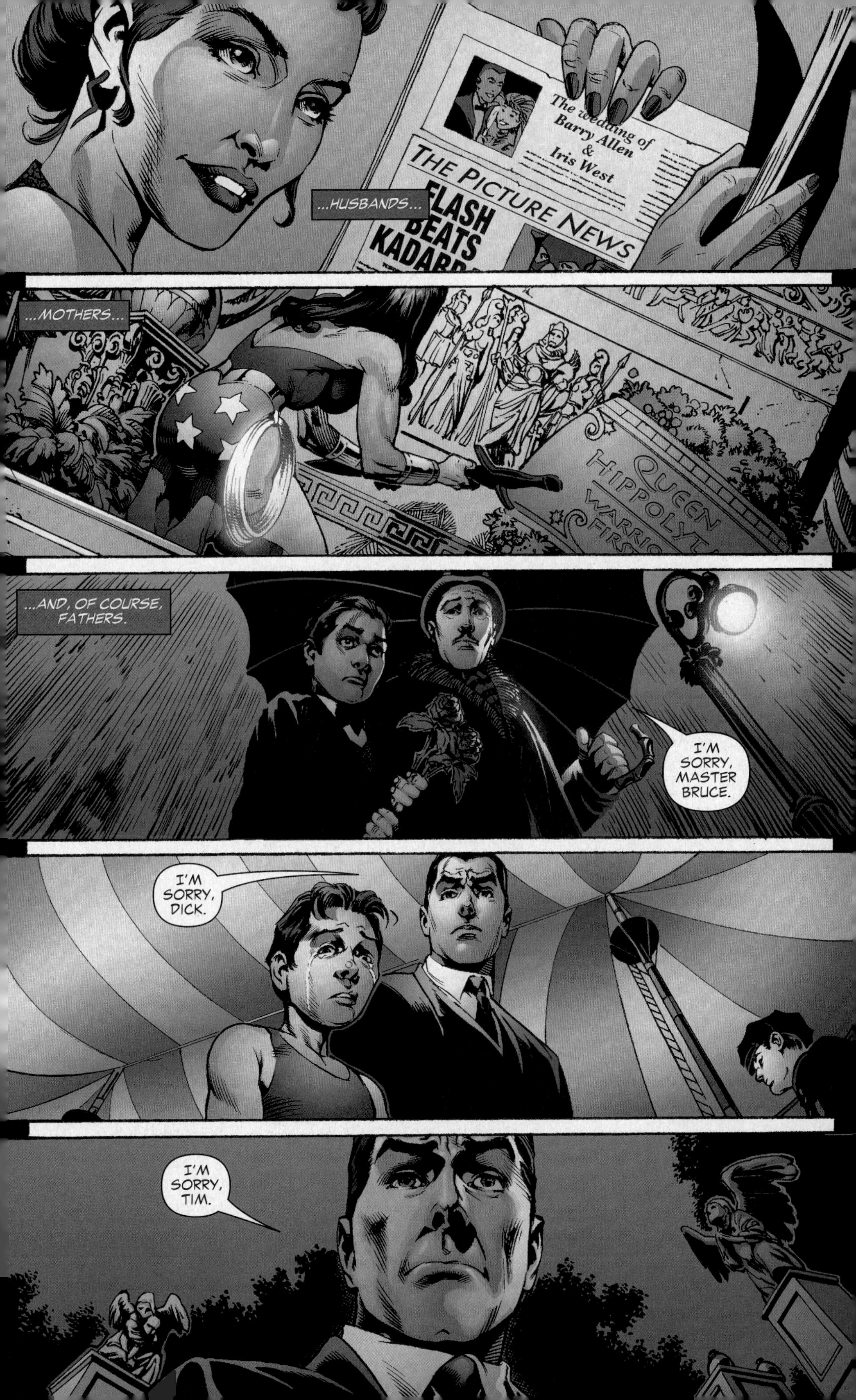
The wedding of Barry Allen & Iris West
THE PICTURE NEWS
FLASH BEATS KADARB
...HUSBANDS...
...MOTHERS...
QUEEN HIPPOLYT
WARRIO
FIRST
...AND, OF COURSE, FATHERS.
I'M SORRY, MASTER BRUCE.
I'M SORRY, DICK.
I'M SORRY, TIM.

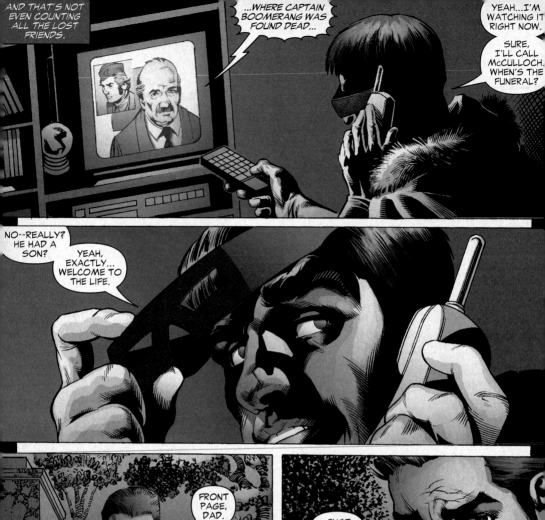

AND THAT'S NOT EVEN COUNTING ALL THE LOST FRIENDS.

...WHERE CAPTAIN BOOMERANG WAS FOUND DEAD...

YEAH...I'M WATCHING IT RIGHT NOW.

SURE, I'LL CALL McCULLOCH. WHEN'S THE FUNERAL?

NO--REALLY? HE HAD A SON?

YEAH, EXACTLY... WELCOME TO THE LIFE.

FRONT PAGE, DAD.

JUST LIKE YOU WANTED.

DIGGER HARKNESS FATHER

Gotham Gazette
CARLINI FAMILY RAIDED

tham Gazette
Captain Boomerang dead in robbe

THE ONLY GOOD NEWS IS, WITH BOOMERANG DEAD, WE DON'T HAVE TO WORRY ABOUT HIM PASSING ALONG OUR PERSONAL DETAILS TO WHATEVER LUNATIC IS SHARING HIS CELL.

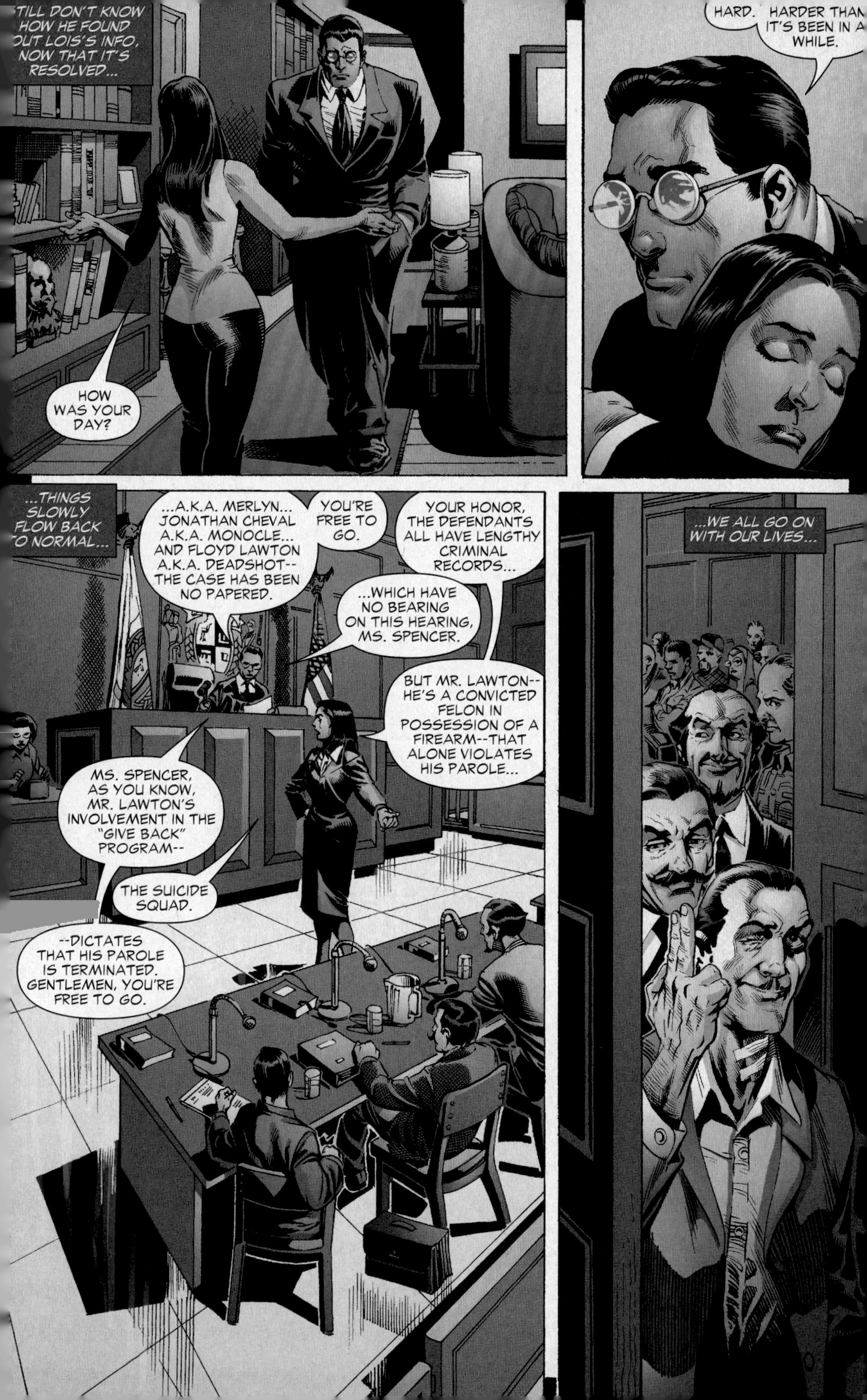
STILL DON'T KNOW HOW HE FOUND OUT LOIS'S INFO, NOW THAT IT'S RESOLVED...
HOW WAS YOUR DAY?
HARD. HARDER THAN IT'S BEEN IN A WHILE.
...THINGS SLOWLY FLOW BACK TO NORMAL...
...A.K.A. MERLYN... JONATHAN CHEVAL A.K.A. MONOCLE... AND FLOYD LAWTON A.K.A. DEADSHOT-- THE CASE HAS BEEN NO PAPERED.
YOU'RE FREE TO GO.
YOUR HONOR, THE DEFENDANTS ALL HAVE LENGTHY CRIMINAL RECORDS...
...WHICH HAVE NO BEARING ON THIS HEARING, MS. SPENCER.
BUT MR. LAWTON-- HE'S A CONVICTED FELON IN POSSESSION OF A FIREARM--THAT ALONE VIOLATES HIS PAROLE...
MS. SPENCER, AS YOU KNOW, MR. LAWTON'S INVOLVEMENT IN THE "GIVE BACK" PROGRAM--
THE SUICIDE SQUAD.
--DICTATES THAT HIS PAROLE IS TERMINATED. GENTLEMEN, YOU'RE FREE TO GO.
...WE ALL GO ON WITH OUR LIVES...

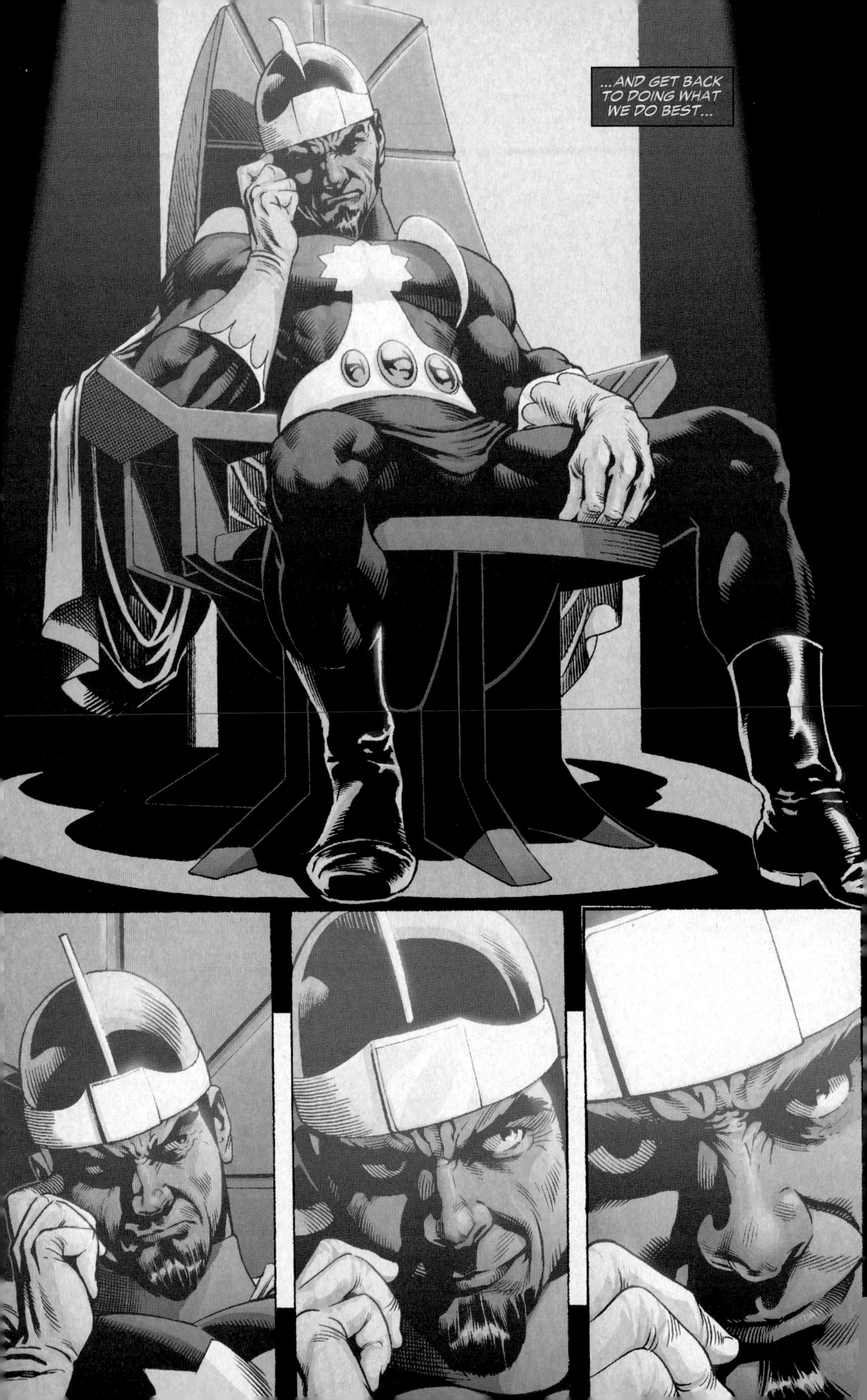
...AND GET BACK TO DOING WHAT WE DO BEST...

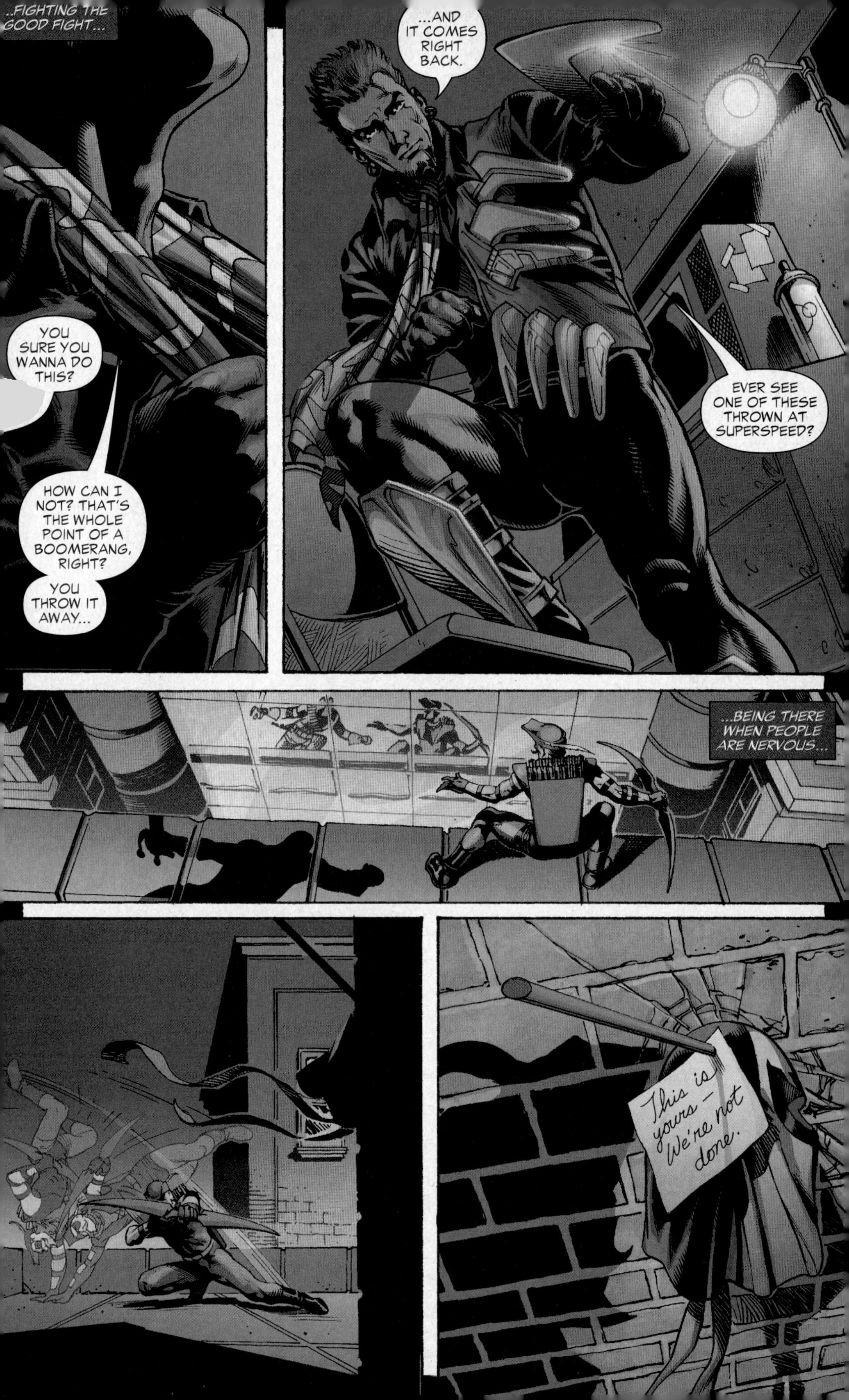
...FIGHTING THE GOOD FIGHT...
YOU SURE YOU WANNA DO THIS?
HOW CAN I NOT? THAT'S THE WHOLE POINT OF A BOOMERANG, RIGHT?
YOU THROW IT AWAY...
...AND IT COMES RIGHT BACK.
EVER SEE ONE OF THESE THROWN AT SUPERSPEED?
...BEING THERE WHEN PEOPLE ARE NERVOUS...
This is yours— We're not done.

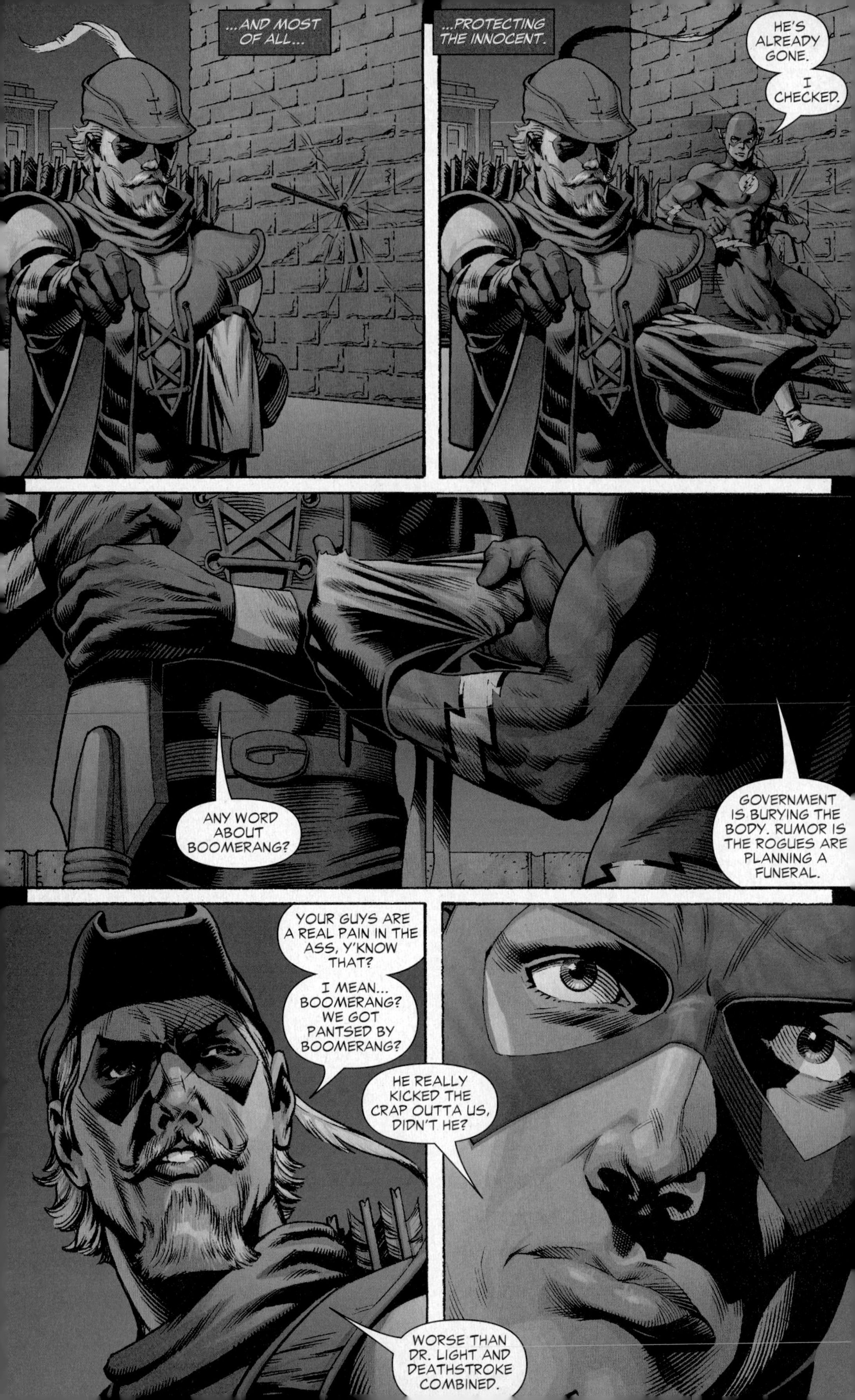
...AND MOST OF ALL...
...PROTECTING THE INNOCENT.
HE'S ALREADY GONE.
I CHECKED.
ANY WORD ABOUT BOOMERANG?
GOVERNMENT IS BURYING THE BODY. RUMOR IS THE ROGUES ARE PLANNING A FUNERAL.
YOUR GUYS ARE A REAL PAIN IN THE ASS, Y'KNOW THAT?
I MEAN... BOOMERANG? WE GOT PANTSED BY BOOMERANG?
HE REALLY KICKED THE CRAP OUTTA US, DIDN'T HE?
WORSE THAN DR. LIGHT AND DEATHSTROKE COMBINED.

YEAH...

THE KID RAN ALL THE WAY HERE.

HE'S A WORSE LIAR THAN HIS UNCLE.

WHAT'RE YOU REALLY HERE FOR, WALLY?

"NOTHING. IT'S JUST..."

DR. ARTHUR LIGHT

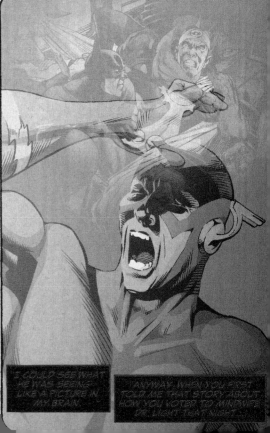

"WHEN WE HAD THAT FIGHT WITH DR. LIGHT AND DEATHSTROKE... AND ALL LIGHT'S MEMORIES FLOODED BACK..."

"I COULD SEE WHAT HE WAS SEEING... LIKE A PICTURE IN MY BRAIN."

"ANYWAY, WHEN YOU FIRST TOLD ME THAT STORY ABOUT HOW YOU VOTED TO MINDWIPE DR. LIGHT THAT NIGHT..."

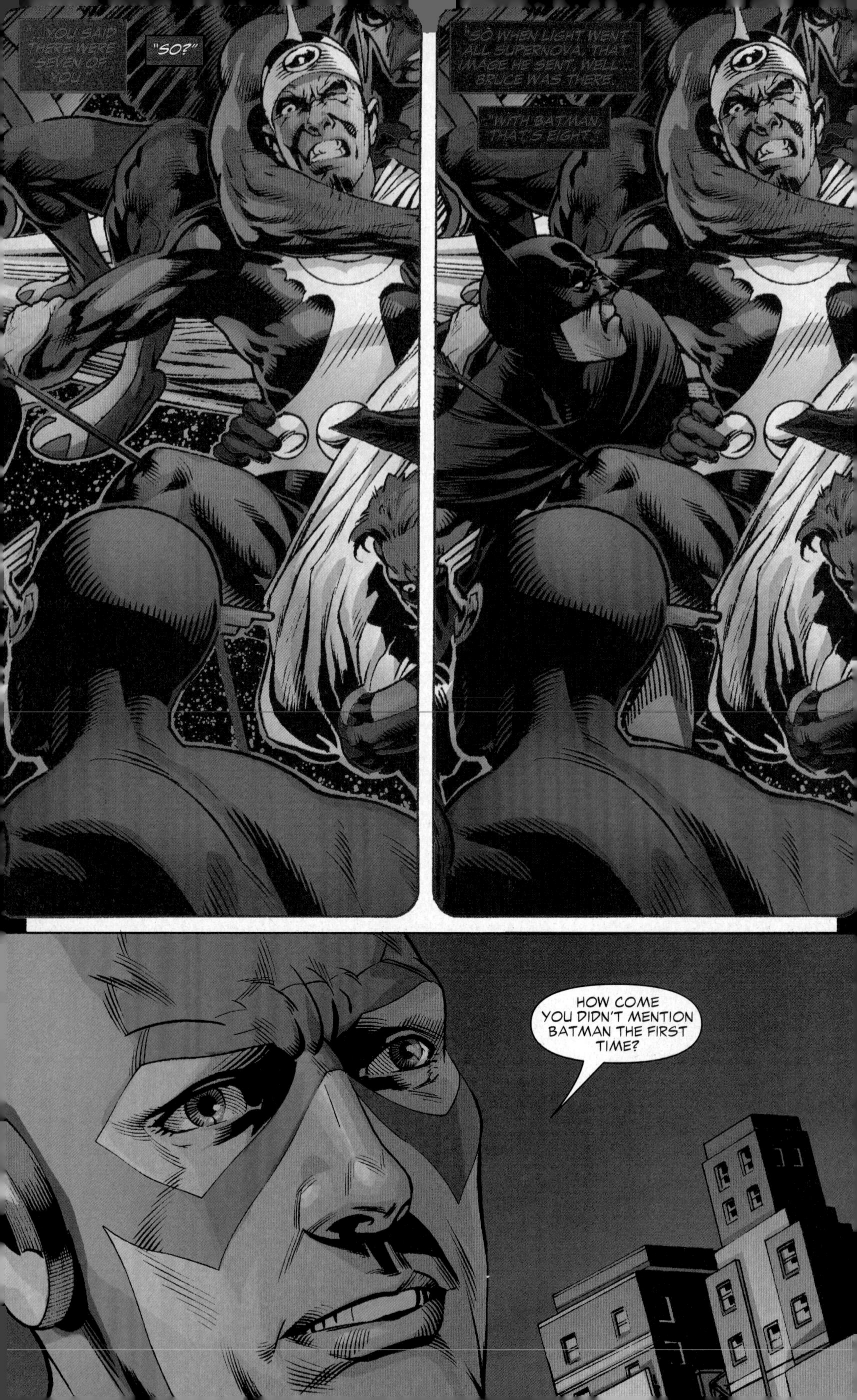
"...YOU SAID THERE WERE SEVEN OF YOU."
"SO?"
"SO WHEN LIGHT WENT ALL SUPERNOVA, THAT IMAGE HE SENT, WELL... BRUCE WAS THERE.
"WITH BATMAN, THAT'S EIGHT."
HOW COME YOU DIDN'T MENTION BATMAN THE FIRST TIME?

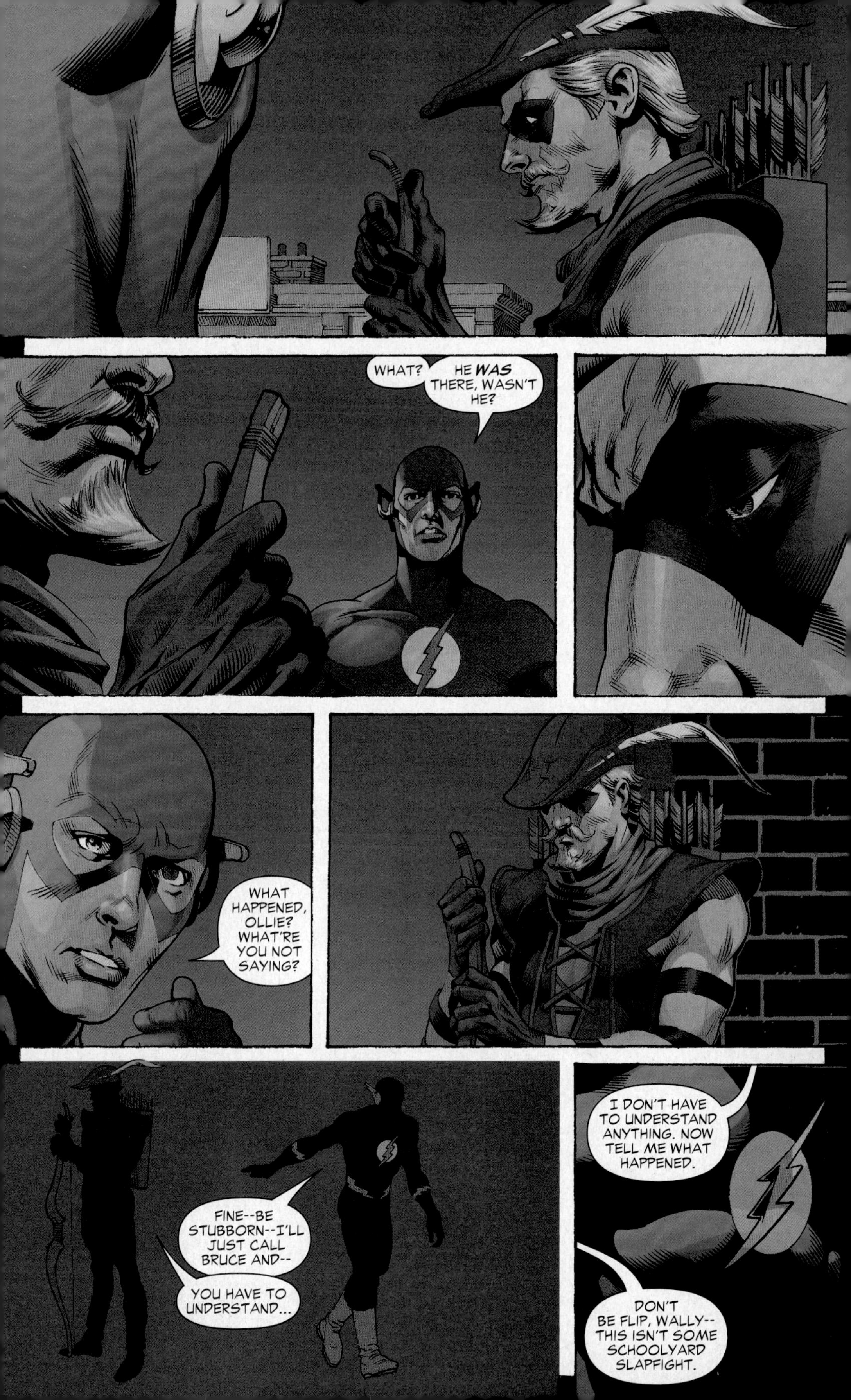
WHAT?
HE WAS THERE, WASN'T HE?
WHAT HAPPENED, OLLIE? WHAT'RE YOU NOT SAYING?
FINE--BE STUBBORN--I'LL JUST CALL BRUCE AND--
YOU HAVE TO UNDERSTAND...
I DON'T HAVE TO UNDERSTAND ANYTHING. NOW TELL ME WHAT HAPPENED.
DON'T BE FLIP, WALLY-- THIS ISN'T SOME SCHOOLYARD SLAPFIGHT.

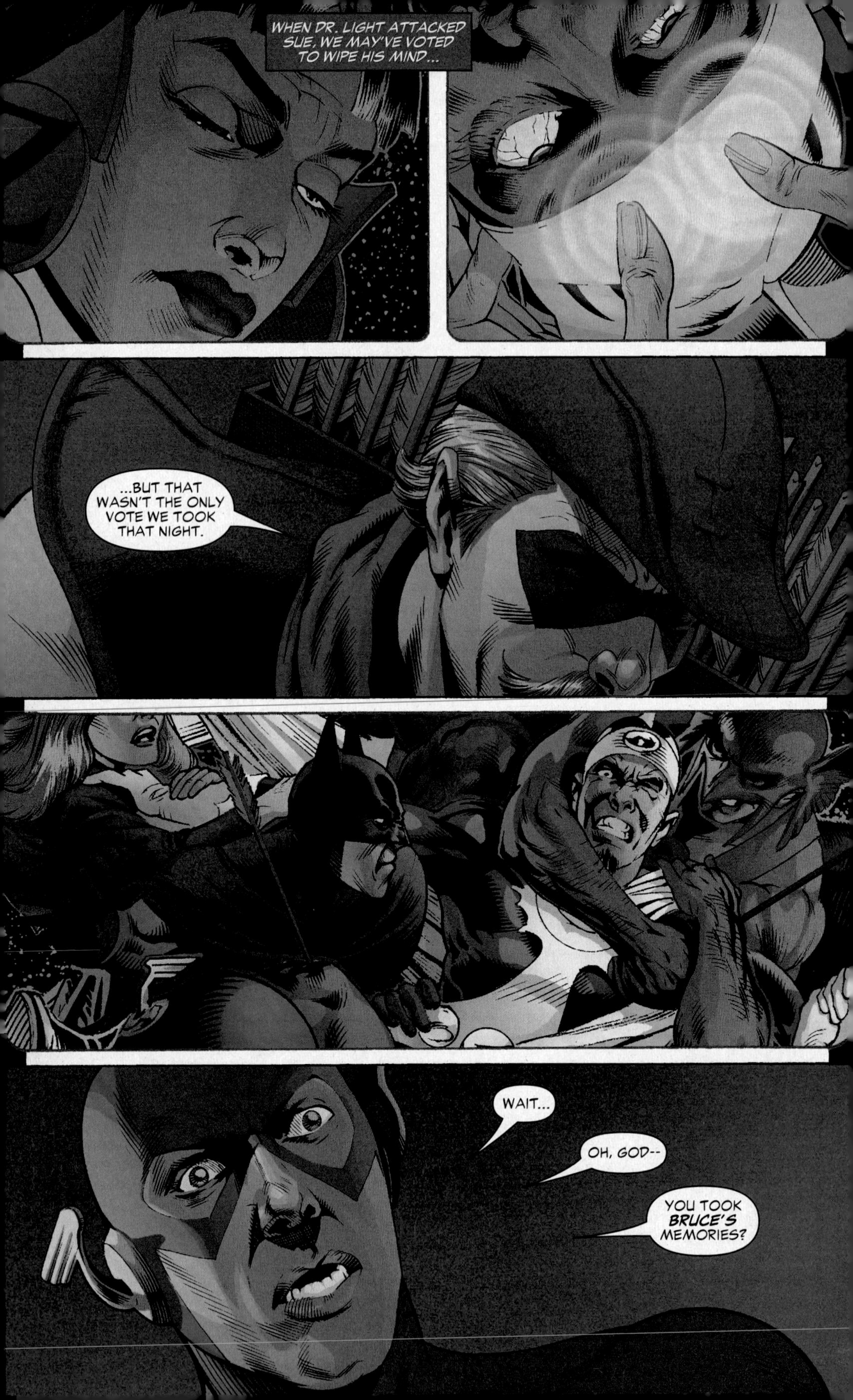
WHEN DR. LIGHT ATTACKED SUE, WE MAY'VE VOTED TO WIPE HIS MIND...
...BUT THAT WASN'T THE ONLY VOTE WE TOOK THAT NIGHT.
WAIT...
OH, GOD--
YOU TOOK BRUCE'S MEMORIES?

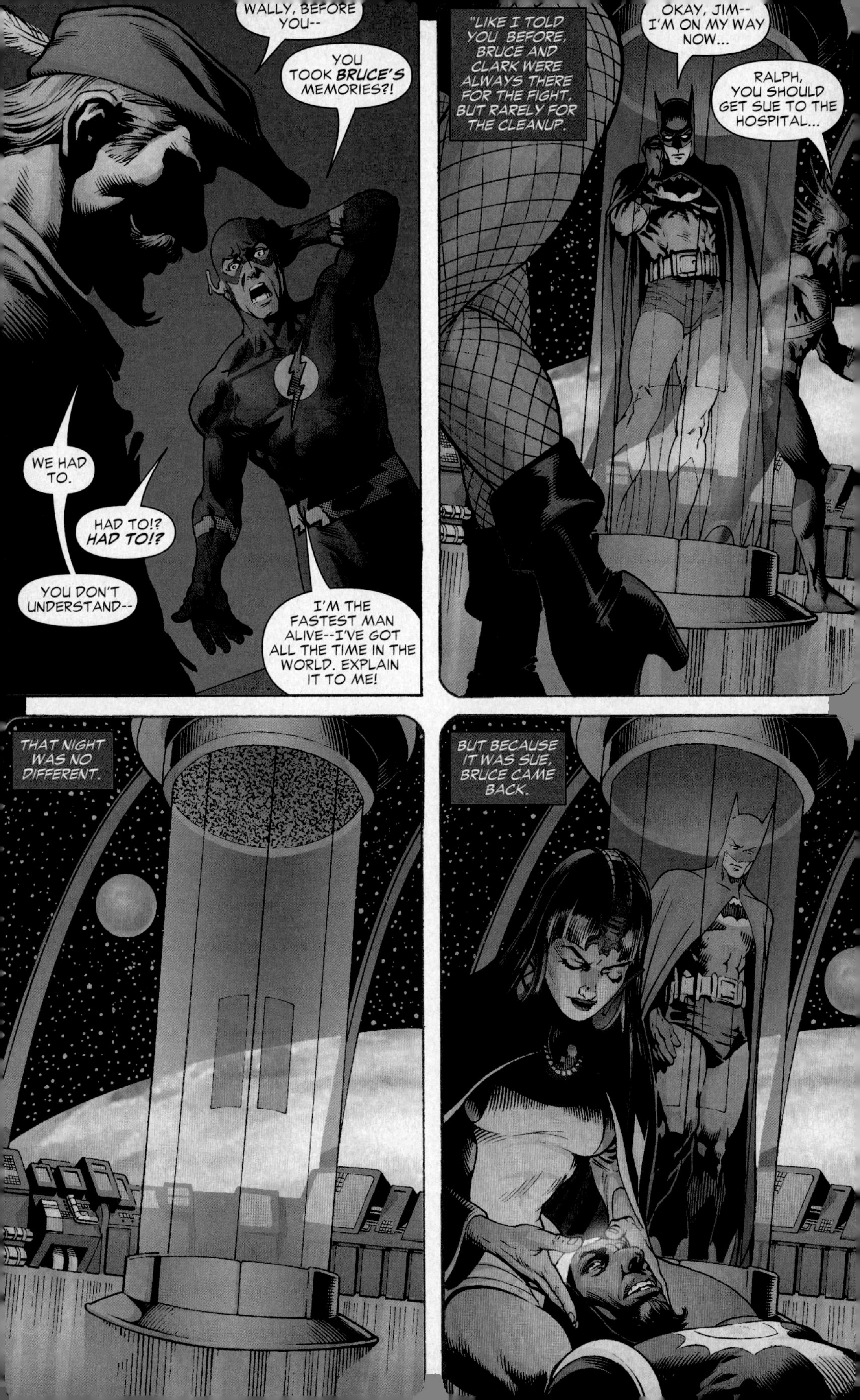
WALLY, BEFORE YOU--
YOU TOOK BRUCE'S MEMORIES?!
WE HAD TO.
HAD TO!? HAD TO!?
YOU DON'T UNDERSTAND--
I'M THE FASTEST MAN ALIVE--I'VE GOT ALL THE TIME IN THE WORLD. EXPLAIN IT TO ME!
"LIKE I TOLD YOU BEFORE, BRUCE AND CLARK WERE ALWAYS THERE FOR THE FIGHT, BUT RARELY FOR THE CLEANUP.
OKAY, JIM-- I'M ON MY WAY NOW...
RALPH, YOU SHOULD GET SUE TO THE HOSPITAL...
THAT NIGHT WAS NO DIFFERENT.
BUT BECAUSE IT WAS SUE, BRUCE CAME BACK.

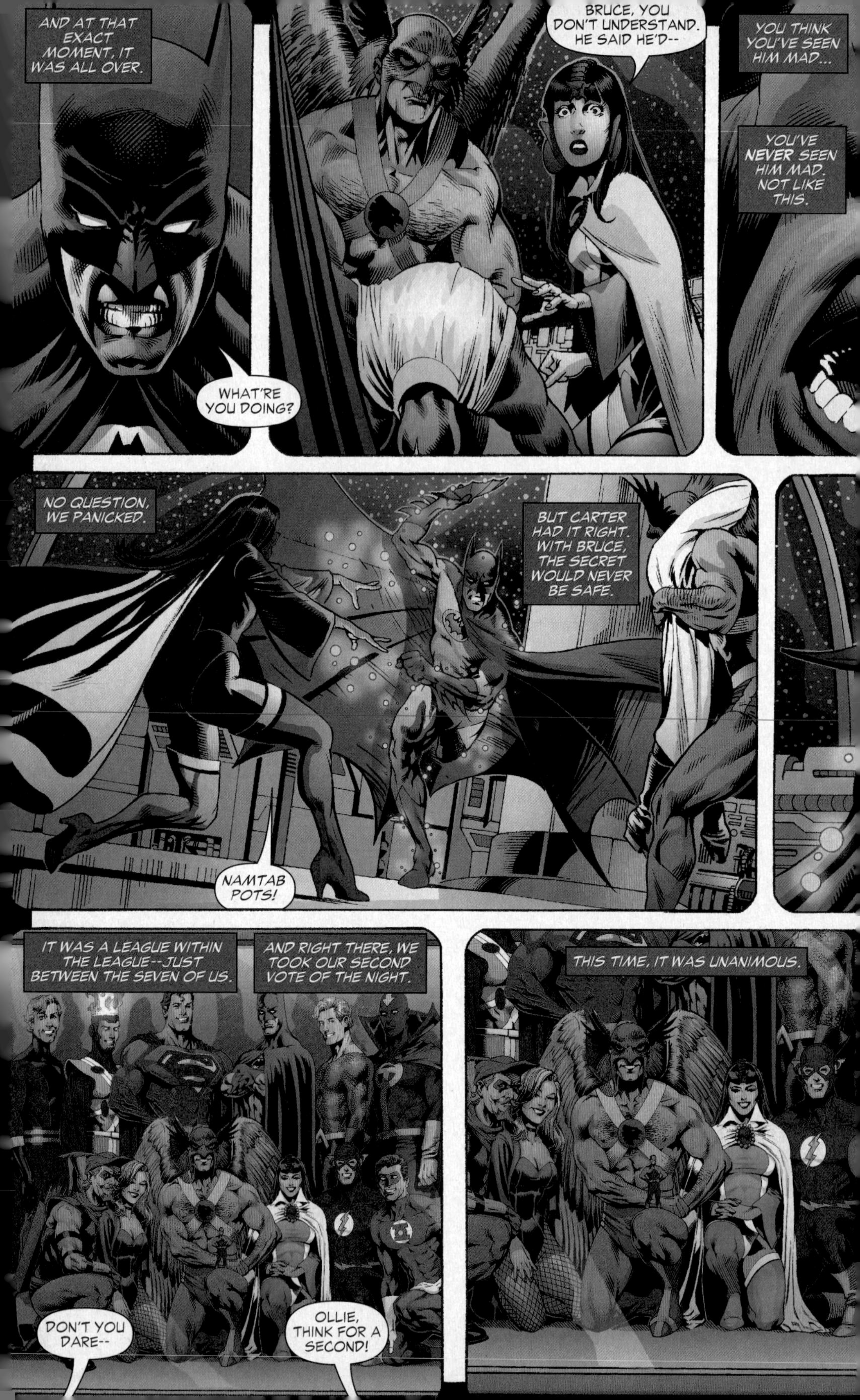
AND AT THAT EXACT MOMENT, IT WAS ALL OVER.
WHAT'RE YOU DOING?
BRUCE, YOU DON'T UNDERSTAND. HE SAID HE'D--
YOU THINK YOU'VE SEEN HIM MAD...
YOU'VE NEVER SEEN HIM MAD. NOT LIKE THIS.
NO QUESTION, WE PANICKED.
BUT CARTER HAD IT RIGHT. WITH BRUCE, THE SECRET WOULD NEVER BE SAFE.
NAMTAB POTS!
IT WAS A LEAGUE WITHIN THE LEAGUE--JUST BETWEEN THE SEVEN OF US.
AND RIGHT THERE, WE TOOK OUR SECOND VOTE OF THE NIGHT.
DON'T YOU DARE--
OLLIE, THINK FOR A SECOND!
THIS TIME, IT WAS UNANIMOUS.

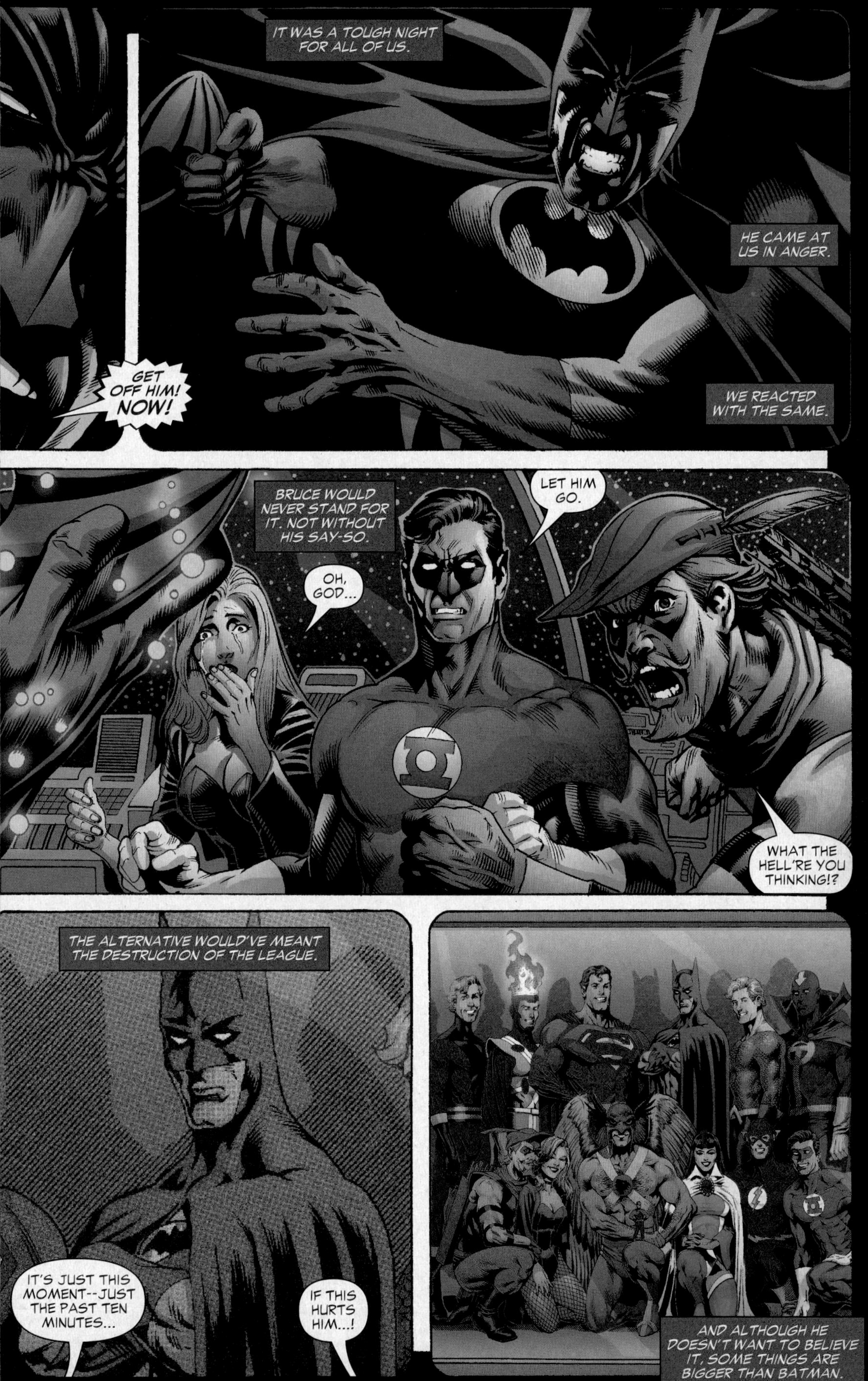

IT WAS A TOUGH NIGHT FOR ALL OF US.
HE CAME AT US IN ANGER.
GET OFF HIM! NOW!
WE REACTED WITH THE SAME.
BRUCE WOULD NEVER STAND FOR IT. NOT WITHOUT HIS SAY-SO.
LET HIM GO.
OH, GOD...
WHAT THE HELL'RE YOU THINKING!?
THE ALTERNATIVE WOULD'VE MEANT THE DESTRUCTION OF THE LEAGUE.
IT'S JUST THIS MOMENT--JUST THE PAST TEN MINUTES...
IF THIS HURTS HIM...!
AND ALTHOUGH HE DOESN'T WANT TO BELIEVE IT, SOME THINGS ARE BIGGER THAN BATMAN.

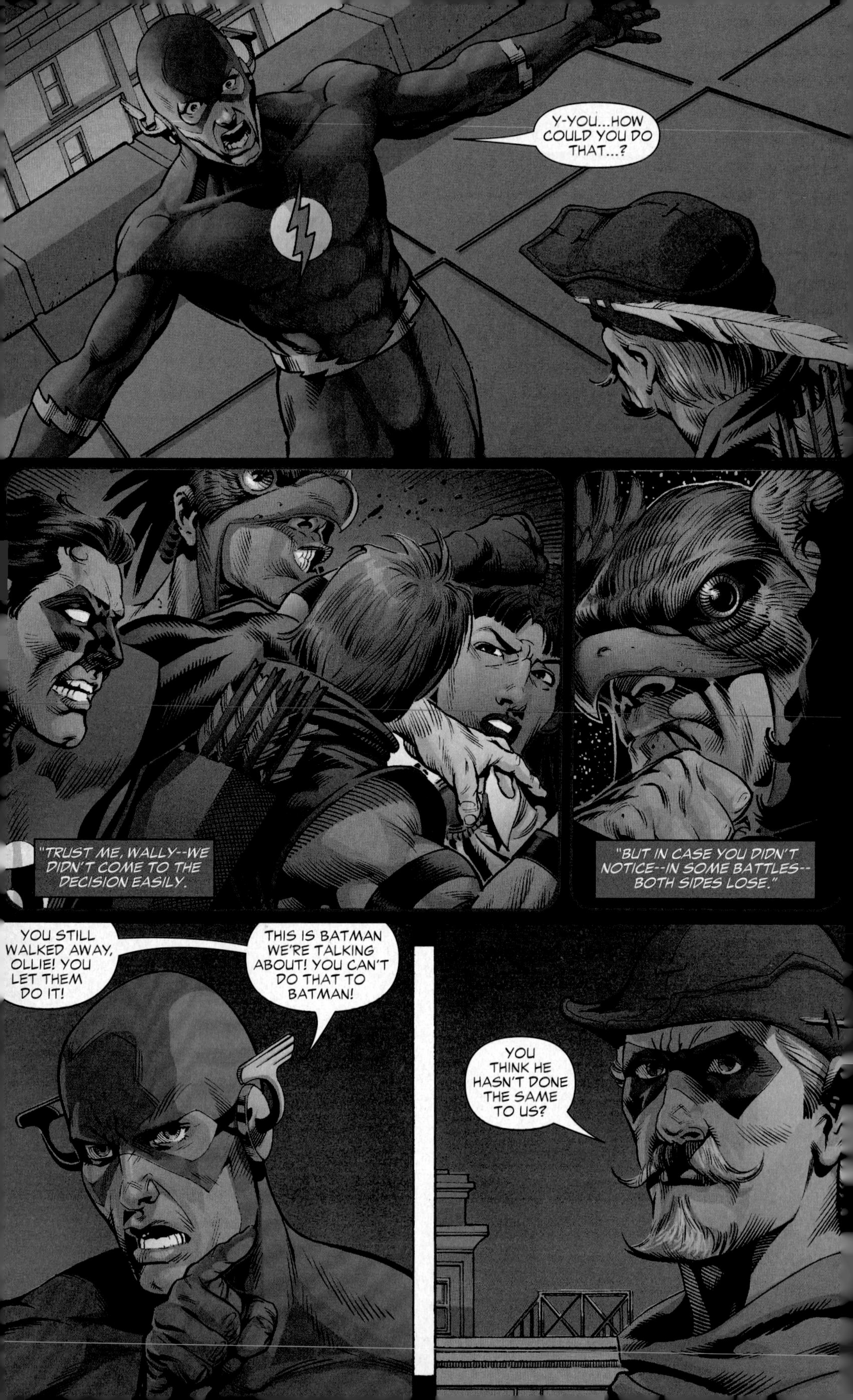
Y-YOU...HOW COULD YOU DO THAT...?
"TRUST ME, WALLY--WE DIDN'T COME TO THE DECISION EASILY.
"BUT IN CASE YOU DIDN'T NOTICE--IN SOME BATTLES--BOTH SIDES LOSE."
YOU STILL WALKED AWAY, OLLIE! YOU LET THEM DO IT!
THIS IS BATMAN WE'RE TALKING ABOUT! YOU CAN'T DO THAT TO BATMAN!
YOU THINK HE HASN'T DONE THE SAME TO US?

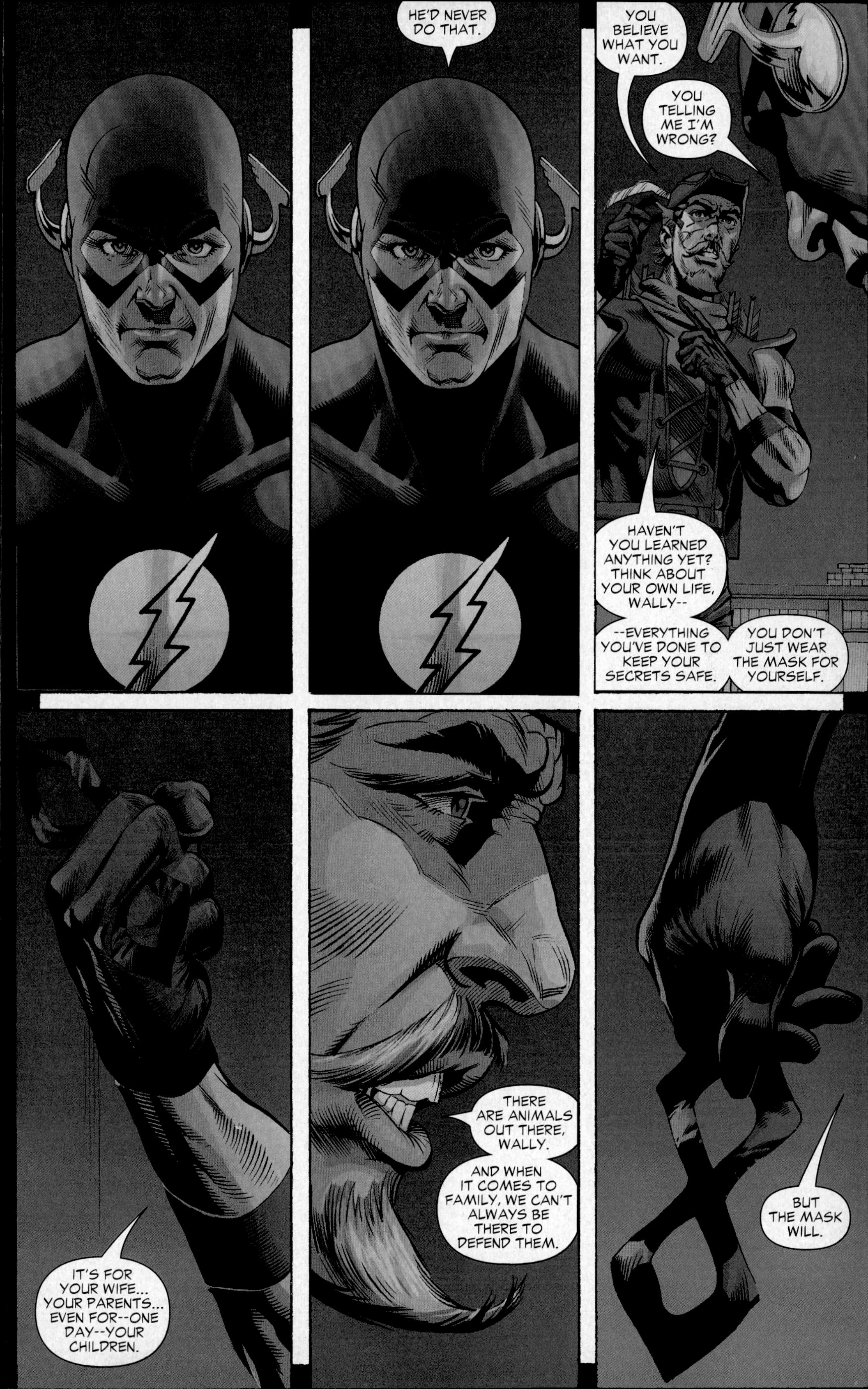
HE'D NEVER DO THAT.
YOU BELIEVE WHAT YOU WANT.
YOU TELLING ME I'M WRONG?
HAVEN'T YOU LEARNED ANYTHING YET? THINK ABOUT YOUR OWN LIFE, WALLY--
--EVERYTHING YOU'VE DONE TO KEEP YOUR SECRETS SAFE.
YOU DON'T JUST WEAR THE MASK FOR YOURSELF.
IT'S FOR YOUR WIFE... YOUR PARENTS... EVEN FOR--ONE DAY--YOUR CHILDREN.
THERE ARE ANIMALS OUT THERE, WALLY.
AND WHEN IT COMES TO FAMILY, WE CAN'T ALWAYS BE THERE TO DEFEND THEM.
BUT THE MASK WILL.

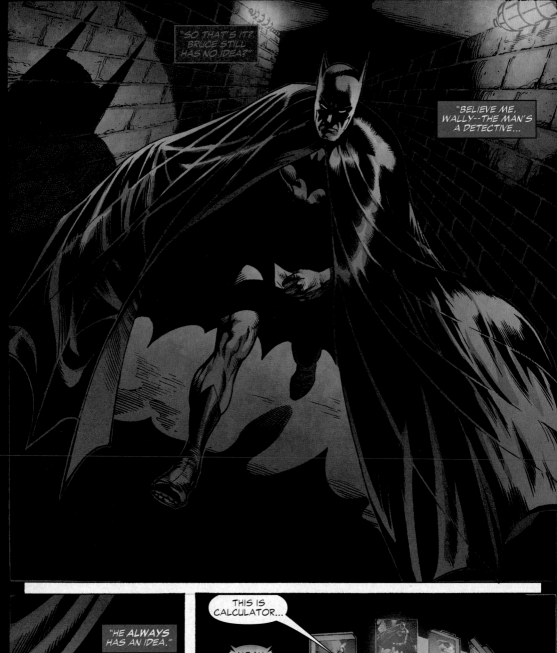

"SO THAT'S IT? BRUCE STILL HAS NO IDEA?"

"BELIEVE ME, WALLY--THE MAN'S A DETECTIVE...

"HE ALWAYS HAS AN IDEA."

THIS IS CALCULATOR...

NOAH, IT'S ME.

MERLYN, WHAT HAPPENED? YOU OUT YET?

OF COURSE--DEADSHOT CALLED WALLER--WALLER CALLED LUTHOR--AND LUTHOR CALLED HIS OLD WHITE HOUSE COUNSEL BOYS, WHO'RE ALL NOW DOING WHITE COLLAR DEFENSE WORK, GOD BLESS THEIR LOAFERS.

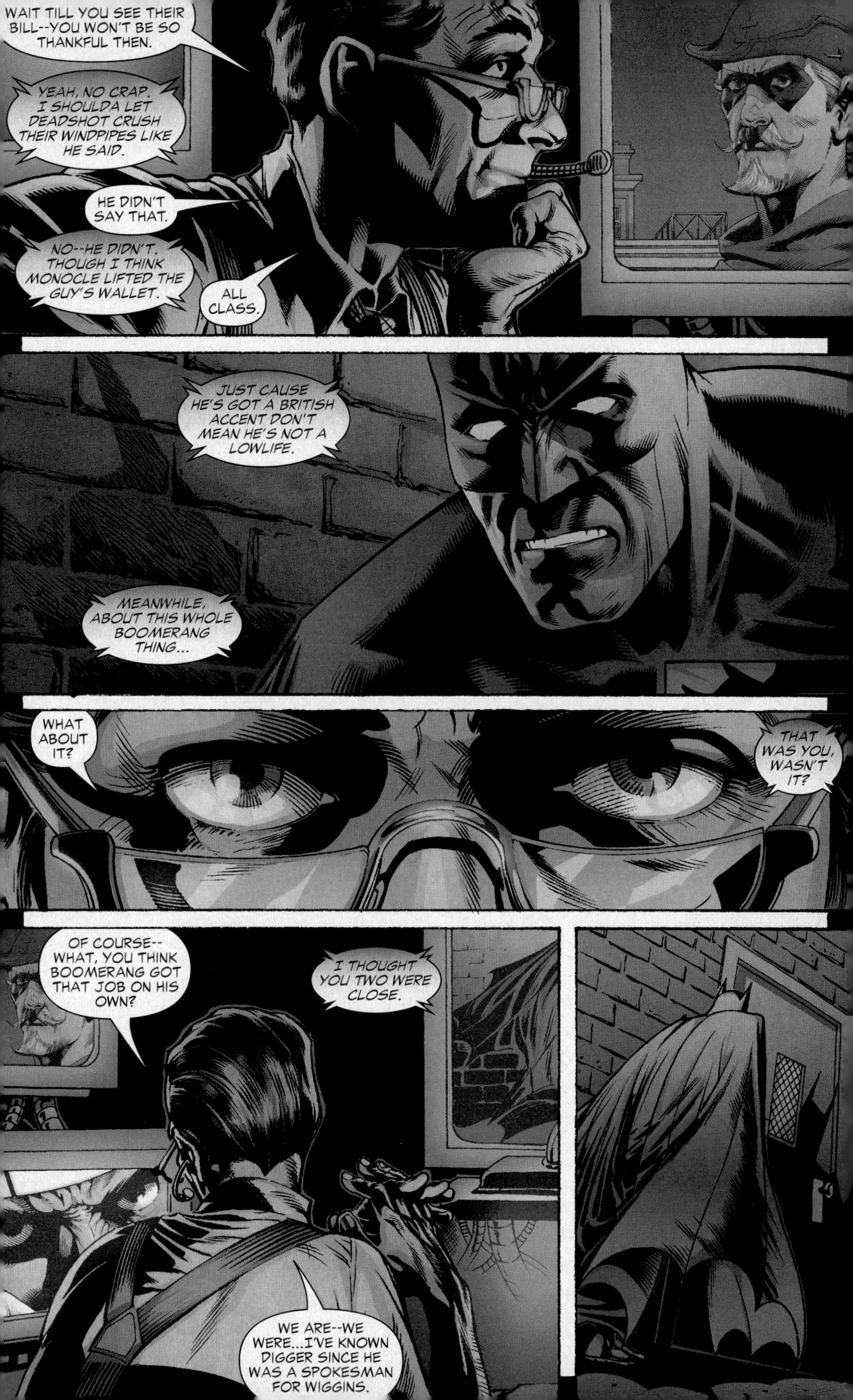
WAIT TILL YOU SEE THEIR BILL--YOU WON'T BE SO THANKFUL THEN.
YEAH, NO CRAP. I SHOULDA LET DEADSHOT CRUSH THEIR WINDPIPES LIKE HE SAID.
HE DIDN'T SAY THAT.
NO--HE DIDN'T. THOUGH I THINK MONOCLE LIFTED THE GUY'S WALLET.
ALL CLASS.
JUST CAUSE HE'S GOT A BRITISH ACCENT DON'T MEAN HE'S NOT A LOWLIFE.
MEANWHILE, ABOUT THIS WHOLE BOOMERANG THING...
WHAT ABOUT IT?
THAT WAS YOU, WASN'T IT?
OF COURSE--WHAT, YOU THINK BOOMERANG GOT THAT JOB ON HIS OWN?
I THOUGHT YOU TWO WERE CLOSE.
WE ARE--WE WERE...I'VE KNOWN DIGGER SINCE HE WAS A SPOKESMAN FOR WIGGINS.

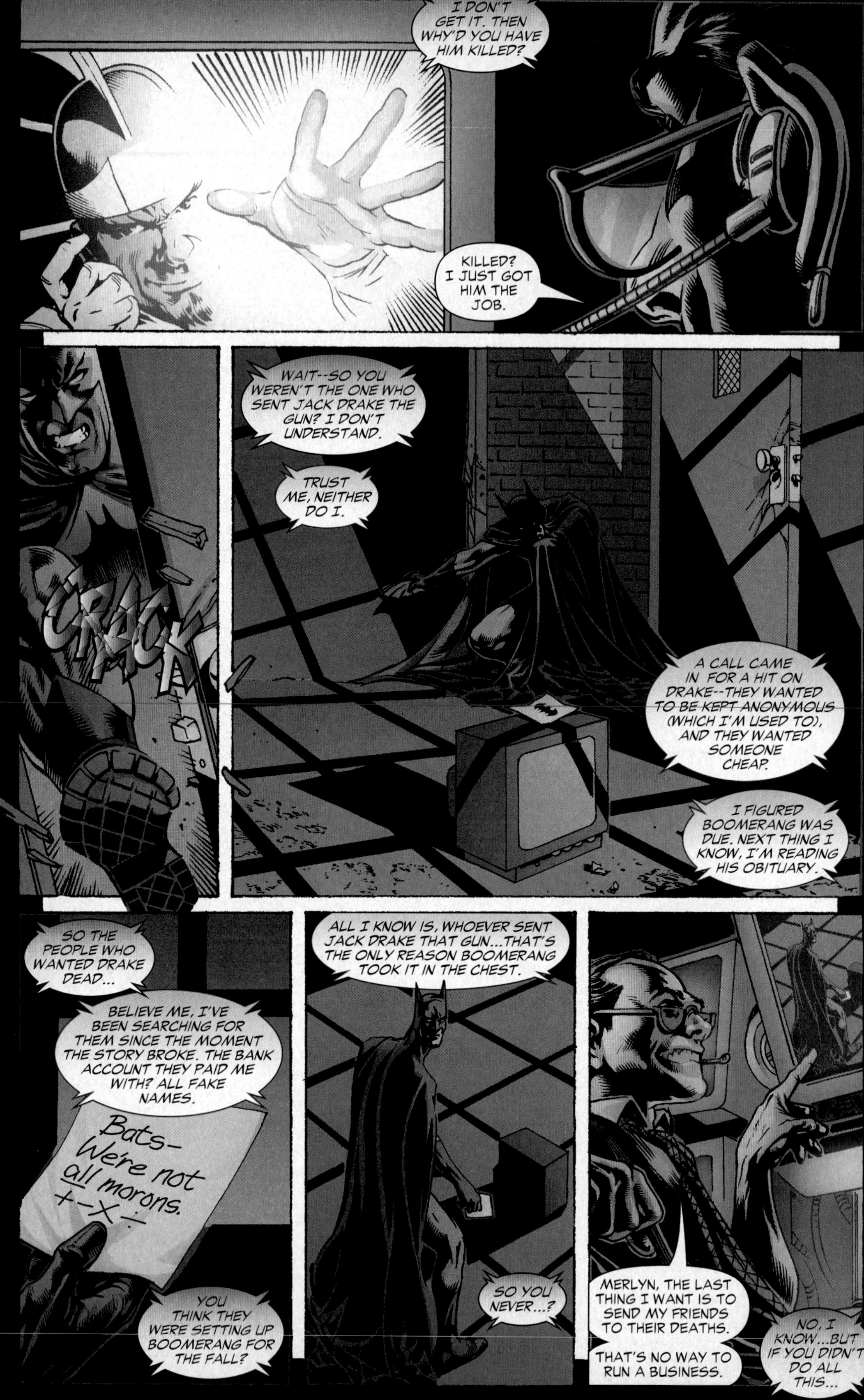

I DON'T GET IT. THEN WHY'D YOU HAVE HIM KILLED?
KILLED? I JUST GOT HIM THE JOB.
WAIT--SO YOU WEREN'T THE ONE WHO SENT JACK DRAKE THE GUN? I DON'T UNDERSTAND.
TRUST ME, NEITHER DO I.
CRACK
A CALL CAME IN FOR A HIT ON DRAKE--THEY WANTED TO BE KEPT ANONYMOUS (WHICH I'M USED TO), AND THEY WANTED SOMEONE CHEAP.
I FIGURED BOOMERANG WAS DUE. NEXT THING I KNOW, I'M READING HIS OBITUARY.
SO THE PEOPLE WHO WANTED DRAKE DEAD...
BELIEVE ME, I'VE BEEN SEARCHING FOR THEM SINCE THE MOMENT THE STORY BROKE. THE BANK ACCOUNT THEY PAID ME WITH? ALL FAKE NAMES.
Bats- We're not all morons. +-x÷
YOU THINK THEY WERE SETTING UP BOOMERANG FOR THE FALL?
ALL I KNOW IS, WHOEVER SENT JACK DRAKE THAT GUN...THAT'S THE ONLY REASON BOOMERANG TOOK IT IN THE CHEST.
SO YOU NEVER...?
MERLYN, THE LAST THING I WANT IS TO SEND MY FRIENDS TO THEIR DEATHS.
THAT'S NO WAY TO RUN A BUSINESS.
NO, I KNOW...BUT IF YOU DIDN'T DO ALL THIS...

"...ELL DID?"

JSA Headquarters.

Sue Dibny's autopsy.

MICHAEL, YOU GOTTA SEE THIS...

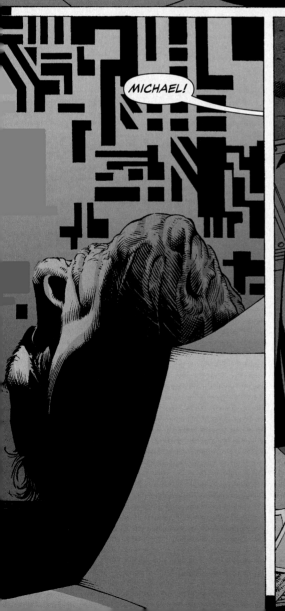

MICHAEL!

I SPEND THE NEXT FEW HOURS IN THE CAVE, STARING AT THE PUZZLE PIECES.

CALCULATOR'S INNOCENCE IS HARDER TO PROCESS THAN I THOUGHT.

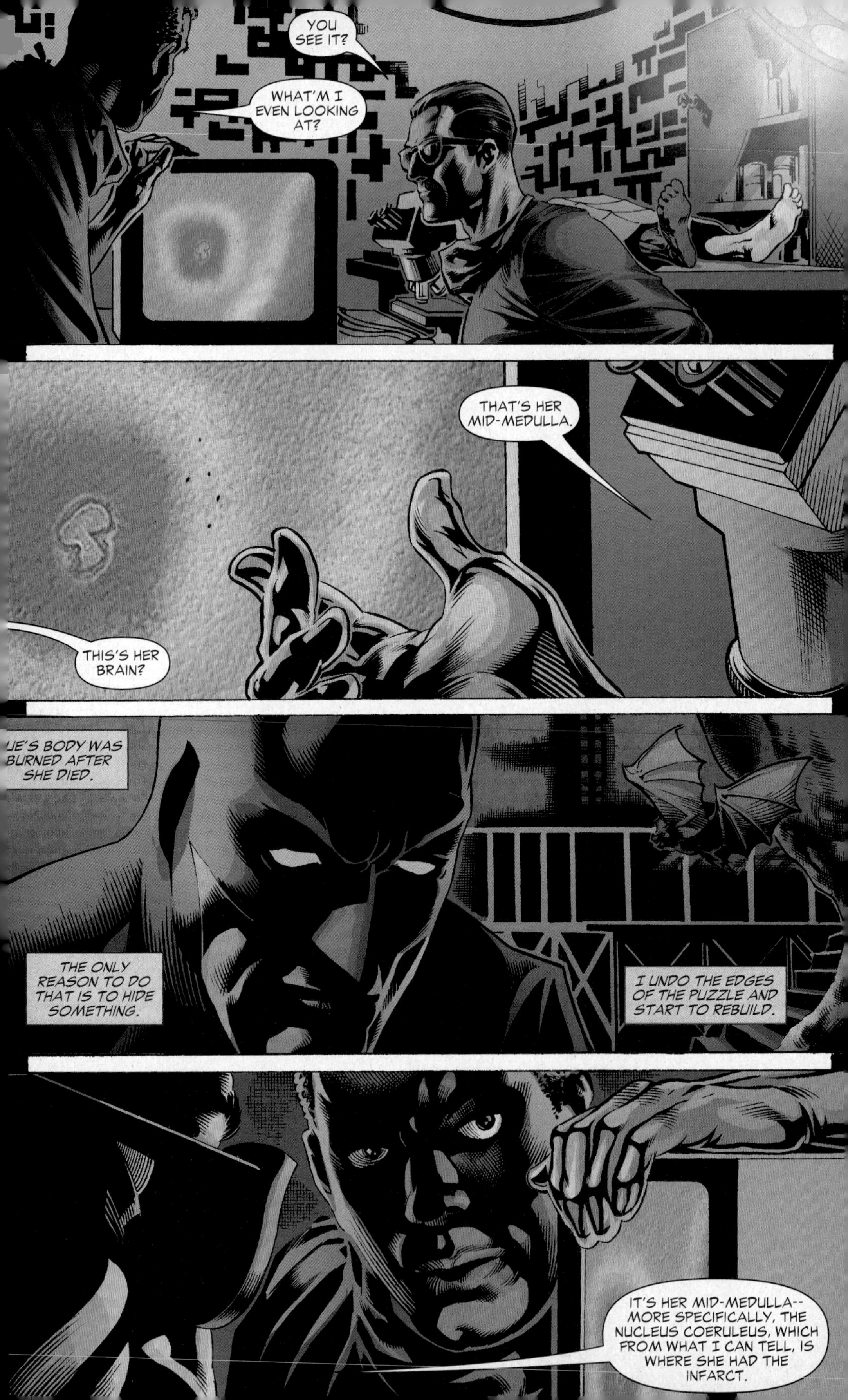
YOU SEE IT?
WHAT'M I EVEN LOOKING AT?
THAT'S HER MID-MEDULLA.
THIS'S HER BRAIN?
UE'S BODY WAS BURNED AFTER SHE DIED.
THE ONLY REASON TO DO THAT IS TO HIDE SOMETHING.
I UNDO THE EDGES OF THE PUZZLE AND START TO REBUILD.
IT'S HER MID-MEDULLA-- MORE SPECIFICALLY, THE NUCLEUS COERULEUS, WHICH FROM WHAT I CAN TELL, IS WHERE SHE HAD THE INFARCT.

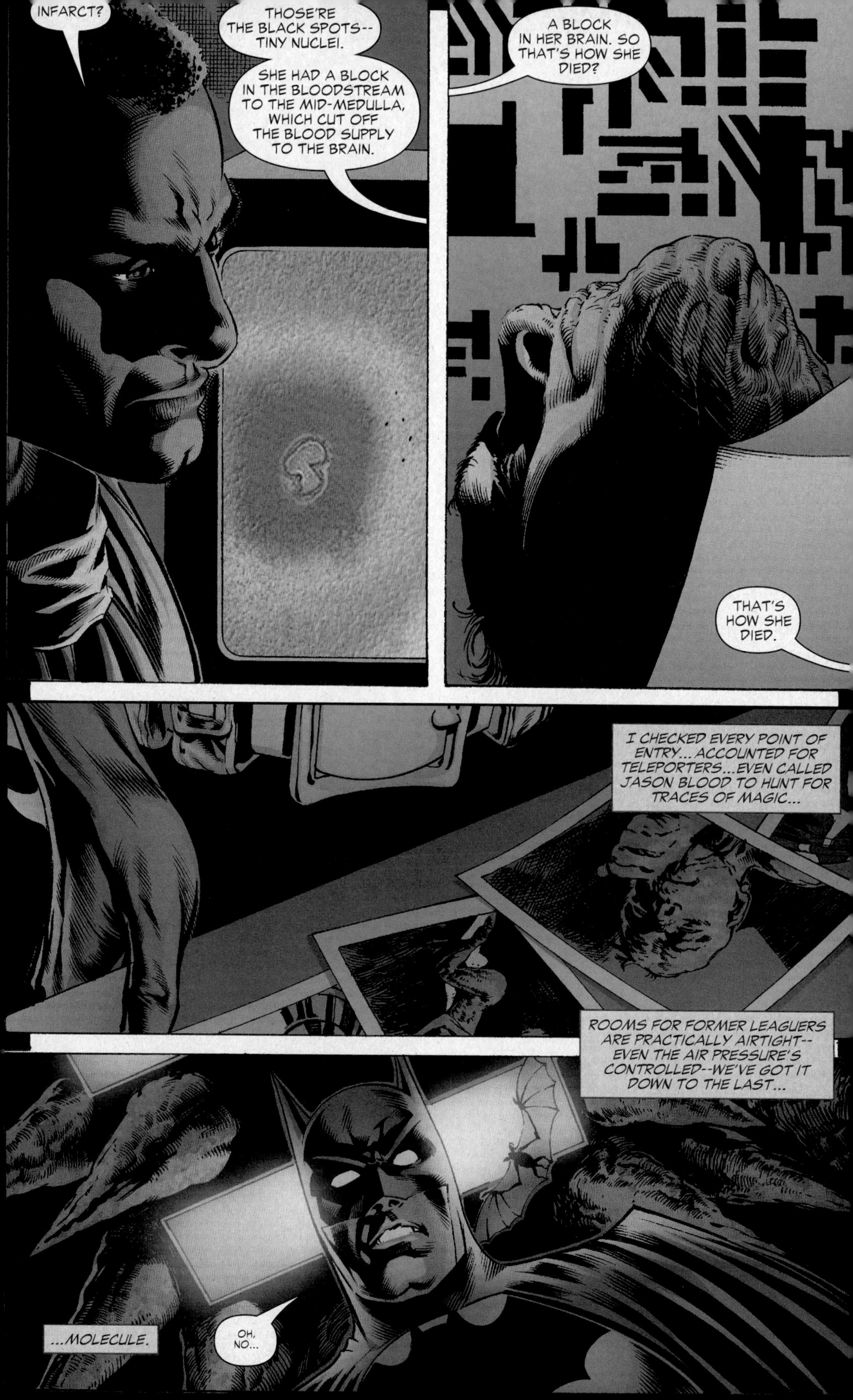
INFARCT?
THOSE'RE THE BLACK SPOTS-- TINY NUCLEI.
SHE HAD A BLOCK IN THE BLOODSTREAM TO THE MID-MEDULLA, WHICH CUT OFF THE BLOOD SUPPLY TO THE BRAIN.
A BLOCK IN HER BRAIN. SO THAT'S HOW SHE DIED?
THAT'S HOW SHE DIED.
I CHECKED EVERY POINT OF ENTRY... ACCOUNTED FOR TELEPORTERS...EVEN CALLED JASON BLOOD TO HUNT FOR TRACES OF MAGIC...
ROOMS FOR FORMER LEAGUERS ARE PRACTICALLY AIRTIGHT-- EVEN THE AIR PRESSURE'S CONTROLLED--WE'VE GOT IT DOWN TO THE LAST...
...MOLECULE.
OH, NO...

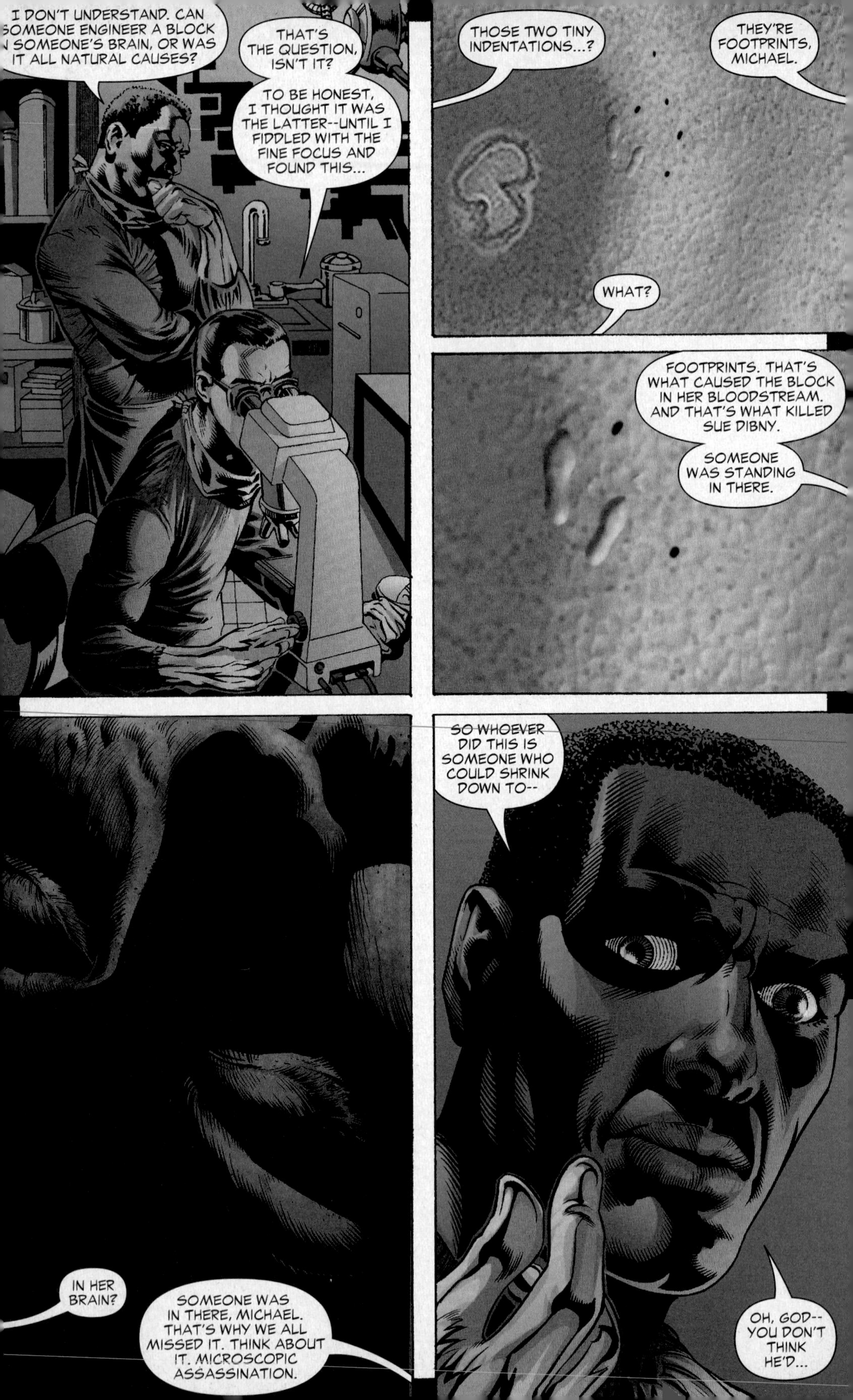
I DON'T UNDERSTAND. CAN SOMEONE ENGINEER A BLOCK IN SOMEONE'S BRAIN, OR WAS IT ALL NATURAL CAUSES?
THAT'S THE QUESTION, ISN'T IT?
TO BE HONEST, I THOUGHT IT WAS THE LATTER--UNTIL I FIDDLED WITH THE FINE FOCUS AND FOUND THIS...
THOSE TWO TINY INDENTATIONS...?
THEY'RE FOOTPRINTS, MICHAEL.
WHAT?
FOOTPRINTS. THAT'S WHAT CAUSED THE BLOCK IN HER BLOODSTREAM. AND THAT'S WHAT KILLED SUE DIBNY.
SOMEONE WAS STANDING IN THERE.
IN HER BRAIN?
SOMEONE WAS IN THERE, MICHAEL. THAT'S WHY WE ALL MISSED IT. THINK ABOUT IT. MICROSCOPIC ASSASSINATION.
SO WHOEVER DID THIS IS SOMEONE WHO COULD SHRINK DOWN TO--
OH, GOD-- YOU DON'T THINK HE'D...

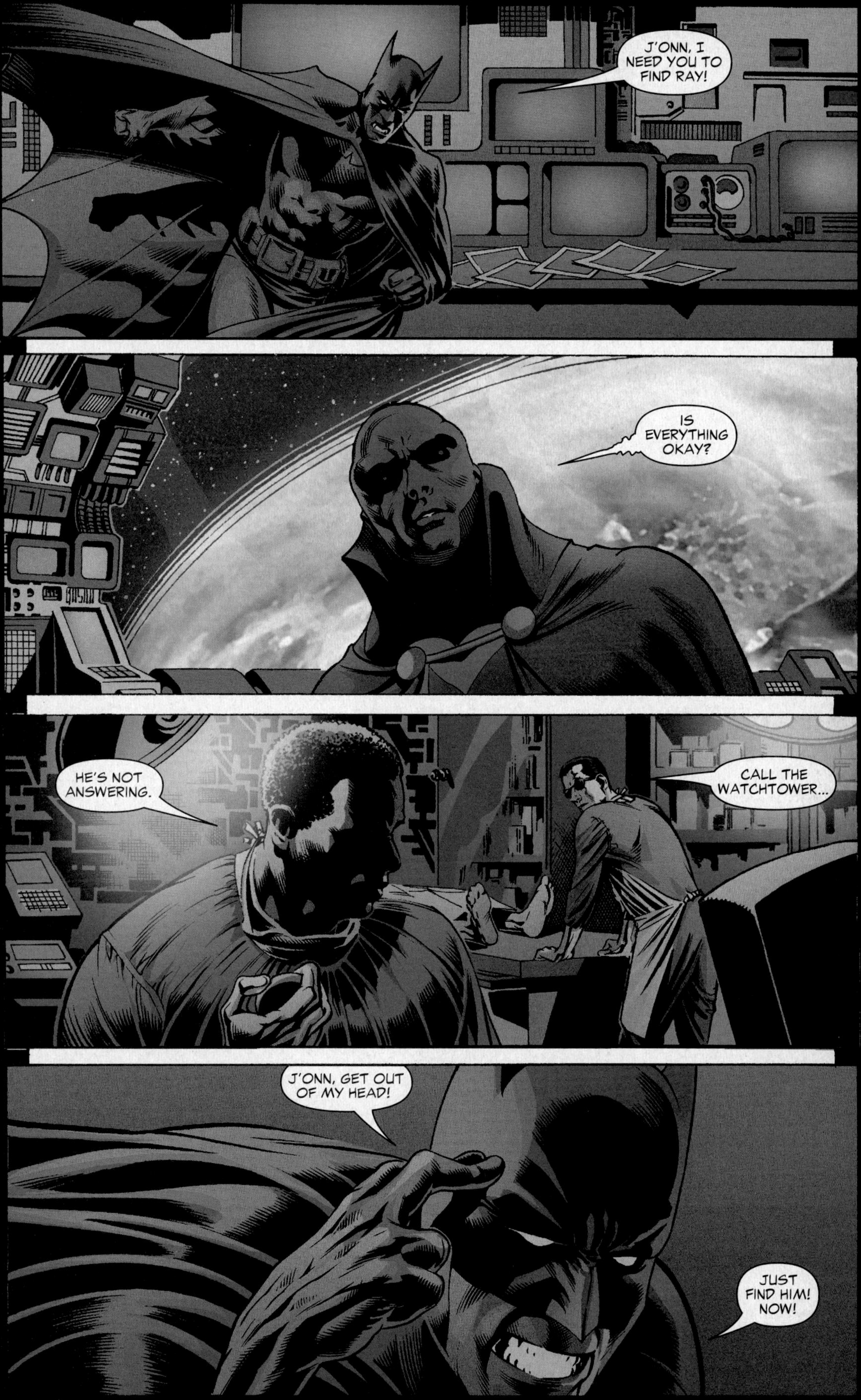
J'ONN, I NEED YOU TO FIND RAY!
IS EVERYTHING OKAY?
HE'S NOT ANSWERING.
CALL THE WATCHTOWER...
J'ONN, GET OUT OF MY HEAD!
JUST FIND HIM! NOW!

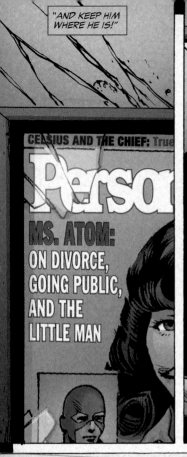

"AND KEEP HIM WHERE HE IS!"

Ray Palmer and Jean Loring.

Lovers.

CELSIUS AND THE CHIEF: True

Person

MS. ATOM: ON DIVORCE, GOING PUBLIC, AND THE LITTLE MAN

I STILL CAN'T BELIEVE IT-- CAPTAIN BOOMERANG...

I MEAN, THAT'S WHO KILLED SUE? THAT'S WHO ATTACKED ME? CAPTAIN BOOMERANG?

BUT CAPTAIN BOOMERANG?

I'M JUST HAPPY IT'S OVER.

WHY'RE YOU SO SURPRISED? HE'S BEEN TRYING TO KILL US ALL FOR YEARS.

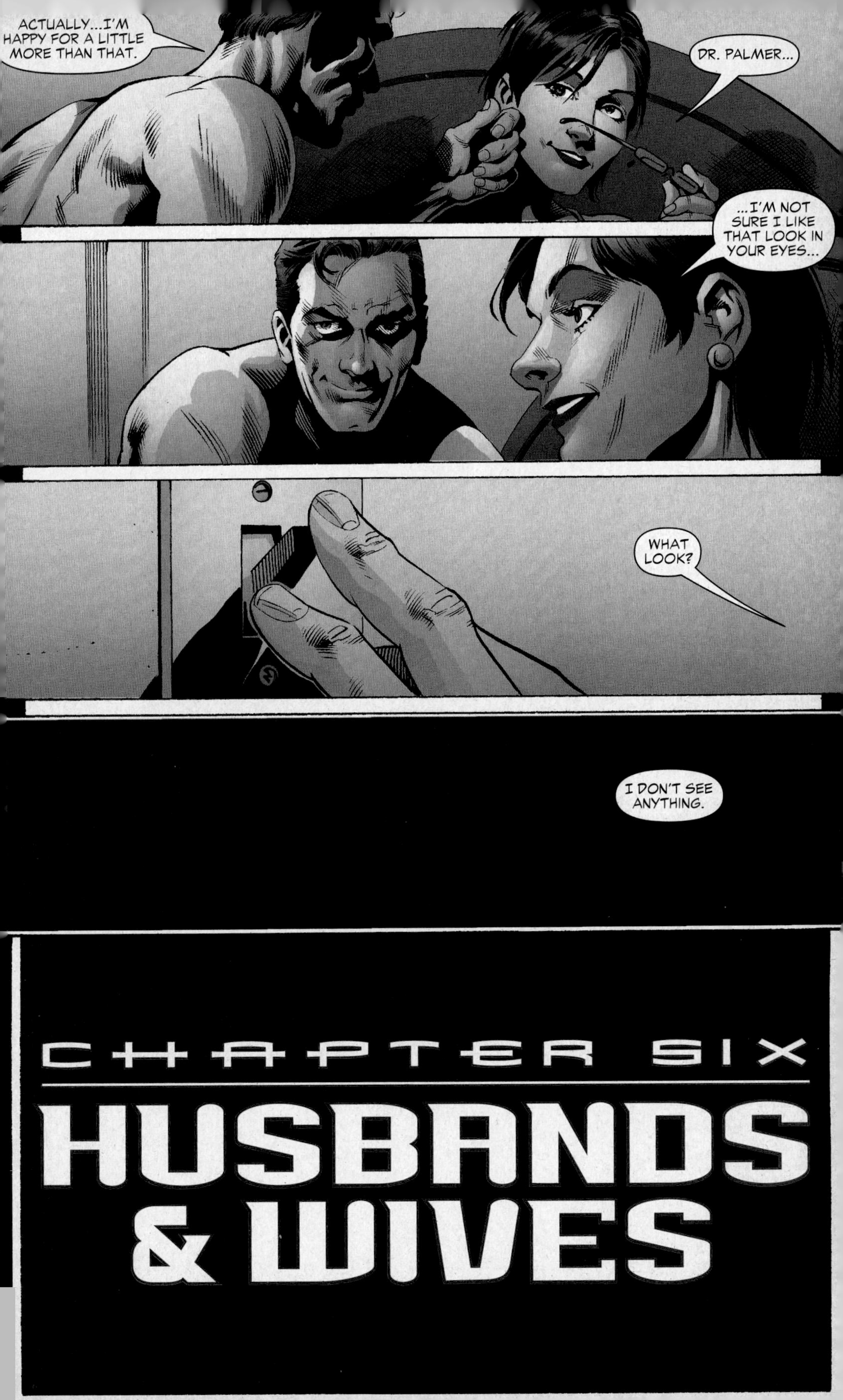
ACTUALLY...I'M HAPPY FOR A LITTLE MORE THAN THAT.
DR. PALMER...
...I'M NOT SURE I LIKE THAT LOOK IN YOUR EYES...
WHAT LOOK?
I DON'T SEE ANYTHING.
CHAPTER SIX
HUSBANDS & WIVES

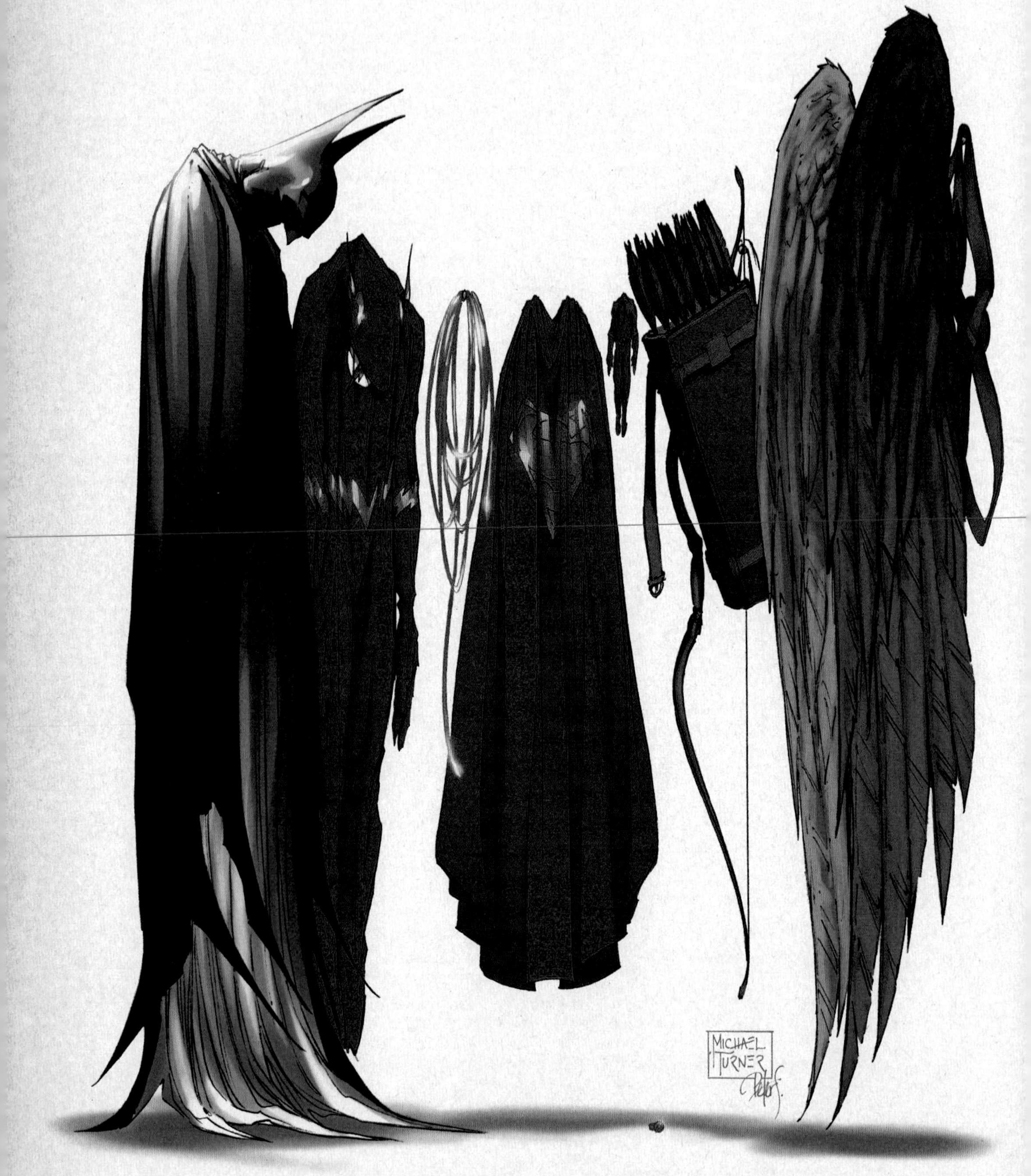
MICHAEL TURNER

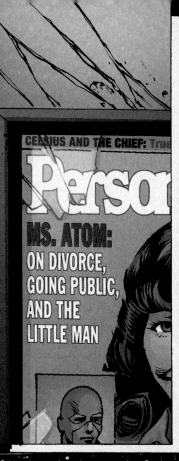

Perso[n]

MS. ATOM:
ON DIVORCE,
GOING PUBLIC,
AND THE
LITTLE MAN

Ray Palmer and Jean Loring.

Lovers.

I STILL CAN'T BELIEVE IT-- CAPTAIN BOOMERANG...

I MEAN, THAT'S WHO KILLED SUE? THAT'S WHO ATTACKED ME? CAPTAIN BOOMERANG?

BY H'RONMEER...

YOU NUTS? YOU'RE TELLING ME THE ATOM KILLED SUE DIBNY?

I'M JUST HAPPY IT'S OVER.

ACTUALLY... I'M HAPPY FOR A LITTLE MORE THAN THAT.

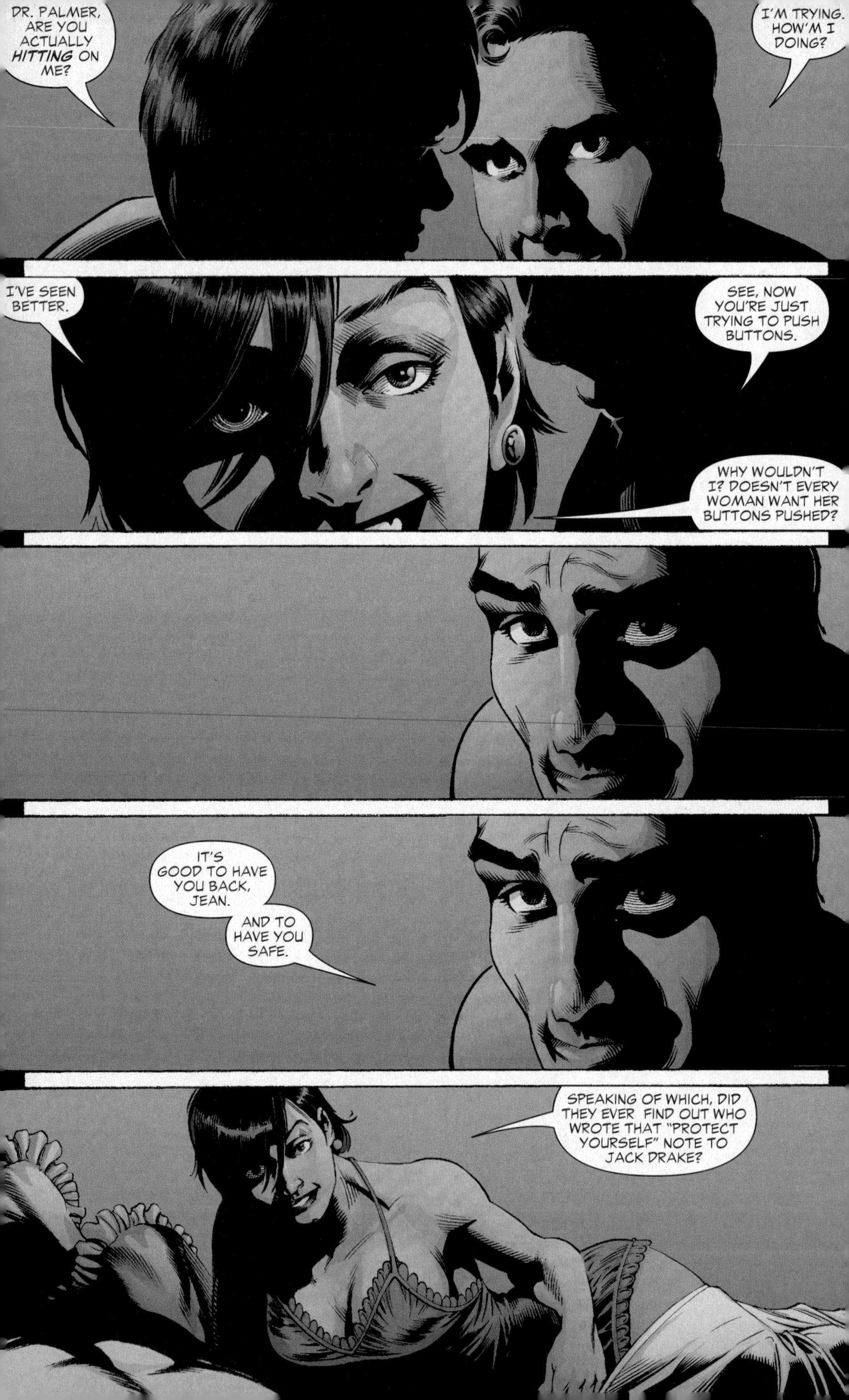
DR. PALMER, ARE YOU ACTUALLY *HITTING* ON ME?
I'M TRYING. HOW'M I DOING?
I'VE SEEN BETTER.
SEE, NOW YOU'RE JUST TRYING TO PUSH BUTTONS.
WHY WOULDN'T I? DOESN'T EVERY WOMAN WANT HER BUTTONS PUSHED?
IT'S GOOD TO HAVE YOU BACK, JEAN.
AND TO HAVE YOU SAFE.
SPEAKING OF WHICH, DID THEY EVER FIND OUT WHO WROTE THAT "PROTECT YOURSELF" NOTE TO JACK DRAKE?

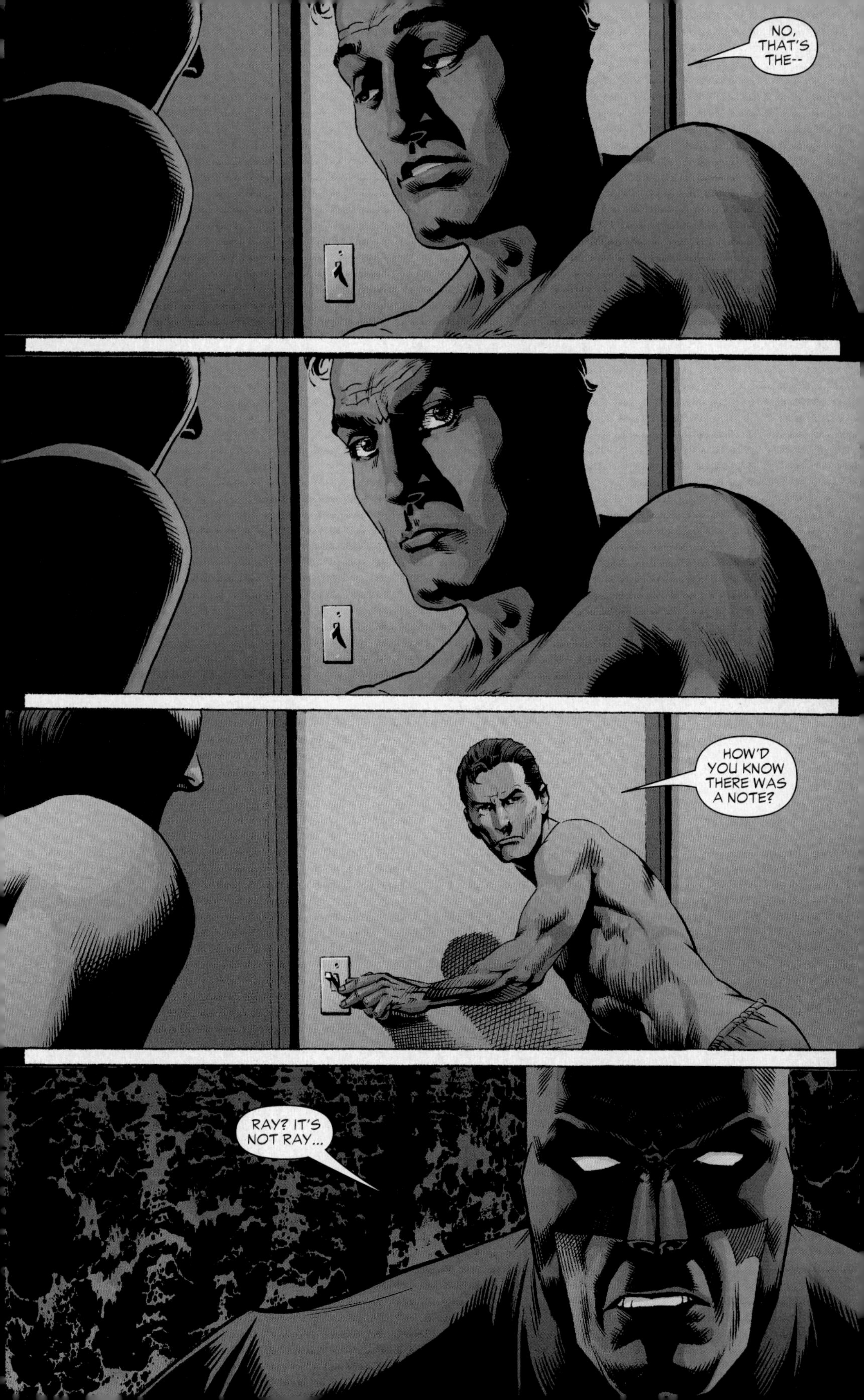
NO, THAT'S THE--
HOW'D YOU KNOW THERE WAS A NOTE?
RAY? IT'S NOT RAY...

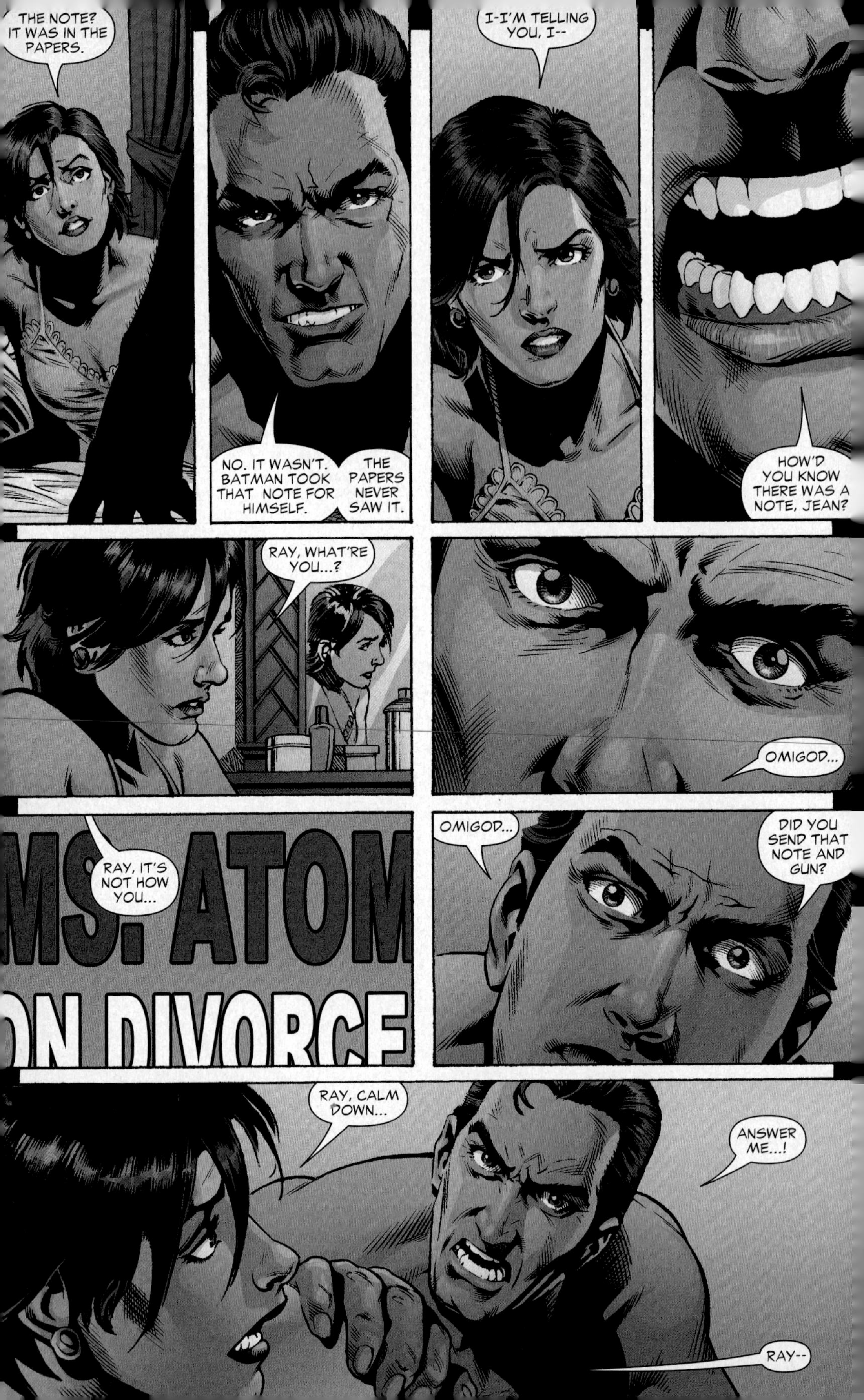
THE NOTE? IT WAS IN THE PAPERS.
NO. IT WASN'T. BATMAN TOOK THAT NOTE FOR HIMSELF.
THE PAPERS NEVER SAW IT.
I-I'M TELLING YOU, I--
HOW'D YOU KNOW THERE WAS A NOTE, JEAN?
RAY, WHAT'RE YOU...?
OMIGOD...
RAY, IT'S NOT HOW YOU...
MS. ATOM
ON DIVORCE
OMIGOD...
DID YOU SEND THAT NOTE AND GUN?
RAY, CALM DOWN...
ANSWER ME...!
RAY--

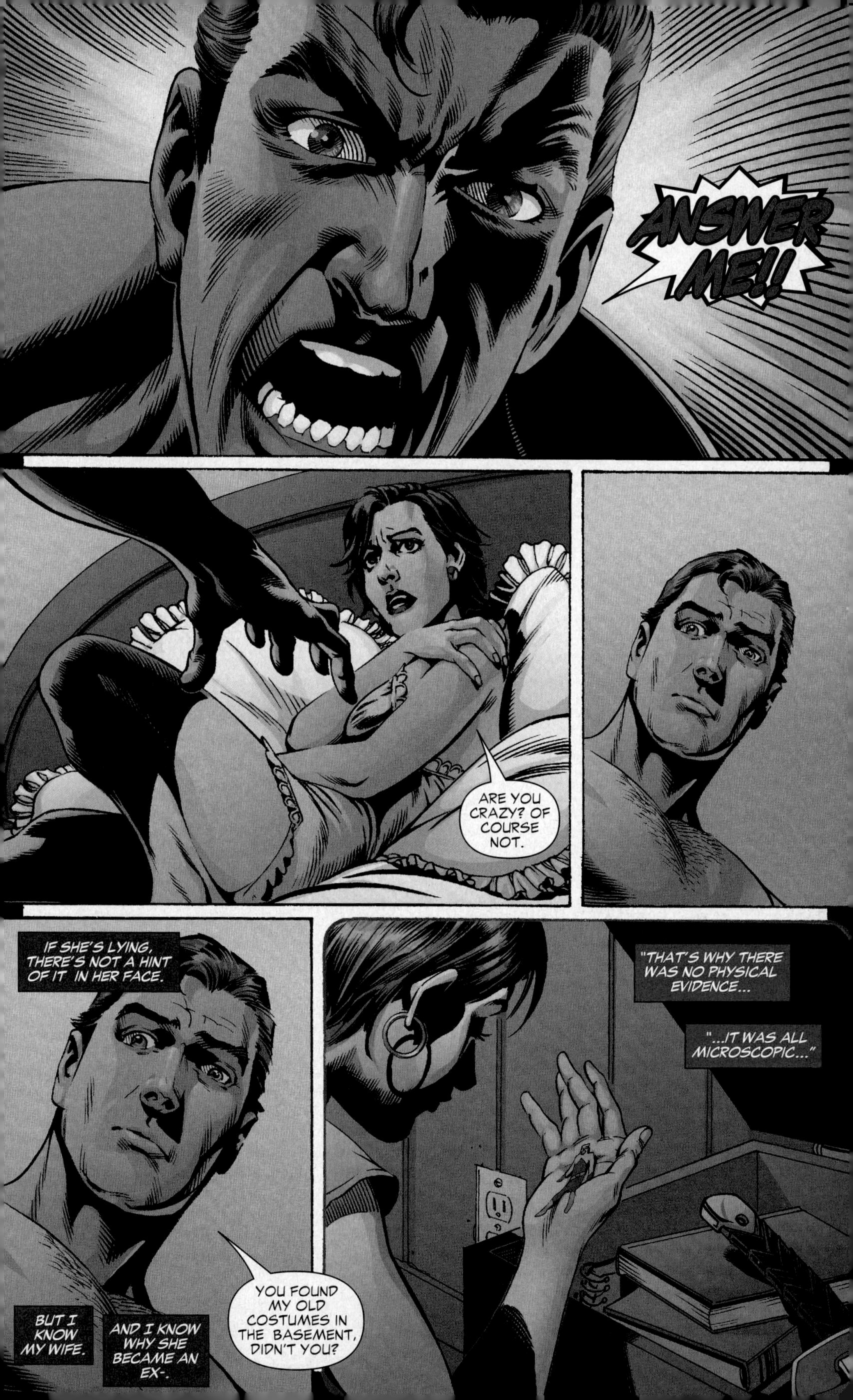
ANSWER ME!!
ARE YOU CRAZY? OF COURSE NOT.
IF SHE'S LYING, THERE'S NOT A HINT OF IT IN HER FACE.
BUT I KNOW MY WIFE.
AND I KNOW WHY SHE BECAME AN EX-.
YOU FOUND MY OLD COSTUMES IN THE BASEMENT, DIDN'T YOU?
"THAT'S WHY THERE WAS NO PHYSICAL EVIDENCE...
"...IT WAS ALL MICROSCOPIC..."

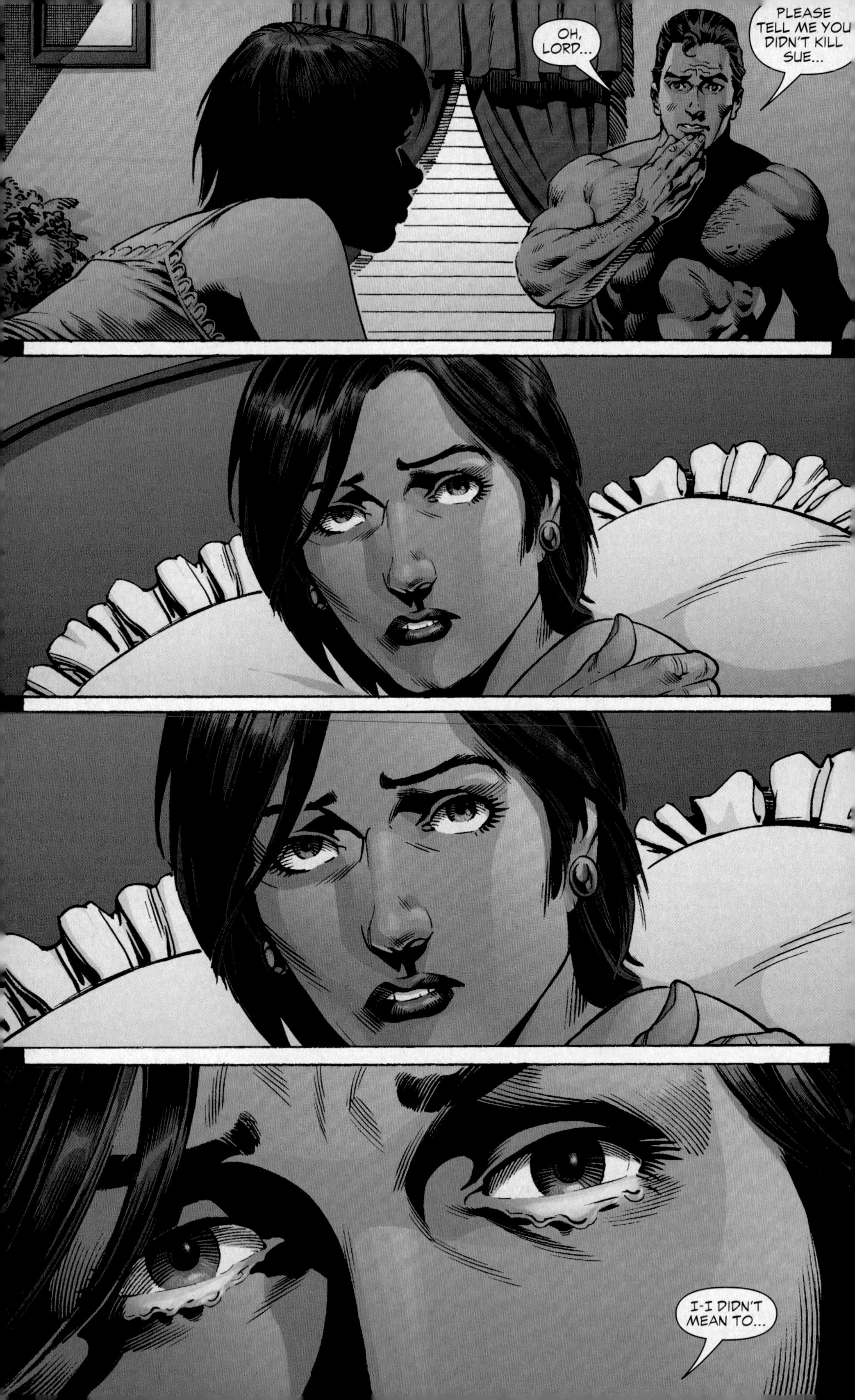
OH, LORD...
PLEASE TELL ME YOU DIDN'T KILL SUE...
I-I DIDN'T MEAN TO...

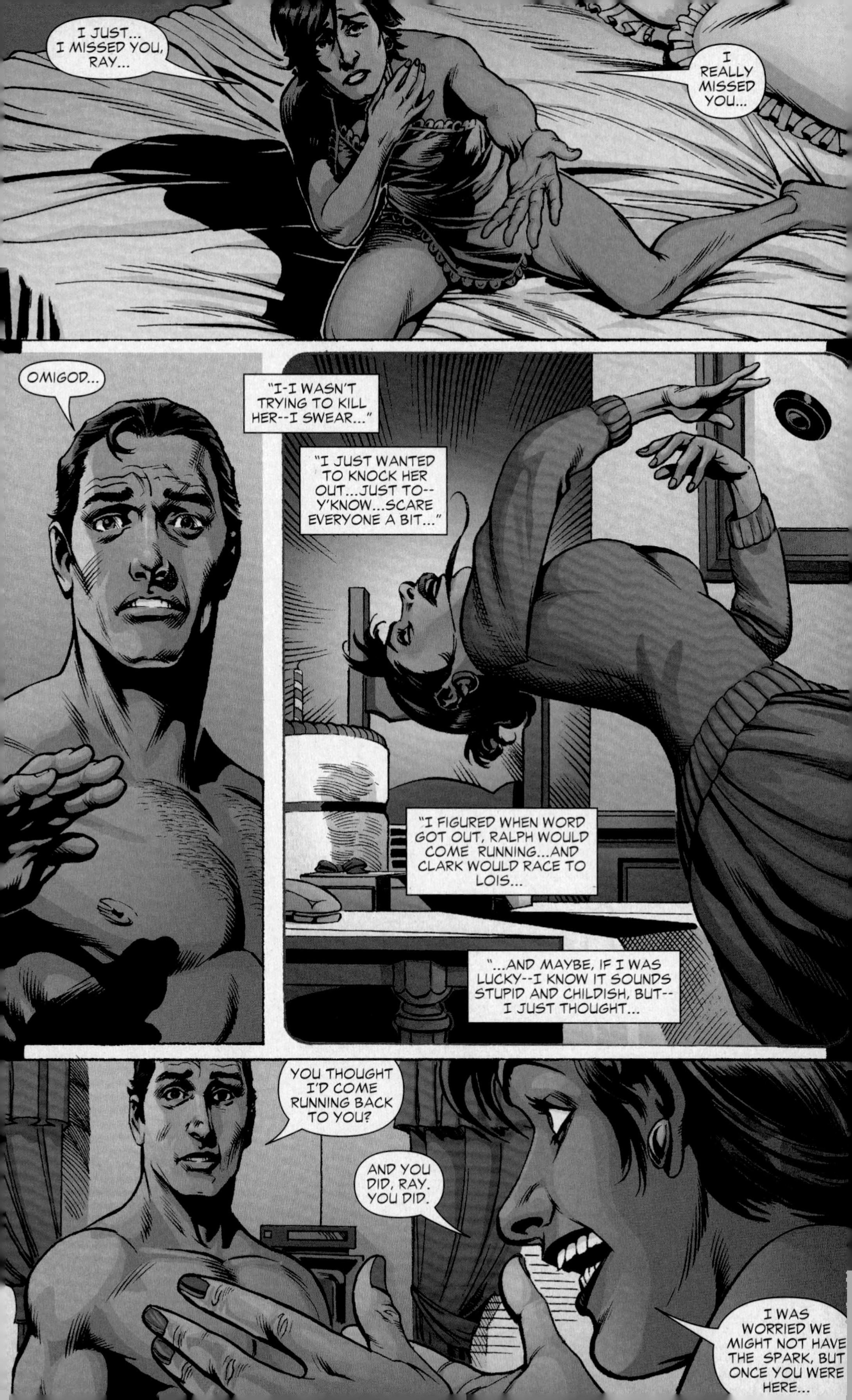
I JUST...
I MISSED YOU,
RAY...
I
REALLY
MISSED
YOU...
OMIGOD...
"I-I WASN'T TRYING TO KILL HER--I SWEAR..."
"I JUST WANTED TO KNOCK HER OUT...JUST TO--Y'KNOW...SCARE EVERYONE A BIT..."
"I FIGURED WHEN WORD GOT OUT, RALPH WOULD COME RUNNING...AND CLARK WOULD RACE TO LOIS...
"...AND MAYBE, IF I WAS LUCKY--I KNOW IT SOUNDS STUPID AND CHILDISH, BUT--I JUST THOUGHT...
YOU THOUGHT I'D COME RUNNING BACK TO YOU?
AND YOU DID, RAY. YOU DID.
I WAS WORRIED WE MIGHT NOT HAVE THE SPARK, BUT ONCE YOU WERE HERE...

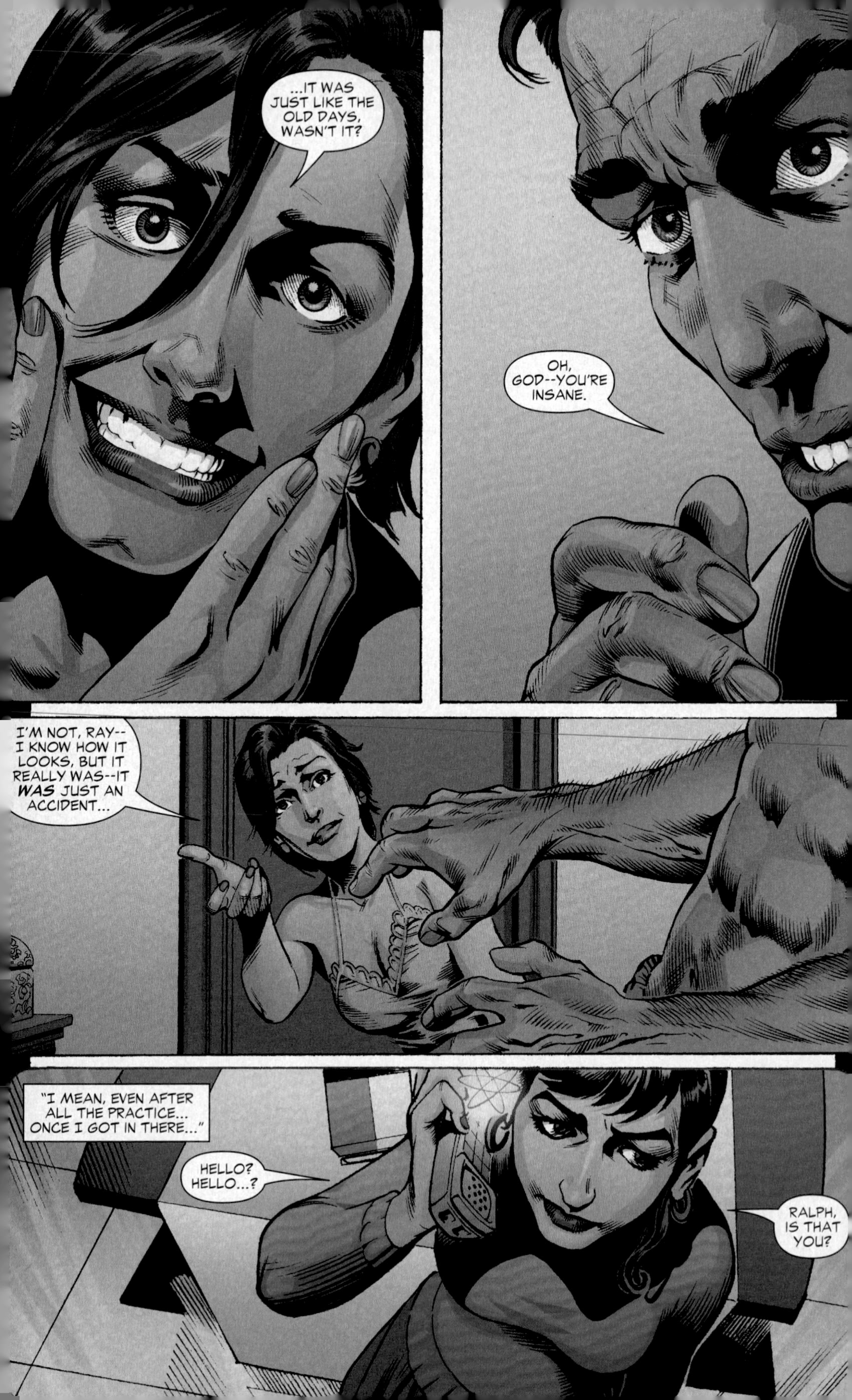
...IT WAS JUST LIKE THE OLD DAYS, WASN'T IT?
OH, GOD--YOU'RE INSANE.
I'M NOT, RAY-- I KNOW HOW IT LOOKS, BUT IT REALLY WAS--IT *WAS* JUST AN ACCIDENT...
"I MEAN, EVEN AFTER ALL THE PRACTICE... ONCE I GOT IN THERE..."
HELLO? HELLO...?
RALPH, IS THAT YOU?

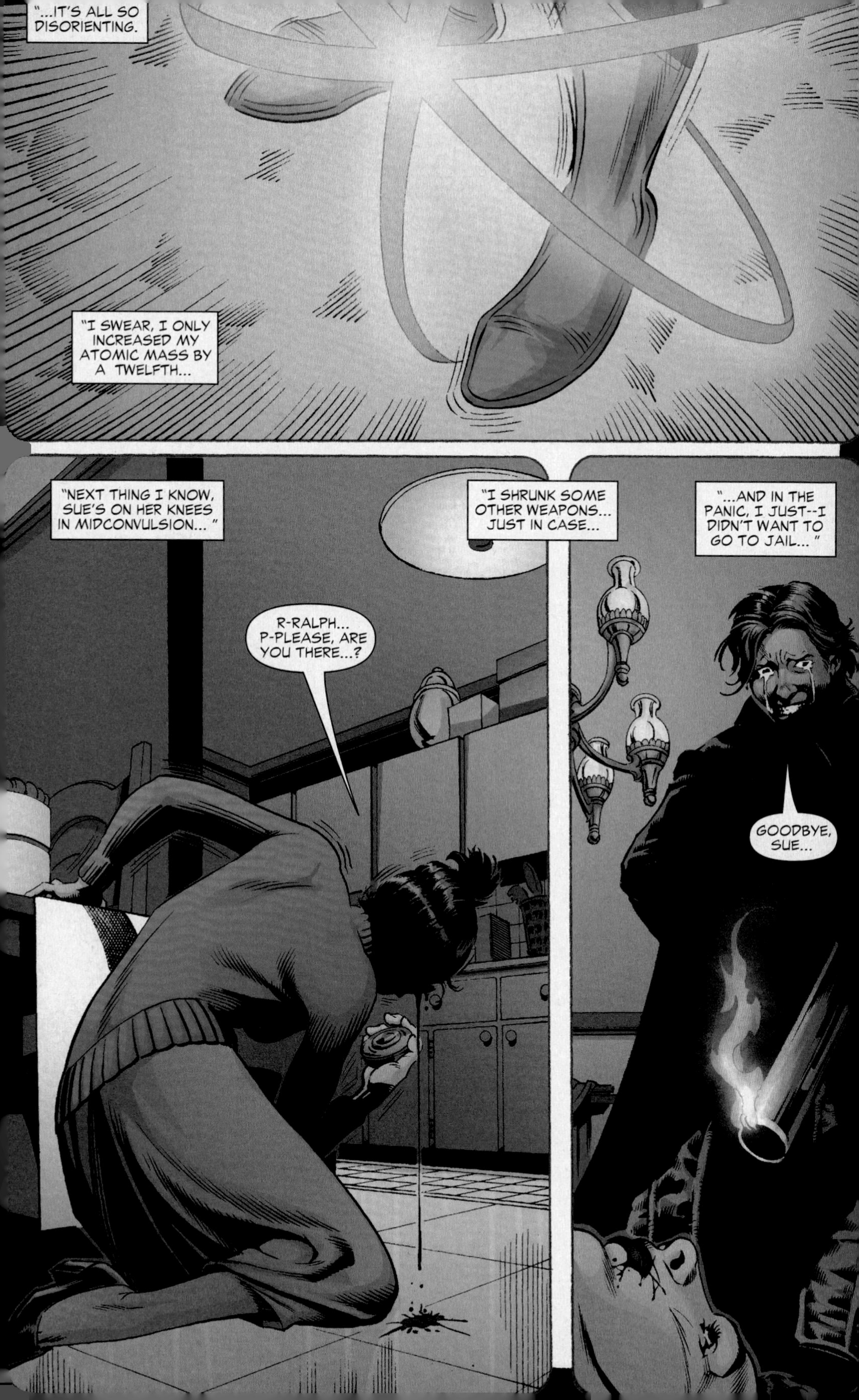
"...IT'S ALL SO DISORIENTING.
"I SWEAR, I ONLY INCREASED MY ATOMIC MASS BY A TWELFTH...
"NEXT THING I KNOW, SUE'S ON HER KNEES IN MIDCONVULSION... "
R-RALPH... P-PLEASE, ARE YOU THERE...?
"I SHRUNK SOME OTHER WEAPONS... JUST IN CASE...
"...AND IN THE PANIC, I JUST--I DIDN'T WANT TO GO TO JAIL... "
GOODBYE, SUE...

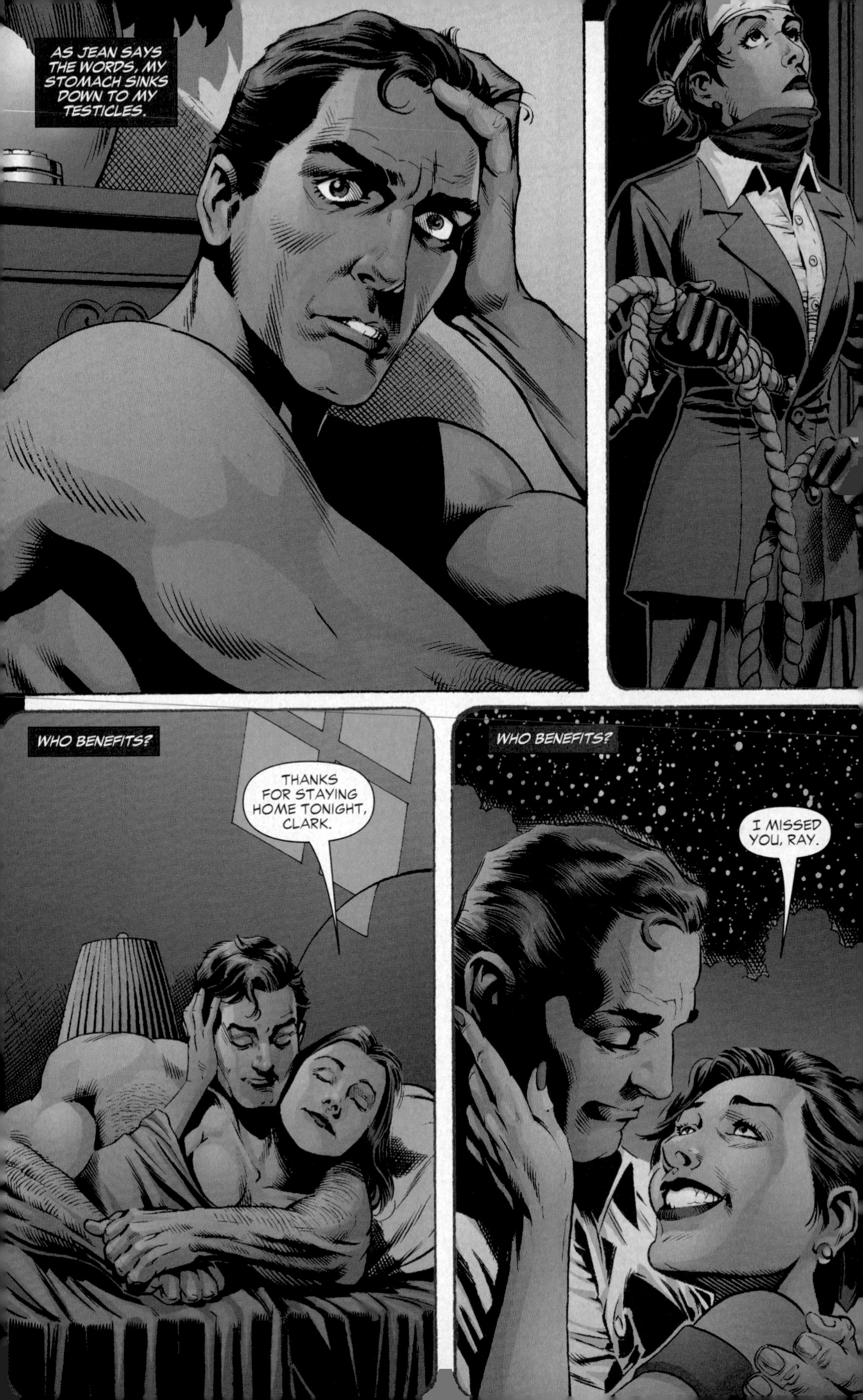
AS JEAN SAYS THE WORDS, MY STOMACH SINKS DOWN TO MY TESTICLES.
WHO BENEFITS?
THANKS FOR STAYING HOME TONIGHT, CLARK.
WHO BENEFITS?
I MISSED YOU, RAY.

FOR OVER A WEEK, BRUCE HAS BEEN ASKING THE SAME QUESTION OVER AND OVER.

THE ONLY QUESTION WE COULDN'T ANSWER.

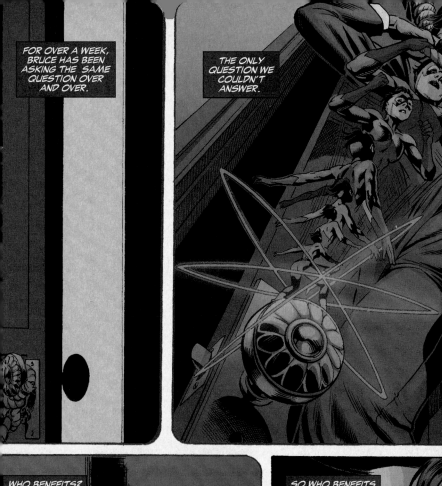

WHO BENEFITS?

I LOVE YOU, DAD.

SO WHO BENEFITS WHEN THE FAMILY MEMBER OF A HERO IS KILLED?

THE FAMILY MEMBERS OF ALL THE OTHER HEROES.

YOU...YOU KILLED HER. YOU KILLED SUE.

JEAN, SHE WAS OUR FRIEND!

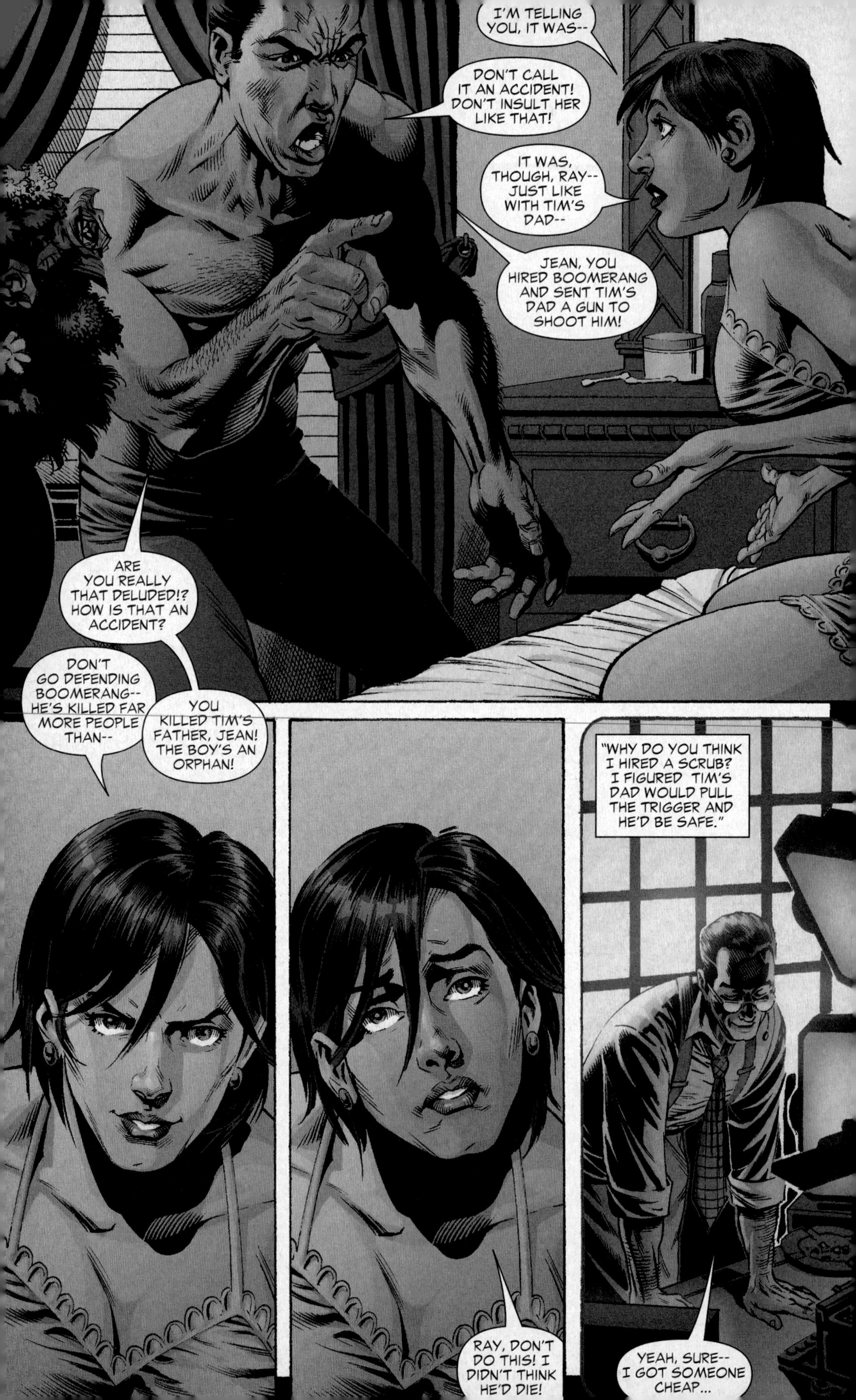
I'M TELLING YOU, IT WAS--
DON'T CALL IT AN ACCIDENT! DON'T INSULT HER LIKE THAT!
IT WAS, THOUGH, RAY-- JUST LIKE WITH TIM'S DAD--
JEAN, YOU HIRED BOOMERANG AND SENT TIM'S DAD A GUN TO SHOOT HIM!
ARE YOU REALLY THAT DELUDED!? HOW IS THAT AN ACCIDENT?
DON'T GO DEFENDING BOOMERANG-- HE'S KILLED FAR MORE PEOPLE THAN--
YOU KILLED TIM'S FATHER, JEAN! THE BOY'S AN ORPHAN!
RAY, DON'T DO THIS! I DIDN'T THINK HE'D DIE!
"WHY DO YOU THINK I HIRED A SCRUB? I FIGURED TIM'S DAD WOULD PULL THE TRIGGER AND HE'D BE SAFE."
YEAH, SURE-- I GOT SOMEONE CHEAP...

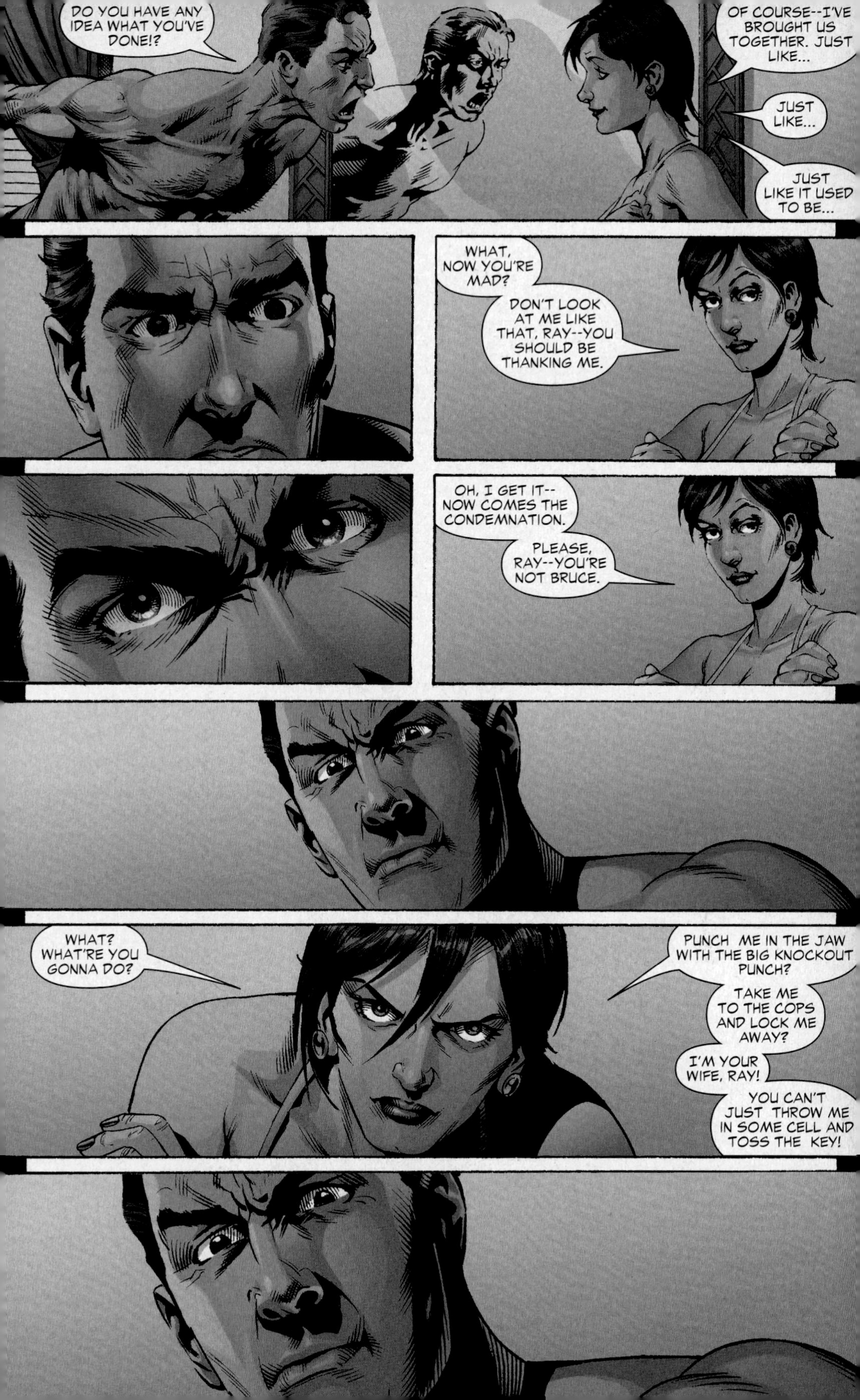
DO YOU HAVE ANY IDEA WHAT YOU'VE DONE!?
OF COURSE--I'VE BROUGHT US TOGETHER. JUST LIKE...
JUST LIKE...
JUST LIKE IT USED TO BE...
WHAT, NOW YOU'RE MAD?
DON'T LOOK AT ME LIKE THAT, RAY--YOU SHOULD BE THANKING ME.
OH, I GET IT-- NOW COMES THE CONDEMNATION.
PLEASE, RAY--YOU'RE NOT BRUCE.
WHAT? WHAT'RE YOU GONNA DO?
PUNCH ME IN THE JAW WITH THE BIG KNOCKOUT PUNCH?
TAKE ME TO THE COPS AND LOCK ME AWAY?
I'M YOUR WIFE, RAY!
YOU CAN'T JUST THROW ME IN SOME CELL AND TOSS THE KEY!

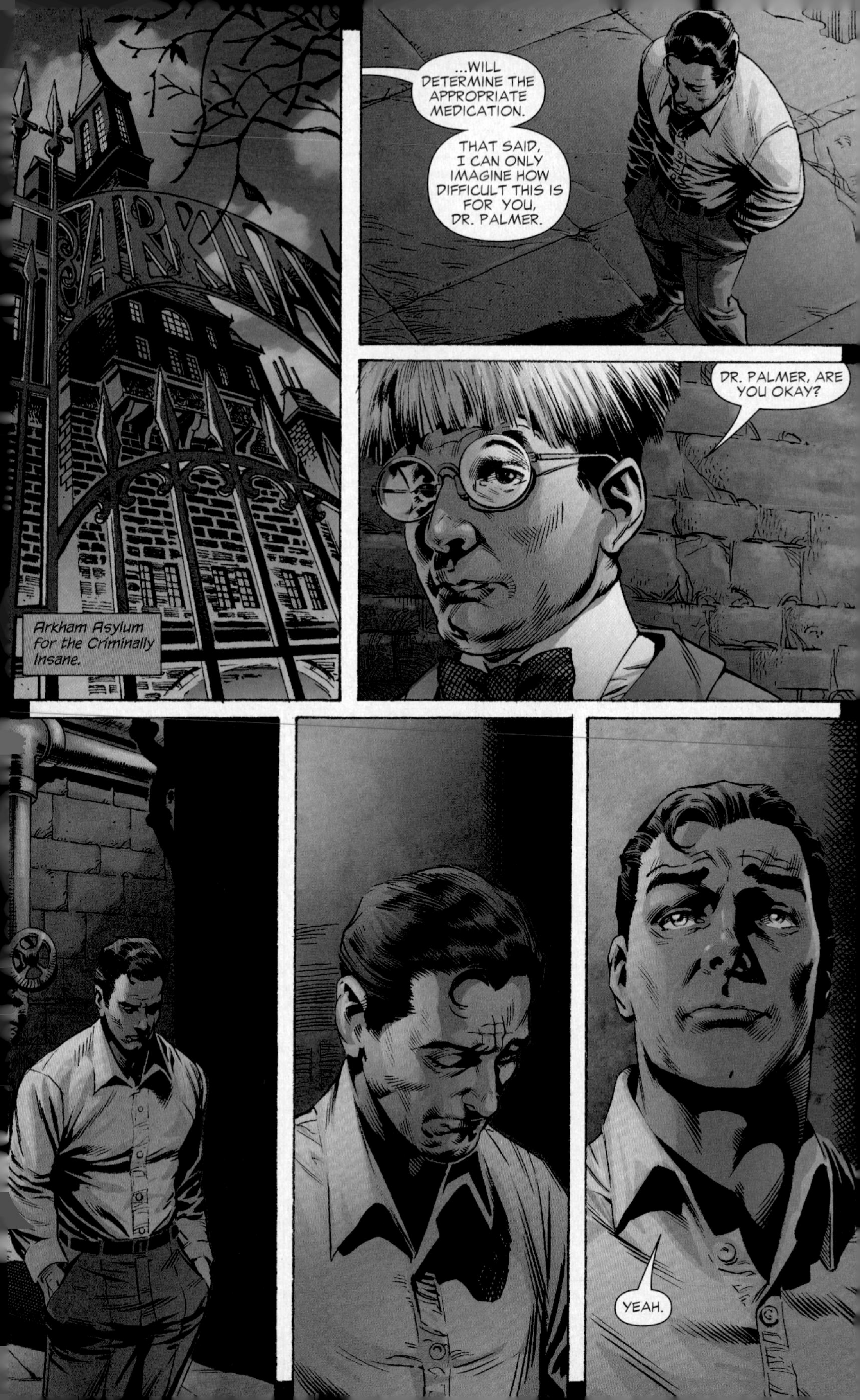
ARKHAM
Arkham Asylum for the Criminally Insane.
...WILL DETERMINE THE APPROPRIATE MEDICATION.
THAT SAID, I CAN ONLY IMAGINE HOW DIFFICULT THIS IS FOR YOU, DR. PALMER.
DR. PALMER, ARE YOU OKAY?
YEAH.

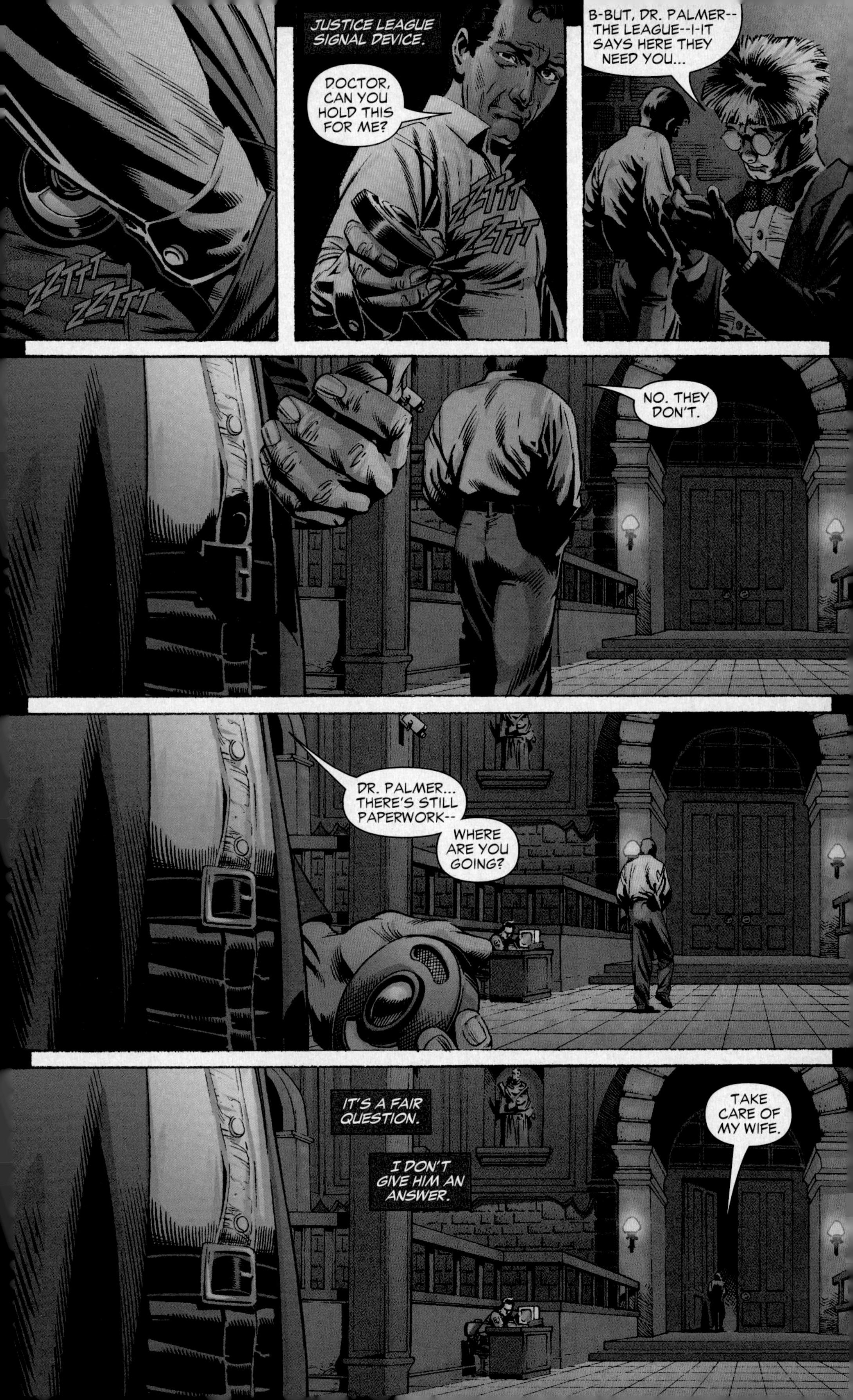
ZZTTTT ZZTTTT
JUSTICE LEAGUE SIGNAL DEVICE.
DOCTOR, CAN YOU HOLD THIS FOR ME?
ZZTTTT ZZTTTT
B-BUT, DR. PALMER-- THE LEAGUE--I-IT SAYS HERE THEY NEED YOU...
NO. THEY DON'T.
DR. PALMER... THERE'S STILL PAPERWORK--
WHERE ARE YOU GOING?
IT'S A FAIR QUESTION.
I DON'T GIVE HIM AN ANSWER.
TAKE CARE OF MY WIFE.

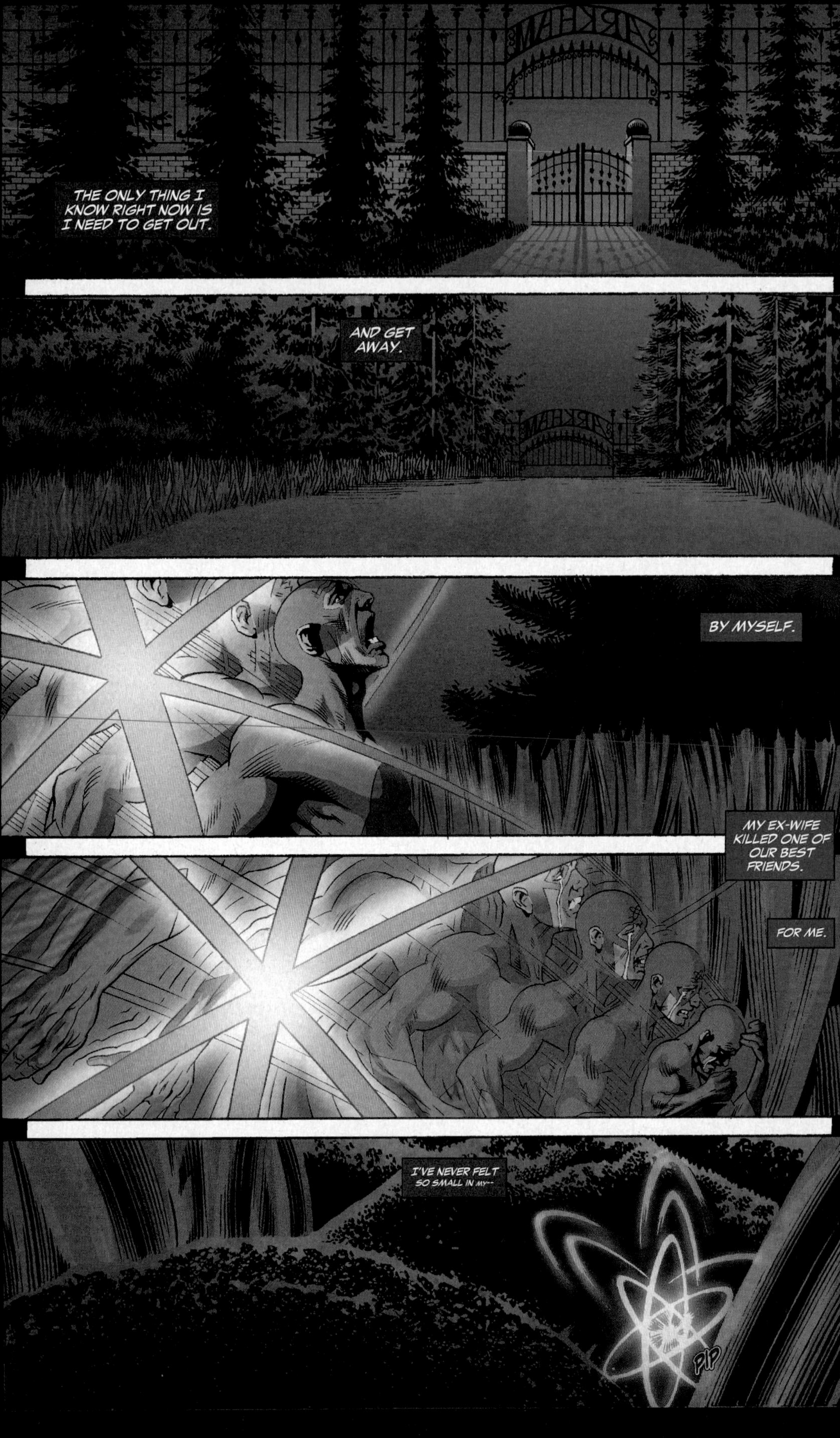
THE ONLY THING I KNOW RIGHT NOW IS I NEED TO GET OUT.
AND GET AWAY.
BY MYSELF.
MY EX-WIFE KILLED ONE OF OUR BEST FRIENDS.
FOR ME.
I'VE NEVER FELT SO SMALL IN MY--
PIP

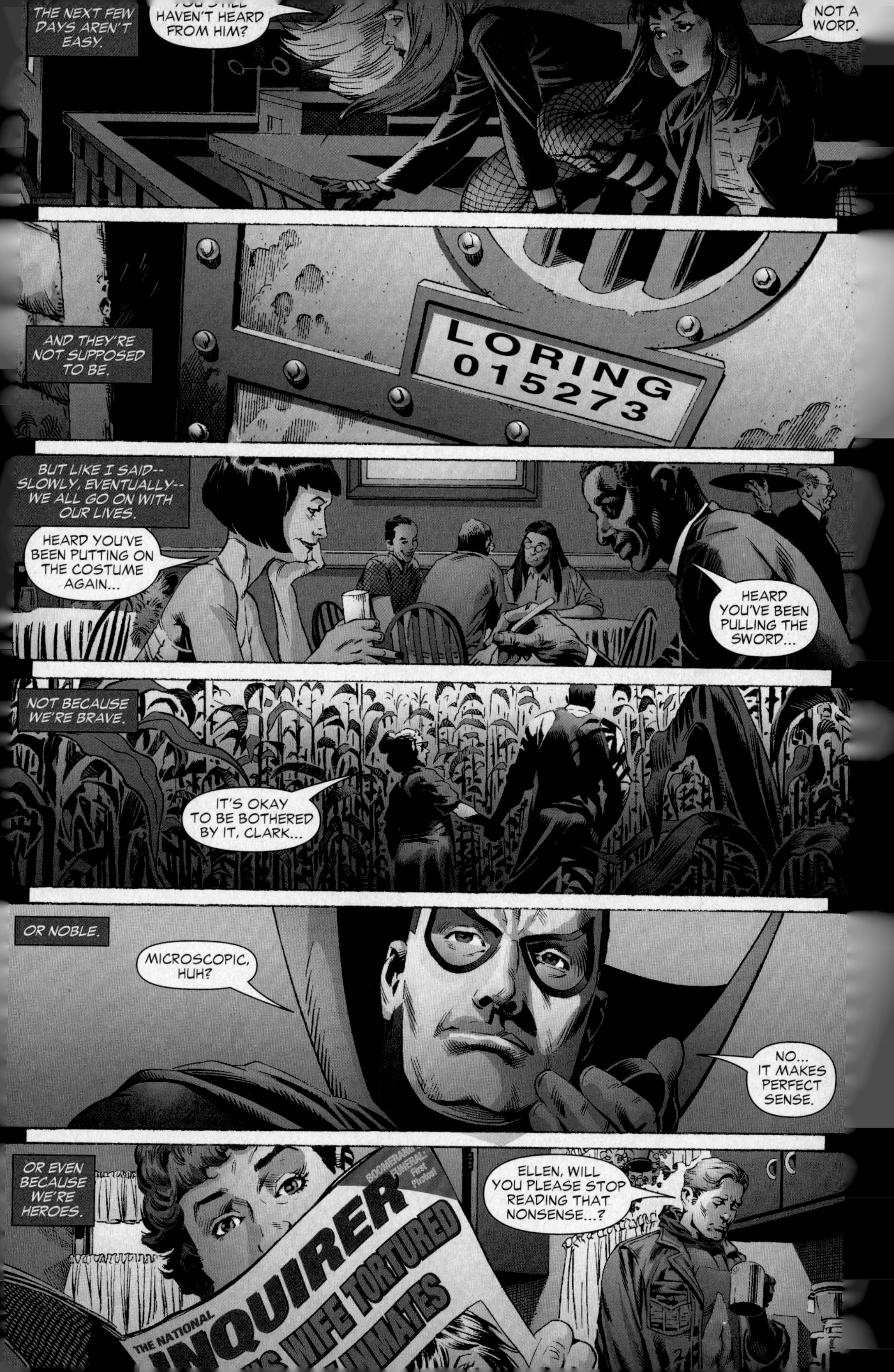
THE NEXT FEW DAYS AREN'T EASY.
HAVEN'T HEARD FROM HIM?
NOT A WORD.
AND THEY'RE NOT SUPPOSED TO BE.
LORING 015273
BUT LIKE I SAID-- SLOWLY, EVENTUALLY-- WE ALL GO ON WITH OUR LIVES.
HEARD YOU'VE BEEN PUTTING ON THE COSTUME AGAIN...
HEARD YOU'VE BEEN PULLING THE SWORD...
NOT BECAUSE WE'RE BRAVE.
IT'S OKAY TO BE BOTHERED BY IT, CLARK...
OR NOBLE.
MICROSCOPIC, HUH?
NO... IT MAKES PERFECT SENSE.
OR EVEN BECAUSE WE'RE HEROES.
BOOMERANG FUNERAL: First Photos!
THE NATIONAL INQUIRER
WIFE TORTURED
ELLEN, WILL YOU PLEASE STOP READING THAT NONSENSE...?

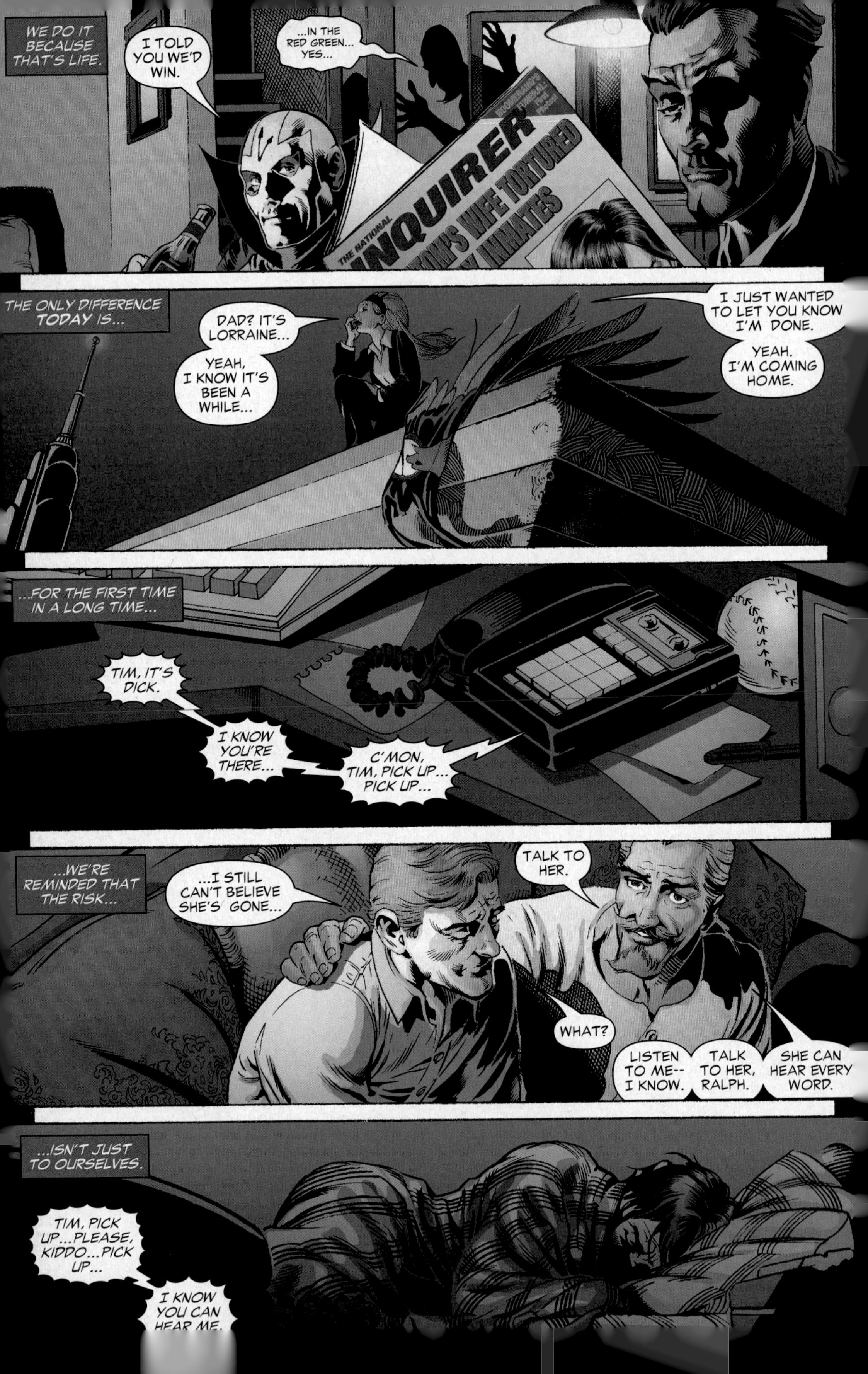
WE DO IT BECAUSE THAT'S LIFE.
I TOLD YOU WE'D WIN.
...IN THE RED GREEN... YES...
THE NATIONAL
INQUIRER
THE ONLY DIFFERENCE TODAY IS...
DAD? IT'S LORRAINE...
YEAH, I KNOW IT'S BEEN A WHILE...
I JUST WANTED TO LET YOU KNOW I'M DONE.
YEAH. I'M COMING HOME.
...FOR THE FIRST TIME IN A LONG TIME...
TIM, IT'S DICK.
I KNOW YOU'RE THERE...
C'MON, TIM, PICK UP... PICK UP...
...WE'RE REMINDED THAT THE RISK...
...I STILL CAN'T BELIEVE SHE'S GONE...
TALK TO HER.
WHAT?
LISTEN TO ME-- I KNOW.
TALK TO HER, RALPH.
SHE CAN HEAR EVERY WORD.
...ISN'T JUST TO OURSELVES.
TIM, PICK UP...PLEASE, KIDDO...PICK UP...
I KNOW YOU CAN HEAR ME.

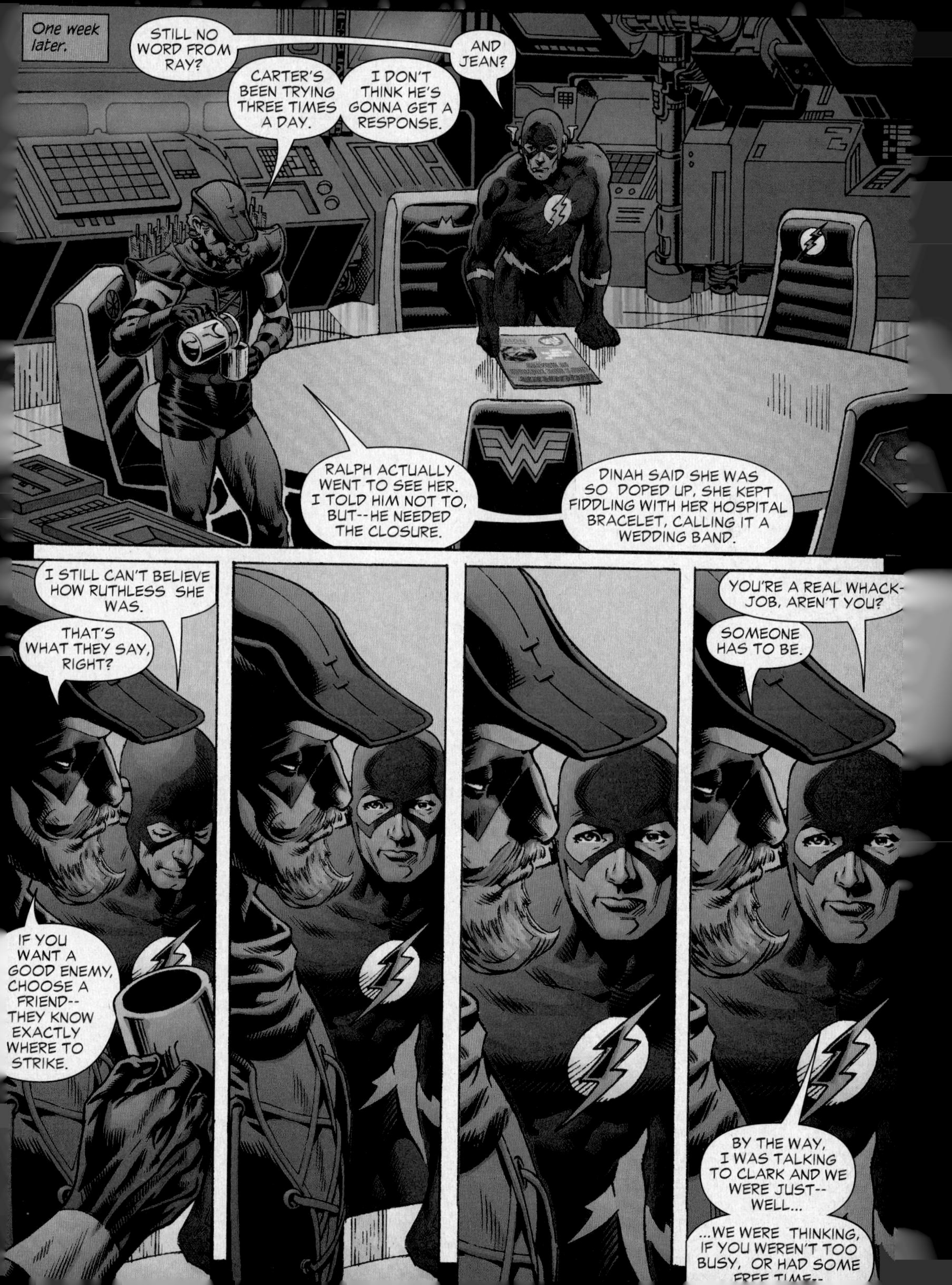
One week later.
STILL NO WORD FROM RAY?
AND JEAN?
CARTER'S BEEN TRYING THREE TIMES A DAY.
I DON'T THINK HE'S GONNA GET A RESPONSE.
RALPH ACTUALLY WENT TO SEE HER. I TOLD HIM NOT TO, BUT--HE NEEDED THE CLOSURE.
DINAH SAID SHE WAS SO DOPED UP, SHE KEPT FIDDLING WITH HER HOSPITAL BRACELET, CALLING IT A WEDDING BAND.
I STILL CAN'T BELIEVE HOW RUTHLESS SHE WAS.
THAT'S WHAT THEY SAY, RIGHT?
IF YOU WANT A GOOD ENEMY, CHOOSE A FRIEND-- THEY KNOW EXACTLY WHERE TO STRIKE.
YOU'RE A REAL WHACK-JOB, AREN'T YOU?
SOMEONE HAS TO BE.
BY THE WAY, I WAS TALKING TO CLARK AND WE WERE JUST-- WELL...
...WE WERE THINKING, IF YOU WEREN'T TOO BUSY, OR HAD SOME

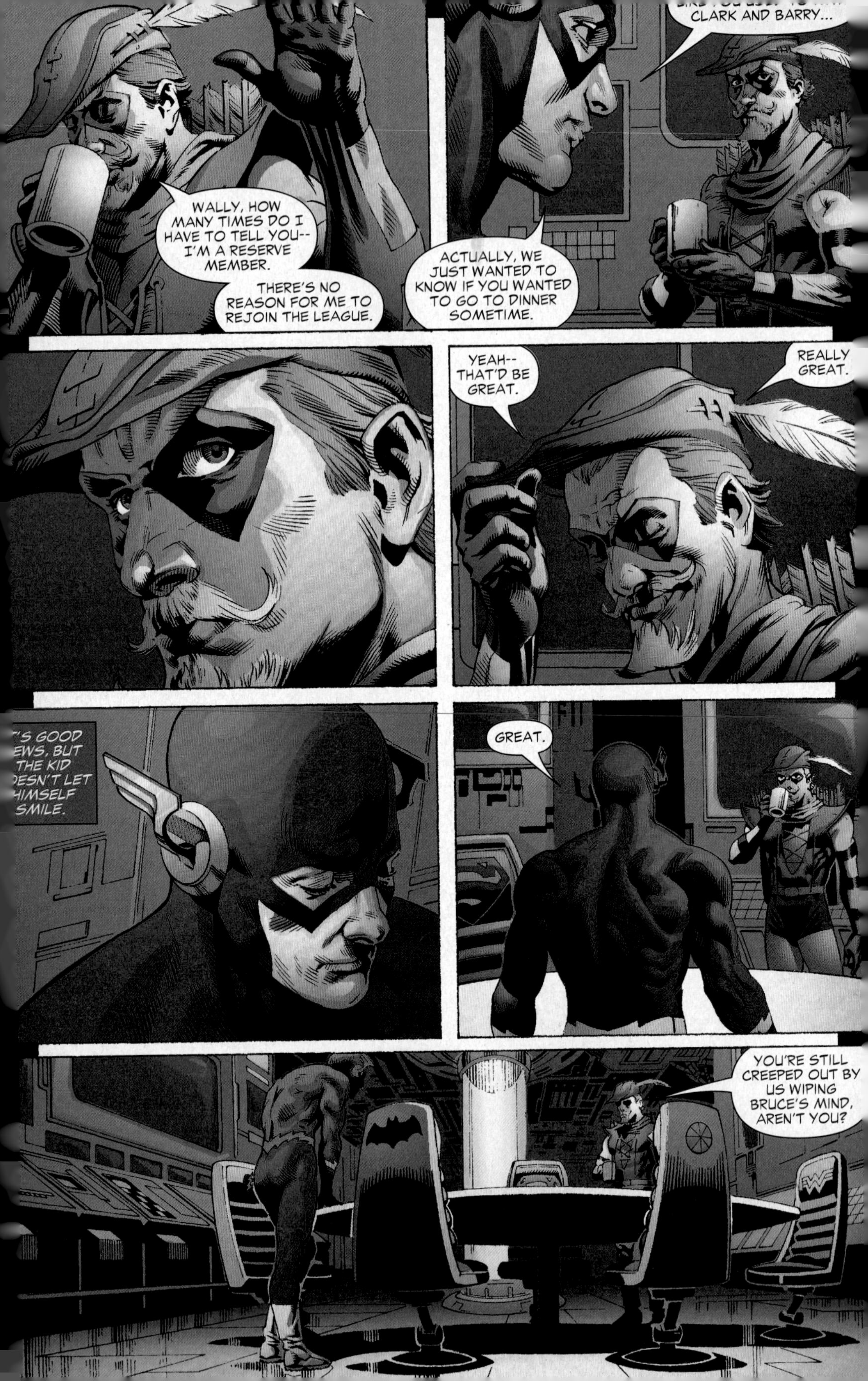
WALLY, HOW MANY TIMES DO I HAVE TO TELL YOU-- I'M A RESERVE MEMBER.
THERE'S NO REASON FOR ME TO REJOIN THE LEAGUE.
CLARK AND BARRY...
ACTUALLY, WE JUST WANTED TO KNOW IF YOU WANTED TO GO TO DINNER SOMETIME.
YEAH-- THAT'D BE GREAT.
REALLY GREAT.
'S GOOD EWS, BUT THE KID DESN'T LET HIMSELF SMILE.
GREAT.
YOU'RE STILL CREEPED OUT BY US WIPING BRUCE'S MIND, AREN'T YOU?

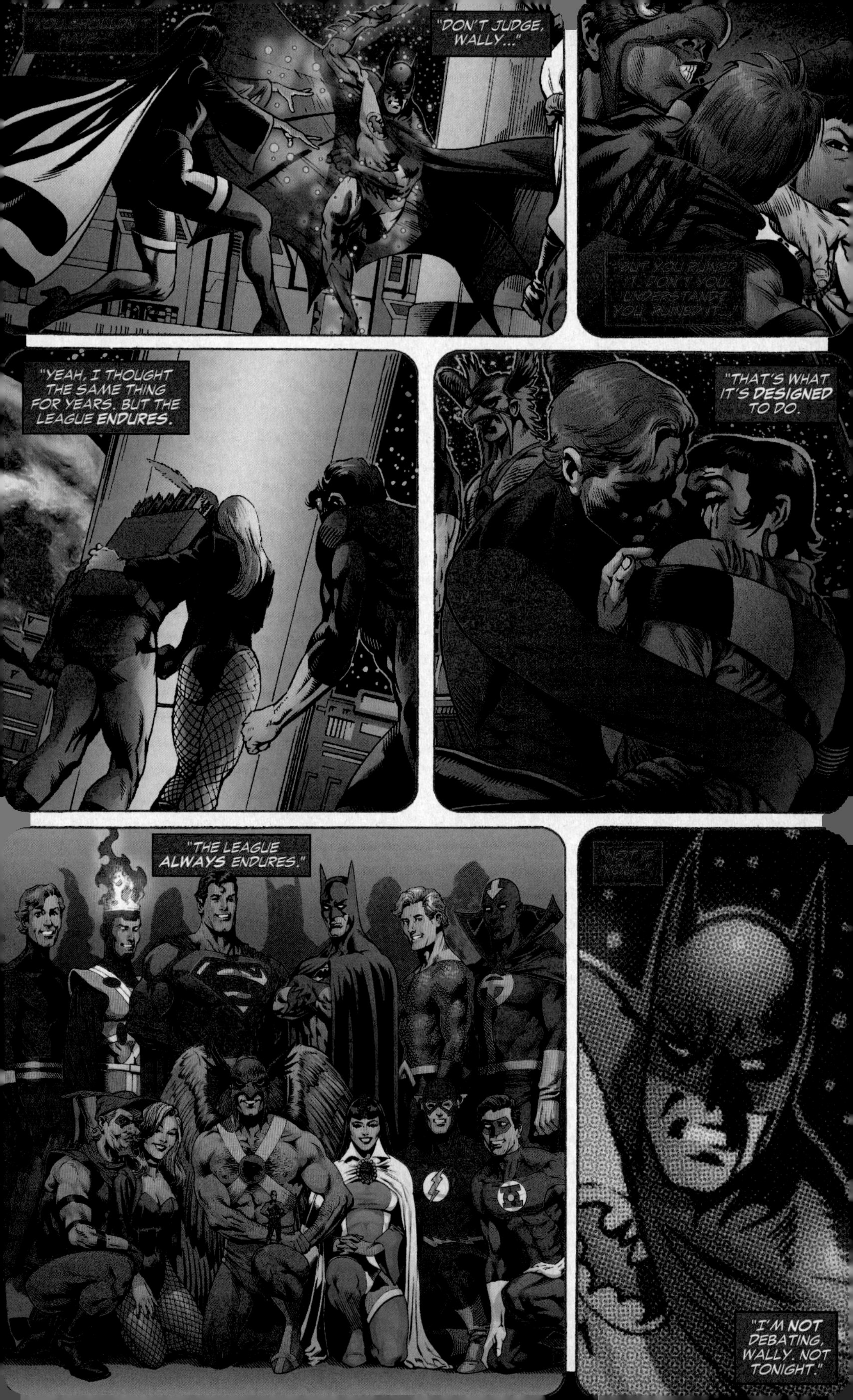
"YOU SHOULDN'T HAVE--"
"DON'T JUDGE, WALLY..."
"BUT YOU RUINED IT. DON'T YOU UNDERSTAND? YOU RUINED IT."
"YEAH, I THOUGHT THE SAME THING FOR YEARS. BUT THE LEAGUE ENDURES.
"THAT'S WHAT IT'S DESIGNED TO DO.
"THE LEAGUE ALWAYS ENDURES."
"I'M NOT DEBATING, WALLY. NOT TONIGHT."

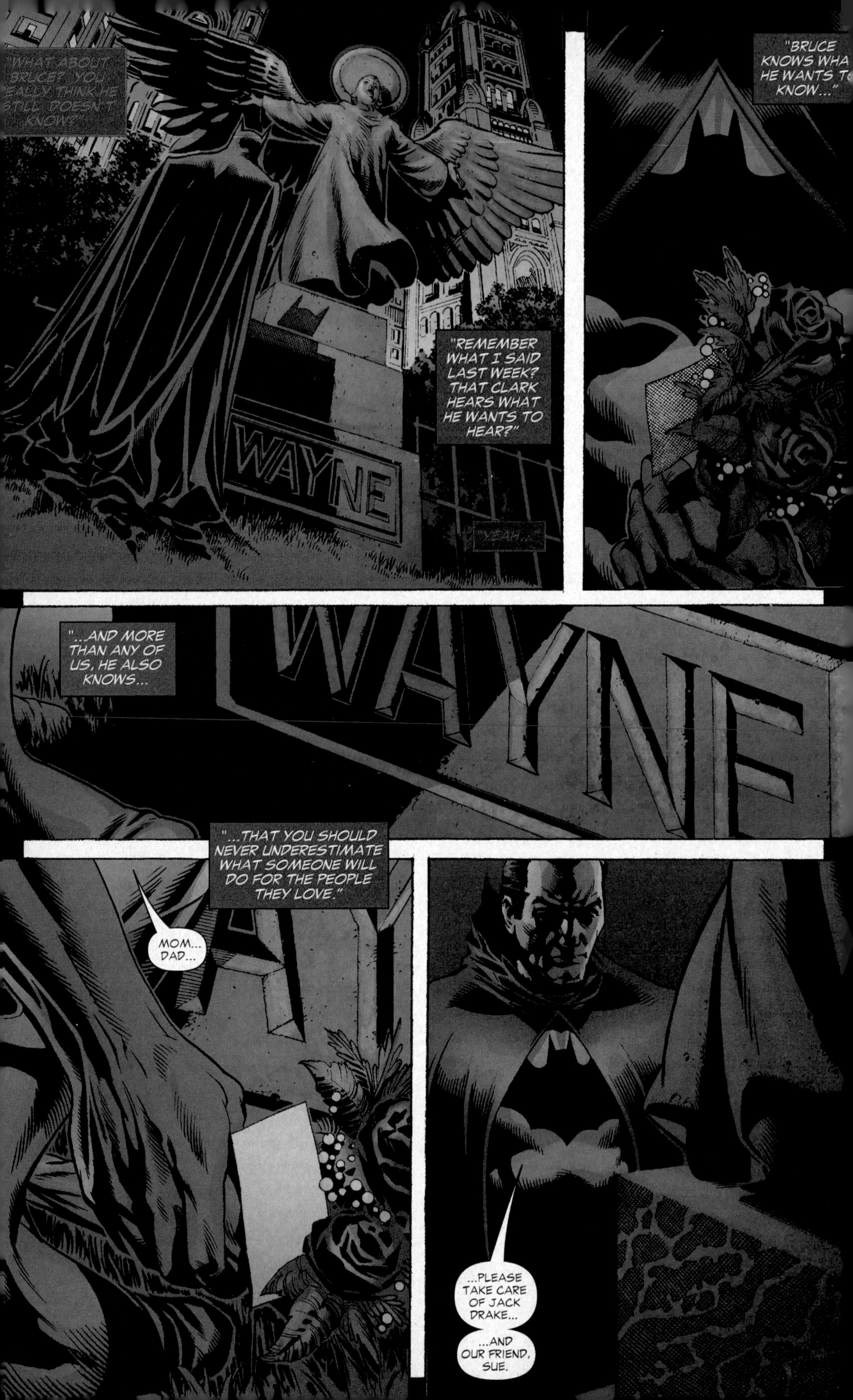
"WHAT ABOUT BRUCE? YOU EALLY THINK HE STILL DOESN'T KNOW?"
"REMEMBER WHAT I SAID LAST WEEK? THAT CLARK HEARS WHAT HE WANTS TO HEAR?"
WAYNE
"YEAH..."
"BRUCE KNOWS WHA HE WANTS T KNOW..."
"...AND MORE THAN ANY OF US, HE ALSO KNOWS...
WAYNE
"...THAT YOU SHOULD NEVER UNDERESTIMATE WHAT SOMEONE WILL DO FOR THE PEOPLE THEY LOVE."
MOM... DAD...
...PLEASE TAKE CARE OF JACK DRAKE...
...AND OUR FRIEND, SUE.

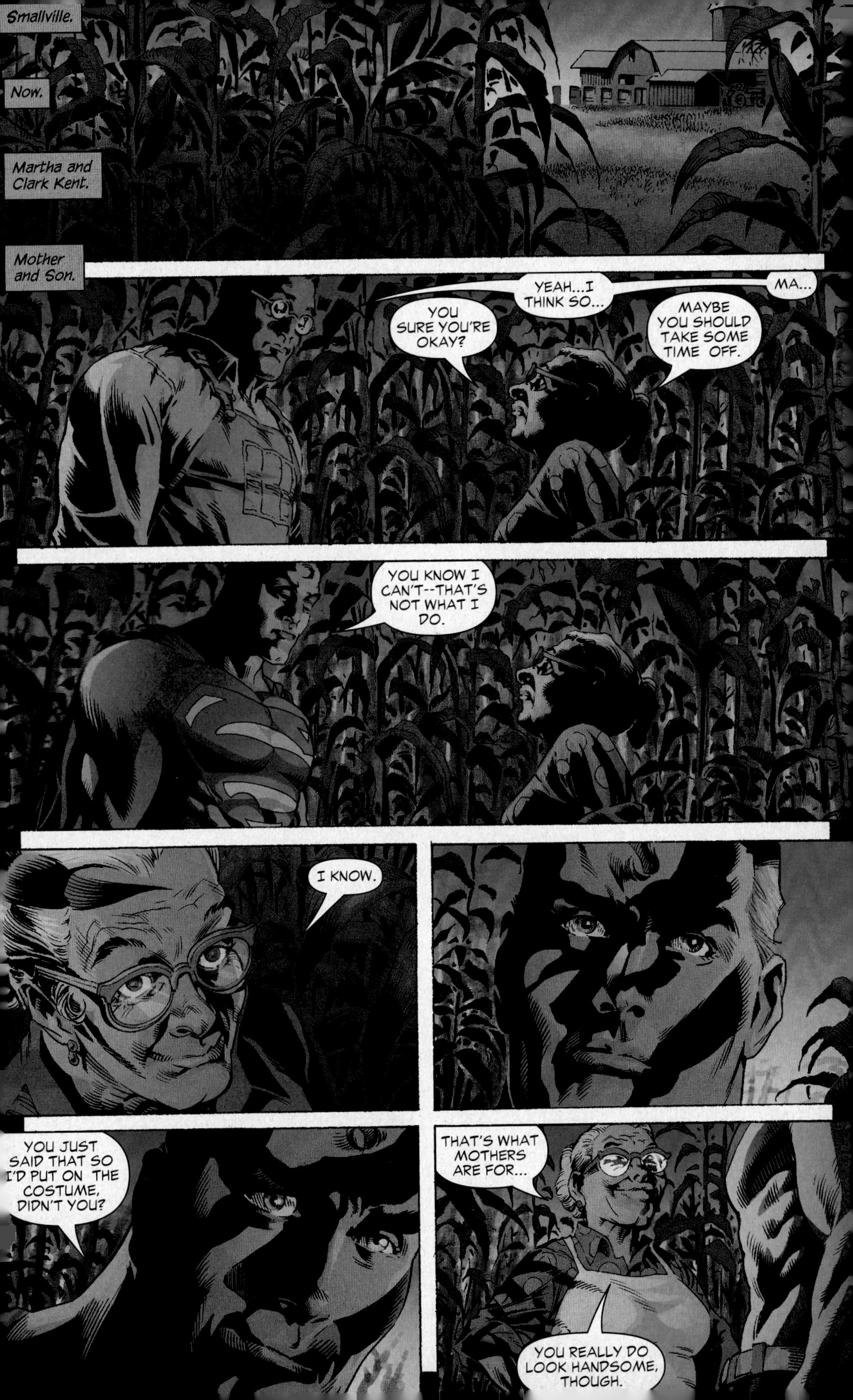

Smallville.
Now.
Martha and Clark Kent.
Mother and Son.
MA...
YOU SURE YOU'RE OKAY?
YEAH...I THINK SO...
MAYBE YOU SHOULD TAKE SOME TIME OFF.
YOU KNOW I CAN'T--THAT'S NOT WHAT I DO.
I KNOW.
YOU JUST SAID THAT SO I'D PUT ON THE COSTUME, DIDN'T YOU?
THAT'S WHAT MOTHERS ARE FOR...
YOU REALLY DO LOOK HANDSOME, THOUGH.

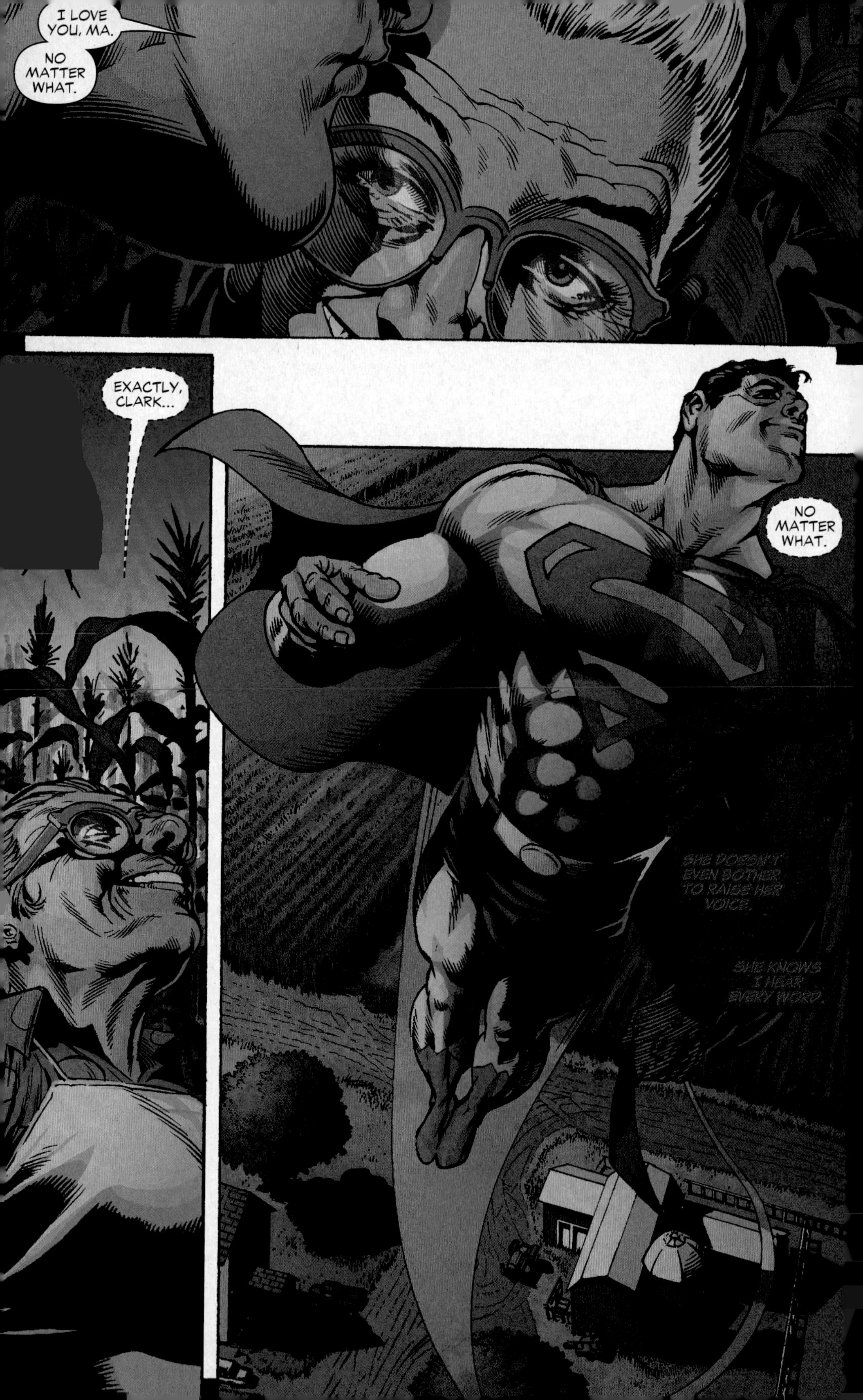

I LOVE YOU, MA.
NO MATTER WHAT.
EXACTLY, CLARK...
NO MATTER WHAT.
SHE DOESN'T EVEN BOTHER TO RAISE HER VOICE.
SHE KNOWS I HEAR EVERY WORD.

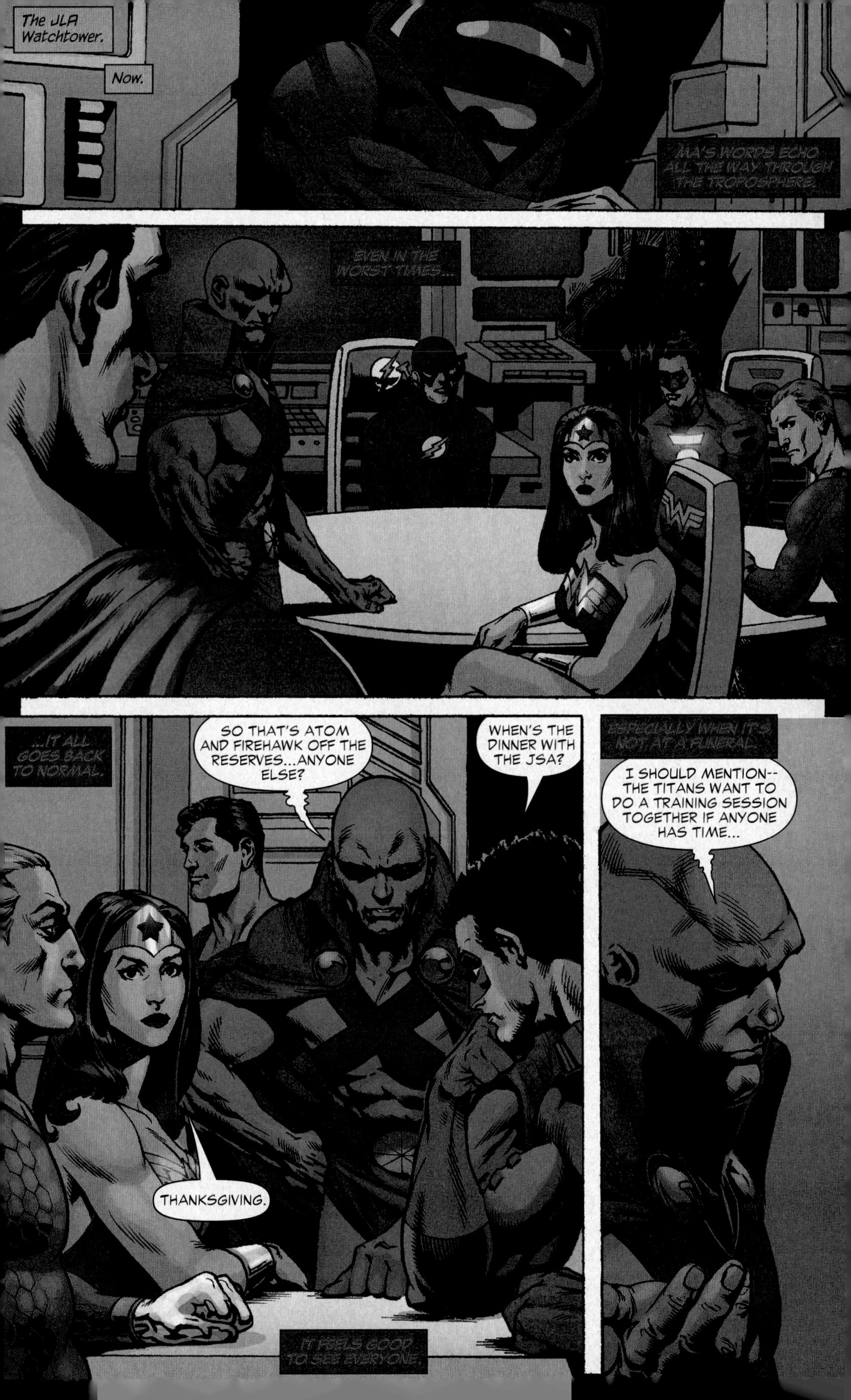
The JLA Watchtower.
Now.
MA'S WORDS ECHO ALL THE WAY THROUGH THE TROPOSPHERE.
EVEN IN THE WORST TIMES...
...IT ALL GOES BACK TO NORMAL.
SO THAT'S ATOM AND FIREHAWK OFF THE RESERVES...ANYONE ELSE?
WHEN'S THE DINNER WITH THE JSA?
THANKSGIVING.
IT FEELS GOOD TO SEE EVERYONE.
ESPECIALLY WHEN IT'S NOT AT A FUNERAL.
I SHOULD MENTION-- THE TITANS WANT TO DO A TRAINING SESSION TOGETHER IF ANYONE HAS TIME...

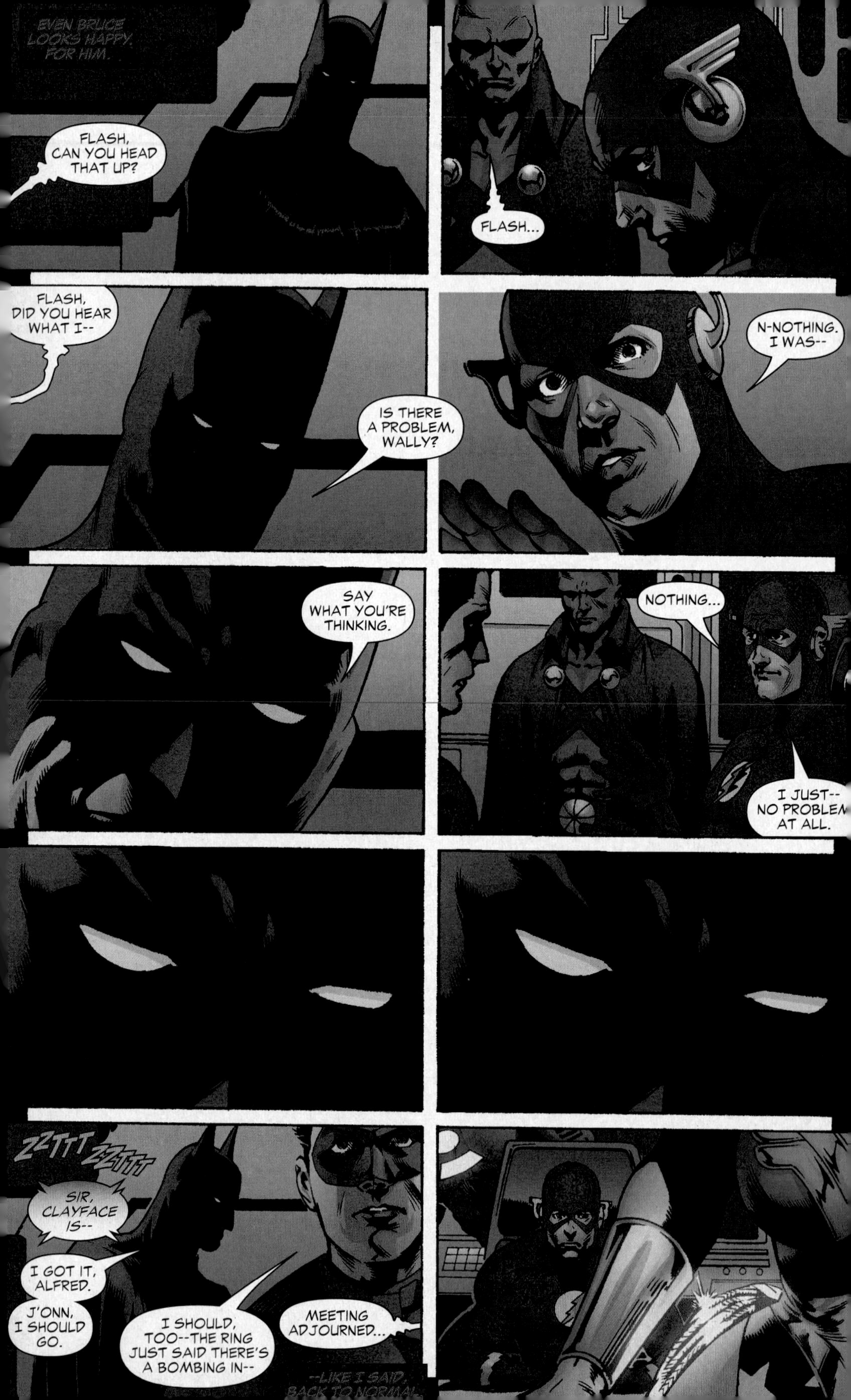
EVEN BRUCE LOOKS HAPPY. FOR HIM...
FLASH, CAN YOU HEAD THAT UP?
FLASH...
FLASH, DID YOU HEAR WHAT I--
IS THERE A PROBLEM, WALLY?
N-NOTHING. I WAS--
SAY WHAT YOU'RE THINKING.
NOTHING...
I JUST-- NO PROBLEM AT ALL.
ZZTTT ZZZTTT
SIR, CLAYFACE IS--
I GOT IT, ALFRED.
J'ONN, I SHOULD GO.
I SHOULD, TOO--THE RING JUST SAID THERE'S A BOMBING IN--
MEETING ADJOURNED...
--LIKE I SAID, BACK TO NORMAL.

Epilogue

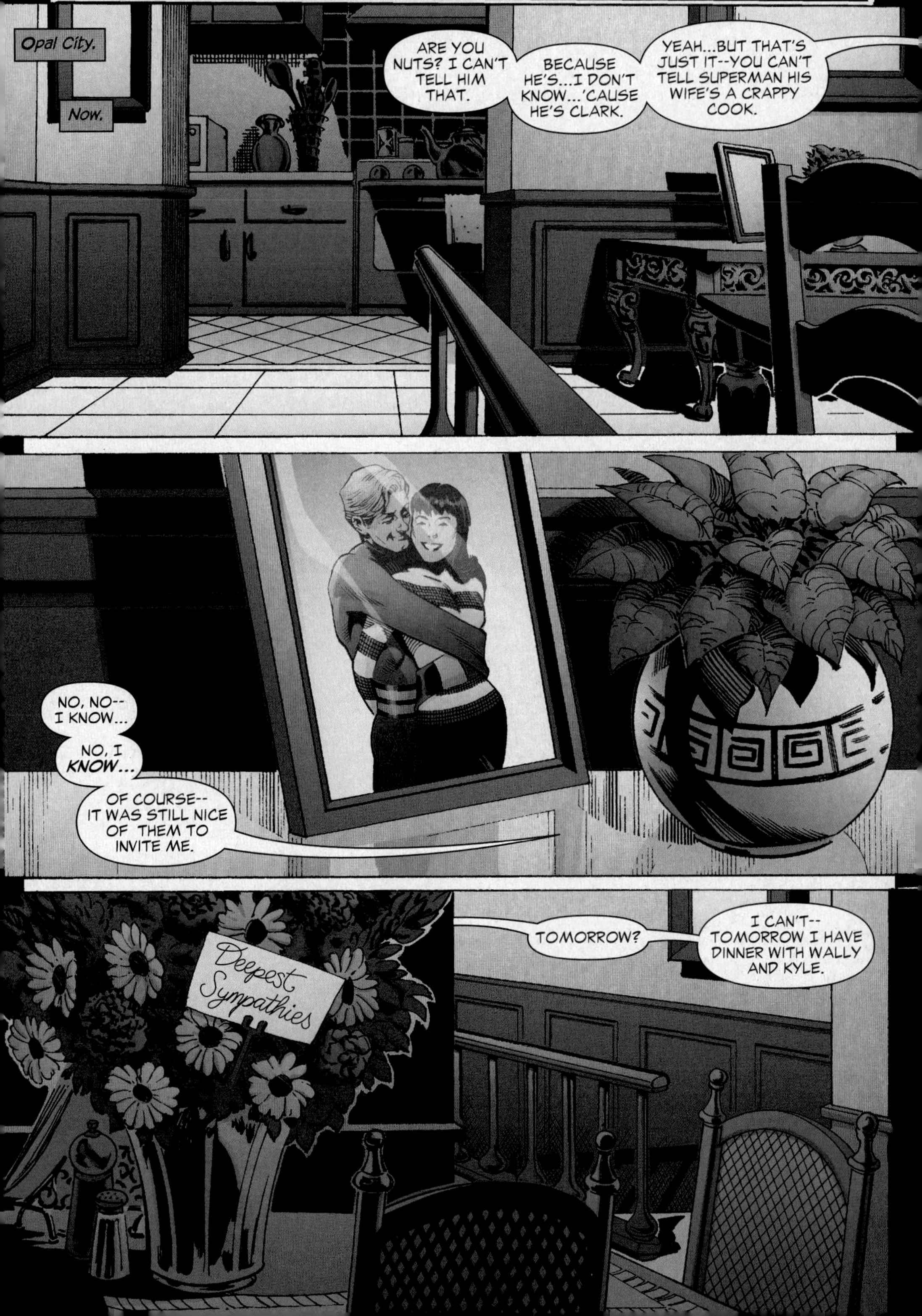
Opal City.
Now.
ARE YOU NUTS? I CAN'T TELL HIM THAT.
BECAUSE HE'S...I DON'T KNOW...'CAUSE HE'S CLARK.
YEAH...BUT THAT'S JUST IT--YOU CAN'T TELL SUPERMAN HIS WIFE'S A CRAPPY COOK.
NO, NO-- I KNOW...
NO, I *KNOW*...
OF COURSE-- IT WAS STILL NICE OF THEM TO INVITE ME.
Deepest Sympathies
TOMORROW?
I CAN'T-- TOMORROW I HAVE DINNER WITH WALLY AND KYLE.

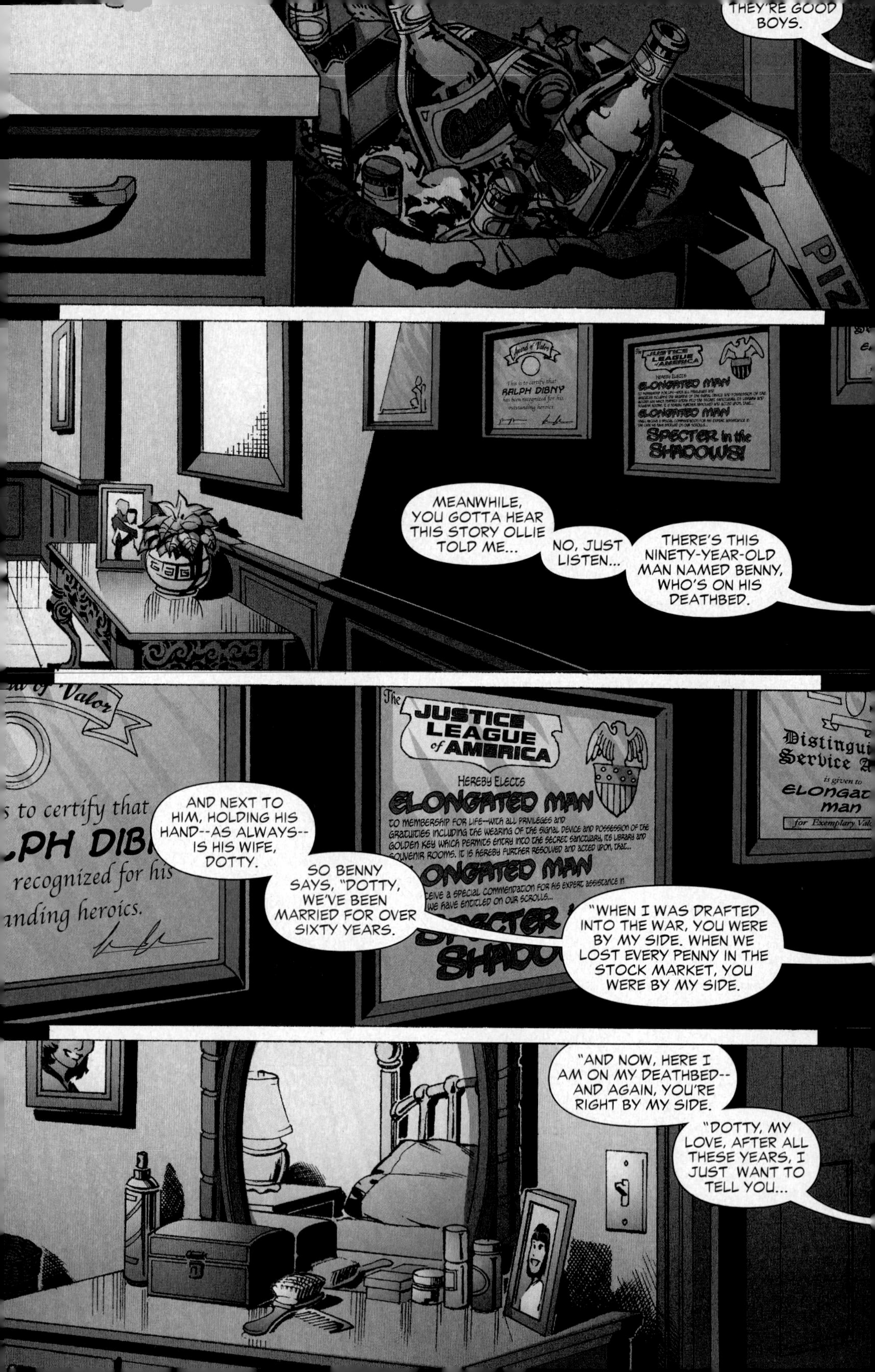

THEY'RE GOOD BOYS.
MEANWHILE, YOU GOTTA HEAR THIS STORY OLLIE TOLD ME...
NO, JUST LISTEN...
THERE'S THIS NINETY-YEAR-OLD MAN NAMED BENNY, WHO'S ON HIS DEATHBED.
AND NEXT TO HIM, HOLDING HIS HAND--AS ALWAYS--IS HIS WIFE, DOTTY.
SO BENNY SAYS, "DOTTY, WE'VE BEEN MARRIED FOR OVER SIXTY YEARS.
"WHEN I WAS DRAFTED INTO THE WAR, YOU WERE BY MY SIDE. WHEN WE LOST EVERY PENNY IN THE STOCK MARKET, YOU WERE BY MY SIDE.
"AND NOW, HERE I AM ON MY DEATHBED--AND AGAIN, YOU'RE RIGHT BY MY SIDE.
"DOTTY, MY LOVE, AFTER ALL THESE YEARS, I JUST WANT TO TELL YOU...

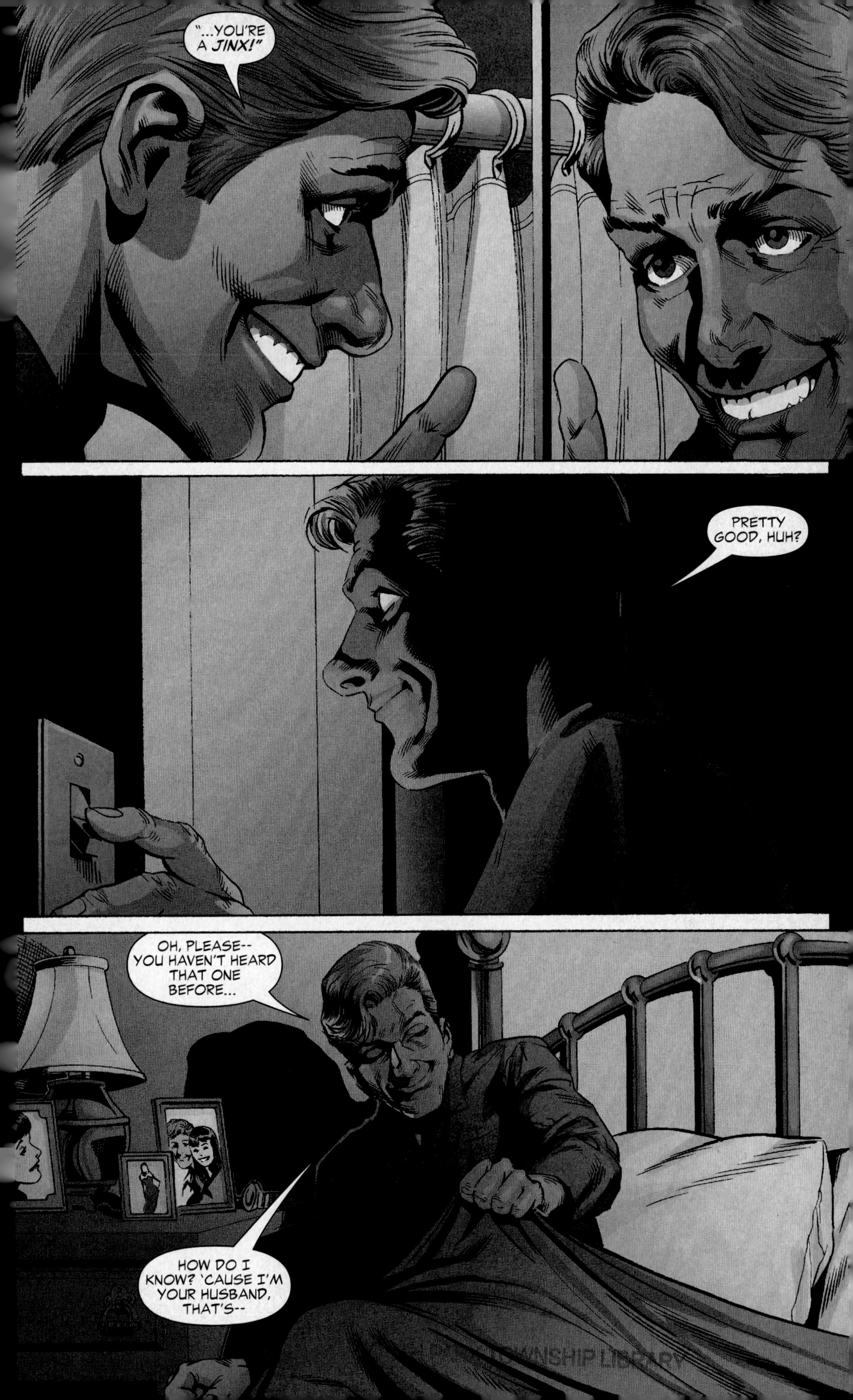
"...YOU'RE A JINX!"
PRETTY GOOD, HUH?
OH, PLEASE-- YOU HAVEN'T HEARD THAT ONE BEFORE...
HOW DO I KNOW? 'CAUSE I'M YOUR HUSBAND, THAT'S--

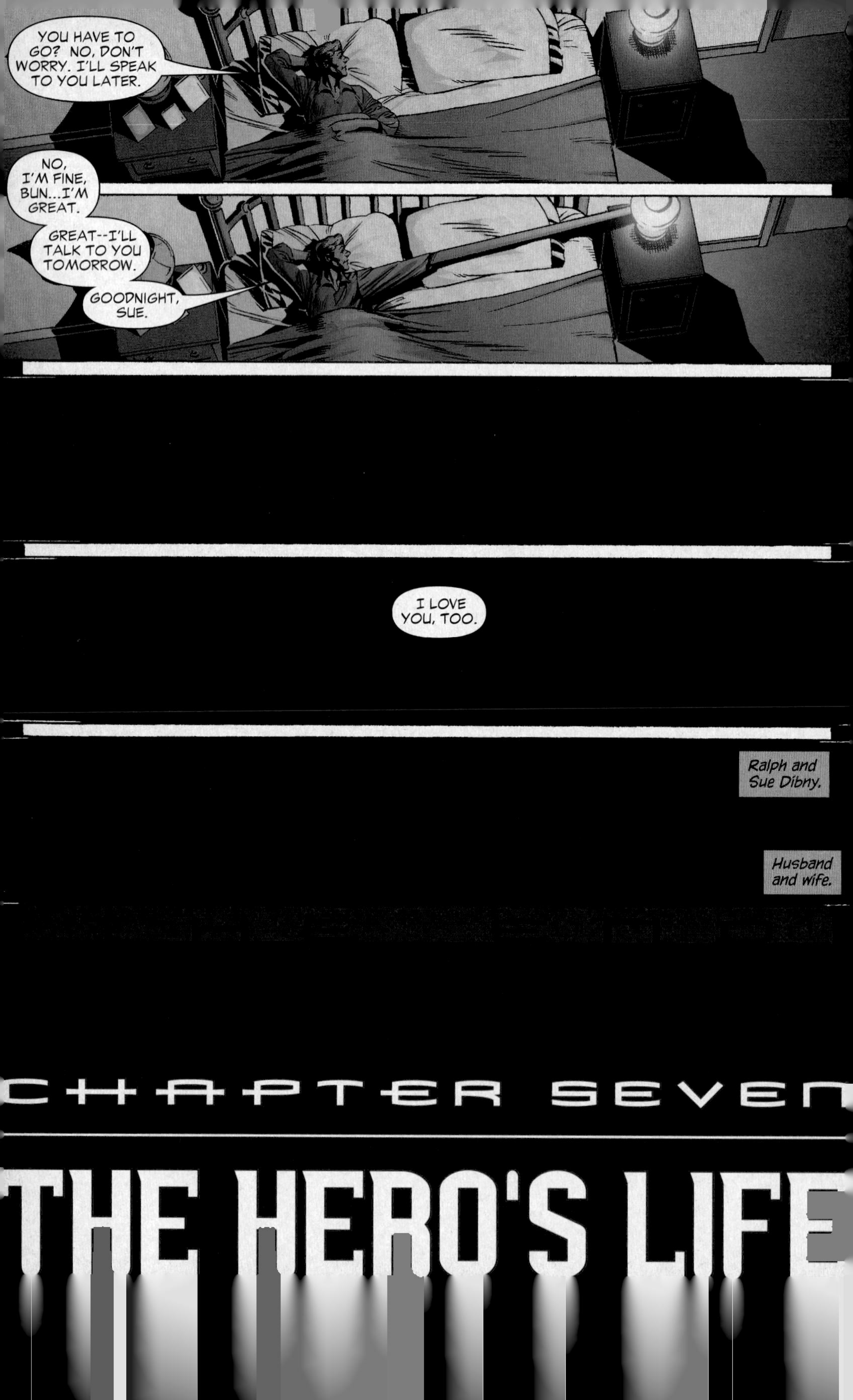
YOU HAVE TO GO? NO, DON'T WORRY. I'LL SPEAK TO YOU LATER.
NO, I'M FINE, BUN...I'M GREAT.
GREAT--I'LL TALK TO YOU TOMORROW.
GOODNIGHT, SUE.
I LOVE YOU, TOO.
Ralph and Sue Dibny.
Husband and wife.
CHAPTER SEVEN
THE HERO'S LIFE

CASTING IDENTITY CRISIS

RAGS MORALES REVEALS THE INSPIRATION FOR THE MINISERIES' KEY PLAYERS

Taking a cue from what's become comics tradition, I've used some Hollywood, TV, and all around pop culture figures to "flesh" out the characters in IDENTITY CRISIS. Now, obviously, I couldn't hire these people to pose for me so I relied on my sense of caricature and artistic license to do reasonable facsimiles of these people. Some actors I've tried to get as close as possible because I felt that if this were a movie, these people must be in my movie. Yet others, such as Firehawk, were pop culture icons that may just have something similar about their background that resembled the character I was drawing. Often times I would combine two people as I did for Captain Boomerang.

However not everyone had a model. I sometimes just went with traditional representation. Those included are: Deadshot, the Monocle, Dr. Light, Deathstroke, Aquaman, Animal Man, the Metal Men, Mister Miracle, Hawkman (c'mon, I did do 21 issues of him...), Black Lightning and Katana, to name a few.

So as you can see, there wasn't any rhyme or reason to everything I did, just running on instinct. Eventually they took on a life of their own and did little to resemble the original models, which is what should happen.

— RAGS MORALES

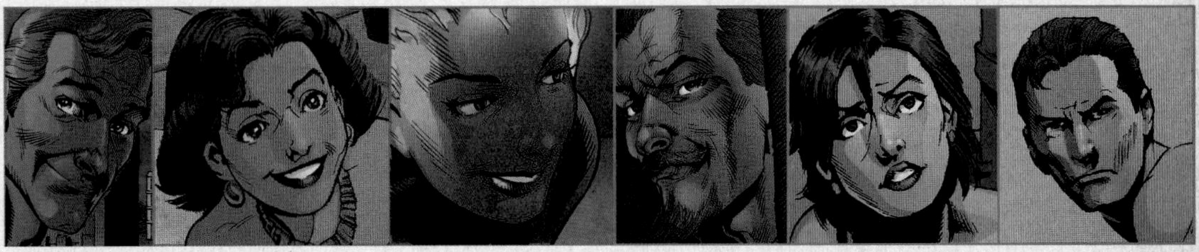

Elongated Man: *Danny Kaye (with Dick Van Dyke, the original model for the character. In fact Dick Van Dyke and Mary Tyler Moore were the actual models for Ralph and Sue. I used a white-haired Dick Van Dyke and a remorsefully hugging Mary Tyler Moore as relatives in the front row of the funerals double-page spread.)*

Sue Dibny: *Dawn Wells (Yes, America's sweetheart. Just a little twist of the knife in your subconscious)*

Firehawk: *Patty Hearst*

Green Arrow: *Layne Staley (Deceased lead singer of Alice in Chains. I liked the shape of his head and face. I originally thought of Steve McQueen, who kinda seeped in when all was said and done.)*

Jean Loring: *Lesley Ann Warren. (Miss Scarlet in* Clue, *among her many roles.)*

Atom: *A young Paul Newman.*

Batman: *Well, at least in the unmasking flashback scene, Tom Selleck sans moustache. Selleck was used for the Wizard as well, with the moustache.*

Flash (Wally West): *Brad Pitt*

Flash (Barry Allen): *John Hurt*

Zatanna: *Phoebe Cates*

Black Canary: *Rebecca Romjin Stamos/Michelle Pfeiffer*

Superman: *I tried to get the original Joe Shuster feel, so I researched Buster Crabbe, but I didn't quite get him. Oh well, it's the pleasure of this business to pursue the perfect piece.*

Nightwing: *Johnny Depp*

Starfire: *Naomi Campbell*

Wonder Woman: *Julie Strain*

Green Lantern (Hal Jordan): *Pierce Brosnan. Mostly for his head shape.*

Green Lantern (Kyle Rayner): *I tried for Freddy Prinze Jr. Then Ethan Van Sciver suggested to think "Calvin Klein model" which is where it ended being, eventually. Thanks, Ethan!*

Vixen: *I was trying for Grace Jones, but somehow she became Geena Davis. Go figure.*

Shining Knight: *John Cleese*

Firestorm: *Josh Myers*

Calculator: *James Woods.*

Merlyn: *Ricardo Montalban (as in* Star Trek II: The Wrath of Khan*)*

Captain Boomerang: *Ron Jeremy (yes, THAT Ron Jeremy)/ Jackie "the Jokeman" Martling (of Howard Stern fame)*

Owen: *Brad gave me this one. Justin Timberlake, but I added a little bit of James Dean in his demeanor.*

Phobia/Dr. Moon: *Carolyn Jones (*Addams Family*)/ Jerry Lewis*

Chronos: *NY Yankees manager Joe Torre*

Felix Faust: *Leonard Nimoy*

Mirror Master: *Eric Roberts*

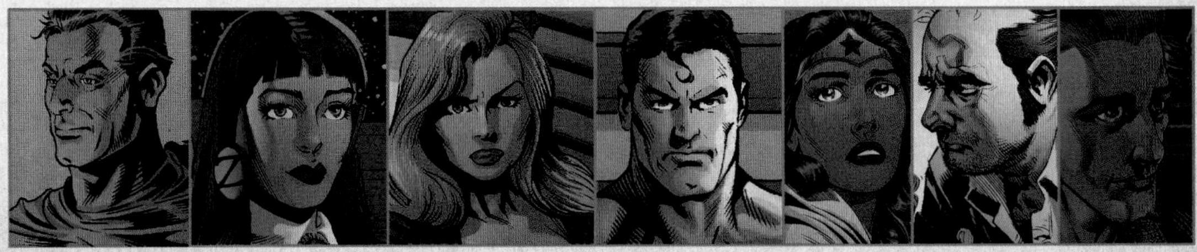

BRAD MELTZER AND RAGS MORALES DISSECT IDENTITY CRISIS

Brad and Rags discuss the series through all seven issues for a true director's cut of how the book was produced. We also hear from other contributors along the way.

THE OPENING VIGNETTES, pages 12-14

Brad: In this story we look at death in all its manifestations — not just the death of a person, but the death of an ideal, the death of a dream, and in the case of Dr. Light, the death of self. As a result, all the vignettes in the beginning touch on death by putting the heroes with the characters whose death would affect them most — and then showing what each hero hides from them — whether it's Clark hiding Bruce's secret, or Nightwing hiding his loneliness, or Ollie (barely) hiding his love for his son. And of course, that's why we started with Superman — the most alien and human of them all in the most mundane and human of situations. When Ma Kent says, "I bet Batman never does this to his parents," we quickly see what Superman's afraid of.

So many super-hero comics look at things through a telescope trying to find giant monsters and whole worlds to punch. *Identity Crisis* is designed to look at these characters through a microscope, pulling in so tight, we can see all their flaws and imperfections.

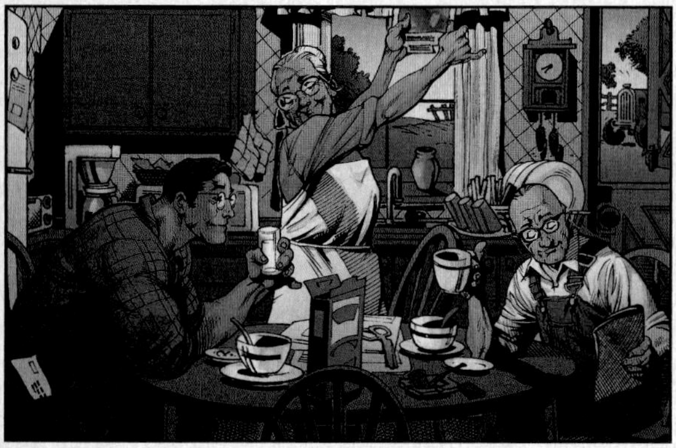

From the script:

Page Four, Panel Two:

Biggest panel on the page. Establishing shot of Ma, Pa and Clark in their kitchen. Ma Kent is standing and looks up from the clipping she's just cut out. She's holding the clip up proudly. Clark and Pa Kent are sitting at the kitchen table, eating cereal and coffee. Clark has a big glass of milk in his hand.

RALPH CRADLES SUE, page 31

Brad: I remember calling up Rags and saying "I'll never do this to you, but can you send me a sketch before you draw it?" because the whole book was going to revolve around this moment. In the script, I said this shot should be just like that shot in *The Shawshank Redemption*, with Tim Robbins looking up at the sky, the rain falling down around him — but instead of joy, I wanted a moment of horror. I wanted to be looking straight down at Ralph and Sue. Rags called me up and said "I really want to do it at a little bit of an angle." I said "No, no, no, you have to trust me on this." He said, "I'll do it my way and if you don't like it, I'll do it your way." I sat at the fax machine waiting for it to come through and when he sent me the sketch, I called him and said "Your way."

The reason we were so lucky to have Rags Morales draw this is, anyone can do the shot. Anyone can draw a husband cradling his dead wife, but it's getting the emotion that's the important part. The look on Ralph's face — the way his jaw is unhinged from his face — it's his super-power giving him the worst agony of his life. I remember showing this to my wife who said, "I feel so bad for them." Needless to say, that was all Rags.

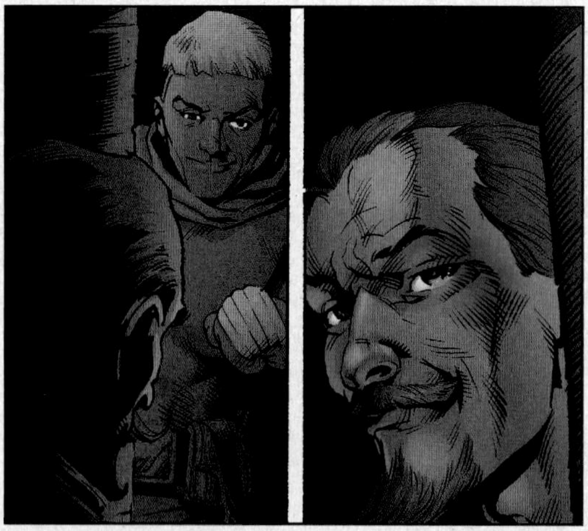

Rags: One of the things I hate is repeating things within my own work, not to mention drawing from other artistic sources. It sounds impossible and it is, but if I can consciously avoid it, I will. So when I tried to conceive this scene via what Brad wanted, all I got was *Shawshank Redemption*, it's all that it felt like to me. I just had to empha-

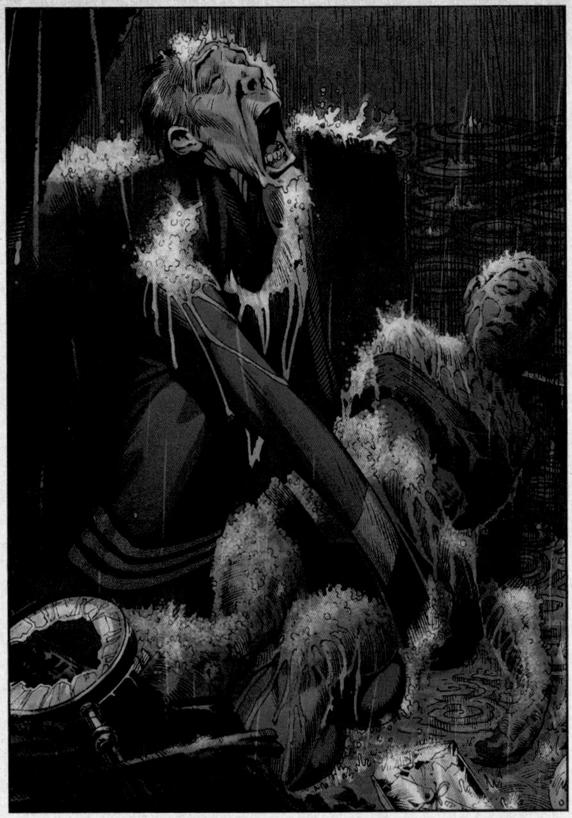

size the "stretch" in that moment. I knew we were going to have Ralph lose control of his face later on in the funeral scene, so for me I thought it was important to set a precedent for that scene. Just to let people know that when emotion takes control, Ralph loses control of his appearance, as we all seem to do. Brad had a distinct vision for this story and I really wanted to oblige, but there are times when two heads are better than one. It's one of the few times where I had to interject, with Brad's brilliant storytelling, this book could have drawn itself.

WHERE'S BATMAN? Page 35

Brad: When I originally wrote the scene at the funeral, this was supposed to be the first appearance of Batman. Batman was going to be there when the heroes dissected Sue's apartment. I waited my whole life to write this scene because Batman had always been my favorite, and not just because I spent most of my youth wearing a Batman cape everywhere I went. But when I wrote the word "Batman" in the script, and I waited to see his first words, I realized — you know what? — Batman would *never* be there. He wouldn't waste time being at the funeral, he wouldn't be there to shake hands and give hugs, he's not a super-friend. He hates funerals. While everyone else is mourning, he's going to be out there solving the crime. This was the first time I realized I wasn't writing the characters — the characters were writing themselves. I took Batman out of the scene, had him leave a note on the door, and moved on. At that moment I made the decision that Batman's *presence* was going to be a true character for the first half of the story. He purposely doesn't even appear until page 118 of this collection — but I think he's felt strongly without ever showing his face. That's who Batman is. A myth. A presence. That's how you strike fear into the superstitious and cowardly lot.

Rags: I remember the Internet community having a problem with Batman's lack of appearance here. I'm glad Brad rethought his original instinct. He should be enigmatic and unpredictable. It just goes to show how little we *all* know about Batman.

From the script:

> Page 35, Panel 7:
> Similar shot, but now, there's a crumpled-up piece of paper on the floor that's obviously Batman's note.

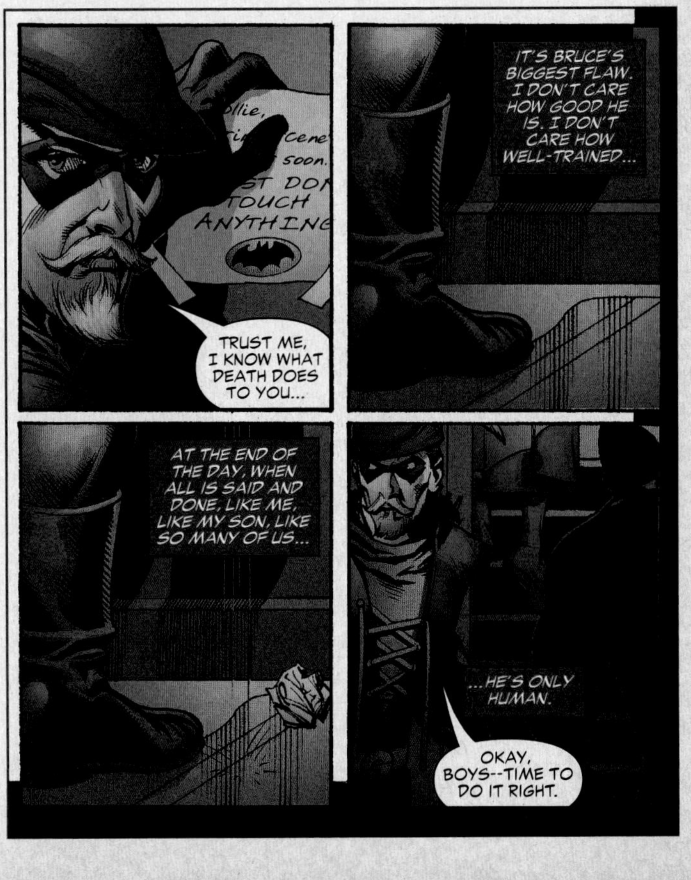
TRUST ME, I KNOW WHAT DEATH DOES TO YOU...
IT'S BRUCE'S BIGGEST FLAW. I DON'T CARE HOW GOOD HE IS. I DON'T CARE HOW WELL-TRAINED...
AT THE END OF THE DAY, WHEN ALL IS SAID AND DONE, LIKE ME, LIKE MY SON, LIKE SO MANY OF US...
...HE'S ONLY HUMAN.
OKAY, BOYS--TIME TO DO IT RIGHT.

THE FUNERAL SCENE, pages 38-39

Brad: The funeral scene is an Alex Sinclair masterpiece. His use of light humanizes the entire scene, and he made it more than just a cheap

double-page, multi-colored splash. I even did a seating chart for every character because I didn't want to do the classic "fill it with all the heroes we have so it'll look cool." I wanted it to make sense where people were sitting and what their emotional response would be: from Starfire crying, to Power Girl enraged and seeking revenge, to Captain Marvel surveying the whole scene through the eyes of a little boy. I even put the League (in all its incarnations) on one side, with the Titans on the other (Roy being the backup to where Green Arrow would be). I know I drove Rags and Michael Bair, and especially Alex Sinclair, nuts, but I wanted it right.

Rags: Heh. I ran into some dead space, so I had to call Brad for some more people to fill in. They're all there on the left side, Snapper Carr, Commissioner Gordon, Gypsy, and of course I had to get Red Tornado in there as well. I just had to make sure he was in the right place, on the right side of the scene.

Alex Sinclair has been on my fave list for some time now. When I conceived the pages for this series I made some pretty concise thumbnails that were done in gray tones for Alex to fol-

low, but not for the double-page spread of the funeral. I think it confused him. It just was too much work for me to do all that intricate detail in gray, so I did a simple thumbnail that no one but me ever saw. Alex had to go by instinct and did a brilliant job of it.

RALPH'S FACE, page 42

Brad: The sequence where Ralph's face melts — this is another moment where I realized how blessed we were to have Rags drawing the story. Someone actually said to me, you should take out the melting face because it'll just look bad, like cheap special effects. I thought, *If it does we'll change it,* but I wanted to see what Rags could do. When I saw the face puddling over Ralph's fingers, I knew we weren't changing a thing.

Rags: I called Brad and said, "I want to twitch his nose here. He should lose control of his nose. It will answer the proposed question at the beginning of the issue where Green Arrow insinuates that his nose twitch is a publicity stunt." Brad said, "Just don't make it silly looking." I suppose it would have been odd and cartoony, but the previous panels were designed to set up the face melt. The rolling of Ralph's eyes was purely for dramatic effect.

From the script:

> Page 42, Panel 8:
> Pull in slightly closer on the shot of Ralph from panel 5. As we get in closer, his skin looks like it's slightly sagging on his cheeks. Please don't overdo this — he's not melting, but he's having a hard time maintaining the form of his face. Maybe his hand is messed up too. Head still down.

ICONOGRAPHY, page 40

Brad: Throughout the series, I tried to focus on just the iconography of the characters — this being my salute to Barry Allen (centered between the male and female as symbols of life). As I say it out loud, I sound like some pretentious film school snob in an L.A. café, but I always wanted the icons to remain larger than the rest of us. Every time they appear, the Big Three are bigger. The rest of us could be small and vulnerable, but the Big Three were different.

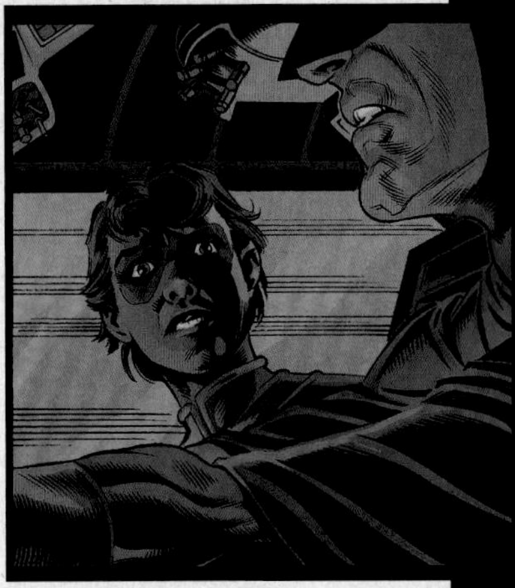

Rags: Brad wrote a lot of these types of panels where we focus on an icon, a prop, what have you. And it's one of those things that struck me so much, that I added it to my own storytelling repertoire. In drawing ADVENTURES OF SUPERMAN #636 I used the same technique, when in the opening sequence, Ruin is reaching out to a picture of Lois Lane, triggering Superman's rage at the thought of her being hurt. Not only did it add punch to the scene, it fit the character better. It spoke of his heroism and his marital impulses as well. I used it again later, when Superman is admitting his guilt to Wonder Woman over this whole Dr. Light mind-wiping thing. Wonder Woman has her hand on Superman's face and he gently pushes it away with Wonder Woman's iconography as the backdrop.

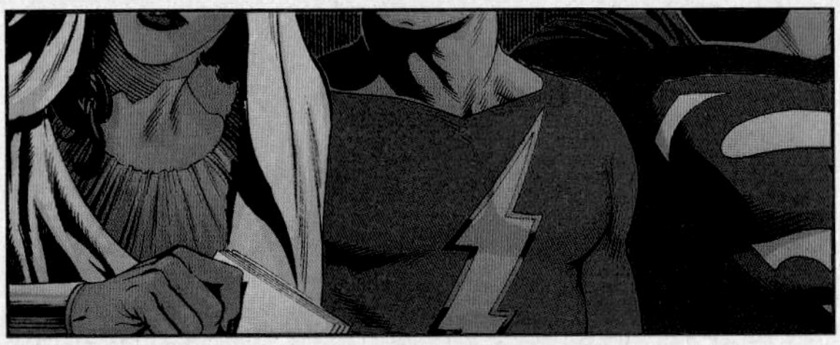

From the script:

> Page 40, Panel 7:
>
> Shot of Superman, Jay Garrick Flash, and Wonder Woman in the front row – but not of their faces. Like page 1, it's just their chests – the iconography. Wonder Woman is getting out of her seat as the other two sit there.

THE LEAGUE WITHIN THE LEAGUE, page 43

Brad: I always said, it's not about the murder, but this is the first time you get to see what the story's really about. It was a very conscious choice to show the group peeling away, the other heroes chasing leads, so that you're left with the final group of five. These five became the centerpiece.

Rags: When I look at those pages of the funeral scene and

FAVORITE MOMENTS
AS SELECTED BY THE STORYTELLERS

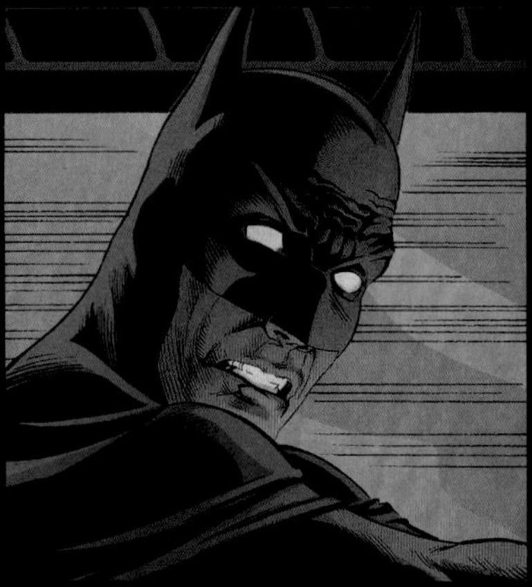

RAGS MORALES

There were many instances that struck me throughout the series. The death of Sue Dibny, the rape scene, the funeral, there are so many, it's unfair to pick just one. But since I do have to pick, I guess the Batman and Robin scene, racing against time to save Jack Drake, was the favorite and most moving scene. I remember reading and feeling my pulse race, my brow getting wet. Brad's most incredible talent throughout the seven issues was not just being descriptive but picking the right words to grab you. It's a shame, really, that the only people who read the script are the ones in the know. I feel that maybe I did the story a disservice by not pouring everything that Brad filled in me on the page. I just don't have that amount of talent to really express as much as I had. At the same time, if I did, then maybe this series would have been shelved waiting for the world to grow up enough to deal with it.

But that scene, the Batman and Robin scene, made me cry. I remember thinking as I drew, about my dad and how much he means to me, from Scoutmaster to Little League coach. I wish there were dedications for this story, 'cause mine would be to my dad. I guess the greatest compliment was reading on the Internet that some readers were so moved, that they just had to call their fathers.

this one, it amazes me that we got this book series out on time. There was just so much involved. Thank God that I had Mike Bair and Alex Sinclair working with me. I think maybe, subconsciously, we all knew how important this story was, that in the end we couldn't let the story down.

From the script:

Page 43, Panel 1:

This page should be set up with a ton of characters in panel 1, and then in each subsequent panel, some of the mentioned heroes will be running/flying out of the panel, so each forthcoming panel whittles down the number of heroes left. Hawkman, Green Arrow, Black Canary, Atom, and Zatanna, however, should not be standing together — so when we see they're the only ones left, it's a surprise to readers. Panel 1: Cyborg, Starfire, Robin, Kid Flash, Metamorpho, Tasmanian Devil leave/fly off panel.

RALPH ANGRY, page 45

Brad: Anyone can draw mean, anyone can draw anger, but Rags had just drawn 37 pages of Elongated Man with that lovable Dick Van Dyke look. And then you get to the last page with all that anger and hate and loss in his eyes. Thank you, Rags.

Rags: OK, OK. You can be my agent; you got the job.

From the script:

page 45, Panel 1:

Just one panel for this page — a thick widescreen rectangle at the center of the page — the space above and below it is black (except for the credits, which can be at the bottom). The shot should be a close-up on Ralph's face as he looks up at us. He's pissed. Ultra-pissed. Eyes angry like Wolverine. He wants revenge.

CAP: "...to Destruction."

ELONGATED MAN: "Help me find Dr. Light!"

ISSUE 2 COVER, page 46

Brad: This was my favorite cover of the series. Barry with his eyes closed — the rest punching through the fourth wall, teasing us with their secret. Michael Turner at his best — and Peter's phenomenal job on colors gives us noir lighting that always evoked *Blade Runner* for me.

THE RAPE, pages 54-55

Brad: We very consciously decided to keep this off panel. To me, the most horrible things in life are the things you can't see. What you have in your head is always scarier than whatever we put on paper. That's especially true here. Also, Sinclair's cold lighting gives it a sterile feel that makes it that much more horrifying.

Rags: This scene was the one that told me I had to make this series as special as I could. I remember reading this script in my bed and beading with sweat. I just got done telling my wife that the script was too dictating and there were just too many panels per page and how this Meltzer guy was killing

me…then boom. I read issue two. I never complained again. It was the moment where I left my professional hat behind me and became not only a fan of the script, but a fan of Brad's craftsmanship. It was just so powerful for me, I really felt bad for Ralph and Sue there. What tragic heroes they became to me.

RALPH YOUNG AND OLD, page 58

Brad: As you can see, from the end of the flashback with young Ralph, to the bottom of the panel with current Ralph, Rags never holds back on the emotional hit. But in this panel, he also tackles the passage of time and the changes in the man. This was why you felt so much for Ralph.

Rags: Just following orders, pal.

From the script:

> Page 58, Panel 1:
>
> Close-up on Ralph's face back then (in the past). He's younger, so his hair is neater, his face tighter. He's got tears in his eyes as they well up. We're looking up at him, as if the camera is on the floor (as if it's Sue's POV).
>
> Panel 3: This is the same exact size as panel 1, but here, we're seeing Ralph in the present (blue sky behind him). His face is aged, weary, longer. His hairline is receding a bit. He looks like he's been through hell.

THE LEAGUE DIVIDED, page 63

Brad: Here it is: the greater good versus the morally right. One giant fight scene — all without a single punch being thrown. When I wrote it, it was meant to be a scale with three

on one side, three on another — with Barry the Saint wedged in the middle — the symbol of the Silver Age being forced to decide whether to step into the darkness.

That the majority of readers agreed with and understood his logic (even if they themselves didn't necessarily condone it), was a complete reaffirmation of the unchanged, enduring strength of these characters.

As for each of the hero's reactions, I just let them be true to themselves. They're self-righteous, noble, hypocritical, selfless, depressed, willful, and heroic — and I didn't create those roles. Those roles have been there for years. That's why they're the world's greatest superheroes. They're us. As writers of these heroes, we're allowed to interact with greatness. All I can ever do is hope to be up to the task.

Rags: The last panel is key. I wanted to put Dr. Light on the floor directly in front of where I placed The Flash. Almost as if he and the others are dissecting a frog for biology class. All the elements are there for a heavy scene. The two sides, Flash in the middle, Dr. Light bisected on the floor, the JLA conference table, the transportation tube, and for the *coup de grâce*, the planet Earth as a backdrop. Not only does this decision impact the heroes, but the people they're sworn to protect.

THE MINDWIPE, page 70

Brad: As I was trying to get into Zatanna's character, I kept thinking: She's the most powerful member in the League, but for some reason never reached her potential. There had to be a reason for that. So I started pulling on the thread of the sweater, hoping to subtly bring those issues to the forefront. The result — and answer — came from the emotional toll of the mindwipes.

Rags: Zatanna is so sweet and innocent a character. Even though she is obvi-

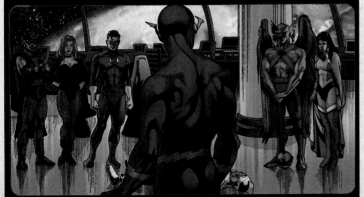

ously concentrating, and you can tell she's trying to make sure it's done right, she seems so out of character here — a witch

doing her craftwork. The Flash being washed out behind her is to signify the loss of innocence and ideology of the heroes. A pain they will live with for a long, long time.

DEATHSTROKE VS. THE LEAGUE, pages 79-91

Brad: The only super-power that works here is brainpower, which is why when the League takes him down, no one is using their powers. What scares me isn't a man who can toss a building at me. It's a man who's been plotting how to slit my throat for the past month. Deathstroke's been thinking about it for years.

Rags: Brad is not just a mystery writer, but a scientist. This scene proves it. I can't tell you how many scripts I've read that take the fight scene for granted.

From the script:

> Page 79, Panel 3: Close-up on just Hawkman's chest-plate. Deathstroke's sword is slicing straight across his chest (from nipple to nipple) — and therefore slicing straight through the X-shaped straps that hold Hawkman's wings on him. We should also see the streak of blood across the chest as it slices across Hawkman.

> Page 83, Panel 4: Close-up on Green Arrow's quiver — more specifically, the ends (the parts with the feathers) of all of Green Arrow's arrows being sliced off (taking off everything that sticks out of the quiver — and leaving him dozens of sticks) by Deathstroke's sword.

> Page 85, Panel 4: Big panel of Slade holding up a weapon that's nothing more than a laser pointer. He holds it in his fist like he's ready to stab someone with it. Out of the laser pointer we see a perfect, thin red beam shooting outward. Atom shrinks even further as he's about to hit the red ray of light.

MICHAEL BAIR

As the pages rolled in from Rags it was obvious this book was special…each page presented a new storytelling challenge [acting, setup, cinematography, etc.], and he knocked it out of the park. Watching him get better page after page was the fun part of the book for me. I love comic art and I hadn't seen anyone since Michael Golden grow so quickly on a book.

The other part of the coin -- Brad's scripts worked on so many levels…the quiet moments being the most engaging and requiring the most subtlety and seeing how like puzzle pieces they moved the story ahead like a sledgehammer. As a fan it was a gas watching it all come together with Alex Sinclair making us all look good.

As a matter of fact, I don't think the book as a whole would have clicked with the public without his colors pulling all the elements forward. And after working at DC for eight years it was nice to finally get to work with Mike Carlin…the iron hand in the velvet glove. The book was a killer on the whole team . . .

. . but we're all proud of it.

DR. LIGHT REMEMBERS, page 92

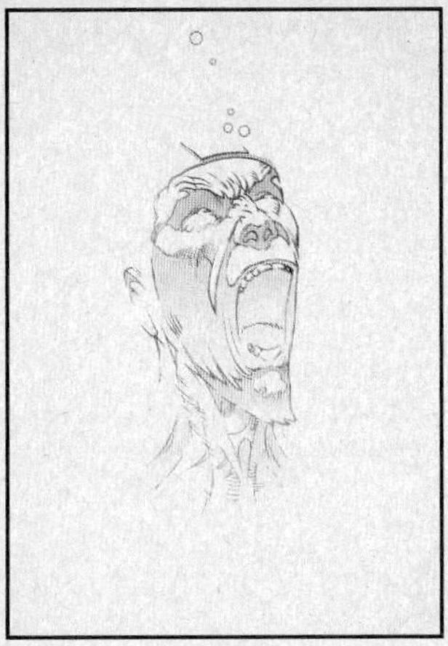

Brad: In the original script, I had the moment where Dr. Light remembers as two blank white pages. I thought it would be much more powerful for the reader to see a double-page spread of white. DC talked me down to one page because they weren't letting me waste two whole pages on my own false notion of artistic importance. So we were down to one stark white page. Rags called and said he'd done this little pencil sketch and if I didn't like it, he'd change it back to the whole white thing. It came in and once again proved why I shouldn't be the artist.

Rags: When I read this part, the first thing I thought of was a Lobo collection that DC put out some years ago. In it was a book of Lobo's deep thoughts. Every page is blank. At first I thought "someone from printing screwed up," but then I got it. I wanted to avoid someone turning to this page and thinking that the printer screwed up so I convinced Brad to let me put in a faint Dr. Light on that page. Besides it just felt unethical to be paid for a page that had nothing on it…damn my moral ethics!

THE MINDWIPES, page 99

Brad: It's easy to say that the mindwipes were there just to let us examine the morality of the heroes. And that's true. But my other goal was that they'd allow us to see the old Silver Age stories in a brand-new way. You look back on those stories now and they're wonderful — nothing tops them — but I think a lot of people chuck them to the side and say, *That's fun, that's cute, but they're a coloring book and we don't need them anymore*. I love those stories. I grew up on those stories, and those stories changed my life. They taught me my values. They engaged me when no one else did. And in my own selfish way, I wanted them back.

Rags: 95% of my artistic heroes come from the Silver Age. I know that Len Wein likes what we did, so that makes me proud.

Here's a little tidbit. I forgot that Wonder Woman was retconned out of the JLA for this remake. Mike Bair was the one that changed her to Black Canary. See why he's so great? You wouldn't know unless I told you.

From the script:

page 99, Panel 1: Big panel with a newspaper (the Daily Planet) as it sits on a table – we only see what's above the fold. On the front page is a shot that recreates the action of Justice League (Mike, is it 166 or 167 of JLA?), where the Secret Society of Super Villains swaps their minds into the bodies of the JLA. Please see that issue to get the costumes then – I know Zatanna and all the villains had different costumes back then. The scene I'd love to recreate is the one where the JLA is lined up on one side, and the Society Villains are on the other – the mystic statue is in the center – and it's like their minds are swapping. The headline reads:

Switcheroo!

(and below that, in smaller font):

Wizard and Others Gather in
Secret Society;
Trade Bodies With JLA

CAP (Green):
People always say it was simpler back then.

CAP (Green): But it wasn't.

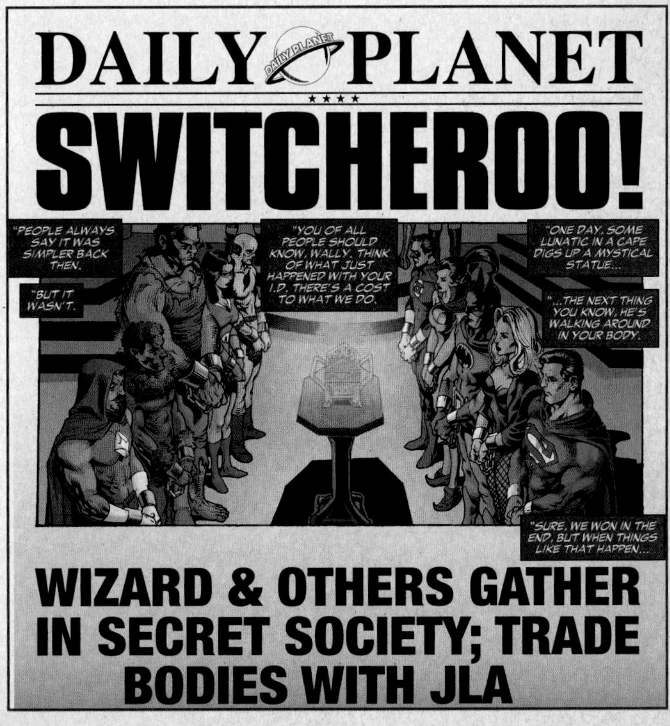

DAILY PLANET

SWITCHEROO!

"PEOPLE ALWAYS SAY IT WAS SIMPLER BACK THEN.
"BUT IT WASN'T.
"YOU OF ALL PEOPLE SHOULD KNOW, WALLY. THINK OF WHAT JUST HAPPENED WITH YOUR I.D. THERE'S A COST TO WHAT WE DO.
"ONE DAY, SOME LUNATIC IN A CAPE DIGS UP A MYSTICAL STATUE...
"...THE NEXT THING YOU KNOW, HE'S WALKING AROUND IN YOUR BODY.
"SURE, WE WON IN THE END, BUT WHEN THINGS LIKE THAT HAPPEN...

WIZARD & OTHERS GATHER IN SECRET SOCIETY; TRADE BODIES WITH JLA

THE CALCULATOR, page 101

Brad: The most important effect the Calculator has on the DC Universe is that, as a concept, it supports the idea of interconnecting relationships, which adds a sense of community to this supposed real universe. One of the things I cared most about with the story was letting the reader feel that all of the heroes' stories — *all of them* — happened in a shared universe. The heroes know each other. The villains know each other. These aren't adventures in a vacuum. They're legends in a complex, interconnected world. That's why Ollie uses everyone's real names. It lets you feel the tapestry of continuity that ties our own lives together.

From the script:

Page 101, Panel 2: Merlyn is sitting at a nice desk in his well-appointed home. The camera is diagonally over his shoulder. He's looking through an oversized magnifying glass (that's attached to his desk like one of those bendable desk lamps). He's looking through the glass at a miniature Red-Coat soldier that he's painting with a tiny paintbrush. Yes, Merlyn has a miniatures collection. A newspaper (that we only see the tip of — see panel 4) should be there as well.

THE ATOM BURSTING THE ROPES, page 113

Brad: When Rags saw in the script that I wanted him to draw all those panels of the rope just waiting to burst, he called me up and said, "Do I really have to draw this same thing over and over?" Feeling guilty, I told him to dupe some of the panels if it made it easier. Two days later, I got the pencils for the page. He drew each rope individually, thread for thread. The result was one of my favorite pages in there — with the Atom doing nothing more than snapping a rope. Look at the Atom's expression. His face tells you everything you need to know about that moment.

Rags: Brad even had the panel layout figured out beforehand. I just couldn't conceive of 21 panels over a two-page spread. Brad faxed me his layout and I followed his every whim. As much as I complained about the tightness of his scripts, I more often than not just did what he wanted. In the end it couldn't have been any other way.

From the script:

Page 113, Panels 8 through 20: Again, this will make more sense when I fax you the thumbnail for the layout, but all of these panels will be tiny in size — each one focusing on just the length of rope above Jean's head (we probably don't even see Jean). In the first two or three panels, the rope looks just like normal rope...in the next few, the twine starts to move slightly...in the next few, a few pieces come undone...and so on... What we're seeing is a slowed-down, frame-by-frame shot of the rope as the Atom is growing within it. The final tiny panel will be the rope almost broken...

Panel 21: This will be the rest of the two-page spread, a big huge panel with the Atom growing, literally, out of the rope as we see it snap in two. He's got gritted teeth, like Kong raging to get out of his chains.

CAP: Physics, as always, takes care of the rest.

ATOM: Rrrhhh!

SFX: Snap

WONDER WOMAN AT THE JAIL, page 121

Brad: Rags was dying to draw her in full figure, and I begged him not to. As before, it's all about the iconography. The Big Three — Superman, Batman, and Wonder Woman — were always dealt with in a way that made them feel bigger than the rest of us. If we saw her in full figure, there's nothing special. She's just another hero. This way, she's so big, she can't even be captured by a panel. Everyone else is human. These were the gods.

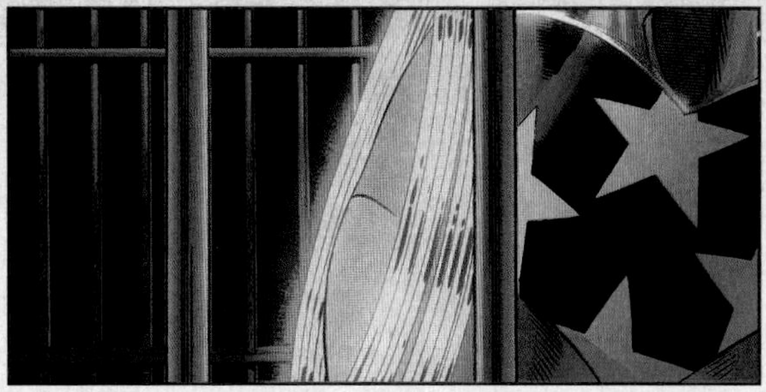

Rags: Brilliant. I didn't know how important that scene was, but now we can play it up. Wonder Woman has had her problems with the mind-wiping (as I stated in the aforementioned ADVENTURES OF SUPERMAN #636), and now that it's dawning on her the scope of what the JLA did, we're having fun playing with that in WONDER WOMAN now and in the next year. Keeping her oblivious and visually absent here, makes for wonderful stories in the future. Just wait and see.

From the script, page 121

Panel 4: POV Slipknot, so we're seeing this all through the bars of the cell. Shot of Wonder Woman, but just her midsection/hips, so the focal point is the magic lasso, which glows on her hip.

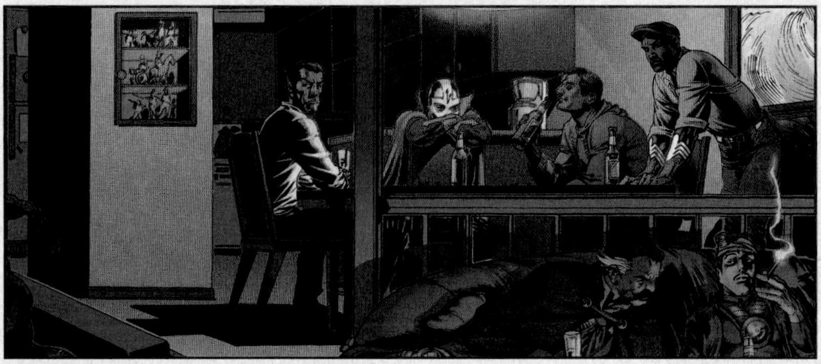

VILLAINS PLAYING RISK, page 127

Brad: This is one of those moments when you see what a wonderful artist Rags Morales is. It's a scene where we could lift out all of the dialogue and you would still see the personalities of the characters. It's so easy to overlook the body language of the characters, and Rags's art uses it to give them so much humanity throughout the series.

Rags: What you're seeing here is my sister's townhouse. The villains are playing Risk where my family has had Thanksgiving dinner. My brother-in-law is a wood worker and he built that glass cabinet on the wall where Merlyn puts his little figurines.

From the script:

Page 127, Panel 1: We're in Merlyn's house. Shot of Mirror Master and Merlyn sitting at a table, playing the game RISK. Make sure we can see the board, so we know what they're playing. In the background is a TV with a newscaster on. Mirror Master has his eyes on the TV. Again, this should all look very normal. Mirror Master should have his mask off, but we can see the costume. He's looking thrilled, leaning back in his chair.

NATIONAL ENQUIRER, page 128

Brad: Kenny Lopez did such a great job here. I was such a pain-in-the-ass since I wanted the typefaces to match perfectly, each little headline adding to that sense of a living, breathing universe. We littered copies of the paper throughout the book, letting it tell its own story to each of its readers.

Rags: Ahh, the luxury of not having to draw copy. Just tell Production what needs to be done and they do all the heavy lifting. Thanks to Ken and the production staff!

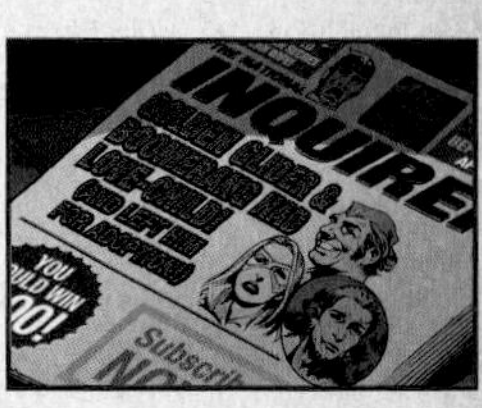
INQUIRER

From the script, page 128

Panel 3: Close-up of the front page of the "Inquirer" from the previous issues. Please pick up the same cover, and photo of 19-year-old Owen, from before: Golden Glider & Boomerang Had Love-Child! (And Left Him For Adoption!)

WHO BENEFITS?, pages 132-133

Brad: Here's where all the chess pieces are in place and you finally get to see the bigger picture. All you have to do is ask yourself the question. Ask that question of every character who's appeared and you'll get your answer.

From the script: Page 132-133

Page layout: These should all be symmetrical horizontal panels — three on each page — to show the same angle on everyone.

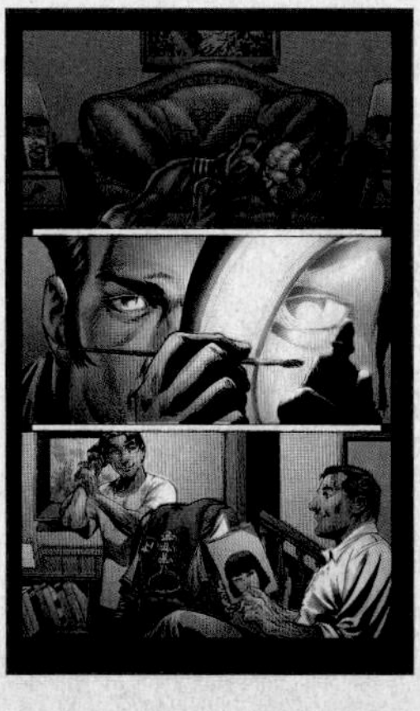

Panel 4: The camera is staring straight at Elongated Man, sitting alone on the sofa in his living room (there's a gap where Sue should be next to him). He's wearing his red

costume. His head is buried in his hands and he's hysterically crying. Rags, let us feel all his pain here. The voice is coming from a nearby answering machine.

CAPTAIN BOOMERANG'S SON, page 156

Brad: Of all the characters in the book, the ones who elbowed their way into more space each issue were these two. The father/son relationship is my own personal obsession, but even I was surprised by how much these two kept

shoving their way in, demanding more space with each passing day.

Rags: All those afternoons of me and my dad playing catch.

From the script:

> Page 156, Panel 4: The camera is diagonally behind Owen (Captain Boomerang's son), who looks young and almost majestic as he stands in the sun, arm arched back to throw another boomerang. It's a glorious day and in the distance, we see Captain Boomerang picking up a few boomerangs that litter the green grass. We also see the smoldering tree in the distance (that they just blew up). Owen's wearing a black leather jacket and jeans, but with the long white scarf from his dad's costume; the Captain is wearing his usual navy peacoat. This is gonna sound crazy, but imagine that scene in Dark Knight, where Superman is standing there (as Clark Kent), his chest stuck out, looking so heroic you'd think he just stepped out of a Norman Rockwell painting? That's the feeling we want here for Owen. He and his dad are having a Norman Rockwell day.

FATHER'S DAY, page 175

Brad: This is just the old Hitchcock quote, "There is no terror in the bang, only in the anticipation of it." As a reader, you know the ending, you know what's coming, you know he's going to die. We're just sitting there with the pin to the balloon.

Rags: Father's Day is my favorite issue. As a dad and a son, it just wrenches in my gut the most. This was my payment for doing this series. Thanks, Brad.

From the script:

> Page 175, Panel 2: The camera is way up at the center of the ceiling looking down at the mess below, where Captain Boomerang is lying on the left side of the room, and Jack Drake is lying on the right side. Tiny pools of blood are just starting to seep below them.
>
> Panel 3: Same exact shot (maybe pull out slightly), but the pools of blood are getting bigger.
>
> Panel 4: Same exact shot (maybe pull out even more), but the pools of blood are even bigger.

ORPHANS, page 182

Brad: There were two moments in the entire series where I forgot I was the writer of the series. This is one of them. If you look at the description in the script, it says Batman should be holding Tim in the pieces of the Robin costume. What Rags did, which was *not* in the description, was he turned Robin's eye toward us. And when you see that eye, it becomes the focal point to the entire page. That's what makes it so eerie. It's my favorite page of the whole series.

Rags: In spite of all his attempts, Batman tragically cannot stop the curse that bears his name. I wanted Tim to look like he is being swallowed up in that curse. It can't be stopped. Often when you do a thumbnail, it looks better than when you translate it to the page. For some reason you lose the spirit of the intention. In this particular instance I was so into the thumbnail and how it worked

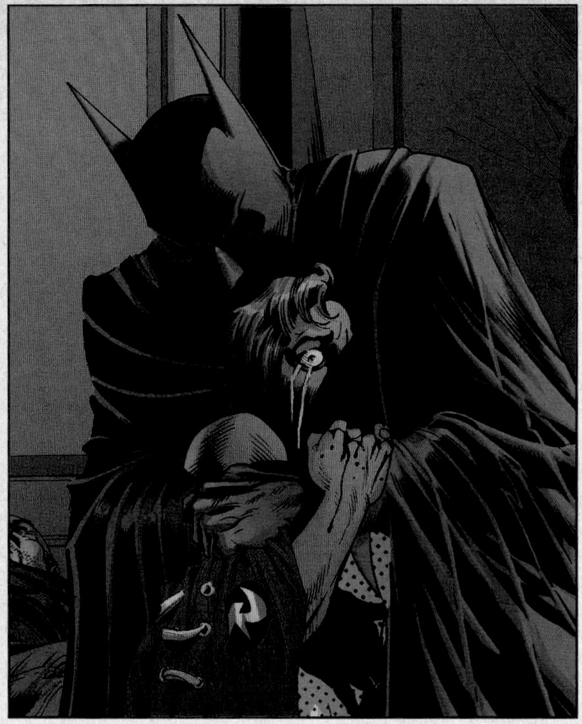

out, that I took particular care to translate it perfectly. If there is one scene that I'm most proud, it's this one.

From the script:

Page 182, panel 1: Full page. Here's the iconic image: Batman (looking enormous) as he takes Tim Drake into his arms, hugging him as if he's saying, I'll keep you safe. The pieces of the Robin costume (that Batman picked up) are still gripped tight in Batman's fists as he embraces Tim (thereby almost embracing him with the dangling iconography of the costume). Tim looks like a little kid again. His back is to us, but his head is turned, so we see his profile as the other half of his face rests on Batman's chest.

BATMAN: ...I've got you...

CAP (at the bottom): Batman and Robin.

CAP: Orphans.

DR. LIGHT AS KING LEAR, page 190

Brad: All I asked Rags for was to make Dr. Light look like King Lear. He also mixed in some John Buscema Mephisto. And the way he's looking away, looking away, looking away...and then looking at you. Only a schmuck lets his words get in the way of that art.

Rags: That last line: *Dr. Light is back.* That was the inspiration for Light looking at the reader. Brad was just communicating with me the atmosphere with that line and I heard it loud and clear. What I didn't anticipate was how it could be used later. There's a scene where Calculator is watching Batman come for him on his monitors. On one of those monitors is a shot of Dr. Light waving his hand to the camera watching him, using his powers to white himself out of view. All I did was duplicate the

FAVORITE MOMENTS
AS SELECTED BY THE STORYTELLERS

KEN LOPEZ

My favorite comes towards the end of the series when we see Batman talking to his dead parents at the foot of their grave.

I got to read it in the script stage and I remember thinking what a great visual this was going to be. Sure enough, when I saw the art for the first time, Rags did not disappoint us. It was a beautiful scene.

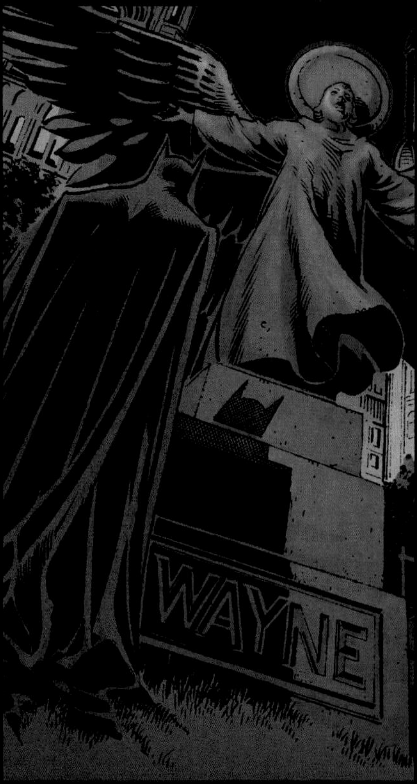
WAYNE

Even without the visuals it's a powerful scene. We always see Batman as the cold, dark avenger, but Brad gave us one of those rare moments when we get a glimpse at the human/Bruce Wayne side.

FAVORITE MOMENTS
AS SELECTED BY THE STORYTELLERS

ALEX SINCLAIR

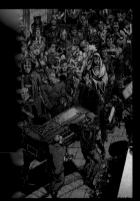

Mine was the Funeral scene for various reasons. I really liked how Brad set up the scene to be so realistic and emotional. Rags and Mike did such a great job with capturing it that it nspired me to go crazy with mood on it. have two versions of this scene. One I colored with everyone's costumes rendered with neutral light, but it looked like someone had spilled a bag of Skittles on the page. I decided to add the golden light from the windows and use those rays to highlight specific characters within the art. I added hat same golden hue to everyone to fix the Skittles problem. I also got to color a bulk of the DC heroes all within those two pages. My desk had stacks and stacks of books and trades that I used for reference, not to mention he set of Who's Who I had to buy on eBay.

MIKE CARLIN

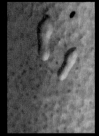

My favorite moment s seeing the teeny, iny footprints on a human brain. Just BECAUSE it's such a CREEPY image!

One SMALL step for Mankind, eh?!

look on Light's face from this scene on the monitor, and it gives the reader more than one reason why Dr. Light gives us that look. It's breaking the fourth wall and serving a purpose for the scene with Calculator's monitors. Sometimes you just get lucky. *From the script:*

Page 90, panel 1: Dr. Light (in costume) sitting slumped back in a high-tech chair (something like the chairs on the JLA satellite). He's not looking lazy – he's looking like King Lear – mulling and scheming. He should look majestic here – his cape draped below him to the floor. His hands gripping the armrests. His eyes are black and we should be terrified by whatever he's planning. Dr. Light is back.

CAP (green):
...and get back to doing what we do best...

Panel 2: Pull in slightly closer on the same shot, so now we see Dr. Light from the waist up.

Panel 3: Pull in even closer, so now we're just on his face.

Panel 4: Pull in even closer, so now we're just on his eyes.

FLASH LEARNS THE JLA's SECRET, page 197

Brad: When I pitched *Identity Crisis* to DC I left this part out because I didn't think DC would let us get away with it. A hero isn't just the person who fights the easy fight — it's the person who fights the hard one. I put the League in an impossible moral dilemma. Watching them make a mistake and battle — for years — to overcome it…watching it test them and destroy them…and then seeing them still try to persevere — that's the measure of a hero.

As for the scene, we could have done it in flashback, but

this is where comics have a clear advantage over novels: I don't have to show Green Arrow or Hawkman saying their dialogue. I can just show that photograph of all the heroes together. Then we just pull in close on Batman. Add Rags's classic picture of the satellite League and you can't help but ask yourself: how can one man possibly be bigger than that?

Rags: I *loved* that scene. Just let the dialogue do the talking and get that creepy feeling while looking at the photo of an innocent bygone era.

From the script:

> Panel 7: Framed group photo of the Justice League (like one of those school photos, with members kneeling in front and everyone looking happy). See Justice League #200, where I think Perez did a photo like it. Here, it's: Superman, Batman, Elongated Man, Firestorm, Aquaman, and Red Tornado in the back row, and Green Arrow, Green Lantern (Hal), Barry Allen Flash, Black Canary, the Atom, Hawkman, and Zatanna kneeling in the front row.
>
> CAP (green): It was a League within the League — just between the seven of us.
>
> CAP (green): And right there, we took our second vote of the night.
>
> Panel 8: Close-up on just the bottom row: Green Arrow, Green Lantern (Hal), Barry Allen Flash, Black Canary, the Atom, Hawkman, and Zatanna.
>
> CAP (green):
>
> This time, it was unanimous.
>
> Panel 9: Close-up on just Batman in the group photo. It's almost grainy, we're so close.
>
> CAP (green): The alternative would've meant the destruction of the League.
>
> HAWKMAN
>
> (off panel)
>
> It's just this moment — just the past ten minutes...
>
> GREEN ARROW
>
> If this hurts him...!
>
> Panel 10: Again, show the full group shot.

BATMAN AT THE GRAVE, page 234

Brad: From the moment I started thinking about Batman, I kept coming back to the fact that his worst wounds are self-inflicted, including the way he copes with the death of his parents. For that reason, I wanted Batman's reaction to be self-contained. It wasn't a cliffhanger — it was his own torturous restraint. So when DC told me they were going to build a year of stories on this moment, that's a nice back-patting compliment, but I cared far more about the actual moment and what it said within the story. If other writers want to build on that moment or see it differently, well, that's the beauty of comics: the tapestry of different interpretations on the same characters/moments/interactions. But in this story, Bruce knows what he wants to know, and more than any of us, he also knows that

you should never underestimate what someone will do for the people they love.

From the script:

> Page 197, panel 5: Same exact angle and size of the last panel, but here, Batman (without the cowl) is standing up again, whispering downward. Both roses are on the grave.

THE MASK, page 201

Brad: So many stories, when contemplating super-heroes, deal with why super-heroes should *not* exist — they become arguments against super-heroes. What I'm proudest of, at the end of the day, is that *Identity Crisis* is an argument about why super-heroes *should* exist. And it does it by embracing one of the greatest conventions of the genre: the secret identity.

Rags: In this scene I wanted to emphasize the nature of the series and the nature of life. I used the dialogue to point out what I was saying by having the rise of Green Arrow clutching the mask and the fall of his holding the mask in the final panel. My attempt at a dramatic Shakespearean moment.

From the script:

> Page 201, panel 6: Close-up even tighter on the mask. Just the mask — it's the symbol of the entire series. It's now every hero's mask (figuratively speaking).
>
> GREEN ARROW:
>
> But the mask will

ATOM SHRINKING AWAY, page 228

Brad: This is all Rags and Bair. Look at the emotion on the Atom's face — you feel for this man. He's shrinking, not just physically, but metaphorically, becom-

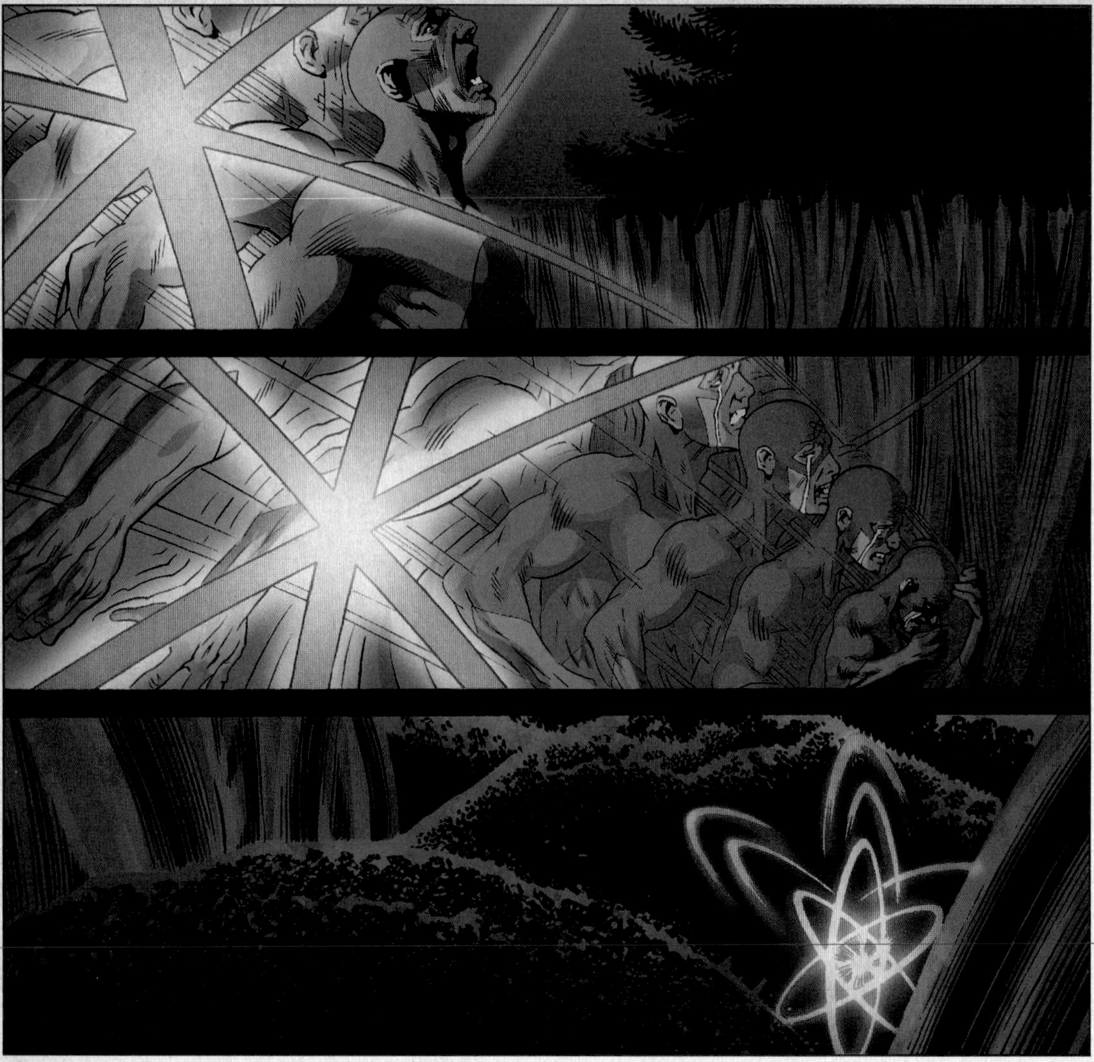

ing nothing and fading into a nowhere world. All the emotion in there is a credit to the art team.

From the script:

> Page 228, panel 3: Headshot of the Atom (he's now in the Atom costume) with the enormous trees, etc. behind him. He's crying hysterically. The tears roll down the outside of his mask, down his cheeks. Rags, this man just turned his wife over to the worst asylum in the country – his friends are dead – let us feel all the pain and regret and sadness he's feeling. If you can show some afterimages of him still shrinking, that'd be best – since we want people to know he's still shrinking even now.

RALPH AT PEACE, page 242

Brad: The last "I love you too" balloon doesn't have a tail on it. On purpose. It's supposed to be read both ways. This couple's love for each other is very much alive, even if Sue isn't. The League endures — and so do human beings as they learn to cope.

As for the design of the page, if you look at the opening sequence of *Identity Crisis*, you see the heroes on top of a building (Ralph with Firehawk). The camera's looking up because the heroes are supposed to be bigger than all of us, like gods. Then when you get to the final pages of the epilogue, the camera's purposely up on the ceiling, looking *down* at Ralph — he's tiny, vulnerable, situated in that most "normal" place (in bed) — all of it telling us that he's just a man.

Rags: I thought it was important to have Ralph reach over and turn out the only lit light, hers. So having Ralph on the left made sense for the motion of his turning out her light. For me, having her light on is like the light in the window, waiting for the sailors to come home. It represents hope. I felt the last scene needed to show this while we cry for Ralph, Sue and the Justice League. It was one of the many poignant scenes in the entire series and it ends so poetically.

From the script:

> Page 242, panel 1: Horizontal panel. Pull out so it's like

the camera is on the ceiling. We're looking down at Elongated Man in bed – but now we see his whole bed: he's on the left side of the bed (our right) – while Sue's half of the bed is completely empty. This should be an immensely stark difference. Ralph's side is lumpy from his body's outline – Sue's is perfectly flat, neat, her pillow round and not slept on. Ralph is looking up toward us. He's clearly talking to himself. (Not sure if you have room for night-stands (which may be too much for the shot), but if you do, Sue's should be empty, while Ralph's is the one with photos, etc.).

ELONGATED MAN: You have to go? No, don't worry. I'll speak to you later.

Panel 2: Horizontal panel. Same shot, but here, he's stretching his arm slightly to shut the light on his night-stand.

ELONGATED MAN: No, I'm fine, bun...I'm great. (cont.) Great – I'll talk to you tomorrow. (cont.) Goodnight, Sue.

Panel 3: Horizontal panel. The panel is all black.

Panel 4: Horizontal panel. The panel is all black.

Panel 4: Horizontal panel. Again, all black, but with just a single dialogue balloon floating in the panel – it has no tail on it – so we can't tell who's saying it.

ELONGATED MAN: I love you, too.

CAP (at the bottom): Ralph and Sue Dibny.

CAP: Husband and wife.

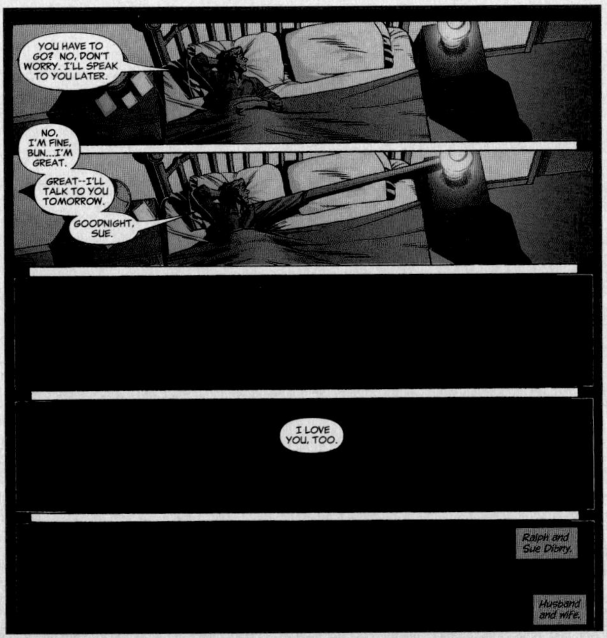
YOU HAVE TO GO? NO, DON'T WORRY. I'LL SPEAK TO YOU LATER.
NO, I'M FINE, BUN...I'M GREAT.
GREAT--I'LL TALK TO YOU TOMORROW.
GOODNIGHT, SUE.
I LOVE YOU, TOO.
Ralph and Sue Dibny.
Husband and wife.

ACKNOWLEDGMENTS

And so, the end. Needless to say, this has been one of the most incredible and humbling projects I've ever been a part of, and so a thank-you must be said to all those who made the journey such a true adventure.

First, to my Wonder Woman, Cori, who only encourages and inspires, no matter the medium. The love Ralph has for Sue — that's me writing my love for Cori. To Jonas and Lila, for reminding me everyday of life's true wonders. To my Dad, for buying all those comics when he would've rather been buying baseballs, my Mom and sister Bari, who always believed, Noah Kuttler, my hero, for reading early drafts and for inspiring the Calculator by being the Calculator (true), Judd Winick, who introduced me to it all — thanks, Max — I owe you forever for that one, Geoff Johns, whose friendship was unwavering throughout, and Bob Schreck, for inviting me in.

Of course, this project only exists because of the incredible team I was paired with, all of whom I'm proud to call friends: my true partner-in-crime Rags Morales let you feel every emotion (and always then some), Mike Bair gave a year of his life making sure all the texture remained, forever improving and enhancing, Alex Sinclair made every scene feel even more vivid (check out Ralph holding the dead Sue, or the funeral spread, or the Dr. Light as King Lear), Ken Lopez put up with all my "voices," and made all the newspapers and tabloids part of the believable landscape, and Mike Turner and Peter Steigerwald, well, c'mon — who else would you want on covers? Also, Valerie D'Orazio and Michael Siglain sought out even my most geekiest of references, while Mike Carlin gave me the true eureka moment (thank you, sir). Most important, Dan DiDio, Mike Carlin, and Paul Levitz let us tell this story with a level of editorial freedom and encouragement that's usually unheard of. It will forever be appreciated. They're the ones who had the initial faith.

– BRAD MELTZER

DC Comics promised that IDENTITY CRISIS was to be a status-quo changing event. Even with that warning, comic shops were selling out of issues very quickly. DC responded to that demand with subsequent printings of the seven issues. To differentiate one printing from another, the following variant covers were used.

VARIANT COVER GALLERY

IDENTITY CRISIS #1, 2ND PRINTING

IDENTITY CRISIS #1, 3RD PRINTING

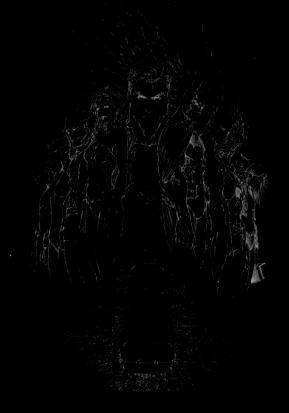

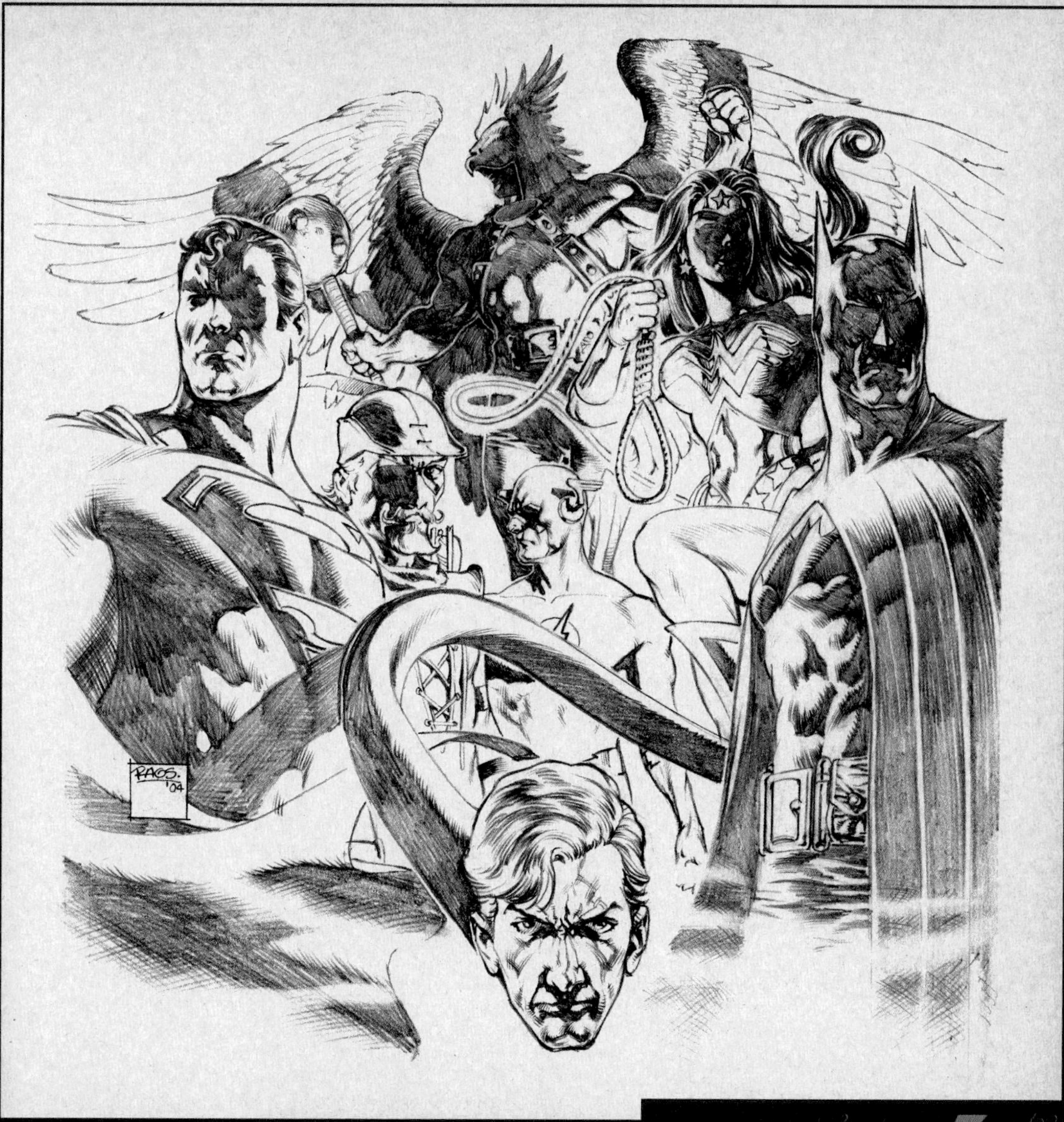
RAGS.
'04

IDENTITY CRISIS #2, 2ND PRINTING

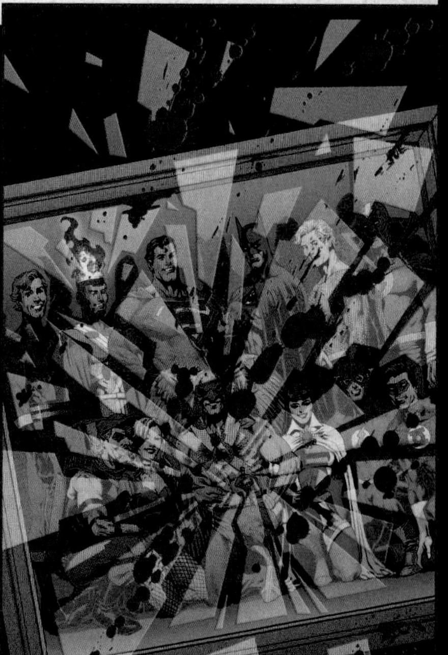

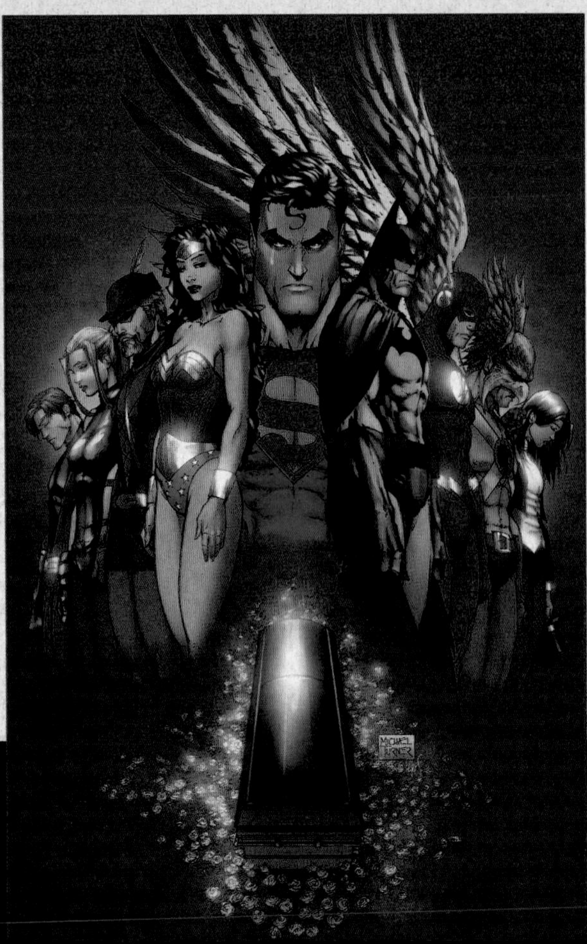

IDENTITY CRISIS #1, 5TH PRINTING

The demand continued through all seven issues and one final printing of the miniseries was released with newly colored covers by Peter Steigerwald.

IDENTITY CRISIS #2, 3RD PRINTING

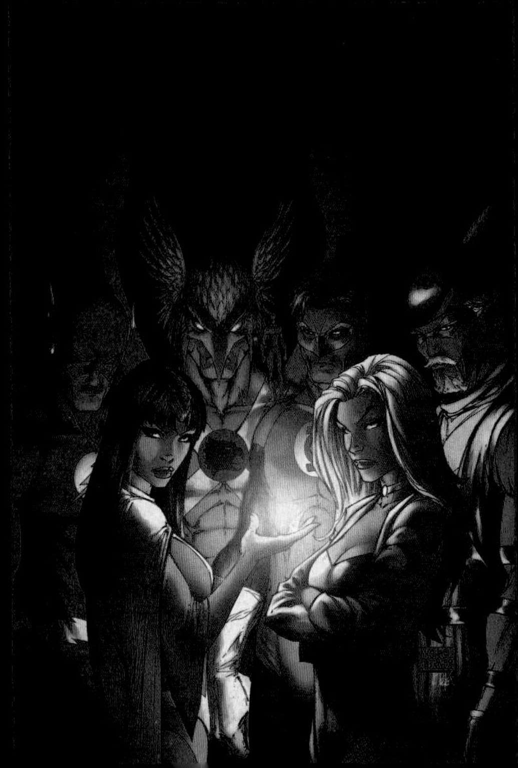

IDENTITY CRISIS #3, 2ND PRINTING

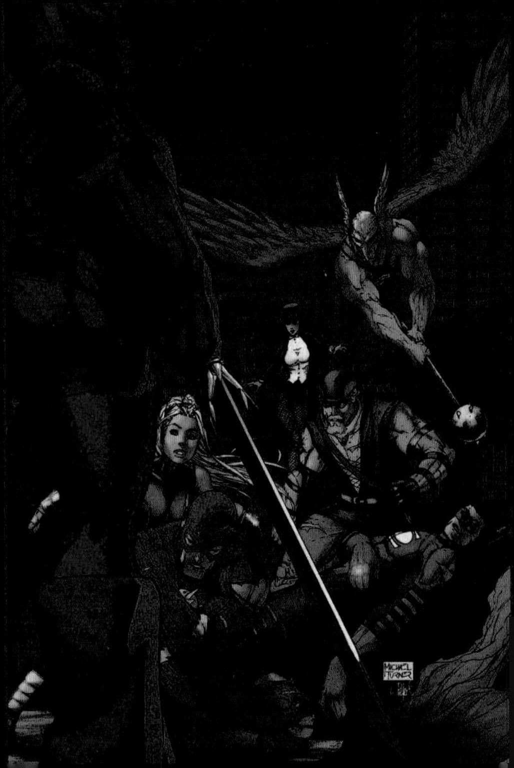

IDENTITY CRISIS #4, 2ND PRINTING

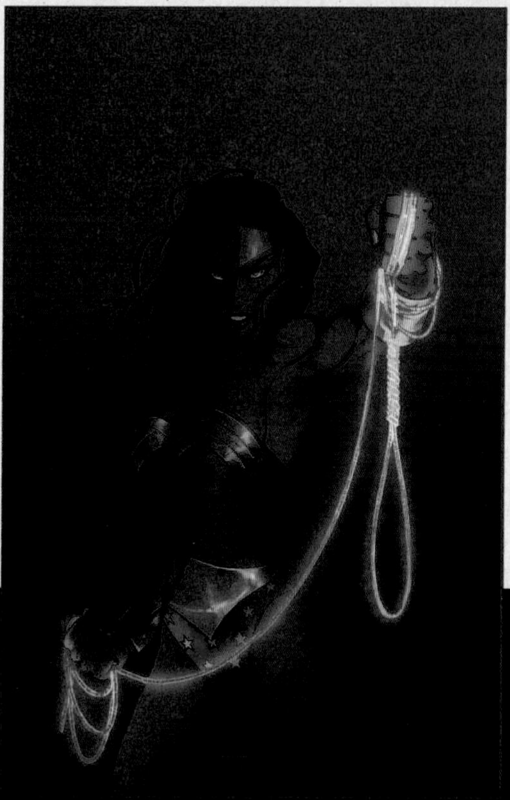

IDENTITY CRISIS #5, 2ND PRINTING

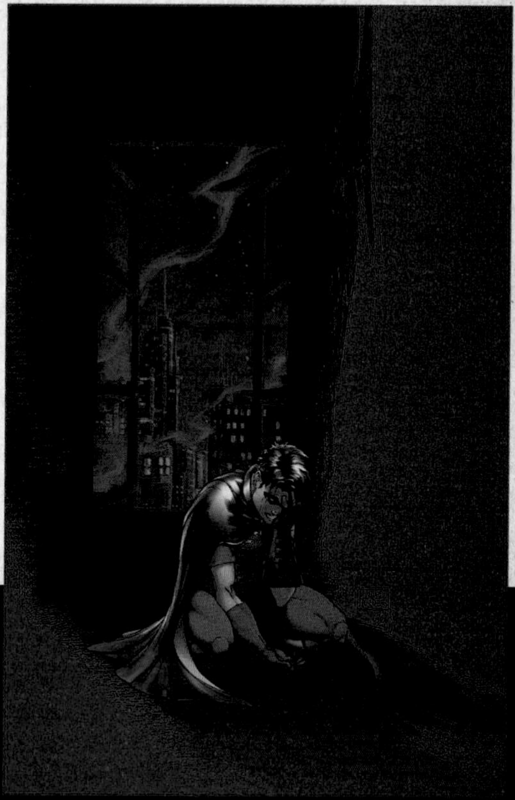

IDENTITY CRISIS #6, 2ND PRINTING

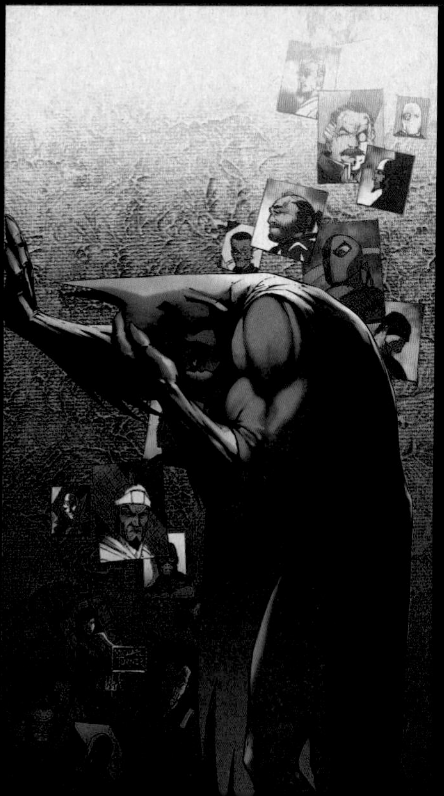

IDENTITY CRISIS #7, 2ND PRINTING

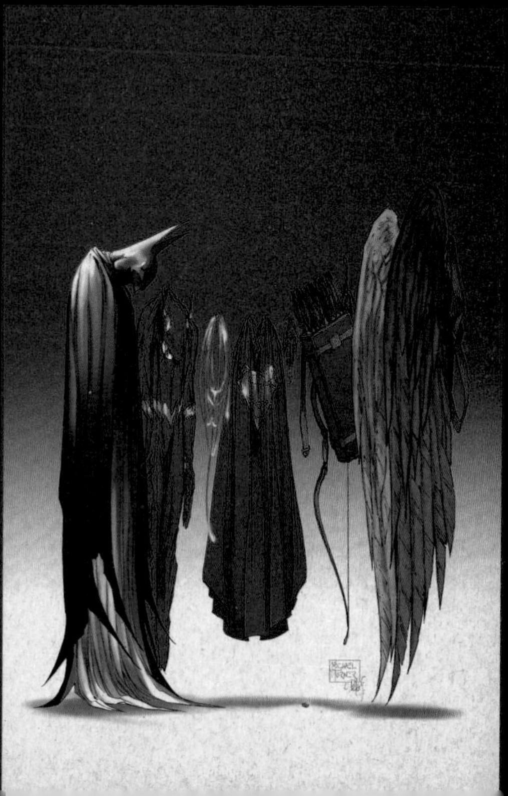

Brad Meltzer is the author of the *New York Times* bestselling thrillers *The Tenth Justice*, *Dead Even*, *The First Counsel*, *The Millionaires* and *The Zero Game*. His first comic book work was GREEN ARROW: THE ARCHER'S QUEST. He is also the co-creator of the critically-acclaimed television series *Jack & Bobby*.

Raised in Brooklyn and Miami, Brad is a graduate of the University of Michigan and Columbia Law School. He's played himself as an extra in Woody Allen's *Celebrity* and earned credit from Columbia Law School for writing his first book, which became *The Tenth Justice*.

The first comic book Brad ever read was JUSTICE LEAGUE OF AMERICA #150 (1978). He was seven years old. In it, Elongated Man saves the League from certain doom. And there's also a flashback with Dr. Light. Really. Needless to say, the comic changed his life. Brad currently lives in Florida with his wife, Cori, who's also an attorney.

Ralph "Rags" Morales started his DC career working on comics based on TSR's role-playing games such as ADVANCED DUNGEONS & DRAGONS. His first super-hero series was the BLACK CONDOR. Since then, he has worked on most of DC's major heroes including a long run on JSA and HAWKMAN, which served as warmups to IDENTITY CRISIS. Since then, he has worked on a story arc for WONDER WOMAN. Married with a daughter, Rags lives in the northeast.

Michael Bair came into the comic business in 1982, first gaining attention for his pencil work on Eclipse Comics' *Aztec Ace* series. Michael continued pencilling until 1989's CATWOMAN miniseries. He illustrated Marvel's *Hellstorm*, *Spider-Man/Dr. Strange*, *Alpha Flight*, *Ghost Raider*, *X-Men* and Harris Comics' *Vampirella* before settling in at DC, primarily as an inker. His other credits include GHOST/BATGIRL, JLA YEAR ONE, YOUNG ALL-STARS, JSA, HAWKMAN and WONDER WOMAN. Michael makes his home in Brooklyn.

Ken Lopez began lettering for Marvel Comics in the 1980s, rapidly rising to prominence for his speed and creativity. In time, he worked with the top names and the top characters at Marvel before adding other companies to his client roster. During the 1990s, Ken was in the forefront of pioneering computer lettering, a skill that landed him a spot at DC in 2004 as Art Director - Lettering. He is currently DC's Cover Editor. He continues to create fonts while training others. A lifelong New

Alex Sinclair has been a longtime fan of DC Comics and its heroes. He fondly recalls going to the local convenience store with his brother to buy as many issues as they could afford and reading through them that same day. He broke into comics with WildStorm in the early '90s and one of his childhood dreams came true when he became the colorist of his favorite title and character, Batman, on the critically acclaimed HUSH story. Sinclair got to color many other, fondly remembered characters on IDENTITY CRISIS. He is also the colorist on SUPERMAN: FOR TOMORROW, ASTRO CITY, and ARROWSMITH. He lives in San Diego with his wife Rebecca and daughters Grace, Blythe, Meredith and Harley, none of whom can perform mind-wipes.

In 1994, Aspen MLT, Inc. founder **Michael Turner** moved from Tennessee to California to begin his comic book career. Working for Top Cow Productions, Michael started off doing background illustrations but soon helped to create and launch the comic book series *Witchblade* in October of 1995. Quickly growing to become one of the most successful titles of the '90s, Michael served as an integral part of *Witchblade*'s immense popularity. Shifting focus, Michael went on to debut his first creator owned series, *Fathom*, in the summer of 1998. *Fathom* was a smash hit and earned the honor of becoming the number one selling comic book of the year.

In the fall of 2002, Michael departed from Top Cow Productions to start his own publishing company, Aspen MLT Inc. With Aspen, Michael produced the SUPERMAN: GODFALL story before returning to *Fathom*.